THE PAPERS

of

JOHN C. CALHOUN

CALHOUN BY CLARK MILLS

Executed in 1845 from a life mask, this bust was celebrated as a true likeness of the South Carolina statesman, by a South Carolina artist, from South Carolina stone. It was acquired by the City of Charleston and is in the City Hall collection.

THE PAPERS

of

JOHN C. CALHOUN

〚

Volume XXII, 1845–1846

Edited by

Clyde N. Wilson

Shirley Bright Cook, *Associate Editor*

Alexander Moore, *Assistant Editor*

University of South Carolina Press, 1995

Publication of this book was made possible
by a grant from the National Historical Publications
and Records Commission.

International Standard Book Number: 1–57003–023–5
Library of Congress Catalog Card Number: 59–10351

Manufactured in the United States of America

CONTENTS

〠

PREFACE

॥

With the end of this volume Calhoun is within exactly four years of the end of his life, though the papers to be edited for the last few years are more voluminous than for any other period except the times when he held Cabinet office. Although he did not speak as frequently in the Senate during 1845–1850 as he had in the period 1833–1843, his preserved incoming correspondence is more extensive.

This is in part due to the accidents of preservation, but also due, perhaps, to an upsurge in political participation and interest among Americans experiencing a dynamically expanding economy, territory, and international involvement, as well as a sharpening sectional conflict. Also, perhaps, because of the stature Calhoun had achieved as an elder statesman.

The support of the National Endowment for the Humanities, the National Historical Publications and Records Commission, the University of South Carolina, and the University South Caroliniana Society makes our continuing work possible. Besides the persons on the title page, Thomas M. Downey participated ably in the production of this volume.

CLYDE N. WILSON

Columbia, May 1993

INTRODUCTION

◫

Calhoun returned to the Senate in late 1845 reluctantly and primarily because he thought he could play a useful role in preventing an Anglo-American war over Oregon. This is the obvious evidence of the record, unless you accept the viewpoint of hostile and jealous contemporaries, and of the many historians who have followed them, that all of Calhoun's actions had a hidden discreditable agenda—by some accounts an overweening ambition, by others an endless conspiring to break up the Union.

Curiously, motivational attributions of this sort are seldom applied to Calhoun's contemporaries and rivals, though if they were, he might fare very well by comparison. Too many commentators have thought that the best or only way to understand Calhoun is to read the letters of his enemies, as if those enemies were unbiased and had no agendas of their own. But, of course, the judgment of enemies as to his motives is only one of the factors that should be considered.

But the negative stereotyping of Calhoun is understandable. He was not only out of step with the main currents of American thought as they later developed, he was also unpopular with both of the major political elements of his own time. Whiggish progressives regarded him as one of the chief obstacles to their desire to develop and profit from the American economy. The organization men of the Democratic party, intent on maintaining a winning coalition of moderate State rights men of the North and South, regarded him as a dangerous rival and disruptive element. They could not fathom his motives and thus gave them attributions they could recognize in themselves—malice and ambition. These attitudes toward Calhoun were held by many, Southerners as well as Northerners, and apart from whether they were antislavery men or not.

It is interesting to follow James K. Polk's Presidential diary in this light. It would appear that at first he was flattered by Calhoun's attentions and held him somewhat in awe. He does not realize, though it is evident to anyone who knows Calhoun well, that the elder statesman was trying tactfully to maneuver him into a more moderate and sensible course on Oregon. Relations cooled gradually, and Polk ended in 1847 with the old slander, his only explanation for Calhoun's opposition to his Mexican policy: Calhoun "is an aspirant for the Presidency."[1]

To those who know Calhoun's mind well, it appears that Polk failed to understand him at all, while Calhoun understood Polk very well. He understood Polk to be a relatively honest and competent politician, good at short-range maneuvering for his objectives, but unable to take long-range and statesmanlike views. Polk brought on a war with Mexico that Calhoun thought was unnecessary. Polk, after much unproductive bluster and brinksmanship, ended in an Oregon settlement on the lines that Calhoun had supported all along. Polk faithfully followed the Democratic platform in vetoing internal improvements on Constitutional grounds, thus fueling a Midwestern revolt that would contribute greatly to the rise of the Republican party and decline of the Democratic party in the North. On the other hand, Calhoun endeavored, as is evident in this and the next volume, to find a way to satisfy those importunate and just demands within the Constitution. Polk regarded the slavery issue as a mischievous aggravation, while Calhoun saw it as "the only question of sufficient magnitude and potency to divide this Union."[2]

The charge that Calhoun's actions in his last two decades were dominated by relentless desire for the Presidency has been repeated so often that it has taken on a life of its own. It has even been argued that he cherished hopes of a nomination as late as 1848. Yet Calhoun always said he was no longer ambitious for the Presidency and knew he could not, except under the most extraordinary event, have it. He had been observing the American political system all his life, and he understood many of its tendencies as well as anyone. He was well aware that the Presidency had become the prize of politicians, not of statesmen.[3] He saw himself as a statesman—a man of foresight and patriotism who pursued what was good for the people, not what

[1] Allan Nevins, ed., *Polk: The Diary of a President, 1845–1849* (New York: Capricorn Books, 1968), pp. 34–35, 41–43, 56–59, 62, 69, 73, 195–196. See the interesting estimate of Polk's character by Senator Ephraim H. Foster of Tenn. in his letter of March 25, 1846, herein.

[2] Remarks against Referring His Resolutions to a Select Committee, January 5, 1838, in *The Papers of John C. Calhoun*, 14:60. See also letter to James T. Austin, December 28, 1837, in *The Papers of John C. Calhoun*, 14:34.

[3] For Calhoun's judgment about the party system and his awareness that he could not be President, see the numerous and convincing quotations collected in Clyde N. Wilson, ed., *The Essential Calhoun: Selections from Writings, Speeches, and Letters* (New Brunswick, N.J., and London: Transaction Publishers, 1992), pp. 331, 342–348, 423–429.

flattered them. His actions from 1845 on, for better or worse, are far more satisfactorily explained by this self-defined role than by the motives ascribed by the shallower of his enemies and critics.

When he left office as Secretary of State in March, 1845, Calhoun entered retirement with the intention of addressing his private economy and working on what would become *A Disquisition on Government*. Later in the year he let it be known that he was willing to return to the Senate. Judge Daniel E. Huger, who had succeeded him, had already indicated that he would resign to make room if the interests of the State required it. This was not so unusual an action as might seem, because Calhoun would actually be taking up again the six-year term to which he had been elected in 1841. Huger resigned, and the South Carolina General Assembly, when it met in the fall, re-elected Calhoun without dissent.

In the fall of 1845 he made his last great public journey, to the Southwest, and then joined the Senate a few days before Christmas, three weeks after the session had begun. According to newspaper speculation, Calhoun was to be named chairman of the Foreign Relations Committee, a reasonable expectation since he was a retired Secretary of State and a senior American statesman. The ultra-expansionists maneuvered hard to avert this and succeeded in naming instead William Allen, the Southern-born longtime Senator from Ohio, a vehement expansionist. Calhoun was elected chairman of the Committee on Finance, which, when he arrived, he declined. In his last four years in the Senate, Calhoun would not play quite as aggressive and active a role as he had during 1833–1843. Rather than taking part in debate nearly every day, as he had earlier, he hoarded his energies for the more important tasks.

The Senate was beginning to change, evolving a new generation of notables who would come to the fore in the 1850's when Calhoun was gone. When Calhoun rejoined, Henry Clay was not there, though he would soon return, and Daniel Webster was in residence. Present as well were old associates like John J. Crittenden, Lewis Cass, Thomas H. Benton, and many others well-known to Calhoun from the battles of the Jackson period.

Among the newer men were the first two Senators from Florida, who had just taken their seats; Calhoun's friend Dixon H. Lewis, now elevated by Alabama from the House to the Senate; and John A. Dix, Senator from New York, who as a young Army officer had been zealous in Calhoun's 1823–1824 Presidential campaign (and would subsequently be a general of the federal army in the Civil War). In March, 1846, the two Senators from Texas joined. One was Calhoun's old enemy Sam Houston, the other Thomas Jefferson Rusk, who, as the son of an artisan in the Pendleton neighborhood, Calhoun had encouraged and aided in his youth. Rusk had since distinguished himself in the Texas War of Independence.

Before Calhoun's death four years later, the Senate would change still more by the appearance of new notables: Stephen A. Douglas, Jefferson Davis, Calhoun's friends James M. Mason and Robert M. T. Hunter of Virginia, William H. Seward, Salmon P. Chase, and many others who would take major parts in the coming sectional conflict.

Oregon

The volume in hand covers some interesting months before Calhoun returned to the Senate and approximately the first half of the first session of the Twenty-Ninth Congress. Such great questions as Oregon, internal improvements, and the tariff are in the course of major developments, although in each case the actual dénouement will come in the period covered by the next volume.

Those who see Calhoun as a shallow and obstructive figure and who like to minimize his importance in his time except in regard to slavery and sectional conflict will have difficulty understanding his role in the Oregon controversy and especially the widespread public appreciation of that role. It seems clear that Calhoun was personally active in a significant way in bringing together Secretary of State James Buchanan and the British Minister Richard Pakenham usefully, to an extent that does not appear in his own papers herein.[4]

---

[4] For detailed accounts of Calhoun's part in the complex resolution of the Oregon question see the following two sources, the first friendly, the second hostile: Charles M. Wiltse, *John C. Calhoun*, 3 vols. (Indianapolis: Bobbs-Merrill, 1944–1951), 3:247–267; Bruno Gujer, "Free Trade and Slavery: Calhoun's Defense of Southern Interests Against British Interference, 1811–1848" (Ph.D. dissertation, University of Zurich, 1971), pp. 242–285. These accounts are by no means exhaustive. The following newspaper reports, among many others, add other material to the story that has so far been written: the Washington, D.C., *Daily National Intelligencer*, December 31, 1845, and April 1, 1846; the Richmond, Va., *Enquirer*, January 2, 1846; the Washington, D.C., *Daily Union*, vol. I, no. 263 (March 6, 1846), p. 1035; the Charleston, S.C., *Mercury*, January 5, 1846, reprinting reports from the New York commercial press; the New Orleans, La., *Daily Picayune*, January 29, 1846, reprinting the Boston, Mass., *Atlas*; the Greenville, S.C., *Mountaineer*, March 27, 1846. And one should not forget Richard K. Crallé's account in Crallé, ed., *The Works of John C. Calhoun*, 6 vols. (Columbia, S.C.: A.S. Johnston, 1851, and New York: D. Appleton, 1853–1857), 5:414–415. For Calhoun's relation to Polk and role in the Oregon question, see also Clyde N. Wilson, "John C. Calhoun and Antebellum America," in

What does appear is his effort to make the Senate a moderating force. He joined the issue publicly with a speech and resolutions on December 30, 1845, and remained active until the settlement was consummated as he had envisioned it.

Polk had indicated in his inaugural address support for giving one year's notice, as required by previous agreement, of intent to end the joint occupation of the vast Oregon territory with the British. This position was reiterated in his message at the opening of Congress in December 1845. There was nothing wrong with giving the notice, which could be seen as a reasonable first step toward a permanent settlement. However, in the context of the militant clamor of Democrats from the Old Northwest (and antislavery men like John Quincy Adams and Joshua R. Giddings) for "Fifty-Four Forty or Fight"—that is, all of Oregon or war—Calhoun was alarmed by the possibility of unnecessary conflict. He hoped to play a role in marshaling the Senate for a more moderate course.

One of the charges made at the time by expansionists was that Calhoun was a sectionalist—that he had gone all out to acquire Texas in the Southwest but was willing to compromise on Oregon in the Northwest. But, of course, the two cases were not alike, and the charge was the typical anti-Calhoun demagoguery of superficial politicians. Texas was an already populated independent republic, anxious to join the Union, and which it was desirable to render safe from European imperialists. Texas could easily be defended by American forces from the Gulf. Indeed, it could defend itself and had already done so. A war with Mexico, though undesirable, would hardly be so serious a matter as a war with the British Empire. And, in a hope of avoiding war, Calhoun had advocated keeping the question of boundary open to compromise in the case of Texas, just as he had in the case of Oregon.

Oregon, however, was already partly occupied by a foreign power and could hardly be defended by the American settlers there. Great Britain had the advantage as a Pacific power, which the United States were not—yet. And a war between the two great Anglo-Saxon powers, which could only be brought on by American bluster, would be a catastrophic setback to a world enjoying unprecedented progress, in Calhoun's view.

It was certainly assumed by many at the time, including a great many observers and commentators who were not partisans of Cal-

F. Kevin Simon, ed., *The David A. Sayre History Symposium: Collected Lectures, 1985–1989* (Lexington, Ky.: Sayre School, 1991), pp. 75–85.

houn, that he played a key role in the compromise settlement. In the upshot, notice was given, but in a moderate form, negotiations were resumed, "Fifty-Four Forty or Fight" was abandoned, and a treaty was made dividing the territory on the lines Calhoun had suggested as Secretary of State. In June, slightly past the end of this volume, the treaty was ratified by the Senate. The key event for Calhoun, so far as these documents are concerned, was his speech of March 16, 1846, surely one of the greatest of his career.

When Calhoun rose for this speech the Senate controversy had been underway for some weeks already and had attracted much public interest. Calhoun was being widely hailed, North and South, as a chieftain of the peace party. The Richmond *Enquirer* reported the occasion:

> Mr. Calhoun made his anticipated speech today in a crowded Senate chamber. Indeed, the ladies had complete possession of the circular gallery by eight o'clock A.M. The forenoon train from Baltimore came in, packed full of strangers, many of whom had journeyed all the way from New York City, solely for the purpose of hearing him. The Alexandria steamboat, which arrived at nine, brought an inauguration day crowd. . . .[5]

Another reporter recorded that the Capitol was overflowing four hours before Calhoun's speech was scheduled: "The crowd was great beyond all precedent, and hundreds of persons were turned away."[6] But more interesting was the crowd's response at the end of the speech, as reported by the New York *Herald*: "Mr. Calhoun sat down. There was no manifestation of applause, as after the war speech of Mr. Allen, but there was a general murmur of approbation and delight pervading the Senate and the galleries."[7]

It was to be expected that Calhoun's friends and admirers would approve of his role in settling the Oregon difficulties. For instance, James Gadsden wrote from New Orleans as early as the fall of 1845 that Calhoun was the only man who could control and settle the question successfully.[8] Calhoun's son-in-law Thomas G. Clemson wrote from Europe, even before the great speech of March 16, that "The position which you have taken . . . has given you a most prominent position on this side of the Atlantic." "The papers in England,"

---

[5] Richmond, Va., *Enquirer*, March 20, 1846, p. 4.

[6] Baltimore, Md., *American & Commercial Daily Advertiser*, March 17, 1846, p. 2.

[7] New York, N.Y., *Herald*, March 19, 1846, p. 3.

[8] Gadsden to Duff Green, November 20, 1845, ALS in NcU, Duff Green Papers (published microfilm, roll 6, frames 213–216).

he added, "as well as the continent have been filled with your name, and if you were in England there is no doubt but that you could arrange the matter with the greatest ease."[9]

But similar sentiments were expressed also by enemies and neutrals. The public and private praise for Calhoun was more widespread and reverent than he had ever experienced, perhaps. A friend wrote Charles Sumner in Boston that his fear of war with England had lessened because Calhoun was to return to the Senate.[10] James Henry Hammond, whose diary for several years previous had been filled with bitter criticism of Calhoun, recorded:

> Calhoun has taken a noble stand. . . . He at once declared himself for peace & breasted the popular current. I . . . really feel as though I may have in my thoughts done injustice to him as a man of firmness & lofty principle. If he goes through this without flinching I shall rank his *qualities* far higher than I have done.[11]

Early in the Senate deliberations the Whig Washington *Daily National Intelligencer* said:

> The recent movements in the Senate of the United States have produced a most cheering effect. In the stand which Mr. Calhoun has taken I am most agreeably disappointed. . . . You can hardly be made to imagine the effect which his resolutions [of 12/30/1845], and the remarks which accompanied them, have already produced . . . .[12]

The Democratic Richmond *Enquirer's* reporter wrote, during the course of the Senate maneuvering against the expansionists: "Mr. Calhoun's views appear to me to be most proper." The *Enquirer* two weeks later editorialized that "we may congratulate the country upon having Mr. Calhoun in the Senate at such an important crisis. He is equal to any emergency and will exert his great talents and influence to bring about a pacific and honorable adjustment of the Oregon difficulty."[13]

The London *Times* complimented Calhoun's major speech: "Mr. Calhoun's declarations were eminently pacific and courageous."[14] The Boston *Post* even made for its readers a joke out of Calhoun's

[9] From Thomas G. Clemson, February 25, 1846, herein.
[10] Jacob Harvey to Sumner, November 22, 1845, ALS in Harvard University Library.
[11] Diary entry of February 14, 1846, in DLC, James Henry Hammond Papers.
[12] Washington, D.C., *Daily National Intelligencer*, January 5, 1846, p. 3.
[13] Richmond, Va., *Enquirer*, January 16, 1846, p. 2, and January 29, 1846, p. 4.
[14] London, England, *Times*, April 11, 1846, p. 4.

current celebrity, by presenting the following "conundrum": "Why is the course pursued by Mr. Calhoun on the Oregon question, like Oregon itself? Because it borders on the *Pacific*."[15]

Calhoun won the acquiescence of the Whigs and the support of many Democrats, but his actions were by no means expedient and designed solely for popularity since he lost ground with many in the party. For instance, a New York Democratic leader had written before Calhoun's public stand:

> Calhoun, who is worth at least two hundred and fifty thousand Polks, is in the Senate once more and if I am not blind to the signs of the times he will make his enemies find their due level before spring melts into summer. He is undoubtedly the strongest man in New York just now and if he does not step wrong on Oregon—which his noble statesmanship renders all but impossible he will be our next President. . . . Two years ago Gov. [Silas] Wright laughed at the idea of Calhoun becoming more popular than himself in this state. He now admits it for an already established fact.[16]

The expansionist who wrote this in late 1845 could not have been pleased with the anti-Polk course that Calhoun took after his arrival in Congress. A Philadelphia reporter gave the following account, suggesting that Calhoun's stand was hardly expedient:

> When Mr. Calhoun reached the city at the commencement of the present session, resistance to the "notice" as recommended by the President, seemed utterly hopeless. A devoted friend of Mr. Calhoun, who knew his determination to oppose it at all hazards, endeavored to impress on him the propriety of a cautious policy, as political rivals would not fail to improve any opportunity of placing him in an unfavorable position before the country, and added that an object was sometimes reached more safely and more certainly by approaching it otherwise than by a direct line. Mr. Calhoun replied, that in consenting to his election to the Senate he had sacrificed his own ease and convenience to what was deemed by many of his friends a public necessity. He would do this regardless of the consequences to himself; and as to his manner of doing it, win or fail, he would approach his object *direct*.[17]

Perhaps the most eloquent tribute to Calhoun's Oregon stand was made by Parke Godwin of the New York *Evening Post*, a member of the reformist wing of the New York Democrats who found Calhoun

[15] Boston, Mass., *Post*, January 27, 1846, p. 1.

[16] J.M. Storms to Mirabeau B. Lamar, undated but *ca.* November, 1845, in *The Papers of Mirabeau Buonaparte Lamar, Edited from the Original Papers in the Texas State Library*, 6 vols. (Austin: A.C. Baldwin, 1921–1927), 4:109.

[17] Philadelphia, Pa., *News* of unknown date as reprinted in the Alexandria, Va., *Gazette and Virginia Advertiser*, April 22, 1846, p. 2.

increasingly uncongenial. Godwin wrote Calhoun after the March 16 oration: "Your speech in favour of Peace, as honourable in its sentiments, to your heart, as the masterly policy it discloses is to your head, has produced a fine and profound impression . . . . Every word of it should be, not fram[e]d in letters of gold, but written on the hearts of the people, which is much better."[18]

To the West

The Union faced, besides Oregon, other large questions in which Calhoun would necessarily play a significant role. Armed conflict with Mexico would break out in the month following this volume's end. The Polk administration had already sent the Slidell mission to Mexico and issued orders anticipating the take-over of California by the Americans there, although this was not public knowledge, and in January had ordered Zachary Taylor's little army to the Rio Grande. Mexico does not appear prominently in the documents of this volume, nor does the outbreak of free soil conflict which followed hostilities. Also, the spring and summer of 1846 would see major actions in regard to the tariff in both Great Britain and the United States, which would help allay the Oregon tensions, but this subject does not loom large in this volume.

A question that does loom large but is not brought to a climax is the perennial one of internal improvements. On this issue Calhoun was positioning himself to take a leading and constructive position. Omnibus rivers and harbors bills, aimed mainly at the Northwest, were to be under consideration in both houses of Congress. It was for this reason that Calhoun accepted the presidency of the great commercial convention held at Memphis in the fall. In his address to the convention on November 13 he laid the groundwork for a new approach to the question of internal improvements.

A memorial from a committee of the convention, headed by Charleston railroad president James Gadsden and including prominent developers from the Southwest, was transmitted to Congress. On February 3, 1846, Calhoun presented the memorial to the Senate and was appointed chairman of a select committee to consider its plea. Calhoun's public position was attacked by strict constructionists, and there was a good deal of public confusion as to what it was until his committee report appeared on June 26, after the close of this volume. The issues raised by Calhoun's initiative and the subsequent controversy will be discussed in the following volume of this

---

[18] From Parke Godwin, March 20, 1846, herein.

edition. (Though it is perhaps worth noting that at one point in his speech he predicted the future greatness of the then village of Atlanta.)

It was this issue that caused Calhoun to violate his customary refusal of public display and take a major trip to the Southwest. He intended to visit, as he had before, his son's plantation in Marengo County, Alabama. However, he let it be known that while in the West he would accept invitations to New Orleans and Mobile and would accept the presidency of and address the convention in Memphis.

It turned into a triumphal public tour which is very amply documented in this volume because it represents such a significant and unique event in Calhoun's public life. Everywhere he was received with great public attention and honor, without respect to party, as all the newspapers pointed out.

He addressed groups at Natchez, Vicksburg, and Montgomery, and traveled the course of the Mississippi twice from New Orleans to Memphis and back. At the convention itself he doubtless met and conferred with numerous prominent men from all over the South and Northwest. The South Carolina delegates included Calhoun's son Patrick, James Gadsden, William Henry Trescot, and the young James D.B. DeBow. Others: Augustus C. Dodge, soon to be one of the first United States Senators from Iowa; such Tennessee dignitaries as John Bell, Senator Ephraim H. Foster, and Governor James C. Jones; Governor Archibald Yell of Arkansas; prominent entrepreneurs from all over the Mississippi Valley; and such young Calhoun lieutenants as Shadrach Penn from St. Louis and Ellwood Fisher of Cincinnati. He was also invited to Tallahassee, Galveston, Jackson, St. Louis, Nashville, Louisville, and Cincinnati, but declined. But Calhoun saw and was seen by a large part of the Union he had never visited before nor would again.

The trip is well documented herein from contemporary sources. A young man who met Calhoun for the first time and accompanied him on the river voyage and during the convention left recollections of the event which, though not contemporary and in error on some details, give vivid impressions of Calhoun that are perhaps authentic enough:

> I was introduced to Mr. Calhoun early in the evening [when the steamboat landed at Vicksburg] and found him very gracious and so like common mortals in his manner and bearing that I soon felt at ease. . . . We all, young and old, found Mr. Calhoun so agreeable and companionable that we were constantly around him, listen-

ing to his interesting talk. . . . Yet he was not undignified, and his conversation was mainly of a serious character. . . . He entertained a group of us for two hours one day in explaining his principals [*sic*] of government. . . . It was a rare treat. I could not have believed it to be within the power of any man to so completely absorb the attention in a simple conversation on so dry a subject.

The account continues with the arrival at Memphis and events there:

A fleet of steamboats had come down the river a short distance, as an escort to our boat, with colors flying and drums beating, and filled with the reception committee . . . while the shore was lined for miles with interested spectators. . . . I stood near him [Calhoun] and watched him as he looked upon the scene. His emotion was quite visible, and he gave a feeling expression of his gratitude for the reception. . . . We landed and Mr. Calhoun was immediately escorted to the point for the meeting of the Convention. . . . A great crowd was in attendance and the desire to hear the great Carolinian was intense. He was escorted to the chair amid deafening applause. . . .[19]

Those who wish to see Calhoun only as a sectionalist and a dark figure fail to allow for the stature he had achieved as an elder statesman of the American Republic at this pregnant moment in its development. In his last few years he would become more and more out-of-step with the main currents, even in the South—would be a Cassandra warning of the portents of wrong turnings and future dreadful consequences. But at this moment he rode high.

A measure of the stature was indicated by William B. Lewis, a former member of Andrew Jackson's "Kitchen Cabinet." Asking Calhoun for a letter refuting misrepresentations that had been circulated about his views, Lewis wrote: "Genl. Jackson[']s letter and one from you are all I desire for the protection of my character and *memory*, when I am no more, as I know they will have more weight, in the estimation of posterity, than any thing *fifty Polks* tho' they should be all Presidents, can say against me."[20]

Or consider this toast to Calhoun at a meeting of Ohio Democrats: "John C. Calhoun, the Cerberus of the constitution—the deathless champion of rational liberty. Too proud to enter the political shambles to bargain for the Presidency, his name will be revered, so long as virtue finds a place in the vocabulary of mankind."[21]

---

[19] H.S. Fulkerson, *Random Recollections of Early Days in Mississippi* (Baton Rouge: Otto Claitor, 1937), pp. 62–63.

[20] From William B. Lewis, August 7, 1845, herein.

[21] Cincinnati, Ohio, *Daily Enquirer*, January 30, 1846, p. 2.

While the Oregon question was in development, Duff Green, who was as practical as Calhoun was idealistic, wrote his old friend and kinsman from the North that he was on the verge of "a triumph for yourself & for the country which will have a permanent influence for good. You have never occupied a more enviable position. The eyes of the world are upon you, the hopes of the country rest on you. Millions are prepared to speak your praise. . . ." However, Green had a warning also: "Not having mingled with the masses as I have done you cannot understand or appreciate the effect which the studied misrepresentation of your views and position . . . has on the public opinion of the North."[22]

The next month, after Calhoun's Oregon speech and the favorable reaction to it, Green wrote again:

> Yours was an appeal to the judgment[,] interests and sympathies of mankind. You have the great advantage that henceforth you are placed at the head of the great movement of the age [free trade and international comity]. You are the man of progress and represent the principle of peace, on which it rests. For the first time in your life you fill your true position and you should not forfeit it.[23]

A New Yorker, evidently a Whig, echoed Parke Godwin's sentiments at the same time, in testimony to Calhoun's standing in the opinion of many:

> Though a stranger to you, I have long known you in the public councils of the Republic as one of those rare and gifted ones who dare be independent, and permit me to add, dare be honest, amid the sycophancy and venality of a corrupt age and country. When I witness these traits of character, so rare in our public men, I cannot but admire them; and though I may differ in opinion on some matters of public policy, still I cannot but hold in high regard one who, I doubt not is conscientious & fearless in the discharge of his public duties—a sure reward sooner or later attaches to such.[24]

The same sentiment in regard to the statesmanlike rather than politician-like esteem that Calhoun held in the minds of many was stated more succinctly by a Kentuckian who wrote to Calhoun that "you form an item of our Moral Capital as a people."[25]

[22] From Duff Green, February 22, 1846, herein.
[23] From Duff Green, March 21, 1846, herein.
[24] From Charles S.J. Goodrich, March 28, 1846, herein.
[25] From Nathan Gaither, January 15, 1846, herein.

THE PAPERS

of

JOHN C. CALHOUN

▥

Volume XXII

JULY 1–SEPTEMBER 30
1845

◫

John C. Calhoun, a private citizen, spent the summer at Fort Hill contending with an unprecedented drought on the plantation and the serious illness of his wife. There was an occasional gratifying letter from members of a far-flung family, including the son who was a young Army officer in New Orleans and the daughter and son-in-law across the Atlantic.

Though he held no public office, Calhoun was a conspicuous public man, one looked to by many for leadership and watched by many others who feared his power to disrupt their agenda. He received frequent reports from across the Union—on the Albany politicians, who, of course, were up to their usual tricks of rule or ruin, and in regard to the Polk administration, which was sounding at times an uncertain and at times a too strident trumpet.

As always, there were the sub rosa slanders assiduously circulated (the stock-in-trade of the Van Burenites) about Calhoun's alleged clandestine manipulations. Those who lived by such could not believe that not everyone did. As Calhoun wrote on August 2: "I do not exercise the least control over the [Charleston] Mercury or any other paper. I leave them to take their own course, as I take mine. It is absurd for anyone, who reads the Mercury to suppose, that it speaks my opinion."

A truer statement of Calhoun's character and standing was given by William B. Lewis, once a member of Jackson's "Kitchen Cabinet" and not always a friend of Calhoun. On August 7 he wrote Calhoun for a testimonial against the slanders that had been used by Polk as a cover for his removal from the post he had long held in the Treasury Department: "Genl. Jackson[']s letter and one from you are all I desire for the protection of my character and memory, when I am no more, as I know they will have more weight, in the estimation of posterity, than any thing fifty Polks tho' they should be all Presidents, can say against me."

Among other public matters that caught the South Carolinian's attention were the division of the Methodist Church into Northern and Southern branches, the prospects for American and British tariff

3

reform, the Mexican and Oregon situations, and the increasing public and private pressure for him to return to the Senate when Congress convened again at the end of the year. Toward that, Calhoun said he was reluctant, but would, as always, do his duty when called upon by his State.

He was doubtless very pleased to receive the congratulations and thanks of the convention which ratified the federal Constitution on the part of the people of Texas, for his role in bringing that Republic into the Union. In his reply on August 12 Calhoun celebrated the triumph and the role that South Carolinians had played in creating Texas. The willing consent of the people of that Republic in giving up their independence to join the Union was, he said, "the highest eulogy ever pronounced in favour of our free, popular institutions."

The ex-Secretary of State was not so good a prophet as usual when he wrote on August 21 that he doubted there would be a war with Mexico. But he was not alone in this judgment. His successor in the State Department, the chief Cabinet officer of the administration that next year would be involved in such a war, James Buchanan, said the same thing in a letter written to Calhoun the very next day.

Calhoun was more concerned by the question of Oregon, and it was this that compelled him to consider re-entry into the Senate. On September 23 he wrote of President Polk's "crowning folly" in forcing the issue with Great Britain. "There are no alternatives left us, but to back out, & settle it by negotiation, or refer it [to arbitration], & fare worse, or to settle it by force. . . . I do not think the administration will have the courage or patriotism to back out [of their folly], & that whether we shall have war, or not, must depend on Congress, & especially the Senate."

In late September plans were afoot for the Calhouns—the statesman, his wife, and their son John—to make a trip to the West to visit son Andrew's plantation in Marengo County, Alabama. It would in fact turn out to be Calhoun's last and largest public journey.

▥

From [Lt.] P[ATRICK] CALHOUN

New-Orleans La., July 1st 1845

Dear Father, I have this moment received your letter dated the 24th of June, and as you desire an immediate answer, I write at once, although the change in the time of departure of the mail from this city will oblige me to make my letter shorter than I desire. Learning from the letter received from you sometime since that so many of your letters had miscarried, I caused search to be made for them in the Post-office, which however proved of no avail for as yet none have been discovered. My impression is that they are notwithstanding the result of the search that has been made, in the Post-office—for I have observed that a degree of carelessness, and want of proper courtesy exists amongst the underlings of the office, which is not at all consistent with its importance. The letters may yet be found.

You desire me to say what amount of funds I shall want in case my marriage [to Miss Kate Wilkins] should take place in the fall. Should nothing prevent I shall go to Pittsburgh early in the fall—but this may be prevented by the stage of the waters, or the sicklyness of the section through which I shall have to pass. As these circumstances cannot now be foreseen, it will be desirable for me to be prepared provided everything should prove favourable. I regret exceedingly that my necessities should oblige me to call upon you for any advance—knowing as I do that you are pressed to meet your engagements. From $800 to $1000 with the salary which I now draw, will furnish me with sufficient means for sometime to come. As for your giving the same portion which you did to brother Andrew [Pickens Calhoun] & Sister Anna [Maria Calhoun Clemson], I do not at all desire it at least for sometime—it had much better remain with you— for if I had it, I could under existing circumstances do nothing with it.

I am glad to hear that John [C. Calhoun, Jr.] and Jame[s Edward Calhoun] are with you—and that John looks so well—if he could only get rid of his cough it would be a source of great happiness to us all— for it would give assurance of continued good health.

No news has been received here since the meeting of the Texian Congress—it is daily expected. The movement of our Troops in Texas within a short period is looked upon as certain—although as yet no orders has been sent through Gen. [Edmund P.] Gaines to that affect. A messenger from Washington passed through her[e] a few days since—his instructions being of a secret nature, nothing definite has as yet transpired in regard to them. As it has been assertained that he went to Fort Jesup, it is supposed that he bears confidential instructions to Gen. [Zachary] Taylor. I would like if I had time, to give you a detailed account of the manoeuvering that is going on in Washington, in reference to the command of the Army to be sent in—but I fear my letter will be too late for the mail. Gen.

Gaines will not for the present go into Texas, unless there should be war between Mexico and this country.

We shall not from present appearances leave here before the middle of this month.

My love to all. I wrote to Sister Anna some days since and enclosed to the State Dep[artment for forwarding]. Your affectionate son, P. Calhoun.

ALS in ScU-SC, John C. Calhoun Papers.

From [Bvt. Maj. Gen.] EDMUND P. GAINES

New Orleans, July 2nd 1845

My dear Sir—In acknowledging the receipt of your letter to our young friend Captain P[atrick] Calhoun—who is with me, in excellent health, and who is all that I could desire my own son to be—I have to request your attention to the enclosed printed copies of two of my letters, one of the 31st of Jan[uar]y to Governor [Silas] Wright of New York, from whom I have received no reply, and the other to President [John] Tyler of the 14th of February, from whom I did not expect a reply. Manuscript copies of these letters were handed by me to our mutual friend Colonel [John F.H.] Claiborne Editor of the [New Orleans] Jeffersonian Republican, that he might avail himself of the contents to correct some misrepresentations of my views— and as I did not expressly forbid their publication, he deemed it proper to publish them. I send also for your perusal a well written article signed "*A Planter*"—together with my letter to Col. C[laiborne] of the [*blank space*] ult.

In respect to the *publication* of these letters I have to remark that although I have never in time of profound peace hesitated to give publicity to my views upon the new aspect of the science of war which the application of Steam power to ships of war and Rail Roads has given to every operation connected with the attack and defence of seaports—in order that they might pass freely for as much, or as little as they were worth—in the hope that the remnant of the experienced men of the war of 1812 to 1815 might follow my example and give publicity to their views—and thus settle the question whether the discoveries of [Robert] Fulton & [Oliver] Evans did not present *a new principle—requiring new means of defence?* I have never thought it proper to publish anything calculated to expose the

6

weakness of our means of defence, when there appeared to be, as now, even a speck of war menacing us. Nor have I ever authorised any such publication even in time of Peace when there was no appearance of disturbance, except when it appeared necessary and proper to sustain my views previously submitted to and in some cases published by the proper authorities of the Government, as the public documents will testify.

In reference to the quotations of the 1st number of "A Planter" from the report of the Honorable William Wilkins late Secretary of War, of November last, I have only to say that however anxious I am to see a sufficient force of U.S. war Steamers to enable us with our present Forts, with such other small Forts & Martello towers as may be necessary to lock up our sea ports upon the Gulf of Mexico, I have never approved or recommended any attempt to have upon the ocean any naval force *in war*—until all our principal seaport towns are secured by small Forts and Martello towers, with Floating Batteries of oak and Iron—principally of Iron—propelled by Steam power, and convertible at any moment into war Steamers for the naval service upon the broad ocean as soon as our sea Port towns are placed in a sure state of defence. (See enclosure D herewith.)

The Ships and Steam Boats always to be found in this Harbour will enable us to provide a temporary supply of Floating Batteries to cooperate with our Forts upon this river in arresting for a time, or repelling any war Steamers that would probably be sent against this city—provided we have a few weeks notice, and are supplied with means and men to do the work. Two merchant Ships placed side by side, and secured together by heavy timbers, bearing a Platform, with a few heavy pieces of Cannon will make a tolerably formidable Floating Battery, to be propelled by one or two good Steam Boats. Twenty such Floating Batteries to cooperate with Forts Jackson and St. Philip, with a few large Rafts of timber anchored between the two Forts—with the Floating Batteries operating above the rafts towed by some of the best of our Steam Boats, would add five hundred percent to our strength and ability to destroy the Enemy[']s Fleet at that point. And wherever we can check the approach of their Fleets & force them to seperate their land and naval forces, at the distance of 50 to 70 miles, we shall every where be safe as they will not willingly venture to attack any place without a combined effort of their land and naval strength.

Hence it is that I consider the whole western frontier as perfectly secure, watched as it will be by western Riflemen under such men as [Henry] Dodge and [Samuel] Houston and others, who will follow the example of [Andrew] Jackson and [Isaac] Shelby and [Richard M.] Johnson & [William] Carroll & [John] Coffee and hundreds of others that I might name. Indeed I consider this city at least *ten thousand times* more important, more vital—and more vulnerable in a military point of view than ["every" *canceled*] all the western Posts from Lake Superior to the Sabine ["together" *interlined*]. *They* need no preparation but what they can receive in two or three days. Whereas this city assailable as it is by war Steamers, with its 300 millions of dollars worth of money and property ["together" *interlined*] with near a quarter of a mil[l]ion of helpless men[,] women & children (including all colours in the city & upon the sugar plantations) would be constantly in jeopardy ["with" *changed to* "without"] means of defence such as I propose.

Some say "let us sink obstructions in the River and in this way prevent the approach of an Enemy's Fleet"—I reply that this river is from 25 to 70 feet deep—generally 45 to 50 feet deep the greater part of the way from the city to the Balize—near 100 miles—and from 600 to 800 yards wide—with a bottom consisting of soft mud & quicksands. If every merchant vessel in America were employed to bring Granite rocks to any section of this river—say to that section between Forts Jackson & St. Philip and all to be discharged in the river at or as near one place as possible, it is doubtful whether any thing like a permanent obstruction would be formed—because the rock would much of it sink in the mud and quicksands—and even if it did not sink, it would force the water to break through the bank on either side and ["form" *interlined*] a new channel, long before the mass of rock would be brought near enough to the surface of the water to constitute any permanent obstruction. Hence I contend that we must have Floating Defences to cooperate with our Forts. I object to none of our Forts except the large ones, such as Monroe and Adams. Fort Calhoun is too large, but as it is judiciously built in an important Position where it will be useful, aided as it ought to be by Floating Batteries, I would not lessen its dimentions. Mrs. [Myra Whitney] Gaines unites with me in affectionate respects to Mrs. [Floride Colhoun] Calhoun and your family. We shall all go to the sea board in two weeks—say to the Pass Christian or the Bay of Biloxi. With the truest regard your friend, Edmund P. Gaines.

[Marginal P.S.] Enclosures marked A, B, C, & D.

ALS in ScCleA. NOTE: Gaines's Ens have not been found.

From Anna [Maria Calhoun Clemson]

Brussels, July 4th 1845
My dear father, We returned to this place day before yesterday, after having spent three or four weeks in Paris, which was agreeable enough, tho' the noise, & heat, were rather unpleasant. The fact is, after nearly a year[']s residence in towns, my wild nature, (of which all we Americans have more or less,) longs for the quiet, & repose, of the country, but that, strange as it may sound, is unattainable, either in this country, or France. Unless you have a chateau of your own or somebody else to go to, as I said before, for human nature could not stand the discomforts of "country lodgings," in either of those countries, & a small village is no better, but if Mr. [Thomas G.] Clemson receives no instructions from the [State] Department, about his treaty, we shall probably go, for a little while, to Blankenberg, a small town on the seaside, much frequented for sea bathing, very quiet, & very cheap, they tell us.

While in Paris we saw a great deal of Mr. [William R.] King, who was very kind & attentive, as he always is, indeed shows really a friendship for us. He desired me, when I wrote, to remember him kindly to mother [Floride Colhoun Calhoun], & yourself, & tell you he hoped to see you in America before two years, as he longed to get back, but if I tell you my own private opinion, it is that is is [*sic*] very much pleased with his position, & will stay there as long as he is permitted, or can afford, which last however will not be very long, unless cotton gets higher, for he told me he spent at least $6000 more than his pay. He lives very well, & entertains handsomely, & is much liked. Paris is full of Americans. There are at least 400, I was told, for I avoided making acquaintances. From what I hear, they do us no credit in any way, & what is worse, many of them have the bad taste, to say nothing ["more," *interlined*] to abuse their country, & lament being born Americans; for my part I lament they were. I was very indignant at some of the speeches I heard of, & only wish there was some law by which they could be punished. They are a pack of people who having made their money easily, or *dirtily*, come to Europe & tag themselves on to the fag end of society, strain every nerve to keep themselves even on its outskirts, & submit to all kinds of ridicule, & contempt, & having spent the money which would have given them respectability, & competency, for life, rightly used, in their own country, retire in disgrace, & either live in garrets in Paris, or return to America, to be miserable. And miserable they deserve to be. There are some exceptions to all this, I am happy to say, & I was

9

quite pleased with one gentleman whose acquaintance we made. He was a Mr. [George] Sumner of Boston, quite a young man in appearance. He has been travelling in Europe, & Africa, for five years, & tho', I should judge, not a talented man, has amassed a quantity of information, which is surprising, & withal, has seen other countries, without despising his own, but I fear there are but few who travel abroad, who do credit to themselves or their country. But enough of them.

You see, by the papers, that our little kingdom of Belgium, is in the midst of, what they call here, "a ministerial crisis." The two parties here, the catholics, & the liberals, are pretty evenly balanced, & *consequently* hate one another bitterly. The late elections went so entirely against the present ministers, that Mr. [Jean Baptiste] Nothomb, (Minister of the Interior,) who was made the scape goat, was forced to resign, & his place there seems some difficulty in filling, to the satisfaction of all parties. In the meantime the King [Leopold I], thinking I suppose it is very little to him, how the matter is settled, has gone frolicking to England, that great visiting ground ["for the crowned heads" *interlined*] of Europe, & leaves his good subjects, to settle the matter as it may be. Some say he has gone for counsel, but I doubt if he cares one iota about the matter. He seems to consider himself a mere state puppet, (as he is,) & acts accordingly; and being, I should suppose, a very indolent man, tho' quite sensible, & well read, seems to like playing king, without any of the responsibilities, or labour of the position, very well. Besides there is no sympathy between him & the Belgians. He is a Protestant, while this is perhaps the most priest ridden country in Europe, & altho' he is permitted to exercise his religion, he is forced to bring up his children catholics. But Mr. C[lemson] gives you all the politics, & I only let this go, to show you that I try to learn & understand something that is going on around me. You know you always liked me to do so, & it is my great pleasure, now that I am so far from you, to recal[l] your ideas & wishes, & conform to them. Oh! if I could only see you for one hour. I was made quite happy, for the time, by the idea that you might come to England, & Mr. Clemson & myself were anticipating the pleasure we should have, in showing you everything worth seeing.

Mr. Clemson & the children [John Calhoun Clemson and Floride Elizabeth Clemson] were all a little indisposed while in Paris, which hastened our departure, but fortunately it has all passed over, & was I think caused by the sudden commencement of hot weather, before one was prepared for it. Mr. C[lemson] gave me quite a fright.

We were walking after dinner, when he suddenly became very faint, & I could hardly get him into a cafe; he came near falling in the street. There it was as much as we could do, to keep him from fainting, by giving him brandy, bathing him with Cologne, &c &c & you may imagine how I felt, speaking french as badly as I do, but I contrived to get him home in a carriage, & tho' feeling badly for a few days, he had no similar attack, & is now as well as usual. He worries himself too much about money matters. He says he sees no possibility of living on what we have, with the present prices of cotton, & makes himself miserable about what he shall do when he leaves here, & the future prospects of his children. Without letting him know I have said this, (for he may blame me for troubling you,) give him advice as ["to" *interlined*] what he had better do, & comfort him all you can, for it worries me to see him so unhappy, as he is, & he often says "if your father being on the spot, would freely give me his ideas, about my position, I should feel better satisfied." He has great confidence in your judgment, & would be relieved by having your opinion. He is such a devoted husband & father, that he can[']t bear the idea that we should want for anything, & frets himself by anticipation, of the arrival of the time, when we may.

Mr. C[lemson] scolds me for writing double letters for he says now you have the postage to pay, we should not do so, therefore I shall not begin another sheet, tho' it is as difficult for me to stop writing, as talking when I once begin. Much love to mother & sister [Martha Cornelia Calhoun] & Willy [William Lowndes Calhoun] & any of the rest of the family who may be at home & do write *me* sometimes. I wrote mother, sister, & John [C. Calhoun, Jr.] from Paris. Mr. Clemson desires love to all & the children send kisses. Your devoted daughter, Anna.

ALS in ScCleA. NOTE: George Sumner (1817–1863) was a younger brother of the more famous Charles Sumner and spent the years 1837–1852 abroad.

From JOHN CARROLL WALSH

The Mound, Harford Co[unty,] Md., 5th July 1845
My dear Sir, The Editor of the "American Farmer" [Samuel Sands] having sent me several extra Nos. of his publication (the 1st No. of the new series) and it containing an article in reference to your estate I have sent you one presuming it might be acceptable, with it I also transmit you a little pamphlet containing the Charter[,] Con-

stitution and By Laws of an Insurance Company which we have had for some time in operation in this and the adjoining County, an Institution admirably adapted to a farming or planting district affording them a safe and economical mode of insurance against loss by fire. You will observe the note given by the insured as the premium of Insurance answers the same purpose as the Cash premium paid to the City offices, and unless the Company meets with a ["heavy" *interlined*] loss the giver of the note has the interest alone to pay. For example, the last two years I have had my property insured in the Company [*one word altered to* "for"] which I gave my premium note for $50—am[oun]t insured on different buildings about $3000— and as we have met with but one loss and that a trifling one which the Company paid without levying any Contribution on the members as there was funds sufficient arising from interest to meet the loss I have had to pay but $6—for insurance for 2 years on property insured for near $3000. If you should deem the system worthy of being introduced into your neighborhood it would afford me pleasure to impart any information in regard to it you may request. With high respect and esteem faithfully Yours &, Jno. Carroll Walsh.

ALS in ScCleA.

To J[AMES] H. HAMMOND, Silverton, Barnwell District, S.C.

Fort Hill, 7th July 1845

My dear Sir, You are now so fairly enlisted, & with so much eclat, as the defender of the institutions of the South against the assaults of the abolition[ist]s, that you will not be permitted to sheath your sword. The object of this communication is to call on you to strike another blow in the cause.

I know not whether you have seen & read the Rev[eren]d Dr. [Henry B.] Bascom's Review of the Manifesto of the Majority. It is a very able production, & fully vindicates the course of the Southern portion of the Methodist Charge, in seperating from the Northern portion. The step is a very important one in a political, as well as in a religious view of the subject. It seems to me, it is very important that the publick attention should be called to Dr. Bascom's Review, and that the praise, which he and his associates, & the whole of the Southern portion of the Methodist Church ["are so well entitled to" *interlined*] for their conduct, in this important affair, should be liberally bestowed on them.

It seems to me, also, that, for that purpose, due notice ought to be taken of the work in our papers, to be followed by an article, of which it should be the subject, in the Southern Review.

There is none more competent to the task than yourself; and I do hope you will not decline it. As you may not have seen the production, I send you a copy for your use, which I received from Tho[mas] B. Stevenson of Frankfort[,] Kentucky. I have acknowledged the receipt of it in a note, in which I expressed, in strong terms, my approbation of the production, and the obligation, which the South was under to the Doctor for it. It accompanies the Mail, which takes this. With great respect yours truly, J.C. Calhoun.

[P.S.] I would not have taken the liberty of asking your attention to the subject, if my leisure had not been engrossed my [*sic*] another subject. J.C.C.

ALS in DLC, James Henry Hammond Papers; PEx in Jameson, ed., *Correspondence*, p. 666.

To THO[MA]S B. STEVENSON, [Frankfort, Ky.]

Fort Hill, July 7th, 1845

Dear Sir: I am under much obligation to you for the copy of the Rev. Dr. [Henry B.] Bascom's Review of the Manifesto of the Majority, which you were so kind as to send me through the Rev. Mr. [William M.] Wightman, of Charleston.

I have read it with much attention and a great deal of pleasure. It is in every respect very ably executed, both as to matter and manner; and is a full and triumphant vindication of the course adopted by the Southern portion of the Methodist Church. Their conduct throughout the whole affair, was such as became patriots and Christians.

Dr. Bascom has displayed the talent and information, not only of an able Divine and Logician, but also of an able Statesman and profound Philosopher. I regard it, taken as a whole, the ablest production which has yet appeared against that fanatical agitation of the subject of Abolition, which exists at the North and North-West, and which threatens both Church and State with so much mischief. The whole Union, but more especially the South, is indebted to him for his clear and full exposition of its character, tendency and object. With great respect, I am, &c. &c., J.C. Calhoun.

PC in the Nashville, Tenn., *Whig*, August 26, 1845, p. 2; PC in the Nashville, Tenn., *Union*, August 28, 1845, p. 2; PC in the New Orleans, La., *Bee*, September 4, 1845, p. 1; PC in the Tuscaloosa, Ala., *Independent Monitor*, September 10, 1845, p. 3; PC in the Washington, D.C., *Constitution*, September 25, 1845, p. 3; PC (from the Huntsville, Ala., *Democrat* of September 10, 1845) in "Documents. 1. John C. Calhoun on the Division of the Methodist Church in 1844," in *Gulf States Historical Magazine*, vol. I, no. 3 (November, 1902), p. 212; variant PC in the Lexington, Ky., *Observer and Reporter*, August 27, 1845. NOTE: Bascom had published *Methodism and Slavery; with Other Matter in Controversy between the North and the South; Being a Review of the Manifesto of the Majority in Reply to the Protest of the Minority of the Late General Conference of the Methodist Episcopal Church, in the Case of Bishop Andrew* (Frankfort, Ky.: Hodges, Todd & Pruett, 1845). Bascom, a native of N.Y., was president of Transylvania University during 1842–1849 and in 1849 was elected bishop in the Methodist Episcopal Church South.

From SAM[UE]L C. DONALDSON

Baltimore, July 8th, 1845

Sir, My impression is, that you made two speeches in the Senate upon the Tariff of 1842, and also two upon the Oregon question. In the volume of your selected Speeches only one ["speeche" *altered to* "speech"] upon each question is given. It is my practice to collect all the more valuable political documents & speeches, and to bind them for the purpose of permanent preservation. Particularly do I wish to make my collection of your speeches as full as possible. Will you, therefore, pardon me for the liberty I take in requesting you to send me a copy of the pamphlet edition of each of the above-named speeches, if you have any spare copies of them?

I remember with great pleasure and satisfaction an evening passed with you in Washington in the latter part of November. That conversation confirmed me in those Free Trade & State Rights principles which I had already imbibed from your writings. But you saw such large numbers of persons in Washington in the same way, that it would be too much to expect that you should retain any memory of such an humble person as myself. It is nevertheless a pleasure to me to refer to it.

In common with most of your numerous admirers, especially among the *young men* of the South, I hope to see you once more in the Senate. The addition of six Senators to the Republican ranks

14

from Texas, Florida, & Iowa, will probably insure the repeal of the Tariff. And who so well fitted as yourself to lead off in the great work of forming a strictly Revenue Tariff, and in establishing "Free trade and low duties" as the permanent policy of the Government? I have always wished to see you the President of this Confederacy, not so much for your own sake (for the cares of the office far outweigh any gratifications it can give)—but for the sake of the Union, that the Government might be put upon the right track, & receive an impulse in the right direction which it would hold for a long time.

Please excuse the liberty I have taken in addressing you, and believe me With sentiments of admiration and esteem, yours &c, Sam'l C. Donaldson.

[P.S.] I send you a pamphlet publication of our [Maryland] Historical Society—the "Journal of Charles Carroll," which I hope you may find worthy of your perusal.

ALS in ScCleA.

From Tho[mas] J. Rusk

Convention Hall
Austin, Republic of Texas
July 8th 1845

Dear Sir, It affords me great pleasure to transmit to you the en-[c]losed copy of a Resolution unanimously adopted by the Convention of the people of Texas now in session. The stand taken by President [John] Tyler and his cabinet upon this question has brought it to a speedy termination—secured to him and to each member of his cabinet the lasting gratitude of the people of Texas, and will entitle them to occupy a bright page in the history of a transaction vitally effecting the interests of the two countries, as well as the great cause of Republican Government. I have the honor to be with the highest respect Your obedient servant, Tho. J. Rusk, President of the Convention.

[Enclosure]
Resolution Expressive of the gratitude of this Convention to
Ex[-]President Tyler and his Cabinet.

Resolved, That the early & resolute stand taken by John Tyler whilst he was President of the United States to restore Texas to the bosom of the Republican family, has secured to him the gratitude & veneration of the people of Texas.

15

Resolved, That the like sentiments are due to the assistance afforded Mr. Tyler by the able members of his cabinet, who with a noble enthusiasm espoused the cause of annexation as a national question, and cooperated faithfully in securing its consummation by the passage of the law which has enable[d] the people of Texas to become a portion of the Union.

Resolved, That the President of this convention be directed to furnish a certified copy of these Resolutions to Mr. Tyler, and to each of the members of his cabinet, the Hon. John C. Calhoun, George M. Bibb, W[illia]m Wilkins[,] John Y. Mason[,] John Nelson[,] Charles A. Wickliffe, and to the families of A[bel] P. Upshur & Geo. [*sic*; Thomas] W. Gilmer deceased.

Adopted, at Austin Texas[,] July 8th 1845.

Attest Tho[mas] J. Rusk, President, Ja[me]s H. Raymond, Sec[retar]y of the Convention.

LS with En in ScCleA; variant PC of En in *Journals of the Convention, Assembled at the City of Austin . . . for the Purpose of Framing a Constitution for the State of Texas* (Austin: Miner & Cruger, Printers to the Convention, 1845), pp. 23–24; variant PC of En in "Convention of Texas, 1845," *William and Mary Quarterly*, 1st series, vol. XV, no. 1 (July, 1906), pp. 41–42. NOTE: An AEU by Calhoun reads "1845, Gen[era]l Rusk's letter covering the resolution of the Texian Convention approbating of the course of the late President & his Cabinet in reference to annexation ["&" *canceled and* "with" *interlined*] a copy of my answer."

From THO[MA]S G. CLEMSON

Brussels, July 10th 1845

My dear Sir, Your favour to Anna dated Fort Hill[,] May 22nd came to hand by the Cambria. She had just written you. We were very much pleased that you all got through so easily with the measles which appeared to be epidemic when you wrote. I hope my people on the Cane Brake will not be troubled.

Your letter was very satisfactory, and explained your position and many things which we did not know. To me Mr. [James K.] Polk[']s course has been incomprehensible. How he could have permitted you to leave Washington is to the world incomprehensible, and that act has been censured universally by foreigners and Americans so far as I can hear. Then his remarks upon the Oregon. It appears such a commencement as he has made, foretells a rugged path for the next four years.

I regretted of course that you could not come to England, on an extraordinary mission[;] tho I never thought it probable still it would have been agre[e]able to have seen you on this side of the Atlantic. Mr. [Francis W.] Pickens should have come if it was possible for, it is absolutely necessary that we should have some one from the South in London. He has wealth & could have spent $1,000 a year more than the government allowance which would have enabled him to live decently, which the government pay does not, as you are well aware of. I hope Mr. [Louis] McLane [new U.S. Minister to Great Britain] may be as orthodox on the negro question as is desirable. I know little of his history or views. He has the reputation of being able and Southeren [sic] in his feelings.

Mr. [James] Buchanan has been at the head of the Department of State better than four months and the only official letter received from him was that notifying me of his appointment as Sec[re]t[ar]y of State. I do not know what is doing at home but we are all in the Wind abroad. Our foreign relations whilst you were at the helm were exceedingly active, and we were all working with effect which has told well, but really we are fast falling into perfect inactivity for want of direction. Mr. Polk appears to be spending his ammunition pretty rapidly, for he has made a great number of appointments in a short time and that course will not satisfy those that want office. I was under the impression that the [Martin] Van Buren party were broken up, but the course that has been pursued by the administration, [indicates] that if such be the case, it is is [sic] only in name. Mr. [George M.] Dallas & Buchanan will kill themselves in Pen[n]-s[ylvani]a and that will be the end of them. Mr. B[uchanan] committed a great error, for himself, in quitting the senate. He will not add to his reputation where he is, and his course during the last canvass has made his best friends afraid of him.

New York will try to make a candidate of Mr. [Silas] Wright, but his being identified with the old hunkers, will prevent his having the weight which he has had heretofore. You are decidedly the strongest man in the Countrey; those that I have heard speak of you say that your friends did you great harm in the last canvass and [Robert Barnwell] Rhett among others is by far the most censured. I feel pretty confident of two things[;] the first is that you [c]an not add to your reputation by going into the senate, and think your position at Fort Hill more elligible than it would be from the senate. If your friends stake themselves on you, and up to the last refuse all communication with others about availability[,] you can be elected by the most triumphant majority, that ever man carried to the presidency. But if there is any talk about availability so sure as you start you are beaten. A few leading men in the different States out of South Carolina that act as I say will whip every clique into your support. There must be no shivering[?], or talk with any other party about men.

My impression is that [Secretary of the Treasury Robert J.] Walker is the man that has had most to do with Mr. Polk. He has a desire to play a part in the next canvass either as principal or second. If he be vice president it will be on the ticket with Wright, and he is courting that party. My impressions are taken from the position of things & not from individuals. From what I have said Walker is politically opposed to you.

The weather here is now quite cool, but we have had some very warm days but owing to the changes the hot weather is very oppressive. Either my long residence in the South or old age has made me very sensitive to cold or I may say the extremes of either. This climate is of all others the most changeable, and humid that I know. The countrey is delightful when the sun shines, the verdure is very green and like all grass countreys it has an agre[e]able aspect.

Both Anna and the children [John Calhoun Clemson and Floride Elizabeth Clemson] are well. We are for the moment at a [*ms. torn; one word illegible*] but propose going to Blankenburg [*sic;* Blankenberghe] on the channel distant about half a day['] s travel from Brussels.

The Elections in Belgium that have just taken place has brought about a change in the ministry. The Cabinet with out exception offered their resignations; that of Mr. [Jean Baptiste] Nothomb the Minister of the Interior and the leader of the Cabinet, was immediately accepted by the King [Leopold I]. After some vain efforts to constitute another cabinet the King went to England where he is at present. On his return he will probably succeed in the formation of a ministry composed of the two parties[,] the liberals and clergy[,] each of which claim a majority. It is believed however if the chambers were dissolved that a decided liberal majority would be elected. You perceive that the Jesuits have been broken up in France & I suppose that Belgium[,] Spain and Italy will have each of them, an augmentation, from that cause.

I know of nothing new.

My love to all the family. Your affectionate son, Thos. G. Clemson.

[*Added in the hand of Anna Maria Calhoun Clemson:*]

Dear father, Do make John [C. Calhoun, Jr.] write me the price of board in the village say at Mrs. [Frances] Lorton's per month or per year with some *statistics* about the price of provisions &c &c in Pendleton. I want them for a purpose I have no room to explain at present but will in one of my letters. Let him give me the price of a good riding horse & anything else he chooses of the kind.

All quite well. I wrote you by this steamer & have nothing more new to say except what is not knew [*sic*] that I love you all dearly & am crazy to see you. Love to all. Your devoted daughter, Anna Clemson.

ALS in ScCleA.

From LEWIS S. CORYELL

Washington, 10th July 1845

My dear Sir, I have been here for 3 days. To give you an outline of matters & things that is now characterized among the Political parties, and Poeple [*sic*] generally is more than time or paper will admit of—Suffice it—Things begin here to react, & with a Violence I had not dreamed of. No doubt [James K.] Polk is not dissatisfied with the departure of the old —— [Andrew Jackson] who was so easily approached by the bad as well as good men, and any cast of Letter obtained that was desired or required. [James] Buchanan[']s Penn-[sylvani]a friends (even) have fell from him, and he is in a very excited state for him to be. He goes on the *Bench*. [Robert J.] Walker [Secretary of the Treasury] is the master spirit & [William L.] Marcy [Secretary of War] unites in his plans. [George] Bancroft [Secretary of the Navy] is satisfied with the prospect that his Report will be more chast[e]ly written than any of the rest. Cave [Johnson] will have to have mills coined to give him a coin comessurate [*sic*] with his circumscribed Views, but to do him Justice he is a better P[ost] M[aster] Gen[era]l than I expected he w[ould] be. [John Y.] Mason [Attorney General] is more firmly a man than many others & to him I talked freely yesterday, but I am worrying you about matters of no importance as you are in your Views far in advance of all I have al[l]uded to. I have from my intimacy with [John P.] Heiss obtained and now enclose what perhaps you may no[t] see in any other way, before the resur[*ms. torn; one or two words missing*] Stone walls, a part of the Depositary [*ms. torn; a few words missing*] in the corner Stone of "Jackson Ha[*ms. torn; a few words missing*]

Tamm[a]ny Juni[or] of this place [*ms. torn; a few words missing*] to ask the favor that you will keep it strictly secret until you have ["it" *interlined*] from another, ["if ever"(?) *canceled*] source. It is too bad to say to you that the cabinet was present (except Mason & Polk) and shouted loudly as [James] Shields' Oration touch[e]d the strings. *So we go.*

The speech of [John C.] Rives was sent to the [Washington] Union to be published, but [Thomas] Ritchie & Polk arrested it (what dunces) and before the Type was distributed this & a few more copies was had.

There is trouble here. The cabinet have sat 6 hours a day ever since my ar[r]ival. There is much allusion to your diplomacy ["which" *interlined*] none now condemn & all applaud. McLean [*sic*; Louis McLane] gives great dissatisfaction to the [Martin] V[a]n B[ure]n men, and I am pained to say that Mr. Polk has been very unfortunate in his appointments so far as making friends is considered, for all seem dissatisfied. Yet I pity more than blame him, after seeing those extracts from the Old ——— letters which explains much & shows what a malicious old ——— he was to the end. You are daily triumphing in your retirement leaving them to their troubles. Penn[sylvani]a['s] Leg[islatur]e will be anti Polk [and] so [will] New York next winter. Then they will begin to feel desirous for the association of friends of strength. I have written you in much haste not caring as I expect & rely that tis for your own eye. I leave for New Hope [Pa.] in a day or two. When you choose write me. Sincerely your friend, Lewis S. Coryell.

ALS in ScCleA. NOTE: The proceedings described by Coryell involved the laying of the cornerstone of "Jackson Hall," which was to be a Democratic headquarters in Washington. This occurred on July 4 and is reported in the Washington, D.C., *Union*, July 7, 1845, p. 3. The chief orator was James Shields of Ill., just appointed Commissioner of the U.S. General Land Office.

From W[ILLIAM] A. HARRIS

Washington, 11 July 1845

My Dear Sir: I have been postponing for three months past, the purpose of writing to you; hoping each day, that I might have some striking fact to communicate, worthy of your special notice. I shall, in as few words as possible, endeavor to put you in possession of such facts and inferences, as I may think will be of some interest to you.

In the first place then, I have seen nothing in the course or conduct of Mr. Polk, public or private, that changes in the least my opinion of him, somewhat warmly expressed to you, before you left; but, on the contrary, much to confirm it. In a single word, he is not equal to the station; and, it will operate forever hereafter, as a caution to us, to compromise ["on any" *canceled and* "on no" *interlined*] second or third rate man for the presidency. A second rate man might indeed do, if ["he" *interlined*] were thoroughly honest and disinterested—free from prejudice and that little ambition which attaches itself to small minds in such a situation, of desiring to be thought above the reach of even Cabinet influence. Such persons most probably at once pass under some other influence less worthy to be trusted. These remarks find a practical application in the present head of our national affairs.

The policy of the President seems to be to forget his friends and buy up his enemies. Hence [Thomas H.] Benton, [Francis P.] Blair, and the New York regency can command any thing. I say so, because they have done it. The [Martin] Van Buren-[Silas] Wright men got every thing in New York that they wanted, till they came to the Custom House. In that case, Mr. [Cornelius P.] Van Ness seemed to be in all respects so unexceptionable, so fitted for the office by every necessary and proper qualification, that every body said, let him be retained. Mr. Polk seemed for a while to appreciate this feeling, and to be fully influenced by the common sentiment. But, the spoils-men were not to be put off so. They commenced agitating and moving upon the President with the most energetic pertinacity. Though their ward meetings failed them, still they continued to agitate. The President for a time seemed unmoved by their efforts and importunity, and less persevering men would have desisted; but they persisted in their purposes, till they ascertained the assailable ["pint" *canceled*] point—they touched it—and the work was accomplished. They ascertained that the great object of Mr. Polk was to give the [Washington] Union the public printing. They at once got the members elect from New York, through the commanding influence of a few distinguished names, to say, that unless Mr. Van Ness was removed, they could not vote for [Thomas] Ritchie and [John P.] Heiss as public printers. That hint was enough. Mr. Van Ness was an avowed Calhoun and free trade man, and had to share the fate of all others of that way of thinking.

They recently offered Mr. [Francis P.] Blair the mission to Spain. He growled his refusal, by telling them he "wanted none of their missions." They then beseechingly asked him if his son Montgomery

Blair of Missouri ["would" *interlined*] not accept a chargéship, which was also refused; but, leave was given him to fill all the offices in Missouri, which he has availed himself of to the fullest extent.

The Benton-Blair-Van Buren party intend to make war upon the Administration and upon the free trade party—or in other words, upon Polk, yourself and friends. They will have a press, it is said, established here in a month from this time. It is also asserted, that at a recent meeting of Van Buren, Wright, and other dignitaries at [John] Coddington's in New York [City], these arrangements, and God knows what else, were decided upon. The story goes, that Mr. [Churchill C.] Cambreleng alone subscribed ten thousand dollars to establish the press. They can certainly make it a formidable engine every way. But, can they get the public printing? They are certainly going for it. Preliminary to this open outbreak, John C. Rives, who had just been elected President of the Democratic association, read a sort of inaugural address upon taking the chair, in which he exhibited to the fullest extent, his hostility to the Administration and to yourself. It was sent, with the Proceedings of the meeting, to the Union to be published, and was actually set up, but the proof reader called the attention of Mr. Ritchie to it, and he in consternation ran to the President, and it was actually the subject of a Cabinet meeting. They determined to suppress it; and thereby showed ["their" *canceled*] great shortsightedness and bad policy. Heiss showed me a copy of it in confidence, and its bitterness may be considered as a fair illustration of the general feeling of the Van Buren party. Rives invited the President and Cabinet, and the editors of the Democratic press here, to be present on the 4th of July, at the ceremony of laying the corner stone of "Jackson Hall." This is to be a very large building put up by Blair and Rives for a printing office, and to contain a Hall for the meetings of the Democratic associations and other democrats of the District. Well, the Cabinet and the editors were present, and, with many other things, Mr. Rives announced that he deposited a copy of that speech in the corner stone. I laughingly told them, that I thought we had all been made to play a very silly part, in coming to see Mr. Rives lay the corner stone of opposition to the present or any future administration, that did not exactly please his clique. Chagrin was upon the face of the whole party, and they could not conceal it.

The signs of dissatisfaction with the administration, are showing themselves on all sides. It was but the other day, that ["they" *canceled*] they were about to hold a public meeting in Cincinnati to express their dissatisfaction with the administration, and it was only by the efforts of Col. [William] Medill, 2d assistant Postmaster General, that it was suppressed. He told me himself, that he had made promises on behalf of the administration, which, if they did not fulfil, would only make the dissatisfaction the greater, and the outbreak when it did come, the stronger. The democratic papers in Mississippi are ["fiercly" *canceled*] fiercely assailing Mr. [Robert J.] Walker. They make his improperly withholding the Governor's Commission appointing [Jacob] Thompson a senator, the ground of the attack upon him; but, it is palpable that they have lost confidence in him. They believe him to be concerned with Dr. [William M.] Gwin and Col. [John] McLemore in extensive Indian speculations of some sort, now in progress, and over which the Treasury Department may perhaps exercise some peculiar control. They fear that he is unsound upon the tariff and the Independent Treasury; and, I am sorry to say, not without reason. I understand that he and Ritchie are cooking up some sort of a league of State Banks, which is to be offered instead of the subtreasury. And the bill of Gen[era]l [James I.] McKay, is to be offered as a compromise upon the tariff. I have taken, on the part of the friends of free trade, the strongest grounds against all compromises upon the subject of the tariff; consenting to nothing but rigid and exact justice in the premises. And, at the same time going for the subtreasury and a total separation of the government from the Banks, as declared at the Baltimore convention, before we entered upon the Canvass. I know that the people, and especially the great west, are entirely and fully with us on these questions. At the same time, I have treated the subject as if I did not ["doubt" *canceled*] for a moment doubt the intention of Mr. Polk and his Cabinet to go for these measures. For, whatever may be my private opinion upon the subject, I consider it the best policy to exhibit the greatest show of confidence now—to hold them to the conditions of the Baltimore resolutions and the natural expectations of the Party—so that, if they should falter or fail in the hour of trial, we may have the fullest justification to denounce the treachery and the injury. [Robert M.T.] Hunter, [James A.] Seddon, and [Henry] Bedinger, who have just been here, fully concur in the propriety of this course.

In regard to the prospects of the [Washington] Constitution press, it is hard to tell whether we shall be able to keep it going till the meeting of Congress or not. I have completely exhausted my pecuniary means to keep it up, and it has placed me in a very unpleasant situation. Unless our friends come to our aid, in the only way which can be really useful—for money is the sinew of the press as well as ["of" *interlined*] war—we must in the end be crushed by the efforts of the administration, who are using all the patronage and all the influence which they can command, to give the Union, not only the public printing, but the control of every thing. This is the object and the interest, both of Mr. Polk and Mr. Ritchie. For let me say emphatically, that notwithstanding the disclaimers of Mr. Ritchie, in his own peculiar way, *Mr. Polk will be a candidate for reelection, if by any [*"means"* canceled] means he can procure a re-nomination.* I have seen enough and heard enough to convince me of that. No one doubts it here. A communication in the Richmond Enquirer, (from [William] Selden the Treasurer [of the U.S.] I think—Ritchie's sense keeper, as the Indians have it) will convince any one who may doubt. If, then, our free trade friends will stand by and see us thrust aside by Mr. Polk, and the whole patronage of the legislative departments given to a press in which his own family is interested, why so be it. We must submit with the best grace we can—though we should be satisfied with the printing of the Senate.

You probably do not know the partners in the Union. Ritchie owns half, Heiss a fourth, J. Knox Walker the President[']s nephew and private secretary a fourth, and Senator [Simon] Cameron of Pennsylvania did hold the other fourth, but for some reason or other they made him sell out, and it now stands in the name of L[ewis] S. Coryell of Pennsylvania, who has from the first been a very active agent in the business; though he assures me that he really has no pecuniary interest in it.

An idea prevails here, and I think it took its rise in the latitude of the Union office, that from your interviews with Mr. Ritchie when passing through Richmond on your way home, that you had such assurances of his friendly dispositions towards you, that you are really desirous that he should succeed in his purposes here. I do not even ask to know of you whether he made you any of his diplomatic promises; but, this I know, that the whole course of his policy now, is against your interests and the interests and hopes of your friends. And furthermore, in a letter from him to his son-in-law Thomas Green, written soon after you had passed [*"through"* interlined] Richmond, and which was shown to me for a different object, he there took credit to himself, for having in no way committed himself to you; and no little credit for his firmness in suppressing some manifestations of enthusiasm in your favor. His whole mind and energies are bent on uniting the interests of [*"the west"* canceled] New York with the interests of the West. He goes for [John W.] Davis of Indiana as Speaker of the House. The South and Southwest, they seem to think, as Hunter remarked the other day, "already bagged";

and of course no further ["effort" *interlined*] is necessary in that respect.

Thus I have, at greater length than I intended, jotted down just as they have occurred to me, various facts and circumstances as they appear here. You will draw your own conclusions from them. If it would not be taxing you too much, I should be most happy to hear from you. You might afford me important suggestions for my government, in this, I must believe, very important crisis in our affairs. I need scarcely say, that whatever you may communicate, will be with me, under the seal of inviolable confidence. Most sincerely & truly, Y[ou]r ob[edient] Ser[van]t, W.A. Harris.

[P.S. George] Bancroft is the soundest and best man in the Cabinet. The general impression is that the Cabinet must dissolve before long. Mr. [James] Buchanan told me himself, not long since, that he was sorry that he ever left the Senate. They have Cabinet meetings nearly every day. W.A.H.

ALS in ScCleA; PC in Jameson, ed., *Correspondence*, pp. 1038–1043. NOTE: The "communication in the Richmond Enquirer" mentioned by Harris appeared on July 11, 1845, p. 4, under the heading "The Presidency—Faction—The Result." It was signed by "A Republican of '98." Among much else, the article stated: "I know that Col. Polk has said that he would not be a candidate for re-election . . . . But those were the individual opinions of Col. Polk, in which I do not concur, and in which the people do not. . . . If the people again call upon Col. Polk, I have too high an opinion of his devotion to them, to doubt that he will not resist their voice." William Selden had been appointed Treasurer of the U.S. by Polk and had advanced Ritchie $13,000 for the Washington *Union*.

From THOMAS R. SMELIE

Mobley Pond P.O.
Scriven Co[unty] Ga.
July 12th 1845

Honor'd & respected Sir, I dare believe, in the kindness of your heart you will pardon the intrusion a Stranger is guilty of in addressing you, when you know the purport.

A Kind Providence bestow'd ["on me a family" *interlined*] of Children Six in ["number" *interlined*] who bid fair to be all a fond parent's heart could wish. Among them are two boys: the oldest from my exalted opinion of ["your" *interlined*] moral worth & political service in our Country, I named in full after you Jno. C.C., altho' I knew not what the C in your name stood for, with a hope that it may be an incentive to emulation in endeavoring to Assimilate his character to yours.

My object in addressing you is not to parade before you my naming a son from your name but to solicit of you at some convenient ["season" *interlined*] a letter of advice to him on the course of life to pursue to obtain a name among his fellow men & a hope of a name in Heaven also.

His age 10 years, is that when the mind like ductile wax receives its impression for weal or woe. This will tend to exalt his mind above the groveling sensual[i]ty of most youth of the day. To be noticed by a letter from one whom he has ["heard" *interlined*] lauded as a pattern of men & that from his earliest remembrance will be no ordinary spur to urge him on to be a man in the just sense of the word. Not only him, but his brother will also reap its benefits. I've endeavor'd to pourtray to his mind what a Carolinian, he being in immediate descent (I being one) from them, should be. Altho' self-expatriated I feel an ardent love "for my own, my native Carolina" of all places the first in ["my" *interlined*] Affection.

I will with God[']s blessing endeavor by example & precept [to] teach them the Rocks on which I split, & fearful indeed were they, and the way to avoid them. His Jno. C.C.'s disposition is ["of" *interlined*] a mild, tractable nature, tenderhearted, almost to a fault, easy to be entreated, Assi[mi]lating in temper to my dear ["departed" *interlined*] & ever to be remember'd mother. His brother Thomas W. is of ["a" *interlined*] more sanguine ["&" *interlined*] ardent nature requiring a steady hand to control & guide him. Should you be pleased to accede to my solicitation be pleased to address him Jno. at this office.

Let me entreat of you not to regard what I said of you as intending flattery or adulation, but the sincere sentiment of my heart. And please accept Hon[ore]d & respected Sir my sincere & heartfelt wishes for your present & future welfare, and I subscribe myself with sentiments of the highest Respect Y[ou]r most ob[e]d[ien]t Serv[an]t, Thomas R. Smelie.

ALS in ScCleA. Note: An AEU by Calhoun reads "Mr. Smelie. I promised to send a volume of my speeches to his son, if he can contrive the means of transmitting it." Smelie was postmaster at Mobley's Pond.

From J[ames] M[artin] Calhoun

Richmond [Ala.] July 14, 1845
Dear Uncle, I see that you contemplate visiting Andrew [Pickens Calhoun] this Fall. Now whether you travel in a Public or private conveyance I beg you not to pass us by. If you come down the River in a Boat get out at Centerport and I will go with you in my Carriage to Andrew[']s. I am about the same distance from him now as when I lived near Selma. I wish you to see one of the most pleasant neighborhoods in Alabama and one in which you have a great many warm and worthy Friends. If you travel in your own conveyance it is none out of your way from Montgomery to come by my House. It will give us great pleasure to have you and Aunt [Floride Colhoun Calhoun] with us and I will take great pleasure in sending you over to Andrew[']s & going with you. My Family are all well and have been. My Sister Sarah [Calhoun] is with us in good health. We returned a short time since from a visit to John [Alfred Calhoun] and his Family who were all well. He seems to be doing very well where he is.

We have had one [of] the severest droughts I have ever known[;] it will be nine weeks day after tomorrow since we have had any thing like a season. And of course our crops must be greatly injured. I can not make ten Bushels of corn where I live to the acre. The cotton is in full bloom to the top and of course can make but little more. I had a fully matured and uninjured bowl of Cotton open on the 12th Inst. In less than two weeks we shall be able to do a good day[']s picking.

Of Politics I can say nothing, as all is quiet and no manifestation of interest about any thing. I fear there is too much apathy.

Susan [Pickens Calhoun] & Sarah join me in affection to yourself[,] Aunt, and the children. With every wish for your health and happiness with sincere affection I remain Your Nephew, J.M. Calhoun.

ALS in ScU-SC, John C. Calhoun Papers.

From Dr. J[osé] M. Caminero

Port Plate [Dominican Republic,] July 16th 1845
Sir, On addressing you these few lines not only I feel very happy by paying you this attention, as a proof of my gratitude for all your

Kindness, but still I think to be an agre[e]able complyence of duty on my part to inform you of the return of the U.S. Commissioner John Hogan Esq[ui]re after having visited our Towns, places and principal counties, and examined our organisation, our political and moral situation, the means we actually possess, those to be soon expected by encrease of commerce and agriculture, and our capacity of maintening our Independance.

It will be of no use for me to enter into any particulars about the prolixes investigations entered [in]to by said Commissioner in the fulfilment of his mission; his report and the documents he carryes shall speak more than what I could say to you; but allow me, Sir, to submit to your consideration some ideas, which, in my opinion, may strongly contribute to examine the question of recognition of the Dominican Republic in a proper light, and to prompt the U.S. cabinet to give their decision with the shortness of time That such a question requires, leaving the making of a Treaty for an Special[?] period of time, say for the month of October.

I say First, That the Two villages on the line of boundaries, *Caobas* & *Hincha* [that is, Lascahobas and Hinche], which were occupied by the haytians troops, at the time of the landing of the U.S. Commissioner in the City of St. Domingo, have been taken in the month of June last by the Dominicans after fighting, and compelling the haytians forces to enter their territory; and by these victories the Dominican Republic is in full possession of her bounderies, and has augmented her forces on the line to secure the same.

Second: That the general feelings and sympat[h]ies of the whole Dominican people are in favour of the Government and citizens of the U.S. in preference to all foreing [sic] European Powers, for whom they entertain the greatest repugnancy, and dislike to be united, being monarchical governments.

Third: That with respect to Spain, the ancient holder of Hispaniola, by the civil dissentions, by the sectional parties, by the exhausted political and financial state under which That Nation has been and is still labouring, by her silence about the Dominican Republic since the declaration of her independance on the night of 27th february 1844, and by the recognition lately made by Spain of the Republic of Venezuela after being aware of the Dominican revolution, it is to be expected That she will be disposed to acknowledge the independance of Hispaniola obtained by the Dominicans, whose courageous determination has put [an] end to haytian usurpations, from which event a real benefit shall arise in favour of the tranquillity of the Islands of Porto Rico and Cuba, having nothing to fear from the Dominican Government, and injoying such good results without any expences on the part of Spain.

Fourth: That in said Two Islands, it exist great dispositions and desire to become Independants, particularly in Port Rico, where the best informed inhabitants are exalted and cry up against the system of Spain and the heavy taxes they are obliged to pay for the payment of European officers and army; and by the U.S. acknowledging the independance of the Dominican Republic They will haste their political change, being by that assured That they will obtain the same without any hesitation, and so all the colonies will consider the U.S. as the only Nation to protect them.

I hope these ideas will meet your approb[ation] and please to communicate them to the Hon. Ex Pres[ident] John Tyler as you were the authors of Mr. Hogan's mission to this country prepossessed of Those feelings That humanity and Cristendom commands in favour of op[p]ressed people. And although neither of you are now to decide on the question I avail myself to beleive That you both will contribute to bring the question of the Dominican Republic to a favourable conclusion, for which the Dominicans shall be gratefully indebted to the most high gratitude.

Expecting the honour of hearing soon from you I remain Sir with respect and true affection your most ob[edien]t Serv[an]t, Dor. J.M. Caminero.

ALS in ScCleA; PC in Jameson, ed., *Correspondence*, pp. 1043–1045.

To "Col." J[AMES] ED[WARD] COLHOUN, [Abbeville District, S.C.]

Fort Hill, 19th July 1845

My dear James, When I was down[,] myself and others of the family made arrangement to enclose with a stone wall the burial ["ground" *interlined*] at the old place; 60 feet square, 4 feet high above ground, & 18 inches thick; and authorised me to employ a mason to do the quar[ry]ing & put up the wall.

I left a note with Dr. William Calhoun for you; requesting you to let me know, whether you could spare Andrew to do the job; and, if so, at what time. It would take I suppose 2 months, and we would expect to pay the usual rate for such work. I also requested you to ascertain from him, what quantity of lime it would take, & to let me know. Not having heard from you, I conclude, that by some accident my note has not reached you, & now write to obtain an answer from you. I would be glad to hear from you at your earliest convenience, as we wish to make preperation to errect the wall, as soon as the crop is laid by.

Your sister [Floride Colhoun Calhoun] has had a very severe attack of the Nerveous complaint to which she is subject. She is now better, but is very weak & reduced; & is still confined to her bed, although it is upwards of two weeks since she was attacked. The rest of the family are well.

We are now very seasonable & the corn much improved. The cotton looks very well.

We all would be glad to see you & hope that you will make us a visit ere long.

All join their love to you. Yours affectionately, J.C. Calhoun.

ALS in ScCleA.

To LEWIS S. CORYELL, New Hope, Pa.

Fort Hill, 19th July 1845
My dear Sir, The mail of yesterday brought me your's of the 10th, with its enclosure, for which I am obliged to you; & shall observe the confidence you request. It is a singular production, & is clearly intended to frighten Mr. [James K.] Polk into unqualified submission. That is the present scheme of the Albany politicians, and the prospect is that they will succeed. The end would be the overthrow of the party & the success of the whigs, unless, indeed, the portion of the party, who rallied at Baltimore to save the party, shall again raise the standard, & make another rally to save it, before it is two [sic] late. The New York Deynasty [sic] may destroy the party, but can never again rise to power. That is fixed.

You give me much curious information, &, I hope, you will continue to write me fully & freely.

From present appearance things ["will" *interlined*] fall into inextracable [sic] confusion. I apprehended it before I left Washington, & what has since happened, has but confirmed my apprehension. Mr. Polk had a clear course. If he had relied on those who elected him, without making war on those who opposed, or coldly supported him, & shaped his policy by the Baltimore resolutions, he would have had a brilliant & successful administration; but, as it is, the prospect for him is far from flattering. With much respect I am yours truly, J.C. Calhoun.

ALS in PHi, Society Collection; PC in Jameson, ed., *Correspondence*, pp. 666–667.

From J[AMES] H. HAMMOND

Silver Bluff, 20 July 1845

My Dear Sir, Although I consider myself now as promoted to the veteran rank & bound to serve only in emergencies, with a view to comply with your wishes as well as to do honor to the methodists as far as in my power, I commenced a careful perusal of Dr. [Henry B.] Bascom's Review ["as soon as I received your letter" *interlined*]. I had scarcely begun when the last Southern Rev[iew] came to hand declaring that in its opinion it would be unbecoming the South to say more on the subject of Slavery—thus virtually excluding it from its ["colu" *canceled*] pages. A course prompted perhaps as much by selfish policy as Southern feeling. I read on however to see what the book contained & what might be made of it through some other channel. I find it full of valuable information which is calculated to work well in the methodist society & certain other classes. But it is a rude, undigested, disconnected & confused mass—enlivened occasionally by peircing [*sic*] interrogatory, & burning sarcasm; & overwhelming—as much by the ponderosity as the keen[n]ess of its logic. It will require much resolution in a reader to get through it. The very purpose however of a review would be to organize & popularize its materials. This I have already done to the extent of my ability in the [Thomas] Clarkson Letters. Dr. Bascom furnishes many cumulative facts & ["some" *canceled and* "much" *interlined*] striking illustration but he scarcely makes a point not made in my Clarkson & Glasgow letters or your Letter to [William R.] King. To re-cook the whole & make one dish with any novelty in it would require a fresh artisan & any one might do it perhaps better than you or I. Besides the Doctor's is fundamentally wrong on the subject of Slavery. He admits & declares it to be an evil in every way & that it is only *permitted* & *regulated,* not *ordained* by God. "The Bible" he says "is neither *pro* slavery nor *anti* slavery." To make these admissions is to admit all—& in fact to justify all. No argument for Slavery [that "is" *interlined*] worth a copper can be built, if these

31

foundations are knocked from under it. And though the Doctor with ingenious causistry [*sic*] has introduced a great deal of argument going to prove that these very admissions are false, still they are recorded in the "Review," & I do not think it is entitled to have the *Southern stamp* put upon it any more nor so much as [Richard] Fuller's Letters. Our only safety against the torrent of abolition is to drive our piling to the rock—the "rock of ages"—the Bible, and the wings of our abutments must exclude the evil of Slavery in every point of view save as every thing in this world is according to our Creator[']s apparent design *both* good & evil. With these views I don't see what I could make out of the Dr.[']s arguments in favour of our institutions.

An article taking a view merely of the religious & *political* consequences of the division of the methodist church, embodying occasional striking paragraphs in regard to Slavery[,] might be made. But who would publish it, if written? I doubt my fitness to write it also. I should be afraid to trust myself on the religious aspect, & the political one could not I fear be treated as thouroughly as it deserves. I will however think more of this. It always affords me great pleasure ["to" *interlined*] carry out your suggestions when I can & I should be glad to do so in this matter. But I should do it anonymously—strictly so. I ought not to have published my Clarkson Letters—I hesitated long about it—& regret it. If my ideas were worth any thing they might have been put forth in some other shape, without attracting to me that public notice, which is any thing but to my taste. I am so convinced that *I* never can as a public man effect any thing for the *real* relief of our proscribed & down-trodden South which is alone *our country*, that I turn with utter disgust from every thing connected with public affairs & wish only to bury myself in un broken solitude. Let those who have heart, hope & a love for the excitement—& there are enough of them—fight the battle & wear the laurel, if won. This ["is" *interlined*] sorry patriotism I know. But I do not pretend to be one of the Decii.

I have extensive plans of agricultural improvement on hand. Besides marl, peat, plaster & manure[,] all of which I am using to my utmost ability, I have draining projects in process of execution which if I live to perfect will revolutionize agriculture in this district at least & quadruple its profits. Should you come down the country this winter I should be most happy to see you & shew you what I am at. By the by A[nthony] B. Allen of New York who publishes one of the best agricultural papers in the Union [the *American Agriculturalist*] wrote me the other day that if it was not an intrusion he would be glad [to] send you his paper free. And added that it would be a great gratifi[cation] to get from you an article on Hill side draining as practiced on y[our farm]. I told him I had no doubt you would read his paper with pleasure, but I had never heard of your writing agricultural articles. I confess I should myself like very much to see a developement of your plan of H.S. draining. I have some slight use for such drains & my brother in Burke County [Ga., Marcus C.M. Hammond] has a very valuable place requiring them extensively. If you could throw off such a thing in a leisure hour I would undertake to make it of use without exposing you. I write much myself for the agricultural papers, always anonymously. I have much at heart a scheme deveolped recently in the [Columbia South-]Carolinian about fencing. I am almost hopeless of effecting much in my day, but mean to press it. An association has been just formed I am told to try the "abolition" of fences between Enoree & Tyger rivers.

The drought has ruined us. I did hope to make half a crop of corn & cotton. But we are again suffering so severely from drought & heat that I fear cotton here will be cut even shorter than corn & that down to one third. Very sincerely yours, J.H. Hammond.

[Marginal P.S.] I paid *my* tribute to the methodists in my last message.

ALS in ScCleA.

From F[RANCIS] W. PICKENS

Edgewood, 20 July 1845

My dear Sir, I returned last night from Mr. [Thomas G.] Clemson's place. I took Mrs. [Marion Antoinette Dearing] P[ickens] with me and I endeavoured to see to his matters. They are all as well as possible. The Dr. has been on the place but once since Mr. Clemson left. The crop is as good as could be expected considering the dreadful drought. They will make a plenty. I think the cotton will make about 50 bags & the corn is good in the low land. I took the responsibility not to [*partial word canceled*] remove the negro houses but to repair them. I fear they would be sickly where Mr. C[lemson] desired them to be moved, that is if I can understand exactly where he intended. They had sowed the oats badly, that is where they could not be pastured, but it was according to his direction. The consequence is that the stock cannot be pastured & the dry weather has ruined the grass out. I found he had ordered all the stock to be kept in a pasture enclosed with woods &c. When I was there last I took it for granted that they would be turned out before this without enquiry. His cattle some died & many of his hogs. I turned them all out & they will do better now. He ordered clearing &c—but I stop[p]ed it as there is now more land open than his force can cultivate. All these orders were in his plantation book with the overseer. I hope you will approve of what I have done. The house is not near finished & the mills have many of them been ["with" *canceled*] without water, but I have ordered lumber[?] from the sand hills to finish the house. He directed the chimnies to be built of rock entirely except the top. He of course wanted fire places in the back rooms adjoining his drawing & dining rooms, & if the chimnies are of Rock—I think it would take up too much space and thus make the two back rooms very small, as they are now quite narrow. It seems to me that this would injure the house & that bricks would be most suitable as they are inside chimnies entirely. Perhaps I am mistaken & Rock chimnies would take up no more space than brick. I wish you therefore to judge of this & write me immediately as I can haul the rock now the crop is laid by. If you think Rock will do will you be so good as to engage a rock mason in Pendleton & send him down as there are none good in this dist[rict] & they are high. If you think brick best—do you think the brick had better be made upon the place or bought? If it can be done on the place good it would be cheaper. I think it would take about 12,000 bricks. Would it be worth while to put up a kill [*sic*; kiln] for this? The greatest difficulty in buying them is the hauling. Be so good as to write me on these points. The ["greatest" *canceled and then interlined*] expence now on the place is the bacon. He has ordered them to be given more than they need, & it has all to be bought. I shall be able to make all the woollen cloth this Summer & Fall as I have the wool on the place, & I have ordered a loom & a woman to be immediately taught to weave, or rather one to be brushed up who says [she] knows how. If I had any hogs on the place I could make the bacon also. However I think I can sell corn enough to buy it. The overseer now is a very steady man. I enquired as you requested whether the place could be sold for what he gave for it. I think it can be. Mr. [Allen S.] Dozier & Mr. [John] Mobley would divide it. But I think there would be no difficulty in selling it for what he gave. I think the part [John] Pow bought injured the place very much. Land is rising & it could be sold. I rec[eive]d a letter the other day from Mr. C[lemson] & all were well there. We are all well here & join in love to Cousin Floride [Colhoun Calhoun]. Susan [Pickens] has been sometime in Athens but will return day after to-morrow. The hot & dry weather is intense, but notwithstanding I believe I have the best crops I ever had—the cotton particularly so. Very truly & sincerely, F.W. Pickens.

ALS in ScCleA.

From F[RANKLIN] H. E[LMORE]

Charleston, July 21, 1845
My Dear Sir, We have begun a quasi action here on the Tariff, or rather we have acted on the action of Mr. Sec[retar]y [of the Treasury Robert J.] Walker in a way that I think you should know & give us your counsel on. A few days ago Mr. [William J.] Grayson [Collector of Customs] rec[eive]d a circular, covering a series of printed questions on the operation of the Tariff, with instructions to hand them over to "reliable sources" of information for answers—requesting the answers before the 1[?] Oct. These questions contained in 40 but very few, if any, that could give an opportunity for developing the action of the protective system either upon the foreign or domestic transactions of commerce, or upon the interests of agriculture as depending on the exchanges of its products. A copy was, on the suggestion of some of us who consulted on it, sent by Mr. Grayson to the Chamber of Commerce, with a requ[e]st that that Body would give the information asked for. The Chamber replied by Resolutions stating that they would at all times be ready as in duty bound to give such information as they possessed to aid the functionaries of the Govt. in adjusting the Tariff ["& and(?)" *canceled*] by developing its operation on those branches of the business of the Country affected by it, but that in consequence of our not being manufacturing people, but agricultural & commercial & these questions relating almost wholly to manufactures & the influence of the protective system on them, that they could give no useful answers to them. But that if questions calculated to develop in a similar manner the action of the Tariff on commerce & agriculture were propounded they would most cheerfully respond to them. They appointed a committee of seven to attend to the matter.

Before the Chamber met, two days—I wrote a "Private letter" to Mr. Walker & stated that a number of the merchants in whose hands his questions had been put had called to see me. That they were dissatisfied—but that I hoped & so said to them that other questions would be propounded by him which would allow *all* the great interests of the country to be heard in like manner. That if I was right & could be of any service to him in procuring proper answers, or in devising any plan of action I would be most happy to aid[?]. This was intended to let him know, if his long boasted movements preparatory to the adjustment of the Tariff were to be no more than these "questions" implied, that we were not blind nor inattentive, but had an organization ready to begin the contest ["with" *canceled*] for our rights with. I do not know what are his intentions. If he meant to send no other inquiries out to the country, then he puts us at every disadvantage—the only interest heard is the manufacturing interest. They may & will accumulate all their views in the *shape of testimony*, while we[,] bound as it were, will be silently delivered over to the sacrifice. But I cannot believe this is the case—it would [be] the coldest blooded treachery ever yet dealt out to a confiding people—the most ungrateful abandonment of true hearted & effective friends. I cannot believe it & am sure that other questions are intended, by which the other great & oppressed interests shall also be heard. It cannot be that only the plea of the Robbers shall be recorded, while the plundered & wronged victims are denied a hearing.

The course we adopted here was intended to meet either aspect of the case. The Secretary had opened the door & we resolved that it should not be shut against us, without a palpable disclosure of the real intention—while if the Secretary really desired to be armed at all points he should have no excuse so far as we are concerned for *excluding us from the witnesses stand.*

I have suggested to Mr. [Moses C.] Mordecai our Chairman to send you, along with a copy of the "questions" & the proceedings of the meeting as ordered, also some suggestions of such points of inquiry as would draw out a proper developement of our side of this question, with a request to you to put in shape & send us such points in the form of interrogatories as would fully & effectually draw out such answers as would expose the action of the Tariff on commerce & agriculture. That these questions might then be sent to some person at Washington (who would you advise?) who might procure their adoption & dissemination by the Secretary to the planting & Commercial interest. Pray give us your views.

Would it think you be of any service to bring the matter up before the Agricultural Convention at Newberry [S.C.] on the 30th inst.? If so you had better see or write to some one on the subject.

I leave the City today for Aiken & then to Columbia—not to return until fall. I go to Limestone—so that while I will be happy to hear from you there on this subject, I would advise you to address your suggestions as to what should be done here to our friends.

I have counselled the [Charleston] Mercury to exhibit as trustful a tone towards the efforts of the administration on this subject as possible, so as if they act right we have nothing to repent & if they are faithless we at least can't be blamed. Y[ou]rs truly, F.H.E.

P.S. I forgot to say that Mr. Connors [sic; Henry W. Conner's] move is I think a most useful one. If you think so would it not be well to write to some of your friends in Mobile & N[ew] Orleans to cooperate & send Delegations?

ALI in ScCleA.

From M [oses] C. Mordecai

Charleston, July 22, 1845
Dear Sir, I beg leave to Enclose to you several Questions sent out by Mr. [Secretary of the Treasury Robert J.] Walker, and Rec[eive]d thro Mr. [William J.] Grayson our Collector, and the action of the Chamber of Commerce thereon, with the Resolution of Mr. [Henry W.] Conner.

The Committee would Respectfully ask your advice as to their future proceeding, and would solicit you to arrange a series of Questions, as we aught to have sent us with your views, that may assi[s]t us in making the answers most Effective on the action of the tariff on Foreign Commerce & Domestic consumption. It may be of importance if Mr. Walker could be got to take a few[?] Questions and make them his Circular. Mr. Grayson has sent the Secr[etary] our Resolutions and Col. [Franklin H.] Elmore wrote him a "private letter," and at the suggestion of the Col. I wrote the Hon. David Levy [Yulee, Senator from Fla.,] who is now at Washington, and sent him our proceedings. He may learn if Mr. Walker intends sending out other Questions, or will ask for our's. I have been told that Mr. Gouge and Mr. Kittell were to be put in the Bureau of Statistics authorised by Congress at its last session, and were to be set at work preparing matter on the tariff, if so would there be any advantage in having our Questions & answers pass through their hands[?] Could it be arranged[?] Very Respectful[l]y Your Ob[edient] Ser-[vant], M.C. Mordecai.

[Enclosure]
The Charleston Chamber of Commerce.

Charleston, S.C., 18th July, 1845

At an extra Meeting of the Chamber held this day, at the Hall of the Bank of Charleston, the President stated the object of the Meeting, and submitted a communication received from the Hon. W.J. GRAYSON, Collector of this Port, accompanied by a Circular from the Secretary of the Treasury of the United States, containing a number of Questions relating to manufactories, and to the effect of the tariff upon the manufacturing interests of the country, whereupon, on motion of Mr. M.C. MORDECAI, seconded by Col. F.H. ELMORE, the following Resolutions were unanimously adopted:

RESOLVED, That the Questions made out at the Treasury of the United States, intended to draw answers from reliable sources, as to the operation of the tariff on the pursuits of our citizens, and sent by the Hon. R.J. WALKER, Secretary of the Treasury, to the Hon. W.J. GRAYSON, the Collector, and by him submitted to this Chamber, have been received and examined; and that this Chamber finds that they contain very few points on which they, as men engaged in commerce and connected with agricultural industry and exchanges, can give any information, as the Questions relate almost exclusively to manufactures, and the effect of the protective system on their interests.

RESOLVED, That the Chamber of Commerce feel it their duty as connected with the best interests of the country, at all times, if requested, to give all the aid in their power to the functionaries of the General Government, in developing the action of the protective tariff upon the commercial and industrial pursuits of the people of this country.

RESOLVED, That a Committee of seven be appointed to which shall be referred the Questions of the Secretary of the Treasury, with instructions and full power to take all such steps as in their judgment may be advisable for procuring the necessary information to be asked for, and to have it collected, properly embodied, and laid before the Secretary of the Treasury, for the use of his department and the Government.

The President appointed the following gentlemen on the Committee:

M.C. MORDECAI, Esq.
Col. F.H. ELMORE,
H.W. CONNER, Esq.
CHARLES EDMONDSTON, Esq.

T.J. ROGER, Esq.
Col. J. GADSDEN, Esq.
A. McDOWALL, Esq.

The following Resolutions were moved by Mr. H.W. CONNER, seconded by Col. F.H. ELMORE, and unanimously adopted:

RESOLVED, That it is highly expedient that a Committee of two or more skilful and experienced Merchants of this City, be delegated to Washington, (whenever the consideration of the tariff is before Congress) for the purpose of aiding and assisting the delegation from this State, with their counsel and advice, in adjusting the details of such tariff bill as may be before Congress.

RESOLVED, That the importance of the subject recommends itself particularly to the attention of the Charleston Chamber of Commerce, and that the selection of the proper persons as delegates, and all other things necessary to further the object be made the special duty of the President; and a Committee of five to be appointed by the Chamber for that purpose.

RESOLVED, That the President be directed to communicate these Resolutions to such other Chambers of Commerce as may be deemed necessary, respectfully inviting their co-operation in carrying out the object of the Resolutions, by the appointment of similar Committees, requesting from them any suggestions they may see fit to make, with the view of obtaining such modifications of the existing tariff as will ensure justice and equity to all interests and all sections.

Ordered, That one hundred copies of the Resolutions and the Circular, be printed for the use of the Committee.

Extract from the Minutes.   WILLIAM B. HERIOT, *Secretary.*

QUESTIONS.

1. State and county in which the manufactory is situated?

2. Kind or description of the manufactory; and whether water, steam or other power?

3. When established; and whether a joint stock concern?

4. Capital invested in ground and buildings, and water power, and in machinery?

5. Average amount in materials, and in cash for the purchase of materials, and payment of wages?

6. Annual rate of profit on the capital invested since the establishment of the manufactory; distinguishing between the rate of profit upon that portion of the capital which is borrowed, after providing for the interest upon it, and the rate of profit upon that portion which is not borrowed?

7. Cause of the increase (or decrease, as the case may be) of profit?

8. Rates of profit on capital otherwise employed in the same State and county?

9. Amount of articles annually manufactured since the establishment of the manufactory; description, quality, and value of each kind?

10. Quantity and value of different kinds of raw materials used; distinguishing between foreign products and domestic products?

11. Cost in the United States of similar articles of manufacture imported from abroad, and from what countries?

12. Number of men, women and children employed, and average wages of each class?

13. How many hours a day employed, and what portion of the year?

14. Rate of wages of similar classes otherwise employed in the same State and county, in other States, and in foreign countries?

15. Number of horses or other animals employed?

16. Whether the manufactures find a market at the manufactory; if not, how far they are sent to a market?

17. Whether foreign articles of the like kinds enter into competition with them at such place of sale; and to what extent?

18. Where are the manufactures consumed?

19. Whether any of the manufactures are exported to foreign countries; and, if so, where?

20. Whether the manufacture is sold by the manufacturer for cash? and if on credit, at what credit? if bartered, for what?

21. Whether the cost of the manufactured article (to the manufacturer) has increased or decreased; and how much, in each year, from the establishment of the manufactory, and whether the increase has been in the materials or the labor, and at what rate?

22. The prices at which the manufactures have been sold by the manufacturer since the establishment?

23. What rate of duty is necessary to enable the manufacturer to enter into competition in the home market with similar articles imported?

24. Is there any change necessary in levying or collecting the duty on such articles, to prevent fraud?

25. What has been the rate of your profits, annually, for the last three years? and if it be a joint stock company, what dividends have been received, and what portion of the income of the company has

been converted into fixed capital, or retained as a fund for contingent or other objects, and therefore not divided out annually?

26. What portion of the cost of your manufactures consists of the price of the raw material, what portion of the wages of labor, and what portion of the profits of capital?

27. What amount of the agricultural productions of the country is consumed in your establishment, and what amount of other domestic productions?

28. What quantity or amount of manufactures, such as you make, are produced in the United States, and what amount in your own State?

29. If the duty upon the foreign manufacture of the kind of goods which you make were reduced to 12½ per cent., with a corresponding reduction on all the imports, would it cause you to abandon your business, or would you continue to manufacture at reduced prices?

30. If it would cause you to abandon your business, in what way would you employ your capital?

31. Is there any pursuit in which you could engage, from which you could derive greater profits, even after a reduction of the import duties to 12½ per cent.?

32. Are not the manufactures of salt and iron, remote from the points of importation, out of foreign competition within a certain circle around them, and what is the extent of that circle?

33. Amount of capital; and what proportion the borrowed capital bears to that which is real?

34. What amount of reduction in the duties would enable the actual or real capital employed to yield an interest of six per cent.? and how gradual the reduction should be?

35. If minimums should be abolished, and the duty assessed upon the actual value of the imported article in the American port, what rate of ad valorem duty would be equivalent to the present with the minimum?

36. What would be the operation of this change upon the frauds at present supposed to be practised?

37. Proportion which the production by the American manufacturer bears to the consumption?

38. Extent of individual and household manufactures in the United States, and how much it has increased since the tariff of 1842?

39. Average profit of money or capital in the United States?

40. Average rate of wages?

ALS with En in ScCleA. NOTE: An AEU by Calhoun reads "Mr. M.C. Mordecai."

To THO[MA]S G. CLEMSON, U.S. Chargé, Brussels

Fort Hill, 26th July 1845

My dear Sir, I would have written to you by the last packet, in answer to your's of the 22d May & 14th June, had not the state of Mrs. [Floride Colhoun] Calhoun's health, when the latter was received, prevented. She then was labouring under a severe ne[r]veous attack, such as she had some two or three years since, when I was absent, & Anna [Maria Calhoun Clemson] attended her. She was attacked on the 3 Inst. and although passed all danger, as I hope, she has not yet left her bed. She has had not much fever, but has been under constant apprehension of d[y]ing. The rest of the family are well. It has been, as yet quite healthy, although the wheather [*sic*] has for the last 2 weeks ["been" *interlined*] very hot, & the river & smaller streams very low; more so, than I ever saw them. The whole year, thus far, has been remarkable for the small quantity of rain that has fallen. Provisions must be very scarce & dear next year over a great part of the Union. Unless there should be a fresh, I shall make enough & something to spare, although one half of my corn crop is on upland, which I do not think will yield more than a third of its usual production. My cotton, with the exception of a 20 acre field, which has had very little rain, looks uncommonly well; I think better, than I ever had it as yet, at this season. I had a letter from Andrew [Pickens Calhoun] yesterday of the 11th Inst. They have been dry in Alabama, but our crop of corn and cotton is uncommonly good. He will make, unless something unexpected happens, between 6 & 7 hundred Alabama bales, & 4 or 5 ["thousand" *interlined*] bushels of corn, beyond our ["supply" *canceled and* "want" *interlined*]. Margaret [Green Calhoun] had just been delivered of a fine boy [Andrew Pickens Calhoun, Jr.], & was doing well.

Col. [Francis W.] Pickens writes, that you will make sufficient provisions, & a pretty good cotton crop [at your place in Edgefield District]. He states, that he had assumed the responsibility of giving such orders about the place, as he thinks your interest requires; & I shall without hesitation give my approval. He can form a far better opinion, as to what ought to be done, than you possibly can, at the great distance at which you are. He thinks, that you can sell the place for ["what" *interlined*] you gave; & I have no doubt you can your negroes, and all your other property, which ["you" *interlined*] may feel disposed to sell; & I have come to the conclusion, that it would be best for you to do so, if you should not think of returning in a short time, unless you can get a first rate overseer, which

I fear would be very difficult. Col. Pickens is too much engaged to give ["it" *canceled and* "your place" *interlined*] his superintendence; it is too far from me to give ["it" *canceled*] mine; & I know [no] one in the neighbourhood, that would agree to give ["it" *canceled*] his. Indeed, there is but little property vested in any agricultural pursuit, which at this time gives as much profit as good bonds & mortgages bearing 7 per cent interest; and from Col. Pickens['s] opinion, I have no doubt your property can be converted into such ["securities" *interlined*] without loss, especially if time is allowed for payment.

I am very glad, that you have retracted in in [*sic*] your last, what you had said in reference to Andrew, in your first. I read your letter with very great regret. You must permit me to say, that you permit yourself to yield too readily to your feelings on partial, one side statements. The letter of Col. Pickens was, indeed, calculated to create unpleasant feelings; and I must say that I am not a little surprised, that he should ["give" *interlined*] such a one side view, with my letter before him, or that he should have troubled you about it, when he knew it would be all settled before his letter could reach you. I had not the least information, that there was any difficulty until I learned by Col. Picken[s]'s letter, that Arthur [Simkins] was about to proceed under the mortgage, when I took immediate steps to take up the note. Arthur[']s conduct throughout was reprehensible, and Col. Pickens ought to have laid the blame on him, and not where he did. It is a case, which strongly illustrates how important it is to hear both sides before opinions are permitted to be formed, & unkind feelings indulged. You must also permit me to say, that you have not, in my opinion, throughout your transaction in reference to the Alabama purchase[,] duely appreciated the motives of Andrew, or the difficulty under which we have had to struggle, in consequence of the great & unexpected fall of the price of cotton. I say we, for I cannot permit myself to be seperated from him, in the transaction. I know, that his proposition to unite you in the purchase, originated in a sincere desire to benefit your interest, & that he is gratified, in thinking that you have ["been" *interlined*] a gainer & not a loser by the connection; while he deeply regrets, that there should have been any delay in meeting the debt due you. We have had, ["indeed," *interlined*] great difficulty in consequence of the great fall of cotton; but such is the fertility of the soil; the ease of cultivation, & the health of the climate, & consequent increase of our force & productive power, ["that" *interlined*] we do not dispair of overcoming it, even at the present price. All we want is time. The place can be made to produce upwards of 1000 Alabama bales annually, with an ample

43

supply of provision, & reserve of uncultivated land for timber & pasture. If we can hold on, until the present pressure shall have passed away, it is good, even with our present force, at 8 cents the pound, for a clear income of $15,000 annually, and may be raised with an increase of hands to $25,000, which ought to be ample for the whole family. You all have a much deeper interest in holding on to such an estate, than I can possibly have, individually. I feel myself to be but a trustee for you all, with a small share of a few short years of individual interest.

I feel assured, you will appreciate the motives with which these remarks are made. I have felt much pain at the ill feelings & harsh expressions you indulge in towards Andrew. It is due to him to say, that he indulges in neither towards you, at least to me, or that comes to my ears. I hope you will irradicate such feelings, and avoid similar expressions hereafter, at least to me.

All join their love to you, Anna, & the children [John Calhoun Clemson and Floride Elizabeth Clemson]. Kiss them for their Grandfather & say to them, how much I wish to see them. Tell Anna her's to her mother written at Paris was received by the last steamer. Your affectionate father, J.C. Calhoun.

ALS in ScCleA.

From ISAAC N. DAVIS

Panola County, Miss.
Near Rice[']s X Road P.O.
July 28th 1845

D[ea]r Sir, Knowing your ever-abiding interest in the institutions of the Country & especially the South, I am induced to tax your indulgence & patience with this letter. The Government having heretofore made appropriation in Land &C. for a State University or Seminary in this State, the Legislature at its last session passed a Law appointing a Board of Trustees to carry the same into effect, under which we are now taking steps. A proposition is before the Board to organize & erect a University upon the European plan in preference to the American close College. As one of the Trustees I am desirous to adopt such a plan as will be the most likely to succeed & at the same time will be the most suitable to the habits & feelings of our people.

Owing to the mismanagement of the Bank & other causes the fund which otherwise would have ["been" *interlined*] ample, will now likely be reduced to one hundred & fifty or two hundred thousand Dollars, with this we propose to make such a commencement as we can. As at present advised[?] It strikes me that the European University would not suit us, but I confess I do not possess the requisite information upon the subject to have confidence in my opinions. I therefore desire, if it will not be too much labour to you to get your Views as much at large upon the subject as convenient. The next meeting of our Board is in Jan[uar]y next. Will you therefore have the goodness to let me hear from you as early as convenient.

As to General matters, We the Whigs have little or no expectations of disturbing the success of the Democrats in the present Canvass as their majority is too large to over come.

Ex Gov. [Alexander G.] McNut[t] has commenced a general Canvass before the people for Senator in Congress. Gen[era]l [Henry S.] Foote & Gen[era]l [John A.] Quitman & others are aspirants for the same office. There are now some indications that the Democratic party will take another step in repudiation towit, the Planter[']s Bank Bonds. I suppose they will not be united in favor of that as many of their prominent men have declared in favor of paying them. So it was however when Gov. McNut first broached the repudiation of the Union Bank Bonds.

There is some excitement in the ranks of the Democrats relative to R[obert] J. Walker[']s conduct in suppressing the commission of [Jacob] Thompson to the Senate. You doubtless have seen his statement, & also Gov. [Albert G.] Brown[']s. One or the other of them, It seems to me, is in an awkward position. You will allow me to say that although I have differed with you in some matters in politics, of late years, yet I have the greatest pleasure & interest in hearing from you at all times & upon all matters. Y[ou]r ob[e]d[ient] Ser[van]t, Isaac N. Davis.

ALS in ScCleA. Note: In the spring of 1845 Jacob Thompson received an interim appointment from the governor as Senator from Miss., to succeed Walker who was resigning to become Secretary of the Treasury. Walker apparently never delivered the credentials to the Senate and Thompson was not seated. Funds intended for the State university had been invested by the Planters' Bank in the Natchez Railroad Company, which had gone bust.

From LEWIS S. CORYELL

New Hope [Pa.,] 29th July 1845
My dear Sir, Y[ou]rs of the 19th is rec[eive]d. Since I wrote you
I had a conference with [James K.] Polk. He wishes to act for the
very best, but neither knows that course himself, nor has he any one
in confidence to enlighten him. He is far from easy in his feelings or
confidence in those about him. Buck [James Buchanan] will go on
the Bench [of the U.S. Supreme Court] in [Henry] Baldwin[']s place.
His modest and increasing timidity is becoming very notorious, and
he has lost all power. Politically, [Robert J.] Walker is Heir apparent and is deporting himself accordingly, and is a perfect St.
Paul[']s man. Cave [Johnson, Postmaster General,] refused to dine
with Mr. Packingham [*sic*; Richard Pakenham] (rudely) and by
which he expects to render himself acceptable to the very Democracy for the highest station. I wish I knew [John Y.] Mason [At-
torney General]. I c[oul]d talk to him I presume in my own way
and humble as I am, I could in some things enlighten him. Miracles
will never cease. My son Ingham is in the custom House in N. York.
He was with McKenzie [*sic*; William L. Mackenzie] (the outlaw)
placed in an upper story to arrange years of confusion & in overhaul-
ing the mass, they came to a box, which proved to be Jesse Hoyt[']s
private papers. Curiosity & duty both they say induced them to
examine them closely. It proved to be a mass of correspondence
organizing and carrying out the burst and dis[s]olution of [Andrew]
Jackson[']s Cabinet. It is very rich, & proves a recklessness & stock
gambling to an astounding degree.

The letters are from M[artin] V[a]n B[ure]n, John V[a]n
B[ure]n, [William L.] Marcy, Bennet [*sic*; James Gordon Bennett],
[Mordecai M.] Noah, [James Watson] Webb, Maj[o]r [William B.]
Lewis &Ct. &Ct. John V[a]n B[ure]n[']s is very profane and vulgar.
Among other matters old Jackson[']s levy of black mail on the office
holders to establish the Glove [*sic*; the Washington, D.C., *Globe*].
Marcy own[s] the charge true for mending his breeches, and is
ready to do any thing to arrest the matter!

McKenzie has quit the Custom House & is going to establish a
paper in N. York. [He] has copies &Ct. and in due time the Public
will have a new dish to digest. Duff [Green] knows all about this
matter. I am going to New York next week & will write you from
there, but I fear my collection of odds & Ends so bordering upon
scandall will induce you to think me a very Paul Pry, but be it as it
may I am determined to know all about things find them as I may.

Y[ou]r fr[ien]d truly, Lewis S. Coryell.

[P.S.] By the way the man who "can't lye" must die at the Senate[']s door. [Simon] Cameron, & [James D.] Westcott, [Senators from Pa. and Fla.], may be relied upon.

ALS in ScCleA.

From F[RANCIS] W. PICKENS

Edgewood, 30 July 1845

My dear Sir, I was sorry you omit[t]ed in yours to let me know whether I should build brick or stone chimnies to Mr. [Thomas G.] Clemson's house. I gave my reasons for differing from Mr. Clemson & desired your opinion. I also desired you to send a stone mason from Pendleton if we were to go on with stone. But since the rec[ei]pt of yours I have determined to go on & execute the directions of Mr. Clemson exactly and have employed a stone mason. I will have it done the best I can.

I was very sorry to hear of the sickness of Cousin Floride [Colhoun Calhoun]. Do present me affectionately to her, & I hope sincerely her ill-health is but temporary.

I was glad to hear of your crop in Alabama. I hope you may realize the full amount of your anticipations, but to sell 7,000 bushels of corn from a *cotton plantation* such a season as this, will require a great deal of land or great yield—unless where there are several hundred hands—or but little cotton planted to the land. The crops are very different in different sections of this Dist[rict of Edgefield]. Some places never better, & some nothing made. I have had no rain on the [Saluda] River, and fortunately planted some of the best low grounds in corn or it would have been a failure there. I shall have no difficulty in fulfilling my engagement as to corn. I am told above this in Abbeville & Laurens [Districts] the prospect is dreadful. The cotton is good with us & opening very much.

My horse fell with me last week and nearly broke my elbow & wrist both backwards & hurt me in several places. It gave me great pain for some days but is now improving fast although not able to use yet. I fear I never will recover the entire use of it. Day before yesterday I stood over the cider press put[t]ing up crab cider and directing the negroes ["longer than I ought" *interlined*], so that the exposure threw me back a little. With that exception we are all very

47

well, & I never had more [*one word canceled*] general health amongst negroes.

I have rec[eive]d letters from our friends in Ala: and they give a gloomy account of their prospects as to bread there this year, but seem to be in good cheer as to politics &c. I suppose [Arthur P.] Bagby [Senator from Ala.] has acted disgracefully. They will instruct him out. Judge [Thomas S.] Mays of Montgomery complains very much of the course of the [Charleston] Mercury in [*one word or partial word canceled*] reference to its correspondence & Editorials in relation to Mr. [James K.] Polk—Says it injures *your friends* in Ala: and throws them back in their movements in your favour to be consummated this winter. He says it *"hurts you far more than all that the old Hunkers can do."* He stands high & was from this State & a devoted friend of yours. I understand also the same complaint is made by your friends in Va., as the Mercury is considered out of the State your confidential organ.

I see it stated you will visit the ["Fall" *canceled and* "West" *interlined*] this Fall. I sincerely hope you will do so. You ought. Go to New Orleans & then up the *River to Nashville*, & then to St. Louis, & Cincinnatti [*sic*]. It will make a great sensation & do more to produce & effect upon the gov[ernment] at Washington in *settling the Tariff* than any thing that can be done. Go early in Oct: so as to get back by the Middle or first of December. More people will meet you at Nashville than ever came out to meet any one man in America. I know it. I hope you will go, & if you could go to Pittsburg[h] & thence to New York, & then home it would make a great impression & I believe for the public good.

Present us kindly to all. Truly & sincerely, F.W. Pickens.

ALS in ScCleA.

From P. GWINNER, "Private"

Philad[elphi]a, August 1st/[18]45

Dear Sir, As I was prophetic in my former epistle, which I infer[r]ed, from what my friend Mr. Hay said to me, you received before you left Washington, I will again venture to opine, as comeing events are said to cast there Shadow before. There is now quite a fued [*sic*] among the officers appointed by the President [James K. Polk] & their subordinates in this district. There are three different Cliques nearly equal in numbers, towit the [James] Buchanan, [George M.] Dallas & [John] Tyler, the latter (feel that they have been proscribed, the other two are pressing the claims of their respective leaders for the Succession, the latter uniting with those who have been disappointed in obtaining office, are now the most numerous, there were more than fifteen hundred applicants for about one hundred offices) are determined to prevent their confirmation if possible. The majority of whom from their complexion & character, were made no doubt, from the most corrupt motives, through the influence of B[uchanan] which the President admitted to an acquaintance of mine, who said the persons appointed were all the friends of Mr. B[uchanan] save one. Mr. B[uchanan]'s ambition has destroyed the dull prospect he ever had to the Succession, he is on the wane here. Mr. Dallas has acquired some little strength from his position & the prospect as some of his friends say of becoming President ["from" *canceled*] like Tyler, supposing Mr. Polk to be in a rapid decline. Judging from the present excitement, the natives [party] will succeed in the City & County at the approaching election, owing to the discontent which prevail in the Democratic ranks.

There is an under current perceptable in favour of S[ilas] E. [*sic*] Wright among the Old Hunkers, a shrewd set of politicians, who will abandon both Dallas & Buchanan & even [Robert J.] Walker whom they feign to believe a strong man, & support the former. Many of your friends here are anxious for your return to the Senate. Mr. Polk's Cabinet is not considered a strong one, many think Mr. B[u-chanan] cannot long remain in it, & that he has neither tact nor talents suffic[i]ent to a successful termination of the important negociations now pending. The annexation of Texas will change the political complexion of affairs. The Oregon & California questions may also be settled before the next Presidential contest, in that event it will give additional strength to the South.

In case you should return to the Senate, which your friends in this quarter very much desire, It would make some of the aspirants sink to their proper level, & would place you in the front rank of the party throughout the Country. The rejection of the appointments, here, would be received with acclamation by a large portion of the Democratic party, & prevent the leaders from rallying their forces again. You have no idea of the discontent that pervades the party, the papers endeavor to conceal the fact because of their apprehension of the defeat of the party in October next, caused by the folly & ambition of Mr. B[uchanan] who is openly denounced as a Hartford Convention federalist, & I believe him to have been one of the principal conspirators against you last winter.

My former letter was from Bucks County, since which I removed to the City & reside at No. 16 Sansom Street; some of our friends have proposed to form a Calhoun association in the City—if they do, you must expect to be annoyed, by occasional communications. I think a scheme of that Kind premature. Very Respectfully Your most ob[edien]t S[er]v[an]t, P. Gwinner.

ALS with En in ScCleA. NOTE: Gwinner enclosed a clipping from the Philadelphia, Pa., *American Sentinel and Mercantile Advertiser* of 7/31/1845, entitled "Rotation." The article contrasted the "democratic principle" of rotation in office with removals from office for political reasons.

To J[AMES] H. HAMMOND, Silverton, S.C.

Fort Hill, 2d Aug[us]t 1845

My dear Sir, Although I agree with you that there ["are" *interlined*] several points, on which Dr. Bascomb [*sic*; Henry B. Bascom] does not agree with us on the subject of abolition, yet his defence is so full and abounds with so much that is good & well said, that it is calculated to do a vast deal of good in portions of the South particularly, that are not as sound, as our State, that I thought it highly desirable, that publick attention should be called to it. I think it the more desirable on account of his high standing & influence in his church, and as the head of the Kentucky [Transylvania] University, where we need strengthening. It is a powerful antidote to the poison, attempted to be desseminated by C[assius] M. Clay in that State. He would feel the compliment of a well written article, & I still hope, you will prepare one for the [Charleston] Mercury or some other of our papers, if the [Southern] Review should be closed. It need not occupy more than a column; & some general expression might be used to except the parts, we do not approve, to which he could take no exception. The object of the article might be ["limited to" *interlined*] a complimentary notice & to attrack publick attention.

I am gratified ["that" *canceled*] to learn, that you have turned your attention, with so much zeal, to agricultural improvements, & wish you the greatest success; but you must not think of looking on with indifference on publick affairs. As often as we have been disappointed, we must still persevere to put & keep the Government right. Perseverance & boldness are the two great qualities, without which nothing can ever be effected ["in politicks" *interlined*], that will be permanently useful. I may well claim the right of retiring & closing my publick life; but you younger men, who are still in the prime, & are capable of rendering great service, must not think, that you have served out your tour of duty yet.

I take great interest in agricultural improvements, and will certainly make you a visit, should I ever be in your vicinity. So far from considering it an intrusion, I should regard it quite a compliment to receive Mr. Allan's [*sic*; Anthony B. Allen's] publication [the *American Agriculturalist*]. I have never yet written any thing on agriculture. I regard myself but an undergraduate; to receive & not to give instruction. Indeed, if I were inclined to write, I have not leisure amidest [*sic*] my other occupations. I would give you such a sketch of my Hill side draining, as you desire, but it is with me so much a matter of mere application to my particular place, that I should find it very difficult to lay down any, but a very few general [*mutilated*; directions], by which to construct ["the drains" *interlined*]. I make it, in every case, a mere matter of good sense. I have never seen its application, but on my own place. The descent must be just such, as to carry sand, which, I suppose, to be [*one word canceled and* "usually" *interlined*] about 3 inches in 10 or 12 feet, but it depends a good deal on circumstances, particularly the volume of water. The greater the [volume of water], [the] less descent is necessary, but the ditch, in that case, must be made proportion[al]ly large & strong. If your brother [Marcus C.M. Hammond] takes much interest in the subject, he had better make a visit & inspect mine. I would be glad to see him, & he could better understand the subject, by one day's inspection, than by reading a volume. I have succeeded so well, that a field, which is very rolling, has now the 13th crop; the two first in corn, and the other 11 in cotton, with the exception of one, in wheat, and is free from gullies or gald [*sic*] spots. But what is still stranger, the present crop is equal to any it ever bore, although it has not been manured, except a small piece of old ground, I took in. Its yield, for the last three years, has not averaged less, than 240 pounds of clean cotton to the acre, & I expect as much this year, as dry as it is. It was oak, hickory & pine land of good quality; more light than [*one word canceled*] heavy. Yours truly, J.C. Calhoun.

ALS in DLC, James Henry Hammond Papers; PC in Jameson, ed., *Correspondence*, pp. 667–669.

To F[RANCIS] W. PICKENS, Edgefield, S.C.

Fort Hill, 2d Aug[us]t 1845

My dear Sir, The omission about the chimnies was accidental. I answered your letter without having it before me, & it slipt my memory at the time. It occurred to me after I had sent it to the [post] office, & [I] intended to notice it in my next, but hoped, at the same time, that you would consider my general approval of ["what" *interlined*] you had done & my readiness to indorse whatever you might think proper to order, as extending to an approval of your suggestions about them. As to a mason, there is not one in all this region that I know of who could be got.

Mrs. [Floride Colhoun] Calhoun's health is still bad. She is very feeble; & for the most part confined to her bed. I regret to hear of your injury, & hope it may pass away, without permanent effect. You were fortunate, in so ugly a fall, to escape as well as you did.

It still continues with us excessly dry. At no period have the streams been lower or the ground dryer. I have a forty acre feild [*sic*], partly in corn & partly in cotton, on which there has not fallen since March rain enough to run. The rest of my place has faired a good deal better. In estimating our Alabama corn crop, I add the old corn we ["will" *interlined*] have on hand, which will be about 1500 bushels I understand. The present crop is good, & we have planted 350 acres. The ordinary product has been about 50 bushels to the acre. Our present, is more, than a third larger than, we ever planted before. We have always had a surplus since the second year.

I do not exercise the least control over the [Charleston] Mercury or any other paper. I leave them to take their own course, as I take mine. It is absurd for any one, who reads the Mercury to suppose, that it speaks my opinion. It is well known to all its readers, that it has differed from me on many important points for the last 2 years.

I do not contemplate going beyond Mobile or N[ew] Orleans, at the fartherest, when I visit Alabama. My repugnance to travel, as ["a" *interlined*] mere show, is very strong, and that is the only way, that publick men can now travel. Besides, my publick life is terminated, as far as it depends on myself. I shall never return to it, unless the country should demand my services, & then only on the principle of duty. I wish to have the rest of my days under my own control. I can fill them up more pleasantly, & I hope not less usefully to the country, even if they should extend beyond the period usually allotted to the life of man. Such being my determination, I am averse to doing any thing, which may be construed as a seeker of

52

publick favour, as travelling would certainly be. I am satisfied with the share which has been allotted to me; and retire at a time & under circumstances with which I am entirely satisfied. In looking back, I see little to regret or correct, had I to go over life ["again" *interlined*].

All join their love to you, Mrs. [Marion Antoinette Dearing] P[ickens] & family. Yours truly, J.C. Calhoun.

ALS in ScU-SC, John C. Calhoun Papers. Note: An AEU by Pickens reads: "J.C. Calhoun denying that the Mercury *represents him* &c. *August 1845.*" A second AEU, added probably by Pickens at a later time in the margin adjacent to Calhoun's paragraph about his proposed travel, reads: "Went on to N[ew] Orleans & up to Memphis—presided at a great internal improvement convention—came out for appropriations for waters of the Miss: River being Constitutional there but not in the Atlantic States."

To A[rmistead] Burt, [Representative from S.C.], Willington, S.C.

Fort Hill, 3d Aug[us]t 1845

My dear Sir, I received a few days since a note from Col. J[ames] Ed[ward] Colhoun, in which he states, that his Mason estimates, that it will take 40 barrels of lime & one of Hydraulick cement for the wall to enclose the grave yard. He also states, that he cannot do the quar[ry]ing, but expects to be able to spare him in time to put up the wall. He desires, that Frank [Calhoun] should see him on the subject. I will thank you to let ["him" *canceled and* "Frank" *interlined*] know, that he desires to see him, in reference to it & request his attendance to it.

We are all well, except Mrs. [Floride Colhoun] Calhoun. She has been ill ever since the 3d July, with a severe nerveous attack, and is still confined to her bed the greater part of her time with it. I hope, however, her health will be shortly restored.

You & Martha [Calhoun Burt] must not fail to fulfil your promise to make us a visit. We shall all be very glad to see you.

We have suffered throughout all this region sever[e]ly from the drought, with very partial exceptions. I have a forty acre field in corn & cotton, on which there has not fallen rain enough to run, since March. The rest of my place has fared better; and if there should be no fresh, I shall make an ample supply of provisions, & not a bad crop of cotton. My up land corn will not yeild [*sic*] a third it ought.

I hope you have succeed[ed] in making a good crop. Andrew [Pickens Calhoun] writes me very favourable accounts from Alabama.

All join their love to you & Martha. Yours affectionately, J.C. Calhoun.

ALS in NcD, John C. Calhoun Papers. NOTE: Frank Calhoun (b. 1820) was a son of John C. Calhoun's brother Patrick Calhoun.

To "Col." J[AMES] ED[WARD] COLHOUN

Fort Hill, 3d Aug[us]t 1845

My dear James, Your Sister [Floride Colhoun Calhoun] still continues quite unwell, and is confined to her bed the greater part of her time. I some times feel very uneasy about her; but hope she may be able in a few days to set out for Glenn Springs, from which she derived great benefit from a similar attack two years ago.

I have sent word to Frank [Calhoun] to call on you, on the subject of the wall round the grave yard, agreeably to your request.

I am glad to learn, that you have the prospect of being a seller, & not a buyer of provisions this bad year. There will be, but few in the State so fortunately situated. The impression is, that this District cannot possibly supply itself next year; let the season hereafter be what it may. I shall make enough, & something to spare, if there should be no fresh. My upland corn will not make a third of a crop.

We have not yet heard from Mr. Toomy [*sic*; Michael Tuomey]. Willie [William Lowndes Calhoun] is going to s[c]hool & cannot go down. All join their love to you. Yours affectionately, J.C. Calhoun.

ALS in ScCleA.

From W[ILLIAM] A. HARRIS

Washington, 4 Aug. 1845

My Dear Sir: I tender you many thanks for your kind letter of the 19 July. It happened, singular enough, that on the same day that I received it, the President [James K. Polk] had sent for me, through Mr. [James] Buchanan, to inform me of his kind intentions. He told me that it had been his purpose from the moment of his coming into office, to confer upon me some appointment worthy of my qualifications, as he was pleased to term it, and such as my friends would approve. That he had determined in his own mind to give me the mission to Buenos Ayres, and sh[oul]d have offered it to me immediately, but that Mr. [Henry A.] Wise had written some months ago that Mr. [William] Brent [Jr.], the present chargé to that government, was dying of consumption, and that he had been withholding the appointment, till he should hear further concerning Mr. Brent's health. He had determined, however, to make the appointment now—and that upon mentioning it to his Cabinet, ["that" *canceled*] they had, with the warmest expressions of kindness towards me, unanimously sanctioned it. He said that it was necessary, however, to withhold the commission a couple of weeks, for reasons that he was not at liberty to explain. He enquired when I had heard from you &c., in the kindest manner. As he lead [*sic*] the way into political topics, and endorsed with his entire approval the course which the [Washington] Constitution had pursued, I took occasion to express myself very freely. And, I told him plainly, that unless he placed himself upon the measures and principles advanced by the Baltimore convention, that he would not and could not be sustained by the country. He declared, in the most emphatic manner, that it was his most firm and settled purpose to carry out to the fullest extent, every measure and principle therein indicated; and, that, as he was inflexibly determined not to be a candidate for re-election, that his highest ambition, was so to administer the the [*sic*] affairs of the government, as to enable the democratic party to elect to the Presidential office, such candidate as they might choose. I told him very plainly that he had been suspected of leaning too much to the influence and purposes of the politicians of New-York and Pennsylvania, and that unless he placed himself upon the true doctrines of the south and west, he w[oul]d find himself in a minority before the middle of next December. He affirmed that he relied upon the south and the west for support, and that they would find him leading the way in the great measures for which they are contending. A great deal to the same purport was said, which it is of no importance to repeat. A wonderful change has come over the policy of the administration, depend upon it. What has wrought this sudden change, I think it were not very difficult to immagine. The signs had begun to be alarming. The President admitted that New-York had given him more trouble since he had been in office than all the rest of the union put together, and yet was not satisfied.

Immediately after this conversation, I met with Mr. Buchanan, then with Mr. [Robert J.] Walker, and then with Judge [John Y.] Mason [Attorney General]. I talked very freely with them, even more so than with the President; and, I soon found that they had become alarmed, and they all made the same patriotic professions which had just been announced by the President. Judge Mason, who is an exceedingly pure minded and honorable man, is greatly attached and devoted to you. He told me that he took no active part in Cabinet matters—that the President treated him as a confidential friend, and that he preferred to occupy that position. Well, upon coming home from this scene of exciting argumentation, I found your letter upon my table. It may be now, that its invaluable suggestions may no longer be applicable, since Mr. Polk seems determined to place himself on southern ground. He has made Mr. [Thomas] Ritchie announce his purposes in regard to the Subtreasury—and, in a previous article, *which was written at the White House*, headed "the Administration—its prospects &c."—he had more clearly defined his position and announced his purposes.

But the subject at present ["mostly" *altered to* "most"] deeply interesting to your friends, is the propriety of your coming to the Senate again. Upon the most mature reflection, I have not changed my opinion as to the policy of your remaining at Fort Hill, till the people move in the matter. But I confess that many weighty and strong reasons are urged on the other side. It is insisted that the whigs have never been so strong on the score of talents, in the Senate, whilst the only man that can pretend to cope with them, and upon whom we can depend, is Mr. [Levi] Woodbury. Col. [Thomas H.] Benton and [William] Allen will go against the Administration and against the South, as far as they can do so. It is insisted, therefore, that were you in the Senate to sustain the principles and defend the measures of the democratic party, ["it" *interlined*] would so enlist the sympathies of the people, by drawing their attention upon yourself, ["and" *canceled and* "as" *interlined*] to make you stronger ["than" *canceled*] than ever. I am willing to say that this is the opinion of a majority of your friends, so far as I have seen and conversed with them. But I know that it will be the policy of Benton & Co. to level their shafts at you on all occasions, and if possible to obstruct the increasing current of public feeling in your favor. [Robert M.T.] Hunter, [James A.] Seddon, [Henry] Bedinger, William Smith, and [David] Levy [Yulee] of Florida, all seem to think that you ought to come to the Senate, yet admit the force of the reasons which I urge against it. It is indeed, difficult to say, what is best. Perhaps after all, your duty to your country and your party, will be best for yourself. Most sincerely, W.A. Harris.

[P.S. in margin of first page:] Senator Levy of Florida is here now. [James D.] Wes[t]cott the other Senator is one of your warmest friends. Levy will hear to nothing else but your returning to the Senate.

ALS in ScCleA; PEx in Boucher and Brooks, eds., *Correspondence*, pp. 300–302. NOTE: Harris was appointed by Polk as U.S. Chargé d'Affaires to Argentina and served 1846–1851.

From M[OSES] C. MORDECAI

Charleston, Aug[u]st 6/1845

Annex[e]d I hand You a copy of a letter rec[eive]d by Col. [Franklin H.] Elmore from Mr. Secr[etary] of the Treasury Robert J.] Walker.

I must say I do not like the substance, more particularly as I learn that there is a seeming Acknowledgment that no change can be made on the free List, indeed rather a conjecture that they may be increased [*sic*] in number. With Great Respect Yo[ur] Ob[edient] S[ervant], M.C. Mordecai.

[Enclosure]

R[obert] J. W[alker] to F[ranklin] H. E[lmore], "(Private)"

July 21 /45

Dear Sir, I have rec[eive]d your letter of the 17th & would be very glad indeed if under the general interrogat[or]ies the Chamber of Commerce or any of our friends at Charleston would give us the information to which you refer. Every thing it seems to me is favourable to a *very great Reduction* of the present Exhorbitant duty, nothing shall be wanting on my part to accomplish this Object. I would be much rejoiced if you would give me your views fully on this great question. It is due to Cander to say that I do not think we can reenact in form the Compromise act, but we can make a substantial reduction approximating it very closely. Y[ours] resp[ectful]ly &c, Sig[ne]d R.J.W.

ALS with En in ScCleA. NOTE: An AEU by Calhoun on Mordecai's cover letter reads "Mr. Mordecai, encloses a copy of Mr. Walker's letter to Mr. Elmore."

From P[ATRICK] CALHOUN

Biloxi Miss., August 7th 1845
Dear Father, Yours of the 24th of last month was received the day before I left New-Orleans—and having been on the move ever since I have had no opportunity of writing. Gen. [Edmund P.] Gaines with his staff and family left New-Orleans on the 3d inst., intending to take up his Head-Q[uarte]rs at this place for a few weeks. The mail boat—the Fashion—on which we left New Orleans could not get into this place on account of the depth of water—and therefore had to land her passengers on a Pier-Head some two miles from the shore. On reaching this Pier-Head it was found that it would be difficult to get to shore as it was late at night and the Gulf quite rough—the Gen. therefore concluded to continue on to Mobile and return from there to Pass-Christian—from which latter place a high-pressure boat of light-draught came to this point. As the boat from Pass-Christian was not a daily one we were obliged to remain there more than twenty four hours. The trip in all amounted to more than four hundred miles—and afforded me an opportunity of seeing and learning much of this part of the Gulf of Mexico and its shores. We arrived here day before yesterday & as it is a small village—some five hundred inhabitants—found it difficult the hour being late to find quarters for the night. Since then we have changed our quarters and are now quite comfortable. The village of Biloxi is situated near the extremity of a peninsula about a mile wide, run[n]ing for some distance into the Gulf—and being the summer resort of many of the wealthy families of New-Orleans. A portion of it—that occupied by these families—is well built and improved—and presents a pretty appearance. The climate is delightful—and the sea-bathing beneficial to the health—the improvement of which I began to find very necessary to me—before leaving New Orleans—as the atmosphere although not actually poisonous, was still injurious and enervating and had affected ["me" *interlined*] considerably. I feel however much improved since breathing the pure air of the Gulf.

After getting on board the boat at Pass-Christian, General Gaines found papers and letters giving him information of later news from Mexico, which rendered it more than probable that war would be declared in a short time. The morning after our arrival—yesterday morning—he sent for me but I was out, having left the house for a few minutes. Capt. [John C.] Reid the Gen[era]l['s] other Aid[e] was therefore sent for—and rec[e]ived instructions to return to New-Orleans and get all the authentic information on the subject he

58

could. Capt. Reid returns this evening and should the information he brings corroborate in any degree what has been stated—the Gen. will I suppose return immediately to New-Orleans. Should it be true, as has been stated, that ten thousand Mexican Troops are on or near the Rio Grande—General [Zachary] Taylor's command will be in a very critical situation. But Gen. Gaines' hands are in a me[a]-sure tied—as he has no instructions on the subject—and has never even been informed from Head-Q[uarte]rs that any movement was to be made into that country. He will however I think from what he says go to the assistance of Gen. Taylor if necessary—if he does not and war is declared, I shall join my Regiment [the 2nd Dragoons] if possible. I have no idea of remaining at Biloxi under such circumstances.

Having written to Brother Andrew [Pickens Calhoun] several times [with]out receiving an answer, I took advantage of my [*mutilation*; trip?] to Mobile to write and mail a letter to him from that place, which I think he will be likely to get. In my letter I mention to him what you desired me to—and also that if he could make the arrangement with some House in Mobile, I could draw on it from whatever point I might be at.

I regret to hear that Mother [Floride Colhoun Calhoun] is unwell—and hope she has recovered ere this. My love to all. Your affectionate son, P. Calhoun.

P.S. Capt. Reid has just returned and brings such information that the Gen[era]l has determined to leave for New-Orleans in the morning. P.C.

ALS in ScU-SC, John C. Calhoun Papers. NOTE: This letter was postmarked in New Orleans on a day that appears to be 8/18.

From W[ILLIAM] B. LEWIS

Nashville, 7th Aug[us]t 1845

Dear Sir, It has been intimated by the President [James K. Polk], as you have doubtless seen, in a letter which he directed to be shown to Gen[era]l [Andrew] Jackson, that it was necessary to remove me from office [as Second Auditor of the Treasury], because my position made me dangerous to the Government, in as much as it enabled me to impart information to a certain foreign power to the disadvantage of my own country—which I interpret to mean, "that

59

at *heart* I consider Major Lewis a *traitor* willing and ready, when occasion offers, to betray his country to a certain foreign power." A high compliment this to the sagacity of Gen[era]l Jackson, Mr. [Martin] Van Buren, yourself and Mr. [John] Tyler—particularly you and Mr. Tyler not to perceive the risk you ran in having your plans for annexation, and negotiations with the Texan ministers, completely broken up by keeping me in office! Not having seen the President[']s list of grievances, I do not know the precise *ground* upon which this imputation against my patriotism and honor has been ["made" *canceled and "*placed" *interlined*] by him, but have reason to believe it is in referrence to the annexation of Texas to the U. States. Gen[era]l Jackson, in his letter to me of the 10th April last, which I have had published, alludes to it and pronounces it, upon *his own knowledge*, to be unjust. The General might well deny the truth of such an allegation, for he had evidence of its falsity in the numerous letters I had written him—some of them at your suggestion—upon that great and deeply interesting Question. No man, with the exception of yourself, knew so well my feelings and wishes in relation to that matter as he did—and here I will say if there is a single individual in America who more ardently desired the accomplishment of that great measure ["than I did," *interlined*] without regard to the wishes of either England or *France,* I should like to know who he is; yet this is made a pretext for an attempt to *dishonor* me in the eyes of the Nation by the President!

This is a matter of importance to *me,* in as much as it deeply involves my character and honor, and may be equally so to my *descendents,* after I shall have gone hence, should the letter of the President, referred to above and written to Gen[era]l [Robert] Armstrong with directions to be shown to Gen[era]l Jackson, containing a long list of *grievances* &c, ever be published, as was originally ["intended" *interlined*] I have no doubt ["intended" *canceled*]. Recollect, this letter was ["written" *interlined*] by the *President himself,* carrying with it the weight and sanctity of his official character, in which he intimates that he feels it to be his duty to remove me from office, because my position enabled me to betray my government and, having no confidence in my patriotism, was afraid I might do so! Gen[era]l Jackson, it is true, says that *he knows* the imputation is unfounded and unjust; but, my dear Sir, in addition to this I want *you* to state what you know of my course in relation to the annexation of Texas to the U. States which, from your well known love of justice, I am sure you will not decline. I had more private and confidential conversations with you, upon that subject, than with any

60

other person and you, therefore, know better what were my real feelings. Allow me then to ask you to state whether, *at any time*, you ever saw or knew any thing of me that could induce you to think, for a moment, that I was more inclined to favor the views of a certain foreign power, supposed to be hostile to annexation, than I was those of my own Country? Whether I did not frequently call at the State Dept. to communicate such information as I thought might be useful to you, and particularly to show you letters from Gen[era]l Jackson? These things must be fresh in your recollection and I am sure you will take pleasure in stating them in answer to this letter. Gen[era]l Jackson[']s letter and one from you are all I desire for the protection of my character and *memory*, when I am no more, as I know they will have more weight, in the estimation of posterity, than any thing *fifty Polks*, tho' they should be all Presidents, can say against me.

The State elections take place in this State to day. The contest it is thought will be close, and the result consequently doubtful. [Ephraim H.] Foster is the candidate of the Whigs for Governor, and A[aron] V. Brown of the democrats. The Whigs for the last four or five years have had a majority of some three or four thousand, and if there has been no change, as contended by them, the probability is that Mr. Foster will be elected by a small majority. On the other hand I incline to the opinion that the democrats will have a majority in the Legislature, on joint ballot, which will give them the Senator. This, as regards the great Texian measure, is of more importance than the election of their Governor. However, as the election is at hand, there is no use in speculating upon probable results.

I am afraid, my dear Sir, that the new administration *we* helped to bring into power will prove a failure! The selection of Mr. Polk was a great mistake. It should undoubtedly have been either you or [Lewis] Cass; but it cannot now be helped, and we ["have now" *canceled*] must make the most of it. He is not a man suited to conduct the affairs of this country at such a crisis—he has neither the mind nor the weight of character that is requisite. Nor has he the moral courage, or firmness, to resist the importunities of the jacobins and desperate men who daily crowd the halls of the presidential mansion and clamor for the *spoils*. I have often said to Gen[era]l Jackson that if the Government should ever be considered worth nothing only on account of its offices, it *would not* in fact be worth a button. It is fast coming to this, if it has not already reached that point. The truth is, the use which is now made of the Government patronage ["have" *altered to* "has"] a most corrupting and demoralizing effect upon the whole community and unless it [*"can" interlined*] be arrested must end in the overthrow of our political system. This is no recent opinion of mine—I have entertained it for the last ten or twelve years and have done all I could, since the latter part of Gen-[era]l Jackson[']s Administration, to check it; but *my* efforts [*"ag" canceled*] to arrest this continually swelling torrent [*"of corruption and abuse" interlined*] were vain and futile. Indeed, I might with truth say perhaps, that they brought my own head to the block, for I have very little doubt it was my opposition to the infamous *spoils* principle, that led to my expulsion from office—and not the fear of my *betraying* my own Government, as has been alledged by our *sagacious* President!

My friend of the Washington Union [Thomas Ritchie], I see stoutly denies that Mr. Polk desires a reelection. This may be so, but some of the sta[u]nchest and most sagacious democrats belonging to the party thought differently when I left Washington, and that I confess was and *is* my own opinion. If, however, he finds this cannot be effected, he will then, I have no doubt, favor the election of a northern man [*Interpolated:* "Mr. (Silas) Wright, most likely"] with the hope of being taken up again in 1852, as he will still be young enough, not even then having reached his sixtieth year. I have lived too long and seen too much, to place any *very great* confidence in friend Ritchie[']s denials for the President, and so, I am sure, have *you.* With my best wishes, I am, my dear Sir, very Truly yours, W.B. Lewis.

ALS in ScCleA. NOTE: Lewis had been a member of the "Kitchen Cabinet" during Jackson's Presidency.

From B[ARTHOLOMEW] R. CARROLL

Charleston, Aug[u]st 8 1845

Dear Sir, The frankness of your favor of the 3d inst. emboldens me to challenge your indulgence again on the subject of my last communication. Should my scheme for the institution of an Academy at the Limestone Springs be consummated, the outline of studies will probably be the following[:]

3d Class. Arithmetic, Algebra, English Grammar, Geography, History, English Exercises, French[,] Duties of the private soldier, and exercises on the farm.

2d Class. Geometry descriptive and analytical, Surveying, To-pography, History, Elocution and composition, Book Keeping, Moral philosophy, French[,] Tactics and exercises on the farm.

1s[t] Class. Calculus, Natural and experimental philosophy, Chemistry, Mineralogy and Botany, Rhetoric, Moral and Political philosophy, National and constitutional Law, French, Tactics, Theo-retical and practical Agriculture.

To instruct in the above branches five professors will be (perhaps) employed. 1 A professor of Modern Sciences, 2 One of Mathematics, 3 One of English Literature, 4 One of Chemistry, Mineralogy and Botany, 5 One of French. J[ohn] A. Leland Esq[ui]r[e] of So[uth] Car[olina], myself and Dr. Lawrence Smith of this State would fill the 2d[,] 3d and 4th professorships respectively. W[illiam] Spenser Brown Esq. a former distinguished graduate of West Point, and for many years an officer in the Engineer's Department of the U.S. [Army], is a candidate for the first place. This gentleman's friends present his name as one whose capability, character and temper eminently qualify him for the chair.

The regulations of the school would be under the strictest disci-pline—in many respects similar to the regulations of the Academy at West Point and that of the Citadel in Charleston.

Your experience has doubtless suggested, that our Carolina Youth are only not inferior to the Northern in the advantages of a business education. Most of our graduates come from college good critics and theses-writers, but is it venturing too much to say, a majority of them are totally unfit to commence life with proper business habits[?] How few for instance are prepared to draw out or examine an ordi-nary ac[c]o[un]t—to draft the most ordinary resolution, or even to write a common business letter. Trivial as these matters appear they are such as renders one very awkward in not possessing them. At our colleges, students are taught Political Economy—and most of them call [*sic*; can] readily tell at what page this or that principle may be found, expounded—but how to apply those principles—very few can tell. And yet; I have seen a class of sixty boys, none of them over sixteen, who could each readily apply every principle of the science, & properly use each of its terms, in application to any article of trade which might be presented. If the teacher will examine, and not merely listen to the recitation of the student; if he will teach how to apply—and not merely how learn, science will then become ["as" *interlined*] useful to the recipient, as tools are to the mechanic.

I am persuaded we loose [*sic*] too much time on the Classics. If I had spent less time in discovering the *under derivative* of Latin and Greek words, in assorting and fitting them into their proper places in a sentence, and had devoted more to my native tongue—in learning for instance to imitate the euphonies of Milton and Shakespear[e]—in denouncing or invoking like [William Pitt, Earl of] Chat[h]am—in probing like Junius [i.e., Sir Philip Francis]—in argumentatively narrating with the perspicuity of [William] Pitt—in rambling with the apparent straight forwardness of [Charles James] Fox—or adorning with the statuesque simplicity of Irskine [sic; Thomas Erskine], or to venture on a personality—in giving, like yourself, to the condensation of comprehensive thoughts, the light and flame of self interpreting words—if I say, I had been taught to imitate such models, I feel that I would have lost nothing, never to [have] scanned Homer or Virgil—nor to have learnt to parse and construe Demosthenes, Cicero, Tacitus or Livy.

And what, Sir, would half the world say, did it know, I had ventured to write thus familiarly to the venerable Statesman of Fort Hill. But if the world will not pardon[,] the Statesman will, and I even venture to trespass on his patience a while longer. Within my limitted acquaintance I know of some 30 or 40 boys who are now being educated out of the State. I am not averse to send our men abroad—it not unfrequently makes them better satisfied with home—but I protest against sending our youth out of the State to be educated. In my own case, I can attribute to such a mistake, the entertainment of early-imbibed errors which years of a different experience have been scarce able to obliterate. We know little of the human heart—nothing of the powerful effects of associations, who cannot appreciate what I maintain.

If our men of influence will come forth to the task the reform can at least be commenced. I know I need not ask where you may be found. You have already frankly and directly stated what you are willing to do—not to talk but to place your jewels where you would have them [one word canceled] as a part of the capital required. But Sir, you can do more. Examine the plan I lay before you—give (to you an easy labor) a proper digestion of it—and favor me the encouragement of your suggestions and advice. You shall find me willing to receive and to serve.

In all of this matter, I console myself with the reflection that I am not too much actuated by a selfish motive. At this very time I have a professorship tendered me out of the State but my heart is in Carolina, and I cannot but confess the ambition of wishing to serve her first. The State is my birth place—has ever been my home, her people have honored me in their service and the dust of my kindred and children is mingled with the soil. The chain that will drag me from so dear a spot, may carry the body—but will surely leave behind the spirit and the heart. I have trespassed long enough—and yet cannot conclude without asking another indulgence—that of being permitted to subscribe myself with profound respect Y[ou]r ob[edien]t serv[an]t & friend, B.R. Carroll.

ALS in ScCleA. Note: Carroll was the son of an Irish immigrant to Charleston and with his brothers, Charles Rivers Carroll (a close friend of William Gilmore Simms), and Edward Carroll, was active in Charleston literary circles. His interest in promoting a new school at this time was apparently related to the fact that his term of office as South Carolina State Treasurer for the Lower Division would expire in 10/1845 and he had not been reappointed.

From W. R. B. DORTCH

La Grange Ala., August 8th 1845

Dear Sir, I avail myself of this occasion & method of announcing to you in the name of the Dialectical Society of La Grange College College [*sic*] Ala. your election as honorary member. The Society tenders to you this mark of their respect in the full confidence that you will receive it as an offering of their sincere friendship and permit them to enrol your name among their honorary members Knowing that all True patriots & noble hearted men feel a lively interest in the promotion of that cause for which they are striving. As the advancement of Knowledge and the cultivation of the mind are their primary objects, they feel emboldened from the signal displays which popular education is making. The society unite in offering you the best wishes of their hearts for your health[,] happiness & prosperity. If it pleases you to accept this mark of the society's regard make it known by addressing the Undersigned at La Grange Ala. W.R.B. Dortch, Sec[re]t[ar]y of the Dialectical Society.

ALS in ScCleA.

From THOMAS R. SMELIE

Mobley Pond P.O. [Ga.,] Aug. 9th [18]45

Dear Sir, Your esteem'd favor of the 24th ult. has been rec[eive]d & [I] feel honor'd. Jno. C. C[alhoun] [Smelie] feels elated at your noticing him so much as to proffer the books you speak of, which I can receive for him thro the Mail. Packages not more than 3 lbs. are admitted, and as I have the office here in charge I shall be enabled to receive them safely.

As you very truly Observe Xample [*sic*] has more influence than precept & I will endeavor to set such an one as after I am call'd hence he may not have reason to blush for his father. I have thus far endeavor'd to instill into the minds of children some of whom are grown, that the first duty they owe is to their Creator & then to their fellow beings, & that they were placed here ["not" *interlined*] for self alone.

In hopes your truly valuable Life may be spared many years to your country & friends, & every blessing of life attend you I subscribe myself Y[ou]rs with great respect, Thomas R. Smelie.

ALS in ScCleA.

To J[OHN] R. MATHEW[E]S, Clark[e]sville, Ga.

Fort Hill, 11th Aug[us]t 1845

My dear Sir, I was much engaged when I received your former letter, which with a severe illness of Mrs. [Floride Colhoun] Calhoun with an attack of a nerveous character, which confined her to her bed for more than a month, will explain the appearant neglect of not more promptly answering your letter. She has so far recovered as to be able to leave for Glenn Springs [S.C.]. She left a few days since.

Mr. [Thomas G.] Clemson has return[ed] to Brussels from his visit to Paris & a letter addressed to him will reach him there.

Unless the [James K. Polk] Administration shall greatly misconduct the Government, the fate of the Whig party is sealed for the present, not only in Georgia, but the Union. Thus far but little wisdom or firmness have been exhibitted by it. It is to be hoped it may change its course, & act with more wisdom & firmness. I understand, from a very reliable source at Washington, that its members have become alarmed, and will change their tack, but I must say, from what I know of them, I expect but little good. The truth is, that the office holders & the office seekers govern the country, & the struggles between the parties have degenerated into a mere contest for the spoils, without a particle of regard on either side for principles or country.

I think it now too late to publish my letter [of 2/8 to John W. Jones, Speaker of the House of Representatives, on the alleged errors of the Sixth Census] & the statistical tables you refer to. The time has passed by, & the publick cannot again be called with any vivacity to their contents. My letter had at the time to work its own way. When it was published, it was pretty generally condemn[ed] at the North by both parties, & was received with dead silence by the press of the South, except a ["few" *canceled*] favourable notice from the Charleston [Southern] Patriot. Both the Richmond Enquirer & the Charleston Mercury published it without the slightest notice; & the [Columbia South-]Carolinian did not publish it at all. [James G.] Bennet[t]'s [New York] Herald was the only paper which anticipated its effects, & it was not until the response came from Europe, that the publick attention, even in the South, was directed to it. Your's was almost the only letter I received which noticed it at all. I do not mention these things with any feeling of discontent or censure. Far otherwise. My feeling is that of deep greif [*sic*] to think how dead the South is to its most vital interests.

We have suffered most severely from the drought. I have one field on which there has not been rain enough for water to run, until day before yesterday since March, & then it was not wet above two [inc]hes. The rest of my place has fared better. My upland corn will make about a third of [the expected] crop, but my low grounds will make a pretty fair yield. I shall make enough for my use. Cotton has done better. I shall make not a great deal short of an average yield.

My respects to Mrs. [Elizabeth Jenkins Whaley] Mathew[e]s & your family. Yours truly, J.C. Calhoun.

ALS in DLC, John C. Calhoun Papers.

To T[HOMAS] G. CLEMSON

Fort Hill, 12th Aug[us]t 1845
My dear Sir, I receive[d] by the last steamer yours of the 10th & Anna's [Anna Maria Calhoun Clemson's] of the 4th of July, and am happy to learn that you are all well. We are all in the enjoyment of good health, except Mrs. [Floride Colhoun] Calhoun. Her indisposition proved more obstinant, & severe, than I expected. It was of the same discription with her illness two years ago, when Anna at-

tended ["her" *interlined*], but I infer, from what I heard of it, more severe. She had so far recovered, as to be able to go to the Glenn Springs. James [Edward Calhoun] accompanied her, & by a letter from him, received yesterday, I learn that they had arrived safely, & ["that she" *interlined*] stood the journey very well; & that her health had improved by travelling.

We have had the most remarkable drought ever known in this region, for its extent & duration. It has embraced all the Atlantick States with Alabama, but its intensity seems to be limited by the Delaware & the Alabama rivers. It still continues, although there have been partial rains of late. The scarcity will approach a famine.

I have suffered, as far as I can hear hereabouts, rather less than the average. My upland corn will not yield a third of a crop, but the bottom land will do pretty well. [With] What it will yield, with the old corn on hand, and a good crop of small grain, I shall have enough, & something to spare, if there should not be a fresh. To form some idea of its severity, the fort hill field, including Cobb's (the Low ground part) has not had sufficient rain to run since March, until ["yesterday" *canceled*] three days ago, & then it was not wet two inches.

I have not heard from your place lately; but from what I hear of rains in Edgefield, within the last ten days, I hope you are doing well. My cotton crop with the exception of the part in the fort Hill field, is surprisingly good for the season. With showers now, it would not fall much below an average. The last account from Alabama was good.

You have formed a very correct opinion of the state of political affairs with us. The Administration is very weak. Its course has neither indicated wisdom nor firmness. My letters from Washington, (one from a very intelligent & well informed observer) says, that there is to be an entire change of policy; that the [Martin] V[an] Buren party remain discontented, notwithstanding that they have been the recipients of almost all the executive favours, & that the Administration now see it, & are resolved to take an independent course. It is strange, that they did not see, from the first, that the proper course was to command, & not to purchase them; that they stood in a position from their passed [*sic*] misconduct, to be command[ed], with ease & certainty; but that to attempt to purchase them, was but [to] give them power, & that to do that, was but to change ["their" *interlined*] relative condition, & to enable them to command the Administration, instead of being commanded.

All join in love to you, Anna & the Children [John Calhoun Clem-

68

son and Floride Elizabeth Clemson]. Tell them that I wish to see
them much & kiss them for their Grandfather. I will write Anna
next. Yours affectionately, J.C. Calhoun.

ALS in ScCleA; PEx in Jameson, ed., *Correspondence*, p. 669.

From T H O [M A] s G. C L E M S O N

Terveuren [*sic*; Turvuren, Belgium] August 12th 1845
My dear Sir, Your favour of the 23d of June arrived by the Acadia.
With the exception of an occasional letter which comes by the sail
packets all ["our" *canceled*] are brought by the steamers, and they
come in bunches. It appears strange to hear you talk of drought,
whilst we are inundated, or rather saturated by constant rains. I
scarce recollect two successive days with out rain since the commencement of the year and I might add since our arrival in Belgium.
So wet has been the season that the Irish potato crop is threatened
with destruction. In some districts a disease seizes and destroys the
plant and tubercles [*sic*; tubers] in a day or two, and that without
further notice than a rapid withering & dying of the tops. The papers have spoken of the subject with a good deal of uneasiness & tho
the wheat harvest is spoken of as being very fine and abundant, apprehensions are felt for its safety, so that the price of wheat is higher
now than it was a month since, and is still on the increase.

I am glad to hear you speak of your fine grain crop and hope
your cotton may be equally good, but I fear the price will continue
to be low; if the crop is large, that will certainly be the case. Planters
should combine for the purchase of no other bagging than Cotton
bagging, use no other blankets than those of cotton in [*sic*] use no
article that can be replaced by that staple.

The consumption of cotton on the continent might be increased
if our diplomatic agents were to use their exertions in the several
states where they may be accredited. A desire is manifest every
where to increase manufactures and the subject should be agitated
and kept warm, but to effect that end we must strive at home to do
something for ourselves. The linen trade in Belgium is languishing
and will be eventual[l]y almost entirely replaced by that of Cotton,
and it is very possible to hasten that moment. European governments as you are aware take a much more direct influence upon internal affairs than we do, so that if a proper course be pursued on the

part of our Sec[re]t[ar]y of State [James Buchanan] by urging the diplomatic agent abroad to exert himself with that view a great deal may be done. Certainly neither Austria nor other parts of Germany want the desire to compete with England. The duties on cotton are now nothing and I should not be surprised to see a premium given for the greatest ["ex-" *canceled*] importation. But I fear we in the Southern States want Union, and the Secretary of State appears to me to be taking a profound sleep. Judging from what I see the Department of State pays very little attention to us her agents abroad. The project of a treaty which I sent home last spring I know reached Washington but so far as the Department is concerned I am not the wiser of it. It is impossible for the best of us to do good, or be active, if we are unattended to or unnoticed. I hope that I may be wrong and that the apparent negligence arrises [*sic*] from the Texas and Oregon questions[,] the first of which is settled, the other if rumour be true is nearly so. The whole Department I am sure wants change or reforming or remodeling.

I recieved [*sic*] the [Charleston] Mercury with Gov. [James H.] Hammond[']s letters on slavery. I read them with much pleasure, and if they could be circulated abroad would do infinite good. English periodicals will not publish them, but they may be gotten into some of the continental journals in the way of reviews and extracts. I shall do what I can and perhaps will have them struck of[f] in pamphlet form for circulation. We must not decieve [*sic*] ourselves at home that we are either loved or respected as a nation, and in England that hatred to our Governments both Federal and State descends to private individuals. We will have to depend on ourselves, and we must go our own road, but in pursuing that course we should have regard to the capability of our public officers.

I am much obliged to you for the advice you give me about my plantation. I have a great desire to do what is right in all things, and am too much interested in the independence and well being of my family not to wish to do what is right with my plantation. My uneasiness arrises from the want of the very thing you speak of. The overseer who is on the place may be very good but I know nothing of him, and the letters I have recieved from those who write me, are not calculated to inspire me with much confidence as to the manner things are progressing, or will progress. I know you have your own affairs to attend to. I do not ask you to see after my business but I would be pleased that you should ["do"(?) *canceled*], if you can make it convenient to visit the place, is to give such directions as you may think necessary and see that the overseer is such a one as he ought to be. I was not long enough in the countrey to form intimate acquaintances upon whom I could depend in my abscence; therefore if you could visit the place as you pass up and down, or in the healthy season your presence will be of infinite good. I have no intention of keeping the place if it is either det[er]iorating, or is likely to bring me in debt. I have too much decision to permit either, but I should like to be informed of the truth of the case that I may act. I have no very particular ["idea" *canceled*] inclination to retain this position because it is in Europe. If I had a situation in the United States which would give me an income sufficient for the support of my family, and from which I could direct my own business I would not trouble any one on the subject. I remain here now because I can support my family (with economy) and may perhaps be useful. If I retire from this position I can neither do one thing or the other. I had hoped in leaving my place that my stock would increase and things be ready for a future day. But since having left my overseers have been changed, and really there is positively no one to say do this or that, find fault or direct, and I wrote you on the subject with a view to make you feel really what I wish. Mr. [Francis W.] Pickens writes me that things are not doing well &c &c so that I am at a loss on all hands. My health is now much better than it has been for years. This climate is very humid & much colder than Carolina, but there is no comparison as to the healthfulness of the inhabitants. If I return to the United States and am obliged to depend upon the manner in which I employ my capital to give my family a support I will have to increase my force of every description; and to do that I must have a greater promise of gain, than is held out by what I have done already on the Cane Brake. More negroes and fresh lands will increase the percentage on the outlay, but if I am to strive there in spite of health and comfort I had better sell out and go elsewhere. My experience tells me that the Institution of slavery is at all times good for the negro (no labourers in the world are so well off). At times good for the master, but very bad for the State. The States north of the Ohio & south of it are examples of the effect of the two systems of labour. If the Institution lasts there is a kind of security in lands and negroes which other property does not possess, and ["when" *interlined*] one has children an investment is made with a view to their interests[;] in that point of view a plantation is desirable & I should regret its loss. But there is no doubt of one thing, if the interest of capital is considered the manufactures of the North have been, and there is a promise that they will be more prosperous with all their risks than the planters of the South. The North understand their interest and act with concert and Union no matter how much they may be divided on minor matters. This gives prosperity to the whole countrey. Planters have been exhausting the richness of a virgin soil, a richness that has been accumulating for ages. The North has been penetrated with one great truth[,] that it is easier to accumulate wealth already created than to create it. The Iron business is lucrative all over the world except the South and I am at a loss to know why it is. But I am sure of one thing after my little experiment and the conversation I have had with others engaged in the same business, that is, that he who engages his property in that kind of enterprize does it at his peril. When the South finds it necessary to improve their lands by manures, it will be a less profitable business to plant cotton than it has been heretofore, and if negroes continue high, lands increase and cotton falls[,] an entire change must come over the countrey. Is it true that the Tariff is the entire cause of the impoverishment of the South? The North has profit[t]ed it is true by the lavishness of the South, & the latter have had too much confidence in the virgin wealth of the soil, in the prolific influence of climate &c in fine in the gifts of the Almighty. They have not helped themselves. The North has been the recipients of the created wealth of the South. There is much more energy in the frugality & economy of the North than the South has heretofore manifested, at least.

We are living at the present time at a little village situated about seven miles from Bruxilles called Terveuren. There is here a beautiful Palace and a fine Park formerly the property of the prince of Orange. It is now the property of the Government and is used for the keeping of the Government Stallions. There is about a hundred of them in the stables at this time. The Government seeing the necessity of care & learning to prevent the perdition of the breed of Horses, have taken the subject into their keeping. They have individuals of learning in charge of the establishment who have made the subject one of great usefulness. I have acquired a good deal of information on the subject from inspection of horses, their product & the conversation of those in charge. When I first saw those large Norman horses I was of the impression that all that was necessary was the introduction of one of them to insure a like of[f]spring. This is a great mistake and I am convinced now that the introduction of one of those large horses would produce deformed animals. There would be too great disparity. But there are several varieties of the Norman horse, and among them there are [some?] whose introduction into the Southern States would be attended with the best possible advantages. We should by this means have a cross on our part blooded mares, that would be suited for all work. Strength, size, endurance and fitted for draft, which is wanting with us. How much the prosperity of an agricultural countrey, depends upon the race of horses, and when I see around me the daily evidence of the good results of a judicious crossing of horses, and knowing the absolute necessity of attention to this matter to produce proper results I can not otherwise than dwell upon the subject. For use we have the poorest race of horses in the world, which arises alltogether from a blind infatuation that obtains in the English blooded racer[—]admirable as he is for the course, he is most unfit for ["the" *canceled*] *all work.* We want a strong well built animal that will do for carriage, plough, or saddle, and that end will be acquired I think indubitably by the introduction of a horse constituted as are those of which I have spoken. The Norman horse is a variety of the Flanders mare celebrated for a long time. The English draft horse comes from a cross of the Norman or F[*ms. mutilated;* Flanders?], with those of their countrey having some blood. The English buy a great many of these animals for the purpose of improving the breed of their draft horses.

I was glad to hear that the Devon Bull was doing so well and I hope that he will be of service to the breed of cattle in the countrey. The cattle in the state of New York owe their superiority to a Devon Bull that was introduced into that many years back by Mr. [James] Wadsworth. All the show [*ms. torn; several words illegible*] in the environs of Phil[adelphi]a & N. York cities owe their fattening properties to that origin and the fine oxen that are seen in the interior of Pen[n]s[ylvani]a have the red colour and distinctive marks of Devon blood.

I hear you say nothing of the gold mine from which I infer that it is producing little. Mr. [John R.] Mathewes at my request forwarded a box of Iron ores taken from different localities about Clarkesville. I took them to the school of mines and I find that they contain some gold but not all alike. The ores became mixed & it is impossible to tell which are rich or contain gold & those that do not. I have no doubt but that there are ores of Iron in that region of countrey that are very rich.

It gave us great pleasure to hear of John's [John C. Calhoun, Jr.'s] improved health, but we are anxious about Patrick [Calhoun] whose position at N. Orleans is calculated to give apprehensions for his safety. Your affectionate son, Thos. G. Clemson.

N.B. You wrote me some time since about a bill for mending the

Dearborn. I have the most distinct recollection that the bill was settled. I paid for it in person, and have the receipt at home & Mr. Christian knows the fact for it was into his hands that I paid the money in gold.

ALS in ScCleA.

To Tho[mas] J. Rusk, "President of the late [Texas] Convention"

Fort Hill, 12th Aug[us]t 1845

Dear Sir, I am in the receipt of your letter [of 7/8], covering a certified copy of a series of resolutions of your convention, unanimously passed, approbatory of the course of the late President [John Tyler], & his administration, in reference to the Annexation of Texas, & communicated by its direction.

I accept this highly honorable approval of the distinguished body over which you presided of the part I performed, towards the consummation of this great measure, with sincere pleasure & gratitude.

Taken altogether, it is one of the most memorable events of our history; and I am proud to have my name associated with it. One of its most striking circumstances, is the Unanimity & enthusiasm with which the people of Texas returned into our great and glorious Union, in spite of every obstacle thrown ["into" *altered to* "in"] their way, and every seduction presented to influence their decision. It speaks a volume in favour of their intelligence and patriotism, & is, at the same time, the highest eulogy ever pronounced in favour of our free, popular institutions; and will be so felt throughout the civilized world. This high evidence of the devotion of her sons to the land of their birth & its institutions, gives assurance, that she will shine, as one of the brightest stars in our brilliant Constellation.

I avail myself of the occasion to tender to [you] my congratulation at the high honour conferred on you by the Convention, in selecting you to preside over its deliberations. It is, indeed, a striking, & to me a gratifying coincidence, that an old acquaintance & native of the District I reside in, should be called to preside in the Convention, which, on the part of Texas consummated, this great measure, in reference to which it has been my fortune to take not an undistinguished part, & that another old acquaintance & law student of mine, & native of the same district with myself [Abner S. Lipscomb], should be the Chairman & organ of the Committee, which reported the resolutions by which it was consummated. With great respect yours truly, J.C. Calhoun.

ALS in TxU, Thomas Jefferson Rusk Papers; PC (from the Washington, Texas, *Register*) in the Washington, D.C., *Daily Union*, vol. I, no. 135 (October 7, 1845), p. 538; PC in the Richmond, Va., *Enquirer*, October 10, 1845, p. 2; PC in the Charleston, S.C., *Mercury*, October 11, 1845, p. 2; PC in the Edgefield, S.C., *Advertiser*, October 15, 1845, p. 2; PC in the Pendleton, S.C., *Messenger*, October 24, 1845, p. 1; variant PC (dated 8/20) in *Niles' National Register*, vol. LXIX, no. 7 (October 18, 1845), p. 100; PEx in Wilson, ed., *The Essential Calhoun*, pp. 157–158.

From J[OHN] S. BARBOUR

Catalpa [Va.] Aug[us]t 14th 1845
My Dear Sir, I agree to all that you have written me of the untoward course of events, & more than that, the ingratitude & injustice to you, of the prominent men of the [Andrew] Jackson party, from their leader down & since his election in 1828. I agree too that you have been constrained to oppose them on leading measures, & to give them the benefit of your exertions, to prevent their sinking, with little advantage to our principles & with treachery on their victories, to the pledges they made in the conflict that preceeded ["their" *changed to* "them" *and one or two words canceled*]. I shou'd not think well of the morality personal & political of the man who cou'd overlook & excuse all this, nor of the indignation which an honest patriotism should kindle in reproach to this baseness. With this admission in advance I arrive at opposite conclusions with you as to your path for power & duty. I attain these conclusions, not by impugning anything that you have urged but by overruling it with matter of ["known"(?) *canceled and* "better" *interlined*] & graver import. Bear in mind that we are not acting by will; *to establish good, but to remedy evil*. It is not a political condition to be formed of prepared materials & with plastic hand[?], but the removal of a burthen grown so heavy & portentous, as to threaten the structure already existing, by an evil bad ["&" *canceled*] in itself, with every tendency to ["greater evil" *canceled and* "grow worse" *interlined*]. Bear too in mind that positive rules apply only to morals & to mathematicks. If we wait until positive evil is overcome by positive good, we realise the fable (by Phaedrus) of the Rustic & the River. In sustaining right & resisting wrong, if we cannot inspire others with the loftier motives, we must

be content to avail ourselves of those which already exist, & where better is hopeless, we may cause Evil to sacrifice on the altar of patriotism. This Administration is so situated that it is obliged to act with us if we sustain them, & sustain them with any rational hope of ultimate triumph. Looking to them as men, there is no reason to suppose them to be worse in the haphazard of motive than the common race of selfish politicians. Of that great combination which came together by the cohesion of patriotism and of selfishness, of courage & of fear, by the hope of rescuing our institutions from the dangers that growl'd over them or of feeding low ambition with the pap & spoils of party, Mr. [James K.] Polk is the *organ*, not the master. They are not *his* party; he is its creature. He is the drop in his own ocean—but unlike the Revolutionary stock of Presidents, he is powerful only when he responds to the sustaining power from without. Conformity to this discord & discrepancy of party & principle, weakness & strength, good & evil, is the necessary effect of his taking power from such a [*one word changed to* "combination"]. His natural & derivative tendencies are all good. His interests identical with ours. His principles with us, if that which is timid to peril, & weak in the wrestle, can be called principle. He must be with us, if we assure him that he is not to be crush'd, by the *avalanche* that hangs over him. He must have this assurance, & he must give it undoubting *confidence*. Politicks is the science of circumstances, & it has grown into our selfish philosophy that victory is never call'd to a strict account. Imprint what characters you please upon your standard, if there be no breeze to unfold it, no numbers will cluster around it. You may raise it for good, but it is the chance of success that lends to it both its attraction & its charm. Without this, you present the saddest of all spectacles, that of powerless virtue—recruits will flock to the enemy & the renown of Curtius in the gulph, [*one word canceled and* "points" *interlined*] an incident in history. Feeble as those in power may be, they see all this and anxious as they are to act our principles & redeem & fulfil our expectations, they are utterly & hopelessly powerless without our aid—Nay, without *your aid*. It is *your* power (inherent & not transmissible), that stands out in the South—like the Fort above the valley—for its protection, & not for your elevation. It is your character & strength alone, that ["can" *interlined*] give hope, & overawe treachery. It is your virtue & disinterestedness that now make so large a part of your power—larger because of the contrast striking & amazing to the degeneracy & rottenness of the public men of the day. What man but you is without some dishonouring blot—some weakness that fell beneath temptation, or some sinful & sinning strength that drove him into reproachful wrong? If a question of selection for personal integrity, & the "*detur digniori*" were propounded by interrogatory to the American people without distinction of party, what other name cou'd fill the true & full response[?] The power which belongs to this high & exclusive position, is associated with high duty. A duty that is the more pressing at this moment, both from our hopes & our wants. Mr. Polk is *with us* & *with you.* Cautious & timid but with you—fearful of owning it, because you are away with your strength—doubting his duty, because he knows not on what to rest. Altho', "the drop in his own ocean," yet is that drop endued with the power to ferment or tranquillise the waters.

You ask how is the organ? *With you*—but he ([Thomas] R[itchie]) wants the public printing. His poverty may restrain him. I have done my part in alleviating his necessity. *He is obliged to be with you.* Let [*one word canceled and* "him" *interlined*] have the printing. He is far worthier than any other—*far more to be trusted.* If I had my wish, with all my regard for [Robert M.T.] Hunter I wou'd earnestly implore him to with[h]old & abstain from the Chair [of the House of Representatives]. Disinterestedness is power. By abstaining for a time, every thing that a selfish ambition cou'd desire will come to them. "*Festina lente*" [make haste slowly] was the Augustan maxim, and wise for the ["true" *interlined*] use [*one or two words canceled*] of Expectation.

If you are not in that Senate we shall fail of everything. If there & defeated, the defeat will be glorious to you. We shall ["go" *interlined*] forth cleansed of the impurities of ambition—neither taking nor desiring office, struggling to reclaim the Constitution, to lighten the burdens of the oppressed, & restore Justice to Injury & wrong; if you succeed, you "read your history in a nation[']s eyes." And if you fail—the indignation of the injured, will award you, its richest trophy. There is ample time for your work on the Constitution. Doctor [Benjamin] Franklin[']s ["faculties" *interlined*] were improving to the last. It is *interest* that will keep them alive. The interest, which patriotism & duty lend to the intellect, will be yours whilst life lasts you. Rescue the federal structure from the evils that are like to crush it, & measure it with Ezekiel[']s reed hereafter. If I had more *space* I cou'd *write more.* God Bless you. Y[ou]rs truly & faithfully, J.S. Barbour.

You see my *hurry.*

ALS in ScCleA.

From M[oses] C. Mordecai

Charleston, Aug[us]t 15, 1845

Dear Sir, I have the Honor to acknowledge receipt of your letter of the 6th inst. I am requested by the Committee to solic[i]t You to prepare a list of the Questions, & your Views, to aid them in making up the statement they are now at work upon. We shall Endeavour to bring about concert of action as you suggest, for altho Mr. [Secretary of the Treasury Robert J.] Walker has signified his desire to receive our Communication, I do not believe he will seek answers to our Questions ["&" *canceled*] from any other Quarter. With Great Respect Your Ob[edient] Ser[vant], M.C. Mordecai.

ALS in ScCleA. NOTE: Calhoun's AEU reads: "Ans[were]d 21th[?] Aug[us]t."

From F[rancis] W. Pickens

Edgewood, 17 August 1845

My dear Sir, I regret to hear that Cousin Floride [Colhoun Calhoun] is still sick. I hope she is better by this time. Present me kindly to her.

I regretted to hear also that you could not think of taking a tour through the West & N. West. I thought such a trip would not only benefit you but would produce a favourable impression upon public sentiment in adjusting the Tariff and other measures. The philosophical and resigned tone of your letter was such as to command my deepest respect. I have long seen that in time of peace the heartless and selfish pursuits of Politics were ill callculated [*sic*] to create resignation or contentment, and it is grateful to see one like yourself furnishing such a prominent example to the contrary.

I see there is some prospect of war with Mexico, but suppose there will be nothing serious. Even if they declare war it will only be a nominal thing to cover their imaginary honor, and well knowing that G. Britain will interpose as a pacificator and reconcile difficulties. This will give England an enviable position. I have no idea there will be a serious war.

I rec[eive]d a letter the other day from Mr. [Thomas G.] Clemson—all well—and I judge from its tenor that he has no idea of returning for some years to this country. His crop is good—& there will be a plenty, & more[?] too, made of corn. This is something these dry times.

My crop is also good. I am just in the upper edge of the rains & so is his place—just enough rain to make very fine crops. From here to the Sea coast, crops good—towards Edisto fine—above towards Columbia[,] Fairfiel[d], New Berry [*sic*] &c, very bad, & from here to the mountains bad. My cotton seems to be all opening at once.

I have out about 35,000 lb[s]. & the crop will be very good, but all of it nearly in good fresh lands. Those who plant old lands & red or clay lands, cotton very triffling indeed.

Susan [Pickens] & [E.] Clark [Simkins] have just returned from Athens & they say there are no crops in Georgia at all. We all join in kindest regards to you & yours. Very truly, F.W. Pickens.

ALS in ScCleA.

From J[AMES] H. HAMMOND

Silver Bluff, 18 Aug. 1845

My Dear Sir, It always affords me so much satisfaction to concur with you in opinion & it is so unpleasant to differ, that in deference to your judgement I chalked out an article for the [Charleston] Mercury after receiving your last letter & began to take quite an interest in it. But when I came to fill it up I became so convinced that it would do far more harm than good that I desisted. If I could have written merely a complimentary notice of Dr. [Henry B.] Bascom[']s book it might have passed, & if there had been little or no point in it, would have been thought of no more. But every thing from So. Ca. in relation to the Slave question attracts attention & must have some weight. To compliment Dr. Bascom for this book, without noticing its unsound & dangerous doctrines in *strong terms* would have had a bad effect in more ways than one, & to notice it in such a manner would have been I think imprudent just now. Judging by the difficulty I had in reading his confused & long spun essay, ["I" *canceled*] which I did solely with a view to meet your wishes, I am pretty certain you have only looked at it here & there & cannot not [*sic*] have seen many passages in it. Besides saying that the Bible does not sustain Slavery & that it is an evil, he declares that it is "on all hands admitted to be an evil," that if any way of getting clear of it ["of" *canceled and* "was" *interlined*] pointed out & shown to be safe ["it" *interlined*] "would find few opponents here," that to say the Southern methodists are in favour of Slavery is a "libel & an outrage," that they have been doing & will continue to do all they can to get rid of it &c &c. Now if his book is noticed *in South Ca.* such sentiments as these must be peremptorily denied & sternly rebuked, or the whole body of sound methodists ["will have" *canceled and* "who are" *interlined*] neither abolitionists nor *colonizationists* will have a damper thrown over them, ["They will" *canceled and* "& may be inclined to" *interlined*] yield to the powerful influences at work to make Bascom a Bishop, to retain the very gross & offensive Chapter ["of" *canceled and* "on" *interlined*] Slavery in the Discipline book, to locate the Book concern as well as Missionary Treasury in Kentucky & in short ["to" *interlined*] give these *pseudo* friends of the Slaveholders an overwhelming domination over So[uthern] Methodism, which would soon become as dangerous to us as that of the North. I do not mean to say that so insignificant an article as I might write would materially aid in bringing about these results, but it would tend in that way & coming from So. Ca. might have far more influence than it might otherwise have. At this moment such an article *in the Mercury* would probably be caught up in Kentucky. There is growing up a powerful abolition excitement there. Cassius Clay, differing no way *in principle* from Dr. Bascom & Henry Clay & doubtless looking to them for support in an emergency & likely to receive ["it" *interlined*], is making the most powerful appeal in his new paper "The True American" to the nonslaveholders of Kentucky, & preaching insurrection to both black & white. He could not be tolerated a moment, if Kentucky was sound or his friends less powerful. The people however are waking up. Abolition entered largely into the canvass between [Garrett] Davis & [Thomas F.] Marshall [for Representative from Ky.] & will become a leading question in elections very soon. I hope & believe in a short time the Clays, Bascoms & all of that stamp will be put down completely & Kentucky redeemed. It is not then a time for So. Ca. to give Bascom a wing. I think also that the true Southern Methodists are displeased with his Review. They praised it in advance, but have received it very coldly. There are reasons for this besides his unsound views of Slavery. He has placed Dr. [William] Capers rather in the light of an officious meddler in his early attempts in the General Conference to reconcile the North & South, & has without necessity dwelt upon the fact that Bishop [James O.] Andrew was elected by the North, "imposed upon the South against her wishes." These flings shew no good feeling & the Dr. evidently aims to absorb for himself all the glory of ["the" *interlined*] action of the South. Our Methodists see what this leads to & have their eyes on the consequences I have mentioned above. To elevate Dr. Bascom would be at their expense. I think therefore every thing considered that a mere complimentary review of his work, slurring over his dangerous opinions[,] would in every point of view be impolitic, as well as a dereliction of our own duty considering the position South Ca[rolina] occupies.

On the other hand to rebuke him severely is not perhaps called for now & would be equally impolitic. The Methodist controversy has by no means ended. The seperation of the Church is inevitable, but the great question remains whether it will be a Division or a Secession, & that involves a very large amount of property. The share of the Southern Conferences in the various methodist funds is not short of $300,000. The North will undoubtedly endeavour to cheat them out of it. Their Editors & writers have already taken the ground that the South has *Seceded*. I have little doubt that a great Lawsuit will be carried on. Pending that & the whole controversy, it would be better to let the Southern Church get on with what harmony it can & sow no seeds of dissenssion. I do not doubt, the methodists would prefer to be allowed to manage the whole matter for themselves. Their So[uthern] papers have carefully abstained from ["noticing or" *canceled*] responding to or noticing any ["po" *canceled*] expression of opinion by the politicians. You saw how ready & anxious the North was to catch them in this trap by charging a correspondence between you & Dr. Capers.

On the whole I trust you will believe that ["if" *interlined*] I have not good reasons for declining to comply with your request, I have not done it without looking all round the matter with what circumspection & judgement I possess, & that my convictions are sincere that it had better not be done.

The Northern papers are making a handle of the political portion of my [Thomas] Clarkson Letters. In New Hampshire they are pushed directly at [Levi] Woodbury & for affect a much more conspicuous position in the Democratic ranks has been assigned me than I ever occupied. I am not sure it would not be good policy to have me read out of them ["ranks" *canceled*]. I propose to have so little to do with politics hereafter—have always so disliked the *name* of Democrat—& really have so little feeling in common with the great body of Democrats out of So. Ca., that such a black balling would cost me very little. If it would do any body any good I would cheerfully submit to it. If I were in public life I would of course adhere as far as I could to the party whose principles & purposes were nearest my own. Being out of it & probably forever, I don't see why I should belong to any party & should certainly be sorry to embarrass any in the least. Lewis Tappan & I are corresponding & have been for some time. I never thought of such a thing as a publication of ["it" *canceled and* "the correspondence" *interlined*] until he suggested it in his last. I declined, but I fear that I may be served as [James G.] Birney served [Franklin H.] Elmore. To prevent it if possible I have taken the matter up in earnest ["with him so as" *canceled and* "& with a view" *interlined*] to drive the notion out of his mind. There are many views of the matter not yet fully treated. Among them is to deprive the Abolitionists of the clap-trap of the "Golden Rule of Christ," "the laws of nature & natural rights" & to make them enure to our cause—to shew that the "compact" between master & Slave is Just & to the advantage of the latter & to trace "Southern decay" to other causes ["at work(?)" *canceled*] than Slavery which in fact is all that saves us. I don't wish to publish any more on the subject however & shall not do it voluntarily.

I cannot write any thing about planting. The season has been so utterly disastrous as to make the whole theme a painful one, unless to one on the spot, to whom I could point out many hopeful signs of the value of marl, plaster & peat notwithstanding the season. If I had not written you so long a letter I might make a good apology, which I can only give as the reason why I have not answered yours sooner. I turned off both my Overseers within the last few weeks, & have no white man now on my premises. My chief manager was the best I ever had if left to himself, but he would not keep the track in *executing orders*, & as I have some dozen of nice experiments in all the branches of farming & stock raising going on, he worried me beyond endurance & continually thwarted all my views in detail. The present race of Overseers are far the greatest curse under which our agriculture labours. I see no hope of being relieved from it until every planter manages his own business & employs mere agents to obey orders instead of crack planters to manage him & his business. We should then soon have valuable assistants. Probably you do not suffer from this evil to the extent we do below. I shall write to [Anthony B.?] Allen as soon as the river rises & I get a cargo of 135 barrels of plaster from ["him," *interlined*] now below. Rolling my seed in plaster 1 peck to the acre has improved my crop when it is done 33 p[e]r c[en]t this year, *on marled land*, & a *bushel* to the acre broadcast has done about the same. Very truly & Sincerely Yours, J.H. Hammond.

P.S. To prove how sincerely I approve the Division of the M[ethodist] Church & the course of the *body* of So[uthern] Methodists thus far, I will state, that soon after the Gen[era]l Conference broke up last year, I got the circuit preachers to make a station here, which I support entirely myself. They preach in my School House (& at my plantation also), but I ["am" *interlined*] now completing a handsome church for them which will cost me $1200. Nor will I fail to contribute my mite to make up any pecuniary losses that may accrue to them from the *Secession*, if it be so decided. In fact my advice will be not to sue, but give up the money if the North refuses to divide the funds, & to throw themselves on Southern generosity.

P.S. Do give me your views of the Mexican war. That is whether it is likely to take such a turn as to interrupt our commerce. I presume we might consistently with the Law of Nations instruct our Naval officers to *refuse quarter* to Privateers if we found they were making a piratical affair of it.

I am one of those who seriously apprehend an Oregon war. If it is revealing no state secret, I should be very glad to know your views, simply for the shaping of my private affairs & my own gratification.

ALS in ScCleA; PEx in Jameson, ed., *Correspondence*, pp. 1045–1049.

From M[oses] C. Mordecai

Charleston, Aug[u]st 18, 1845
Dear Sir, I have the honor to acknowledge rec[e]ipt of your letter of the 14th inst. The Committee [of the Charleston Chamber of Commerce] rece[ive]d today the Enclosed Communication from Mr. [Robert J.] Walker through Mr. [William J.] Grayson the Collector— which they have requested me to forward You.

As Mr. Walker's letter will afford us the oppertunity of placing before him, at once, Questions in the Sh[ape?] we most desire, the Committee w[ill?] await your advice on the same with a list of interrogatorys thay [*sic*] would be pleased if you would prepare for them. With Great Respect Your Ob[edient] S[ervant], M.C. Mordecai.
[Enclosure]
R[obert] J. Walker to W[illia]m J. Grayson
Washington City, August 15th 1845
Dear Sir, Will you oblige me by conferring *immediately* with your Chamber of Commerce and obtain from them such questions ["as they" *interlined*] would desire to have propounded by me to show

the operation of the tariff on the Commercial & Agricultural, navigating & Ship building interest and enclose them to me at the earliest practicable period. Very respectfully Your Ob[edien]t S[er]v[an]t, (Signed) R.J. Walker.

ALS with En in ScCleA. NOTE: An AEU by Calhoun reads "Mr. Mordecai."

From ELIZABETH A. R. LINN

St. Louis, August 19[?], 1845

My Dear Cousin, Indulging the hope, that you still feel, an interest for me, & my bereaved family, I cannot refrain, from sending you, the enclosed New[s] Paper. The vengeance of Col. [Thomas H.] Benton, has tryumphed against me, although I was sustained, by so many noble Friends, & by the united Voice of our State Legislature, for all, the Democrats in that Body signed a Petition, to President [James K.] Polk in my behalf for obtaining, the P[ost] O[ffice] in this City, & every Whig, in the Legislature, would have also signed the Petition, had they hoped, to aid me, with their *Names* as asking a favor, of President Polk—but there is one consolation to me, in all my Troubles, that is, that I hear of you, my noble & greatly gifted Cousin, constantly spoken of, as our next President, and deep, is the regret, of a Vast Majority, of the Missourians, that you are not now, at the helm of our Government, then, indeed, we might confidently trust, in the prosperity of our beloved Country.

Should dear Mrs. [Anna Maria Calhoun] Clemson, be with you, will you have the kindness to present me affectionately to her, & Mr. [Thomas G.] Clemson, although I have never had the great pleasure of seeing Mrs. [Floride Colhoun] Calhoun, yet I will take the liberty of sending her, my respec[t]ful Compliments. With sentiments of the highest regard I am Most truly, your sincere, & very grateful Friend, Elizabeth A.R. Linn.

ALS in ScCleA.

From S[AMPSON] H. BUTLER, [former Representative from S.C.]

Florida Madison Co[unty], Aug. 21, 1845

My dear Sir, I have designed for a long time to trouble you, with a line, but have hitherto been deter[r]ed from doing so, by the belief, that you already were overburdened with your correspondence. I claim however to be one of your sincerest political as well as personal friends, and know your goodness of heart, will excuse me, for the wish, I have to hear some of your thoughts and suggestions.

When I first came here, I was broken down in health, and had no intention of embarking warmly into the excitement of politics, and hence I committed an error, which has weakened my position. You see I speak frankely. I looked to you as the only proper candidate of the Republican party, and when you were Juggled out, by the political intrig[u]ers, I felt so indignant at the manner & mode of it, that I declared I would hurra, for [Henry] Clay, sooner than for any other man, though I at the same [time] avowed I would not vote for him, if we were in a State government. I did not however, say this much longer, than I saw his letter on the Tariff. I abandoned even the ground I had assumed towards him, but all this has injured me, & prevented me from being elected one of the Judges of the State, at the late session of our Legislature, it was the only ground urged against me, & although I had frequently a majority on joint vote, and 36 ballotings were necessary to make a choice, yet this Clayism defeated ["me" *interlined*]; but for that I should have rec[eive]d the concurrent vote of both Houses, by a large majority. The man who was mainly instrumental in defeating me, is one of the U.S. Senators, who has a good deal of talent and active industry, but is an unscrupulous liar and intriguer. He is one of the "old Hunkers," and secretly, as I am well assured, desired my defeat because I was a Calhoun man, and a friend of [David] Levy [Yulee]. This man [James D.] Westcott [Jr.] may be compelled from the public Sentiment here, to be in your favour, but he is adopting every means, to put down your friends here, and a variety of circumstances favoured him, at the last legislature. In that legislature, you have a majority of warm, enthusiastic admirers, and I feel confident of taking the lead of him, hereafter as I did in Convention last spring. His election to the Senate, was effected by his artful combination of the various candidates, for the State offices, in his favour. He was known to possess a certain am[oun]t of strength, and this made all the candidates anxious to secure his good will, and fearful of encountering his opposition. He has engendered an opposition to him, by his tortuous & treacherous conduct, which must tell against in all future time. Levy I know does not like him, or have any confidence in him, and I apprehend a split between them, this winter. If Levy, who is thoroughly your friend, remains firm, I have no doubt, we shall be able to overcome any opposition to you in this State. I think I am pretty fairly over the charge of inconsistency now, and shall be able to do something, when the proper time comes. We design to start a press this winter, advocating your views and ours, and to make a fair issue upon all the great questions of national politics, and especially on the tariff.

I hope from some intimations dropped by Levy, that this winter, if the Administration does not take high ground against the tariff, that our friends in Congress, will take ground for themselves, and maintain their principles against all parties. If this is done, all things will go right in Florida, and your name will be, with your principles, dominant beyond all others. I hope to see such a state [of] things, because I am tired of truckling to a portion of the Republican party who use ["us" *interlined*] only for their selfish purposes.

I have written you, a hasty, and I fear an uninteresting letter, but I shall be satisfied if you can find leisure, to give me a few of your thoughts in return. I should take it as a favour also, if you ["would" *interlined*] advise what line of policy you think best to pursue, what issues to make, and any suggestion, which your experience, and wisdom may point out. I hope I need not assure ["you" *interlined*], how much interest I feel in your prospects and your policy, and that I shall be discreet enough not to disclose any thing which ought to be kept to myself. I repeat you have many warm decided friends in every part of the State, more than any man living, and all we want to shew our strength is organization, and union. I do not despair of your being the next nominee for the Presidency, notwithstanding my small share of confidence in the "old Hunkers," and I hope you will pardon me for saying you did wrong in leaving the Senate; you ought to go back; every speech you made there, was producing a powerful impression, throughout the Union. I hope you will review your decission in this respect, & return to the field of your renown. Respectfully and Sincerely Your Ob[edien]t Serv[an]t, S.H. Butler.

ALS in ScCleA. NOTE: A S.C. native, Butler had been a Representative from S.C. from 1839 to 1842.

To F[RANCIS] W. PICKENS, Edgefield, S.C.

Fort Hill, 21st Aug[us]t 1845

Dear Sir, There will probably be no war with Mexico, or if one, of little consequence, unless there should be a prospect of a rupture between us & England in reference to Oregon. She is averse to war with us; but I do not see how war can be avoid[ed], in reference to it, unless the Administration should back out from the grounds taken in the Inaugural, so untimely & so improperly. The west & the mid-[d]le States seem determined that Mr. [James K.] Polk should not back out, and I am sorry to see, some of our papers, & especially the [Columbia South-]Carolinian, chiming in with them. The question was in our hands and under our entire control, until the Inaugural appeared. It threw away, to use a gambler's phrase, our trump card; & gave England the control. I saw my way clearly & had the whole in the fairest train; and ["apprise" *canceled and* "informed" *interlined*] Mr. Polk & [James] Buchanan how to manage ["it" *interlined*] to ensure success; and the danger of taking any other course. The whole territory, or at least all drained by the Columbia river might have been had. They have acted directly opposite to the course I was pursuing; and I hazard nothing in saying, that it must end in backing out, or a most disasterous & disreputable conflict to us.

It still remains very dry in this region generally. I have not had my ground wet 2 inches in six weeks. My cotton crop which was very promising a month ago, will fall short a third at least. I shall make bread, although my upland, which is more than half my corn crop, will not make more than a third of a crop.

Mrs. [Floride Colhoun] Calhoun is at Glenn Springs. She writes that her health is rapidly improving. James [Edward Calhoun] accompanied her.

The rest of the family join their love to you all. Truly, J.C. Calhoun.

ALS in ScU-SC, John C. Calhoun Papers; PC in "Letters from John C. Calhoun to Francis W. Pickens," in *South Carolina Historical Magazine*, vol. VII, no. 1 (January, 1906), pp. 14–15. NOTE: An AEU by Pickens reads "Mr. Calhoun—on Oregon & war[,] Polk &c—1845." Two notations were added by Pickens, evidently at some time well after the receipt of the letter, in reference to the last two sentences of the first paragraph. The first notation reads "This is exactly what the Adm[inist]r[ation] did gain and the treaty was made exactly on that basis. That was all Polk ever contended for, as he offered those *precise terms* and the British minister rejected them with these remarkable words—until terms more reasonable are offered no further proposition could be considered, & then in less than 6 months accepted the identical proposition. This proposition was then pending shewing beyond controversy what Mr. Polk was for—at the same time the Adm[inist]r[ation] Press & some imprudent Senators assumed 'The whole of Oregon or none,' but Mr. Polk did not—and when he said the just & entire rights of the country should be maintained fully we know what he meant—that was the country drained by the waters of the Oregon (never Frazier's river) & this is exactly what he did gain & assert & no more." The second notation reads "There was no backing out & there was no war, & the truth is the only danger of war was from pursuing the course of Mr. Calhoun—as he would have left it to time & emigration to settle up the disputed territory—& the conflicts between the settlers & the British Hudson Bay company would have brought on war, & we would have been drag[g]ed into it by reckless adventurers whose interest it would have been to produce war."

From JAMES BUCHANAN, [Secretary of State]

Washington, ["23" *altered to* "22"] August 1845
My dear Sir, A short absence at the Bedford Springs has prevented me from returning you an immediate answer to yours of the 24 ultimo. It was mislaid & did not come to my notice until ["the day before" *interlined*] yesterday. ["The" *interlined*] enclosed statement contains the information which you requested.

Nearly all our information from Mexico would indicate war; and yet I doubt whether this will be the result.

I have been prosecuting the Oregon negotiation in pursuance of the plan on which you had progressed; but I doubt ["very much" *canceled*] whether the question will ["at this time or" *interlined*] ever be settled by ["a Treaty" *canceled*] the parties. I am exceedingly desirous that it should.

This office is one of hard labor & great responsibility. I never had any fancy for it & now less than ever.

Hoping to see you in the Senate & asking you to present my kind remembrance to Mrs. Calhoun, I remain Sincerely & respectfully your friend, James Buchanan.

ALS in ScCleA; PEx in Boucher and Brooks, eds., *Correspondence*, p. 302.

From H[AYM] M. SALOMON

New york [City,] August 22d [18]45
Dear Sir, Notwithstanding some time has elapsed since my last to you be assured that your claims for perpetual consideration among the true friends of the Country will never be obliterated, your case is ever present to my mind whenever I think of the extraordinary Chapter of events that has befallen the most eminent of our Statesmen[.]

Mr. [Hiram] Ketchum on the part of Mr. [Daniel] W[ebster]

and myself as the confidential friend of the other party discuss repeatedly the subject already understood by you—we cannot or rather he cannot satisfy himself as to which of the many ways that have presented themselves is the best for its annunciation as to manner and place[.]

I enclose by today[']s mail under a seperate cover some ["printed" *interlined*] scraps of recent facts continuing the proofs of those unanswered and unanswerable arguments so ably written by you in the letter to Mr. [William R.] King at the French Court[.]

My friends have often asked me how it was that I, who had been devoted to your cause from the first through all the Storms and calms have not yet been tendered a cent of patronage while yet so many others men of but yesterday were well provided for while Mr. [Cornelius P.] Van Ness held the Collectorship. I have told them it was the "natural History" of a republic whose institutions were at length seen to be so imperfect that unfortunately its government could be carried on and alternately managed by factions of various denomination for the last twenty odd years even to the deterioration of its character and of numbers of millions of its true resources[.]

It appears at this moment that without being considered unreasonable I might suggest something for your consideration which if adopted might indirectly advance my just views and promote an action the general tendancy of which would be a reproof to those venal men who have been malignantly opposed to your personal interests and to those of the nation for the last twenty years[.]

Mr. [George] MacDuffie can and will from his profound understanding and its consequent influence, *certainly control those* ["Southern" *interlined*] *senatorial votes* that will be required by the governing party to carry out their rewards and punishments and will it be possible for upright statesmen holding their position to refrain giving an admonishing vote on the presented names of the political chiefs and their subalterns who were active from first to last in stifling ["the voice of" *canceled*] the voice of the people by means of their interminable intrigues so as to hinder your nomination either with or without a convention either before or at the Convention? Several of these inveterate men, among the headmost is the Jessuit [Benjamin F.] Butler have procured nominations to valuable offices and by voting in favour of those chiefs of of the enemies of the country Mr. MacDuffie and his friends would thus bestow an enormous premium as encouragement to such traitors to the country[']s good tending to an inducement to their renewal of the work of evil against you, to the end of time.

And now sir as I never have had the advantage of ["the"(?) *canceled*] personal friendship or acquaintance with Mr. McD[uffie]—and your possessing a knowledge of my devoted and lasting attachment to your immediate interests and those of the south and thus of the general union for full twenty five years at the expence of every chance of patronage from both of the other political divissions of the country, and that if personally known to Mr. McD[uffie] *could give him that kind of unalloyed intelligence respecting facts, men and measures in this quarter of which that distinguished man might* ["put"(?) *canceled and "have" interlined*] *a just value on my coming to Washington and putting myself in communication with him*[.] I say that a letter which it seems would be proper for you to give me to him in such a special case would be very pleasing to me *and* ["would" *interlined*] *have the best effects* under the guidance of a good and just Providence. It could state ["in addition" *interlined*] that you had the satisfaction of seeing last year testimonials of my character[,] capacity and integrity from ["our" *canceled*] the Judges of our several Courts[,] from our several mayors for years past[,] from *all* our Magistrates, Common Council—Aldermen & of all parties as well ["as well" *canceled*] as from the two chief Houses in the shipping interests of both parties but such (as he no doubt was aware) was the manner in which appointments were procured that altho the President promised me the rightful consideration of my irresistable claim showing its connection with revolutionary loss of [$]300,000 and that I positively should have an appointment still so evident was it that in nearly all the cases, it was management and not Merit that had its reward that in the end I was an entire ["suferrers"(?) *canceled*] sufferer ["an"(?) *canceled*] as in addition to this neglect Dr. [John] Miller writes to me that Mr. [John] Tyler lost A Box in which with other papers most of my documents and autographs of distinguished men familiar with my case, was lost!

As the tax on epistolary intercourse is now with great propriety much reduced I trust you will indulge me with an occasional line in addition to one specially in reply to this, to which allow me to beg your reasonably and conveniently prompt attention. And believe me as ever your devoted friend & Ser[van]t, H.M. Salomon.

[Enclosure]

Additional and seperate memorandum

I owe it to my general wish of putting you in possession of the conduct of the different persons in this quarter who have occasionally from time to time ["professed" *canceled*] been permitted to call themselves prominant advocates or leaders of your cause.

John J. [*sic*; A.] *Morrill.* You doubtless saw months ago the death of Mr. Morrill. For the last two or three years he had been so extremely attached to drink owing tis said to severe anguish from a private and domestic family misfortune that finally it ended in a total incapacity for business—a loss of all his property and final and sudden death one morning from the effect of drinking more than a quart of Brandy over night.

Alex[*ander*] *Hamilton.* Is yet engaged in stock jobbing speculations but of so little credit among the dealers in Wall Street that his responsibility ["is not good"(?) *canceled and* "would be taken" *interlined*] for 500 Doll[ars]. He and [Greene C.?] Bronson tho the latter is a man of property seek the intimacy and confidence of prominant political and influential statesmen solely to obtain information *to profit in their Speculating*[.]

[*E*]*Manuel B. Hart*[.] This chief among the genteel Rowdy soap locks, has been to the surprise of all good & moral citizens placed among the Common Council of our City. Perceiving that the republican party were nearly divided as to a candidate—in a ward where they had a majority and that the Whigs were determined to run a Candidate—He hired a parcel of turbulent ["young" *interlined*] men in a remote tavern of the ward to call out his nomination. And his supporters altho' Seven Hundred less than a majority of the Voters of the ward carried his name in as the highest of the three to the astonishment and regret of the good citizens who now sees a man sitting ["occasionally" *interlined*] as an adjunct to the recorder on the Criminal Bench who was himself condemned and sentenced not long ago by the same Bench, for felloniously trying to put out the Eyes of his adversary in a conflict[.]

The Van B[uren] men have by divissions in the native & Whig party got a temporary advantage in the City Councils[.]

The chief part of those individuals whom Mr. [Robert Barnwell] Rhett and Gen[era]l [Duff] Green thought were sincere and disinterested friends to your Cause turned out as I at the time from my long acquaintance with [*ms. torn; one word missing*] City affairs was able to predict as men who would disappoint them, and did disappoint them in toto.

General Politicks[.] I perceive there are several under currents at work running strongly and various directions. One is to ["favour" *canceled*] persuade Mr. [James K.] Polk that notwithstanding his promise to the people that he would only be once a Candidate—he ought to be, and can be, with the aid of Mr. [William L.] Marcy as Vice [President] on his ticket successful. This fact I gather from conversations with certain men in regard to appointments and actions at W[ashington]. My Son Col. D[avid] Salomon, aid[e] to Gov[erno]r of the State of Alabama passed thro W[ashington] last week on a visit to us for the hot Season. he had a long conversation on southern—mexican—and *political* affairs as far as prudence would allow. My son D[avid] was introduced by a letter from D[ixon] H. Lewis as one journeying north, and *no* office seeker. ["They" *canceled*] My son D[avid] endeavoured to draw out the P[resident's] intention as to his Views of the next candidate of the D[emocratic] Party and observed to the P[resident] that he hoped no opposition would be made by the General party to Mr. [Thomas] Ritchie as printer because it might endanger the union of the party in respect to a nomination of Mr. [Silas] Wright as, he was understood to be the intended Candidate of the north for a nomination in '47. As to presidential Candidates replied the President—"Sir it will be time enough fully in two years to name such a a one or such a thing["]—then some other matters dropped [*ms. torn; one or two words missing*] which made my son think, that Mr. P[olk] did think that he might himself be a candidate again—altho he named no direct fact leading to it.

In speaking last week with Judge [John B.] Scott who has been in our State Senate and legislature for Several years as the representative of the Van B[uren] party and was *recommended by them* for Post M[aster] of N. York *by the electors* by *Several personal friends* of the P[resident]—["& t"(?) *canceled*] and said Scott[,] "I tell you that *he promised I should have it.* Still, says he, It was given *to* [*Robert H.*] *Morris.* Now says he There is [John] Coddington. *The President* to my knowledge promised to make this man *Collector* at four Several times in conversation with Coddington *provided* that he turn out Van Ness. He turned out Van Ness and made *Mr. Laurence* [*sic*; Cornelius Van Wyck Lawrence] a respectable but unlearned and party man Collector. Scott who knows all the movements, ["Says" *canceled*] Said to me, that Marcy is at the bottom of these movements which he manages by Causing Polk to suppose, that if the Patronage is given out rightly—They can secure the next nomination & the Election[.]

Therefore you now can judge that matters are So situated & such a combination of antagonistical events as to aspirants for the next campaign—that you must not be surprised to find—matters fully as undetermined as to final party action as at any time since the adoption of the Constitution. Van B[uren] is obliged to hide himself from the friends of these several men as it might commit himself. And it is said that he and his immediate supporters are crying out—that Polk is a second John Tyler and for his refusal to attend to the direction given to him by the Select dictator of that School—he Mr. P[olk] shall be blown to ["attoms"(?) *canceled*] atoms.

["Mexico my" *canceled.*] But if my plan can be adopted it will cause all these president makers and their candidates to fall as prostrate as if striken by a ["World" *canceled*] whirlwind.

Mexico[.] In respect to this question I think our people are prematurely frightened. My Humble judgement is that *their* Congress will not declare war before 1s[t] October—and more likely *not at all*— as a majority of them, Know they cannot get the 15 Mile, and that *they would be overcome* quietly[.]

ALS with En in ScCleA.

To A[RMISTEAD] BURT, Willington, S.C.

Fort Hill, 23d Aug[us]t 1845
My dear Sir, I think I may safely say, that Mrs. [Floride Colhoun] Calhoun will be at home in the next ten days. We had letters from her by the last mail. She is much better, but does not state particularly when she will return, but ["I" *interlined*] conclude from what she says, it will be within the time I state. I expect to leave for Alabama, as soon as it is safe & have written to Andrew [Pickens Calhoun] for his opinion on the subject. I hope I may set out by the 1st October.

I trust you will not delay your visit. I wish to see you on several subjects ["before" *canceled*] before I go.

I regret to learn, that you have suffered so much by the drought. It has been intense with us; but I shall make provisions sufficient and about ⅔ of a cotton crop.

We are all well & all join their love to you & Martha [Calhoun Burt]. Truly, J.C. Calhoun.

ALS in NcD, John C. Calhoun Papers.

From B[ARTHOLOMEW] R. CARROLL

Charleston, August 27/[18]45
Dear Sir, Your favor of the 21st is before me. Since writing my last the Limestone Springs have been sold to the Rev[eren]d Dr. [Thom-

as] Curtis, who intends establishing there a Female Academy [Limestone Springs Female High School]. I hope he may succeed, but I am fearful he will realize nothing but hopes. I offered for the property as fair a price as he did—but wanted a refusal of the sale until October next, as the consummation of my plans depended upon procuring fifty scholars to commence with. I now have no reason to believe under the present pressure of the country, I would have been able to procure the number desired. So it is perhaps as well that Dr. Curtis has superceded me in the purchase.

For your hint about the Pendleton Academy I sincerely thank you. Were the buildings sufficiently numerous, I think it would be in many respects a more favorable position for prosecuting my original plan. A principal objection to the Limestone Springs, would have been the want of a sufficient population of citizens to act as a restraining public opinion over the students in cases of rebellion or insubordination. In Pendleton such an objection could not exist. But to the point.

Could the Trustees of the Pendleton Academy be induced to offer me the school upon the terms you suggest and at the same [time] insure 25 scholars from the up country at a liberal price I could pledge myself to establish there such an institution as would be useful to the State and of no little honor to myself. I do not promise it would be on so complete a plan as that promised for the Limestone Springs But it should be such an one as would educate the student to become the well informed gentleman and useful citizen. Upon this matter I am willing to place myself at your disposal.

Meanwhile I am compelled to turn my thoughts to another State. I have reason to believe by December next I will receive an invitation to accept of the professor's chair of English Literature in the Alabama University. Strong friends in that State, some of them of the board of trustees, have been urging me to apply. I feel the conscientious persuasion that I possess the ability, the inclination and temper to discharge the duties of that professorship with usefulness to the institution and honor to myself. Under such ["an" *altered to* "a"] persuasion, I think I may leave the State, unless strong inducements are held out to me to remain.

In the event of my going, your name will greatly serve me. If it has been my good luck to be favorably known to you by report or otherwise, a line from you to that effect, to be used by me in Alabama, will serve as a valuable introduction of me. For such a favor, I need not assure you how sincere will be my thanks.

As a specimen of the materials with which I sometimes hurr[i]edly build, I send you an article of mine on the life and character of the late Mr. [Hugh S.] Legare. Bear in mind, if you please, it was published several months before Mr. [William C.] Preston's eulogy on that gentleman was pronounced, as you will discover a striking similarity in the criticisms of the two productions. With Sentiments of profound respect and regard I am dear Sir Y[ou]r ob[edien]t se[rvan]t, B.R. Carroll.

ALS in ScCleA.

From SETH SALISBURY

Pennsylvania State Library
Harrisburg, Aug. 27, 1845

My Dear Sir: It has been my intention, for some time past, to write you. I am aware, that your correspondence is oppressive, at least, that it is very extensive, and necessarily commanding a portion of your attention: this is the inevitable consequence, under our free system of government with a citizen, whose talent & integrity have earned for him an high reputation with his countrymen.

In writing you, Mr. Calhoun, I hardly feel as though I was addressing a stranger. The first vote that I ["have" canceled] ever gave, was for John C. Calhoun, Vice President of the United States; and, permit me to say, in all sincerity, that notwithstanding years have passed by, I have never given a vote with more pleasure.

In Pennsylvania, *especially* in my own portion of it, ("Northern Penn[sylvani]a") your name & high services have been familiar with the people and dear to the *Republican party*. My father, who was a Revolutionary patriot (died last October in his 87th year) although unknown to you personally, had taught his family to know, & respect your character & services.

Perhaps, you will remember, Sir, the name of William Salisbury, who, for many years was a merchant at Pendleton Court House, South Carolina; he subsequently moved into the State of Georgia; and in the summer of 1832, he was attacked with fever, and although he had a fine constitution; after a few days sickness his constitution yielded & he sunk under the disease.

He was a favorite brother, and my heart is pained in going back to his sickness & death. Permit me to say, that John C. Calhoun never had a more devoted friend; one more sincere and true, South of the

Potomac, than *my own dear brother*. His *letters*, which I have now on file, *speak* the language of his heart, and I never read them, without feeling a warmth of affection and regard toward yourself. In the fall, Decem[ber] 1832, when on my way to Georgia, I had the pleasure of being introduced to you, in Washington City, by *Gen. Samuel McKean*, a Senator from Pennsylvania, my near neighbor when at home, and I am happy to say, that, (although he is now no more), I can claim him as having been my friend.

I have been honored, by the Legislature of Pennsylvania, with the appointment of State Librarian, which office I now hold. It is my intention to be a candidate for the office of Sergeant at Arms, of the United States Senate at the opening of the present Congress; and I very respectfully, refer you to the Hon. C[harles] J. Ingersoll of Philadelphia, & the Hon. John Snyder, late Member of Congress from this State, for any information, touching my qualification, &c, ["to" *canceled*]. The Hon. Levi Woodbury of N.H. has, also, known me for many years.

If you should regard it, as not improper, to interest yourself in my favor, I shall remember it with grateful feelings. Living a retired life and not visiting Washington during Congress, it is not my happiness to know, personally, many Southern members of Congress.

I felt, however, as if I could be pardoned for writing you in the matter. Although in my humble capacity, having been a private in the ranks of Democracy, it has not been in my power, to render you great and essential service, yet, I will yield to none, in the sincerity of my friendship, and honest admiration of your talent, patriotism, and devotion to great doctrine of Democratic truth. I am trying to collect together for the *Pa. State Library*, the portraits of our eminent men, our Presidents & vice Presidents. If it is in your power, without too much trouble, to inform me where I can procure your portrait, or if you have it already engraved and could spare one, it will be regarded as a special favor to myself; and, I know Sir, that I am fully authorized to say, that it will be most acceptable to the people of Pa. who are manifesting a becoming interest, in the prosperity of their State Library.

I am happy to hear that Gen. [George] M'Duffie is recovering his health. I have not the pleasure of knowing him personally.

The war talked of with Mexico, it seems to me, cannot be very alarming; although, if persisted in may be some what annoying & harrassing to a portion of our commerce.

I enclose this letter to my friend, the Hon. Mr. Ingersoll, with the request that he may forward it to you. With great Respect, I am very truly your friend & obedient Servant, Seth Salisbury.

ALS in ScCleA.

From C[HARLES] J. INGERSOLL

Forest Hill, Philad[elphia]
Aug. 29, [18]45

Dear Sir, Dr. [Seth] Salisbury whose letter herewith he desires me to send you, is a warm & thorough going adherent to whom ever he takes an attachment, and otherwise deserving of your good will. I do not know whether the place he seeks is vacant or attainable. But he would fill it very satisfactorily.

In a few days my first Volume—events of 1813—of the war will be published. It has made me work hard for several months, withdrawing me entirely from current affairs, so that party politics will be new to me when called to Congress as I expect to be, for I don't see how Mr. [James K.] Polk can make war without that help. I am always very sincerely y[ou]rs, C.J. Ingersoll.

ALS in ScCleA.

To JAMES BUCHANAN, [Secretary of State]

Fort Hill, 30th Aug[us]t 1845

My dear Sir, I enclose a letter to Dr. [José M.] Caminero, the minister appointed by the Dominican Republick to our Government, which I will thank you to have forwarded to the address.

He informs me, that Mr. [John] Hogan's report will shortly be made. I hope, if it should be favourable, the administration will not hesitate to recognize the independence of the Republick, as soon as it can be done according to what has been usual in such cases. S[an]t[o] Domingo is, perhaps, the most fertile & best of all the West India Islands. ["which, however, have been" *canceled and* "It was" *interlined*] lost to civilization & commerce through the insane movements of France during her revolution. Should the Dominican Republick sustain itself, it opens a prospect of restoring the Island

97

again to the Domains of commerce & civilization. It may one day, or another be one of the great marts for our products. It can sustain a population of many millions.

It belongs to us to take the lead in its recognition. I have good re[a]son to beli[ev]e, that our recognition would be accep[t]able to both France & spain.

I am much obliged to you for furnishing me with the statement I requested in reference to the first census. The delay has subjected me to no inconvenience. It came in time for the purpose I desired it.

I regret to learn, that the prospect is so discouraging in reference to the settlement of the Oregon question by the parties. I regard it as very important, that it should be settled. If it should not be, there is great danger of its leading to a rupture between the two countries, which ["will" *canceled and* "would be" *interlined*] equally disasterous to both. It is beyond the power of man to trace the consequences of a war between us and England on the subject of Oregon. All that is certain is, that she can take & hold it aga[in]st us, as long as she has the supremacy on the ocean & retains her Eastren [*sic*] dominions. The rest is rapt in mystery.

As to my going again into the Senate, I do not contemplate to return ever again to publick life. I am entirely content with the portion of the publick honors, which have fallen to my share, and expect to spend the rest of my days in retirement, in my quiet retreat near the foot of the mountains. I find ample & agreeable occupation both of mind & body. With great respect Yours truly, J.C. Calhoun.

ALS in PHi, James Buchanan Papers (published microfilm, reel 9, frames 352–355); PC in George Ticknor Curtis, *Life of James Buchanan* (2 vols. New York, 1883), 1:576–577; PC in John Bassett Moore, ed., *The Works of James Buchanan* (12 vols. Philadelphia: J.B. Lippincott & Co., 1908–1912), 6:230–231.

From M [ATTHEW] ESTES

Columbus Miss., August 30th 1845

My Dear Sir, I take the liberty of enclosing to you a letter of introduction from my friend the Hon. W[illia]m M. Gwin of this State. It sufficiently explains the object that I have in view in seeking your acquaintance.

I am aware that several able treatises have been written on the subject of Slavery, but none, so far as my knowledge extends, embraces a full and satisfactory view of the whole subject, such a view as is necessary to satisfy the minds of the Southern people. In my opinion the subject can be so presented as to satisfy all reasonable men, that slavery is not only in accordance with revelation, but with the laws of God as revealed in nature. Our writers in general have granted too much. They have most generally conceded to our opponents that Slavery is a moral and political evil, which of course should be removed as soon as possible.

I shall present prominently one idea which I have no where met with in the writings of others. It is this—Slavery depends on the condition of the Globe, and must continue so long as the Globe continues, as at present. The greater part of the Globe is yet in a rude uncultivated state; its energies and resources yet in a measure undeveloped. To subdue the earth, polish its surface, develope i[t]s energies and resources, rough hands and strong arms are necessary, and these will never be applied to such purpose with energy and effect unless directed by superior heads.

To meet the demands of the world we have the African race—a race organized by nature for the work assigned them. I do not deny the Scripture doctrine that all men originated from a common parentage, but I do utterly deny that climate and other circumstances have produced the differences that we see among men. I conceive that there is a radical, fundamental difference between the white and black races which no change of circumstances can ever materially alter. The black man is greatly the inferior of the white man. I make these remarks in order that you may have some idea of my pro[po]sed work.

I am greatly desirous of obtaining your assistance, and should have written to you if I had not so opportunely met with my friend Dr. Gwin. Any papers or documents bearing on the subject will be thankfully received; but more especially any hints or suggestions in reference to any part of the [wor]k will be highly welcome.

I should be pleased to learn your view as to the best arrangement of such a work—the size, and other matters of a like nature.

As a public man you have long been known to me; and you will not I am sure deem me ["as" *canceled*] a sycophant when I assure you that I highly approve of your entire political life: I have been with you in every trial, and unless you change I expect to continue with you until death. I have written for you, and spoken for you, but never until now sought your acquaintance. I could have been in political life but have declined. Your friend Dr. D[avid] Lipscomb is a candidate for the State Senate in this county with a certainty of being elected. The Dr. is one of your most ardent friends.

Be pleased to write to me as soon as you can with convenience.

Please inform me whether you will visit Ala. this fall and if so whether it will suit your convenience to extend your visit to Columbus. With the highest Regard your Ob[edien]t Serv[an]t, M. Estes.

ALS with En in ScCleA. NOTE: An AEU by Calhoun reads "Dr. Estes." Estes published in 1846 *A Defence of Negro Slavery, As It Exists in the United States.* In 1856 he wrote under the pseudonym "A Lady of New Orleans," the proslavery novel *Tit for Tat, A Reply to Dred.*

From W[ILLIAM] M. GWIN, [former Representative from Miss.]

Columbus Mississippi, August 30th 1845

My dear Sir, I take the liberty of introducing to your acquaintance my friend Doctor Matthew Estes of this city a gentleman distinguished for his intelligence & moral worth[.]

The Doctor is engaged in a work on the subject of slavery and is anxious to collect facts to make it as complete as he can. I have assured him it would afford you pleasure to aid him in his undertaking and have recommended him to correspond with you on the subject[.]

My friend the Doctor is a Democrat of the South Carolina school & has been so through sunshine & storm. Need I add that he is an enthusiastic admirer of yours? Wishing you many years of happiness and prosperity I remain very truly your attached friend, W.M. Gwin.

P.S. If you ever have a leisure moment it would afford me pleasure to receive a line from you directed to Vicksburg. Will you visit the South West this winter[?] I am engaged in a contest for the United States Senate & if elected should above all things like to have y[ou]r views on the present Tariff & Texas question[.]

ALS in ScCleA.

To J[AMES] H. HAMMOND, [Barnwell District, S.C.]

Fort Hill, 30th Aug[us]t 1845

My dear Sir, You state some facts, that are new to me, in reference to circumstances connected with Dr. [Henry B.] Bascom's pamphlet,

& the feelings of the Southern Methodists towards it, and which are entitled to much consideration in relation to the subject of your letter. I had read it cursorily, and although there was a good deal, that I could not approve, yet it was so much sounder on the subject of abolition, than what I had expected from him, & that quarter, that it ["seemed to me to" *interlined*] deserved [*sic*] an encouraging notice from the South, with an allusion, that would not be offensive to the parts, which did not accord with our opinion. I, however, acquiesce in the conclusion to which you have come, as you have paid much more attention to the contents of the pamphlet, than I have, and are far more familiar with the connected ["circumstances" *interlined*]. You must, however, permit me to say, that I think you do not do the Doctor justice, in identifying his opinions either with Cas[s]ius [M.] or Henry Clay on the subject of abolition. The former is one of the most rabid of the fanaticks, and goes all lengths against the South and its institutions. I do not think the latter an abolitionist, but I should be glad to think him as sound, as Dr. Bascom on all points. But enough of this.

You are right in taking all possible precaution in your correspondence with [Lewis] Tappan. If you give him the least chance to pervert what you write, and misrepresent you, he will be sure to use it. A fanatick, to promote his object, regards neither truth, justice nor honor. The course you think of taking is the right one. The last of the topicks, you think of discussing, to trace to its true cause the decay of the South, deserves an elaborate investigation, which I hope you will give it. It has been often touched on, but has never yet been discussed & presented in the full light, it ought to be. Abolish custom Houses & let the money collected in the South be spent in the South and we would be among the most flourishing people in the world. The North could not stand the annual draft, which they have been making on us 50 years, without being reduced to the extreme of poverty in half the time. All we want to be rich is to let us have what we make.

I made several years ago, the experiment of rolling cotton seed in plaster, which was very satisfactory, & nothing prevented me from following it up, but my great distance inland. I am glad you are making such experiments. You are setting a highly useful example to our large educated planters, in being doubly engaged; in defending our institutions, and improving our agriculture. It is what all owe to the State & the South, & I hope your example will be extensively followed. I am endeavoring to do something both ways.

If the Administration should act with firmness & discretion, we either shall have no war with Mexico, or one, that will give little trouble, unless England should countenance her, & that she will not do, unless she should calculate on having difficulties with us about Oregon. That & not Texas has all along been the dangerous question; & I, from the first, so regarded it & acted accordingly. England is exceedingly averse to war with us on many accounts, as we ought [to] be with one, with her. It would be calamitious in the extreme to both countries. But, if we should force her, she will resist us on the Oregon subject. Mr. [James K.] Polk made a profound blunder in alluding to it at all in his inaugural. The last administration said all that should have been said in a short Message to the Senate in answer to a call of Mr. [William] Allen, just before the close of the session. Nothing could be more imprudent, or more improper, than the remarks he made. It has left the subject in the worst possible condition. As it stands, I cannot see any other alternative, but for him to back out, or a conflict with England, if Congress should sustain the inaugural. I left the subject in a fair way, and felt confident of conducting it with success. The [*one word canceled and* "annunciation" *interlined*] of the inaugural alarmed me, & I fear the worst. Much will depend on the course taken by the Southern Senators. My fear is, that England will dispair of settling it, & run it into the Texian question. If so, she will secretly encourage ["her" *canceled and* "Mexico" *interlined*] to take hostile measures. Yours truly, J.C. Calhoun.

ALS in DLC, James Henry Hammond Papers; PC in Jameson, ed., *Correspondence*, pp. 669–671.

From R[OBERT] BEALE

Baltimore, Aug[us]t 31, 1845
My Dear Sir, I should have replied to your favour of the 13 inst. ere this but I was anxious to see Mr. Keller whose judgement I desired in aid of my own before writing you relative to the straw cutter &c &c; unfortunately Mr. Keller was absent and while waiting for his return I was taken sick and confined to my bed for several days. As soon as I recovered I called on Mr. Keller and we are now endeavouring to select for you the last and most used & approved machines. In consequence of having no machine shops in our city I have come to this place to examine such machines as you desire in your letter.

So far I have not determined which to select, except the saw. I find that Page[']s circular saw which saws through any thickness of log is most in use, & saws four times as fast with moderate power than the common whip or up & down saw—all the farmers in this section of country are using them to saw out post[s] for fencing & rails to suit the posts; the posts are mortised with an [a]uger that can be attached to the saw. This saw is usually driven by steam but water will answer quite as well. The farmers use horse power all together 3 horses are sufficient for ordinary work and you must increase it to 4 or 5 or 6 for sawing very heavy timber. As for the straw cutter, and the threshing machine I shall decide upon them in the course of a few days. The cob crusher has not been improved so that the old fashion will have to answer. So soon as I can get the lowest price of each with a horse power that can be applied to all at once or seperately as may be required I will write you. I hope Mrs. [Floride Colhoun] Calhoun is well.

[James K.] Polk is rather going down. The [Thomas H.] Benton anty [*sic*] Tiler [John Tyler] Democrats wants to know how Polk can reconcile to himself the keeping of [John Y.] Mason in as one of his Cabinet and turn out a thousand little petty officers who Tyler appointed.

All the disappointed Democrats are turning anty pro[s]criptionists & those who have obtained office join in with them, & the whigs are roaring against ["it" *interlined*] like all the world, so that so far as proscription goes it is almost without an advocate. Very many of the whigs are for you upon the ground that you are opposed to proscription, all the Tyler men are for you, and the disappointed & to be disappointed Polk men are for you. This last convention has made the ["Politicians & the" *interlined*] people sick of conventions, and I think in future the ["people" *interlined*] will take the offices into their own hands, and if they do the young Democracy look to the South. New York is growing stronger for us every day, & very strong feelings ["is" *canceled and* "are" *interlined*] getting up in this city & in the lower counties of this State both with the young whigs & Democrats in our favour. They say that Mr. [Henry] Clay is no more and that they have no other chance to have any influence in the administration of the government than by aiding in the election of some distinguished man of the the [*sic*] democratic party who scorns party trammels and the traterous business of selling the public offices to purchase his election to the presidency. I do not write you often but I do not see a news paper that your name is not associated with it in my mind. Let all your friends who love their country & wish its future prosperity do but half the little that I do and ["have" *interlined*] half the zeal & they will do much & not faint by the way side. We can & we must ultimately succeede—ruin is too palpable if something is not done. Your friend, R. Beale.

ALS in ScCleA; variant PEx in Boucher and Brooks, eds., *Correspondence*, p. 303.

From Tho[ma]s G. Clemson

Terveuren [Belgium,] September 1845
My dear Sir, Your favour by the Cambria dated Pendleton July 26th arrived about the first inst. It must have remained some fifteen or more days in Washington. Judging from the weather here, for the last two weeks, it has been dry; you may have had a change in the United States. The past year here, has been remarkable for the quantity of rain, whilst with you the drought has been as remarkable. The harvest is finished generally, in the North of Europe. Some of the grain had germinated in the fields, but on the whole the grain crop is abundant. Not so with the potatoes; that crop will be a failure throughout the continent. The public prints are filled with discussions on the cause of the failure, and means of preventing a recur[r]ence of the misfortune. The cause appears to be a disease, which first attacks the stock, and rapidly descends to the root. This disease is a variety of fungus, and the means of obviating its continuance, and preventing its recurrence, are to cut & burn the stock, and import seed from the United States, or some other countrey, where the disease has not made its appearance. Preparations are also making to plant for a winter crop, which appears feasible, even in this climate, so that you might succeed better during the winter in Carolina, than during the summer. The great point appears to be to avoid the effects of frost, which is done by planting deep or covering well with straw.

We regretted very much to hear of Mrs. [Floride Colhoun] Calhoun[']s indisposition, but were as much gratified to hear of her recovery. We are all well, and now that the winter is coming, I hope we shall be better fixed, and get through the cold weather with more comfort, than last year. The house I have taken is more comfortable, and has a southern exposure which in this climate is a great point. It gives us great pleasure to hear that your crops are so promising, and we hope you may realise all you anticipate. My experience tells me that all planters make abundant calculations in the spring, and summer, but unfortunately something always intervenes between the calculation and harvest, at least as regards the cotton crop.

I am very much obliged to you ["for your observations" *inter-lined*] about my planting interest in Carolina. My plantation [in Edgefield District] is the most valuable I know in the State. Its healthfulness, its position in the district, the beautiful manner in which it lies, and happy constitution of its soil, which for fertility, endurance, and recuperative energy is not surpassed, whilst its facilities for manuring, are only equal[l]ed by the kindness with which it recieves [*sic*], responds to, and retains it. Besides the nature of the soil, and its position, are such that when the crops in the neighbourhood are destroyed by drought, those on the Cane Brake are unscathed. It is truly a place possessing a rare combination of ["cir-cumstances" *canceled*] advantages, and if it were stocked as it should be, it would be unrivalled. There is a very extensive range in the neighbourhood, which would sustain a large stock of cattle &c which would so manure those beautiful fields, as to carry their production as high as any land in the United States. If my place had equal force to what you have put upon your place in Alabama, my place would give a greater interest, (considering the cost) than yours. I have not been able to carry into execution what I anticipated doing, when I purchased the place. My force & stock are in no wise sufficient to cope with the difficulties, and as it is there is too much dead capital in the land for me to carry. The price of negroes has changed, so that ["on the whole" *interlined*] I did well to come here, and would do badly if I relinquished this place at present, without I could get some position in the United States that would give me support, when I should return with pleasure.

When the next instalment on the place shall have been paid, I will have expended near about $24,000 including negroes, & every thing as it stands, and to put it in a condition to be agre[e]able or profitable, it would require every cent I have in the world, and more besides. As it is I should be governed by my plantation, instead of my governing it, and this is the rock upon which hundreds of thousands have been wrecked in the United States, and as many more will be swamped from a like cause, ["to" *canceled*] which end I ["have inclinations" *canceled and* "am desirous" *interlined*] to avoid if possible. From what you say, there appears to be a probability of my being able to sell the plantation with out loss; It can not go on satisfactorily without my presence, which under the circumstances I can not give. If my property were securely invested, I should have the interest, and my living out of this position in Belgium. I have therefore concluded to sell the plantation, stock, and implements, and if I can, retain the negroes, at least for some time. They are good, were selected out of many, and according to the size of the gang I doubt if a superior one could be found any where, so that if I can avoid the necessity of selling them, I should much prefer it. By selling the plantation, safely investing the proceeds, and recieving regularly the interest thereon, together with the money in your hands ["it" *interlined*] would give a sum of not far from $25,000 bearing interest, and if I return to the United States, I should like the option of having my negroes, in case I should desire to purchase a home in the South. I have now been living in S. Carolina some years, and if I were to go to another State I should be loosing [*sic*] palpable advantages.

I shall explain my views at large, and you will judge of the practicability of the plan. If I shall have proposed either in part or entirely that which is not feasible, you may yourself have some ideas that will be equally agre[e]able to me. If the negroes can be retained, I do not wish them to leave the State, or to be hired where they would be badly treated or their lives jeopardised in an unhealthy position. The Gang consists of 37 in all. Of these 24 are workers and 13 children. The following are the names of the boys. Bill Laurence, Waddy, Joe, John, Dick, Hamilton[,] Tom, Daniel, Polydore[,] Jim, Jack, Charles[,] Spencer, Nim, and William (Carpenter). Women Dido, Delia, Mary, Jane, Monimia[,] Betzy[,] Daphne, Susan and Susan. Perhaps my having mentioned their names will enable you to form a better idea of the force of the gang. Some of these men might be hired out, if it were thought practicable. Of these, William the Carpenter has a complete set of tools, and he I suppose could be hired for 25 or 30 dol[lar]s a month. He is not only a carpenter but cabinet maker. I should suppose that Bill Laurence would bring good wages any where. Charles is an excellent cook [and] takes pride in it. He is stubborn and wants to be kept up to the mark. He is a very handy fellow and one of the best hands I have on the plantation. I presume the reason why Mrs. Calhoun did not like him was, that he wished to return to Edgefield to his wife, and did not wish to give satisfaction. Jack is a rough blacksmith, a remarkably quiet, orderly, negro. Charles, Spencer, and Jack, I purchased in Charleston. They cost me about $1700 and if they gave any trouble might be sold, for I have less objection to parting with them than any of the others. By hiring the men out in Pendleton, or the environs; I say Pendleton because it is healthy[,] I could afford to take less for the rest of the gang, if they were hired together. Now, Sir, as you have a plantation in Alabama, where your negroes would produce more than they can do in Pendleton, I thought it might suit you to send some more of your own negroes there, and take such of mine as you pleased to select and work them on your place, at Fort Hill, as your own, and in order to effect this, you might hire land of [Andrew F.] Lewis, if you have not enough, paying him in kind so as to make the operation a sure one, and make the payment to me to depend upon the net income which you might derive from their labour. Without you can make a safe operation, one that would in no wise embarrass you, I would not desire it. In thinking the matter over, I thought you might be pleased to make some such operation. My plantation being converted into cash or securities, I should not require the funds in your hands, until perhaps you would wish to fund it, (at least not more than the interest for some time). Your gang and product in Alabama would be increased by the number you would send there and your force at Fort Hill as strong as you desire it, without you being liable for more than they produced. If they produced nothing, I would bear the loss with you, and only recieve in proportion as the crop is good. Or, if my men could be hired well, the women would support themselves, and children at all events. If some such arrangement suited you, and more horses, or waggons, were wanted take of those I have at the Cane Brake, & let the rest be sold. I shall now proceed on the supposition that the plan be accepted by you. In that case, or at all events, take Cherokee and her colt to Fort Hill, for your use. There is also one very fine cow, which you would do well to take up. And as my flock of sheep, are fine and their wool would clothe the negroes, they might be driven up also. There is several Gallons of very fine Brandy, Gin, Rhum [*sic*], & Wine, which you can have if you think it worth accepting. (There is none better.) There are some valuables, in the House which could be easily packed up, & sent up in the waggon, and what ever Mrs. Calhoun might desire, she can take, & use, and if we should require it again & it be in existence there it is, or if gone it would make no difference. Two or three of my Women are first rate weavers, and they during the winter season might clothe the rest, out of the wool from the sheep, which would thus save an important item of expense.

If the plan I have suggested should not be practicable Anna [Maria Calhoun Clemson] suggests another, to which she attaches no more importance than she would an idea in conversation. She says that Patrick [Calhoun] (by Cornelia[']s [that is, Martha Cornelia Calhoun's] letter) is to be married in September. If he leaves the Army and wishes to plant, I would make an arrangement with him somewhat of the character spoken of above. I would sell my place to him[,] making the payments suit. He can purchase some more negroes which together with mine might manage the place and make it profitable.

If there be any come out in the South, my negroes are worth keeping. They ["negroes" *interlined*] are the most valuable property in the South, being the basis of the whole Southern fabric and I should like to see a few years more before I part with mine. If you should object to the proposition I have made on account of the uncertainty of my tenure here, I can only say in answer, that if I thought I should be deprived of this situation shortly, I would not sell the plantation. Even suppose I be deprived of the situation, before the end of the year, some time must elapse, after I return, before I can make a change in the matter. My means are too small to live on my income, and I not only wish to make my property give a regular income, but wish to occupy myself profitably. My family and my health requires that I should do both. Least of all my desires are to solicit pecuniary favours and if you can not make the transaction a business one &, of advantage to yourself, in that case I should not be satisfied if you were to enter into the arrangement. I would rather do you service, ["and should regret" *canceled and* "than" *interlined*] giving you difficulty or embarassement [*sic*], and with such feelings, frankly submit the proposition. The distance is far too great to correspond upon minor differences; the season is fast coming, when it will be propitious to change, if change is to be made. If provision be scarce, my corn & other articles will bring a good price, for if the place be sold all that is on it, (save those things you may require,) had better be sold on such terms as to bring the greatest amount of money. My object now is to get my funds into certain, perfectly secure investments, so that I may have a regular income, upon which I can calculate to the day. (Without the investments are undoubted, the change had better not be made.) If no arrangement can be made for retaining my negroes, I should like to be informed of the fact, and be more particularly advised as to the price, & terms, for which they would sell. If they can be retained, then I suppose plantation crops of all kinds, tools &c had better be sold, and these will swell the amount of assets to be realized. If my proposition suits, and goes into action, things will stand thus. My place cost me $10,000, (when the last & next instalment shall have been paid). Since its purchase I have built & made other improvements, so that the $10,000 will scarce clear me, consequently it must not be sold for a less sum. The grain and all such articles which you may not want, had better be sold. The purchasers to give the best and most undoubted security. You will use your discretion in selling the negroes, I have specified; they were purchased for cash, & if sold for cash the money they bring and all other assets, (if any there be in cash,) to be invested in State securities or some other investment, in which the money will be perfectly secure, & yield a regular interest. You will reserve Cherokee, & her colt, the Cow I mentioned, and any thing in the way of Stock, or other articles, which you may think desirable. As to the things in the house Anna writes her mother her ideas concerning them. You then hire out those ["of the" *canceled*] men ["you may select" *interlined*] on the best conditions, you can make, calculating interest, health, & convenience to yourself. William, (the carpenter,) in a short time would give little trouble as he could look up work, ahead, after becoming acquainted with the neighbourhood. In his leisure time he could make himself useful to you & Mrs. Calhoun. The balance of the hands you will keep and work on your place, using your discretion as to those you will hire, & those you will keep. The Debt to me from Andrew [Pickens Calhoun], & yourself, in that case, can be reduced to a bond, bearing yearly interest, and the principal can still continue with ["you" *interlined*] until I I [*sic*] require it, or it suits your convenience to pay it. (Except the instalment due A[rthur] Simkins in January next, which of course I expect to be met.) By this means, you will have time, and so far as I am concerned, be tranquil and easy. I should regret very much if some such arrangement can not be made. I wish you to know, & feel, that my desires to serve you, are such as they are. Mr. [John Ewing] Bonneau has kept an account of the moneys I have recieved from yourself, and Andrew; you have the same, & I have also an account: by procuring a statement from him, making your observations on it, & forwarding it to me, the whole matter can be easily arranged without my presence in the United States, but if that be necessary, I suppose there would be no difficulty in my getting permission to run over, and settle all that would require my presence, & then return, but for this I do not foresee the necessity. There will then remain between us, I believe, only the carriage and horses. The Carriage cost including harness $350 (not counting freight from Phil[a-delphi]a to Augusta). You had it at $300. Of that there can then be no difficulty. As to the Horses, I am utterly unacquainted with the manner they have turned out, tho I have had some curiosity to know, after what Mrs. Calhoun said to you in her letter to you, to

109

Washington, before I left. I have no inclination to hold you to the original price, tho it is what I gave for them, did you not find them all that I said, and should much prefer bearing the loss if there be any. I thought them every thing I said, and would not have offered them could I have supposed you would not have been satisfied. Had you not taken them, they were sold for $50 more than what you got them at. You will set the price on them which you think them worth, and I shall be contented, & incorporate that sum in the general bond and thus our whole business will have been simplified, to my satisfaction. So that if I die my property will yield a regular income to my family, without much trouble, and if I live I may enjoy as I think proper the usefruct [*sic*]. ["On your part, you will be set at ease and I hope to your advantage" *canceled.*] My negroes, I do not think, can give much difficulty if any. They will be placed in a simple form, between us, and about which there can not be the shadow of a shade of difficulty, or misunderstanding. On thinking over the plan, I am so well convinced of the advantage to my position, of selling the place & keeping the negroes, that I beg you, should you think none of my above mentioned plans feasible, to turn over in your own mind, for some other arrangement, by which they could be safely & comfortably placed for the next year at least, so that I shall not lose by them, even if I make nothing. That length of time will give me the opportunity of looking about me, or of at least seeing how I stand in regard to my present position here. I am sure that any arrangement you would think satisfactory would content me. On reflection I should prefer if the place is sold that Charles & Spencer be sold also. They have both given some difficulty which will be a reason to the rest if they are sold, & the price I gave for them is too high to permit me to retain them as mere field hands. Love to all. Your affectionate son, Thos. G. Clemson.

[P.S.] What think you of the following terms for the sale of the Cane Brake? $1000 down on day of sale or Jan[uar]y 1846: $2000 in January 1847: $2000 Jan[uar]y 1848: $2000 Jan[uar]y 1849: $3000 Jan[uar]y 1850: $3000 Jan[uar]y 1851—making $13000 with out interest in five years.

ALS in ScCleA; PEx in Boucher and Brooks, eds., *Correspondence*, pp. 303–305. NOTE: An unrelated marginal endorsement by Calhoun reads, "Count Hompeth[?] the President of a company for cutting a canal [*one or two words illegible*] wants an engineer recommended."

From JOHN HASTINGS, [former Representative from Ohio]

New Garden, Col[umbian]a C[ount]y Ohio
Sep[tember] 1, 1845

With this, my dear Sir, you will get the ["first" *canceled and* "Ohio Patriot containing the first" *interlined*] of a series of essays on the tariff which I intend to progress with until Congress convenes. We have all along been dealing with, and discussing effects, without exposing causes. I commence with the latter, and before I have finished, will have went far I hope, towards satisfying the People that the whole impost scheme should be abolished, and the government expences paid in proportion to means, instead of the producers paying some ten times as much as they should through their consumption of dutied articles. The cry must ultimately be—sweep off the custom houses and give us free trade! And we will, and must, come to it, in a shorter time ["too" *interlined*] than may be imagined. Nothing less will satisfy me for one: and to assist towards the consummation, I will do my best to expose the indirect tax simulations and delusions to the plain sense of the People.

As I live by work, and write "jus bono publico," I will not prepay postage in writing to those who are equally interested with myself. With the highest esteem Yours as ever, John Hastings.

ALS in ScCleA. Note: The *Ohio Patriot* was published at New Lisbon.

From J[AMES] B. MOWER

New York [City,] 1st Sept. 1845

Dear Sir, I have long contemplated writing to you Sir, and am now impelled, the sooner to do so, on account of hearing, that it is intended very soon, to establish a Calhoun press, in this city. All your friends here, that I've seen, say no. And all the same friends too, most respectfully, and most earnestly desire, your return to the Senate, of the U.S. at the proper time, say, next winter. The casting aside such men as you Sir, and electing a 2d, or perhaps more properly speaking, a 3d rate man, is what I do not believe in. And although Mr. [James K.] Polk, may be right on several national affairs, such as, Texas, Oregon, Tariff, and the Land question, and on all which, we are with him. Yet, his strange conduct, in the appoint-

111

ments, in this ["city" *interlined*] particularly, and in the State generally; has caused great disappointment, dissatisfaction, murmurings, and heart burnings, among the most respectable, influential, and decided friends, of Mr. [Martin] Van-Buren, and yourself. He has violated his most sacred promises, both oral, and written. And all these appointments, (save Mr. [Michael] Hoffman's) appear, to make Mr. Polk, the mere automaton, of Mr. [William L.] Marcy! ! ! This state of things, most assuredly, cannot last long. I think Sir, you may rely on one fact, that Mr. Van Buren, is as much out of the question, for the Presidency, in '48 as old [Andrew] Jackson. Gov. [Silas] Wright, has a disease, that very easily besets him, and his friends say, that it is incurable, and they think also, that it may be very improper, in 2 or 3 years, to bring him ["out" *interlined*] as a candidate in '48. These things being so, your friends and the old friends of Mr. Van Buren, will from the very nature of circumstances, be brought together. First, from sympathy, then the talking over of grievances, and the last, and perhaps the most important cause of all, interest, will make us all, one family. Then on whom can we rally, but you? But should some of your indiscreet friends, and who do not reside among us, undertake to establish a press here now, purely your advocate, I think it needs no prophecy, to foretell its downfall. The very reunion, we desire to build up, would be in fragments. Never was the old saying more true, "Let well enough alone." It is alarming to see already, the movements at Washington, through Marcy, to affect the elections in this city, by means of the patronage, of the Customs; used corruptly. The first indication, of Marcy's interference here, is the selection of a Senator, from this city, to our State Legislature. His candidate, is a Mr. [Edward] Sanford, a son of the late Chancellor [Nathan Sanford], whom you may remember in the U.S. Senate, and "Aristedes" [*sic*] (W[illia]m P. Van Ness) used to call him, an "elastic puppet." This son, is a large "chip of the old block." We must put a stop to such manoeuvre's, in our elections, or, our elective franchise, is a perfect farce.

We want such men as you Sir, in the Senate of the U.S. as a check to mad ambition, and profligate Secretarys.

I tender you Sir, my most friendly salutations, for your health and happiness, Most truly your friend, J.B. Mower.

ALS in ScCleA.

From ABNER PRATT

Marshall [Mich.,] Sept. 1st 1845

Dear Sir, Your communication is received, and in consummating the *decree* in the cause of Adams vs Kirkland I shall endeavor to carry out your wishes, as expressed.

Not having had the pleasure of your personal acquaintance it may be regarded impertinent in me to touch upon matters not relating to the subject of your communication; but having long known you by reputation, and having long taken a deep interest in your public and political life, I must be permitted to avail myself of this opportunity, to say, that your leaving the counsels of the nation, at the time when you did, has been a source of regret, not only to me; but also to many others. I fear that many of the leading politicians of the day, are substantially loosing sight of great fundamental principles—principles which, as it were, constitute the very *bases* of our national compact—principles which are essential to the living existance of our Republic, and which must be kept constantly in view, steadily adheared to, and faithfully carried out, or our government cannot be maintained, nor the blessings of liberty and equality perpetuated. The most of our leading politicians, and especially editors and conductors of political journals, are apparently becoming entirely *remiss* on this subject. They are too much engaged about *party*, or *party tactics*, or too completely entangled with the various *political cliques* of the day to study thoroughly the correct principles of the government, and much less to understand and fully appreciate their importance. It is not therefore surprising that their political action is not always governed by fundamental principles, or sound political policy. Again; we have a great many *pretenders* in our country—men who profess great regard for democracy—great regard for the cardinal principles of democracy; and yet, in their political action, they boldly violate them, almost every day of their lives. The *press* in the *North West* and particularly in this State, is completely *muzzled* on this subject. Almost every *news paper press*, being owned, or entirely control[l]ed by, ["some" *canceled*] political demegouges, or ["some" *interlined*] corrupt clique. Since 1840 I have made several efforts to have some person establish a press in this section of country, and publish a political paper upon correct principles—a paper (*to be frank with you*) that would advocate your principles—adopt your political measures and otherwise do you justice for the ["many masterly" *canceled*] ideas and measures, your mind has generated; and for the invaluable services you have, in various ways,

113

rendered to the country. But thus far, my efforts have been unavailing, though I have not the least doubt that such a paper could be ably conducted by your friends in this section, and would have in the course of a year, a great circulation. I am still in hopes of being able to accomplish my desire, before [18]48. Your friends I believe are not generally ["the" *canceled*] *trading politicians*, at least I am not one of that class, and therefore have about as much as I can do to live and support my family at this time in Michigan, by my legitimate business, otherwise I would have had *one independent paper* in Michigan long ago. I trust for the good of the country that your retirement to the domestic pleasures of private life, may be temporary, much as you may desire to continue its enjoyments. I fear that *Mr.* [James K.] *Polk* has in many instances been too much under the selfish influence of the [Martin] *Van Buren* politicians. Gen[era]l [Lewis] Cass, by pursuing the course he did, to obtain the election of Senator in Congress, has been constantly loosing ground ever since. It is entirely clear to me, that he is on the wane, of not only his intellect, but his political popularity. And I *predict*, that he cannot sustain himself in the U.S. Senate. My personal acqua[i]ntance with Gen[era]l Cass has satisfied me of three things; 1st. that he is *vain* & *ambitious*—2d. that he has but very little moral firmness, & 3d. that ["he" *interlined*] is sometimes disposed to vacillate in his political course. A *President* of the U.S. should be selected by the people, for his principles & qualifications and not because he resides at the North or the South—not because he resides in Michigan, ["or" *canceled*] Virginia [*sic*; "or any other section of the Union" *interlined*]. This is a subject not sufficiently commented upon by political editors. No sectional, or clan[n]ish feelings, should ever be indulged in by the people, in the selection of their *Chief Magistrate.*

Your correspondents are undoubtedly numerous, and any thing like ordinary attention to them, must operate as a severe tax upon your time, but ["at any time" *canceled*] when you cannot employ a leasure moment, with any more pleasure, or profit to yourself, be assured I ["shold" *altered to* "should"] be happy to hear from you. With great respect I am Yours &c, Abner Pratt.

P.S. Your friend Gen[era]l [Isaac E.] Crary is in the Lake Superior country, and your friend Maj. [Francis W.] Shearman is at this time temporarily confined by sickness.

ALS in ScCleA. NOTE: Francis W. Shearman (1817–1874) had come to Mich. some years before to assist Henry R. Schoolcraft in Indian negotiations. He was a State legislator, judge and editor of the Marshall, Mich., *Democratic Ex-*

pounder. Pratt (1801–1863) was a native of N.Y. resident in Mich. since 1839. He was a justice of the Michigan Supreme Court 1850–1852.

From JOHN G. BOWMAN

Columbia [S.C.,] Sept. 2, 1845

My Dear Sir, During my visit to Pendleton, Gen. [James] Gillam requested me to make enquiry for you, of Mr. [James S.] Boatwright of this place, in relation to his corn & cob crusher, its price and capacity of being attached to a Grist Mill.

Since my return, I made the enquiry stated above, and have ascertained that the "Crusher" which Mr. Boatwright has, will not answer your purpose, inasmuch as it cannot be so attached, the Drum wheel being necessary. A Mr. [E.A.] Knowlton, as I am informed, was the original patenter of the crusher you want, and sold his right for this State to Mr. J.W. Burn of Cheraw, S[.]C. I am well acquainted with Mr. Burn, and will take pleasure in making any enquiries of him which you may authorize, or desire.

I directed the S.C. Temperance Advocate to be sent to your address. I hope you will excuse the liberty I have taken in so doing. I intend it merely, as an expression, however imperfect, of the high esteem I feel towards you both personally and otherwise, and should you deem it worth the postage, I shall be altogether satisfied. My paper is the organ, not only of the State *Temperance*, ["Society" *canceled*] but of the State *Agricultural* Society, and you may possibly find, occasionally, an agricultural article of interest. Most Respectfully, John G. Bowman.

ALS in ScCleA.

From ELLWOOD FISHER

Cincinnati, 9 mo[nth] 2, 1845

Dear friend, I send herewith the Cin[cinnati] Enquirer containing the proceedings of our late county convention. As this is the most populous county and city of the State and now votes probably the largest Democratic majority, its opinions have great influence throughout the party in the State. Our friends therefore considered

115

it very important to secure on this occasion the triumph of the true doctrine. Thee will perceive the resolutions were reported by a friend of thine. The tariff question we have long since settled in this quarter, and on that there is not much said. We concluded it would be well through the Committee which is appointed to transmit [to Robert J. Walker] the Sec[retar]y [of the] Treasury on behalf of Western agriculture and commerce a strong free trade paper. The Banks give us here much more trouble than you experience from them in the South, where the entire city and mercantile influence is so subordinate to the agricultural. There has been a long and severe struggle here for the establishment of the metallic doctrine, in which thy friends have taken the lead, and this is their first complete triumph in the county. Appearances indicate their triumph in the State also.

We could have nominated a Calhoun man to the State Senate very easily if we could have prevailed on him to accept the office; but being extensively engaged in business he could not ["accept" *canceled*] consent. It was W[illiam] F. Johnson, a young man of superior talent.

There is a serious evil resulting from the superior pay and chances of preferment to be found in the service of the Federal government over that of the States. The consequence is that State offices are almost considered derogatory to their incumbents—and scarcely a man of talent and standing can be found to accept one. The debasing action of the Convention system also has degraded the standard of qualification for office so much, that office, no longer confer[r]ing honour, is sought chiefly for emolument—and this is not sufficiently attainable under our State government, to countervail the attractions of the federal service.

The leading presses of our State are undergoing improvement. The [Columbus *Ohio*] Statesman has been sold by [Samuel] Medary (who was a coarse imitator, in every thing, of [Francis P.] Blair) to [Charles C.] Hazewell[,] a person of much more ability and decorum, who has the confidence of [Levi] Woodbury, [Senator from N.H., David] Henshaw & [Edmund] Burke [former Representative from N.H.] from whose section he comes. The change excited the fears and jealousy of the ultra [Martin] Van Buren men who taking advantage of some ill-advised manifestations by the new editor of indulgence for Banks succeeded in creating an unfavourable impression against him. He has however corrected that error and will I think triumph.

We made a very strenuous effort to secure the Demo[cratic] paper at this place. One of our (thy) friends came forward and offered himself alone to contribute $5000 to secure it—but we had been anticipated by a purchaser from the East who not having yet taken possession has not disclosed his preferences. The gentleman who acted so liberally is A.G. Sloo a very cordial and devoted friend of thine.

I met Senator [from Fla. David] Levy [Yulee] the other day at Louisville with whom I had a long conference on the present posture of our affairs—and among other things we discussed very earnestly the expediency of thy return this Winter to the Senate. I was at first unfavourable to the suggestion, on the ground that the existing issues and thy present attitude in relation to them were extremely favourable—and that thy presence in the Senate would facilitate the enemy in presenting new questions of such character as to have at once a false yet popular aspect, in order to take advantage of any action of thine which however correct and patriotic might not correspond with the first impressions of the people, and might bring thee into needless conflict even in that body with members who might otherwise be friendly. I also suggested that there was at present a partiality for the selection of those out of power and unconnected with office. I did not conceal from myself that great services might be rendered by thee in the Senate to the Union, and that this consideration rendered it at once a duty of thy friends to urge and of thine to accept that station. But I countervailed that view by reflecting that any course now adopted that would operate against thy being soon called to the first station in the country would on that very account be possibly more calamitous to the country than any probable senatorial service would compensate. On the other hand Senator Levy insisted that the Democratic party were although numerically strong, otherwise recently much weakened in the Senate—and required very much a leader of pre-eminent ability and weight of character. That such an one would concentrate at once in his favour the popular sympathies of the party—and direct not only the councils of the party aright but exert a salutary influence on the Administration. That if thee were absent [Thomas H.] Benton would be too prominent and pernicious. I was forcibly impressed with these views, and have since reflected much upon them. I am satisfied that it will be the policy of thy enemies to present new and false issues, and in this they will be assisted by the Whigs. It seems to me also that thy absence would not avail to exempt thee from the effect of such movements—for thee would be held responsible for the action of thy friends. Every vote of [George] McDuffie[']s would be considered or represented as thine, and the indifferent or prejudiced would be persuaded. In this view of the case it is of the highest importance for thee to have the direction of affairs as well as the responsibility. Great as are the number and abilities of thy friends in the next Congress I know of none to whom I could with sufficient confidence commit the leadership of our cause surrounded as it must be with open and secret and powerful foes. If thee were present thee might not only prevent the enemy from changing adversely to us the position of the party—but thee might also thyself present such new measures as the succession of events might render expedient and add to the strength we have already acquired.

I am confirmed in these views by learning as I did the other day that there will probably be no necessity of dispute on the Tariff— [James] Buchanan having already signified his willingness to accede to [James I.] McKay[']s bill, whilst [George] Bancroft insists on the entire abandonment of protection. I suppose that even McKay[']s bill would be better than a rupture of the party, although the West demands more. Benton was here the other day. I am told he said that Texas was not yet annexed. He however thought there would be no war. Said that our proper position at such a time as this would be mediatorial between Texas & Mexico! Thee will have seen from recent proceedings in Kentucky that my prognostic in the Winter concerning the agitation is being verified. Lou[isville] Journal is for emancipation. Judge [John] McLean is to be the Whig Candidate.

P.S. I have received no letter from thee since my last. I perceive from the results in this county as at Baltimore, that the Van B[uren] men lose faith in the Convention system when their friends are not nominated. With [grea]t regard, Ellwood Fisher.

P.S. Our friends intend to present themselves in force at the Convention in Columbus on the 8th Jan[uar]y next.

ALS in ScCleA.

From M[oses] C. Mordecai

Charleston [S.C.,] Sept. 2/1845

Dear Sir, I have the Honor to acknowledge Rec[ei]pt of your letters of the 21 & 22 ult[im]o [not found]. In place of handing Mr. [William J.] Grayson the list of Questions asked for by Mr. [Secretary of the Treasury Robert J.] Walker, the Committee have addressed him direct. Enclosed I hand you a copy of the letter & the list of Questions, the Committee have added to your list, and I have made a cross x, in your copy, where additions have been made.

I do not believe Mr. Walker intended to issue any other Circular than the one to the manufacturers. The last communication he sent to Mr. Grayson asking the Chamber for the Questions they wished propounded I feel satisfied originated thro the instrumentality of the Hon. [Fla. Senator] David Levy [Yulee]. I must say I have no faith in the President [James K. Polk] or his Cabinett [*sic*], we shall look to the next move and be prepared to act upon it. The Committee have [*sic*] introduced the Question on the Establishment of the warehouse system, connected with the abolition of Drawbacks.

I think the South would be benefit[t]ed by it, in as much as our own vessels would be Enabled more frequently to return with full cargoes, as well as ships now coming in ballast for our staples, and having a market for the purchase of suitable articles for Export would have the tendency to increase our direct trade & give more facility to smal[l] capitalists, but I am not satisfied, and I would Respectfully beg your opinion in what manner it may likely act upon us in our No[r]thern Cities. With great Respect your Ob[edient] S[ervant], M.C. Mordecai.

[Enclosure]

Committee to R[obert] J. Walker, Secretary of the Treasury

Charleston, 29th August 1845

Sir, The chamber of Commerce of this City has been applied to by the Collector of this Port, the Hon. W[illiam] J. Grayson on your behalf to obtain from them such questions as they would desire to have propounded by you, to shew the operation of the Tariff on the Commercial & Agricultural Navigation & Ship Building interests with a direction to inclose them to you at the earliest practicable period; & the Committee of the chamber to whom the questions heretofore officially propounded by you have been referred, and who are charged with the whole subject with full power to take all necessary steps, and adopt all advisable measures, in relation to it, have in compliance with Mr. Grayson[']s application prepared the series of questions herein enclosed, with as much promptness as a careful & deliberate consideration of the extensive & important subject to which they relate would permit. In one particular however, the Committee have ventured to deviate from the request conveyed to them through Mr. Grayson, which they trust you will pardon. The momentous bearing of the inquiries you have intrusted relative to the operation

119

of the Tariff upon the vital interests and prosperity of the Southern States, have induced them to transmit the questions, they have prepared, directly to yourself, instead of sending them through Mr. Grayson, in order that they might have an opportunity of expressing their views on the vast importance of propounding & extensively circulating such questions in conneccion [*sic*] with those which you have propounded in relation to Manufactures. The Hon. F[ranklin] H. Elmore who is a member of the Committee has submitted a letter to them which he received from you in reply to one from himself, from which they are truly gratified to learn that you regard the present as a favorable moment "to make a very great reduction in the tariff." The Committee not only concur in this opinion, but is acompaned [*sic*] with the belief, that unless such reduction is *now* vigorously pressed, this highly favorable opportunity will be irretrievably lost. They deem it too, indispensable for that purpose, that all the other great interests—the Agricultural, Commercial & Navigation—Should be as fully heard on the subject of the reduction, as the manufacturing. The former are suffering severely under the exorbitant & oppressive duties of the present tariff, and have as deep an interest in having these duties eaqualized & reduced, to the lowest standard, consistant with the fiscal wants of the Government, as the manufacturers can possibly have in keeping them up at the present rate, or at any other above that standard; and they are far better entitled to insist that the Government should make such reduction, than the manufacturing interests can be to insist on keeping them above that standard. Now it seems manifest to the Committee that it is only by hearing both sides, that the operation of the system can be fully brought to the knowledge of Congress, and that a partial statement of one side, without hearing the others, is calculated to mislead and impose upon Congress & the Country. It will be impossible therefore to give to these great and suffering interests, which include those of nine tenths of the whole Union a full & fair hearing hearing [*sic*], without preparing and propounding questions by the Treasury Department, eaqually minute and searching and to be as widely circulated as those addressed by the Department to the manufacturing interests; and the Committee respectfully submit to you, that these great interests are justly entitled to claim it as a right, that the same course which has been adopted by the Department to bring out the views and opinions of the manufacturing interests, in relation to the Tariff, should be afforded to them to bring out their views. With a strong conviction of the correctness of this view of the subject the Committee after the fullest deliberation have come to the conclusion that they could not with propriety attempt to furnish answers to the questions heretofore propounded by you. These questions contain very few points on which they can give any information, and the Committee felt bound on behalf of the Chamber of Commerce to decline volunteering informal & irrelevant answers to interrogatories which on their face plainly shew, that they are intended to bring out the opinions & views of the manufacturing interests only. Self respect no less than the inefficiency of answers so volunteered, especially to interrogatories from so high a quarter, forbid their responding to any, which are not as directly addressed to the other great & suffering interests, and eaqually well calculated to bring out their views & opinions, as those received are in relation to the manufacturing interest. The committee have felt confidant that upon reflection you would concur in these views, as absolutely necessary to insure even handed justice to all the great interests of the Country, and that you would ultimately therefore adopt a course similar to that, which they have suggested; and they are highly gratified to learn by the communication received through Mr. Grayson, that these expectations have not been disappointed. The Committee however are so deeply impressed with the importance of these views, that they could but feel as though they had fallen short of the duty they owe to the great interest they represent, if they had transmitted the questions they have prepared in conformity to them, without urging distinctly upon your attention the great considerations of justice and eaqual rights among all the great interests of the Country, which seem to them imperitively to require the concourse they have suggested. It remains to add that the questions now sent are such as are calculated to bring out the views of that portion of the Commercial[,] agricultural and Navigation interests, with which the Committee are most intimately acquainted & which in fact most nearly concern those interests as far as relates to the Southern States.

It would be going beyond their proper field to have attempted more, but it is manifest that similar questions calculated to bring out the views of the great interest refer[r]ed to in the Northern[,] Eastern & Western States, ought also to be propounded.

This the Committee must leave to yourself, but on behalf of the Interest they represent, they respectfully request, that the questions now sent, may be printed and circulated as widely as those already sent forth by the Department, and they on their part will furnish answers to them with the least possible delay.

The Committee beg leave to subscribe themselves with great respect Your Ob[edien]t S[er]v[an]t, Signed by the Committee.

[Enclosure]

"Questions to be propounded to the growers of the great agricultural Staples, Cotton, Rice, and Tobacco, and the Commercial, Mechanical, manufacturing and ˣNavigation interests, immediately connected with, and dependent upon them."

1st   Which of these Staples are grown in your State?

2nd   What portion of its Capital is engaged in their production?

3rd   To what extent is its Commercial, Mechanical, Manufacturing, and ˣNavigation interests, immediately connected with, or dependent upon them?

4th   What has been the average annual profit on Capital employed in their production on well conducted estates for the last three years, since the passage of the tariff of 1842, including the Crop of that year, and deducting all expenses incident to the production of the articles, their preparation for market, their transportation to the place of Sale, and the Sales themselves?

5th   What has been the annual profit of the Capital so employed, for the ten years preceding 1842, under the reduction of the duties by the Act of 1832, and the Compromise Act of the next year, estimated in the same way?

6th   What has been the Annual Average price of these Staples during the same periods respectively; and what the annual average income per hand, deducting all expenses during the same periods, respectively?

7th   ˣHow far have prices and profits during the periods referred to been affected by the operation of the Tariff Laws, and how far by the state of the Currency?

8th   Does the State raise a sufficient supply of horses, mules, and of Cattle, meats, and other provisions; if not from what places does it draw its Supplies: and what has been the average annual amount for the last three years, and also for the ten preceding. If there has been a difference between them, to what do you attribute it?

9th   Are the Commercial, Mechanical, Manufacturing, and ˣNavigation interests of the State so immediately connected with, and dependent upon the Staples, that their profits increase, or diminish, in the same, or very nearly the same proportion with them?

10th   Have the average prices of what are called the protected articles, been as low in proportion to the average prices of the Staples for the last three years, as in the preceding ten, making allowance for the effects, which the average prices of the raw materials, during the respective periods referred to must have had, on the cost of making such articles: if not, to what do you attribute it, and to what extent has it affected the growers of the Staples, and the State at large, in the increased cost of their production and the general expenses of living?

11th   Does the State export any other articles of its own product, besides the Staples; if it does of what description are they, and to what extent have their prices, and the aggregate amount in value been comparatively affected, during the same periods?

12th   What proportion of the aggregate amount of articles of every kind, that the State makes for export, are exported, and consumed abroad; are their prices governed by the foreign, or the home demand; to what foreign markets are they principally shipped; do you meet competitors in them, from other countries with similar articles for Sale; do the high duties imposed by the present tariff lessen your ability to meet them successfully; and if they do, state how?

13th   Is there any such immediate connexion between imports and exports, that a Country cannot continue to import for any great length of time a greater amount in value than it exports, or *vice versa*, export for any great length of time, more than it is permitted to import, estimating fairly the value of each: and if there be, to what extent must the present duties affect ultimately the value of the exports of the Country?

14th   Have you any manufacturing establishments in your State; and if so, of what kind are they, what is their number, & what amount of Capital is invested in them; what descriptions of goods do they make, and what has been the profit on their investment for the last three years?

15th   ˣIs your State now, or have its Citizens been at any former period, engaged in the business of Ship-building, or that of navigation, and to what extent; what is the present condition of those interests; how have they been affected by the tariff laws; and what is the effect of the present duties upon them?

16th   ˣWhat proportion does the Capital invested by your Citizens in commerce, bear to the value of its Staples: have the commercial interests of the State been affected by the tariff laws; if so, how; and to what extent?

17th   ˣWould the establishment of a Ware-house System promote the trade, and increase the Commerce of your State?

18th ˣHow would the abolition of drawbacks, in connexion with a Ware-house System, operate upon the Commerce of your State?

19th ˣAre there any, and what articles, on which a debenture, or drawback, ought to be allowed on their re-exportation, which would operate beneficially upon the trade of the Country, and equally to all classes of Citizens, but on which no debenture or drawback is now allowed?

20th ˣWhat articles are there of foreign manufacture, which come into competition with similar articles manufactured in the United States, the duties upon which are so high as to amount to a prohibition of the foreign article?

21st ˣHow are the interests of the several great interests of your State affected by the minimums of the present tariff, and the rule requiring duties to be paid in Cash, without the establishment of a Ware-house System, or admitting goods en entropot?

22nd ˣWhat would be the effect in your State of a duty upon Coffee & Tea?

23rd ˣWhat other articles are there now in the list of those duty free, on which a moderate duty might be levied, without being onerous to any class, and which would operate equally on all; and what amount of revenue might be levied by such a duty on these articles?

24th ˣWhat is the comparative operation of the present tariff, upon the manufacturers, and the other classes of our Citizens, as to articles used in manufacturing, and other articles consumed by them respectively? State the particular articles.

25th ˣWhat is the effect of the present System of duties upon articles, especially those extensively consumed, which are manufactured only to a very limited extent in the United States; and how do these duties operate upon the interests of the other industrial classes of the country?

26th ˣAre there are any, and what descriptions of goods or other commodities consumed in your State, which are either very greatly enhanced in price, or altogether excluded by the operation of the present tariff: for what prices might such goods or commodities, be imported, independently of the duty; and what are the prices actually paid by the consumers for these articles, or such others as are substituted for them: is the consumption of these articles, or their substitutes, extensive in your State, and is it peculiar, or nearly so, to your State, or any other particular States: what is the aggregate amount of duties now paid to the Government on such articles; and what amount would be paid under a tariff graduated entirely with a view to revenue?

27th   Do the present duties benefit in any respect those engaged in growing the great Staples referred to; and if not can they be so modified, in any other way than by reducing them, so as to benefit the growers: Has the State prospered or not, under those duties; if not, to what do you attribute its cause; if the high duties, explain to what extent, and in what manner, they have affected the prosperity of the State?

ALS with Ens in ScCleA. NOTE: The members of the Committee were Mordecai, Franklin H. Elmore, Henry W. Conner, Charles Edmondston, Henry Gourdin, Thomas J. Roger, James Gadsden, and A. McDowall.

From S. C. KELL

Huddersfield [England,] 3d Sept. 1845
Sir! I have just received your favor of 12th July and in reply to it have made inquiries concerning the missing Nos. of the Economist. I find that they have been regularly forwarded to you since the time of my last letter, but addressed to you at Washington which accounts for your not having received them. I have however now given instructions that the missing Nos. be sent you by the steamer which takes this letter & should any irregularity occur in future I request you to be so kind as to inform me of it.

I think that every day's experience of passing events tends to teach us that nothing is so likely to keep the world at peace as the binding of nations together by the ties of *commercial* intercourse, & that *Free Trade* is destined to be henceforth the chief instrument in the progress of civilization and happiness, and as I believe your views on this subject are the same at all events to some extent perhaps it would not be taxing your complaisance too far if I were to request that in case you are acquainted with any societies or even influential individuals, or indeed any other channel where you think that the spread of sound commercial knowledge would be promoted by ["our" *interlined*] forwarding copies weekly of the Economist, that you would be so obliging as to furnish me with the addresses of such parties, influential members of your government or legislature, and editors of leading Newspapers. Reading Societies & News Rooms in large towns are the channels through which the Society has chiefly circulated the Economist. Of course we could not lay claim to the sacrifice of a moment of your valuable time to forward the plan we have at heart but thinking that you might possibly at once be able to give us a few such suitable addresses and that with little trouble to yourself it might possibly happen that a word from you to such parties would insure an attention to what we have to offer that might otherwise in vain be hoped for. I have taken the liberty of making this request & which I trust you will excuse. Remaining Sir! With great Respect, S.C. Kell.

ALS in ScCleA. Note: An AEU by Calhoun reads "Mr. Kell, Huddersfield England. To be attended to."

From JAMES E. BROOME

Tallahassee [Fla.,] September 4th 1845

Dear Sir, I am a native of your State and a resident until within eight years, and feel as lively an interest in her sons, and her measures of policy as I could have done had I have continued to reside within her borders. I apprehend that there are troubles and divisions ahead to be encountered by the Democratic party. I fear that the just expectations of the South are to be disappointed by the action of the next Congress on the subject of the Tariff. If so we should understand our position, and be prepared to unite on the policy to be pursued. Some of us here desire that our infant State shall not be backward in the struggle, through which I fear we are to pass. We have elected Senators who will vote right in the Senate, but should the South be defeated on that question, and decide to take high ground there is one of them (Mr. [James D.] Westcott) who will fly the track; he is a New Jersey Politician, and will go with the Pen[n]-sylvania & New York Democracy. He is a man of talents, and an addroit [*sic*] manager, and I fear his influence in the State; he has managed himself into the Senate very unexpectedly to many and in fact to a majority of the party here. It is not to be concealed, that the South must rally in 1848 ["if not earlier" *interlined*] and that you must lead them. What influence Mr. Westcott may be able to command will be exerted against you, and there are some of us here who desire to forestall him by getting his friends committed before he thinks it necessary to take ground.   He will be absent at the session of our Legislature in November and we wish to procure the passage of a set of resolutions placing the party here on proper grounds, and committing them to the principles and policy which the South should advocate, and on which the Presidential canvass in forty eight must be conducted by us.   For this purpose I have intruded myself upon your notice, which I hope you will excuse, and ask of you should it not be inconsistent with your ideas of propriety to draw a set of resolutions which you ["may" *interlined*] conceive proper to be adopted, and transmit them between this time and the 1st of December to some confidential friend here or to the Hon[orab]l[e] D[avid] Levy [Yulee] one of our Senators.   As a stranger to you I would not ask so important a trust, but should you send them here I would suggest the Hon[orab]l[e] S[ampson] H. Butler near Madison Court House who is one of your warmest friends.   Should you decline complying with this request I would suggest the propriety of your intimating the desire of the South Carolina School of the Democracy here, on the subject, to some discreet friend of ability who would probably undertake to draw them.   I am induced to present these considerations and requests to you not because we have not the talents here, nor yet because I have not acquaintances to whom I could address myself in my native State, but because I feel assured that when ground is to be taken, South Carolina will lead, and I wish Florida committed to follow and when committed I desire that there shall be no mistake in the position which she assumes.   South Carolina can trust Mr. Levy, he is with us on all points but Mr. Westcott is a man of superior ability.   We are about to elect Mr. [William H.] Brockenbrough to Congress.   He will go right on the subject of the Tariff, and in respect to remedies, he will be a Virginian, and go probably with [Thomas] Ritchie of the [Washington] Union.   He is a man of Talents and character.   The South Carolina School have not the most implicit confidence in him.   He was nominated by a legislative caucus composed principally of Mr. Westcott[']s adherants.

I hope you will excuse the length of this epistle and pardon me for thus intruding myself upon and allow me to be Your Ob[edien]t Servant, James E. Broome.

ALS in ScCleA.

From Sam[ue]l W. Dewey

Washington D.C., 4th Sept. 1845
Hon[ore]d Sir, I am aware that you have no time to bestow upon
ordinary communications from ordinary sources upon subjects of
little or no importance, but, Sir, I cannot believe that you will refuse
to answer this letter after you shall have duly reflected upon its purport & upon the effect that may be produced on the welfare of untold
generations to come, by a simple statement of your views in regard
to the matter now submitted to you.

You cannot have forgotten the testimonials of Judge [Mordecai
M.] Noah which I laid before you, nor can it have escaped your mind
that I told you President [John] Tyler left it entirely with you to
decide upon the appointment of Judge Noah as Minister to Turkey
or Special Agent to Egypt.

You no doubt recollect the deep interest & solicitude which was
expressed throughout the testimonials in question. I endeavored
particularly to draw your attention to the letter of Sir Moses Mont[e]-
fiore, who unequivocally stated that *the appointment of Judge Noah
as Minister from this country to Constantinople would be highly
beneficial to the interests of the United States & that it was anxiously
looked for throughout Europe.* The petitions from all the Syna-
gogues in this country & from all of your wealthy & respectable
Hebrews, were also submitted to your inspection, & well do I remember the beaming intelligence that shone forth in your countenance,
as you said *"Well, the Major certainly has reason to consider himself
as the Head of his people."* This remark of yours, coupled with your
reply to my stating, that "to me it was grievous & humiliating to reflect that men who like yourself & Mr. [Henry] Clay, had done so
much for this country, should be passed over & one that has comparatively done nothing, should be placed in the Presidency," will
ever be remembered by me. *"Perhaps we have done too much!"*
These few words express volumes, & convey more than it would be
possible for me [to] put upon paper were I to write from now till
doom's day.

Calling a Negro Convention in Canada to prepare an address to
the Slaves of our Southern States, requesting & urging them to rise
in favor of Mexico; the siezing [*sic*] upon & occupying of Oregon;
the taking of mortga[g]es upon Mexican lands in Upper California
& the doing of many like acts on the part of England & the English,
the more & more convinces me, that sooner or later we shall be
brought fairly into collision with that country.

Now that Texas has been annexed solely *to protect the South* & Southern interests, I trust that the North may not be accused of being the only[?] favorites of government protection. In my former letters to you (which I fear have seriously annoyed you) I have given my views on the subject of what I consider would be the effect that would follow the appointment of Judge Noah as Minister to Constantinople. I will not again trouble you with a repetition of them, but I would respectfully request you to reperuse the Discourse of my good friend the Judge on the Restoration [of the Jews to Palestine] before you decide to refrain from complying with the request I now make of you. President Polk now sees that he has not treated you even civilly, his conscience fairly smites him, & he is most anxious to make amends. Already he begins to tremble & to fear as to his success with the coming Congress. A troop of competitors have sprung up for public printing & public favor, hence there will be no end to the abuse which one will heap upon the other. Should the [Washington] Union, lose the public printing, that paper would probably be suspended before the close of the Session. Amidst all the cross firing of these cliques, I imagine that the chance is now better than ever for getting Judge Noah appointed as Minister to Constantinople. That office, has not been promised, & like many others, it is reserved probably to be used as an inducement to operate with upon refractory parties next winter, should it become necessary to resort to such expedients. As already stated, I know that President Polk is extremely desirous to conciliate the South, as the only dangers which he has to encounter lie in the troubled waters of that section. He is straining every nerve to make himself popular in that quarter, for can he but command the Souther[n] influence in next Congress, he will be perfectly safe & have his own way.

For one, I do heartily approve his course in regard to Texas, & I feel that we are at this moment to all intents & purpose at war with Mexico. She threw down the gauntlet, we took it up when we passed the Texas Annexation Resolutions, hence there can be no occasion for her to make a further declaration of war. Mexico has murdered in cold blood, our citizens whose widows & orphans cry aloud to high Heaven to be avenged; they have robbed, plundered, despoiled, insulted & abused us to a degree that forbearance, patience & long suffering have ceased to be virtues, & I see no good cause why we should not "carry the war into Africa."

When once our Troops get started, when once a little blood is spilt, I no long[er] fear as to the result. We will make Mexico forthwith indemnify us for all the robberies she has perpetrated upon our defenceless citizens; make her pay the expense of ["the" *interlined*] war, & in other respects treat her as England & France treat the nations who commit robberies upon them. England towards China, & India; France towards Algiers, Moroc[c]o, Tahiti &c. &c. have set us examples which if we follow will reinstate us in the estimation of civilized nations. Our national pusillanimity has become the by word of the world. We allow the weakest Government to insult, abuse, rob, & plunder us with impunity. True, we did have the hardihood to chastise the poor Malays of Sumatra & the Negroes in Africa. I beg pardon for wandering from my subject. I do wrong in taxing your time, therefore I will at once proceed to the point. In my heart I do solemnly believe that you consider Judge Noah peculiarly fitted to fill the office of Minister to Constantinople, & I likewise feel persuaded that his appointment to that office by President Polk, would be gratifying to you. I am sincere in this belief for I know that your discernment is such, that you cannot have been an inattentive observer of his course ever since the period when he was Editor of a Newspaper in your native State [and] was among the first if not the very first to place your name before the country as a candidate for public office. His prompt & energetic conduct in Africa where as U.S. Consul he purchased a number of American citizens from Slavery & sent them rejoicing on their way home; his indefatigable labor in the great cause of our Country[']s welfare & in short his whole career as a man, a citizen, a patriot & a real friend to the cause of humanity must be known to you to an extent that warrants me in believing his appointment by the present Administration as Minister to Constantinople would meet your warm approbation & hearty approval. I trust you may be pleased to give me your views on this subject, provided I am correct in the above mentioned belief. A few words in your pointed & laconic style, is all I ask. I might then submit those words, with other papers I have, to President Polk, & mer[e]ly call his attention to the fact, that you know Judge Noah personally, know his merits, & know the nature of the lost testimonials which his friends sent to the late administration, & that knowing all this, you deem him well calculated to fill the office in question, & that his appointment would be pleasing & satisfactory to you.

I await a reply at your earliest leisure. I beg you will pardon my importunity. I am aware that it has exceeded all bounds of propriety, but, Sir, the present case is without a parallel in the annals of history. *Perseverance* is my motto & when I have a good cause, continued defeat tends but to make me the more confident of ultimate success. Requesting in behalf of the *great Cause of humanity*, that you will favor me with the desired reply, I remain with Sentiments of unfeigned Sincerity your Ob[edien]t & Humble Servant, Saml. W. Dewey.

ALS in ScCleA.

From ANNA [MARIA CALHOUN] CLEMSON

["Brussels" *canceled and* "Terveuren" *interlined*]
Sept. 5th 1845

I believe, my dear father, this letter is due to you, tho' it is difficult, writing thus at intervals, to keep exactly the order I have prescribed myself of writing by turns each steamer, to either you, mother [Floride Colhoun Calhoun], or sister [Martha Cornelia Calhoun], that I may be certain you are not made anxious by my silence. Even with all my punctuality, & regularity, I find sister in the letter I received, by the Cambria, complaining of my silence to her. How this has happened I cannot say, & beg you will tell her so, for I have always endeavoured to divide my letters as accurately as possible, & I am sorry to see she supposes, for an instant, I could neglect her. Your letter to Mr. [Thomas G.] Clemson, & hers, have made me very unhappy, by the account they give me of mother's illness. Absence from those we love is always painful; & never more so than when we hear they have, & may still be suffering, but I do hope, from what you say, that she has ere this entirely recovered, & ["enjoying" *changed to* "enjoys"] her usual health. She should be careful of herself, & change the scene occasionally, which is positively necessary for her health, of which one cannot have a better proof, than the benefit her health received from her visit to Washington last winter. But I will speak no more of her illness, lest thinking of it should render my whole letter sad. I am glad to find all the rest are so well, & that John's [John C. Calhoun, Jr.'s] health continues good, tho' I should have liked to have had a more particular account of him, whether his cough still continued, &c &c but I suppose had it been sufficient to render you uneasy, you would have mentioned it.

Sister mentions that Patrick [Calhoun] is to be married in September, which surprised me, as it did not agree with what he says in his letter to me. Is it so? & does he intend continuing in the Army after his marriage? You none of you give me details enough about *anything*, because you do not consider what you deem trifles worth

131

writing, but that is exactly what I read with pleasure, & the most common place occurrence connected with any of the family, or even with the State, has for me a charm of home, & I really felt melancholy, for several days, after hearing that some South Carolinians, who knew me, had been in Brussels, & enquired for me, tho' the person had forgotten their names. It so happened that we had had so much rain, that Mr. Clemson did not go into Brussels the week they were there, so we knew nothing of it till after they had left. I have missed seeing a good many Americans, who have passed through, by being here, but Mr. Clemson has seen several of them, & amongst others a Mr. & Mrs. Kirkpatrick, who saw mother last winter, & brought a message from her to me, but as they left the very day he saw them, I missed them also.

We are are [*sic*] still, as you see, at this little village, tho' now only waiting on these intolerably slow Belgians, who are furnishing our house. They promised it to us the first day of the month but there is not the least certainty we shall have it by the last, which is very provoking, as cold weather is coming on, & it is positively necessary we should get into town, for many reasons, but we must even have patience, when we have to deal with the people of this country, for besides being the slowest I ever saw, their [*sic*] is no truth in them. I positively have never yet met a Belgian, of the working classes, (for the others I cannot say,) who had apparently the slightest idea of the difference between truth or falsehood, or had any shame in performing the meanest action. This is a hard character to give of a people, but my observation so far proves it to be just. However, when one considers the working of ["the laws of" *interlined*] society here, this state of things ceases to be so surprising. Tell mother I think six months experience of the white slaves of this country, would make her consider our negroes perfection. For my part I don[']t know what I should do, were it not for our negro Basil, who proves to be really a treasure, & is not, as yet, at all spoiled; indeed he seems to hold the servants of this country in perfect contempt.

We have nothing stirring, just at present, but Queen Victoria's trip up the Rhine, where, from all I hear, she has been making herself perfectly ridiculous, & acting the part of a spoiled child, showing herself utterly ignorant, or neglectful, of the commonest rules of politeness, & the decorum incumbent on her high station. I should think if the tenth of what I hear be true, that there can be no doubt of the truth of the rumour, that she had exhibited symptoms of the insanity of her grandfather. From all accounts, poor prince Albert pays dearly for his high station, but really I am ashamed of having wasted so much of your time, & my ink, on these state puppets, who inspire me at a nearer view, or rather hearing, with the most profound contempt, both for themselves, & the people who permit themselves to be governed by them. I speak now pretty much of all crowned heads, & dignitaries, tho' to be sure there are some exceptions.

Speaking of dignitaries, what are ours at home about? We know nothing, except what we see by the papers, for not a line has Mr. Clemson received from the [State] Department, or even from Mr. [Francis] Markoe, since you left, except the official announcement of Mr. [James] Buchanan's installation, tho' he has heard *through the ministry here,* who got it from Mr. [Charles] Serruy's [*sic*; Belgian Chargé d'Affaires in the U.S.], that Mr. Buchanan expressed himself much pleased with the treaty, & told him (Mr. Serruy's,) it only needed the signatures, & this Count [Albert Joseph] Goblet told Mr. Clemson two months ago. Is it not mortifying, that Mr. Clemson is obliged to reply, to the constant questions of the minister, whether he has heard, *no?* They all see, & speak of the change in our foreign policy, since you left, which of course is very gratifying to me as a daughter, tho' it mortifies me as an American.

It is time to tell you something of ourselves, tho' fortunately what I have to say can be compressed into a few words. We are all uncommonly well, & even Mr. Clemson is *"taking on flesh"* quite rapidly. The country air has been of great benefit to all of us, & I really regret being obliged to return to the trammels of the town, after our free, & tranquil, life here. It is *needless to repeat that I have the two smartest & best children in the world,* for I have told you often enough to convince you, if you are ever to be convinced, of the fact, tho' I had much rather you could have the opportunity of judging for yourself, & then I am sure you would agree with me.

Mr. Clemson seems to be writing you quite a despatch, so I will have pity on you & stop at this sheet, hoping you will be able to read what I have written, for really my hands are so uncomfortably cold, as to prevent my writing as well as usual. What think you of that for the 5th of Sept.?

My best love to mother, sister, & the boys, & beg mother to write me as soon as she is able, that I may be convinced by the sight of her handwriting, that she is well again. Mr. C[lemson] sends love to all & the children kisses. Your devoted daughter, Anna Clemson.

ALS in ScCleA.

From J[AMES] HAMILTON, [JR.]

Savannah Geo[rgia], Sept. 6[t]h 1845
My Dear Sir. A variety of engagements have prevented my writing you for some time and I have now merely a moment to say that I shall leave this for New York tomorrow. I shall stop at ["Richmond" *canceled and* "Washington" *interlined*] for a day on my way on and at Richmond for a day on my return about the 15[t]h Oct.

Whilst I am in New York I will see what can be effected as to an organization of your friends there which will enable ["me" *interlined*] to confer more ["efficiently &" *interlined*] intelligently with your friends in Richmond on my return.

Should I gather anything of interest, whilst at Washington, I will write you from that place.

Pray let me hear from you whilst in New York, more especially if you have any suggestions to make. I shall expect to meet you at Columbus [Ga.] about the 15[t]h Nov. on my way thro Alabama to N[ew] Orleans.

I met Dr. [William C.] Daniel[l] & Seaborn Jones, at Merriweather Springs [Ga.], last week, with our friend [John H.] Howard[;] they think you ought to return to the Senate of the U. States. They ["likewise" *interlined*] think the [Charleston] Mercury is doing us injury with the Democracy of the South by its constant attacks on [James K.] Polk[,] rather carping & captious than serious & argumentative.

I have long thought they ought to have reserved their fire until the administration showed their hands. I shall say [so] to [John Milton] Clapp next week on my way thro' Charleston.

In the mean time My Dear Sir believe me as always with the highest esteem faithfully & respect[full]y Your devoted friend, J. Hamilton.

ALS in ScCleA.

From N[ICHOLAS] P. TRIST

Department of State
Washington, Sep[tember] 8, '45
Dear Sir, The mail received here on yesterday, (Sunday) I found this morning upon my table: a portion of it having been opened by

Mr. [James] Buchanan; but the greater part, in the state in which it came from the post-office. I proceeded to open the letters; and whilst engaged in this task, I cut & tore, in the way you see, the enclosed envelope of your letter to Mr. [José M.] Caminero, before I became aware that it was not directed to the Secretary of State. This I perceived, whilst in the act of taking out the letter, the face of the envelope being then towards me; and (I need not, I hope, say) I proceeded no further. The inside of your letter has not met my eye; and I should at this moment be no less ignorant of the subject, and of the writer's name even, than I was before committing the blunder, had not both become known to me afterwards, upon my coming to your letter to Mr. Buchanan, in which this one ["for Mr. C(aminero)" *interlined*] came enclosed; & which, had it arrived on any other day but Sunday, would have been opened by myself, thereby securing me against the oversight.

The letter for Mr. Caminero has been put under a new cover, and will go forward to the Despatch agent at New York by this evening's mail. I am, with great respect & friendly regard, Y[ou]r ob[edient] Serv[an]t, N.P. Trist [Chief Clerk].

P.S. Private & confidential. Among the papers which I found upon the table of the Chief Clerk, upon taking charge of it at the end of last month, were two, of which the following are copies. The list referred to in the second is quite a long one, covering nearly two pages of large letter paper. It is evident from the man's tone, that the delivery of these articles cannot be obtained from ["him" *interlined*] (except on payment of his claim, which there is no authority to make on public account) otherwise than by a recourse to legal compulsion; and if this were resorted to, there would be no end to the fuss growing out of it. Should it become necessary to act upon the subject before I hear from you, I will pay him the $30 "on Mr. Scoville's account," believing that it will be more agreeable to you to throw away this amount, than to have the case made a subject of public talk & newspaper tirades.

[P.P.S. in margin:] *No* one has the least intimation (or will have) of my intention to bring this subject to your notice. Should it be your wish that the man be settled with, I will have this done by some third person, who will apply to him as if on behalf of Mr. Scoville; and, in the same way, cause the things to be delivered to the Department. If there be any person now in the city, to whom you could entrust the management of this business, the best way of all perhaps would be to adopt this plan, so that I should have nothing at all to do with it.

(Copy)

Jackson City D.C., July 12th '45

Sir, There are various Books & Documents in my possession belonging to the State Dept.; left by Mr. J[oseph] A. Scoville, private Secretary to Mr. J.C. Calhoun. Mr. Scoville was a boarder at my house, and created a bill to the amount of $30. I presume these articles are liable for the amount of the bill, as they were in his possession. I shall be pleased to know if the Secretary of State is authorized to pay the bill and receive the articles. I have the honor &c, (signed) James H. Bennett.

(Copy)

Aug. 21, 1845

Sir, This is a correct list of the Books & Documents about which I wrote to you some time since. I understood from the chief of the Dept. yesterday that a letter had been sent me, containing your views on the subject, which letter I could not find in the Post office. These articles must be valuable to the Department of State, and none to me, but I am of opinion they are bound for the board of Mr. Scoville as much as his trunk & other baggage, and although I know these articles properly belong to the Departm[en]t, Mr. Scoville should make arrangement to pay his bill and deliver them—or if of the value I suppose they are to the Department the bill can be paid by it and recourse [had] to Mr. Calhoun for the acts of his private Secretary. I have the honor &c, (signed) James H. Bennett.

ALS in ScCleA. NOTE: An AEU by Calhoun reads "Letter from Mr. Twist [*sic*], relating to Books & doc[umen]ts said to be left by Mr. Schoville [*sic*] with a Mr. Bennet[t] & a rough draft of my answer."

From W[illia]m P. Duval

[Pal]atka [Fla.], Sept[embe]r 9th 1845

My dear sir, I had intend[ed] sooner to have answered your last letter but thought to wait the result of certain elections to be made by the Legislature. The most disgusting scenes have occur[r]ed at our seat of Government. A certain party with James D. Westcott at their head, who bye the bye, is the most faithless and unprinc[i]pled man in Florida, had organized secretly to defeat Mr. [David] Levy[']s [that is, David Levy Yulee's] election to the senate, and finding him too strong had the cunning then to unite upon him, and thus induce the friends of Mr. Levy to support Westcott, who is a disgrace to the Senate of the United States and to Florida[.]

This man came out last winter as soon as he saw Mr. [Martin] Van Buren[']s letter, against the annexation of Texas. He was sent to this State by Mr. Van Buren and he will carry out his views and wishes—altho, he had from necessity, to declare he was in your favour, but not untill he found such was the public opinion. Westcott could not now, or for years past, ["have" *inserted*] been elected to the Legislature from his own, or any other county in this State. He induced certain men who are utterly without principle, but cunning rascals like himself, to offer for the Legislature in many of the counties pledged to go for him if required against Mr. Levy—twelve of these fellow[s] all of ["who" *changed to* "whom"] were to have offices—and most have succeed[ed], were thus elected, and these twelve voted against Mr. Levy in caucus hoping the whig members and some stragglers from our own party would defeat Mr. Levy. This bribery & corruption succeeded in making the [*ms. torn; a few words missing*]se in our State a senator. The people are m[*ms. torn; one or two words missing*]tified, and now an outdoor nomination for member of congress in the person of W[illia]m H. Brockenbrough has been made at Tallahassee through the intrigues of Westcott, when but 3 members from East Florida and but one member from West Florida, and two out of eight from his own county would attend the causus. Mr. Brockenbrough is no more your political friend than Mr. Westcott. They will exert themselves to entrap, and break down Mr. Levy. we are to be divided in this State. Mr. Westcott (& Brockenbrough if he is elected) will join the northern democrats. Mr. Levy will be for the South. I write you frankly, so you may understand these men and if you should be sent back to the senate, that you may be g[u]arded in what you utter before them. Westcott will endeavour to worm himself into your confidence to betray you. This is his usual game, and the more he avers he is your friend then rest assured he intends to play the spy & hippocrite. I have heard this man by the half hour discribe the various tricks and deceptions he has practic[e]d and boast of the artful lies—that he has propagated in order to accomplish his objects. When told in public company of some infamous act he has committed and denounced as a rogue, & rascal I have heard him say to his accusor, "That is nothing new, if you will go to the business part of our town you can find fifty men who will prove your charge[."]

Last summer this man was horsewhip[p]ed in the streets of Tallahassee for slandering a lady—he did not even resist. At this moment he is a defaulter for near $2,000. Some years since congress made an appropriation, to have a revision of our laws, and Westcott applied for, and obtained the work, he drew the money & has never performed any part of the work, and for several years a suit has been pending in middle Florida to recover back the money but his brother in law Mr. [Charles S.] Sibley was the district attorney, and never has urged the case. This man is to honor to our senate, because he is a swindling defaulter, and for the distinguished flogging he received for slandering a lady. It was the only chance he ever had to cheat the Territory of Florida, & use her money, on his contract to revise the laws, and he has taken advantage of that first opportunity[.]

I was a candidate for no office. Mr. Levy and myself both live in East Florida. I feared if my name was proposed for Senator it might, defeat his election. I therefore desired my friends not to nominate me although many in middle & West and some in East Florida desired it. I also refused to permit my name to [be] used before the Legislature for any office. The judgeship in this district was pressed upon me strongly, but I refused to take it or any other office under the State while such disgraceful proproceedings [sic] stain our character[.] I will either go to Texas this fall or settling in Tallahassee to kill off the rascals. Yours sincerely, Wm. P. Duval.

[P.S.] I write this in confidence. If I determine to settle at Tallahassee, I will organise the best and ablest of the democratic party that sustain the southern interests, and if I live at another congressional election, a man, worthy of the confidence of your friends will represent us in congress[.] I will as certainly break down Westcott and his junto as I live. I fear that Levy wants that sort of moral courage necessary to protect him & his friends—and even now these men that have out generaled him & his his friends are at work, living[?] upon him & setting to the people against him—by saying he played them false by pretending he would serve them, as their representative when he knew, he would not, as he would go into the senate and leave them to hold another election—and I tell you this slang is having its effect[.] Wm. P. Duval.

[P.P.S.] your friends must be more on the lookout in this State, or cunning, & intrigue will trap the people. you shall hear from [me], as soon as I decide where I shall locate myself. The temptation is on me, strongly, to remain at Tallahassee & If I do you shall in due time, know the course I shall pursue[.]

ALS in ScCleA.

138

From [Lt.] P[ATRICK] CALHOUN

New-Orleans La., Sept. 11th 1845
Dear Father, I received a few days since from Brother Andrew [Pickens Calhoun], a letter in reference to the money which you had the kindness to authorize him to advance me. He informs me in the same letter that but one of my many letters had reached him, which accounts for his long silence. I have written on the subject of the manner of its transfer—and to render his receiving my letter more certain I gave it to a friend going to Mobile, to be mailed in that city. The only letter which reach[ed] Brother Andrew was mail[ed] in Mobile. All mailed in this city miscarried.

Nothing of any great importance has transpired since my last letter. All the information from Mexico on the subject of war, is for the most part little more than rumour—and as you have doubtless seen them in the papers of the day I shall not mention them in detail.

As far as can be judged from these rumours and what little authentic information has reached us, there appears much less prospect of a war than some weeks since; indeed unless some great change takes place in Mexico, there is much greater probability of a civil war amongst themselves, than that they will declare war against us. The authorities in Washington very properly continue to strengthen the army of Occupation by supplies of men and military stores—thus preparing for any contingency. The course adopted will moreover go farther to prevent hostilities than any other.

Gen. [Edmund P.] Gaines as you have seen by the papers has sent into Texas some Volunteer Troops furnished on his requisition by the Governor of Louisiana [Alexander Mouton]. In ordering these Troops to Texas he has drawn upon himself the animadversion of many of the public prints, and in some degree the disapprobation of the War Department. The Secretary of War [William L. Marcy] did not at first approve or disapprove the General['s] requisition, but left the matter open until the papers began to censure it—when the Secretary came out and joined in the cry. Gen[era]l Gaines ["has" *interlined*] not only been improperly but outrageously treated through this whole affair. I had no idea that the authorities at Washington could act in the informal and illegal manner in which they have, with impunity. They have managed to make his command a military mockery, informing him only on what points it suits their convenience—and keeping him in ignorance on many subjects that interest his Division—and of course himself. Gen[era]l [Zachary] Taylor's Brigade formed, and still forms a portion of his

(Gen[era]l Gaines['s]) Divisions; no order has ever been issued taking Gen[era]l Taylor or his command from this Division—and yet Gen[era]l Gaines is censured for sending even assistance. I will not enter further into the details of the case. Some investigation will I suppose be made on the subject. As it appears to be the intention of the authorities that be, to keep Gen[era]l Gaines out of Texas—under all circumstance—I shall be obliged to leave him in case there is any active service in Texas. I shall not join my Regiment [the 2nd Dragoons] unless there is a stronger probability of war than at present. If there should be no difficulty with Mexico, Gen[era]l Gaines will spend the winter in Washington, as the law suit in which himself and Mrs. [Myra Clark Whitney] Gaines has for some years been engaged, comes before the Supreme Court for final decision this winter. In the event of the General's going to Washington I shall apply either for leave of absence, or permission to joint [*sic*] my Regiment temporarly, as I am anxious to visit Texas, and moreover have a desire to see so many Troops together as Taylor has under his command.

The Yellow-fever has been officially reported by the Board of Hea[l]th to be in the city—it has not however as yet spread much, and it is the opinion of some that it will not.

New Cotton is coming in rapidly and commands ready sale and fair prices. The Levee already presents the appearance of the return of the business season. The report of the Board of Health has however cast a damp on business, many having left the city as soon as the fever was reported—they will however soon return should it prove false.

My love to all. Your affectionate son, P. Calhoun.

ALS owned by Bruce W. Ball of Miami, Fla.

From B[ARTHOLOMEW] R. CARROLL

Charleston, Sept. 11[t]h 1845

Dear Sir, You were kind enough in your favor of the 21[s]t ult. to offer to negotiate for me with the Trustees of the Pendleton Academy for their school house &c. My relatives are so anxious that I should remain in the State, and I am so much inclined, to gratify their wishes, that I am induced to address you again on the subject.

If not inconvenient to yourself, will you oblige me, dear Sir, in assertaining of the trustees whether their academy will be vacant during the next year, and in such an event upon what terms they would be willing to let it.

Should the terms be favorable, I can guaranty the establishment of such an institution as will I am confident meet their approval. I should prefer to exclude the classical branches, but would not insist upon that should the Trustees desire otherwise.

Be pleased to let me hear from you at your earliest leisure, and for this and other favors hold me Y[ou]r ob[edien]t ser[van]t, B.R. Carroll.

ALS in ScCleA.

From JOHN G. BOWMAN

Columbia [S.C.,] Sept. 13, 1845

My Dear Sir; I received your favor of the 9th inst. and promptly availed myself of the earliest opportunity of obtaining the information you desire, in giving which, I will follow the order you observe in your letter.

The price of a machine is $75. Freight to Hamburgh $3.50. Mr. [James S.] Boatwright will therefore deliver one at Hamburgh consigned to whomsoever you may designate for $78.50.

Col. B[enjamin] F. Taylor of this place, has had one in use for a length of time, is much pleased with its performance, does not regard it as liable to get out of repair, and should it do so, thinks, from its extreme and admirable simplicity, that it could be very easily repaired. With regard to the duration, that is yet to be tested—with proper care and management however, it is believed by competent judges that it will ["last" *canceled*] do service 20 years, with little, or no repair. They are regarded by all who have tried them as superior to any other machine with which they are acquainted. Indeed, it is difficult to conceive any thing better adapted to the purpose intended. Mr. Boatwright does not know the precise weight, but is confident that it does not exceed 400 lbs.—say 350. Waggoners haul freight from this place to Greenville, (upwards of 100 miles) at from 75c. to $1.00 per hundred. I do not know the distance from Hamburgh to Pendleton, but think it cannot exceed 100 miles—and the whole cost delivered to you, ought not therefore to exceed $83 or $84.

Mr. Boatwright I assure you, is no *"humbug."* I repose entire confidence in his integrity, judgment, and even *disinterestedness*, for although he has these and various other machines manufactured, yet, he is by no means dependent upon his success in this branch of his business, (for he is among our wealthiest citizens) and I believe it ["is" *interlined*] more a natural *penchant* ["for such things" *interlined*] than the desire of gain, particularly, that induces him to carry on this business. Mr. B. too, is a native of Columbia, and deserves much credit for having reared a large and respectable family, and the only fault I find with the old gentleman is, that I cannot prevail upon him to give up his occasional [*ms. torn;* gl]ass[?].

It will afford me much pleasure to serve you in any way I can, and I sincerely trust, that you will not hesitate to command my services whenever you desire them. Should you see Dr. [Frederick W.] Symmes, be so kind as to present him with my most respectful compliments—also, his interesting lady, in which Mrs. Bowman unites with me, and be pleased to accept for yourself the assurance of my sincere and most respectful consideration. John G. Bowman.

P.S. We had a fire yesterday evening, which destroyed some 5 or 6 houses in the "business" portion of our town.

ALS in ScCleA. NOTE: An AEU by Calhoun reads "Mr. Bowman[,] relates to the corn crusher." Benjamin Franklin Taylor (1791–1852) was one of the largest planters in the Columbia vicinity.

From SETH SALISBURY

Pennsylvania State Library
Harrisburg, September 15, 1845
Dear Sir, Some time since I took the liberty of writeing [*sic*] you, and mentioned that it would be most grateful to my own feelings and in accordance with public sentiment ["If" *canceled*] if I could procure your Portrait for the *State Library.* I am quite happy, Sir, in being able to say—that I have been able to procure your likeness from the "Democratic Review"—and that it has been framed elegantly and placed in the Pennsylvania State Library by the side of your friend Mr. [Levi] Woodbury.

I only regret Sir, that I have not your *Portrait* for myself and family.

Our elections in Pennsylvania this fall will be close, and I am sorry, Sir, to say there is much danger that the whigs will elect their Legislature.

You can barely imagine, Mr. Calhoun, how much pleasure a visit from you would afford the people of Pennsylvania; especially, in my own section of the State, "Northern Pennsylvania," where your political sentiments are and always have been highly popular. With great respect Yours, Seth Salisbury.

ALS in ScCleA.

From John A[lfred] Calhoun

Eufaula [Ala.,] Sept. 16th 1845

Dear Uncle, From your last favour to me, received sometime since, I was much pleased to learn that you were in the full possession of your former taste for agriculture; and that instead of missing public emplo[y]ment as a source of happiness, you felt relieved from its tram[m]els. That you may continue to enjoy a full measure of happiness in your retirement, and that you may live to see your political opinions, and principles fully understood & appreciated is my most sincere desire.

As to that portion of your letter, which is a reply to my suggestion, that you might occupy your leasure [*sic*] moments in writing a history of the U.S. I can only say that although I should be much pleased with the history; yet if you can write a treaties [*sic*] on the "elementary principles of political science, preparatory to a discourse on the Constitution of the United States" it will be a good substitute for the history. I hope you will be able soon to accomplish this much at least. Although I fully agree with you, that posterity will do you justice, as to your peculiar opinions, whether the present generation does or not: yet I feel that ["that" *canceled*] there is a something wanting yet to *complete* the whole—though it should be nothing more than a capstone still I think this should be added. Your views are ahead of the age, and hence the necessity of your having your task fully completed, in order to prevent any future pretender from laying violent hands on your labors, and by a few additions, to claim the whole as his own.

I think you sometime since promised your friends in this State to visit them in the course of this fall. What have you determined on? In making your arrangements I hope you will not forget us. In a letter which you wrote me sometime since, you will recollect you promised on your next visit to to [*sic*] Ala. to visit us. I have had many persons to inquire of me when you would be out, and to express a strong desire to see you here. You will find many warm friends in this section of the State. If you will inform me when you will be in Columbus[,] Georgia I will meet you there & bring you to this place in my carriage; and will return you to the West Point & Montgomery railroad; & if I can spare the time from our Courts, will carry you to my Brother James [Martin Calhoun's home in Marion, Ala.]. Let me know your mind on this subject at your earliest convenience, in order that I may be able to arrange matters.

We have fine health in this section of country; and now that the season for fever has begun to pass away, I [am] in hopes it will continue he[*ms. torn; a few words missing*] some sections of the country [*ms. torn; one or two words missing*] are exceedingly bad; But in other sections we have fine crops. There will be I think an abundance of provisions raised here for our own wants, but not much for foreign supply. My own crop is tolerably good especially my grain crop. My cotton will yield about 800 lbs. per acre.

My family are all well. Sarah [Morning Norwood Calhoun, my wife] desires to be kindly remembered to yourself and family. I remain your nephew most affectionately, John A. Calhoun.

ALS in ScCleA.

To A[RMISTEAD] BURT, Willington, S.C.

Fort Hill, 17th Sep[tember] 1845

My dear Sir, Since you left me, I have received several letters from different parts, some expressing their regret, that I left the Senate, & others pressing my return. One in particular, from one of the most intelligent & devoted friends from Ohio, who last winter advised me by no means to return to the Senate, but whose impression now is entirely changed.

My own impression is, that as far as I am personally concerned, I have nothing to gain by returning, while I may lose much for *the present*. I think, the approaching session will be one of great confusion & conflict of opinion. Nothing can prevent it but more nerve & wisdom, than, I fear, those in power have. It will be difficult to go through, on my part, without giving & receiving blows, & losing for the time, much of the good feelings now felt by all. But be that as it may, I owe it to myself & the country to be governed by higher considerations. If it be my duty to return, & such should ["be" *interlined*] the decision of my friends & the State, I ought not to decline, however opposed to my inclination. To yield our desires & interest to the good of the country is the essence of patr[i]otism.

I write now principally to say, that in writing to [Franklin H.] Elmore & other friends in this State, it would be prudent to abstain from making any remarks, from which it might be infer[r]ed, that you had conversed with me on the subject of my returning to the Senate. It would be better, it seems to me to rest your opinion on the ground of the necessity of my doing so; from the state of Mr. [George] McDuffie's health; the want of experience on the part of Judge [Daniel E.] Huger; and the great magnitude of the crisis & the necessity of having some one, who ["would" *interlined*] have the confidence of the South & the State rights party in the Senate, where the great pending issues must, in a great measure, be decided. You might state that it is well known, that Judge Huger has been at all times ready to make a vacancy, if it should ["be" *interlined*] thought that my services in the Senate were needed, & that from my known principles, I would hardly decline, if the State should deem it to be my duty to serve.

You will regard this as mere suggestions to be adopted or not, in whole or part, as your judgement may dictate.

Mrs. [Floride Colhoun] Calhoun ["returned" *interlined*] on Monday. Her health is not restored fully. She is still of a very nerveous habit, but otherwise well. I hope she will agree to accompany me to Alabama. She regret[t]ed much that you & Martha [Calhoun Burt] left before ["she could see you" *interlined*].

Since you left, I selected three ears of corn, that were dry, impartially as possible, of the medium size. I think they were, if any thing, below, rather than above. They yielded 1⅛ quart, dry measure, which would require but 86 to the bushel, which corresponds very much with previous experiments, as I stated [to] you. The yield per acre of the Mill pond, at that rate, would be 74 bushels to the acre. I do not think it will be below 70.

All join in love to you, Martha & [her brother] George [McDuffie Calhoun]. Yours truly & sincerely, J.C. Calhoun.

ALS in ScU-SC, John C. Calhoun Papers; variant PC in James Elliott Walmsley, "The Return of John C. Calhoun to the Senate in 1845," in the *American Historical Association Annual Report* for 1913, 1:163–164; variant PC in the Columbia, S.C., *State*, September 13, 1925, p. 27.

To T[homas] G. Clemson

Fort Hill, 18th Sep[tembe]r 1845
My dear Sir, The last Steamer by the Boston line brought me yours of the 12th August. Your seasons have been the very reverse of ours. Instead of rains, & clouds & chilly weather, we have had almost one continued drought & sun shine, with intervals of exceedingly warm weather, since the last of March. The streams are all lower than ever remembered; so much so, that it is difficult to get grain ground, even in this well watered region. The drought still continues, so that the crops of turnips & potatoes are in a fair way of failing to the extent of that [of] corn. It will be difficult for this and the other Southern Atlantick States to get through the next year. It is thought, that this District may, with close economy, & the advantage of a fine mast, supply itself, but I doubt it. The upland corn, except in spots, will not average 5 bushels to the acre; the bottom lands on the creeks & rivers will make nearly an average crop. I shall make enough & to spare. Between corn, wheat, Rye & Oats, I expect to sell between 1500 & 2000 bushels, which, I think, speaks pretty well for my farming this dryest of all years. My cotton crop was much injured by the intense drought of August. It is all matured & will in two weeks be all opened. It will yield something less than ⅔ of a crop; say 450 or 500 pounds round instead of 750 or 800.

From Alabama I have very favourable accounts. Andrew[']s [Andrew Pickens Calhoun's] last letter is of the 21st August. He then had picked & packet [sic] 70 bags; and was picking out daily about 11,000 pounds of seed cotton. He estimates the crop at the lowest at 600 bags, say 320,000 pounds of clean cotton. His corn crop is equally good. We shall have a very large surplus for sale. The general estimate is, that the crop will be (of cotton) far short of the general average, say, 2,100,000 bags. If so, & the provision crop of England should not be short, we may expect a fair price, say from 8 to 10 cents.

Gen[era]l Gilliam [sic; James Gillam] writes me, that he hears favourable accounts of your crop, both of corn & cotton. I would make your place a visit, but am making my arrangement to leave for Alabama, in the course of 8 or 10 days. If we can find a house keeper Mrs. [Floride Colhoun] Calhoun will accompany me, & probably John [C. Calhoun, Jr.]. We will take our own carriage, & take the upper route, which will keep us in a healthy region. I shall be gone to the mid[d]le of Nov[embe]r.

My gold mine is yielding moderately. The stream has been so

low, that the mill could do but little. I have renewed the lease to [Benjamin M.] Milner on condition, that he puts up one on a larger scale on the river. It will yield in toll this year about $800 or perhaps $900, if there should hereafter be a sufficiency of water. I have not been over, but the prospect is, I understand, that it will hold out for a long time. The coinage, it is said, will be greater at Dahlonega ["in this" *interlined*], than in any preceding year.

As to politicks, I can say little. I am much urged to return to the Senate. My inclination is ag[ai]nst it; but the state of our affairs, external & internal, is so critical, that I should feel it my duty to serve, if the State should request me. I fear the Oregon question will lead to difficulties with England. The Administration, I fear, will not meet it, as it ought to be. In its present entanglement it requires not only great skill & prudence, but great firmness & decision to avoid a conflict between the two countries. Whether we shall ["have" *interlined*] war with Mexico or not, in my opinion, depends on the fact, whether we are likely to have one with England or not, in reference to Oregon. It cannot be doubted, that Mexico is entirely under the control of England; & that she will be strongly opposed to a war between us & Mexico, unless she should conclude, that she will be forced into a war with us about Oregon. In that case, she will, of course, desire to unite Mexico with her, as an ally. With the aid of British gold & British officers, she would be a very useful one to her & not a little formidable one to us. I say forced into a war; because I believe she is exceedingly desireous, on many accounts, as we ought to be, to avoid a war; yet folly & weakness may force the two countries into deadly conflict.

We are all well. The whole Union, indeed, seems to be blessed with health. Mrs. Calhoun['s] health is quite restored. We are happy to hear of your good health, & that of Anna [Maria Calhoun Clemson] & the children [John Calhoun Clemson and Floride Elizabeth Clemson]. I hope your weather is better. Ours is delightful; clear & moderately cool.

All join their love to you & Anna, & the children. Kiss them for their Grandfather. Your affectionate father, J.C. Calhoun.

ALS in ScCleA; PEx in Jameson, ed., *Correspondence*, pp. 671–672.

147

From R[OBERT] B[ARNWELL] RHETT

[Charleston] Sept. 18th 1845

My Dear Sir, I passed through Washington on my way home; and took the occasion, to see Mr. [Secretary of the Treasury Robert J.] Walker[,] Mr. [Secretary of State James] Buchanan & the President [James K. Polk] on the subject of the Tariff. My purpose was to ascertain what the administration really proposed to do, and [I] informed them severally of my object. The President was prepared with no details—He went for ["a" *interlined*] reduction, of the Tariff, but on no principles that I could understand—unless a mere reduction might be supposed to be a relinquishment of any reformation of principle in the existing Tariff. Mr. Buchanan talked fairer. He said he was indifferent to the principle—believing that a revenue Tariff would afford all the protection required. But still I got from him no details, excepting that he thought the Tariff might be reduced to 25 per cent. To this however he distinctly declared that Gen[era]l [James I.] McKay[']s Bill of the last Congress ought to be the standard of reduction and reformation. Mr. Walker was more explicit. He went into details and all his details with one or two exceptions, were previously Gen[era]l McKay[']s Bill. After hearing all, I am satisfied that that Bill substantially is all the administration will propose—and that is all we will get, from the Democratic Party, if we get that. I do not think we will obtain however even that.

Under these circumstances—connected with the course of the administration towards our wing of the Party, it is necessary to determine before Congress meets, what course we shall pursue. Shall we act out the confidence we expressed in the Presidential election, and take it for granted that the administration is about to be true to us[?] With this line of policy we ought to vote for Mr. [Thomas] Ritchie as printer—go into Caucus as to who shall be Speaker &c. The [Washington] Constitution must stop without the printing of the Senate; and we have no organ, in case the Government proves false. Or shall we take the contrary course—take it for granted that the administration ["& the Democratic Party" *interlined*] are about to be false to us—refuse to go into Caucus on the Speakership &c.— and run in the Senate for the printing for the Constitution. The two [South] Carolina Senators [George McDuffie and Daniel E. Huger] & [Ga. Senator Walter T.] Colquitt & [Ala. Senator Dixon H.] Lewis can reverse it. For my part, I shall not be found again as at the opening of the last Congress, ["with" *canceled*] attempting what our friends have not courage to execute. I must be sure of my game before I attempt it. You know my opinions of the Democratic Party. Circumstances since Mr. Polk[']s election has [*sic*] not at all altered them; on the contrary every movement at Washington I think have [*sic*] tended to prove my estimation true. Mr. Reverdy Johnson [Senator from Md.], informed me in London that a Senator told him that Walker the Sec[retar]y of the Treasury, had boasted to him, that he was the real author of the Kane Letter; and his questions sent on here, have occasioned great surprise & dissatisfaction. I have no faith in them, in carrying out correct principles. All we can expect on the Tariff, is a modified Protective Tariff Act. And if this proves to be true—what course then shall the Delegation pursue in Congress? Shall they support it and vote for it? or shall they act towards it, as the So[uth] Ca[rolina] Delegation did towards the Act of 1832—vote against it—denounce it, and come home to resist it? These are questions that we ought to be prepared to meet at the opening of Congress—for they must shape our line of policy at the beginning.

Write to me at your earliest leisure and believe me Dear Sir, Yours truly, R.B. Rhett.

ALS in ScCleA; variant PC in Jameson, ed., *Correspondence*, pp. 1049–1051. NOTE: This letter has a Charleston postmark of 9/18. The "Kane Letter" referred to by Rhett was written by Polk to John K. Kane of Philadelphia on 6/19/1844 and widely publicized at the time. In response to an inquiry about his views on the tariff, Polk stated that he was in favor of a tariff for revenue, along with "such moderate discriminating duties" as might "afford reasonable incidental protection to our home industry." It does not appear that Walker wrote the letter, although his stated views were very similar.

To N[ICHOLAS] P. "TWIST" [*sic*; TRIST], Chief Clerk, Department of State

Fort Hill, 18th Sep[tembe]r 1845

Dear Sir, Your explanation is entirely satisfactory in reference to the envelope of my letter to Mr. [José M.] Caminero. Accidents of the kind have not unfrequently occur[r]ed to myself.

I fully appreciate your kind intention, in writing to me about the books & documents belonging to the State Department, & said to be left by Mr. [Joseph A.] Scoville at the House where he boarded, & which its owner refuses to deliver up, unless the amount, which he alleges to be due him, should be paid, & the course you propose to take, should the demand be pressed.

I hope, if it has been, you have not complied with it; for I cannot possibly reconcile it to my feelings to pay it. The amount is nothing; but I cannot consent to buy off a swindling demand in any case, much less one under the circumstances of this.

To give a plausibility to his demand he calls Mr. Scoville my private Secretary. He had no relation whatever of the kind towards me. He was simply a copying Clerk in the Department, and as such was paid for the actual amount copied, if my impression is correct. Mr. [Edward] Stubbs the disbursing officer of the Dept. can inform you whether my impression is correct or not. I had no private Secretary, nor ever had while at the head of a Department. The law authorises no such officer. Nor had I any officer ["of" *canceled*] or person about me of a confidential character, but my chief clerk [Richard K. Crallé]. Mr. Scoville had no authority from me to remove any book, documents, or any other article of property out of the Department; and I cannot consent to establish the precedent, that the Head of the Department, should be held responsible in such cases for the unauthorized acts of his clerks, or that the ["keepers" *canceled*] keepers of ["a" *canceled*] boarding houses have a lien on publick property so left, for debts alledged to be due to them from clerks, much less to expose myself to the the [*sic*] imputation I would, should I buy off this, or any other swindling demand.

I avail myself of the occasion, to congratulate you on your appointment to your highly respectable station. With great respect yours truly, J.C. Calhoun.

ALS in DLC, Nicholas Trist Papers, 20:59232–59233; variant autograph draft in ScCleA. NOTE: The first paragraph of the draft concludes with a section, omitted in the ALS, that reads: "Indeed, the contents of the letter was of a character, I would have been glad if propriety would have admitted it I would have been glad [*sic*], had you read it. It related wholly to the Republick of Dominica; and its struggle to maintain its Independence, which I regard of vast importance to us & this continent. It is a reaction against barbarism, and an important step should it succeed to maintaining the ascendancy of the more civilized portion of what may more truly[?] be called Spanish America over the less civilized. No one will more readily understand its importance in this respect than yourself." An EU on the ALS indicates that it was received on 9/27.

From FERNANDO WOOD

New York [City,] Sep[tembe]r 18, 1845

Dear Sir, We are gratified to hear that you will consent to be returned to the Senate. Your friends here are not satisfied that at this important crisis in our foreign, as well as domestic affairs the country should lose your sagacity—practical talents, and great experience. We all feel "at sea, without a rudder." No man like JCC can strengthen public confidence in getting through the agitated waters safely.

Our mer[c]hants hesitate in their business. Commercial men generally forbear hazarding their capital, owing to an apprehension that the administration is too weak to carry us through, and that the Senate—(a part of the admini[s]tration, so far as our foreign relations goes) contains so few men of wisdom—moderation and patriotism. A general want of confidence pervades this community. We know not what to do[.] We have gained a bootless victory indeed! Therefore let us again rally around those on whose oft tried patriotism has led us safely through labrynths equally dangerous and gloomy.

Politically, your friends see many reasons why you should again appear upon the theatre. Matters are tending towards a correct feeling and appreciation of the distinguished services which you have rendered the party and the country. In short, in behalf of the great liberal democracy of this city and State I beg to express the hope that you will not desert us. The future looks bright—our hope is great[.] We are determined to work on! work forever!! We will rid ourselves and children of the tyran[n]y which for forty years has born[e] down our energies in this commonwealth. We want a head—a front on which to rely. Very Truly Yours &, Fernando Wood.

ALS in ScCleA.

From LEWIS S. CORYELL

Washington, Sep[tember] 19/45

My dear Sir, I have been here for 3 days. Saw and heard much, but there is no news as the Poeple [*sic*] are up to, if not in advance of the Adm[ini]s[tration]. I had a long and satisfactory talk with [James K.] Polk who has assured me most solemnly that he will carry out not only the letter but spirit of the Baltimore resolutions, and that he considers that his Election was carried on the admitted necessity of reducing the Tariff—and that in no event would he be a candidate for a 2nd term. *These are my facts.*

I send you a commercial Statement and a Circular &Ct. Now my dear Sir you have as a humble Individual the opportunity to give this nation a Text book on the subject of the Tariff, and I do hope you will not loose [*sic*] the opportunity to bennefit the nation, & at the same time gratify your many friends in every State. There is war threatened. [Levi D.] Slamm has established a paper in N.Y. and will deal daggers to [George] Bancroft [Secretary of the Navy] and [William L.] Marcy [Secretary of War] to begin, and although opposed to the ultra V[a]n B[ure]n men yet he is mainly supported by them by way of Virginia.

[William A.] *Harris of the Constitution is to have a charge*[?] *after Congress meet but a very secret.*

Things look threat[e]ning in the Senate for many confirmations and Penn[sylvani]a & New York will both be in the minority this fall. Ohio also, but by ultras.

You will excuse my hasty letter, as I am within a few minutes of my departure for home, but thinking of you have taken the liberty to thus inflict my mark[?] upon you. By the bye [Thomas H.] Benton is here & trying to infuse ["o" *canceled*] the fact of Southern opposition to the Adm[ini]s[tration] & that their Support must come from the North & West. Y[ou]r fr[ien]d truly, Lewis S. Coryell.

ALS in ScCleA.

From JAMES GADSDEN

Charleston S.C., Sep[tembe]r 19, [18]45
My Dear Sir, I have recently returned for a somewhat extensive Tour North & East: and particularly through Pen[n]sylvania where I encountered many of your old acquaintances, and among the number Lewis S. Coryell, and a Mr. [Samuel S.] Haldeman of Lancaster C[oun]ty. The latter I found a very decided Free Trade man and very sanguine of the ultimate triumph of the Cause. A Revolution he says among the Farmers, as having been humbugged by the manufacturers has commenced: but still such a shield do the manufacturers & Politicians continue to throw between us and the great body of the People who are affected by the system of protection that it is difficult to reach them with the truth. The Press—and I presume they are paid belong to the monopolizers; and how to be heard by the Tax paying citizens is our difficulty. If we could only reach them by facts and results the game would be up & it is for you among others to devise the plan.

I found a strong anxiety everywhere expressed for you to return to the Senate. Mr. [James] Buchanan informed me that he had addressed you on the subject. Having on a former occasioned [*sic*] added my influence with others to a request that you should go into the State Department I feel reluctant to unite again in any expressions in favor or against a movement of which you must be the judge. I will say however that my opinion remains unchanged on one question. That you should never again place yourself in the power of the treacherous northern democracy, who can by organization always pack a ["nominating" *interlined*] Jury against you. Had you denounced Conventions (instead of arguing on their organization) as you once did Caucusses with suc[c]ess: and stood boldly & immoveably on the Platform of Free Trade, Retrenchment, & Texas before the People & not the party you would most probably have been in [James K.] Polk[']s seat. These are my views unchanged; and without regretting the past, let us look to them as our beacons for the future[;] but to return to the Senate.

You see [Thomas H.] Benton[']s position & game. More than half what nous ver[r]ons says in his correspondence with the [Charleston] Mercury may be credited I fear[.] Benton is in Washington like a mad Bull—and I do not believe that the [Administration] Organ [the Washington Union] has nerve enough to stand him. He will have possession of that paper (if he promises the [government] printing), as he had of the Globe. Besides [Lewis] Cass & [Levi] Woodbury, who are looked to as leaders in the Senate have not nerve enough, particularly the first to stand Benton[']s overbearing impudence. The Democracy will need a Leader to contend with [Daniel] Webster & Co. & will I fear fall into Benton[']s lead: for the want of one in Cass or Woodbury. If you were present Cass & W[oodbury would] fall into your ranks with all who prefer following them; leaving Benton with a Corporal[']s guard growling & opposing the very Administration he professes to sustain.

These are speculations for you to think on. I am in doubt—["and" *changed to* "but"] willing to view the whole ground and act as our judgements, at the crisis, may approve. Besides at this session some action must be had on the Tariff & to you should be the honor of forcing it down to the principle of *Revenue* alone. The period for a triumph is propitious. Yours Truly, James Gadsden.

ALS in ScCleA.

From THO[MA]S J. GREEN

New York [City,] Sept[embe]r 19th 1845

Dear Sir: You may have noticed in the papers that I have been north some months. My opertunity for assertaining public opinion hereabouts has been good, and it gives me great pleasure to say, that your strength has increased, and increasing beyond the most sanguine expectations of your warmest friends. Even many *Ultra* Whigs now say that, "since the comeing in of Florida & Texas with the democratic gains of Tennessee and North Carolina, and as we are to have a democratic *Next* President we want the best one and ["they" *canceled*] prefer you."

My particular object in now writing is to give my unhesitating opinion in favour of your comeing into the next Senate. I have consulted many of your friends and they all agree with me in this opinion—all, except Colo[nel] Ja[me]s Gadsden, he at first objected, but I learned afterwards came into the opinion. Gadsden, at first thought that your present unexampled popularity was owing to your retirement. I told him on the contrary that it was your bold action upon the Texas question and your still bolder meeting European impertinence in attempting to control the destiny of this continent. Thus, with this exception, your friends agree with me in saying that, you must not at present "hide your light under a bushel"— that you must meet the English & Abolition *ultraism* of the Mas[sachusetts] Senators. Make the question with them of English control *vs* the extension of freedom upon this continent. In doing so you have nothing to fear, and you rely upon it, that the latter is the great growing principle which will soon be as resistless as was the annexation of Texas.

I feel, my most esteemed Dear Sir, like running into a long Letter and must stop it, & hope to say in person to you at Washington city, what would be troublesome for you to read in a Letter.

I have just published a work which I wrote while in prison in Mexico and would be glad to send you a copy if I knew how it would reach you. In haste, Your devoted friend & h[u]m[b]l[e] Serv[an]t, Thos. J. Green.

ALS in ScCleA; ALS (retained copy, dated 9/18) in NcU, Thomas Jefferson Green Papers. NOTE: Green's publication was his *Journal of the Texian Expedition Against Mier . . . .* New York: Harper & Brothers, 1845. The recipient's copy bears Calhoun's AEU reading "Gen[era]l Green of Texas."

From R[OBERT] BEALE

Washington, Sept[embe]r 20, 1845

My Dear Sir, I have at length obtained the prices of the most approved machines for which you wrote to me—they are all used by our Maryland planters & farmers and they are entirely satisfied with them, in addition I have engaged a man by the name of F[.] Grieb a german who has put up the horse power & threshing machine for all the rich planters in the vicinity of this District & they all speak highly of them—he has agreed to come out with your machines for nothing but his travelling expenses and to put them up for nothing. I have no doubt that he will be enabled as he takes the machine with him to make a bargain for his passage & the transportation of the machines for what it would cost you to get the machines to Charleston.

The corn crusher will be	35 doll[ar]s
Straw cutter " "	30 [dollars]
The thresher with the horse power	140 [dollars]
making in all	205 [dollars]

This I consider cheap—he has also a corn sheller which when applied to the horse power will shell double if not threbble [sic] what the common sheller does by hand—he says he will fix the horse power to work all these machines at once or seperately as you may need them.

The saw I can not select until I could ascertain what head of water you can get. Mr. Grieb says when he sees your stream he will be able to decide at once whether a circular or an up & down saw will suit you best—the circular saw requires considerable power say 4 horses at least. I could not obtain drawings of the machines but they are simple & if per chance they should get out of order they are easily put in order.

I should like to hear from you as soon as possible & if you think proper I will send Mr. Grieb out[;] he is anxious to put yours up in complete order so that he may be able to sell the power & threshing machine of which he is the proprietor. So much for the machines. I have one of the straw cutters & it is the best I have seen—it will cut by hand 500 bushles [sic] per day easy.

A week or two since Mr. [Edward] Dyer the Sargeant [sic] at Arms of the senate died & I am entitled according to the uniform usage of the senate to the place & if it would not be asking too much I should like you to write to Mr. McDuffy [sic; George McDuffie] and Judge [Daniel E.] Huger. I shall send them a circular in a day or two & I am quite sure they will vote for me but they can do me great good besides if they will exert themselves a little. There is a man from N[ew] York who is the only opponent I have, he if supported at all will be by the old hunkers. *The position has its advantages.* I feel quite sure Mr. [James] Buchanan will not long be sec[re]t[ar]y of state & Mr. [George] Bancroft will vacate his seat [as Secretary of the Navy]—in short I believe that their [*sic*] will be an entire new cabinet in less than 8 months. [Robert J.] Walker will be the last to go but go he must. Tis rumoured here that you will come to the senate & lead the party. Some of your friends do not desire it as they think Col[o]n[el Thomas H.] Benton will do all he can to thwart you & defeat your measures. It is needless for me to say anything upon this subject. You are better advised of how things stand & ["a" *interlined*] better judge with a knowledge of facts than any one else. Tis growing so dark I can[']t see to write. Yours, R. Beale.

ALS in ScCleA; PEx in Boucher and Brooks, eds., *Correspondence*, pp. 305–306. NOTE: Beale was elected Sergeant-at-Arms of the Senate when it convened in 12/1845.

From SAM[UE]L R. THURSTON

Brunswick, Me., Sept. 20, 1845

Sir: It will be recollected by you, that I have written you frequently before. I now write you in relation to a matter in which you may think you have no interest. The present Incumbent of the office of collect[o]r of customs for the port of Bath Maine, is Amos Nourse. It will be recollected by you, that while you was Secretary of State, and in the latter part of Mr. [John] Tyler's Administration, Col. Alfred I. Stone of Brunswick was appointed to that office, and that upon the induction of the new Administration, Col. S[tone] was removed, & Mr. Nourse appointed. Perhaps you are not familiar with the immediate causes which caused the removal of Col. Stone. There are two classes of Democrats in this State, or two who call themselves so. The one class composes or is composed of, those who are half federal in their notion[?], half abolition, three fourth[s] high tariff—in a word, are at he[a]rt of the federal party, and opposed to every southern man & measure, continually crying out against southern influence. The other class are radically democratic, whol[l]y opposed to the abolition spirit & movements, forever set against a high tariff, and friendly to southern policy, & willing to see the advancement of any deserving southern man. Of the first class named is Nourse, only more federal, abolition, & anti-south & Southern men, than any. Of the other ["or 2d" *interlined*] class is Col. Stone. When the canvass was first opened relative to our last State candidate for President, Col. Stone was foremost among your friends in this State, always taking the ground, which all admit now to be true, that Mr. [Martin] Van Buren could not be elected if nominated. He was first & foremost in the Cumberland Co[unty] can[vass?] to struggle to cho[o]se a delegate in your favor, and through out has been opposed to what is rightly denominated the old hunkers of the north. Dr. Nourse, on the other hand was fierce for Mr. Van Buren, loud & long in his denunciations of Southern men & measures, and of you in particular. For the part Col. Stone took in that canvass, he drew upon his head the enmity & persecution of the old Van Buren clique, of this grade[?] happens to be John Fairfield [Senator from Maine]. F[airfield] is trying to hang to [Thomas H.] Benton[']s coat tail, while Benton ["is" *interlined*] hanging to Mr. Van Buren[']s alias Silas Wright[']s. Col. S[tone]'s case had been taken up in Mr. [James K.] Polk's cabinet & considered, & he had been informed that he would not be removed. Not supposing there was any danger, he remained at home, had no one at Washington to see that he suffered no wrong, and meanwhile Fairfield with other candidateates [*sic*] than Nourse, of the same stamp, however, went to Washington, & a bargain was struck, between the candidates, under the supervision of Mr. F[airfield] I suppose, that all should push for one of the candidates, and he appointed should appoint the others to sub-offices. The result was, that after this violent push, by deceiving Mr. Polk, Col. S[tone] was removed. Nourse thereupon beheaded, immediately, as he supposed, all of Col. S[tone]'s officers, than whom a better set of Democrats never lived, but for some good reason appearing to Mr. Secretary [of the Treasury, Robert J.] Walker he has refused to make any alteration at all, so Nourse[']s appointments are so only in expectancy. Nourse's confirmation is to come off at the next Congress. My object, therefore, is to let you know the facts in miniature, so that, holding intercourse with the senators from S.C. as you do, you may take it into consideration, whether or not it will be policy on the part of your State to go into the confirmation of such a man as Nourse, who, when he has received the favor at your hand, will turn about & rend you, and use all his efforts to thwart both Southern men

& measures—who being in such a capacity will exert his utmost to throw upon you the curses of an oppressive Tariff, and send the brands of abolition among you.

We hope you will consider these matters, and if it should appear so to you, we believe it will be for your interest & for the interest of your section of the country to speak out by your vote against such a man as Nourse. And should your opinion harmonise with mine & the hosts of democrats upon the same subject, in our State, we hope you will not confine your influence to your own State. If Nourse is not confirmed *Stone will be appointed to that office,* and if there or any where else, you may rely upon him with the utmost confidence. Should you feel at Liberty to reply to this, *Confidentially,* expressing your views, or indicating them so far as prudent, they will be treated by ["me" *interlined*] with all the sacredness due to such correspondence, and the notice will greatly oblige your sincere friend and fellow citizen, Saml. R. Thurston.

ALS in ScCleA. NOTE: Calhoun's AEU on this letter reads: "S.R. Thurston[,] Maine[,] to be attended to." Thurston was Delegate of Oregon Territory to Congress, 1849–1851.

From **Walker & Pearson**, Hamburg [S.C.], 9/20. "Above we hand bill of items in favor G. Walker from the dates of which you will perceive was made after your settlement with Mr. Walker and previous to the opening of your a/c by Walker & Pearson except one or two small items." The attached bill shows charges for sugar, coffee, and candles in 9/1844, plus a charge of 50 cents "for disc[oun]t on check" in 7/1844. The charges total $51.25. Calhoun's AEU reads: "Mr. Walker. W[illiam] H[enry] Calhoun owes for his share of the freight $8 which added to the cost of the tomb stones for his father [James Calhoun] & child makes $38.50. I requested him to pay ["the" *canceled*] it to Walker & Pearson & have my ac[coun]t credited with it[.] Paid." LS in ScU-SC, John C. Calhoun Papers.

From F[RANCIS] W. PICKENS

Edgewood [Edgefield District, S.C.] 21 Sept: 1845
My dear Sir, I regret to see that you think a war with England probable on the Oregon question &c. I had thought differently. If she brings it to a conflict, the Oregon question will only be the pretext. Her real objects will be the region of the Gulph of Mexico, Cuba,

Texas & Florida. I have long thought that the two countries must have another appeal to arms sooner or later. Our systems are at issue and the contest will be for mastery over the world. One or the other must go down or yield. Our policy is to postpone the final appeal as long as possible, as we are growing in strength & she is stationary.

I hope Cousin Floride [Colhoun Calhoun] has returned before this much improved in health. We have had an exceedingly healthy Summer. I suppose we had the Equinox last night & to-day. I hope it is over as more rain would ruin our cotton. I think our cotton will be lighter than we anticipated some weeks ago. The corn will be better. This Dist[rict] will make enough to do. I hope it will turn out better in the upper country than was anticipated some time since. [George] McDuffie came down & spent two days & nights with me some two weeks since and he says his crops & the neighbourhood [in Abbeville District] is better than common. He looks dreadful. It is melancholly to see him & think of what he was. It is cruel to allow him to exhibit himself in public, and it will sacrifice his noble fame. It ["is" *canceled*] stood heretofore as a bright example to our young men in the State. And I am told [Daniel E.] Huger is not much better. They say in Charleston that he is in his dotage. He attended a public meeting on the death of Gen[e]r[a]l [Andrew] Jackson & introduced resolutions calling upon the legislature this winter to erect a monument to his memory worthy of the State &c. I am told he spoke like a crazy man. I suppose he was induced to make the move at the instigation of [Joel R.] Poinsett in order to try & divide the old parties this winter in the Legislature. As a Senator from Edgefield I would cut my right arm off before I would vote for So. Ca. raising any monument to Jackson. We had better first burn the records of nul[l]ification which stand out as the most glorious chapter in our history.

Mr. [Thomas G.] Clemson's people are well—not a doctor on the place since he left. The crop will be tolerable.

My own crop is pretty fair for the season. From what I have gathered, I think I will have about 15,000 bushels of corn. You know I have to measure several thousand bushels which I have sold, so I can come pretty near the amount.

Present us kindly to the family. I am very sorry to hear from J[ames] Edward [Colhoun] that he is still as much depressed in spirits as ever. Truly & sincerely, F.W. Pickens.

ALS in ScCleA.

From JOHN HOGAN

Washington City, Sept. 22, 1845
My dear Sir, In conformity to the instructions that you gave me on the 21st Feb. 1845 I went to the Island of St. Domingo to examine into the situation[,] reso[u]rces[,] ability &c of the Dominican Republic. I remain[ed] in that Republic for nearly three months[,] had many interviews with the President Gen. [Pedro] Santana an old Spanish Gent[leman] also with his Cabinet Tho[ma]s Bobadilla Sec[retar]y of State[,] R[icardo] Mena [*sic*; Miura,] Sec[retar]y [of the] Treasury & Jamenies [*sic*; Manuel Jimenez] Sec[retar]y of War[,] the Sec[retar]y of the Interior & the Roman Catholic Arch Bishop. I met the Chief Justice & associate Judges of their Supreme Court. Their Congress is composed of 15 members their Senate of 5 members Elected by the Whites, three of ["them" *interlined*] Gen[eral]s. *All* of them Spanish Gent[lemen] or at least of Spanish de[s]cent & very fair complexions. The city of Santo Domingo has about 9000[,] two thirds white. It is a walled city defended by four Forts with 12 Cannon in each fort with Powder and Ball in abundance & a good Port that was the city built by [Christopher] Columbus. The city is well fortified. The Dominicans occupy about three quarters of the whole Island of St. Domingo where an extent is about the size of the State of Maryland, with a population of I should think of 25,000. There are three Whites to two Blacks & mulat[t]os ["put" *canceled*] together. As you are aware the Spanish Black are a more civilize[d] race than either the French Black or our Black. They are a peac[e]able quiet submissive C[r]eatures entirely unassuming and obedient. they yeild [*sic*] implicit obedience to their White rulers & they have the utmost veneration & respect for their White masters. There [are] 7260 Regular Soldiers under arms—Twenty five thousand [*sic*] National Guards with about 250 pieces of Cannon of from 64 pounders to two pounders[,] thirty thousand stand of Arms. All their Ports are well fortified on their frontier Ports along the Black Government or Haitians and on the boundary they are well fortified as they desire to be. They have Four Schooners of War carrying 10 Guns each. They are as united a People as lives in their determination to maintain their Independence or die in the contest. They have an income of duties on Imports & Exports & other things of over $620,000 & will have next year one million. *In short* their Govt. is on as firm a basis as ours & will stand beyond all doubt & will with good management Conquer the French part of the Island [and] all become one Govt. I have to contend with the French & English

Intent. They were bitter toward me at first. That Governm[en]t must be taken care of with the efforts of that Governm[en]t in the overthrow of the wretched & im[m]oral Blacks & their Governm[en]t. Our Southern States are safe & England is sorely beatten in her wicked efforts. You now have the substance of what my report will be. That Island is composed of the fines[t] soil in the World. I have brought with me incontestable proofs of their capacity to sustain themselves & to conquer the other part of the Island. I have got the report of the Sec[retary] of War there[,] Sec[retar]y of the Treasury & State. I reviewed their Troops & Inspected their Cannon & Guns & other Equipages and I went into eight of their Ports or harbours & visited their frontier Forts & Inspected the Implements of War. I will send you a copy of my report & all the papers that you may see for yourself. I will go down to see you if my health will permit. I am feeble since my return. I had a narrow escape from the fevers. You will see when I give you the papers that I carri[e]d the whole question ["be" *canceled*; and] defeated England & France. Yours respectfully, John Hogan.

P.S. Mattie[']s [Martin Van Buren's] herd[?] are in a Strange State. I am fearful that [James] Buchanan will put me back. You know him better than I do myself. I will remain here for two weeks longer. Will you come to the Senate[?] It is said that you will. The Interest of the Country demands of you that you should come. Could you write me[?]

ALS in ScCleA.

From R[ICHARD] K. CRALLÉ

Blue Sulphur Springs [Va.] Sept[embe]r 23rd 1845
My dear Sir, When I received your letter of the 7th of June I was just on the eve of starting to the salt works in Kanawha [County, now W. Va.], and had not time to acknowledge its receipt. Indeed I was unwilling to do so before I had seen our friends in person or ascertained their opinions on the views contained in it. I saw Judge [William?] McComas and [Robert A.?] Thompson, (with some others) in the western part of the State during my stay in Kanawha; and, fortunately, on my return to Lynchburg, six weeks since, met with [William O.] Goode who was then on his way to Richmond. We had a full conversation on all the topics suggested, and it was

agreed that he should see our friends in Richmond, and after obtaining their views communicate with me here. A few days since he passed by this place, (having in the meantime been westward as far as Kentucky) and gave me a pretty full account of all he had been able to ascertain.

There is much diversity of opinion in regard to the main question as well as to *time*. [James A.] Seddon and [Robert G.] Scott, (and Goode *after* he had conversed with them) incline to the opinion it would be hazardous to venture a rupture with the old clique at this time; believing it better to wait the meeting of the Legislature in order more fully to ascertain the views and wishes of your friends generally. To move now, and more especially in opposition to the cherished system of the Party might, they think, give them the vantage ground, and place formidable weapons in their hands for future use. The course they recommend is, (for the present) to wait the progress of events, to rally the Party during the next Legislature, and organize for the spring campaign in the State. To effect this it is proposed to start a State Rights man in every County *avowedly* to test the strength of the Party, and bring out its full power. Goode thinks we can carry the State openly under the *"Calhoun Flag"*—and tells me to say to you that he shall insist upon the open avowal of our determination to sustain it at all hazards. Seddon believes that you are gaining strength every day, and fears to hazard the prospects before us by any decisive movement at present; while he is fixed as steel to run our ticket at all events when the proper time arrives. On this point there is no hesitancy, no diversity of opinion whatever. McComas and Thompson are inclined to the views I expressed to you in my last, and are willing to go into the contest at once. Such also are the wishes of Judges [Daniel A.?] Wilson, who openly declares he will support no other ticket, and I believe Talliaferro [*sic*; John Taliaferro?], though I have had no communication with him. I have remained here six weeks, and been able to sound the feelings of a large number, not only from the State but from abroad. On the whole I see nothing to discourage, much to stimulate us. Your friends are firmer than I have yet known them to be; and the miserable conduct, and weak fetches at reform of the Administration have greatly tended to disgust the Country and turn the eyes of thinking men towards you. The Whig Party, too, is destined to add to our strength, partly from ultraism of its Leaders at the North, and partly from having lost its most cherished head [Henry Clay]. It must disband. The change of Leaders always tends to division, and more especially when a favourite is to be supplanted. Clay has been on here no doubt for the purpose of rallying his friends and saving himself from being [*one word canceled*] thrown over board. His confidence was strong when he went on to the White Sulphur [Springs]; but he was, (as I was fully assured) miserably disappointed. Tired of fighting under a leader so often defeated, the managers of the Party had resolved to raise the banner of another. His travelling companion, Maj. [John] Tilford, gave me to understand so much; and, indeed, Clay's fallen countenance and sad forebodings of the future, told, in very intelligible language, that his hopes were gone. He conversed with me in quite a friendly way, and spoke kindly of you, as did also Maj. Tilford, who publicly declared, as I understand, that he went for you after Mr. Clay. This *feeling* will not be confined to him. Many disappointed in their first choice, will follow in the same course. [John] McLean, who is to be the Candidate, will be unable to rally the Party. I hear that [Andrew] Stevenson at the White Sulphur, as well as two or three others of the old clique, have been speaking quite favourably of you. This, however, may be but hollow *seeming*. On the whole I think, without some untoward circumstance, we shall carry the State Rights flag triumphantly in the State. The Tariff question, I fear, may be used to prejudice us. Some such arrangement as that of [Louis] McLane's bill in 1832, may probably be resorted to more for the purpose of acting on your State than of settling the question. [Robert J.] Walker will probably push it at you, in order to further the views of [Vice-President George M.] Dallas, or even [Silas] Wright or himself. If they can drive S. Carolina into Nullification, they will give you, as they expect, the *coup de grace*. Such I fear is the scheme. *Entre nous*, I am told that Mr. [Robert Barnwell] Rhett declared at the Salt Sulphur that if the Tariff was not brought down to the Revenue Standard at once, the State would nullify, and that if you did not go to the full with them, they would throw you overboard. Such I was told by some gentlemen here was the purport of his remarks.

I am disposed, on a full view of the whole matter, to accede to the views of Seddon, and to wait the events of the next session; though not clear that the present time is the most unfavorable. We shall not lose, however, by the delay, as there will be time enough to organize after the spring. All that I desired to guard against was the falling of our friends into the [*ms. torn; partial word missing*]tion snare. This I believe may not now be apprehended and *en passant*, allow me to caution you against writing on the subject but in the most confidential way, and to friends not only *true* but *discreet*. Your letter to [Franklin H.] Elmore was forwarded to Seddon and

Scott, and seen by both. Now Scott is as true and warm a friend as any in the Union, but he is not *discreet*. [Thomas] Ritchie, I am told, can *worm* anything out of him. For this reason I did not allow him to know the contents of your letter to me. Seddon is quite the reverse, and you can communicate with him freely. I suppose Mr. Elmore is not well acquainted with our friend S[cott]. This, of course, is *between us*.

I shall leave this the day after tomorrow for Lynchburg; having been detained by surveying a tract of land which I have purchased in the neighbourhood, and will settle this winter. I am sorry to hear that Miss [Martha] Cornelia [Calhoun] was so little improved by her Physicians in Philadelphia, tho' I was by no means sanguine. To her & to Mrs. [Floride Colhoun] Calhoun, Bettie [Elizabeth Morris Crallé] joins me in offering the kindest regards, as well as to yourself. She is *somewhat* improved tho' still delicate. The next summer will be passed at our farm here; and she *will* flatter herself that she will have the company of yourself and family. I cannot but unite with her in the hope. With high regard and affection I am truly yours, R.K. Crallé.

ALS in ScCleA; variant PC in Jameson, ed., *Correspondence*, pp. 1051–1054.

To F[rancis] W. Pickens, Edgefield, S.C.

Fort Hill, 23d Sep[tembe]r 1845

My dear Sir, I do not think, if war should grow out of the Oregon question, that it will be only the pretex[t] on the part of England, and that her real object will be the Gulf of Mexico, Cuba, Florida & Texas. I do not doubt, that England feels an intense jealousy towards us; but I believe, & think I cannot be mistaken, she is exceedingly averse to a war with us at this time. If there be war about Oregon, she may certainly aim to strike blows at all the points, which you designate; but they will not be the object. The war, if it should come, and there is great danger it will, will be forced on her by the most besot[t]ed folly on our part, that a people & a government ["ever" *interlined*] committed. The whole territory would have fallen into our hands, if we had only had the sense to stand still, & adhered to the convention for its joint occupancy. The greatest simple ought to have seen, that, if we made it a question of force (as the rescinding of the convention would) ["be" *canceled*] that we would

164

lose the Territory, & that, if ["it" *interlined*] was settled by negotiation, we could not get the whole; and that the only possible mode by which we could get the whole, was to leave it to time. But folly, instead of the last, resorted to the two first, & Mr. [James K.] Polk by the ["consumate" *canceled and* "crowning" *interlined*] folly of alluding to it, as he did in his inaugural, has made them the only alternative; and has united England, & Russia & France against us in reference to the ["question" *canceled and* "territory" *interlined*]. There are no alternatives left ["us" *interlined*], but to back out, & settle it by negotiation, or refer it, & fare worse, or to settle it by force. It is, as it now stands, both a question of pride & ["profound" *canceled*] policy ["on the part of England" *interlined*] to resist our claim. He who commands the ["North" *interlined*] Western coast of this Continent, including California, commands the Pacifick. I do not think the administration will have the courage or patriotism to back out, & that whether we shall ["have" *interlined*] war, or not, must depend on Congress, & especially the Senate; &, let me add, the Southern Senators. In my opinion the fate of the country, on this & on other questions is in their hands. If war comes, it will begin with Mexico. If England concludes, that she will be forced into war about Oregon, we shall have war in due time with Mexico, &, if not, we shall not. The latter acts under her advise & will be ready to do whatever ["the former" *canceled and* "she" *interlined*] bids her to do.

The state of Mr. [George] McDuffie's & Gen[era]l [Daniel E.] Huger's ["health" *interlined*], & their total want of experience & ["great" *interlined*] liability, in consequence of both, of being acted on by the cunning & designing, is deeply to be lamented. It causes great uneasiness with our friends every where, & greatly distresses me. I know the extent of ["the" *canceled and* "their" *interlined*] uneasiness better, perhaps, than any other, as I receive letters by almost every mail from all sections, pressing my return to the Senate. I mention, in strict confidence, what I have to no other individual, but one, that he, ["(Gen[era]l Huger)" *interlined*; has] written to me, that he would resign, if I thought my services would be required in the Senate at this time. I received ["it" *canceled and* "his letter" *interlined*] some time since, &, in acknowledging its receipt, I made no allusion to ["it" *canceled and* "that part" *interlined*] as I did not know what ["would" *canceled and* "might" *interlined*] occur, and thought it prudent to keep ["it" *canceled and* "my answer" *interlined*] under my control, until events should more fully develope themselves. It has been a question of deep solicitude and much reflection ["with me" *interlined*] to determine, what answer to give. I am exceedingly adverse to returning again to publick life; and yet when I look at the momentious character of the present juncture, the great strength of our friends in Congress, if it could be brought to act in concert, the good it may possibly secure, & the calamities it ["would" *canceled and* "might" *interlined*] advert [*sic*], & the utter *incompetency* of our two Senators from the causes ["I" *canceled*] mentioned, to take the lead & give unity to the action of our friends, I feel, that there is a heavy responsibility ["on" *canceled*] on me, in determining the course I ought to take. I hold it certain, that as things now stand, the Administration will fall, almost by necessity, under the control of Col. [Thomas H.] Benton & his partisans, who will give it a direction most fatal to us & our principles & policy. Indeed, that is one of the strong reasons urged by many of my friends out of the State, why I should return to the Senate. Looking at the whole, as dispationately as I can, with a strong desire to remain at home, for many reasons, I do not see, under all the circumstances, how I could decline the duty, if it should be the desire of the Legislature & the State, that I should again serve them in the Senate, until the country has passed through the present difficulties, which I hope might be by the next session. Write me & let me know your opinion, & what answer you think, I ought to make to Judge Huger.

I would be glad to ["learn" *canceled and* "hear from you" *interlined*] by the return of the mail, or before the 1st of next month, when I expect to leave on a visit to Andrew [Pickens Calhoun in Ala.], as I wish to answer his letter before I go. If you find, that your letter cannot reach me before the 2d or 3d Oct[obe]r, address me at [*partial word canceled*] Faunsdale, Marengo County, Alabama. Mrs. [Floride Colhoun] Calhoun & John [C. Calhoun, Jr.] will accompany me.

I am glad to learn that your corn crop is doing so well. I shall make enough & to spare. Between corn, wheat, rye & oats, I expect to be able to spare between 1500 & 2000 bushels & 5 or 6 thousand pounds of Pork. My cotton like yours, will fall short. It was, with the exception of a field of 20 acres, promising until the mid[d]le of August. I shall make round between 450 & 500 pounds per acre, which is more than a third less than the average of the last 3 years.

Andrew has made a fine crop of cotton & corn. He estimates his cotton at the lowest at 600 Alabama bales, say 320,000 pounds of clean cotton. He had out at the date of his last letter (21st Aug[us]t) 70 bales & was averaging in picking out 10,000 pounds of seed cotton daily. Yours truly & sincerely, J.C. Calhoun.

[P.S.] Mrs. Calhoun & family join their love to you, Mrs. [Marion Antoinette Dearing] P[ickens] & family.

ALS in ScU-SC, John C. Calhoun Papers; variant PC in "Letters from John C. Calhoun to Francis W. Pickens," in *South Carolina Historical Magazine*, vol. VII, no. 1 (January, 1906), pp. 16–19. NOTE: An AES by Pickens on the first page of the letter reads: "If the joint occupancy treaty had remained our frontier adventurers would have constantly been brought into conflict with the British subjects in the employment of the Hudson Bay company, as there were no ascertained boundaries between us, & the frontier population would, in fact have drag[g]ed us into a war as they were interested for one to force an army with its disbursements. The only way to prevent certain conflict was to give notice to terminate the joint occupancy treaty & fix the boundaries which we had an express right to do by the terms of the treaty itself. This notice was what compelled a settlement, which the British desired to avoid, because with no fixed boundaries, their people had a right to trap for furs over the whole territory, whereas[?] when fixed they would be restricted to the line. It was therefore a peace movement & not war as Mr. Calhoun supposed, and as after facts proved for it settled the question & saved us from a war forced on us, by an aggressive frontier population. This was the real object of Mr. Polk—& he was wise in it as events prove. F.W. Pickens." An AEU by Pickens on the address sheet of the letter reads: "J.C. Calhoun's Sept: 23 1845–his return to the Senate & his reasons–my answer."

From J[OSEPH] N. WHITNER

Anderson [S.C.,] Sept. 23rd 1845

Dear Sir, Mr. Barkley [*sic*; William K. Barclay] now engaged in portrait painting in our Village is very anxious if an opportunity may be afforded of executing a painting of yourself. He is a native of our State[,] a Scholar of the Celebrated [Thomas] Sully, a man of worth & I think an artist of more than ordinary promise. He is fully aware of the manner in which your time & patience have been & yet are taxed by the public to whom you have principally belonged and that such a request therefore may be inconvenient to grant. As I think his ambition laudable and from his painting heretofore I should feel strong confidence in his executing a painting that would be creditable to himself as an artist & gratifying to your friends & acquaintances that might have an opportunity of seeing it, I have thought it not amiss at least to inquire for him whether it would suit your inclination & convenience to afford him some two or three Sittings including perhaps as many hours altogether in the course of the next week to take your Portrait. He intends locating himself in Charleston permanently. I am sure no apology is necessary for the request made & that you will at once & without hesitation decline if it does not suit you for you cannot at least mistake the spirit in which it is made.

I send to you by the mail a number of the Central Democrat handed to me in Harrodsburg Kentucky by President [James] Shannon [of Bacon College] formerly of Athens Georgia who I found to be a warm political admirer. It contains an address pronounced by himself on the occasion of Gen. [Andrew] Jackson[']s death of the merit of which I know nothing not yet having read it. He was formerly a professor in the Franklin University of Georgia, a Brother-in-Law of Judge [Charles] Dougherty, but an exceedingly staunch Democrat of the Southern, State-right stamp.

I avail myself of the occasion to bear to you the most hearty good wishes & assurances of affectionate remembrance from an old gentleman in Kentucky whose name I am ashamed to have forgotten who served with you many years in Congress[,] has been ever & yet is an ardent friend & supporter of every prominent measure I think you have been known to advocate. He recounted to me many incident[s] if I could repeat I have no doubt would bring him to your mind. I think he was of your mess probably as far back as during the war. He is a man of stout person now quite an old man & I most[?] think has probably since he left public life written a history of Kentucky. I hope you may be able thus to remember him for his heart beats most warmly toward you. I shall not be able to visit you as I promised before I go on the Fall circuit & shall be glad to receive a line at your earliest convenience. With sincere esteem Y[ou]rs &, J.N. Whitner.

ALS in ScCleA. NOTE: Of a number of Kentucky friends from Calhoun's earlier career, the one most likely to be the "old gentleman" referred to by Whitner in his last paragraph is George Robertson. No portrait of Calhoun by Barclay of this period has been identified, although one exists which is attributed to 1831, about the time Barclay reportedly began his painting career in South Carolina.

From H[ENRY] A. S. DEARBORN

Hawthorn Cottage
Roxbury Mas[sachuset]ts, Sep[tember] 24, 1845
Dear Sir, Allow me to introduce Doct[or] Augustus Mitchell of Portland [Maine] to you, as he intends to pass the winter in the south,

chiefly for the purpose of extending his researches in natural History, & particularly in ornithology. He is a young gentleman of great merit, & is universally respected for his scientific attainments & excellence of character.

Any attentions you may be so kind as to extend to him, will be gratefully received, & you will also confer a great favor on me, as I feel a deep interest in a gentleman who has evinced such a highly commendable spirit, for increasing our information on the various branches of the natural history of the United States.

No man has been ever more active & zealous, to promote all the branches of letters, science & the arts, than yourself, & therefore it is, that I have taken the liberty of recommending Doct[or] Mitchell to you. With sentiments of sincere respect, I have the honor of being your most ob[edien]t S[ervan]t, H.A.S. Dearborn.

ALS in ScCleA. NOTE: Lacking a postmark and address this letter was perhaps hand-delivered to Calhoun at Fort Hill. Henry A.S. Dearborn (1783–1851) was the son of Gen. Henry Dearborn. He held a variety of federal, state, and local offices in Mass. and was a prolific author.

From DUFF GREEN

Washington, Sep[tembe]r 24th 1845

My dear Sir, I am met at every corner with the enquiry of whether you will come to the senate. I do not know that my opinion will have any influence and I may be deemed impertinent but I venture to give you a few suggestions.

I believe that Mr. [James K.] Polk real[l]y feels pledged to exert his influence to reduce the tariff, to the revenue standard & to establish the subtreasury and that he intends to fulfil his pledges in good faith. But this is more than I can say for all those who are about him.

I believe that [Thomas] Ritchie would sell the democratic party and Virginia too for the public printing and I have no doubt that he is laboring to get up a coalition with [Thomas H.] Benton for that purpose, and that Benton's object is to bring [James] McDowell into the senate [from Va.], when with [Arthur P.] Bagby [Senator from Ala.], [William] Allen [Senator from Ohio], [John] Fairfield [Senator from Me.], & [John A.] Dix [Senator from N.Y.] and the chances for the Senators from N. Hampshire, Indiana & Tennessee he will be disposed to set up for himself and by throwing himself between you & the administration assume the control of the Government.

169

My belief is that if you come to the senate you will find the President sincerely your friend, and that the fact of your coming, especial[l]y if you are here at the commencement of the session, will enable your friends to control the elections in Virginia and to give the printing of the Senate to the Constitution & the House to Ritchie, that the publication of McKensie's [*sic*; William Lyon Mackenzie's] book in which he gives the confidential correspondence of the Albany Regency will create a crisis that will induce the party to rally on you as the only means of saving the party, but to do this you must be here.

I saw [Senator Edward A.] Hannegan of Indiana yesterday. He says that the West will be united and will demand funds for the the [*sic*] improvements of their harbours, rivers & the Cumberland road— & the graduation of the price of the public lands and that if the South will give these to the West the West ["South" *canceled*] will go with the South on the tariff. This is Benton's card. I write that you may understand it.

McKensie's book discloses a mass of corrupt intrigues, the equal to which has not been before disclosed in this country, and the contrast with your public life will endear you to the country.

The foolish declaration in the [Washington] "Union" that the President wishes to use your friends to elect his successor will react on Ritchie & force him into an early declaration that he prefers you to all others if you are here to control your friends.

I have seen the correspondent of the Charleston Mercury and he has promised me that he will be on his guard and always bear in mind that Benton's object is to throw himself between you and the administration. I have been a looker on and gratified to see this controversy take a turn that will, as I hope defeat the purposes which Benton has in view, and can see that if treated with judgment by the Mercury, it will prevent the mischief which the coalition with Benton would otherwise have done. The coalition with Benton is so infamous that Ritchie will be compelled to deny it in terms that will do Benton injury and the public mind being aroused will see & condemn any attempt to execute the purposes which Benton has in view.

We are anxious to hear from Mrs. [Floride Colhoun] Calhoun, as the ["last" *interlined*] accounts said she was very ill. Mrs. [Lucretia Maria Edwards] Green & Eliza [M. Green] wish to be affectionately remembered to Mrs. Calhoun & [Martha] Cornelia [Calhoun]. Your sincere friend, Duff Green.

ALS in ScCleA; PC in Jameson, ed., *Correspondence*, pp. 1054–1055. NOTE: The book to which Green referred was by the refugee Canadian patriot William

Lyon Mackenzie, *Lives and Opinions of Benj'n Franklin Butler, United States District Attorney for the Southern District of New-York; and Jesse Hoyt, Counsellor at Law, Formerly Collector of Customs for the Port of New-York* (Boston: Cooke & Co., 1845). It is an elaborately documented portrayal of the corruption, spoilsmanship, and self-seeking that had prevailed among the N.Y. Democrats over the previous two decades. Benjamin F. Butler had been Martin Van Buren's law partner and Attorney General. Mackenzie, who had for a time held a post in the New York Customs House, followed this work up with another the next year from the same publisher, a further exposé entitled *The Life and Times of Martin Van Buren* . . . . In the latter work, the author wrote: "I have been a warm admirer of John C. Calhoun. . . . Calhoun is frank—he has nothing of the fox or weasel in him, as he said of Van Buren . . . ." (pp. 64–65).

To J[OHN] A[LFRED] CALHOUN, [Eufaula, Ala.]

Fort Hill, 26th Sep[tembe]r 1845

My dear John, I am happy to hear, that you & your family are well & that your crop is a fair one.

I write at this time to say, that I expect to set out on a visit to Andrew's [Andrew Pickens Calhoun's] the 1st or 2d of next month. Mrs. [Floride Colhoun] Calhoun & John [C. Calhoun, Jr.] will accompany me, & we will travel in our own Carriage. I shall take the upper route by Decatur [Ga.], as it is too soon in the season to take the lower. I expect to be about 12 days on the road, & will probably remain with Andrew until the 1st week in Nov[embe]r.

On my return, if I can possibly make my arrangement to do so, we will call on your brother James [Martin Calhoun] & yourself.

I am much occupied & you must excuse the shortness of my letter.

We are all well, & Mrs. Calhoun & family join their love to you, Sarah [Morning Norwood Calhoun] & family. Yours affectionately, J.C. Calhoun.

ALS in ScU-SC, John C. Calhoun Papers.

From J[AMES] H. HAMMOND

Silver Bluff, 26 Sept. 1845

My Dear Sir. I am very glad you approve my not reviewing Dr. [Henry B.] Bascom's work. I am more & more satisfied it should not be done & that all half way & compromise views of that question come from whence they may if not openly denounced should be altogether discountenanced. Our greatest danger arises from fear & doubt among ourselves. Every Slaveholder is ready to do battle for Slavery & far more willing to do it for that than any other cause. All that is necessary to render each man immoveably & undauntedly firm is to know that every other Slaveholder is of the same opinion as himself & will stand by him to the last. Every thing therefore that looks like misgiving, hesitation, apprehension of ["the" *canceled*] our want of strength either in argument or ["power" *canceled and* "actual fight" *interlined*], is dangerous in the extreme. It encourages the abolitionists & helps to create among us fears which may end in panic & ruin us. In fact no other means can ever really endanger us. All our risk is that we may not prove true to our own interest. A Slave holder then or Southern man who falters, who apologizes, much less who denounces Slavery & regards abolition as inevitable is in my opinion our *very worst enemy*, the man who saps our strength at the core & does more to destroy us than a brigade of abolitionists could. You have seen the blow up with Cassius [M.] Clay. That he survived so long can only be accounted for by the reasons I have suggested. Had each man *felt sure of his neighbour* the first no. of the [Lexington, Ky.] T[rue] American would have been the last. But these very half way doctrines had paralyzed the community & but for his audacious imprudence he might have stood long & done serious mischief. Neither the abolitionists nor *ourselves* have yet put forward with sufficient prominence the true ground on which the permanence of Slavery rests—*interest*. They cannot conceive of it. We are ashamed to avow it. But *we* should not be for our interest is not only that of individuals but of Society, of the Caucasian race, of Civilization. But all these things you know. [Lewis] Tappan has not answered my letter. I fear I gave him an overdose. I did not suppose that any strength of reasoning or coarseness of abuse (in which I did not indulge) could have prevented a fanatic from coming back with his balderdash. He is probably working underground somewhere. I have reason to believe that our abolitionists will try to draw something from [Lord Henry Peter] Brougham or [Thomas B.] Macaulay on American Slavery on the pretext of answering my letters to [Thomas] Clarkson. I shall regret such a thing for besides that they would be rough customers in any controversy, aided by the researches of the English Anti-Slavery Society, they may prove an overmatch for my limited information & still more limited abilities which would prove an injury to the cause. In such a contingency can you help me to facts & illustrations or will you take mine & come into the rescue?

It seems a settled thing—I fear it is so—that the [James K. Polk] Administration does not intend to move heartily on the Tariff. For one I always apprehended it. What are we to do? As the great Southern & Free Trader Leader you will be beset on all sides I presume before Christmas. Are the free traders to take a bold, violent, & of course dangerous line of ["pol" *canceled*] action or to subside into a tame, safe & prudent policy at least equally dangerous to our principles & the aspirations of those identified with the cause? The question is knotty. While the Free Trader doctrines are rapidly advancing in England & gaining north & west of us, I fear they are losing ground in the South. The whole body of Southern Whigs are tainted & will not lift a finger against the Tariff. The Union men of course eschew every thing but shrewd discussion—the Nullifiers are dispersed to the four winds while the Southern manufacturers are rising to importance & distilling poison in every neighbourhood. The prospect looks gloomy. If I were in public life I should have no hesitation about my own course, but I confess my hopes of a triumph for Free Trade for many many years to come are slight. You will have to chalk out a course. The ardent spirits actively engaged in politics must have a plan of action & if you don't furnish one, they will seize one from hasty & perhaps from unsure councils. As the world goes there is no spot on which one can find a *stand still*, but in agriculture, *my* haven of quiet. You have done too much to find or at least to be allowed to enjoy such a haven. "Bubble, bubble, Toil & trouble" to the end is for every one who passes 30 years or even half that many in public service. I thank my stars that I have been engaged in it but two & a half as yet & trust I am secure against more. I have therefore only *curiosity* to gratify, & this leads me to inquire of you how we are to meet our present difficulties, & to watch the game as it is played.

Speaking of agriculture, all the plagues of Egypt seem to have beset those of us who are under the curse this year. Half a crop of corn & one third of a crop of cotton (all I shall make) was too [*one word canceled and* "good" *interlined*] for us. We [in Barnwell District] have almost had frost & the worm after ruining our pastures is devouring cotton, peas & even fodder stacks. I do not see what is to become of ["us" *interlined*]. Having luckily planted corn largely I have housed enough to keep off famine from myself & the poor around me. But the river forbids marling & the season prevents ditching. Others have far greater evils to complain of. Have you tried Berkshires? If not let me advise you to be cautious. In your colder climate they may do better, but they have injured me seriously. For five years I have cultivated them to the neglect of all other breeds. The consequence is that but for my stock of cattle I should have to buy meat this year & the next—a thing I have never done. They are as tender as ["young" *interlined*] turkies [*sic*]. One in ten farrowed is all that can be put into the smoke house in this region, & they do not breed more than half so well as the common hog. After much experience & great loss in hogs, cattle & horses, I am decidedly of opinion that in all cases half native blood is indispensable to any substantial profitable use & I would prefer three fourths of it. Very truly & sincerely yours, J.H. Hammond.

P.S. You confirm my apprehensions of war. Yet a friend from whom I have just purchased 22 negroes is counting the money by me. Is not this very imprudent in me[?] I have misgivings about it. There is no interest but the cotton interest that will oppose war I fear. And if England does not back out I don't see how we shall escape. Have you any hope that England will? We Bullied France but John Bull, the great father of bullies, is not to be beat at his own game.

ALS in ScCleA.

From H[ENRY] W. CONNER

Charleston, Sept[embe]r 28, 1845
My Dear Sir, I have just returned from New York [City] where I have spent the last month.

The people there, without exception as to party are extremely desirous of seeing & communicating with you personally & it does seem to me that there are reasons more numerous & powerful at the present time to induce you to do so than at any former period & with all possible deference to your better knowledge & experience I now venture to recommend your visiting the city of New York & Boston & stopping at Richmond in Virginia on your return[.] You will understand my motive better when I state my reasons.

There is at this time a complete breaking up & disorganization of old combinations & machinery of party. There is no principle of cohesion amongst them except the common loss of plunder & so corrupt have the politicians of both parties become that they dare not confide long enough in each other even to commit an act of party pillage[.] The truth is both parties are tired of their own leaders & party practices & are ripe for a reorganization upon better principles & upon better men—if they had them. Towards yourself there is a feeling of confidence both as regards your personal character & political principles that surpasses that of all other men and it is not confined to one party alone. It is common to both—in fact it is nearly universal[.] Your putting yourself into easy & familiar personal intercourse with the people generally at this particular time would in my opinion lead to a reorganization of the democratic party in New York upon sounder princip[les] & with more elevated views than has heretofore been the case & which would result in maintaining & preserving the ascendancy of the party, without which defeat would be the consequence—you would serve as a neuclus [sic] around which ["all" canceled] would rally the better & greater part of the democratic party—with a considerable body of the whig party— many of whom have been forced into the whig ranks from a dread of the disorganizing & levelling tendencies of some of the ultra doctrines of the ultras of the party. This is one reason requiring you, as I conceive, to visit New York, & it has for its object the general good of the country & the party.

In addition to this I perceived I think a decided change coming over the minds of the people upon the subject of the Tarriff [sic] & abolition questions. The free trade principles have evidently gained ground from the late movements in England as well as from a better understanding of the subject & the minds of very many—heretofore decidedly Tarriff—are a good deal unsettled latterly, particularly amongst the manufacturers themselves—while as regards abolition the opinion is becoming settled that the two races cannot exist together except in subjection, one to the other, & that it is philanthropy misapplied to attempt to interfere with the subject of slavery. The public mind to the North is in a condition now to be shaped & directed by your personal intercourse with the people there, in such a way I think as to insure the modification of the Tarriff & peace upon the subject of abolition, except from the Fanatics alone. The deep & abiding interest which the South has in these two questions furnishes abundant reasons to recommend your visit to New York, for these objects alone.

There is another reason—personal to yourself & on that account held by you as very secondary in importance to the other public considerations—yet should surely not be without its weight. I allude to your position before the public in reference to the next Presidency. It appears to me you are the only man upon whom all that portion of the party who look to the good of the country can unite. If this be so it appears to me it is a duty you owe the people to give them an opportunity of seeing & knowing you personally. In New York the desire to see & hold communion with you is so great that your withholding yourself from them has been viewed almost with resentment. They begin to think you have no feelings or sympathies in common with the people—altho all your acts & speeches go to prove the contrary. The present condition of things in New York renders it peculiarly desirable that you should go amongst them—talk with them—hear them talk & explain yourself in your usual free happy way to them. The feeling already is strong & powerful in your favour—particularly amongst the young democracy but a personal intercourse with them would ripen the feeling into a confidence & enthusiasm that no selfish or designing combination of corrupt partizans could ever remove.

I have spoken of the present time as favourable for the visit. I mean before the meeting of Congress—after that time circumstances may have been changed & the occasion in a great measure lost.

If you prefer[re]d to go by invitation the slightest intimation from any quarter that you could be induced to go would bring instantly the warmest kind of an invitation. My impression is that an informal visit is preferable[.] I would be glad to know your views.

I sent you by Friday[']s mail "The life & correspondence of B[enjamin] F. Butler & Jesse Hoyt late Collector of New York." It is in fact the private history of the politics of N. York for the last 10 or 20 years. It contains details of a system that you have known to be in operation amongst that class of politicians for many years. With great respect Yo[ur]s &C, H.W. Conner.

ALS in ScCleA; variant PC in Jameson, ed., *Correspondence*, pp. 1056–1058.

To J[AMES] H. HAMMOND, Silver Bluff, S.C.

Fort Hill, 28th Sep[tembe]r 1845
My dear Sir, I have just received your's of the 26th Inst., and you must excuse a hasty answer, as I am on the eve of leaving home on a visit to my son in Alabama.

I concur in the opinion, that we ought to take the highest ground on the subject of African slavery, as it exists among us; and have from the first acted accordingly; but we must not break with, or throw off those who are not yet prepared to come up to our standard, especially on the exterior limits of the slave holding States. I look back with pleasure to the progress, which sound principles have made within the last 10 years in respect to the relation between the two races. All, with a very few exceptions, defended it a short time since on the ground of a necessary evil, to ["be" *interlined*] got rid of as soon as possible. S.C. was not much sounder 20 years ago, than Kentucky now is, & I cannot but think the course the western Baptists & Methodists preachers took, in reference to the division of ["the" *canceled and* "their" *interlined*] churches has done much to expel C[assius M.] Clay & correct publick opinion in that quarter.

I think you ought to rejoice, if the abolitionists should bring out [Lord Henry Peter] Brougham or McCaulla [*sic*; Thomas B. Macaulay] against you. It would open a fine field & give you the audience of the world. You would have nothing to fear from the rencountre; nor would you have need of any one to come to the rescue. If any assistance should be needed ["on my part" *canceled and* "from me" *interlined*], as to advice, or information, it would be cheerfully given.

I fear the Tariff question will not be met by the [James K. Polk] administration as it ought; but I am of the impression, that it is too soon for us to say yet, what course we ought to take, except that we shall withdraw all support from those in power if they should deceive us. We war against both the principle & the oppression, & ought never to be satisfied until we have put down the one, & freed ourselves from the other. When we shall see the whole ground & know our position in reference to those in power, and the Northern wing of the party, we shall then be able to say, what course we ought to take; & that we shall before the session is over, if our delegation shall do their duty, as I trust they will.

As to Oregon, my hope for preserving peace mainly relies on the indisposition of England to go to war, & the possibility of getting a majority in the Senate to take the proper course in reference to it. I am of the impression, that the whole of the Atlantick States are opposed to war, if it can possibly be avoid[ed], and the administration too, if they could get out of the scrape. We cannot bully England; but if a majority can be got in the Senate against re[s]cinding the Convention of joint occupancy on our part, I doubt whether England would re[s]cind it on her part; & time may extricate us from our difficulties. All I think depends on the Senate. Yours truly, J.C. Calhoun.

ALS in DLC, James Henry Hammond Papers, vol. 12; PC in Jameson, ed., *Correspondence*, pp. 672–673.

From JA[ME]S GILLAM

Homestead [in Abbeville District, S.C.,] 29 Sep[tember] 1845
My Dear Sir, I rec[eive]d yours by Mr. Golding—also your very handsome present for which I tender you my sincere thanks. I have just rec[eive]d intel[l]igence from Mr. [John] Joiner of Union on the subject of the cutting machine which I send you—also one from Mr. [James S.] Boatwright about the cob grinder. The latter implement I have had an oppertunity of seeing since my last to you. I think it a very simple and very complete Machine. It g[r]inds the corn in the year [*sic*] converting the cobs and corn into hominy (and if desired) into fine meal—or it will grind shell'd corn into meal, as may be desired. It is capable of grinding forty bushels of corn into meal in a day with 3 horse power, or double the quantity of horse hominy in the same time. It is propell'd by a band and may ["be" *interlined*] attach[e]d to mill gear or an ordinary cotton gin—it has no other gearing but a permanent iron whirl. Its inventor intended ["it" *interlined*] for a mill to grind corn, the stones running vertically and forc'd together by screws—with a horizontal ["shaft" *interlined*] extending through them. In the end of that shaft (which is a square bar of iron about 1½ Inches in diameter) 2 holes are drill[e]d or punch[e]d into which crooked steel hooks are inserted. Just over these hooks a small form hopper suited to the size of a year of corn is fix[e]d—the year is drop[pe]d in, the hooks break it into small pieces—these fall into the stones and are converted into meal.

There is another invention I understand for converting ears of corn into meal—which is still more simple, Viz, a hole is drill[e]d in the upper millstone of a common corn mill about the size of a[n] ear of corn—into which the ear is drop[pe]d & at each revolution of the stone, the rapid motion of which tears up the cob against the furrows—it is thus (with the corn) ground into meal—each of these plans have their advocates. Of their comparative merits I cannot speak haveing [*sic*] only seen one. With *that one* I was pleas'd which is Mr. Boat[w]right's.

I send you the letters that you may have all the light on the subject. Should you conclude to purchase you can order them yourse[l]f or instruct me to do so.

I hope to be at Pendleton at the meeting of Synod in November and should I come ["I shall" *canceled*] I shall again do myself the pleasure of calling on you & hope to see your *labor savers* and *oeconomizers* in operation.

My family is in health and join me in respects and kind regards to yourself and family. Very respectfully Yours, Jas. Gillam.

N.B. My mother [Elizabeth Caldwell Gillam] tenders her special regard—is about to apply for a pens[i]on for the revolutionary services of my father [Robert Gillam]. But on account of the very few revolutionary soldier[s] that survive, she has not been able to particularize but few of his services. She has obtained the affadavits of Col. Z[achariah] S. Brooks of Edgefield & of Hugh Oneall [*sic*] of Newberry (the father [of] the Judge [John Belton O'Neall]). She bids me say to you that if [you] could be serviceable at all to her in the matter, either by letter, or a certificate as to the credibility of the witnesses, and her own respectability and family, and that ["there" *interlined*] is no fraud directly nor indirectly in the application, but that it is just and meritorious—or any thing else that you could feel free to do—that it would be thankfully rec[eive]d—and gratefully remembered.

[Enclosure]

John Joiner to Gen. James Gillam, Lodi Post Office, S.C.

Unionville [S.C.,] 13th Sep[tembe]r 1845

D[ea]r Sir, I received your favour dated 12th August not untill three days ago. I also rec[eive]d another today making enquiry respecting my cutting machines & in answer to which I will say that I will deliver a cutter at the Columbia Depo[t] for fifty dollars and hope to be successful in selecting Materials of best quality and shall be carefull that the work is faithfully done. As to delivering ["a" *interlined*] cutter at Greenville I know of no chance at this time except at a verry considerable cost & likewise to Hamburgh. About 6 or 8 weeks ago when waggons were going toward the mountains for corn I expect I could have had a cutter carried to Greenville for a trifle. Waggons are going from this to Columbia for corn & I expect I can get one carried to that place upon good terms provided there is not too much delay in the matter. An order either from yourself or friend in my line of buisiness will be thankfully received & punctually attended to By yours verry respectfully, John Joiner.

[Enclosure]

James S. Boatwright to James Gillam, Lodi Post Office, Abbeville District, S.C.

Columbia, Sept. 16th 1845

Dear Sir, Yours of 10th Inst. has been rec[eive]d & contents noticed. Your letter was the first I had heard of the mill[.] Mr. [John G.] Bowman spoke to me for one for Mr. Calhoun but said nothing about you. With regard to the mill—I can give you my views of the matter. To run it by Horse power—it will take about 3 Horses—and can be attached to the ordinary gin Gear. It is worked by a band and to run by water you will have to have a drum. Speed is very requisite to do work. As to their durability I believe they will last 10 or 15 years—and the cost of them is $75. The nearest point I can send to you is Hamburg—and the cost is of freight is [sic] $3.50 to Hamburg. Yours Respectfully, James S. Boatwright.

ALS with Ens in ScCleA. NOTE: Gillam's letter is addressed to Calhoun "private p[e]r[?] Golding." An AEU by Calhoun reads "Gen[era]l J. Gillam." Elizabeth Caldwell Gillam was a sister of John C. Calhoun's mother, Martha Caldwell Calhoun.

From F[RANCIS] W. PICKENS

Edgewood, 29 Sept. 1845

My dear Sir, I only rec[eive]d yours to-day—dated *23d inst.* but Postmarked *27th Sept.*, so that this may barely reach you on the 3d as you requested an answer by that time.

I am glad to hear Andrew [Pickens Calhoun] has made so fine a crop. His energy and intelligence as a planter with his fine lands are a great blessing to you.

I cannot entirely agree with you as to the Oregon question & its tendencies. I think the President [James K. Polk] was imprudent or undiplomatic in the language he used in his inaugural as to it, but he was bound in honor to allude to it as it formed a great point in the canvass that elected him. He ought not to have used such ultra language nor ought he to have proclaimed that we were going on to consum[m]ate our *title by settlement.* But as to our title, according to all the laws & usages of nations from discovery, settlement, proximity, purchase &c—I hold it to be clear and beyond dispute, and England has not a particle of title. I believe she desires to avoid a war with us at present, because she is no more prepared for a rupture than we are. She looks forward to a state of things that must be presented upon the death of *Louis Phillippe* [*sic*] and the struggle that may take place to establish his dynasty & thus preserve the peace of Europe. In this she has a deep stake and desires to husband all her resources to meet that event. Therefore she desires to avoid a rupture with us now as a conflict might give us the control of the Commerce & wealth of the world, particularly if a convulsion should take place at the same time in France & thereby bring a war on in Europe. But as to her deep and embittered hostility, engendered by the history of the past—by the rivalship of our institutions, commerce & power—I entertain not a ["shaddow" *changed to* "shadow"] of doubt. And I have no idea but that there must be a rupture sooner or later. Our policy is to avoid it as we are growing in all the elements of power more rapidly than she is. I hope & believe war may be avoided for a long time to come because it is obviously the interests of both countries to avoid it at present. But I confess I cannot bear to see her ar[r]ogantly claim what she has no right to, simply because she knows it gives her the control over the Pacific, and under an idea that the point is too distant to be defended by our arms. And this is the true cause of the almost universal feeling of the country in favour of Oregon, not that much is felt for Oregon itself at present as a ter[r]itory, but because England assumes a right to it simply because she has the force and because the point is a strong one in the adjustment of power over the Pacific.

As to the propriety of your returning to the Senate upon which you desire me to write you my opinion &c—I can only say—you have already weighed the reasons with great power; and I infer that your mind is made up pretty much, as you say "I do not see under all the circumstances how I could decline the duty if it should be the desire of the Legislature & the State, that I should again serve them in the Senate." I have always spoken my sentiments candidly to you when at all consulted. If you go back, you ought to have it authoritatively an[n]ounced that you would ["not suffer" *canceled*] under no ["circumstances" *canceled*] consideration whatever allow your name to be *spoken* of in *connexion with the Presidency.* That matter ought to be stop[p]ed beyond all doubt. If it is not there will be division and distraction. Amongst other reasons you mention why you ought to return is—"the great strength *of our friends* in Congress if it could be *brought to act* in concert." If you do not take the most decided steps and forbid your friends to speak of your name for the Presidency your return to the Senate instead of producing concert will produce the reverse. You could not move even on the Tariff without being misconstrued and opposed. [Thomas H.] Benton, [Silas] Wright, and *perhaps* the Adm[inist]r[ation] would be enlisted to divide what you now call "the great strength of our friends in Congress." This is my candid opinion. But if you go simply as a Senator from So[uth] Carolina and *never* for *any other post*, then your great fame, enlarged experience, and magnificent abilities, would add lustre to your State & produce a profound impression upon the institutions of your country. In this view my opinion is that you ought to go—it suits your habits and temperament. Looking as you would do to truth alone you could glory in the triumphs of your own genius and scorn and defy the opposition of heartless and selfish partizans around you.

As to the results to be produced, I think it probable you will not be at all satisfied with them. The North West will to a great extent control all the great questions to which you ["have" *interlined*] alluded, and although they may do what is pretty nearly right, yet it will be very difficult to bring our system to work upon the exact principles which your views might require. Modification & compromise have always been adopted under our complicated & conflicting interests, and your views & habits of mind are so devoted to abstract truth that it is difficult for you to embrace and be satisfied with the middle ground. Yet you can always make landmarks and sign posts by which others hereafter may be guided, and although a practical and selfish world at present may pass them by, nevertheless Posterity may look to them with admiration & wonder. I think if you go back to the Senate (as I take it for granted you will) you ought to spend the balance of your life as a Senator & build up your system to the end, and even if it be not adopted by the government it will have great control over the destinies of a free people hereafter.

Now as to the private happiness you may enjoy in old age by this kind of life that is a matter for your own consideration and no human being can advise you as to that.

You are mistaken if you suppose that your going to the Senate now is a new thing to be considered or that no one has known of it. It was said months ago that you would go. And it was said that [George] McDuffie would also resign provided he was sure that [James H.] Hammond or [Franklin H.] Elmore could be elected, he preferring the former, but that he would not trust the matter to this "infamous Legislature." [Daniel E.] Huger has kept no secret in the lower-country that he would resign for you to go, and I think it has been the general wish & expectation of the whole State that you would do so.

I confess that I had anticipated with certainty ["that" *canceled*] a large portion of the country bring[ing] forward your name for the Presidency and it did seem to me with a reasonable prospect of success. I do not say that it would be better that it ["should" *canceled*] should be so. I rather think there is more happiness to you & ["perhaps" *interlined*] a higher fame in purely *a Senatorial career.*

I have written you candidly & frankly my opinion. I may be wrong but I could say nothing less consistently with my judgement.

Present us kindly to Cousin F[loride Colhoun Calhoun] & family & also to Andrew [Pickens Calhoun]. Truly & sincerely, F.W. Pickens.

ALS in ScCleA; slightly variant ALS (retained copy) in ViLxW, Francis W. Pickens Papers; PEx in Boucher and Brooks, eds., *Correspondence*, p. 306. NOTE: This letter was addressed to Calhoun in Pendleton and was forwarded to Marengo County, Ala.

From WILLIAM P. SIMPSON

St. Clairsville, Ohio
September The 29th AD 1845

Dear Sir: In addressing you these fiew lins I am aware That the amount of Correspondence you receive has already Become Oppressive to your honour.

This however cannot nor ought not to prevent your friends at A grate distance on ocations as we think important to ask at your Pleasure & own time a *diffident* answer as we expect it out of your power to know certainly wether it will be possible For You to Comply with our requst.

Many of my accuantances and doubtless your *political friends* Has requsted me to write to your *honor* and requst you to take A *travel* threw the west asspechaly Ohio. These men refird To Resids at Cin[cinnati] Cleaveland & other points in our State &C: Since receiving divers letters requsting as above stated I have Convirsed with B[enjamin] G. Wright Esq. who informs me that he Had Requsted the Same thing. I must comply with the request Of our friends You will pleas *excuse* the second letter on the Same Subject from Old *Belmont* [County]. If you can comply of corse You must fix the time. We would respectfully recommend The Summer of

AD 1846. Our congressanal Election will take Place in October 1846. Our friends Seams to *Lack* Confidence In our choice of *men* of any Section of the *Union* ever tryumphing And Seam to feare the total defeat of our Principels. We here In Ohio & doubtless So threw the Union Look to you and at you as the Origionator of most of our Important national meashurs &C. Hence my dear Sir, you see that It would give a new impulce To our friends in the west. I think it also due to yourSelf & Asspechaly you principels and carractor as an amarican Stats Man, to travell threw a part of this new & grate valley of the Father of Warters in this Union of Stats. Dear Sir you see The hole ground at a glimps. Your position sence (32) has Never bin as well identified with the Old [Andrew] Jackson party. And the State right men will ralley at all times with grate Warmth. Your *Celebrated* Letter to *Col.* [William R.] King *also* to *Gov.* [Wilson] Shannon—in this I mean your *bold* and Amarican Like—or [Thomas] Jefferson like Deplomacy. With difrent men on The Subject of our Liberty and rights has in a grate degree Alayed that *demond* Sperit of persicution that prervaded this Land from 32 *untill* 37. When your King letter made its Appearance the contents was denounced as *Treason.* Deselution must be the result of that letter *Desalution certain.* It would be *Vain* to dwell on the affects these questions must have On the Amarican Freemen. The doctrins set forth will In my oppinion ["will" *canceled*] have moor affect on *Europe* Than *Napoleon's* victorious *armies* from 1795 To 1815.

The high character you have preaviously gaind is lost[?] compaired with the *flood* of light cast upon the world by displaying *Genius* in that never to be forgotten Letter. In truth our Polititions always acknoledged that Britten had Som grate object In view on the Subject of Slavrey the affects of their oppaerations Was sean & felt by many but the *cause* was known by *none.* Remember our request and when conveanance pirmits let Me here from you as our friends will continue to inquier. All will be kept confidential You nead have no fears on that subject. All matters of corse is left to you to deside. On ["that" *interlined*] desition much depends As I beleave on the results of 48. The organ of Hunkerism is Sold *To a Liberal.* The Ohio *Statsman* [and] other presses is changen hands. The contest with the presses has bin anamated untill they must Halt untill after the 14 october the day of our Election. I think We will be beaten owing to devisions in our ranks. Hunkerism Prevaild with the *capts*: Successor on the 4th of march but we will Be able to defeate them hereafter we are all united *Calhoun* & [Lewis] Cass men against the *Hunkers* the Cass men is *No.* 2 of *Hunkerism.* They are much moor honourable men then then [*sic*] the old [Martin] *Van* [Buren] Dinasty the *Leaders* of both I mean. Gov. Shannon is here yet Not desided to stay or goin to *Cincin*[*nati*]. Personaly & Politicaly he profeses a grate regard for you what corse he will take is uncirtain. As to 48 Cass he thinks is the only man can take Ohio. He fels *soar* at Cass for folding his arms to the Hunkers In the Senate in the appintments and asspechaly placing W[*illia*]*m* Allen on the *Com*[*mittee*] of feron affairs &c.

What ever may happen in this Union of Stats I hope the old Hunkers will grant us *Libertas loqundi*—with that condesention On their part we will hope to sirstain our selves better In *48* then we did in *44*. My friends would & did ask Col. [James K.] Polk For the Marshallship for me. I dislike that I consented but Was compeled to yeald to their demand. I am well satisfied that It caused the hunkers truble to defeat me of corse all Liberal Men in Ohio was defeated. My practice at the *barr* here suits me best although I would have bin glad to have received The appintment to have a position to brake down *hunkerism*. I have the *hon*[*or*] to be yours Respectfully, William P. Simpson.

P.S. Pleas direct to St. Clarsville. I am at Wheeling [Va.].

ALS in ScCleA.

From JAMES GADSDEN

Charleston 30 Sep[tembe]r [18]45
My Dear Sir, Yours of the 23d instant has just been received. I concur with you in all the political views you have presented. Our situation is critical—Distrust abroad—and ignorance, imbecility and cupidity in our Councils at home. We have reversed the order of things. The Goths & Vandals left sterility and frigid Regions to enjoy the refinement and milder climate of the South. We abandon Refinements, prosperity, and all the goods that a bountiful soil can afford to seek a new home in distant lands: or to rove like the Beasts of the field over endless Prairies.

The spirit is false; & like the Revolutionary impulses in France, must bring us in conflict with Foreign Powers. You will see in our last papers a notification of the Russian Government as visiting the N[orth] W[est] coast above the 54° latitude which looks ominous. Our Mad Caps however confident in American Prowes[s] will find that the war they are [*one or two words canceled*] encouraging is widely different from that which Revolutionary France excited. But your own sagacity must comprehend all the difficulties which our wild and extravagant pretensions may lead to.

I have been in correspondence with the Gentlemen[?] of Memphis, & would like to attend the meeting if possible. But I am a slave, overburthened with details in an office, every hour[']s absence from which creates embarrassments.

[Mitchell] King I will endeavor to have there. We will attempt to get up a deputation from this place, but it is difficult to find Individuals willing or able to go. Our Business men who would be most important at such a convention, will all object.

I am pleased to hear that you possibly could go. I will have you requested to represent So. Carolina, which I hope will remove the scruples of appearing as a volunteer. If therefore you should leave Pendleton for Alabama before you hear again from me proceed in time to Memphis where your credentials shall meet you. Shall I have it published that you will represent our interests in that quarter by particular request[?] Yours truly, James Gadsden.

ALS in ScCleA.

From CHRISTOPHER HUGHES

Baltimore; 30th Sept[embe]r 1845

My dear Mr. Calhoun, This must be a very hasty & short letter; but it positively *shall* be written—as it ought to have been several days ago: that is on my *return* home [from Europe] & *arrival* in my Native Town. It was my intention to write to you on landing: it was my *duty* & my impulse *so to do!* to announce to you that not very important fact: to pay a becoming respect & Courtesy to you—sentiments which I do, & ever shall entertain—& ever *have* entertained, for you; and to thank you for your most kind & invariable[?] courtesy to me—when I had the honour to serve under you—and to claim you as my Chief.

Now my dear Sir—I do *all this*—though tardily—sincerely. I have the truest esteem—respect & admiration & confidence in you as a Man—a Gentleman—a Countryman—a Statesman & a Patriot: & I say this, at home—as I have ever *said* it abroad! I say it—moreover—without any *arriere penseè*; any *calculation*—for you are in retirement—and *so am I* (forgive the impertinence of this presumptuous *juxta*: and, certainly, I have no projects; and, before God! excepting the ambition, to live cheerfully—honourably—happily & in harmony with my fellow-men (I mean the *good humoured & pleasant* portion of them, & the *clever* ones of them) I have *never known what ambition means!* I have never comprehended it! I can quite comprehend that a true & gallant man—is always ready to serve his Country—even *to die* for his Country! (I'd rather *live* for it—however; & I *mean* to live *in* it. On this point I have not been *consulted*.) I can, I say, understand *this* but I positively cannot explain to myself—the torment—& worry & *misery* men consent to undergo—& even ["to" interlined] seek—& good & clever men too! under the impulse of what is called ambition—in the ordinary practice and developements of Life. The world—all that it inherits—Men in general—are not *worth* this turmoil & this strife! This is my honest—perhaps not very lofty view of the world & my fellows.

I am admonished to stop. I am overw[h]elmed with calls & household occupations and all manner of business—on my return to my native Town; in which—if you *ever visit* Baltimore I shall be most happy to see you, & may I say? how highly I should feel myself—and my simple house—to be honoured (in such a Contingency—& if you ever be in our Town) if you would allow me to be your host—& consent to be my Guest. I am proceeding very far—in my familiarity; but I know how to value the kind & favourable opinions of such men—as I am now writing to! I know—by my own knowledge—by my own conviction—& by my valued Friend—Mr. Clemson—the friendly & favourable opinions, you expressed for me—when I served under you! & I *assure you*—I was & I am—most highly gratified, at knowing this. Let this excuse the freedom I now exercise.

I shall be too late for the Mail! I saw Mr. & Mrs. Clemson—& their noble Boy (*your image*) at Brussels—in July! I stopped & lodged there a week, with my old[?] & dear friend Marquis de Ruvigny[?]— French Ambassador—& I was also at Brussels—in January! *I think* I wrote this *last*, to you. In July—Mr. & Mrs. Clemson were well!—and as kind to me & my Daughter as possible. I need not say that Mr. C[lemson] is held in high Consideration by His Colleagues, by Society & by the King [Leopold I of Belgium]. His Majesty is (I may say) an old *friend* of mine.

I have been for many years—quite on easy & amiable & even *free* terms with King Leopold (as I *was* with his Brother—the Father of Prince Albert, who corresponded with me *autograph*) who spoke to me—in the highest terms of satisfaction of Mr. Clemson.

187

I must stop—apropos I wrote a *very long* Letter (some 30 & more Note paper pages) from the Hague—in the month of January or Feb-[ruar]y (I think) of *this* year—to my Friend *Joseph R. Ingersoll.* I sent this letter ["open" *interlined*] (historical of a then late *sojourn* of a few days at Paris) in a short *open* Letter to you; & I requested you to *read* & then *to send* my long Letter—to Mr. Ingersoll! *He* never got it; & I *got* into a *scrape* for forgetting my friend & for *not* writing to him.

Did you get this Letter? It must have reached you shortly before you left Washington; You *must* have *got* it. Where can it be? it was *sewn* together as this is! Did you *leave* it at the State Department (*I hope not!*) it is quite a little Book! If you can find it—I pray you—to send it *by Mail,* "to J.R. Ingersoll—Fourth Street—Philadelphia." You will much oblige me—& *Him*; & now, my dear Mr. Calhoun—forgive all this freedom from Y[ou]r obed[ient] Ser[van]t & friend, Christopher Hughes.

ALS in ScCleA. NOTE: Hughes had returned home from a diplomatic career of almost twenty years under five administrations as U.S. Chargé d'Affaires in Denmark, Sweden, and the Netherlands.

OCTOBER 1–NOVEMBER 30
1845

◫

Calhoun's neighborhood newspaper, the Pendleton *Messenger, reported on October 3 that the statesman and family had left the previous day on a visit of six weeks to his son in Alabama. The paper very obligingly provided the public with his mail address during the absence: Faunsdale Post Office, Marengo County, Alabama. The* Washington *Daily* Union *repeated this useful information for the whole country on October 10.*

From then on Calhoun's trip was a media event, nationally and in every place he passed through. The Calhouns were sighted in Decatur, Georgia, on October 8 and in Wetumpka, Alabama, on October 13, and must have arrived at Andrew's plantation about October 15. There he found all healthy and the crops good. In the first letter written from Marengo, on October 18, he informed an old friend that he had consented to return to the Senate, "though much against my inclination."

The media event exploded when this fact was learned, along with the news that Calhoun had, uncharacteristically for him, agreed to visit Mobile and New Orleans and to accept election as a South Carolina delegate to the great Southwestern Convention to assemble in Memphis in November. This brought a proliferation of invitations from all over the Southwest, including a plea to visit Galveston signed by two former Presidents of the Texas Republic.

The journey from Marengo County to Memphis and back became a triumphal procession, greeted everywhere by crowds, decorations, distinguished committees of reception, the tender of special trains, boats, and accommodations. Calhoun was accompanied by Francis W. Pickens, who was also a delegate, his son Andrew, and from New Orleans on by his son Patrick of the Army.

He reached Mobile on November 4 by boat downriver and after a two-day celebration left by coastal steamer for New Orleans. In that festive city he was greeted on November 6 by the governor, the militia, immense crowds, and flag-draped ships and buildings. He endured two huge receptions and numerous other attentions and departed up the Mississippi on the night of November 8.

Because of engine trouble a visit ashore at Natchez had to be canceled and at Vicksburg cut short, to the disappointment of hundreds. On the evening of November 12 he reached Memphis, met by the by-now-customary reception. The next day he entered the convention of which he had already been elected presiding officer. On the 13th and 14th he addressed the 564 delegates of fifteen States and Territories, inaugurating a new and controversial internal improvements movement.

On November 16 he left Memphis on the downriver voyage, speaking briefly at Vicksburg on November 18 and stopping to visit a sugar plantation above New Orleans on November 20. He again passed through Mobile and back to Andrew's to collect Mrs. Calhoun. On the stage and rail journey home he was unable to avoid speaking at Montgomery on the 25th. However, he had declined pressing invitations to visit St. Louis, Jackson, Nashville, Cincinnati, and many lesser places in the West. The papers pointed out often that the honors that had been tendered Calhoun on his journey had been bestowed by Democrats and Whigs all, "without distinction of party."

The Calhouns were back at home at Fort Hill around the first of December. Meanwhile, the General Assembly of South Carolina, in joint session on November 27, had elected Calhoun Senator of the United States in place of Daniel E. Huger, resigned. He received this news, which could hardly have been a surprise, while passing through Athens, Georgia, on November 29, according to the Athens *Southern Banner of December 2.* The vote was 135 yeas out of a membership of 139. Calhoun was in fact simply resuming the term to which he had been elected in 1841 and from which he had resigned in 1843, a term to end March 4, 1847.

▥

From ROBERT PATTERSON

Office Concordia Intelligencer
Vidalia La. [*ca.* October?, 1845]
Sir, In the absence of a personal acquaintance with yourself, but prompted by the same earnest desire for the weal and advancement of "*our South*" the developement of her vast resources, the unfolding of her splendid capabilities—that has formed one of the

characteristics of your course during your long public service, I am induced to address you in relation to a matter of highest importance to the *whole South* and of especial interest to your own State.

It is in relation to the connection of the Atlantic with the Mississippi by Rail Road from Charleston to the best available point on our glorious stream.

A native of this immediate vicinity—of Natchez, and a resident from birth to this hour, with a full thorough practical knowledge of the region bordering the Mississippi from its mouth to that of the Ohio, and with an eye directed to the developement of its resources, its improvement and the ["advocacy of the" *interlined*] just claims its Citizens have upon the General Government for having wrested *the Lowlands, the Garden Lands of the Valley, from the Waters*—I am decidedly of opinion that the best, most feasible and profitable point that could be fixed on for the Western terminus of the Road, or rather its intersection with the Mississippi, is the *City of Natchez.* My knowledge of the region and the foundation of this fixed opinion is based upon a personal examination of the region named, made on horseback, in steamboats—horse boats—canoes, skiffs etc.—a trip of some six hundred miles was made in this manner by myself during the overflow of '44 through the overflowed district; and when the waters subsided I followed the same route on horseback through that portion which had been most deeply covered.

Natchez possesses advantages superior to Memphis in every respect, Western freights can be landed here as cheaply as at the latter point—the health of the region is better, the surrounding country and the City are filled with a permanent, settled population—fixed and identified with all ["shemes" *altered to* "schemes"] intended for her benefit.

She holds a position preferable to Vicksburg from the fact that she controls a larger portion of the Lowlands of Louisianna opposite her, and bordering the Mississippi in her vicinity—and in case a continuation of the road *west* to Texas is contemplated, *"and it should be by all means"* the route via Natchez is in every respect far preferable for crossing the Lowlands, to any other point whatever on the Mississippi. The valley here is narrowed to 28 miles, and Red River is intersected by either route that may be selected from the mouth of the *Ouachita*, at such point as would command its trade almost entirely. The line to central Texas is direct, the route most favorable, and such as to control the entire trade and travel of Northern, Western and Central Texas—and if yet farther West it should be deemed wise to [*one word altered to* "push"] the Car of civilization—the "Star

191

of Empire," the route to Tamaulipas, Chihuahua and the rich and populous Intendencies of New Mexico, would offer inducements for an early consummation of *this, the most splendid enterprize of the age*, one that belongs properly ["peculiarly" *interlined*] to minds such as yours, to men wielding the vast influence that you do, and which directed to an end noble as this, must the more ennoble the gallant champion who would conquer the wilderness, not by fire and sword, but by the *arts of peace, the genius of civilization, the elevation of man.*

A glance at the map exhibits the fact that the route from Charleston west, strikes *centrally* across the entire Cotton region, truly and emphatically the only cotton growing portion of the Globe—the fact being by the present state of things *proven*, that *overgrowth* can never occur, no limit can be fixed to the flood of prosperity that must within few years flow in upon the South—*the wealth producing portion of the Union.* The increase of value in this article in the face of the surplus now on hand, and the (*unfounded*) reports of a large crop, is an extraordinary ["great" *canceled and* "event" *interlined*], and originates, I doubt not, in the increased demand and the competition growing out of the appropriation of large means to Manufacturing purposes in this Country and Europe.

No single inducement offers for connecting the Road with Memphis, when the fact is known that a branch of your road—*is demanded by Nashville*, that is a continuation to that point from Chattanooga, a distance of about 260 miles—*an admirable idea*, for your route from Nashville points to the Ohio at *Louisville* as the best possible means of securing all the Western trade that can be brought South. This is the true course for giving your State and your City the stand, their wealth, position, and more than all, their high intelligence entitle them to. Your *right arm* is stretched through the interior regions of your own State ["through" *canceled and* "across" *interlined*] *Georgia, Tennessee, Kentucky* centrally—while *the left* with long sweep stretches west and gathers tribute from the States of *Georgia, Alabama, Mississippi, Louisiana* a line of 700 miles with a population of near ["700,000" *altered to* "800,000"] *souls* and a region capable of admitting an increased population of ten fold its present numbers.

Here then you have the *key of the West*, the *key of the South-West* and the *whole* South in your hands—for who would ascend or descend the Mississippi or ship valuable cargoes of Merchandize either way, *when* by your steam Cars he could accomplish half the distance to New York in *20 hours.* Besides all these considerations, ["stricking" *altered to* "striking"] the Mississippi at Natchez, gives you control of the Valley of the Ouachita and the vast region border-ing ["bordering" *canceled*] the *Arkansas* throughout its course of 1200 miles!

Aside from all political results, and these alone are of sufficient interest and importance to demand of the citizens of the South that they should be bound and banded together as brothers—The mere pecuniary considerations are so vast as to present to your City and State opportunity for placing the former in the same relative po-sition toward the *Mammoth Mart of the South,* New Orleans, as that now occupied by *Boston towards New York*—a proper applica-tion of means to this end would redound to the advantage of Caro-lina, of Charleston of the several important points on the route—Montgomery—Decatur—Natchez—Austin—and others which this en-terprise would build up in the wilderness and waste places to be found at intervals on the route—its consummation would enure to the benefit of each State through which this line would pass, for instead of one market half a dozen would be opened to each State—Charleston—Augusta—Savannah—Mobile—Natchez—New-Orleans—all would be open, and honorable competition between the *first* and *last named* would determine which is in reality the Emporium of the South despite the *boasted natural channels* behind which the Cres-cent City now seems to rest as securely as did her defenders behind their Cotton bales in 1815.

The fact would again be made manifest that *natural channels* (a mis-nomer by the bye) may be most successfully competed with by artificial means of communication.

I take the liberty of referring you to the accompanying papers—articles prepared by myself for the purpose of awakening the citizens of Natchez to the importance of early action—the statistics are gath-ered from late authorities and may be relied on—upon the route through Georgia, Alabama, Mississippi and Louisiana I have taken a range of 40 miles on each side of the road as being directly influ-enced by the road, this however will prove too small an estimate for the influence to be exercised in Alabama and Mississippi upon the Northern tiers of counties—it will be felt by them to the extent of 60–80 and even 100 miles, while a hundred short lines, the smaller arteries of this grand line must come into existence, gathering from each settlement, village, town, its tribute, as our noble river in his far reachings gathers the chrystal treasures from every clime and a range of region containing 30,000 miles of navigation, which is con-centrated within his banks before my eye at this moment.

I shall continue to stir the subject in the columns of my own paper and others, with the hope that ere a decision is given by your company in regard to the location of a route, that this *via Natchez* may be examined fully and fairly—if this is done I rest confident that its superiority over all others will give it decided preference.

I have just now returned nervous from excitement caused by attending a large and enthusiastic meeting of the Citizens of Natchez and vicinity including our Pari[s]h of Concordia and other parishes of Louisiana, assembled for the purpose of responding to the Call of the Southwestern Convention at Memphis. Their action will be seen by you at Memphis—one of the largest and most respectable delegations ever sent from this quarter is appointed to attend, with the personal pledge to do so.

A full array of facts will be laid before yourself and your friends from Carolina [who] may accompany you, as your attendance is looked for *without fail*—the assurance of your presence is an inducement with many.

To any one but a devoted friend of the South such as I know you to be, I should apologize for this long letter—but the glorious scheme is one worthy the consideration of the giant minds of the day, worthy the liberality of the South and best calculated to make her what she should be *Independent*—if need be. Truly your ob[edien]t S[er]-v[an]t, Robert Patterson, Editor[,] Concordia Intelligencer.

[Enclosure]
Statistical Items
Charleston and Natchez Rail-Road
Distance to Montgomery Alabama from Charleston—

to which point the Road is now *nearly completed*	400 miles
distance from Montgomery to Natchez— — —	300 "
total	700 miles

Population on and adjacent to the route
from Charleston to Natchez—to be directly
operated on by the Road—

The Counties of *Carolina* extending from Charleston to Augusta—	162,532
The Counties of *Georgia* within 40 miles on either side of route through that State	235,605
The Counties of *Alabama* on route and to be affected by its completion—	261,280
The Counties of *Mississippi* to be affected by its completion— — — —	86,281
The Parishes of *Louisiana*—	51,000
Total	796,698.

194

This estimate includes for Carolina only the population of the Counties, through which the route passes—others there are that must be operated on, upon this and other portions of the route and we may safely assert that a direct influence will be exercised upon the active Capital possessed by a population of one Million individuals, residing permanently in the *wealth producing portion of the Union*—the *floating population*, the summer travel, would probably amount to Five Hundred Thousand. For all convenient internal improvements have given evidence of the fact that *facility* for travel will *increase* travel.

LS with En in ScCleA. NOTE: Patterson wrote only the last three paragraphs of this letter in his own handwriting. The rest is in another hand. An AEU by Calhoun on the back of the En reads "Relates to the Natchez rail road." Patterson was a La. delegate to the Memphis Convention. The dating of this letter is conjectural.

From M[OSES] C. MORDECAI

Charleston, Oct[obe]r 1st 1845

Dear Sir, I duly received your Letter of the 9th Ult[im]o and was pleased to find that you approved of the course persued by the Committee.

Herewith I beg leave to hand you the questions sent by Mr. [Secretary of the Treasury Robert J.] Walker; he has left out No. 22 in our list & added 27 & 28.

We received them through the Collector [William J. Grayson], with a request that answers would be handed in by the 1st Prox[im]o.

The Committee respectfully solicit your aid in answering them. With great Respect Y[ou]r Ob[edien]t Ser[van]t, M.C. Mordecai.

ALS with printed En in ScCleA. NOTE: This letter was addressed to Calhoun in Pendleton and was forwarded to Faunsdale, Marengo County, Ala. See below Mordecai's letter to Calhoun on 10/7.

To "Col." J[AMES] ED[WARD] COLHOUN, [Abbeville District, S.C.]

Fort Hill, 2d Oct[obe]r 1845

My dear James, We start for Alabama tomorrow, & ["are sorry" *canceled and* "regret" *interlined*] you could not make us a visit before we set out. Your sister's [Floride Colhoun Calhoun's] health is quite restored, & I hope your's [sic] is much better. I expect to return about the mid[d]le of Nov[embe]r.

James [Edward Calhoun] & William [Lowndes Calhoun] go down with the intention of going to the Erskine College, at Due West Corner. I have had good accounts of it; & have selected it, because it is situated ["situation" canceled], where there will be nothing to divert their attention from study, & where their morals will be safe. One or two years there will do much, I hope to give them studious habits, and also to prepare them well to finish off in some other institution, with greater literary & scientifick advantages.

They are both talented, & only need application to make good scholars. They are disinclined, I find, to latin & Greek, which I regret, so much so, that it would be, in a great measure, a loss of time to continue them at it, unless there should ["be" interlined] a change of inclination; & I have accordingly written to Mr. Pressley [sic; Ebenezer Erskine Pressly], the President of the institution, ["not" interlined] to force them to their study, unless he should find them more inclined to their study, than I fear he would, at least until I could see & converse with him after my return from Alabama. I wish you would speak to them, as to the importance of their study. Yours affectionately, J.C. Calhoun.

[P.S.] The term at Erskine commences the 1st Nov[embe]r, & I hope you will see that they leave in time to be there two, or three days in advance, to obtain boarding, & make their arrangement before it commences.

Your Sister, John [C. Calhoun, Jr.,] & [Martha] Cornelia [Calhoun] join their love to you. J.C.C.

ALS in ScCleA.

F[RANKLIN] H. ELMORE to [Armistead] Burt, [Abbeville District, S.C.]

Limestone Springs [S.C.,] Oct[obe]r 2 1845

My Dear Burt, I was away when yours of the 18th ult. was rec[eive]d & I lost the mail yesterday, the only one since my return. Having an opportunity to send this to Columbia to be mailed, I embrace it to reply.

I am heartily glad to hear from you that Judge [Daniel E.] Huger has written to Mr. Calhoun proposing to resign if he will go to the Senate—and I agree with you most fully that Mr. Calhoun ought to accede to the proposition. It seems to me that every thing calls him to Washington. The manner he has been treated will give him immense power for good. No man can so effectually curb & rein in this administration & save them, if they are to be saved, from falling into [Thomas H.] Benton[']s hands; or if they surrender to him, can so effectually give the rally to the country. I fear the worst while I will still hope until hope is folly.

We are in the utmost danger of all sort of confusion at home. Next winter will be as fruitful of discordant views & schemes of politics, as last was if we are not saved by the Pilot—All confide in Mr. Calhoun, or will be controlled by his views. He can nowhere give them so well as at Washington & in the Senate.

My present opinion as to his course is this—He should answer Judge Huger & say "I will accede to your proposition, but do not resign now—wait till the beginning of the Session of the Legislature or about that time." If [George] McDuffie can[']t go, then the Judge may still hold on or resign as may be advisable or he wish. This will save the appearance of calculating on McDuffie[']s ability. I have feared that he could not go—but I have heard he was resolved if possible to do it.

Mr. Calhoun should come through Columbia during the Session, or indicate clearly what should be done there this winter. There will be rash moves I fear. It seems to me that we never needed caution more, to maintain firmly our principles & keep up to the proper point & yet to avoid taking ground on which we shall not be able to stand. If for instance we drop below the proper point, our own spirit is lost, & the Tariffites & the administration will bear the more boldly against us—and if we go beyond, it may be construed into bullying & vaporing ["& we lose friends & sympathy" *interlined*]— or if again ["if" *canceled*] *we assume* that the administration & Party intend to prove false & betray us ["& act on this presumption" *interlined*] we shall lose a position of advantage, for it will be charged (& many will believe it), that we never were sincere in our association with them & have *always* intended to make war—or, at the very best, that since Mr. Calhoun was left out of the Cabinet, it has been our intention to break & make war. It seems to me extremely difficult to fix upon our line of action; & now, more than ever since I have had a share in politics, do I feel the absolute necessity of the Master Mind to work out & define our line of movement. All the weight he has with his friends will be required to keep *us united*. He *only* can do

197

it—and he must, at once, make up his mind, & either set about putting the *field in order*, or give up the whole matter.

If possible see & confer freely with Mr. Calhoun—fix on the course that should be taken—and do not lose time in putting your & his friends in possession of it. If he hesitates we are in danger I tell you of confusion. If he decides & sets his course, & the course the State sh[oul]d take, be known early, all will go well.

Now as to himself I have said what I think—as to us, the rank & file—the State. What is the Legislature to be at next winter? Something must be done, by the Master or the Boys. There will be plenty of moves—Resolutions &c. &c. Could not Mr. Calhoun & yourself put in form some that should go. [William F.] DeSaussure is chairman of [the Committee on] Fed[eral] Rel[atio]ns in the House [of Representatives]. I forget who is in the Senate. We could get them to DeSaussure very easily so as ["not" *interlined*] to commit him—and a letter from Mr. [Calhoun?] to [Ker] Boyce w[oul]d keep him up & he will be *none* the *worse* of a *little* touching from *that* quarter.

It seems to me we have not yet played out our part with this administration. We can not say they have failed to fulfil their pledges, until their policy is developed next Congress: Would we not be awkwardly situated if we were to predicate any movements on the assumption of their faithlessness, before we have the act to point to? As yet we have only such things to justify us, as, however strong to us, would be to the masses, mere speculations. We will have to wait the developement of their course & so hold ourselves if possible, as to lose nothing while standing still. Give them a fair trial & act as they act—faithful & true if they are so—if not be prepared to expose them at every step & to act afterwards as the occasion requires—the next Session will show all.

For this it seems to me no man living is capable of guiding us unitedly but Mr. Calhoun—and if any thing could add to his power in guiding us & controlling others in this great struggle, it would be something of this sort. On the first proper occasion after taking his seat, if he were to declare that he put aside all considerations of self— he threw up all ideas of office & should devote himself & all his powers to the adjustment of this great question, it would arm him with immense moral power. I should look on his exclusion from the Presidency as a great public calamity—but I have no idea that *his taking* this course would have that tendency—on the contrary that the effect of such a course would be to render him more popular, & to make his friends more resolute & able to urge his claims. He would be no candidate, but they would run him only with the more zeal.

I have written rapidly offhand my thoughts to you & you must do as you think best. I am so engrossed here I have no time for any thing but work. My respects to Mrs. [Martha Calhoun] B[urt]. Yours truly, F.H. Elmore.

P.S.   Oct. 3, '45
I have time this morning for a word or two. I can't write to Mr. Calhoun perhaps for some time. If you think it [at] all advisable the letter I write you is intirely at your disposal to be shown to him or sent to him. He should be doing something to let us have light. All the questions of the day with which his name & services are associated, the acts of the last administration & all are to be up in the next Congress & he should be there. Y[our]s truly, F.H.E.

ALS in ScCleA. NOTE: An AEU by Calhoun reads "Mr. Elmore," indicating that Calhoun received this letter.

P[ATRICK] CALHOUN to Andrew P[ickens] Calhoun, Faunsdale Post Office, Marengo County, Ala.

New-Orleans La., Oct. 3d 1845
Dear Brother, I leave tomorrow evening for the Bay of Aransas in the Steam-Ship Alabama and shall most p[r]obably be absent from this city for three or four weeks. The Alabama ["goes" *interlined*] over quite full—she carries some five hundred additional Troops—among which will be nearly fifty officers. Should there be any active service I shall of course remain—but if not return and continue with Gen[era]l [Edmund P.] Gaines. From appearances and from what authentic information has been received the likelihood of any serious difficulty with Mexico, seems to be less and less probable every day. I did not determine to visit Corpus Christi so soon until a day or two since when being in conversation with Gen[era]l Gaines I accidentally mentioned that I had some curiosity to see so many of our Troops together. He said to me that I had better take advantage of the opportunity which offered—as, if I put it off until next month, he might not be able to spare me for so long a time.

I received by Barnard [E.] Bee, who is on his way to Texas, a letter from Father, in which he mentions that Mother and himself would leave home about the first of this month on a visit to Sister Margaret [Green Calhoun] and yourself. Barnard also mentions

199

that John [C. Calhoun, Jr.] intends spending the winter in New-Orleans—for the purpose of continuing the study of medicine. In some respects the idea is a good one. A fine Medical-College has in the last few years been established in this city, which in some respects has great advantages over any other in the Union. There are however objections to New-Orleans in other respects. It is one of the most, if not the most expensive city in the country, there are too more inducements to dissipation than in any other city. John cannot however do better than try it.

It is at present very doubtful at what period I shall get married—indeed I have reason to doubt if I shall ever be married to Miss [Kate] Wilkins. Unless some explanation is made by her in reference to some circumstances which have passed, I certainly shall not go to Pittsburg.

As Father comes so far as Mobile I might as well come to New-Orleans. Many person[s] are anxious that he should visit this city—And I shall on my return visit Alabama as much to induce Father to come here as anything else. The fact is he has never mixed half enough with the people—and owes it to himself to visit the valley of the Mississippi.

I have not time to say anything more. My love to all. Your affectionate brother, P. Calhoun.

P.S. Mr. Carter—or rather his House—negotiated the draft on the House of Allen and Haden which you sent me. P. Calhoun.

ALS in ScU-SC, John C. Calhoun Papers.

From EDWARD DIXON

Warrenton [Va.], October 3rd 1845

My Dear Sir, I send you a number of the Warrenton Democratic paper containing some remarks which I have appended to a paragraph prepared by Mr. [John S.?] Barbour expressing a wish on the part of your Virginia friends for your return to the Senate. This is anxiously desired for your own sake as well as for the advancement of the important interest alluded to in the editorial. After your long and valuable service in the councils of the country, it is natural enough that you should want some rest, but we think that while it is important for the South that you should be in the Senate at this critical period, your presence there is essential in another point of view.

Mr. [Thomas H.] Benton, with his power of commanding popular attention, may endeavor by insiduous [*sic*] attacks to arouse sectional prejudices against you, and thus seek to weaken your claims with the Democratic party. Your presence in the Senate would render his malice impotent, and give consistency and organization to your party. We think that you ought at least to be there during the next two sessions. You know best what course to pursue, and will pardon me for the liberty I have taken. In conclusion, I beg leave to renew the assurances of my very sincere regard, and to say that although you are in retirement, I have not ceased to remember you with gratitude and affection. Edward Dixon.

P.S. Major [Robert?] Wallace desires me to tender to you his best respects. E.D.

ALS in ScCleA. NOTE: This letter was forwarded from Pendleton to Alabama.

From WILLIAM AIKEN, [Governor of S.C.]

Charleston, Oct. 4th 1845

Dear Sir, At a meeting of Citizens held this day at the City Hall— the following resolution—among other's—was passed.

Resolved that the Governor of the State be particularly requested to nominate Two Delegates for the State at large to represent her interests on the leading questions which are to form the subjects of deliberation and action at the Memphis Convention.

Under the above resolution—I take the liberty to ask you—to accept of the appointment of one of the Delegates, to the proposed Convention. With the highest consideration and respect, William Aiken.

ALS in ScCleA. NOTE: This letter was addressed to Calhoun at Pendleton and was forwarded from there to Faunsdale, Marengo County, Ala., on 10/9. The Charleston *Mercury* and the Charleston *Courier* of October 6, 1845, both contain accounts of the meeting referred to. James Gadsden announced the convention to be held in Memphis on November 12 for the promotion of internal improvements. Resolutions were passed asserting Charleston's approval of the goals of the convention, establishing a committee of correspondence, recommending district meetings throughout the State for the selection of delegates, and requesting Governor Aiken to appoint two delegates-at-large. (Calhoun and Franklin H. Elmore were so appointed.)

To R[OBERT] BEALE, [Washington]

Aquila P[ost] O[ffice] Georgia, 4th Oct[obe]r 1845
My dear Sir, I am thus far on my way on a visit to my son [Andrew Pickens Calhoun] in Alabama, accompanied by Mrs. [Floride Colhoun] Calhoun & one of my sons [John C. Calhoun, Jr.]; and hasten to answer your letter [of 9/20], which I received on the road yesterday by a messenger who I dispatched by the Post office at our Village [of Pendleton], with directions to follow after me until he overtook me.

I regret, I did not receive your letter sooner. I waited a long time to hear from you, before I decided to take a cutting machine & a cobb grinder, made in a distant part of the State. The latter I ordered, shortly after I received your first letter [of 8/31], in which you stated, that not much improvement had been made in that discription of Machinery of late, & the former not until the day before I left home, waiting to hear from you. They are both said to be well calculated for the purpose, but cost a good deal more than the price you ["gave" *canceled*] state. I have concluded for the present to dispense with a thresher. Indeed it would not be worth while for Mr. [F.] Grieb to come so far to put ["up" *interlined*] one; and I am in hopes, that I can fix my present one, which is excellent, with gear so as to enable me to move it from field to field. It now goes by water.

For your trouble in the business, I am much obliged to you.

It will give me much pleasure to afford you all the aid I can to obtain the place you desire, and will write as you desire. Yours truly, J.C. Calhoun.

ALS in PHi, Society Collection.

From J[OHN] S. BARBOUR

Catalpa [Culpeper County, Va.] Octo[ber] 5th 1845
My Dear Sir. I rec[eive]d yours of the 12th Sep[tembe]r about a fortnight since, when I was confined to my bed with a severe attack, which prostrated me for ten days. Three days since I was from my bed for the first time.

The night I rec[eive]d your letter I wrote hastily to [William F. Ritchie and Thomas Ritchie, Jr.,] the Editors of the Enquirer &

to Mr. [James A.] Seddon. The Enq[uire]r briefly & strongly as you will have seen alluded to the expectation of your return to the Senate. My daughter [Sally Barbour] wrote a communication for the Fredericksburg Recorder over the signature of John Taylor of Caroline, which was doubtless sent you, & the Editor of that paper (by request) seconded very earnestly, the appeal to you. The communication has one marked defect in its mat[t]er[?], which I w[oul]d have corrected had it struck me. At my instance my youngest son [Edwin Barbour] wrote ["by my dictation" *interlined*] a brief paragraph for the Warrenton Flag of '98 & sent it that night to Major Wallace, to have it inserted editorially in the next morning[']s paper. It did not reach Major Wallace in time for *that* paper (of the next morning) & before the following weekly paper issued Gen[era]l Wallace the real Editor returned from the Military Institute at Lexington Va. & added as you will see. I send you the paper: And ["the" *interlined*] paragraph sent over ["from here" *interlined*] is the first in it—& marked within x marks.

I would have sent you the communication from Fred[ericksbur]g as soon as the paper arrived, but I was too ill to do so, and now the paper is mislaid. The printer was requested to send you a paper.

The publick voice is almost unanimous for your return so far as I can learn. My Eldest son [John S. Barbour, Jr.] returned from Orange Supr[eme] Court last night where he has been some days. He saw some of your friends there & he reports but one feeling, & that strongly for it. If you are there ["(in the Senate)" *interlined*] we shall succeed. *Not otherwise.* I think [Henry] Clay will be there too. His drunken *pun*, when stepping on board the Steam Boat *"The Senate,"* shews the drift of of [*sic*] his [*one word canceled and* "thoughts," *interlined*] in the unguarded expression of a wayward moment.

If the Tariff is to be adjusted, this crowning honour should be yours. *The responsibility too shou[l]d be yours.* Rashness will not mingle its deeds with the deliberation & its result; & no one can so well harmonise by fair & legitimate concession, this distracting subject as you. By being present you will command the administration, instead of having your popularity the sport of its freaks[?]. If Destiny itself were revealing to you the good fortune of the *antient* Goddess *"Opportunity,"* it cou'd not have more happily hit the appointed hour. (I believe the feigned Goddess *"Opportunity"* was painted with but one lock of hair, & that in front, standing on a wheel in perpetual rotation, & offering that lock of hair but once. J.S.B.)

Your position will command the cause you sustain, & subject others to its power. The difficulty will be in the vacancy to be created at home. Judge [Daniel E.] Huger will hug the ruling passion strong in death & refuse to abandon his seat. With [George] McDuffie there are considerations both of delicacy & tenderness, that cluster over your relations with him. Made now more sensitive from the weakness & decay that environ him. I will write Mr. [Isaac E.] Holmes [Representative from S.C.] before I go to rest from the labour that now engages me. He had last Feb[ruar]y no hope of any favourable action by this adm[inistratio]n. The sombre hue of his thoughts, were akin to the valicinations[?] that sometimes cast their shade over the Charleston Mercury. Gen[era]l [George] Washington[']s remark to [Henry] Knox at crossing the Delaware, has ["as" *interlined*] much of the truth which belongs to the natural phenomenon he referred to, as of the energy which *despair* inspires, & which is often the great instrument of Conquest. "The darkest hour of the night is just before the break[?] of day." With kind Respects to Mrs. [Floride Colhoun] C[alhoun] & all around you, I am Sincerely y[ou]r friend, J.S. Barbour.

[P.S.] I send the Warrenton Flag, and when I can find the Recorder I will send that too. The manuscript of Sally I send you so you will see *in substance*, what it is, if the paper fails to come to you.

[P.P.S.] I found "the Recorder" & do not send the manuscript (original) which ["Sally had written" *canceled*] my daughter wrote for it. You have it in the Recorder, & the strong editorial preface. J.S.B.

ALS in ScCleA.

From Lewis S. Coryell

Washington, 6th Oct. [18]45

My Dear Sir, I directed my son [Ingham Coryell] who lives in N[ew] York to send you a [William Lyon] M[a]ckenzie book but for fear he may not succeed I have procured one & now send it by this day[']s mail, & will try and get it franked. The Edition has run out; besides there is injunctions that prevents the open sale in N[ew] York and they now sell for from One to $5 a piece. There will however be a new Eddition with new *matter*.

I think the Adm[ini]s[tration] is decided to carry out Southern views as to Tariff altho' [James] Buchanan is feebly opposed, & report says he will go on the Bench & [Attorney General John Y.] Mason [will be put] in his place. I sincerely hope you will not come to [the] Senate, but next year make a Tour through the middle & Eastern States & become familiarly known &C &C for our next nomination will be by acclamation. I am here for a day or two & as yet have seen nobody, but will. Y[ou]r fr[ien]d, Lewis S. Coryell.

ALS in ScCleA.

From JAMES GADSDEN

Charleston, Oct[obe]r 6, [18]45

My Dear Sir, You will see from the Charleston papers what we did on Saturday [10/4]. The meeting was well attended and the enthusiasm of 1836 began again to boil. Now that our Western friends are in motion we must keep up the steam. The currants [*sic*] were never more in favor of our Long conceived views of a Rail Road Connection with the West than at present. It is our fault if we do not consummate the Great Work.

The Governor [William Aiken] has sent you the nomination as Delegate to represent the State [in the forthcoming Memphis convention]. [Franklin H.] Elmore is associated with you. You must and ought to attend. I look to this meeting as calculated to begin to bind the bonds of union between the South & West and your presence must have a powerful influence.

I hope you will not only attend but take part in the debates and particularly on the Leading questions of Improvement of Western waters & connection by Rail Roads to the Atlantic. By the by[e] I am on the Committee to report on the latter subject & really am so overwhelmed by details in my office that I have little time either to collect facts, or to embody ideas. Still as the labouring oar is put on me I will endeavor to use it to the best advantage through the aid of Friends. Now can you throw together your Ideas of the benefits of the Connection in a political[,] social & commercial point of view. I mean the speculative & enlarged views. The details as to commerce I must put into the hands of a Commercial man & I shall get one of our Medical faculty to give me a Report on the health of our City compared with other Atlantic & European Ports. Yours truly, James Gadsden.

[P.S.] The Committee on the Tariff (the Secr[etary]'[s] Questions have been sent you) are of the impression that our Cause may be assisted by the Memphis Convention. If we are present we will seize the occasion of turning the currents into our freer channels of Free Trade. [Moses C.] Mordecai wrote you on the Warehouse system which he wishes you to examine into on your comments on the other questions. The Ware House system as I comprehend it is to give greater facilities to trade & Traders without taxing it beyond the duty on consumption. Now what [*sic*] of the difficulties with Charleston is the want of a sufficient supply of Commodities to make up an assorted Cargo. Thus all our Shipments are in mass of but one articl[e]—Rice or cotton & if either should be depressed on the Foreign Market when the Vessel enter[?] a loss by the voyage is encurred. In Boston[,] N.Y. & elsewhere, Cargoes are assorted—Yankey notions as expressive of the idea & if one article fails another makes the loss up, so that in the aggregate Few vessels sail from there [*sic*] Ports which do not make a safe return. It does seem to me if the ware house system in the general is favourable to active Trade it must assist Charleston, as well as elsewhere. It will be fault of our Enterprising merchants if they do not take or avail themselves of its benefit. Yours, Jas. Gadsden.

ALS in ScCleA.

From P. J. SULLIVAN

Washington City, Oct. 6th 1845

Dear Sir, The motives which induce me to brake in on your retirement at this eventful crisis, are various and complicated. The unyealding remonstrance which I made, against your leaving the State Department, is well known to your friend, Mr. Crawlé [*sic*; Richard K. Crallé]: And is the only proof, *til further in my power*, of my devoted attachment to, and desire to promote the interests of *"the firm* ["friend" *interlined*] *& supporter*," of States rights and free trade. Imagine not, sir, that I now call your attention to *that fact*, with the imbecile idea of biasing you in my favor—I have none to ask.

From a boy I have been taught to study your political course, have always been an admirer of your incorruptable integrity, and of your unweavering, pure republican, democracy. In you, have I perceived, that vast superiority of mind, that sublimity of right reasoning and justness of ideas; which you have acquired, not by studying the speculative theories of visionary abstractionists, but, in contemplating the wise & wholesome laws of the genius of liberty—the spirit as well as the letter of democracy. Democracy and liberty are synonymous: their votaries, will yet raise, an imperishable monument, to the patriotism, morality and unrivaled talents of the "*Cincinnatus*" of young America: who, when intriguing, unprincipled ["political demagogues" *interlined*] are overwhelmed, in the whirlpool of, the disaffection of a "*dis[c]erning people*"; will stand forth as the land mark of his countries genius; the democratic party.

I honor the head that conceived—the hand that executed and the patriot that *superintended*, with success, the true move of rean[n]exing the lone Strar of Texas to the bright constel[l]ation, composing our Heaven born Union; whose brilliancy are attracting the admiration & esteem of the world—and in fifty years hence, I should not at all be surprised if the spirit of liberty were to extend to the extremities of the earth, and varied nations lie down and repose beneath its shade. The *idea* is prophetic, and what is prophecy, but a narrative preceeding the fact.

The young men of the country are banding together, under the propitious cognomen of "Texas," or "Young democracy." All eyes are turned towards you; some with the fond hope, others with fear, of your becoming the leader of "*that irresistable party*" in 1848. The time is not far distant, when flattery and falsehood can no longer be ["misled" *canceled*] of use, and "youth" can no longer be "misled." When meetings will be called, associations & clubs formed—the political ball, of the Texas or young democracy, set in motion, and wo[e] be to those shall attempt to stop it! !

My intimate acquaintance with President [James K.] Polk, and with all, but two, (C[ave] Johnson & G[eorge] Bancroft,) of his Cabinet, has given me an opportunity of forming a pretty correct estimate of their present, as well as future course of policy. To deep observers, the "*picture*" presents dim but prophetic shadows. To a mind so well capable of conceiving as yours, it must naturally appear evidently ["just," *interlined*] that, in the "*language of Gov.* [William L.] *Marcy*," to the "*victors belong the spoils.*"

We have yet to learn, whether the Gov. will carry out *those* principles for which ["he" *interlined*] has always contended, or not. Is it a true principle, founded in the nature of things, to take to your confidence and support, your bitter and reviling enemies and cast off those faithful friend[s], who spent their time and means for the promotion ["of principles" *interlined*] & men, to perish & decay? I forbear, at present, to pursue any further the train of *"foreboarding"* that forces itself upon me.

Let us, in the language of a friend, turn from the blight and ruin of this wintry day, to the fond anticipation of a happier period: when bleeding democracy will stand erect, with a bold, independend and *just* leader. Then we will ask but what is right, and will not submit to what is wrong.

I was recommended to the Secretary of State [James Buchanan] and to the President, for an appointment. They *satisfied* me with flattery and fine promises only. How the Missouri delegation, several of the leading members of the south and west, by whom I have been recom[mende]d will reconcile this as well as *similar* matters, I am at a loss to conjecture.

I ask your forgi[ve]ness for having, *thus*, trespassed on your attention. I remain, dear Sir, most assuredly your *friend*, P.J. Sullivan of Missouri.

ALS in ScCleA.

From JAMES GADSDEN

Charleston S.C., Oct[obe]r 7[t]h 1845

My Dear Sir, From your last letter to me I did not anticipate so early a departure on your part to Alabama. The documents therefore in relation to our Public meeting in Charleston [on 10/4] may not be forwarded. I therefore enclose you a duplicate.

The Governor [William Aiken] has written to you to Pendleton and sent you an appointment, as State Delegate to the Convention at Memphis. You must not fail of being there. I have labored hard to get up what we have done and I will find it very difficult myself to attend. Still I will make every possible sacrifice if I am seconded by those who have as deep an interest as myself in the subjects which will engage the attention of the Convention: but who can render more service than myself. I have said you will attend and I will therefore take no denial. The Labor of preparing a Report on the Rail Road has been devolved on me and I almost regret having promised to endeavor to prepare one.

Will you give me your views directly, by mail on the enlarged consequences socially, commercially & politically of such a Connection[?] I will prepare the details, collect the facts but the embodiment of thought I would wish to have from you. In haste Yours truly, James Gadsden.

[P.S.] You may rest assured that your presence at Memphis will do more to forward all the Great interests & questions we have so long been laboring on than your seat in the Senate. It will bring bring [*sic*] you in closer alliance with the People—with the Great Body of Western men, without which communion we can never have a triumph of our principles.

The Reform can only come from the People. Hitherto they have been in the hands of Politicians moulded at Conventions to suit their designs. We must reach them with the Truth if we expect or desire a triumph.

ALS in ScCleA.

From M[OSES] C. MORDECAI

Charleston, Oct. 7, 1845

Dear Sir, I had the honor of addressing you on the 1st inst. Enclosing the Questions received from the Secretary [of the Treasury, Robert J. Walker], and directed my letter to Pendleton. I notice by the morning papers, that you had left on a Visit to your Son [Andrew Pickens Calhoun] in Alabama. I fear my letter may not reach you, and as our Committee depend greatly upon your aid, and Entirely as relates to the Questions propounded by yourself, I take this opportunity to forward you another Copy and remain with Great Respect Your Ob[edient] S[ervant], M.C. Mordecai.

[Enclosure]

[Circular letter] from the Charleston Chamber of Commerce

Charleston, S.C., 1st October, 1845

THE QUESTIONS annexed having been received from the Treasury Department, through the Collector of this Port [William J. Grayson], in order to obtain information on the subject of the Tariff, the Chamber has to request your aid in answering such of the Questions as relate to your own particular business, or pursuit; and the Chamber would further ask any other information, that you may be enabled to furnish in connection with the Tariff, and its bearing upon the interests of this State. Your answer is requested by the 20th instant, if possible. M.C. Mordecai, F[ranklin] H. Elmore, H[enry] W. Conner, Cha[rle]s Edmondston, Henry Gourdin, Tho[ma]s J. Roger, James Gadsden, A. McDowall, *Committee*.

ALS with printed Ens in ScCleA. NOTE: The enclosed list of Walker's interrogatories, headed "Questions Propounded by the Secretary of the Treasury," differs in a few questions from those sent by the Committee to Walker on 8/29. (See Mordecai's letter of 9/2 to Calhoun.) Walker's questions begin with, "What agricultural products are raised in your State, and which, if any, of the staples of Cotton, Rice, or Tobacco?" To the fourteenth interrogatory concerning the operation of manufacturing establishments, Walker added, "Are the present duties necessary to keep them in operation with profit; if not, what amount, if any, would be required to give a profit equal in amount to the average profit of growing the great staples of the State, for the last three years, or the ten preceding?" Walker omitted from his list the question "What would be the effect in your State of a duty upon Coffee & Tea?" The final two questions were added by Walker and read: "27th. What quantity of Wool is raised in your State, what is its price per pound since the Tariff of 1842, and what its price per pound for the ten years preceding? 28th. What mines are worked in your State, what quantity of metal or mineral has been produced, what has been the price since the Tariff of 1842, and for the ten years preceding?" Enclosed with Mordecai's letter of 10/1 to Calhoun was a different printing of Walker's questions.

From JOHN TYLER

Sherwood Forest
Charles City County Va., October 7, 1845

My Dear Sir: Your esteemed favor of the 30 August in consequence of my absence from home did not reach me until last Saturday. I have read Dr. [José M.] Caminero's letter which is herewith return'd, and fully concur with you in the policy of recognizing the independence of the Dominican Republic should Mr. [John] Hogan's report satisfactorily establish the fact of its perfect ability to maintain itself against the Haytian govt. and people. The experiment which the blacks have made of governing themselves has resulted in bloodshed and anarchy—and the most fertile Island in the world is almost converted into a waste. Apart from the considerations adverted to by Dr. Caminero, this would constitute with me a sufficient reason for desiring to see the Dominican Republic free and independent. But my D[ea]r Sir I do not feel myself warranted as the Doctor would seem to desire, in urging upon Mr. [James K.] Polk the adoption of any particular policy. I must content myself with the reflection that we have through the labors of Mr. Hogan plac[e]d him in possession of all necessary information on the subject. To volunteer to him an opinion might be considered as going too far. The settlement of the Texas question fills me, I declare to you, with a pleasure greater than

I can express—not so much from the fact that the finishing hand was put to it by my administration, as from the consequences, incalculably great, which are to flow from it. Nor can I ever forget the important aid which you afforded me in all that related to it after your accession to my Cabinet. I call[e]d you from a retirement which it pain[e]d you to leave to assist me properly to adjust the important matters which then occupied me, and in the spirit of a true and lofty patriotism you answered the call satisfactorily, and to say nothing of other matters the country will long have cause to rejoice in the great measure which our conjoint labours assisted by those of able and patriotic associates enabled us to consummate. I never doubted the wisdom of the prompt decision in favour of the House resolution. A mere feeling of courtesy to my successor could alone cause a moment's hesitation and that was easily gotten over. The doubt arising from a new organization of the Cabinet and a knowledge of the extreme solicitude of the British govt., plainly indicated the policy of leaving nothing undone that could be done.

I left the govt. with but one wish remaining unfulfilled, and that related to the Oregon Question. I wish[e]d you to terminate that negociation. I entered upon it with reluctance ["however"(?) *canceled*] believing that under the ["convention of" *interlined*] joint occupation we stood on the most favorable footing. Our population was already finding its way to the shores of the Pacific, and a few years would see an American Settlement on the Columbia sufficiently strong to defend itself and to protect the rights of the U. States to the territory. L[or]d Aberdeen however express[e]d in some despatch a regret that that matter remained open, and the Treaty of Washington was assail[e]d by Mr. [Thomas H.] Benton and others upon that ground and finally a clamour was raised in relation to the subject throughout the country, which was loudest in the west, and nothing seem[e]d to remain but that negotiation should be attempted. With Prudence and fortitude on the part of the administration my hope is that it may result in an amicable termination—but it requires firmness to do what is right on the part of those in power. What their views may be concerning it, I have no means of ascertaining. With England a mere point of honor is involv'd which she will go ["any lengths" *canceled*] to war upon if urg[e]d to that extremity, but peace with us is so important to her, that she will be ready to make concessions in order to secure it. If however it be the intention of Mr. Polk to make no concessions, he should without delay demand of Mexico an explanation of her ultimate intentions, while he procrastinates the negociation with Great Britain. But my hope is that wise councils will prevail, and that an actual collision with Great Britain will be avoided.

I give my attention but little to public affairs and am devoting myself to the cultivation of my farm. The turmoil through which I have pass[e]d serves only the more to render acceptable my present repose. Should you ever pass near my residence it would give me the truest pleasure to receive you within my doors.

Mrs. [Julia Gardiner] Tyler desires to be remember[e]d to Mrs. [Floride Colhoun] Calhoun to whom present my best respects, and for yourself accept sincere assurances of my regard. John Tyler.

ALS in ScCleA; slightly variant PC in Jameson, ed., *Correspondence*, pp. 1058–1060. NOTE: An AEU by Calhoun reads: "Ex-Pres[iden]t Tyler returning the ["enclosing" *canceled*] letter of Dr. Caminero."

From W[ILLIAM] A. ELMORE

New Orleans, Oct. 8th 1845

Dear Sir, Accompanying this letter, you will find, the "Jeffersonian Republican" published in this city, containing an editorial in reference to the propriety and necessity, of your once more re-entering the Senate of the United States, and upon the subject of the Tariff, to which I beg to invite, your serious attention. With the view expressed in that article, I concur: and such are the views of your friends here generally—they all think that your appropriate place, at this moment and under present circumstances, is the Senate of the U.S.

Since, the retirement, of Mr. [Levi] Woodbury [as Senator from N.H.], we have become doubly anxious upon the subject. We feel that the States' rights' branch of the party, has no such representative in the Senate, as the crisis demands. Our principles are truth, and we should have some one there to enforce their truth; and you are *now* looked to, as the only person in any quarter of the Union, that we think can do justice to them. We very much fear that Mr. [Thomas H.] Benton is to have the sway; and if so, we know very well, what to expect from his tender mercies—our principles will be sacrificed upon the altar of his vindictiveness, and you will be one of the first victims, that will be offered up to glut his vengeance.

I look at the question, in two aspects. First as to the service you can render the country in the reduction of the Tariff to the revenue standard—and secondly in reference to the influence, it will have upon your prospects for the Presidency in 1848.

There is a deep distrust existing in the minds of the people of ["the" *interlined*] South, as to the sincerity of the administration in its' [*sic*] efforts to reduce the Tariff to the revenue principle. If this opinion, is well founded, it is all important, that we should have such friends in the Senate, as will be able, by the weight of their influence and talents, to oppose, resist, and expose, such departure, from the true principles of the party, and in open violation of solemn pledges; and rally the country in opposition to it. If on the contrary, the administration is sincere, which I will not permit myself at this time to doubt, your services in the Senate, will be indispensable to the administration, in carrying out it's [*sic*] views. I look with great suspicion, upon the course that Benton & his followers intend pursuing— for if the administration should bona fide, attempt to bring down the Tariff as it ought to do, and as it is pledged to do, then I look out for a storm, from him, & his suite; and in that case, the administration will require all the assistance, that can be had, to enable it to withstand the shock of their opposition. And this brings me, to the consideration of the question—how will it affect your position in reference to the Presidency in 1848.

The Tariff is now, the only vexed question, between the two parties. Consequently, that party must triumph or fail, as that question is strong or weak. It is very certain, that if we succeed in reducing the Tariff, it will be after one of the hardest and fiercest ["battles" *canceled*] political battles, that ever was fought in the Halls of Congress: and if success crowns our efforts, that candidate for the Presidency in '48, who most largely participated in achieving that victory, will be to a certainty, most prominent. But, whether, this be so, or not, your success depends upon the triumph of your principles. With you and your friends, there can be no concealment, no deception, no double dealing, no equivocations. Who then, so fit and proper as yourself to assist in securing and carrying out these principles? It is evident, to my mind, that ["the war" *interlined*] against you is to be continued—that every prejudice, that malignity can excite, and hostility arouse will be resorted to, to break ["down" *interlined*] you and your friends. Upon the whole, therefore, I think, you have more to lose in retirement, than in public life, and my best judgment induces me, to express the hope, that you will once more enter the Halls of Congress.

The above suggestions, are but the outline of the reasons, that have brought conviction to my mind; and are submitted to you with proper diffidence and in the utmost frankness—without of course any knowledge of your personal wishes upon the subject, for all which,

213

excuse the liberty, I have taken; and refer it to the deep interest, I feel in the establishment of our common principles, and your election to that only other earthly station, that ["can" *interlined*] reflect, any credit, upon you.

I received some time since, a letter, from [Dixon H.] Lewis, suggesting the grounds, your friends, should take in reference to the election in '48. With the views you express to Lewis, I assent; and think, that we must run you as an independent candidate, and not trust to caucus or convention. I find, that such is the opinion of your friends ["here" *interlined*], several of whom, I have consulted upon the subject. Without intimating, that it was the opinion of any one, but, myself, I approached Col. [John F.H.] Claiborne (Editor of the Jeffersonian Republican) upon the subject; and expressed to him my views, to all which he assented, and avowed his readiness to sustain your election, in spite and in opposition to a convention candidate; and re-iterated what he had often told me before, that you were his first and only choice, for the Presidency in 1848. Without having any reason to doubt his sincerity, in the declaration of these opinions, we have not the fullest confidence in the stability of his views, or the independence of his position. But, I doubt, not, you know him well, as he was in Congress several years, from the State of Mississippi.

I think, your position in Louisiana, is highly favorable, and that you are gaining strength, every day. Our candidate for Governor, Judge [Isaac] Johnson, tho' he does not understand the Tariff system *perfectly well*—is one of your most enthusiastic admirers and friends. There can be, no doubt, about your being stronger for the Presidency with us, by far, than any other man—whether we shall be able to cast the vote of the State, in your favor, in case, there is a regularly nominated Democratic candidate, I cannot at this time venture to express an opinion.

When we separated in Washington, you intimated, a possibility, that you might extend the visit you contemplated making to Alabama this fall, to this city. I have spoken of this fact, to some of our friends, and they express themselves, delighted at the prospect of seeing you and making your acquaintance. I think, the visit, would be mater[i]ally agreeable. You would see this great Metropolis of the South west, in the midst of the business season and you could, if you were so disposed, go without inconvenience into the interior, upon one of the sugar estates, and witness the grinding of the cane, which I am told is exceedingly interesting.

If not too much pressed for time, it would afford me, great pleasure to hear from you.

I have the pleasure of subscribing ["myself" *interlined*] your sincere friend and ob[e]d[ien]t Serv[an]t, W.A. Elmore.

ALS in ScCleA.

From S[AMPSON] H. BUTLER

Florida Madison Co[unty,] October 9, 1845

Dear Sir, I have scarcely any thing, to reply to your letter of the 15th ultimo, but to thank you for the attention, given to my own letter. I cannot however permit this occasion to pass without correcting, an erroneous impression under which you lie, touching myself. I never was a [William Henry] Harrison man, and I supposed my course in Congress [from South Carolina], for nearly four years, under your observation, would have disabused your mind of any such impression. I have been with you on all Public measures, for the last twelve years, except for a few months, last year. My indignation at the shuffling of the last Baltimore convention in reference to yourself, did cause me, for a few months to say, I would take [Henry] Clay, next to yourself, under a full conviction that he was in favour of the "compromise", and could do no harm on any other measure, as he would be in a minority in Congress. I abandoned none of my principles & as soon as he shewed his hand upon the tariff, Texas &c I quit him. This is the sum and substance of my deviation from the right track, and if we had then been in a State government, I repeatedly avowed, I would not vote for him, but was merely willing to see him defeat others, whom I could not admire.

You are right in supposing myself and Mr. [James E.] Broom[e] are acting in concert, we are your friends, and the advocates of your measures. We are desirous to take such steps as shall secure this State for you at the proper time. In your Judgement and foresight, we have entire confidence, and hence our desire to consult you, upon our contemplated movements. The course which you have indicated is such a one, as I supposed best, and the one which I had advised to our friends. It will be right hard, to restrain some of our friends from expressing their preference for you, this winter in the legislature. You have many warm, zealous friends here, and I have no doubt by assuming the proper grounds, upon the Tariff, distribution

&c, we shall carry our whole party with us. [David] Levy [Yulee] is with us, thoroughly, [James D.] Westcott [Jr.] may be or not, as the wind blows; my own impression is, that he will be driven into our ranks nolens volens. The Governor of the State [William D. Moseley], and in fact every prominent man of our party, are your friends. Rely upon it, we shall do all we can as honorable men, to aid your election, not for you, but for the country, and if we fail we shall at least, have the consolation, of having done our duty. Respectfully & Sincerely Yours &C, S.H. Butler.

ALS in ScCleA.

From [James] Gadsden

Charleston S.C., Oct[obe]r 9, [18]45

My Dear Sir, I cannot sufficiently express my regret at any misconstruction I may have placed on your letter of the 23 Sep[tembe]r [*not found*]. Your language was, "I expect to be on a visit to my son[']s [Andrew Pickens Calhoun's] in Alabama at the time, and if I could with propriety, I would make it a point to attend." Now any scruples which you may have had of going to such a Convention as a Volunteer, it seems to me are removed and with "*great propriety*" by the invitation sent direct by those who made the Call; and by the particular request of this State that you should attend to represent her interests on the leading questions which will form the subjects of action at Memphis. Your presence would be very important to your native State, and to all those projects in which she has so deep a stake. We are on the eve of realizing all the fond hopes and expectations of 1836, and this is not the time for our strong and leading men to falter.

I have toiled as much if not more so on these matters. I have very nearly sacrificed myself in the Cause, and to be left alone at the time I need most encouragement, and the strongest backers is cruel. I do not know of more than 6 or 8 of our Delegation that will go from this City. We made our appointments from the Class that we thought would attend & most of them are begging off. If I go it will be at great sacrifice and I certainly will not go if you, [Franklin H.] Elmore & [Mitchell] King Back out. King is lukewarm cold, pretends he has not been invited &c and so it is the laboring oar is to be left in the hands of one who has not the power to use it.

But I come now to the sub[j]ect which seems to have given you some very false scruples on the matter. Whatever may be the designs of the Friends of Reform & Free Trade your name is not at present before the American People, and as much as I appreciate the motives of those who abstain from seeking high elevation, yet those who are the exponents of the Great Political *Truths* we wish to propagate and the Reform we desire to effect must go and be heard by those on whom it is absolutely necessary to operate. So long as the People are not reached directly; so long as an intermediate power by *Organization* and *false pretences* can deceive these People, so long will we the advocates of *Truth* & *honesty* fail. The People must be reached directly. Caucus & conventions, the packed Juries of [Martin] Van Burenism must be exposed and put down. I am not affraid of our cause if the People can hear us. It is the cause of equal rights, and of unrestricted American industry, and if we could only be heard, Van Burenism with all its selfishness and duplicity would be swept into nought. But to do so, to have this triumph you as well as all w[ho] have been true to the cause must put your shoulder to the wheel. The Time was never more propitious for a happy Revolution—For the formation of new Parties, or rather the bringing back of Democracy to its simplicity & honesty—To free it from the snears [*sic*] into which it has been deluded by Conventions and to make it stand erect as speaking the *honest* & *irresistible* voice of the People. I have for years yielded to the views of my friends & have for years been cooperating with them; with the perfect conviction of defeat. My letters to you have spoken unreservedly my views. I know I am right. I have not seen a *True Democrat* North, who has not [proved] what I have long preached; that there is no coalescing with the Northern Democracy. You must shake them off unless you are disposed again & again to be reached and to be placed in a false position. Now is the time to do it. Now is the time to meet our Western friends at Memphis—to set the ball in motion which must bring the Valley to the South, and make them feel as allies of the Great commercial and agricultural interests—instead of the Tax gathering and monopolizing interests of the North. I shall expect to see you at Memphis. Your friend Gadsden.

ALS in ScCleA; slightly variant PC in Jameson, ed., *Correspondence*, pp. 1060–1062.

From F[RANKLIN] H. ELMORE

Limestone Springs [S.C.,] Oct. 10, 1845
My Dear Sir, The last mail brings me a letter from Gov. [William] Aiken appointing me one of the Delegates for the State at Large to a Rail Road Convention at Memphis to assemble the 12th Nov. next. A letter from a friend also informs me that you are the other. I am not a little rejoiced at this movement in all its aspects except as to myself, for it is out of my power to go. My affairs here will engross me entirely until I am compelled to go to Charleston to prepare for the Session. It would be disastrous to me to leave them as they now are. But you I most ardently hope can & will go. In all respects it will be most important that you do. You have been too much secluded from the people. They have an inexpressible anxiety to see & know you & on such an occasion as this, where so much may be done to advance Southern interests—to form & consolidate a right sentiment—to unite our section upon the right policy & principles on which to place their destinies, it would be a sad oversight I think to decline, if you can possibly go. The work in hand, is itself, aside from these considerations, one of the greatest moment. I think more of good would result to South Carolina from its accomplishment than from any ever yet projected. A Rail Road Communication based at Memphis in a slave region & extended direct to Charleston, passing through the most martial portion of our people & who have, as at present situated, the least interest of all the South in slavery, would render their relations with us at Charleston & Memphis so intimate & advantageous, that their interests & ours would be indissolubly united. They would be to us a source of strength[,] power & safety & render the South invulnerable. The influence of free intercourse could not be otherwise than happy & useful. The value of the trade I do not believe could be now estimated—& it would make the stocks of our Rail Road like the shares in the Bank of England, almost without price or the means of computing values in an enterprize to whose gains every moment is adding.

The call upon you from the public to go & attend to their welfare is one too which takes from the occasion all ground of imputation. It is a public duty & to be done at the instance & for the benefit of your State & the Country at large. It is fitting that when a scheme of such grandeur & importance to the South is to be perfected & brought before the Country, that one who has served it so long, so faithfully & so ably should participate in the measure which, if guided aright, will be the most useful of any ever projected for us.

I find our friends in Charleston have forced Mr. [Robert J.] Walker [Secretary of the Treasury] at last to adopt their movement. He has omitted one question which they proposed, in regard to a duty on tea & coffee—being afraid I suppose of its effect. I have a letter just rec[eive]d, but written near a month ago to me at Charleston & forwarded here, from Judge Maysen [*sic*; John Y. Mason], complaining of the Mercury & asking me if the Mercury spoke for you & your friends. He says it does Mr. [James K.] Polk & Mr. Walker great injustice in its giving currency to its correspondent[']s charges ag[ains]t them of insincerity in regard to the Tariff. That they are sincerely & truly for a Revenue Tariff—& ag[ains]t the protective principle & that we will be satisfied with the Pres[iden]t[']s Message & the Sec[retar]y[']s report. I shall answer him, that the Mercury speaks for itself—that it undoubtedly speaks the opinions & ["feelings" *canceled and* "shows the feelings" *interlined*] of many of your friends—but that it commits nobody but itself. That if the President & Mr. Walker come out in the way we can approve, we anxiously desire it & will heartily & thoroughly sustain them. Our principles are first. They separated us from Mr. [Martin] Van Buren when he went against them & must separate us from all others who trample on them. In short that it is Mr. Polk & his administration who will determine our position.

I am afraid from a letter I had from Charleston & from the tone of the Mercury, that attempts will be made to make movements against the administration before we know or rather have proofs of its course. It seems to me it w[oul]d not be wise on our part to predicate & take any action condemning them before we have proofs that they are betraying us. To assume that they will be false is to offend all who are their friends & if they sh[oul]d not be all untrue, would place us in a very awkward position. I fear they will not stand up to principle manfully & would therefore guard before hand against their defection, & take measures to prepare for it—but it seems to me we should lose the vantage ground we now have & put ourselves in the wrong if we branded them with faithlessness, before the action of the administration is developed. I have so written to one of the movement Party Maj. James M. Walker, who wrote to me on the subject.

I have heard from a friend that Judge [Daniel E.] Huger tenders a resignation if you will consent to fill his place. I hope it is so. I hope from the bottom of my heart you will consent. I know the troubles it will bring on you—it may even, (which I do not believe) insure your future prospects for the Presidency—but it will most as-

suredly give you the proudest position you ever yet have held for controlling the action of the Govt. & serving your Country & of advancing
your own fame. You have the confidence of all men, whether they
are your supporters or not. You have a moral power beyond all—
and never in my judgement has this Country stood more in need of
its exertion. [Levi] Woodbury is gone, [Lewis] Cass is you know
too feeble & nervous for great questions & can't face [Thomas H.]
Benton. [George] McDuffie is prostrated by his sufferings—and
Judge Huger is not able to do us the service the crisis demands. We
are without leading & hope if you are away. It is useless to mince
matters—there is not a man in the State can hold it togather [*sic*] but
yourself. This very winter, if you don't take this place & show us
from the Watch Tower, how we are to marshal ourselves[,] we shall
be split up at home & ["fall" *canceled and* "turn" *interlined*] upon
each other all the energies which we should unite upon our adversaries. Not only ought you in my opinion to consent, but you should
indicate to your friends the course we should hold towards Mr. Polk
till he & his administration show us what they will do. I have shown
to you what is my opinion of what that course ought to be, but it is
one which I have not adopted [so] conclusively as not to modify it
for any that may be better.

At the next session Mr. Polk[']s policy is to be settled & he is to
stand by himself or fall to Col. Benton. His only chance of being
saved from Benton is in having one able & bold enough to give him
shelter. He can't stand up without such support & there are none to
give it in his party. The Whigs will have a powerful phalanx—and
they will press him to the wall. You may keep him honest—or if that
can[']t be, you may yet save the country even tho' he fails her. All
your policy in regard to Foreign Governments & Texas will be up, the
Zoll Verein & commercial policy—indeed every thing to open to your
abilities & experience the high road to fame & your Country's gratitude. Y[ou]rs truly, F.H. Elmore.

ALS in ScCleA; slightly variant PEx in Jameson, ed., *Correspondence*, pp. 1062–
1063.

From W[illia]m A. Elmore

New Orleans, Oct. 10th 1845
Dear Sir, Some days since, I wrote you a long Letter; and among the
subjects mentioned, I spoke of the anxiety your friends here, felt and

expressed, that you might be induced to extend your visit, among them. I directed, that letter, to your residence in So[uth] Carolina; since doing so, I learn, that you have left your residence, for Alabama, and I fear, that some delay may be incurred, in its receipt, in consequence of which, I write you again.

When we separated, in Washington, you intimated to me, that you might extend the visit, you contemplated making to Alabama, to New Orleans. I hope, that nothing, has occurred, to change your views, as it would, I assure you, greatly disappoint numerous friends who are anxious to see you, to make your acquaintance. They do not wish, or intend to annoy you, with any officious public demonstration of regard, as they understand, it would not be agreeable to you. But they wish to meet you ["and" *canceled*] socially, without pretension or parade. I cannot but think, that your visit would prove agreeable to you, as I am sure, it would to the great body of our citizens of all parties.

I am particularly anxious, that the creole population of Louisiana, should have an opportunity, of becoming acquainted with you. They have many faults, personal influences frequently controlling their political bias—but they have also, manly and generous qualities; and it is only necessary, to ["their" *canceled*] give them a proper direction to make them fast and firm friends.

There are so many reasons, that will suggest themselves to you, why you should come and see us, that it seems to me, impossible for you to decline coming.

If [you are] not pressed too urgently, ["I should" *canceled and* "for leisure" *interlined*] I should be happy to hear from you. I am with great respect your friend & ob[e]d[ien]t Ser[van]t, Wm. A. Elmore.

ALS in ScCleA.

From DUFF GREEN

Washington, 10th Oct. 1845

My dear Sir, I enclose you a copy of a letter addressed to the Editor of the Charleston Mercury, because it is the best means of presenting the views therein suggested. I am gratified to see that you are appointed one of the delegates to the convention at Memphis. You will see that the question of improving harbors & rivers will in a great measure control the new organisation of parties, and consequently greatly effect the legislation of the next Congress. Your position as a member of this convention will enable you to do much in digesting a compromise which will govern the measure here.

The more I reflect on the subject the more I am convinced that you ought to be here. [Thomas H.] Benton is now shorn of his power if you are here, but if you are not here he will recruit his strength and use for evil.

The contract for the completion of the [Chesapeake and Ohio] canal to Cumberland has given an active value to my property & I intend to make hay while the sun shines. Yours truly, Duff Green.

[Enclosure]

Duff Green to [J. Milton Clapp], "Editor of the
    Charleston Mercury"

Washington, 1st Oct. 1845

Dear Sir, I venture to write to you for the purpose of making a few suggestions relative to your Washington Correspondence, and to make myself better understood I must speak of the state of parties and of the facts & circumstances tending to control events.

The position of the [Washington] Union is an anomaly in our history. The controversy which has grown up between the Globe on the one side and the Constitution on the other, as the organs of adverse interests in the democratic party; and especial[l]y in reference to Texas, made it obvious to all that the President must choose between the two, or receive the cordial support of neither. He resolved to invite Mr. [Thomas] Ritchie to purchas[e] the Globe, hoping that there would be no conflict, between the Union & the Constitution. Mr. Calhoun's friends did not consider that as a measure hostile to them. Their language was that the Globe must not be *the* Organ of the government. They were gratified & Mr. Ritchie who ["was" *interlined*] supposed to have relinquished his previous opposition to Mr. Calhoun was selected, and one reason no doubt for selecting him was that his relations to both parties was such that neither would make well founded objections to him. [Thomas H.] Benton might prefer [Francis P.] Blair but he could make no personal objection to Mr. Ritchie. Mr. Calhoun might prefer Mr. [William A.] Har[r]is but he could not object to Mr. Ritchie. That a desire to become the printer to Congress and a hope that his position would enable him to command that appointment induced Mr. R[itchie] to leave Richmond and submit to the labor and privations of his present position is obvious. He is now an old man. He has laboured long & laboriously as a Republican Editor. I have often had cause to regret his course, but all admit that few men have stronger claims upon the democratic party. Under these circumstances it is natural and proper that the President should sympathise with him and that his election as printer should become an object of earnest solicitude. And again apart from these considerations—I am told that in private life Mr. Ritchie is a pleasant amiable man. It is his duty to vindicate the President & heads of Departments and this necessarily begets in them a desire to serve him. So much for Mr. Ritchie.

Benton in his opposition to Mr. Calhoun, for his course on the Texas question was nothing else, had lost much of his influence with the party. The fact that the Globe was *his* organ, constituted one of the strongest inducements to substitute the Union for it. Finding he was compelled to sell out or to be repudiated by the administration, Blair submitted—bitterly mortified and filled with resentment, he made a merit of a reluctant acquiescence in the will of the President; yet retired on terms that placed Ritchie under personal obligations. In some of the States, and especial[l]y in New York those of whome [*sic*] the Globe had been the organ claimed to be the majority of the party. They urged that they had been proscribed by Mr. Tyler, and demanded as an act of strict party justice that the Executive favour was due ["to" *interlined*] them. The relinquishment of the Globe, gave them additional claims upon the administration and they exerted their united influence, aided by the machinery of party & the powerful combination formed for the purpose of distributing the spoils. The late publication of McKensie's [*sic*; William L. Mackenzie's] book, illustrates the motives which governed the means by which these men accomplish their purpose. Is it surpriseing [*sic*] that they should seek to make the most of Mr. Ritchie's position—that they should make his election as printer one of the means of secureing [*sic*] the Executive patronage?

Their modus operandi, was first, to alarm [Ritchie] by showing him that without their aid he could not obtain the public printing, and next, by persuading him that if he ["obtained" *altered to* "obtains"] it, he will be indebted to them & to them only for it. He saw that neither he nor the administration had any claims on Mr. Calhoun or his friends, and that they would of course prefer Harris & [John] Heart to Ritchie & Hiess [*sic*; John P. Heiss].

The President & his Cabinet saw this too, and hence the seperation from Mr. Calhoun & his friends, & the character & position of the Cabinet necessarily created a state of distrust; ["it" *altered to* "which"] favoured Benton[']s intrigue. His purpose was to alienate

Mr. Calhoun & his friends from the administration, that by comeing [*sic*] in as their champion he might control the measures ["of the" *canceled*] and the patronage of the government.

Hence he himself professed to stand aloof. He muttered his discontent, whilst he pressed for the most important offices those persons who had combined to nominate [Martin] Van Buren. In many cases he was successful. It was the necessary consequence of the position in which the President was placed. In his desire to reconcile all parties, feeling that the Globe faction were disappointed and discomfited, it was natural that he should yield to their organised, constant pressure, the more so as there was no counter pressure on the part of Mr. Calhoun & his friends. So much as to the President and his appointments.

When I reached here in March I found many of Mr. Calhoun's friends much dissatisfied under a belief that the President would proscribe them because they were Mr. Calhoun's friends. I saw that things must necessarily run to a certain point where if there was no imprudence on our part there must necessarily be a reaction. The still small voice must penetrate the Executive mansion, and that having done enough & more than enough to satisfy Benton and his faction, the President must fall back on the south and do justice to the State rights Democrats in the north. What I foresaw did come to pass and I learn from a most reliable source that, the President believes that he has gone too far in that direction & will be careful henceforth to resist the pressure from that quarter. I also learn from a reliable source that the question of the tariff & Subtreasury has been made the subject of a Cabinet consultation & that [*one word altered to* "altho"] there was a difference of opinion, the President himself and a majority of the Cabinet were decided in fulfilling to the letter & in the strictest sense, the pledge given to the south in the Baltimore Resolutions, not a tariff of revenue only, but a tariff on the principal [*sic*] of revenue. So much for the [*one word canceled and* "measures" *interlined*] of the Administration. In the mean time Benton has been West. I learn that a consultation was held at Cincinnatti [*sic*]. That after deliberating on the propriety of a further manifestation of disaffections it was resolved ["by the parties present" *interlined*] to be most expedient to give to Benton the credit of inducing them to take the ground of conciliation—that the success of the administration ["requires" *canceled and* "depends upon" *interlined*] the union & harmony of the party, and that therefore they will acquiesce, whatever cause for discontent, they may have. Benton came on here and among other things his organ in the West announced that the Union was the organ, support of the Union was to be a test of support of the administration & that Col. Benton & his friends could therefore support the Union although ["they" *canceled and* "others" *interlined*] might not do so.

This was placing themselves between Mr. Calhoun & his friends & the administration. Was it matter of surprise that Mr. Ritchie should accept the olive branch, *alliance* if you please, thus tend[er]ed to him? What dose [*sic*] it become us to do in this crisis? Shall we make war on Mr. Ritchie, & the administration, and thus throw Mr. Ritchie and the administration upon Col. Benton & the corrupt Clique of political financiers who consider every Presidential Election as a lottery for the distributing of 130,000,000$ and party services as the price to be paid for tickets? Among the details of Benton[']s plans is a scheme for consolidating the West. This was one of the objects of the meeting at Cincinnatti. The West are to be united as one man. They must unite in ["the" *canceled*] support of men, & of measures. Benton has his Candidate for speaker & clerk of the House, and he has his measure, which is large appropriations for the Cumberland road and for Harbours & Rivers in the West. Upon these he expects to coales[c]e with the East & North and to isolate the South. Is this the time to make war on Mr. Ritchie and the Administration? Benton and his faction are now so much committed that they cannot recede & is not this the time for us to come to the aid of the Administration and secure their support for our measures?

The publication of the [Jesse] Hoyt Correspondence, is a death blow to Caucus dictation if we of the South act with prudence, if instead of diluting the effect by a petty war on individuals, some able writer will take up the correspondence and by an able review of it show the effect which "*the usages of the party*" must have on the destinies of the Republic. It was the Anti Caucus feeling which defeated Mr. [William H.] Crawford in ["1834" *altered to* "1824"]. Mr. [Henry] Clay said "give us the patronage and we will make ourselves popular" and the anti caucus feeling hurled him & [John Quincy] Adams from place. General [Andrew] Jackson unmindful of the ["principal" *altered to* "principle"] which brought him into power, became the instrument of the caucus managers, and although his will placed [Martin] Van Buren in the Presidency, the anti caucus sentiment inherent in the people, hurled Van Buren from office, although Mr. Calhoun threw the weight of his name and influence into his scale, and it was this same sentiment which defeated the nomination of Van Buren at Baltimore. It was not military fame or influence, that elected Jackson or [William Henry] Harrison. It was opposition to political management. It was a belief that corrupt men had combined to enrich themselves at the expence of public liberty. It was a desire to vindicate the ["purty" *canceled and* "purity" *interlined*] of the elective franchise, and a fixed resolve to show that the people are capable of choosing their own public servants without the aid of a corrupt coucus [*sic*] machinery. This feeling will be much strengthened by the late developements, and the connection which Mr. Polk and most of the members of his Cabinet have heretofore had with the parties implicated by the McKenzie's disclosures will weaken the Administration so much that if they were not sincere in their purpose of supporting Southern measures, it makes them depend upon the South for the success of the Administration, ["so much that if" *canceled*] and will contribute greatly to strengthen the South in the conflict for principals [*sic*]. Is this the time & these the circumstances to throw ourselves in hostility to the Administration? The position of Mr. Ritchie is more peculiar. He has been for more than twenty years intimately associated with the men, whose intrigues are exposed by the McKenzie Correspondence ["shows that" *canceled*]. That Correspondence shows that hostility to Mr. Calhoun was one of the articles of their association. Mr. Ritchie is now dependant upon the support of the friends of Mr. Calhoun in Virginia. It is the opinion of some, that his power over the party in Virginia is increased by placing him here as an auxiliary to the Enquirer. But we should remember that Mr. Calhoun's position in Virginia has grown up with the events of many years and in opposition to Mr. Ritchie until Mr. Ritchie, either from conviction or the force of circumstances from an active professing opponent, has become a passive professing friend. We should remember too that Mr. Ritchie's son, the Editor of the Enquirer, grown up in the respect which all admit is due to Mr. Ritchie as an exemplary father is the open professed follower of Mr. Calhoun. He is just entering on a carear [*sic*] the success of which must depend upon the zealous cooperation & support of the young men who, in yielding his nomination in 1844 then declared that Mr. Calhoun was their candidate for 1848 and that he was so because he was the best exponent of the ["principals" *altered to* "principles"] which they pledged themselves to support.

Now under these circumstances it dose seeme [*sic*] to me that we are playing into the enemy's hands by enabling Col. Benton to place himself between Mr. Calhoun and the administration, whether as the advocate of their measures or as the friend of Mr. Ritchie. ["If" *canceled.*]

If I was permitted to advise I would urge that Mr. Calhoun should come to the Senate. I do so because I believe that the President & part of the Cabinet are sincerely desireous [*sic*] to me[e]t his wishes and to give him all ["propper" *altered to* "proper"] aid in such a modification of the tariff, as he desires, and because the peculiar circumstances under which Congress will assemble are such as greatly to increase his influence & usefulness. I would treat the President with confidence, because I can assure you that so far as I can judge and I have been a very close observer, he deserves it. He may not be able to do all that we desire, but he can do much and he unites, with us, I firmly believe, in a desire to do all that we wish.

I would urge Mr. Calhoun to come to the Senate because I believe that he is the only man who can counteract Benton's scheme of a combination among the western members to plunder the Treasury in the form of appropriations for Roads[,] Rivers and Harbours. Something must be conceded, and Mr. Calhoun is the only man who can prevent a cor[r]upt combination by digesting a proper compromise. It is all important to give a right direction to the public sentiment of the West. That section will have a large representation in the next Congress, most of them young men, who are setting out in life. They will probably choose between Benton & Calhoun. How important that our great statesman should be here to be seen & felt and understood for himself. *No one can represent him.* If he comes into the Senate now the Administration will be compelled to cho[o]se between him & Col. Benton, and after the Hoyt correspondence expediency to say nothing of ["principal" *altered to* "principle"] would prompt them to prefer Mr. Calhoun. Again, the annexation of Texas & the increased strength of the West, gives a new aspect to the land question. If he is not here to bring forward his own measures, Benton will bring forward his, with a certainty of win[n]ing for himself fame & popularity if he dose not carry it through Congress.

I will not disguise the fact that you are indebted to your Washington correspondent [Cyril Gray] for this long letter. He thinks that Mr. Ritchie has treated him with unkindness, and I fear that the manner in which Mr. R[itchie] has treated him and the Mercury may lead to an unprofitable controversy. Permit me to suggest that ["suspense" *altered to* "suspension"] of hostilities, for the present at least, may be advisable. There are other matters of equal interest which may be discussed with more profit.

I have been much tempted to write to you on the position and policy of England and explain how it is, that the E[a]st India Company control the government of England but I have been much occupied otherwise. Yours truely, Duff Green.

ALS with En in ScCleA; FC of En in NcU, Duff Green Papers (published microfilm, reel 6, frames 117–128). NOTE: The enclosure is in an unknown hand with corrections and additions by Green.

From H[ENRY] W[HEATON, U.S. Minister to Prussia]

Berlin, 10 Oct. 1845

My dear Sir, I duly received your kind Letter written soon after the change in the Administration, & am much obliged by the continued proofs of your friendly interest in what concerns my welfare. I have received no *direct* intimation as to the P[resident']s [James K. Polk's] intentions respecting this mission, but I have reason to believe that in the midst of the pressure made upon him by the office seekers, he has not yet made up his mind as to what he will do, although he professes the highest respect for my abilities & Services as a negociator. Under these circumstances it has occurred to me that as he has shown, on some occasions, a desire to avoid collision with your political friends, that the desire of conciliating them might possibly influence him if he *knew* that you had any particular regard for me. I therefore venture to submit to you the expediency of making to him, either directly or indirectly, a suggestion as to your wishes on the subject, if there be no insurmountable objections in your mind to such a course. I have *so much at stake on the present occasion*, that I trust you will find a sufficient apology in the peculiar nature of my case for making this request. I have pursued this line so long that I cannot at my time return to my profession with advantage, whilst the experience I have acquired & the aptitudes I possess for diplomacy ["render me capa" *canceled*] may still be utilized for the for the [*sic*] public interest without injury to the just claims of any other citizen. In fact no other has devoted himself to diplomacy as a profession, & to no other of our agents abroad would a recall be so injurious as to myself. There will still be scope enough for the exercise of executive patronage whilst leaving *one* mission untouched where the incumbent has peculiar qualifications for the employment. If the head of the Government is so much the slave of party as to be unable to do this, then our system, so far as respects the working of this part of it, is a practical failure.

I need not say, my dear Sir, that you are one of the very few men to whom I would make such a frank appeal, which I am sure will not be made in vain if it is possible for you to gratify my wishes. Should that be the case you will add very sensibly to the weight of obligation by which I am already bound to you. I will only add that if it is in your power to serve me on this occasion, no time ought to be lost in making known your wishes & those of our friends to the P[resident]. I remain, ever, my dear Sir, your obliged friend, H.W.

ALI in ScCleA. Note: Unlike his five predecessors, Polk removed Wheaton, the most experienced and respected American diplomat of the day, from office.

Receipt from E[noch] B. Benson & Son, [Pendleton], 10/16. "We have rec[eive]d of Mrs. R[ebecca Weyman Foster] Gaillard Six Dollars 25 Cents—which amount we have entered to the credit of Mr. J.C. Calhoun." DS in ScU-SC, John C. Calhoun Papers.

From PERCY WALKER

Mobile, Oct[obe]r 16th 1845
Dear Sir, As Chairman of a Committee of your Democratic fell[ow]-citizens of this place, I had the honour in April last, to address you a letter expressive of our high sense of the value of your public services, and tendering you an invitation to a Public Dinner, as a slight testimonial of our admiration for your character and our gratitude for your distinguished efforts in behalf of Republican principles.

In your reply, you declined the invitation, but informed us that it [was] your intention to visit this state in the Autumn, and would at that time "make it a point to see your friends in Mobile."

The announcement in the public Journals, that you were to [leave] Pendleton on the 10th of this month for Ala., has given us muc[h] pleasure. I write to remind you of your promise, and to say to y[ou] that we *exact* it's fullfillment. In the name of the Comm[ittee?] and of your Republican fellow-citizens, I renew the invitation tendered last April, and trust that you will honour us by an acceptance. Most gladly will you be welcomed to our city.

Your numerous friends, here, count with *certainty* upon seeing you.

I trust, then, my dear Sir, that you will gratify their wishes and that you will at your earliest convenience, inform me of the time at which you will pay us this desired visit. Assuring you of my profound respect and esteem, I remain most truly Yours, Percy Walker.

ALS in ScCleA. NOTE: This letter was addressed to Calhoun at Faunsdale Post Office, Marengo County, Ala. Some letters and words have been supplied in brackets in the above transcription where the ms. is unreadable from a frayed margin.

From R[OBERT] M. T. HUNTER, [Representative from Va.]

L[l]oyds, Essex Co[unty, Va.,] Oct[obe]r 17th 1845
My dear Sir, It has been some time since I wrote to you before because I knew you were overwhelmed with a correspondence which must tax too far your time and patience and because in this out of the way corner of Virginia I had nothing of interest to communicate. I had heard with apprehension I confess that you would probably return to the Senate but I did not write to you because I knew you were a far better judge of the propriety of this step than I could possibly be. Upon passing through Washington lately I fell in with Major Mark A. Cooper of Georgia and others of your friends and I am now induced to believe that if you take this step it will be against your own wishes and judgment and in compliance with the solicitations of your friends. Now if this be the case, I, as one of your friends who ["is" *canceled and* "are" *interlined*] as much entitled to speak as any of them if friendship can give me the title, beg that you will be governed in this matter by your own judgment and not by their solicitations. You are better able to guide your friends than they are to guide you. Nor, do I believe that such is the general sentiment of your friends out of So. Ca. All I know would desire to see you in the Senate if they had no purpose of running you for the presidency. But I cannot imagine how any man who desires you to be elected next time to the Presidency should urge you now to return to the Senate. It was the general sentiment of your friends (if I understood it) that you should retire from the Senate when you left it. Every reason which then existed for that step applies with double force to the continuance of your retirement for the present. You have been so connected with public affairs in another capacity since your retirement from the Senate that the public has not had

time as yet to see and feel the chasm occasioned by your absence from that body. You would immediately become the most prominent object of assault to aspirants of all parties sects and persuasions and every effort would be made to isolate you from the party and especially from the West on the Oregon question. I know they say that [Thomas H.] Benton will seize the opportunity to attack and weaken you. Every such effort on his part in *your absence* would weaken him not you. He being in the Senate and you out of it is the only relative position which your friends should desire. He cannot secure position it seems to me without adopting your principles to a great extent and if he does not he will have to oppose the administration as I now believe. Mr. [James K.] Polk I am now convinced will adopt your line of measures to a great extent. This he will be willing to do in your absence. He will hope to identify himself with these measures and he will regard them as his. In this event Benton[,] [Silas] Wright &c must yield or be broken down. Were you in the Senate your previous connection with these measures and your own reputation would lead the public to regard the measures as yours and not those of the administration. You would be openly assailed and the president would be covertly reached by insinuations that he was guided by you and under your influence. This might have an unfortunate effect on the administration. It might at least make it less willing to risk much on these measures or direct its feeling towards you. If you however are at home and Mr. Polk should take this course, its effect will be to benefit your prospects and to place the party in such a position that you must be its exponent in the next contest.

But will the president take this course? What I now communicate is in the strictest confidence. I have every reason to believe that he will. I had a long and confidential conversation with him about a week ago. I am satisfied with his views as to the Tariff. He is sound too on the negro question. Unless I am greatly deceived he will take a decided course upon these questions. Let Benton & Co. make the war upon him and then we will sustain him and carry the party with us. I do not believe that Mr. Polk will take this course with any view to your benefit. But such must be its effect. I think he is very anxious to see [Thomas] Ritchie elected and I believe that the New York wing are as anxious to defeat him if they decide under these circumstances opposition to Ritchie for that place would be impolitic. Be this as it may, I cannot be mistaken in thinking the course of the [Charleston] Mercury highly injudicious. That makes the war on the President and I really believe does him great injustice on the Tariff. Next winter your friends may do much for you if they are prudent. None of them would rejoice more than myself in your personal presence and advice if it were compatible with the interest which I feel in seeing you elevated to the presidency. But I humbly believe that this object can be better attained by your remaining at home for the present.

I trust you will excuse me for the frankness with which I have presented you my views on these matters. My advice may be wrong, but my motives are such as would excuse even a greater error in judgment. Most truly your friend, R.M.T. Hunter.

ALS in ScCleA.

From S[HADRACH] PENN, JR., "Private"

St. Louis, Oct. 17, 1845

Dear Sir, The views contained in your letter of July were strictly correct, except, perhaps, on one point. I still entertain the opinions I conveyed to you in relation to the conduct and ultimate designs of the Secretary of the Treasury [Robert J. Walker]. He has, in my opinion, been the chief laborer in throwing Mr. [James K.] Polk into the embrace of the [Martin] Van Buren and [Thomas H.] Benton faction—and I fear he will not play fair on the tariff question.

I hope you will return to the Senate, as I believe such a step necessary, since Mr. [Levi] Woodbury has accepted a seat on the bench of the Supreme Court. Much may depend—I fear everything— on the movements that may be made at the commencement of the session. A bold rally of the Annexation Democrats, may "systematically frighten" the President back into the path of duty; and if you cannot be there to lead and counsel them, I trust you will at least write to your friends on the subject.

Those who denounced the course of the Baltimore Convention and the Texas movement may, by a bold and combined effort, be put into the back ground at the commencement of the session; and without such an effort there is reason to fear that the Hunkers, by their discipline and superior management, may again obtain control of Congress, for which they are now making great exertions. If foiled at the outset, the better portion of the faction will come over to the Annexation Democrats, and the other portion will be rendered powerless. In that event the President will change his position, as he is not the man to stand out against the majority of the party.

The men who came to the rescue at the Baltimore Convention should rally at the commencement of the session—on the very first issue that can be made; as political victory or death awaits them—nothing less. They have no alternative but to force the Administration to respect its friends and carry out the policy of the party—or consent to a restoration of those who were overthrown in the Baltimore Convention.

Had the President been firm I should have preferred to see you remain in retirement *for the present*; but in the existing state of affairs I believe your presence at Washington necessary to the success of correct principles and the [*partial word canceled*] ultimate triumph of the party.

Efforts will be made to force [Thomas] Ritchie to pledge himself to the Hunkers before he is elected Printer, if elected at all. This is the position taken by some of the Ohio members, and it is possible that [Benjamin] Tappan's recent visit to Washington is connected with this matter. But, be this as it may, such an early movement as I have discribed is absolutely necessary to save the party—for, if the President is allowed to permit himself to be controlled by the anti-Annexationists a permanent division, and defeat, will be inevitable. A bold and unequivocal indication is necessary at the outset, that full justice must be done to the Annexationists and the Tariff properly modified. If this is not yielded, the sooner the conflict shall be commenced, the better. But a proper onslaught on the *halters* and *balkers* in the late campaign would certainly have the desired effect. Men almost invariably yield when in the wrong. Yours Truly, S. Penn, Jr.

ALS in ScCleA.

To "Gen[era]l" DUFF GREEN, Washington

Cane Brake, Marengo (Co[unty]), Ala., 18th Oct[obe]r 1845
My dear Sir, I received your letter the day I left home, & while on my road to this place, accompanied by Mrs. [Floride Colhoun] Calhoun & John [C. Calhoun, Jr.]. We arrived three days since, and found Andrew [Pickens Calhoun], Margaret [Green Calhoun] & the children well. Andrew has made a very fine crop of corn & cotton. He has gathered 300 bales of upwards of 500 pounds each & is, I think, not half done. We shall make, I think upwards of 300,000

pounds of picked cotton. The place is in remarkable fine order. Mrs. Calhoun is delighted with the country. Indeed, it would be difficult to find any where else within the cotton region health & fertility combined to the same extent.

I find my friends, with very few exceptions, concur with you, that I ought to return to the Senate. I have been, much pressed by them to do so, & have, though much against my inclination, consented to do so, if there should be a vacancy, & the legislature should think proper to elect me. I mention this, however, in confidence. It is better, for many reasons, to leave things in the present state of uncertainty 'till the Legislature meets & acts on the subject.

In yielding, I have been governed exclusively by deference to the opinion of my friends, & what they regard as my duty. I find private life has many charms for me, & it will be difficult for me to retire at any time hereafter under circumstances more propitious to my reputation & standing in after times, than what I did last spring. But be that as it may, if it should be my good fortune, in the event of taking a seat again in the Senate, to contribute in any degree to carry the country & the Government, through their present difficulties, I shall not regard the sacrafice.

Mrs. Calhoun's health is entirely restored; & she joins with me in affectionate remembrance to yourself, Mrs. [Lucretia Maria Edwards] Green, Miss Eliza [Green] & the family. Yours truly, J.C. Calhoun.

ALS in DLC, Duff Green Papers.

To W[illiam] B. Lewis, Nashville

Faunsdale, Marengo [County] Ala.
18th Oct[obe]r 1845
Dear Sir, Your letter of the 7th of August addressed to me at Pendleton, followed me to this place, where it found me on a visit to my son. It came to hand by the last mail, which will explain, why it has not been acknowledged earlier.

You request me to state, what I know of your course in relation to the annexation of Texas to the United States. It affords me pleasure to state, as an act of justice to you, that I found you uniformly a zealous & devoted friend to annexation. I had frequent conversations & interviews with you on the subject, and on all occasions, you exhibited the utmost zeal for annexation. It is also due to you to state, you wrote, at my request, more than once to Gen[era]l [Andrew] Jackson on the subject, and that through your correspondence with him, you rendered essential aid to the success of that great measure. With great respect I am & &, J.C. Calhoun.

ALS in NjMoN, Lloyd W. Smith Collection (Morristown National Historical Park published microfilm, Reel 8).

From RODERICK MACKENZIE

Wetumpka [Ala.,] 18 Oct. 1845

I regret much missing the pleasure of seeing you when passing through this place, if I could not have prevailed on you to remain here a night, I would have certainly done myself the pleasure of accompanying you to the Governor [Benjamin Fitzpatrick] or Mr. [John A.] Elmore both of whom are much disappointed at not seeing you. I am glad however you got the same night into good quarters and spent it with my worthy friend Capt[ai]n [Richard?] Long. Can we expect you to take this on your way back to Carolina? It is the best and shortest route if you travel in your own conveyance. Moreover it would give Mr. [William L.] Yancey an opportunity of seeing you who is a man of tact, energy and ability to forward the good cause dear to every patriot heart. To your views and promotion of the same I have always looked with admiration and delight. Now my dear Sir although not personally acquainted I cannot let your visit to our State pass without making known to you my constant and devoted admiration of you as a christian, statesman & patriot. This may appear silly to you, but really I cannot help it and in view of this permit me the liberty of asking you to give me a few lines over your signature which I purpose to preserve amongst my valued relics whilst I live, afterwards to be handed to the one I like best as the production of one than whom no man in the Republic love[s] more than your Friend, Roderick MacKenzie.

ALS in ScCleA. NOTE: This letter was addressed to Calhoun at Faunsdale, Marengo County, Ala.

From JAMES GADSDEN

Charleston S.C., Oct. 21, [18]45

My Dear Sir, I have just seen [James] Hamilton [Jr.]. He concurs with me that you ought to attend the Memphis Meeting, and has written you a long letter today. I find we agree in many particulars in relation to our political aspect. We can never have a triumph of our principles & integrity, unless the People can be reached, and the delusions under which they are duped by a selfish clique are removed. This can only be effected by your being before the masses, known to them personally, and made to feel the force of truth. I would be one of the last to wish you to take the stump or to travel about for popularity. But on great occasions, where assembl[i]es are made to discuss questions of general & great interest, I see no more impropriety when asked, to attend these meetings: as to go to the Senate if elected. It is only in the West that we can have any hopes of a triumph. If they do not come to us we will be overwhelmed by the power that has combined for our ruin. There is now an opportunity afforded, of being heared [*sic*] and I really hope and entreat that you will not disappoint your best friends, who will feel paralysed if you do not now come to their aid. I shall look confidently at your being at Memphis—and if not there, So[uth] Carolina will not be heard in the Great Enterprise which is to constitute in part the deliberations of that assembly. Respectfully Your ob[edien]t, James Gadsden.

ALS in ScCleA.

From RICHARD ADAMS

Washington, 23rd Oct[obe]r 1845

Dear Sir, Some of your Political friends are urging you to consent to return to the Senate of the U. States. I differ with them. I do not believe you can, under present circumstances, render as much aid to the Anti Protective Party by being in the Senate as you can by remaining in private life. So soon as you are elected you will be secretly assailed and thwarted in every possible manner by the clique of each aspirant for the Presidency.

The Democratic aspirants and there are several, fear you more than any other ["Politic"(?) *changed to* "eminent public men"].

You will stand in their way; remove you they will cost what it may. Your being in public life will furnish them advantages they cannot avail themselves of, should you continue a private citizen.

That I am guilty of presumption in thus tendering, unasked, my advice, I am free to admit. My apology must be a sincere and ardent desire, to serve one, for whom I entertain the most profound respect and admiration.

That you may be possessed of every means of enabling you to arrive at a correct conclusion as to the proper course for you to pursue in the present exigency, I communicate a fact which may be of some importance. I must at the same time request, that, you will confine it to yourself for the present, as I am not at liberty to communicate it to any one save yourself.

You are aware that the Rev[eren]d Mr. [Calvin] Colton is about publishing the life [of] Henry Clay. In it he will state that during the pendency of the Presidential election before Congress, when John Q[uincy] Adams was elected, Mr. Clay and Mr. (now Gov[erno]r) [Robert P.] Letcher of Kentucky were in a room together in Washington and Mr. [James] Buchanan entered it. After conversing on various subjects Mr. Buchanan remarked, "there is a gentleman in this room who can have any office under Gene[r]al [Andrew] Jackson he may select, provided, General Jackson is elected President and that gentleman has it in his power to elect Gen[era]l Jackson President." Mr. Clay remarked, Letcher here is a chance for you; Mr. Buchanan promptly remarked "he is not the gentleman." Mr. Clay then said, "then I must be the man, Mr. Buchanan. I am not the man to be thus approached." There the conversation ended. Colton further states, that, Mr. Clay intended ["to" *interlined*] have mentioned this fact in a speech which he made in the Senate some time after this, and commenced doing so. Mr. Buchanan perceiving his intention went to him and begged he would not, and it was owing to the earnest entreaties of Mr. B[uchanan] that he refrained. This I have from a gentleman who has read the manuscript.

It was Mr. Buchanan[']s intention a few weeks since to have resigned his seat in the Cabinet and take a seat on the bench of the Supreme Court. I know this from two gentlemen to whom he communicated this intention, but some ten days since, he was informed of what Colton relates and now is determined to remain where he is.

Wisely has he determined, for if nominated to the Senate this fact will be at once made known and he would be rejected. I have the honor to be most respectfully your obedient servant, Richard Adams.

ALS in ScCleA. NOTE: Calvin Colton published in 1846 a two-volume work entitled *Life and Times of Henry Clay* (New York: A.S. Barnes & Co.).

From JAMES GADSDEN

Charleston S.C., Oct. 24, [18]45

My Dear Sir, The Citizens of So. Carolina and your immediate friends will take no denial.

You are expected at Memphis and must and ought to go. The elements are in our favor and if we will not take the advantage of the currents and the winds we cannot expect to work our Passage into the Port of Free Trade. I write, in reiterating my requests with those of numerous friends for your attendance at Memphis merely to indicate the Route.

You have been invited to Mobile & probably a similar invitation you may receive from New Orleans. Take those Two places in your way. They are, from your present position, the shortest & best Route. Even from here I am not so sure but it is the best & many of our Delegates will take it. The Assembly will be a large one & there alone can we sound, with the prospects of success the Triumph of Free Trade, Low duties &c. Yours truly, James Gadsden.

ALS in ScCleA.

To T[HOMAS] G. CLEMSON, [Brussels]

Cane Brake, Ala., 27th Oct[obe]r 1845

My dear Sir, Yours by the last Steamer reached me here by the last mail, where I arrived with Mrs. [Floride Colhoun] Calhoun, & John [C. Calhoun, Jr.], ten or twelve days since. I found all well, and the plantation and all connected with it in excellent order. Our corn crop is abundant, so much so, that we shall be able to sell several ["hundred" *canceled and* "thousand" *interlined*] bushels, if we can find in this plentiful region, ["we shall be able to find" *canceled*] purchasers. We have gin[n]ed & packed three hundred bales, of upwards of 500 pounds to the bale, & shall have by the end of the week a sufficient quantity out to make upwards of ["fifty" *canceled and* "sixty" *interlined*] more. After going over the fields several times, I cannot doubt, that the yield will be 300,000 pounds. I think the prospect of exceeding that amount, is greater than falling below. Should the present price continue, we shall be able to apply $15,000 to our debts. Among them, we shall take up your remaining note to Arthur Simkins at maturity, & ["the" *canceled*] pay the amount due John [Ewing] Bonneau, & the interest on what we owe you. We have found Cuba of great service. It has greatly increased our productive powers, by enabling us to plant full crops; & to expand our clearing ["hereafter" *interlined*] with the increase of our force. It has proved, indeed, indispensible to us; so that, what was regarded unfortunate at the time, has turned out the reverse.

Considering the difficulty of getting any one that is competent to take the supervision of your place [in Edgefield District], & the still greater, if possible, of getting an overseer, every way competent to take charge of such an estate as your's [*sic*] in your absence, I think you have decided wisely in determining to convert your property into good bonds, or ["funds" *canceled and* "stock" *interlined*], as you propose. I have duely reflected on the mode, in which you propose to dispose of your negroes, with every possible disposition on my part to meet your wishes, but it will not be possible for me to make the arrangement you propose, in connection with myself. To pass over the great inconvenience & expense of sending my negroes here & bringing them back again, your force would be too large, of itself, for my place. It is stronger than mine, & mine is too strong for it; so much so, that I propose to send out next fall fully one half to this place. The residue will be sufficient to cultivate it in corn, small grain, pease, and a small cotton crop on my best uplands highly manured. I expect to make nearly as much that way, with half the ["amount" *canceled*] hands, as I now do with the whole; while I shall make more by far with the half here, than I now do with the whole in Carolina.

I am of the impression, that there would be great difficulty in hiring your hands advantageously. I do not think there is the least prospect that the entire gang, or any considerable portion of it, can be hired to any one person, who would be responsible, or would probably take good care of them. They would ["have to" *interlined*] be hired one or two or three to this man & that man, & be scattered about in every direction. The process of hiring would be troublesome, & the collection ["of the money" *interlined*] probably still more so. Indeed, there are strong objections to hiring, under any circumstances, a gang of negroes. The object of him who hires, is generally to make the most he can out of them, without regard to their comfort or health, and usual[l]y to the entire neglect of the

children & the sick. With my impression, I think it the last alternative, which ought to be thought of in the disposition of a gang,
especially of an absentee, as you are; unless ["indeed" *interlined*]
they could be hired, as a gang to some one individual, in whom entire
confidence could be reposed; and that, I think, impossible.

I am of the impression, that your only alternative is to sell, either
by publick or private sale, on reasonable credit. I am not prepared
to say how they would sell at present either way. The crop in South
Carolina & all the staple States both of corn & cotton, with little exception, is either indifferent or bad. I hear of no place in this State,
or Georgia, or S.C., which will make average crops, except hereabouts, & it is thought the crops to the West ["of this," *interlined*], including Texas, will be below the average. On the contrary, the
price of cotton is advanced; so that it will ["probably" *interlined*]
give as great an income, as it did last year; and the probability is,
that the price ["of negroes" *interlined*] will not vary much from what
it was then. It is not improbable a gang, such as yours would sell
at $300 round.

If you should conclude to sell, we would give you ["three" *canceled and* "12,000" *interlined*] hundred [*sic*] dollars for the gang,
which is something more than $300 round, ["at one, two &" *canceled
and* "at" *interlined*] three years['] credit, with interest from the time
of taking them in possession; or, if you prefer it, on the valuation of
Col. [Francis W.] Pickens, or any other friend you would choose to
name, to be secured by bond, in whatever manner you might desire,
& the interest to be punctually paid, when it becomes due. We will
also take your wagon & horses, except Cherokee & colt, on like valuation; and will agree to return you Daphne & her [c]hild & Bill
Laurence, and any other two or three negroes you may select, any
time in the three years, you crediting us with a sum equal to their
value, & we paying you hire for the time they may have been in our
service. We feel ourselves perfectly safe in making you this offer.
The sum it will add to our debt will not be equal to the sum we
shall be able to apply to its discharge out of the present crop, while
it would increase our effective negro force, with the addition of
those I shall send out in another year, nearly one third, without the
cost of one dollar for land; ["but" *interlined*] with a corresponding
increase of our cotton crop. With so large an increase, we would be
able to meet all our engagements, including the proposed purchase
easily, at 5 cents the pound, estimating the yield far below the average, since we have been planting in the region; while, in the mean
time, from the great durability of the soil & health of the region, our

capital ["& productive power" *interlined*] would be annually increasing by clearing & ditching our land & the increase of our negroes. Our soil neither exhausts nor washes. The oldest lands cultivated in the region ["is" *canceled and* "are" *interlined*] as productive, as the recently cleared, & our phisican's [*sic*] bill has been but $40 [*or possibly* "$46"] in three years; and in that time, there has been but two deaths, one a child & other by accident. To this may be added, that the experience, of this year of extreme drought, proves, that we have nothing to fear from that quarter; while we are entirely exempt from the hazard of floods. It is on this solid basis, that I feel myself justified in pledging ourselves to perfect punctuality, in meeting our engagements to you hereafter, both the existing & that we propose to enter into.

I will take Cherokee & her colt to Fort Hill; & take the cow you refer to, & your flock of sheep ["their value to be estimated by Col. P(ickens) &" *interlined*] accept with pleasure the wine & liquors, you have at the place.

I would advise ["that" *interlined*] all the other personal property there ["to" *canceled and* "should" *interlined*] be sold, (including grain of every discription, & forrage, & excepting the cotton,) ["to be sold" *canceled*] at publick sale on a credit of a year for notes duely secured. The grain & forrage will prob[ab]ly sell high.

I shall write to Col. Pickens relative to the sale of the land. I think the mode you propose to sell it, very judicious, except ["in" *interlined*] two particulars. Your object, I suppose, is to get as much as you can for it, & that you have not any need of a ["present" *canceled*] payment ["down" *interlined*] of $1000. Under this impression, I would advise you to offer it at a sum, which with interest, would give you the $13000, in the same time, without any present payment; and ["have" *canceled and* "shall" *interlined*] accordingly authorise Col. Pickens, to make the offer to dispose of it either the way you propose, or the one I suggest, as he finds he can most readily dispose of it. Few people estimate discount as it ought to be. They look for the most part to the present sum.

Mrs. Calhoun requests me to say, that she ["wrote" *canceled and* "has written to" *interlined*] Anna [Maria Calhoun Clemson] since her arrival here, & that she will attend to Anna[']s requests. Our present arrangement is to take Edgefield & the place in our way on our return; I to see & converse with Col. Pickens about ["your" *canceled*] the contents of your letter, & she to attend to Anna's requests.

It is desirable, I should hear from you without delay. The present indication is, that I shall be forced into the Senate again by the State, so that you had better write to me in duplicate; one ["of which" *canceled*] to be addressed to Fort Hill, & the other to Washington.

I shall leave this for Memphis to attend the convention there on the 12th No[vembe]r ["before" *canceled and* "will return about" *interlined*] the 25th Nov[embe]r.

All, including Andrew [Pickens Calhoun] & Margaret [Green Calhoun], join their love to you & Anna. Kiss the children [John Calhoun Clemson and Floride Elizabeth Clemson] for their Grandfather. Your affectionate father, J.C. Calhoun.

ALS in ScCleA.

To Sam[ue]l Conner, S. J. Harris, W. E. Pegram and Others, [Dayton, Ala.]

[Marengo County, Ala.] 27 October, 1845

Gentlemen: It is with great regret, that I am compelled to decline your invitation to partake of a public dinner. I am compelled to leave on Friday, in order to be in time to meet the Convention at Memphis, to which I have been appointed a delegate; and I am engaged every day between now and then. Under other circumstances, it would have afforded me pleasure to accept your kind invitation. With great respect, I am, &c. &c., J.C. Calhoun.

PC (from the Demopolis, Ala., *Marengo Ledger*) in the Tuscaloosa, Ala., *Independent Monitor*, November 5, 1845, p. 3; PC in the Richmond, Va., *Enquirer*, November 11, 1845, p. 1. Note: The Washington, D.C., *Constitution*, November 10, 1845, p. 3, reported: "The citizens of Dayton, Marengo county, Alabama, tendered a public dinner to the Hon. J.C. Calhoun, on the 27th ult. Owing to his engagements and preparations to start for the Memphis Convention, he was compelled to decline the honor."

From John P. King

Augusta [Ga.,] Oct[obe]r 27th 1845

My dear Sir, I read your kind favor of the 22nd this evening, and have but a few minutes to answer, by the first mail.

Though you greatly overrate my probable efficacy in the Convention, it would give me great pleasure to attend it. I cannot however do so consistently with other engagements. The time of the meeting unfortunately conflicts with the session of our legislature, where business will probably call me, that I fear would not be so well represented by others, as our interests here will be, in the Memphis Convention. I feel, as you know, a deep interest in ["their" *changed to* "the"; "subjecting" *canceled*] subject of connecting the South, and West, and am much gratified that you have consented to lend your active aid in a cause, in which you can be so efficient. Whilst others have been wild and wandering *you* have been right on this subject *from the beginning*, and had your advice been taken the present meeting might have been called, to celebrate the *Consummation* of this great national object, but would not have been necessary *to devise means* for its accomplishment. As this will probably not reach you I[']ll write you again to Memphis. Y[ou]rs, &c, Jno. P. King.

ALS in ScCleA. Note: This letter was addressed to Calhoun at Faunsdale, Marengo County, Ala. King was President of the Georgia Railroad and Banking Co. and had been Senator from Ga. during 1833–1837.

From Ro[BERT] McCandlish and Others

Williamsburg [Va.], October 28th 1845

Dear Sir, The Undersigned, a committee of invitation appointed by their Fellow Citizens of Williamsburg, request the favour of your company at a dinner to be given at the City Hotel on Tuesday the 11th day of November next, in honor of our distinguished Fellow Citizen President Tho[ma]s R. Dew of William & Mary College. The devotion which you have manifested through a long life to the great principles of Constitutional liberty, has won for you the Confidence & best wishes of all, who love their Country & its present institutions.

The wisdom & ability, which you have evinced in advocating the fundamental doctrines of Political Economy, held in Common by you & the illustrious individual we desire to honor on the present occasion, has created an ardent desire in this Community, to have you in our midst. We venture to affirm, there are none of your Fellow Citizens, who more fully appreciate your public services & the purity of your private life, than those of this ancient metropolis, and none who would derive greater pleasure from your presence. Accept from the Committee assurances of their most respectful & distinguished Consideration. Ro: McCandlish, Ro[bert] M. Garrett, William S. Peachy, John J. Jones, William Waller, Committee.

LS in ScCleA. NOTE: An AEU by Calhoun reads "Invitation to attend the dinner to be given to Pres[iden]t Dew."

From GEO[RGE] W. HOUK

Dayton [Ohio,] Oct. 29th 1845

Dear Sir, You will perhaps remember to have received a letter from the undersigned previous to the last presidential election in relation to questions which were put in issue in that contest. I will not here with[h]old even at this late date an expression of my acknowledgements for your very early & satisfactory answer. It embodied in brief terms the same views which I had so often recognized in your speeches and correspondence and set forth the basis of what I consider the true policy of the American Statesman.

Your apprehension of the consolidation & centralization of power is I fear but too well founded. It has however been the main-spring to your political action and we may find cause for rejoicing in the fact that the views & the policy which you have hitherto sustained have found so able an advocate.

The excitement of the presidential canvass has well nigh passed away—the time for congratulations if limited at all, may also be regarded as past—but in the consummation of that most important political movement of our day, the Annexation of Texas, (and which too I trace to you as its originator) the whole Nation has just cause to be proud. It would have been a piece of blindness and stupidity which the American Historian would have blushed to record had we been unsuccessful in the pursuit of so great an acquisition, so vital to the south, so important to the Republic. All obstacles have however vanished before the majestic popular will & the energy of our ministerial agents. Domestic opposition has even subsided down into the murmurings of applause while foreign intrigues have failed & England & France have been foiled in their diplomatic interference.

There yet remains a difficult question to dispose of. I refer to the Oregon controversy. I do not doubt, myself, that this will eventually lead to a rupture with Great Britain. The West has so far committed itself in relation to 54th degree, that it would be very clamorous were anything less adopted, as a compromise.

The President has committed himself too in language the import

244

of which is easily understood. The tone of the English Journals has been even more violent than our own. In short the controversy has arrived at a crisis from which I think the art of diplomacy will fail to rescue it.

I have never met with your views I believe at any length in relation to this vital question—at least since it has assumed so serious an aspect. Whether we should enforce our claim to the 54th degree or whether a compromise should be effected[;] Whether in the latter case England would be the predominating power on the western Coast & the Pacific, or Republicanism gradually gain the ascendancy? In view of the spirit which prevails among the American People, the love of enterprise & adventure which characterizes especially the citizens of this portion of our Union, and in view too of the Policy which the British Government has for years been so steadily pursuing toward this country, I think the Oregon Question is fraught with more important consequences to the United States & to the great cause of Republicanism, Constitutional liberty, than any one which has ever yet been presented for solution. Probably my views may savor a little too strongly of *westernism* or I may give perhaps the controversy an undue importance. You will oblige me [*mutilation*]h by returning me an answer at your earlie[st conv]enience—now that political excitement has in [a gr]eat measure subsided, your correspondence perhaps somewhat limited. I hope I am not asking a favor which it will be burdensome to grant.

Your name I have heard mentioned in connexion with a seat in the Senate. I hope you will not decline the post. I would wish you however to entertain no scruples about resigning should your country[']s voice call you to a more auspicious station. With solicitations for your health & welfare I am with great respect yours &c, Geo. W. Houk.

P.S. An answer if received will of course be considered private.

ALS in ScCleA; PEx's in Boucher and Brooks, eds., *Correspondence*, p. 307.

From M[OSES] C. MORDECAI

Charleston, Oct. 29/1845

Dear Sir, Your letter of the 18th in[stan]t is at hand, and although it gives us pleasure and satisfaction to learn that you intend being at Memphis as one of the delegates from the State, yet the Committee will be greatly disappointed and much embarrassed should you not answer the questions from the [Treasury] Department, which originated with yourself, when these questions were received from you. We saw that there would be great difficulty in answering them, but relying upon your aid, we did not hesitate to place them in the list sent to the department as among the most important. Gov. [James H.] Hammond thinks that the course of the department has been such, that we should not be drawn in at so late an hour to answer questions so reluctantly put forth, and he declines having any thing to do with it. Mr. [George] McDuffie has been written to by the Committee, and by Mr. [Ker] Boyce asking his aid, but nothing has been heard from him. It is desirable If a report is sent from here it should be most Effective.

You will perceive therefore that we are awkwardly circumstanced in relation to these questions, and If it be possable for you to answer them, we shall still be greatly obligated by your doing so. With Great Respect Your Ob[edient] S[ervant,] M.C. Mordecai.

ALS in ScCleA.

From EDWARD DIXON

Warrenton [Va.], October 31st, 1845
My Dear Sir, The paper which I send you contains a brief article in relation to your return to the United States Senate. I thought it advisable that it should be published as early as possible, and as the subject was not taken up until just before the close of the mail, I could not bestow as much attention upon it as I wished. The sentiments expressed, however, are those entertained by the Democratic party in Virginia without an exception that I am aware of. Your Virginia friends are looking anxiously to South Carolina for her action upon the subject, and should the place in question be tendered to you, we sincerely trust that you will not be embar[r]assed in your course by the apprehension of being exposed to unworthy suspicions. In the event of war, the country would rely much upon your abilities, experience, firmness and patriotism, for a proper vindication of its rights and honor, and in this view of the matter, your return to the Senate may be regarded as of the highest importance. Your position, in any event, would be a most commanding one, and I think better calculated than any other to secure the great end which your friends have so long and ardently desired to accomplish. I would not again

have addressed you upon this subject, but for a desire that you should be advised of the very general wish entertained here by Democrats to see you back in the Senate at this important juncture. I remain, Sir, very truly and sincerely yours, Edward Dixon.

ALS in ScCleA.

To —— Hubbard, Despatch Agent of the State Department, Boston, 10/31. "I am here [in Marengo County, Ala.] on a visit to my son, and enclosed a letter to my son-in-law Mr. [Thomas G.] Clemson [in Brussels] to you by the last mail, on which . . . the postage was omitted to be paid. I write to state the fact, and to ask you to excuse the omission. I hope the letter has been received and that it will be speedily forwarded, as it was on business of importance, to which an early answer is desirable." PEx from an ALS offered for sale by Rendells, Inc., Newton, Mass., as Item 11 in Catalogue 162 (1982), p. 4.

From MIRABEAU B. LAMAR, DAVID G. BURNET, and Other Texans

Galvezton, October 31st 1845

Sir, To the undersigned Committee on behalf of the citizens of Texas present in Galvezton has been entrusted the gratifying task of communicating the Resolution of a public meeting, held this afternoon, tendering you the hospitality of the Country.

Yours Sir is a mind as unassailable to the ostentatious flatteries of public adulation, as it is to the insidious addresses of private corruption. We cannot flatter you, because we feel that no language, however strong, could adequately express the sentiment that prompts it. But in the name of a gallant people who admire, respect and love you, we invite you to come among them as their guest, and to share their hospitality, as a man, who after the consecrated name of Hero of the Hermitage, stands highest in their affections, as their early and steadfast friend. We are Sir, most respectfully Your obe[dien]t Servants and fellow-citizens, David G. Burnet, H[iram] G. Runnels, M.M. Potter, William L. Cazneau, A[lbert] C. Horton, Levi Jones, H[amilton] Stuart, H[ugh] McLeod, Hanson Allsbury, Eben[ezer] Allen, Mirabeau B. Lamar, Chairman of the Meeting.

[Enclosure]
Proceedings of a Public Meeting in Galveston

Galveston, October 31st 1845

The public prints having informed us that the Hon. John C. Calhoun has accepted an invitation to visit the City of Mobile & possibly New Orleans, during the coming month, and recognizing as we do, in that distinguished citizen, the loftiest patriotism, the purest integrity, and the highest ability in his long and [*one word canceled and* "brilliant" *interlined*] public career, and feeling as we do the warmest admiration and gratitude for his uniform justice and kindness towards the people of Texas—Therefore

Resolved—That in the name of ["the" *canceled*] our fellow citizens at large we invite the Hon. John C. Calhoun to extend his visit to us, & mingle socially among our people, who reciprocating his generous friendship will, we know, receive him as their, and his own Country's ablest advocate.

Resolved—That this resolution be communicated to Mr. Calhoun by the Chairman of the meeting with an appropriate letter from the Committee. Mirabeau B. Lamar, Chairman of the Meeting, H. McLeod, Secr[etar]y.

LS with En in ScCleA. NOTE: Lamar and Burnet were both former Presidents of the Texas Republic.

AFFIDAVIT by J[ohn] C. Calhoun

[*Ca.* November 1845?]

I do hereby certify, at the request of Mrs. [Margaret] Carlile, the widow of Col. Francis Carlile deceased, formerly of Abbeville District South Carolina, that I knew her deceased husband. I frequently saw him at my Father's [Patrick Calhoun's] residence, when I was a boy, and often heard him spoken of by my Father & others, *as a brave soldier, and, as I, think, officer also of the revolution.* My recollection of him extends back prior to 1796, the year my Father died.

I do not recollect of having been acquainted with his wife or any of his children, or of having heard them spoken of; *but have no reason to doubt of his being married at the time,* I knew him. I commenced my classical education a few years af[ter] 1796 and have been absent from the District & State the greater portion of the time since. J.C. Calhoun.

ADS in DNA, RG 15 (Veterans Administration), Revolutionary War Pension and Bounty-Land Warrant Application Files, 1800–1900, W10576 (M-804:470, frame 409). NOTE: This was one of several "proofs" enclosed in an ALS of 12/7/1845 from Charles Lewis, Jacksonville [Ala.], to Reuben Chapman [Representative from Ala.], found in the same file.

From JULIUS TIFT

Mobile, 2nd November 1845

D[ea]r Sir, In behalf of the owners of the Steamer "James L. Day" I have the honor of tendering you the hospitalities of said Boat for your conveyance to New Orleans; hoping you may so make your arrangements as to accept of this invitation, I subscribe myself with the highest respect Your very obedient Servant, Julius Tift.

ALS in ScCleA. NOTE: This letter was addressed to Calhoun in Mobile via Percy Walker. An AEU by Calhoun reads "Mr. Tift[,] tendering the Hospitality of his ["boat" *canceled*] Steamer, James L. Day."

From JOHN R. STOCKMAN

City Hall, Natchez, Nov. 3d 1845

Sir: I have the honor to communicate to you, subjoined, a copy of a resolution adopted by the Board of Selectmen of the City of Natchez at a special meeting held this day, tendering you an invitation to partake of the hospitalities of our City at such time, during your western tour, as may best suit your convenience.

Be assured Sir, the resolution expresses truly the feelings and wishes of our Citizens, who, entertaining a just appreciation of your distinguish[e]d & valuable public services, and the greatest veneration for your person and character, would receive your acceptance of the invitation, hereby tender[e]d, to visit them, with the highest gratification.

"Resolved that whereas it is known that the Hon: John C. Calhoun designs shortly to pass the City of Natchez, on his way to the City of Memphis to attend the Convention to be held in that City on the 12th inst. The President of this Board be authorized & requested to tender to Mr. Calhoun an invitation to partake of the hospitalities of the City of Natchez upon his way to, or from Memphis as will most

249

suit the convenience of Mr. Calhoun." I have the honor to be Y[ou]r ob[e]d[ien]t Serv[an]t, John R. Stockman, Pres[iden]t of B[oar]d of Selectmen.

ALS in ScCleA. NOTE: An AEU by Calhoun reads "The proceedings of the board of Select men in reference to my visit to Natchez."

From JOHN G. TOD

Mississip[p]i River, Nov. 3th 1845

My dear Sir, I am now on my way up to the City (N. Orleans) having left Galveston on the evening of the 1st.

We had a very large public meeting at Galveston before the Packet left, for the purpose of inviting you to extend your Visit West as far as Texas! Your numerous friends in Texas, and indeed I may say the People of that Country, would be truly gratified if your arrangements are such as to enable you to respond favorably to their request.

It would not require much time to visit Galveston & Houston and while on your way to the latter, you could take a look at the plains of San Jacinto.

I sometimes thought of writing you a few lines while in Texas giving you the news, but then I judged you had abler & better correspondents, keeping you advised of all that was interesting.

If I mistake not, I forwarded you, one among the first Constitutions that was published of our new state. As it was a necessary result of the great act of annexation, in which your name must forever occupy a prominent position, I trust you were favorably impressed with the first fruits of this measure.

I am now wending my way on to Washington City. I go there to try and find out how far my interest, and that of our few remaining officers of the Army & Navy of Texas, are to be disposed of by the Federal Government. The acceptation of the Resolutions of Annexation as presented by the Cabinet at Washington, debarred our own Govt: from making that provision for our interest that otherwise would have been done.

I would like to write you fully upon this subject, but I fear to occupy your time at present. I cannot help, but add, however, that I do pray, in connection with your numerous friends in Texas, that the report of your being found once more at your old post in the Senate, will prove true; this hope may be partly selfish on our own account: for we look to you, as to a friend, who would cheerfully render your aid and influence, if necessary, in securing to us our rights, heretofore obtained by long and faithful services to the "Lone Star."

I have sometimes thought that my anxiety, in times that are past, to see Annexation accomplished, led me probably to place in an unfavorable light, the views & opinions of some who were not thought, at that day, very favorable to the measure.

I always viewed it tho: as one of those great measures that might be opposed from proper motives.

This will be handed to you by your son [Patrick Calhoun], with whom I have enjoyed a pleasant passage across the Gulf. With great esteem, I remain your obedient Serv[an]t, Jno. G. Tod, Capt[ai]n of Texas Navy.

ALS in ScCleA.

ACCOUNT OF CALHOUN'S VISIT TO MOBILE

[November 4, 1845]

At an early hour yesterday morning [11/4], news was received here that Mr. Calhoun, on board the steamer "H. Kinney," would probably arrive in the city at about 12 o'clock, M. On the receipt of this intelligence, the Committee appointed to provide for his reception immediately engaged the fine steamer Montgomery to proceed up the river for the purpose of escorting him to the city. At half past ten the Montgomery departed, having on board the Committee and a large number of citizens, accompanied by a fine band of music engaged for the occasion. We met the H. Kinney about five or six miles above the city. On approaching the boat Mr. Calhoun made his appearance, uncovered, and was greeted with loud and prolonged cheers from the Montgomery. The two boats were then lashed together and proceeded towards the city. Mr. Calhoun was waited on by a sub-Committee, composed of Col. J[ames] S. Deas, Gen. R[obert] Desha, Dr. J[osiah] C. Nott and Col. P[ercy] Walker, and conducted on board the Montgomery, where he was introduced to the members of the Committee and the passengers generally. On arriving at the city, the wharves were lined with thousands of our fellow-citizens, anxious to obtain a sight of the great Statesman of the South, who for the first time in his life was to honor Mobile with

251

his presence. On the landing of the boat and the appearance of Mr. Calhoun on deck, he was welcomed by the most enthusiastic shouts from the immense concourse of citizens there assembled. An open barouche, drawn by four splendid bright bay horses, having been provided for the occasion, Mr. Calhoun was conducted thither by the Committee, and in company with Messrs. Deas, Desha and Walker, was conveyed to the Mansion House where a suit[e], of rooms had been provided for his reception.

Arrived at the Mansion House, he was waited on by the Mayor, Aldermen and members of the Common Council, who were severally introduced. His Honor the Mayor [Charles A. Hoppin], then, in behalf of the Corporate authorities and citizens made a short address of welcome, extending to him the hospitalities of the city. Mr. Calhoun made a brief, but chaste and feeling reply, eminently and beautifully appropriate to the occasion. This ceremony over, the citizens generally were introduced, and hundreds, of both political parties, availed themselves of the occasion to take by the hand the great statesman and patriot of the South.

The day was delightful, and not an incident occurred to mar the pleasures of the occasion. Mr. Calhoun appears in remarkably fine health, cheerful and happy. His reception, though quiet and unostentatious, we cannot but think was in the highest degree gratifying to his feelings. There was a cordiality, a sincerity and warmth of feeling evinced on the part of all—of those who have differed, as well as those who have agreed with him in political sentiment—that must have convinced him, as well as all who witnessed the scene, that there are times and occasions when the American people can rise above party and do justice to patriotism, talent and moral worth. Thus may it ever be.

[November 5, 1845]

Mr. Calhoun.—We are requested to announce that Mr. Calhoun will be pleased to see as many of our citizens as may be desirous of calling upon him, this day, between the hours of 11 A.M. and 1 P.M., in the parlor of the Mansion House.

. . . .

The Hon. John C. Calhoun, after a visit of two days, left our city for Memphis via New Orleans, on Thursday [11/6] at 12 o'clock, on board the fine steamer Creole. During his stay here he was called on by most of our citizens, and we have no hesitation in expressing the opinion that his visit has left a very favorable impression upon the public mind. It was the desire, we believe, of all parties to extend to Mr. Calhoun some public testimonial of the high estimation in which his character and public services are held by the people of Mobile, and the effort for a gratification of that desire was only abandoned in obedience to the wishes, repeatedly and earnestly expressed, of Mr. Calhoun himself. He however did consent to dine with a small party of gentlemen, composed of the members of our city corporation, the New Orleans committee, the Mobile committee of reception, and a few of the citizens, on Wednesday evening. The dinner was furnished by Mr. Cullum at the Mansion House, and, considering the short notice he had for getting it up, was prepared in magnificent style. His Honor the Mayor presided, assisted by T. Sanford, esq. "Our distinguished Guest" was toasted by the Mayor, and Mr. Calhoun responded in a complimentary sentiment to Mobile—declining to favor the company with a speech. Numerous toasts were drank by the company, the sentiments of which were in fine taste—characterized by the utmost liberality and good feeling. Mr. Calhoun retired in the midst of the festivities, amid cheers "three times three." The occasion was one of the most agreeable that we have ever participated in. Party feeling was entirely forgotten, and not a sentiment, not a word, was uttered calculated to grate harshly upon the ear of any one, or at all inconsistent with the occasion.

[November 6, 1845] On Thursday morning, in a carriage provided for the purpose, drawn by the four beautiful bright bays noticed in our account of his reception, (which were furnished by our friend B.W. Van Epps,) Mr. Calhoun, in company with a portion of the committee, took a view of our city and environs, after which he was conducted to the Creole, where a vast concourse of citizens had assembled to witness his departure. As the boat moved off slowly and gracefully from the wharf, the distinguished statesman was again honored with shouts of applause.

Nothing has ever given us more heartfelt satisfaction than the cordiality with which Mr. Calhoun has been greeted on this occasion by all classes, but particularly by our own [Whig] political friends. They have shown that they can honestly differ with a man in opinion, and still award to him honesty of purpose, integrity of character, and pay a proper tribute to exalted talents and moral worth. The manner of his reception and his treatment while here, we flatter ourselves were also in the highest degree gratifying to the feelings of Mr. Calhoun. There was no display, to be sure, but there was something better—there was an unmistakable manifestation of sincere respect and profound admiration. Our citizens paid him the unaffected tribute which they all felt was his due, as a great American statesman, possessed of many noble traits of character—a true patriot—a pure and upright citizen, and an honest man.

From the Mobile, Ala., *Daily Advertiser*, November 5, 1845, p. 2, and November 8, 1845, p. 2. Also printed (in French and English) in the New Orleans, La., *Courrier de la Louisiane*, November 6, 1845, pp. 2–3; the Washington, D.C., *Constitution*, November 17, 1845, p. 3. Different account in the Richmond, Va., *Enquirer*, November 14, 1845, p. 2, and November 18, 1845, p. 1; the Mobile, Ala., *Register and Journal*, November 5, 1845, p. 2, and November 8, 1845, p. 2; the Washington, D.C., *Constitution*, November 13, 1845, p. 3.

From C H A [R L E] S A. H O P P I N and Others

Mobile, Nov. 4/1845

Dear Sir, The undersigned on behalf of the Corporate authorities of the City of Mobile respectfully invite you to partake of a private dinner to morrow at 5 o[']c[loc]k at the Mansion House. Very Respectfully We have the Honor to be Y[ou]r ob[edien]t S[er]v[an]ts, Chas. A. Hoppin, Mayor, John Hurtel, Ch[ai]r[ma]n of the C[ommon] Council, E. Salomon, Ch[airma]n of the B[oar]d of Ald[erme]n.

LS in ScCleA. NOTE: An AEU by Calhoun reads "Invitation to dine with the Co[r]poration of Mobile."

From W [I L L I A] M L. C O W A N and Others

Eufaula Ala., Nov. 5th 1845

Sir, The citizens of Eufaula in grateful recollection of your long faithful and distinguished public services to the Government and country have appointed the undersigned a committee to invite you to visit their town and partake with them of a public dinner at such time as may suit your convenience.

Under these instructions, we respectfully solicit your acceptance of the invitation. It will be gratifying to them to have the honor and pleasure of tendering to you the hospitalities of their town. With sentiments of respect, we have the honor to be Your Obedient Servants, Wm. L. Cowan, W[illiam] Wellborn, A. McDonald, Jno. Cochran, B[enjamin] Gardner, W[illia]m J. Ridgill, E.B. Fuller, John L. Hunter, Reuben Shorter, J. McNab, T. Cargill, E.B. Young,

254

E[dward] C. Bullock, J. McCaleb Wiley, Thomas Flournoy, John Gill Shorter, J[efferson] Buford, N.M. Hyatt, Z[adoc] J. Daniel, Jacob Smith, Rob[er]t Ferguson, Committee.

LS in ScCleA. NOTE: This letter was addressed to Calhoun "care of Hon. James M. Calhoun, Richmond P.O., Dallas Co[unty], Ala." An AEU in an unknown hand reads "To be forwarded if necessary." An AEU by Calhoun reads "Invitation to Eufaula."

From HENRY P. HOLCOMBE

Mobile, 5 Nov[embe]r 1845

Dear Sir, At the time of my taking leave of you on yesterday, you will remember, that I intimated my desire to entertain a private conversation with you. I now perceive, that in all probability an opportunity may not occur when such conversation will comport with your perfect convenience—so short will be your stay in our city. I have therefore concluded to commit to paper all that I designed to have communicated verbally to you—and in making this communication, I shall acquit myself of a solemn declaration made to a friend of mine, and a most ardent one of yours, some seven years ago.

The history of my political predilections is easily told; and no man in the Union knows better than yourself, how to appreciate them. I was educated in the Georgia school of politics, under *The* [William H.] *Crawford division of that school,* and imbibed strong prejudices against the South Carolina politicians, *yourself always foremost* in my contemplations, from the fact, that we at that period being State Rights men of the straightest sect, doubted the political orthodoxy of yourself and other distinguished men of South Carolina, and from the further consideration, that we were induced to believe, *your influence* had been the means of preventing the nomination of Mr. Crawford by the congressional caucus in 1824—or previously, which as we then thought would have secured to him the Presidency at the close of Mr. [James] Monroe[']s term.

These prejudices from these considerations were strongly entertained up to the year 1831, when your letter on the relation which the States and general Government bear to each other was published—and altho' I was not able to detect, in the premises, erroneous positions, State rights man as I was, and always had been, ["yet" *interlined*] I could not bring my mind to assent to *your conclusions.* I saw, or thought I saw, that the doctrine must result in a fatal subversion of the Government—or, in the necessity of put[t]ing down a sovereign State of the union, by *the military force of the union*—the consequences of which would have been equally disastrous to *the existence of our institutions.* I therefore warmly and zealously denounced the doctrine of nullification as expounded by you, under the Virginia & Kentucky Resolutions—and warred against it up to the final compromise of the difficulty in 1833. It was after this period, when the passions of men had ceased to exert its sway—and reason had resumed its wonted power, that *reflection came,* and induced me to review the history of your public life as exhibited in our country's annals. As my thoughts ran on the general course and tenor of your public career, I soon became impressed with the belief that I may have misconceived your motives, and misapprehended your character. I sought in vain, for *the slightest evidence* of your *unfaithfulness* to the interests of *the South especially*—on questions involving the rights, interests or honour of the South, I found you *always—invariably—firmly at your post.* I accorded too, to your interpretations of the constitution—and the origin of the Government, *full acquiescence.* The doctrine of the sovereignty of the States originally—and the necessity of confining the Federal Government to a strict construction of that instrument, in order to preserve the sovereignty unimpaired, met my hearty approbation. Notwithstanding all this, I could not assent to *the constitutionality* of the doctrine of nullification on *the South Carolina plane—The Georgia practice* I preferred—and still prefer. Still the difficulty remains to be solved. If the States have rights, what is *the remedy* in the last resort for the wilful and obstinate infraction of those rights? I reply in the language of Gov. [George M.] Troup, after "*exhausting* the argument— if the Government *will have it so,* "stand by our arms." I need only say Sir at this time, that I used my pen & my tongue lavishly, in strictures on your *public character,* from time to time, from 1824 to 1834—and be assured you were not spared. Your private character, happily for yourself and your country, stands upon unequalled ground for its elevation & its purity. *This* I always accorded to you, because it was beyond the power of your political opponents to attack you on *that point.*

My mind as before observed had taken the enquiring direction— and the more I examined, the more I became convinced that my early associations with the friends of Mr. Crawford, had instilled into my mind prejudices against you, which *had no foundation* in fact— and gradually brought me up to the point and date of your celebrated speeches on the "Subtreasury" Bill & replies to Messrs. [Henry] Clay

& [Daniel] Webster in 1838—after reading these speeches I lost the last lingering prejudice I had entertained. They placed in my mind *a Key* which unlocked all the apparent imperfections of your career, and I became from that moment convinced that I had been *guilty* of great, and almost *unpardonable injustice* toward you—and I sought & obtained an interview with a warm friend of yours (at that time the Editor of the "Chronicle" in Augusta Georgia) and who had some knowledge of my occasional essays in the columns of another city paper. A man whom I highly esteemed as ["an" *canceled*] honest[,] open hearted & ingenuous—and proclaimed to him that I from that day ceased my warfare against you—that I could never forgive *myself* for having been so weak as to have so far misapprehended your motives & your character. That I would make it a part of the business of my after life to repair all the wrong I had done if it were possible, and that I would if ever an opportunity offered, make to you in person the acknowledgement, that *I had wronged you*—and my determination *to repair that wrong* by all the means in my power. Receive this Sir, as the redemption of that pledge, with the sincerity of (I hope) an honest heart. I am not so vain Sir, as to suppose for a moment, that this acknowledgement can afford you *any gratification.* My strictures were too feeble to affect a character so firmly established in the estimation of his countrymen as yours. But it is for the purpose of *redeeming the pledge* I made seven years ago, that I now trespass on your time to read this ["hasty letter" *canceled*] hastily written letter.

My course in your case, has been a warning to me, never to pronounce a condemnation on a public man without close examination—and above all, not to suffer mere *associations* to warp my judgement—on the estimate proper to be placed on public men.

That I am redeeming my other pledges, I trust Sir you will be the last to doubt. It would be indelicate in me to pursue this subject as I could desire. Besides, I know that my friendship, or my enmity as a politician could not give you much concern.

Trusting that you will consider this communication as entirely confidential—and that you will favor me with an acknowledgement of its reception by you, I am Dear Sir, Your friend & fellow citizen, Henry P. Holcombe.

ALS in ScCleA. Note: This letter was addressed to Calhoun at the Mansion House, Mobile, care of "Dr. W.S. Taylor."

From W[ILLIA]M C. ANDERSON and Others

St. Louis, November 6, 1845
Dear Sir: We, the undersigned, Democratic citizens of St. Louis City
and County, having learned that you will attend the Convention to
be held at Memphis, Tennessee, on the 12th inst. earnestly solicit, in
our own behalf and in behalf of your numerous friends in this vicinity,
that you will extend your visit West, to this place, the commercial emporium of the Upper Mississippi Valley, and accept the hospitalities
of those who are anxious to see among them a statesman for whose
patriotic devotion to sound principles they feel so deep and lasting
gratitude. The citizens of the Great West feel justly indebted to you
for your untiring zeal in behalf of the producing and agricultural
States of the Union, as manifested by your exertions to bring back
the Federal Government to the true principles of taxation, and thus
relieve the South and West of the burthens unconstitutionally imposed on them for the peculiar benefit of northern and Eastern capitalists. As the Champion of the State Rights principles and party,
and the unflinching opponent of consolidation in all of its schemes,
you have conferred the most important and lasting benefits on the
West and the whole Union. As Secretary of War you first directed
general attention to those great national measures in the West,
through the neglect of which by the Federal Government, the people
of this valley have suffered immense losses for a long series of years;
and as a Senator you have firmly adhered to those doctrines, on the
observance of which the continued prosperity of each and all sections
of the Union depends.

Notwithstanding our high regard for the many distinguished
acts of patriotism with which your long public career has been
illustrated, from the date of your fearless advocacy of the War of
1812, and defence of our national honor and rights then assailed,
down to your recent retirement from the Department of State; yet
there is one measure above all others, for the triumph of which the
country is especially indebted to your boldness, sagacity and patriotism—we refer, of course, to the *Annexation of Texas*. Residing, as
we do on a portion of that soil acquired by the Louisiana treaty, and
west of the Mississippi river, we regard the restoration of Texas to
our national domain with peculiar pride and interest; it being the
re-union of the dissevered Mississippi Valley and a vast stride in
National progress. To your services in an eminent degree does the
Country owe the accomplishment of that American measure—an
"extension of the area of freedom"—to be followed, it is hoped, by the

spread of our free institutions, in due time, westward to the Pacific. As Americans we are proud of the bold and lofty stand taken by you whilst Secretary of State in defence of our true national policy and in opposition to and defiance of the intrigues of European monarchs on this Continent.

It has been justly remarked that the South and West are natural allies; and so regarding them, whilst desiring at the same time the prosperity of the whole Union, we are the more solicitous that you shall visit this city, in order that your many friends in this vicinity and State, may have the long desired opportunity of receiving among them a Statesman who though residing in the South, belongs to the whole Union, and is honored wherever sound and liberal principles have an admirer. We have the honor to be with sentiments of the highest esteem, Your obedient servants, Wm. C. Anderson, George Maguire, H. King, W[illia]m Palm, John Dunn, Rob[er]t P. Simmons, Jos[eph] H. Conn, Ro[bert] M.V. Kercheval, Abner Hood, C. Pullis[?], Silas Reed, A.P. Ladew, Jos[eph] S. Crane, James S. Lane, John O. Agnew, Rob[er]t A. Barnes, William Milburn, B.W. Ayres, John Black, Miron Leslie, Sam[ue]l Treat, D.U.[?] Armstrong, C. Garvey, Sam[ue]l Willi, Tho[mas] B. Hudson, Chas. D. Gillespie, Tho[ma]s Andrews, Mat[he]w[?] Elgin, Trusten Polk [later Senator from Missouri], C.B. Lord, Nath[anie]l Holmes, C.W. Edgerly, John Regan, G[regory] Byrne, Elihu H. Shepard, Sylvanus Sanborn, Tom F. Anderson, A.W. Manning, Chr[istopher] Kribben, R. Dowling, E.K. Woodward, John D. Hill, John S. Watson, John Ostrander, H. Walton, Stephen Ladew, Jr., Rich[ar]d S. Blennerhassett, Cyrenius C. Simmons, J.W. Magrear[?], John M. Krum, Rob[er]t P. Chase, James G. Barrey, Edw[ard] Cruft, Jr., Wm. Lindsay[?], J. Warner Ormsbee, A.F. Garrison, William Weber, Ja[me]s Lemon, Daniel H. Donovan, N[athan] Ranney, Nath[anie]l Blackeston, S[hadrach] Penn, Jr.

LS in ScCleA; PC in the Springfield, Ill., *Illinois State Register*, December 5, 1845, p. 2; PEx in Boucher and Brooks, eds., *Correspondence*, pp. 307–308. NOTE: The published list of signers includes the additional name of H[enry] M. Shreve.

From W[ILLIAM] B. LEWIS

Fairfield [near Nashville,] 7th Nov. 1845

Dear Sir, Yours of the 18th Ultimo was received a few days ago, *all in good time.* I had no doubt that the delay was occasioned by your absence from home and, as I anticipated, on a visit to your son in Alabama. It is every thing that I could desire it to be—just such an answer as I was sure your love of justice would prompt you to write—and for which I beg you to accept my sincere thanks.

Can you not, my dear Sir, on your return from Memphis take Nashville in your route to South Carolina? You have many warm friends and admirers here who would be glad to see you. Besides, it would afford you an opportunity of visiting the Hermitage where my young friend Andrew Jackson and his amiable family would give you a cordial welcome; and, I need not say, it would give me great pleasure to be your conductor to that renowned and hallowed spot.

I see from the public Journals that your friends are anxious to have you again in the Senate and I hope, most sincerely, that they may be gratified, as I consider it important for the Country that you should be there. We need, at the present crisis, men in the Senate not only of distinguished ability but of purity and undoubted patriotism. With you from the South and Gen[era]l [Lewis] Cass from the North I should think the Republic safe—for I am sure with both [of] you, its safety and the preservation of our Institutions far out weigh all mere party considerations. The General[']s views upon the Tariff are not entirely coincident with yours; but you and he ["are" *interlined*] not very wide apart—not so far, perhaps, as you may have supposed.

There are several questions of vital importance to the country that must come before Congress and be acted on at the approaching session—particularly those of the Tariff and Oregon. By the by, I have good reason to believe that nothing has been done, or *attempted*, in relation to the latter, since you left the [State] Department! Is not this a little remarkable? It is nevertheless true, as I verily believe.

I cannot conclude without again expressing the hope that your friends may be gratified in their desire of seeing you soon in the Senate—and, in the mean time, I beg you to believe me to be, my dear sir, very truly and sincerely yours, W.B. Lewis.

ALS in ScCleA; ALS (draft) in CtY, Sterling Library, A.C. Goodyear Collection.

ACCOUNT OF CALHOUN'S VOYAGE FROM MOBILE TO NEW ORLEANS

New Orleans, November [7], 1845

[By the correspondent of the Mobile *Register and Journal:*] Dear Sir—In pursuance of my promise, I use the first leisure moment to give you a brief account of the reception of Mr. Calhoun in New Orleans [on 11/7], which was as we expected, a most hearty, enthusiastic and brilliant one, with no useless noise and ostentatious parade, but precisely such as he and his friends could have desired. You know how we left the city [of Mobile], with a large concourse assembled on the wharves, who cheered us as we rounded off for the voyage, and received in reply the parting salutations of Mr. Calhoun, who raised his hat and bowed to the assemblage. We had a delightful time on board. After supper, nearly all who sat down, lingered in a social way about Mr. Calhoun, who sat at the upper end of the cabin, and engaged in the conversation with that ease and affability for which he is distinguished, making each one perfectly at home, and offering, from time to time, easy and pleasant occasion for nearly every one present to suggest topics and engage in the conversation; and thus, without the slightest intermixture of party politics, the conversation glided on until near midnight, when we all rose to retire, only regretting that we had not longer to listen to the striking and original views with which every subject touched upon was illustrated. I need scarcely add, that we all found ourselves supplied with rich and ample food for reflection—materials for many days of thought. And here, before parting with this portion of our delightful excursion, I must acknowledge the obligations of the Mobile delegation to the spirited commander of the "Creole," Captain [R.A.] Hiern, for the admirable manner in which he did the hospitalities of his boat, and I must also record of him decidedly the best and pithiest thing said on the occasion. Captain Hiern, with as much taste as kindness, relinquished his own excellent apartment on the hurricane deck, next to the pilot's stand, to Mr. Calhoun, as the best and most spacious on board; an idea which struck me as being at once original and hospitable. And I took the first occasion that offered itself to express this sentiment, for our delegation, to the Captain. "Why, certainly sir," he replied, "how could I do less? I had that room built there for my own use, because I have to be *on deck at all hours of the night,* and as *the old man* has been *on deck at night* for the last twenty years, I thought *that* was the true place to put him—

261

the place suits the man." We all laughed heartily at the admirable reply, and no one enjoyed it more than Mr. Calhoun, to whom it was soon after repeated. In fact, after a short pause, in which it could be easily discovered there was more of solemnity than mirth, he said it was the highest compliment he had ever received, and one, of all others, that he was most ambitious to deserve. And so I fancy his friends would think. To be *on deck at night*—to be near the helm of state to direct the pilot in the tempestuous hour of darkness and danger, is the station which the patriot and the statesman would, of all others, desire to fill. Is it not that too which *history* will designate, with our Captain, as having been filled by Mr. Calhoun? And is it not that to which a lowering future may induce his country again to summon him. I allude not to the presidency, (a small matter in my opinion for such a man as Mr. Calhoun,) but to those duties of a yet higher statesmanship, which the profound sagacity and far seeing wisdom of such men alone can discharge in the critical conjunctures that seem to await us.

We arrived at the hotel on the lake at day light, where many of the older citizens of New Orleans had already arrived to offer their congratulations to Mr. Calhoun—and who, together with the New Orleans and Mobile delegations sat down at "Bell's hotel," on the lake, to the most tasteful and sumptuous breakfast I ever saw—indeed the market of New Orleans and the lakes seemed to have contributed every delicacy that the season and the waters could afford to please the eye and the palate, and had our distinguished guest been at all addicted to epecurean enjoyments, or, indeed, any thing but the most temperate of men, he must, for once at least, have been tempted to deviate from what is said to be his invariable rule of never rising from a meal with an appetite entirely satisfied. We rose from breakfast at 11 a.m., and took the cars for the city, where, on our arrival, we found assembled at the *Depot* such a mass of human beings as I have never before seen on any similar occasion. Indeed we thought that New Orleans, with its accustomed enthusiasm, had sent forth its entire population, to impress upon us the magnitude and brilliancy of the city, but as we passed through the city we found the streets, the doors, windows and porticoes of private houses and public buildings similarly crowded.

At the Depot we were met by the Governor [Alexander Mouton] and suite, General [Edmund P.] Gaines and his staff, the military and civic associations of the city, who with a large concourse of citizens formed a procession and escorted Mr. Calhoun and the two delegations from Mobile and New Orleans in carriages, provided for the purpose, through several of the principal streets to the St. Louis Hotel; while minute guns were fired on the Public Square by a company of Artillery. At the St. Charles Hotel, which the procession passed in going to the St. Louis, an immense concourse had assembled, both in the street and on the magnificent portico of the former building, and three long and hearty cheers, amidst the waving of hats and handkerchiefs greeted the coach which bore Mr. Calhoun. And this was a degree of enthusiasm, entirely divested of all party motive or party animosity, but with a feeling which no one could doubt was wholly and purely American, Mr. Calhoun was received in New Orleans, and conducted to the elegant apartments provided for him by the corporate authorities at the "St. Louis Hotel." This Hotel was selected in accordance with his known tastes and feeling so often expressed during his present visit, and so uniformly acted upon throughout his life, of appearing in no other light than as a private citizen, and avoiding, as far as it was possible, with a proper respect and sense of gratitude to his fellow citizens for public manifestations of their approval, all improper show and parade. Indeed, I may mention, in this connexion, that on his arrival at the lake hotel, he expressed much regret that the idea of a public procession had been adopted, and said with a degree of emotion which impressed every one present, that he feared he should have hereafter, deeply to reproach himself for not having sufficiently warned his friends as to the line of conduct on this subject, which from his earliest entrance into public life he had firmly resolved to pursue, and that having for near forty years denied himself the pleasure of seeing as much of his own country as he desired, in order to avoid misconstruction, he should deeply lament, now that he felt himself in a purely private capacity, that any thing should be done by his consent inconsistent with his past life, or justly subject to exception. But to this, a whig of the New-Orleans delegation made, we think, a very proper reply that, what had been done was the spontaneous offering of all parties, and that in fact the whigs themselves claimed, and were determined to have the credit, of giving to his reception whatever of a public character it displayed. This was literally the fact, for I was informed in New-Orleans that the proceedings for this cordial and patriotic reception, originated with the "Common Council" of the second Municipality—the resolutions tendering Mr. Calhoun the hospitalities of the city, having been introduced by a whig, and meeting a temporary opposition but from a single member of that or any other Board. Indeed, I may truly say, that the most striking feature in the enthusiasm with which the great American Statesman has been received, both at Mobile and New-Orleans, was its apparently, and I believe, *really* entire freedom from all party character. The men of all parties, and from all sections of our common country, seemed to have vied with each other in those kindly and patriotic expressions which tend to evince the pride of a people in illustrious worth, distinguished genius, and spotless private character. In Mobile, as you are aware, (and in New-Orleans it was not the less so,) in public and in private, in the toasts at the social board and in the columns of the press, this has been the pervading sentiment, expressed in every form which the spontaneous generosity of heart and language could suggest.

At the private dinner provided by the corporate authorities of the city of New-Orleans, about a hundred and twenty persons sat down, including the Governor of the State, his Honor the Mayor [Joseph E. Montegut], and the several Boards of Aldermen and Common Council of the three municipalities. I need not say, the feast was a sumptuous one. You know that the taste of New-Orleans is second only to her generosity, and that her heart is as large as her commerce. I had intended to make memoranda of the toasts, but the time flew too pleasantly to tarry at such an occupation. I only wish I could remember the sentiment of surpassing eloquence and beauty, offered to Mr. Calhoun by the great orator of the Louisiana Bar, Mr. [Pierre] Soulé—expressed in that inimitable manner of which he is the peculiar master. It was in the spirit of broadest and most comprehensive patriotism, and yet pointed with an inimitable felicity to the peculiar graces of Mr. Calhoun's character and his career as a statesman. It brought every one at the table, at once, to his feet, and was followed by a burst of applause as unanimous as it seemed irresistable and spontaneous. Mr. Calhoun rose with great emotion, expressing in a few feeling words his profound sense of the hearty welcome he had received—"so far," he said, "exceeding anything he felt that he deserved, or was prepared to expect, as to rob him, in the deep feeling of the moment, of all power of language to express his grateful acknowledgements." How true this was could only be fully realized by those who saw the glistening eye and heard the deep but tremulous tone in which it was expressed.

Mr. Calhoun retired at an early hour from the table, leaving his hospitable friends to enjoy the festivities at their leisure; and this they did in good earnest; for never did I see a more joyous assemblage. I leave the city at 2 o'clock to-day [11/8], so that I shall be deprived of the pleasure of witnessing a portion of the hospitalities with which it is intended to distinguish the occasion. Mr. Calhoun, at half past 2 o'clock, is to visit the St. Charles, where a collation will be prepared by some of his friends, and which it is said will surpass the sumptuous dinner spread yesterday at the "St. Louis." In fact, the people of New-Orleans seem determined to make Mr. Calhoun acknowledge "*nolens volens,*" in the language of one of the toasts given by a member of the Mobile delegation, "that *New-Orleans,* in commerce the first of southern cities, in hospitality and the generous appreciation of illustrious worth, is second to none in the Union." Nor have these gratifying manifestations been confined to the citizens proper of New-Orleans. As soon as Mr. Calhoun arrived in the city, he received a message expressed in the most tasteful and complimentary language, from the proprietors of the splendid steamer "Maria," placing her at his disposal at any hour he might designate; and it is understood that he will leave the city at 3 o'clock, against which hour, it is understood that preparations are making to give him a *Farewell* as generous and touching as was the *Reception,* which, I fear, I have very poorly described.

In conclusion I will only add, that the delegation appointed to accompany Mr. Calhoun from Mobile to New-Orleans, were afforded in the attention shown them and the hearty welcome and farewell they were received and parted with, another in addition to the many past evidences of the hospitality of the citizens of the Crescent City, and the fraternal feeling they are ever ready to cultivate with us of Mobile. Long may this feeling continue to distinguish the intercourse of the two cities, and to unite them, as on this occasion, in the noble work of doing homage to the great, the wise and the good of our land. It is, indeed, on occasions of this kind that all mankind are made to feel that they are brothers, and have a common property in the fame of those illustrious men whose name and memory a Nation should ever wear, and be proud to wear, on her breast—the most precious of her jewels as they are the bright insignia of the only nobility that freedom tolerates and acknowledges.

PC in the Mobile, Ala., *Register and Journal,* November 11, 1845, p. 2.

ACCOUNT OF CALHOUN'S VISIT TO NEW ORLEANS

[November 7–8, 1845]

Yesterday morning [11/7], at 7 o'clock, Mr. Calhoun, accompanied by a committee of twelve of our citizens, and escorted by a like number of gentlemen from Mobile, arrived upon the steamer "James L. Day," at the lake end of the railroad, and after partaking of a *dejeuner a la fourchette* at the Washington Hotel, took the 11 o'clock train of cars for the city. At the railroad depot, an immense concourse of our citizens were anxiously awaiting the arrival of our distinguished guest.

As soon as the cars appeared in sight, the bands of the military struck up "Hail Columbia," and the cheers and shouts of the assemblage greeted upon his arrival the illustrious statesman. Upon leaving the cars, Mr. Calhoun was welcomed to our city by his honor the Mayor [Joseph E. Montegut], in a few brief and appropriate remarks, to which Mr. C[alhoun] replied in an appropriate and feeling manner. A procession was then formed, headed by the military [that is, militia] under the command of Maj. Gen. John L. Lewis. Next followed a landeau, drawn by four grey horses, in which were seated Mr. Calhoun, his excellency the Governor [Alexander Mouton], and his honor the Mayor. A landeau and four, containing A[ndrew] P. Calhoun, esq., a son of our distinguished guest, and the Recorders of the several municipalities, and a similar establishment in which was seated Major Gen. [Edmund P.] Gaines, of the U.S. Army, and a long line of carriages, containing the members of the General and Municipal Council, distinguished strangers and citizens then followed. The rear of the procession was brought up by some of the companies of the fire department, dressed in their uniform, and headed by their beautiful banners. Upon passing the "Place d'Armes," a salute in honor of the occasion was fired by a company of the batallion of artillery under the command of Capt. Augustin. The flags of the shipping and of the numerous public buildings of the city, were displayed through the day. Upon Mr. Calhoun's arrival at the St. Louis Hotel, he was escorted to the magnificent drawing room of that establishment, and there was introduced by the committee of arrangements to a large number of our citizens.

Mr. Calhoun appears in fine health and spirits, and gratified at the cordial reception he has received in New Orleans.

[November 7, 1845]
Mr. Calhoun. This gentleman received the utmost courtesy, civility and manifestations of respect, during his sojourn in our city. He was waited on during Friday [11/7] and Saturday [11/8] by a large number of citizens. On Friday evening he dined, as the guest of the city, with a numerous party of gentlemen, including the Governor of the State and the city authorities, at the St. Louis Exchange, and on

Saturday at the St. Charles Hotel. On both these occasions, the entertainments were remarkable for the spirit and animation of the company. Mr. Calhoun declined, at either party, to remain long upon the floor, but in both instances returned thanks in a very handsome and feeling manner, for the hospitalities he had received, and closing with apt sentiments.

At the dinner on Friday evening, the health and welcome of Mr. Calhoun having been proposed by the Mayor of the city, Mr. C[alhoun] replied, expressing his acknowledgments, declaring the warm interest he had felt and should always feel in the prosperity of the city, and offered as a sentiment: "New Orleans: What Paris is to the Seine; what London is to the Thames; may New Orleans be to the Mighty Father of Rivers."

On the occasion, Governor Mouton, having been called to his feet by a complimentary toast, offered a very handsome and appropriate sentiment. The Mobile Committee, who accompanied Mr. Calhoun, having been toasted, responded with much spirit through their chairman. A great number of sentiments, nearly all pithy and appropriate, were offered by different gentlemen, but were none of them reduced to writing.

[November 8, 1845]

The Dinner on Saturday evening was even more spirited. Mr. Calhoun, in response to a sentiment in his honor, after declaring that the emotions with which he was inspired by the kindnesses he had received were beyond any words he could express, offered the following: "The Valley of the Mississippi: Take it all in all, the greatest in the world. Situated midway between the oceans, it will yet command the commerce of both, and that commerce may be centred in New Orleans."

This was followed by a number of happily expressed sentiments, and flashes of wit and humor, from different parts of the table, but like those of the previous evening, they were not put on paper, and of course perished in the using.

Mr. Calhoun left the city at 6 o'clock on Saturday evening, in the fine steamer Maria [bound upriver accompanied by fifty delegates to the Memphis Convention elected by the people of New Orleans at a meeting on November 7]. He was accompanied to the boat by a large concourse of citizens.

November 7–8 account from the Washington, D.C., *Constitution*, November 17, 1845, p. 2, reprinting the New Orleans, La., *Bee* of ca. November 7, 1845. Three variant accounts in the New Orleans, La., *Daily Picayune*, November 8,

1845, p. 2; the Richmond, Va., *Enquirer*, November 18, 1845, p. 1, reprinting
the New Orleans, La., *Delta*, November 8, 1845; and the Raleigh, N.C., *North
Carolina Standard*, November 19, 1845, p. 3, reprinting the New Orleans, La.,
Commercial Times, November 8, 1845. November 7 and 8 accounts from the
Richmond, Va., *Enquirer*, November 18, 1845, p. 2, reprinting the New Orleans,
La., *Bulletin*, November 10, 1845.

Toast by Calhoun at the St. Louis Hotel, New Orleans, in reply
to [Joseph E. Montegut], Mayor of New Orleans, 11/7. *"New Orleans*: As Paris is to the Seine, as London is to the Thames, so may
New Orleans be to the mighty Father of Rivers." From the New Orleans, La., *Daily Picayune*, November 9, 1845, p. 2. Also printed in
the New Orleans, La., *Bee*, November 10, 1845, p. 1; the Mobile, Ala.,
Register and Journal, November 12, 1845, p. 2; the Jackson, Miss.,
Mississippian, November 19, 1845, p. 2; the Cincinnati, Ohio, *Daily
Enquirer*, November 24, 1845, p. 2.

From A[LBERT] G. BROWN, [Governor of Miss.], and Others

Jackson, Mississippi, 8th November 1845
Dear Sir, We address you in obedience to the enclosed resolution
passed at a large meeting of our fellow-citizens who having learned
that you would shortly visit the borders of Mississippi depute us to
invite you to the seat of Government as the guest of the State. The
Resolutions express but faintly the general wish of all parties in this
State to greet you on your homeward route and to extend to you the
hospitality of a people who acknowledge with gratitude your vigorous
defence of the Constitution and the ceaseless vigil you have kept
over the rights guarantied to them by that sacred instrument. We
will not point to isolated efforts of your political life and say it is for
these we honor you. We do but express the general sentiment when
we declare that your whole life presents to our minds the single unbroken idea of a mighty effort to sustain the institutions of the Country at every point and against every assault. We address you without
reference to party. Some of us differ with you as to the means to be
employed in attaining good ends but all of us a[ward] you purity of
purpose, vastness of intellect and a patriotism bounded only by the
limits of this great Republic. It is for these we honor you. Visit us
at our homes—every hand will greet you warmly—every heart will
rejoice as you come—not an eye that will not beam with pleasure nor

a tongue that will not welcome you to our soil. *Republics may* be ungrateful but Mississippi acknowledges her gratitude to you, and her sons will not repudiate the debt. Very truly your fellow citizen, A.G. Brown, ch[air]m[an], John Mayrant, C.R. Clifton, A.A. Mc-Willie, W[iley] P. Harris, D.C. Glenn, C[ollin] S. Tarpley, George Fearne, Sam. Matthews, W[illia]m Yerger, W[illia]m L. Sharkey, S.S. Erwin, P[atrick] Henry, W[illia]m M. Smyth, R.H. Buckner, H.A.G. Roberts, Dan[ie]l Mayes.

[Enclosure]

1st. Resolved—That the Delegates appointed by the meeting, act also as a Committee of invitation, with instructions to invite the Hon: John C. Calhoun, and the Hon: F[ranklin] H. Elmore, representatives of the State of South-Carolina to the Memphis Convention, to visit Jackson, as the guests of this State.

2d. Resolved—That His Excellency Gov: Brown, be respectfully requested to act as Chairman of said Committee of Invitation.

LS with En in ScCleA; PC with En in the Jackson, Miss., *Southern Reformer,* November 22, 1845, p. 3. NOTE: All signatures to this letter except Brown's were added in a handwriting different from that of the individual who copied the letter and resolutions. Brown appears to have been the only member of the committee who signed the ms. himself. In printing the above resolutions, the *Southern Reformer* substituted the name of Christopher G. Memminger for that of Franklin H. Elmore (Jackson, Miss., *Southern Reformer,* November 8, 1845, p. 3.)

From Tho[ma]s J. Green

New York [City,] Nov[embe]r 8th 1845

My Dear Mr. Calhoun: Gratuitous advice from a comparatively obscure man like myself, to one very distinguished like yourself, ought ordinarily to be considered impertinent, but in this instance my long and warm friendship for you will take that risk.

In my last letter [of 9/19] I gave my reasons in favour of your returning to the Senate. Since which time I have conversed with your friends the Hon. Mr. I[saac] E. Holmes & Gen. Duff Green, and they believe that if you return to the Senate you will oppose the measures of the administration upon the Oregon question.

Now my advice is, that if this is to be your course, however right it may be in the abstract, for God sake do not come to the Senate. An immence majority of this nation is & will continute [*sic*] to be with the President upon this question—[Thomas H.] Benton will be the champion of that majority, and will place you where the Calhoun's and [William] Lownd[e]s' placed the anti war party in 1812. If we are to have war, then do not destroy yourself by vainly endeavouring to prevent it; and your better patriotism will be, to hold yourself as the nation[']s *corps-de-reserve*, to bring it to an honourable and a glorious termination. I cannot be driven from the impression that, your opposition to the measure will destroy you as effectually as Texas destroyed [Henry] Clay & [Martin] Van Buren. Your *good* Whig friends are very anxious for you to come into the Senate and butt your brains out against this question, and the people north of 36.30° will say that, *Mr. Calhoun & his South Carolinians are very willing to get more slave territory, but are unwilling for us to have more anti slave territory.*

It would be an insult to your intelligence to give you all the reasons which press upon at this time for this advice, but rely upon [it,] My Dear Sir, the popular impulses of this nation will not stop to listen to the nicer reasons for this postponement. They demand immediate and unconditional possession of every inch of what they beleive theirs, and nothing less will satisfy this country. Your friend truly, Thos. J. Green.

ALS in ScCleA.

From W[illiam] B. Lewis

Nashville, 8th Nov[embe]r 1845
D[ear] Sir, This will be handed you [in Memphis] by my friend Jno. M. Bass Esq[ui]r[e], with whom I beg leave to make you acquainted.

Mr. Bass is one of our most respected and useful citizens and has been sent by the city of Nashville as a delegate to the convention at Memphis which is to meet at that place, on the 12th Inst. And, as a further recommendation to *you*, I will add that he is a son in law of your old friend and former associate in the councils of the nation, the late Felix Grundy. Hoping to have the pleasure of seeing you soon in Nashville, I am, dear sir, very Truly yours, W.B. Lewis.

ALS in ScCleA.

From A[LEXANDER] MOUTON, [Governor of La.]

[New Orleans] Nov. 8th 1845

Dear Sir, I have left at your room, a cane made of Bois d'arc, or wild orange, a growth peculiar I believe to the upper part of Red River & Texas; I wish you to accept it as a small souvenir of your visit to New Orleans. Your Ob[edien]t Servant, A. Mouton.

ALS in ScCleA. NOTE: An AEU by Calhoun reads "Mr. Mouton[,] present of a walking stick."

Toast by Calhoun at the St. Charles Hotel, New Orleans, in reply to "Recorder [Joshua] Baldwin," 11/8. "*The Valley of the Mississip[p]i*—The greatest in the world, take it all in all. Situated as it is, between the two oceans, it will yet command the commerce of the world, and that commerce may be centred in New Orleans." From the New Orleans, La., *Daily Picayune*, November 9, 1845, p. 2. Also printed in the New Orleans, La., *Bee*, November 10, 1845, p. 1; the Mobile, Ala., *Register and Journal*, November 12, 1845, p. 2; the Vicksburg, Miss., *Daily Sentinel*, November 13, 1845, p. 2; the Boston, Mass., *Post*, November 19, 1845, p. 2; the Cincinnati, Ohio, *Daily Enquirer*, November 24, 1845, p. 2.

Account of Calhoun's first visit to Natchez, 11/9. "He left New Orleans in the Maria, with the intention of stopping a few hours at Natchez; but in consequence of some accident happening to the machinery of the boat, their arrival at Natchez was so late, that Mr. C[alhoun] did not go ashore. The boat however tarried an hour, and the ladies and citizens rushed on board to see the great American statesman." From the Jackson, Miss., *Southern Reformer*, November 15, 1845, p. 3.

Account of Calhoun's first visit to Vicksburg, 11/10. "Reception of Mr. Calhoun.—Owing to some accident which happened to her machinery, the Maria, on which Mr. Calhoun left New Orleans, was detained at Natchez, and did not reach this place till 6 o'clock yesterday evening. The Ambassador had left our wharf in the morning to meet her, with a large company of ladies and gentlemen; and both boats came up in magnificent style with torch lights and music, and the thunders of cannon in honor of the great Carolinian. The detention of the Maria made it impossible that she could remain for more than a few minutes and reach Memphis in time for the Con-

271

vention; and on this account Mr. Calhoun did not come on shore as anticipated. A large crowd, however, rushed aboard and met him with more enthusiasm than we have ever seen evinced towards any other man except General [Andrew] Jackson. He seemed deeply pleased with the warmth of feeling shown in his reception; and promised to spend a day with us on his return from the Convention." From the Vicksburg, Miss., *Daily Sentinel,* November 11, 1845, p. 2.

From ANNA [MARIA CALHOUN] CLEMSON

Brussels, Nov. 10th 1845

My dear father, If we did not see by the papers that you were coming to the Senate, & therefore nothing could be the matter at home, I should really begin to be uneasy at the silence of all the inhabitants of Fort Hill. Not a line have I received, (or Mr. [Thomas G.] C[lemson] either,) by the last two steamers, from home, & you don[']t know, I am sure, how great a disappointment it is, after counting the days till the steamer arrives, to receive nothing by her. I had, to be sure, a letter from mother [Floride Colhoun Calhoun] the other day, but it had come by a sailing vessel, & had been so long on the road that its contents were of no value as news. I believe it was two months old. With the three boys, sister [Martha Cornelia Calhoun], mother, & yourself, all at home, you might [write] us one letter each steamer. But I won[']t grumble any more, for I am sure after all the silence was accidental, as I know you all love me too much to neglect me, or to forget to write. I suppose this letter will find you in Washington, & you will doubtless get it there, without delay, as they will know in the [State] Department of your arrival in the city. I shall continue to direct all my ["letters" *interlined*] as usual, to you that you may read them, & afterwards send them to their address, for two reasons. In the first place it will avoid worrying you with duplicate letters, for writing by each steamer I use up all my *news* completely & besides, really, you all scatter & change places so often, I am unable to keep up with the different addresses of each one.

I was much gratified to learn you were going to the Senate. In the first place I think the life is one you are so accustomed to, that your health might suffer by the change of habits, &c &c & in the second I really think the country needs you in the Senate. It seems to me that if you do not return there will be literally no head in the Senate, & it will become a complete mob, & they really need you there to keep all straight. I think also you are in a position to do yourself great credit there, & hold the balance of power, if you will, among all the little mushroom divisions of the democratic party, that seem to be springing up on all sides.

We here are busy in our little way also. Mr. Clemson is very busy, & very happy just at present. He has his treaty all ready, & it will be signed tomorrow, or next day, & there is no doubt it will very shortly pass the Chambers with scarcely a dissentient voice. All this is quite a triumph, after fifty years failure to make a treaty on both sides, more especially as Mr. [James] Buchanan['s] letter expresses perfect satisfaction, & forwards the President's [James K. Polk's] full power to conclude the treaty. The Belgians appear very well pleased at the state of things between the two countries, & are sending a Minister Resident [Napoleon Alcindor Beaulieu] to America in the place of their Chargé d'Affaires, Mr. [Charles] Serruy's [*sic*]. He was to have started next steamer, but at present waits to take the treaty with him, after it has received the consent of the Chambers. A great compliment to America.

You see I write you all the Diplomatic secrets, but it is only to you I speak of these things, for you know I am very discreet; but I cannot help telling you of things which redound so[?] much to credit of Mr. C[lemson]. He has really been & still is very active, & has I believe more influence here than any other diplomatic agent, besides being a personal favourite. He has really *come out* wonderfully as a man of business, & is very zealous for the interests of America. I write you all this because I know it will please you to know how much credit he is doing himself here.

We are settled at last in our new house, & quite comfortable, though we have all been a little sick, one way or another, since we have returned to Brussels. The town is beginning to fill for the winter, & I am dreading the commencement of the gaiety.

The Chambers are to be opened day after tomorrow, by the King. This is quite an affair of State, & Ceremony, & a brilliant show. All the Diplomatic corps go in uniform &c &c.

It is getting quite cold now, & if we have another such a winter, as the last, Heaven knows! what will become of the poor, with the failure of the potato crop, & the dearness of all provision. They have admitted Indian Corn here duty free, (amongst other things,) & a Mr. Read, (a New York merchant,) was here the other day, making arrangements to send a cargo by way of experiment. It will be a great thing for America, & Europe, if we can introduce the use of corn into Europe, since it has been proved, by ample experiment, that corn can never be raised with much success here, ["(in Europe)" *interlined*], consequently we shall always be sure of a market for an immense corn crop.

It is amusing to see how they are beginning to open their eyes about America & American products here. An inhabitant of Antwerp sent to New York for one of our carriages. When it first came every one was afraid to ride in it, it looked so light & unsubstantial, after their heavy concerns here, but when they became accustomed to it, they were so delighted with its goodness, & cheapness that several have sent orders for similar carriages.

[John] Calhoun [Clemson] & Floride [Elizabeth Clemson] grow finely & ["continuing" *changed to* "continue"] very interesting. Calhoun says he wants to see America, & all his relations, "so bad," & declares he remembers you & his grandmother. He is a saucy little fellow, & full of fun, & makes some very queer speeches. His father is more devoted to him, if possible, than ever. It is almost painful to see how wrapped up he is in the little fellow. Floride is a great bouncing miss, with a round face, & red cheeks, but pretty & lively. She is a very bright child, & has an excellent memory. They both commit little pieces of poetry to memory with great ease. How I wish you could see them; you would kiss them to death I am sure & It is perhaps as well they are ["at" *interlined*] a distance from mother & yourself, for they would be even more spoiled than they are. I cannot say however, in truth, they are spoiled, tho' much petted, by both of us, but they are on the whole very good & very affectionate children.

If you are in Washington, or if indeed you are still at home, do write me a little oftener, & tell me more how things are going in America. Do tell me by the way what the [Charleston] Mercury is about, & if you approve of its course[;] we only see *it*, the Union, & the Herald. If from time, to time, there is anything in any other paper, of importance, we would be much pleased if you would enclose it to us, & give us a little light on matters & things in politics, for it is very tantalizing not to know what to believe, & what not, for we know too well how little faith is to be placed in newspaper statements.

I must stop as I have no more place. Love to all if you are at home. I hope mother goes with you to Washington. Our love if she is with you. Kisses from the children. Your devoted daughter, Anna Clemson.

ALS in ScCleA.

ACCOUNT OF CALHOUN'S ARRIVAL AT MEMPHIS

[November 12, 1845]

Hon. John C. Calhoun arrived in our city about sun set last evening [11/12], to take his seat in the Convention now assembled, as a delegate from South Carolina. The steamer Memphis arriving from N. Orleans about one o'clock, reported the near approach of Mr. C[alhoun] on board the Maria. Seeing the anxious multitude assembled at the river a good deal chagrined that *he* was not the great Carolinian, and whom he had wickedly seduced into that belief by a *hoaxish* firing of cannon as his fine boat coquettishly pirouetted into the shore, Captain Fretz proposed to the disappointed Committee of reception and people, to wheel the Memphis about and meet the Maria, which he promptly did, several hundred ladies and gentlemen accompanying them.

In about two hours the Memphis and Maria, a pair of nonpareil steamers, announced their coming when some ten miles distant by the firing of cannon, when some 8 or 10,000 persons at least rushed to the river to witness and participate in the reception. Amid the firing of cannon, the music of the bands accompanying the boats and the shouts of the excited crowd, the boats landed, and Mr. Calhoun was received into our city in a manner alike creditable to its liberality and respectful and flattering to Mr. Calhoun. So dense was the mass and eager to catch a glympse of the Carolinian, it was with some difficulty and great inconvenience that a way could be cleared to the carriage waiting at a short distance to convey him to the Gayoso House, where rooms had been prepared for him. All parties united in the flattering reception of Mr. Calhoun; for none indeed could be more so; as thousands we doubt not of his admirers had visited the city mainly in consequence of his expected presence. Hundreds had the gratification of taking him by the hand until the scene was closed by the approach of bed-time. Mr. C[alhoun] it is expected will take his seat in the Convention this morning [11/13].

From the Memphis, Tenn., *Weekly American Eagle*, November 14, 1845, p. 2 (report dated 11/13).

ADDRESS ON TAKING THE CHAIR OF
THE SOUTHWESTERN CONVENTION

Memphis, Nov. 13th, 1845

I thank you gentlemen for the distinguished honor you have conferred on me in calling me to preside over your meeting.

The object of your deliberations, as announced in the Circular of your Committee calling the Convention, is the Development of the Resources of the Western and Southern States. It will be for you to determine, after a full deliberation, what their resources are; how they can best be developed; and how far the aid of the General Government may be invoked for that purpose. But I trust it will not be deemed out of place for me to state my views on those points.

The region occupied by the Western and Southern States is of vast extent. It may divided into three parts. The first and greatest is the magnificent valley in the midst of which we now stand, and which is drained by the mighty stream whose current rolls under the bluff on which your city is located. It extends north and south nearly through the entire breadth of the Temperate Zone, and east and west from the Rocky to the Alleghany Mountains; and occupies in its northern extension a position, midway between the Pacific and Atlantic Oceans. The next is that portion which stretches east from the mouth of the Mississippi River along the Gulf of Mexico and the Atlantic Ocean, as far as cotton, rice and tobacco, are cultivated. The other stretches from the Mississippi westward, along the Gulf of Mexico to the Mexican line. I say the Mexican line, for although Texas, is not yet annexed, the day is near at hand when she will shine as one of the brightest stars in our political constellation.

The vast region comprehending these three divisions may be justly called the great agricultural portion of our Union. Its climate is so various; its extent so vast; its soil so fertile, that it is capable of yielding all the products of that zone in the greatest perfection and abundance. Already much has been done to develope its great resources. Already all the leading articles of food and raiment are produced in sufficient abundance, not only for its own wants and for those of other portions of the United States, but to require the demand of the markets of the world to consume. In addition, it produces the articles of tobacco, lead, tar, turpentine and lumber, far beyond the home consumption; and in a short time the fertile valleys and extensive prairies of the northern portions of this great valley, will add to the list of exports the important articles of hemp and wool, and the southern plains, when Texas is annexed, will add that of sugar.

I approach now, gentlemen, the important question. How shall we, who inhabit this vast region, develope its great resources? For this purpose there is one thing needful, and only one—and that is, that we shall get a fair remunerating price for all that we may produce. If we can obtain such a price, this vast region, under the active industry of its intelligent and enterprising inhabitants, will become the garden of the world! How is this to be effected? There is but one mode by which it can be, and that is, to enlarge our market in proportion to the increase of our production. This again can be obtained only in one way—and that is, by free and ready transit for persons and merchandise between the various portions of this vast region, and between it and other portions of the Union and the rest of the world.

The question then is, How shall we accomplish such a transit? For this purpose Nature has been eminently propitious to us.

I begin with this vast valley drained by the Mississippi and its tributaries. Nothing more is necessary to secure a cheap, speedy, certain and safe transit between all its parts, but the improvement of its navigation and that of its various great tributaries. That done, a free and safe communication may be had between every portion. To secure a like communication between it and the Southern Atlantic cities, the first and great point is, to adopt such measures as shall keep open at all times, in peace and war, a communication, through the coasting trade, between the Gulf of Mexico and the Atlantic Ocean. This is the great thoroughfare which, if interrupted would as certainly produce a revolution in the commercial system, as the stoppage of one of the great arteries of the body, would in the human. To guard against such effects in the event of war, it is indispensable to establish at Pensacola, or some other place in the Gulf, a naval station of the first class, with all the means of building and repairing vessels of war, with a portion of our Navy permanently attached. But this of itself will not be sufficient. It is indispensable to fortify impregnably the Tortugas, which lie midway between Florida Point and Cuba, and command the passes between the Gulf of Mexico and the Atlantic coast. And to this must be added a naval force of steamers or other vessels, which will habitually command our own coast against any foe. It will also be necessary that the bar at the Balize shall be kept at all times open, so far as it can be effected, cost what it may.

But other measures will be indispensably necessary to facilitate the intercourse between this great valley and the Southern Atlantic coast. With all the advantages possessed by the coasting trade between the Gulf and the Atlantic, be it ever so well secured against interruption, there is one great objection to which it is liable. The Peninsula of Florida projects far to the south, which makes the voyage from New Orleans and the other ports of the Gulf to the Southern Atlantic cities, not only very long and tedious, but liable to frequent and great accidents in its navigation. A voyage from this place for instance, to Charleston, would be a distance of certainly not less than two thousand five hundred miles, and is subject to as great losses as any voyage of equal extent in any part of the world. It was estimated some dozens of years since that the actual loss between Cuba, the Bahama Islands, and Florida, was not less than half a million of dollars a year, and it may now, with the great increase of our commerce be put down as not less than a million. While between this and Charleston, or Savannah, there may be a communication by railroad to not much exceed six hundred miles, and which would be free from accidents and losses. What then is needed to complete a cheap, speedy and safe intercourse between the valley of the Mississippi and the Southern Atlantic coast, is a good system of railroads[.] For this purpose the nature of the intervening country affords extraordinary advantages.

Such is its formation from the course of the Tennessee, Cumberland and Alabama Rivers, and the termination of the various chains of the Alleghany Mountains, that all the railroads which have been projected or commenced, although each has looked only to i[t]s local interest, must necessarily unite at a point in De Kalb County, in the State of Georgia, called Atlanta, nor far from the village of Decatur, so as to constitute one entire system of roads, having a mutual interest each in the other, instead of isolated rival roads. At that point the Charleston and Savannah roads, each aiming at a connection with this great valley, meet, and from that point the State of Georgia is engaged in constructing a railroad to terminate at Chattanooga, on the Tennessee River, above the Suck, which passes south of the western termination of that chain of the Alleghany which throws the water on the one side into the Mississippi, and on the other into the Atlantic. With this trunk, the road from this place to Lagrange [Tenn.] will meet with the Decatur Railroad around the Muscle Shoals at Tuscumbia [Ala.], and the extension of that road to the Georgia trunk near Rome. With the same trunk the road projected from Nashville, will meet at Chattanooga, and the Knoxville and Highwassee, already graded, will fall in with it at a point not far from Rome. So, if we turn south from this place to the railroad from Vicksburg to Jackson, and the projected roads from Grand Gulf

[Miss.] and Natchez, it will be seen, by reference to the map, that they must all unite in their eastern extension at some point on the ridge between the Mississippi and Tombigbee, and thence in their extension towards the Southern Atlantic ports, must necessarily unite with the railroad now partially completed between Montgomery on the Alabama, and West Point [Ga.], on the Appalachicola, and unite at the same place with the Charleston and Savannah road, and the Georgia trunk. So again, the short railroad from New Orleans to Lake Pon[t]chartrain, leads by navigation through Lake Pon[t]chartrain to Mobile, and thence by the Alabama to Montgomery. To the same point the projected railroad from Pensacola leads through the Montgomery Railroad. If we cast our eyes further to the north-east, we shall find that the projected railroad from Richmond [Va.] to Kanawha, or the Ohio, in its south-western branch, must necessarily pass near Abingdon [Va.], down the valley of the Holstein to Knoxville, and thence to the same point. The whole thus constituting, from the remarkable formation of the country, one entire system of roads, uniting at a great central point, through which the whole have a common interest—each in the completion of the other—each increasing its particular prosperity from the prosperity of the whole. All of which will no doubt more fully appear from the report of the Committee on Railroads.

I have limited my remarks in reference to railroads to the region east of the Mississippi, as I do not feel myself sufficiently acquainted with the subject to offer any views in reference to their extension through the region lying west of it; but I am confident, from a general knowledge of the country, that in their extension west the interest of all the roads will be found to be in like manner harmonious. When the various roads alluded to have been completed, the coasting voyage between the Gulf and Atlantic coast, secured against the interruptions of war, and the navigation of the Mississippi and its great tributaries sufficiently improved, then there will be between all parts of the Southern and Western States a facility of intercourse which, for expedition, safety and cheapness, will be without equal in any country of the same extent on the globe. It will furnish a great internal market within itself through the exchange of the great staple commodities of the southern portion, with the bread-stuffs and other provisions and products of its northern parts.

But, gentlemen, it is not sufficient that the market of this vast region shall be open by safe and ready transit within itself. Our productions are far beyond our own wants; and the object of the present meeting is their further development. We must look to other portions of the Union, and establish between us and them the same facility of transit as between the different parts of ours. For that purpose, much indeed will have been done by accomplishing what has already been proposed. By securing the coasting trade in the manner already stated, between the Gulf and Atlantic, and the improvement of the navigation of the Mississippi and its great tributaries, and the completion of the railroad between the Mississippi and the Atlantic, there will be opened at all times, in peace and war, in summer and winter, a free, cheap and ready communication between the Northern and Eastern States, and Southern and Western. But something more must still be done; our great valley must be intimately and closely connected with the valley and lakes of the St. Lawrence, by a canal which will permit the vessels which navigate one to pass, if practicable, into the other. That, with the various communications already established or now in progress by railroads and canals between the two valleys, will unite in the closest commercial ties every part of our great and glorious Union.

But how is all this to be effected? This, gentlemen, brings us to a more delicate question, and that is, How far we may invoke the aid of the General Government for that purpose? I cannot be wrong in supposing that there must be a great diversity of opinion in this assembly in reference to the extent to which it may be constitutionally invoked. It is well known that my opinion is in favor of a rigid construction of the Constitution, while there are others in favor of a more enlarged view. But I trust that we shall be all agreed on one point, and that is to abstain from pressing our views on all subjects, where there is a diversity of opinion. It is only by such forbearance that we can avoid conflict and preserve harmony; and I for one am prepared to set an example of such forbearance. Let us then all agree to touch no subject on which any portion of the body entertains constitutional scruples. With these impressions, I read with particular approbation the circular of your Committee calling the Convention, which stated that no subject upon which a diversity of opinion existed on constitutional grounds should be discussed. It evinced a regard for that sacred instrument which augurs well for the success of our labors. Indeed the first step towards the accomplishment of the objects for which we are convened—the development of the resources of the South and West—is the preservation of our liberty and our free popular institutions; and the first step, towards that, is the preservation of our Constitution. To them we owe our extraordinary prosperity and progress in developing the great resources of our country, and on them we must depend for their full and perfect development, which would realize the anticipations of all the founders of our Government, and raise our country to a greatness surpassing all that have gone before us.

With these remarks, I begin with asking, How far the aid of the General Government can be invoked to the improvement of the navigation of the Mississippi and its great navigable tributaries? And here let me premise, that the invention of [Robert] Fulton has in reality, for all practical purposes, converted the Mississippi, with all its great tributaries, into an inland sea. Regarding it as such, I am prepared to place it on the same footing with the Gulf and Atlantic coasts, the Chesapeake and Delaware Bays, and the [Great] Lakes, in reference to the superintendence of the General Government over its navigation. It is manifest that it is far beyond the power of individuals or of separate States to supervise it, as there are eighteen States, including Texas and the Territories—more than half the Union—which lie within the valley of the Mississippi or border on its navigable tributaries.

But, gentlemen, while I am in favor of placing its navigation and that of its great navigable tributaries under the supervision of the General Government, I am utterly opposed to extending its supervision beyond the limits the grounds on which I have placed it would carry it. It is the genius of our Government to leave to individuals what can be done by individuals, and to individual States what can be done by them, and to restrict the power of the General Government to that which can only be effected through its agency and the powers specifically granted. Indeed, setting all constitutional objections aside, it would be improper, as a mere matter of expediency, to invoke the aid of the General Government in the execution of any one object which could be effected by the agency of individuals or States. In a country of such vast extent as ours, local expenditures [by the General Government] are liable to great abuses. They are seen to lead to a system, to use an undignified phrase, of *"log-rolling,"* and to terminate in useless and wasteful expenditures of public money.

As to the measures necessary to keep open at all times a coasting voyage between the Gulf and Atlantic, there is no one who will question the Constitutional competency of Congress to adopt them, and I accordingly pass them over without further remark.

I come now to the question, How far the aid of the General Government may be invoked to execute the system of proposed railroads between the Mississippi and its tributaries and the Southern Atlantic ports? And here I must premise, that, according to my opinion, the General Government has no right to appropriate money except to carry into execution its delegated powers, and that I do not regard the system of railroads or internal improvements as comprehended under them; but it may still be in its power to do something directly in aid of their execution where the roads pass through lands belonging to the United States. I do not doubt the right of the Government, regarded in the light of a proprietor, to grant lands in aid of such improvements when they are calculated to enhance their value; and have accordingly never hesitated as a member of Congress to vote in favor of acts granting alternate sections to railroads or canals under such circumstances. Acting on that principle, I cheerfully, as President of the Senate, gave the casting vote in favor of an act granting alternate sections to the canal intended to connect Lake Michigan with the Mississippi through the Illinois River. But though it may not be in the power of the General Government to give any considerable direct aid in execution of the system, yet it may give indirectly very essential aid. It is well known that the principal expense in constructing railroads is caused by the price of iron; but perhaps it is not as well known that a large portion of the price consists in the duty laid on the importation of iron. The duty alone on heavy T iron, I am informed on good authority, is more than two thousand dollars a mile. A repeal, then, of the duty on it would, in effect, be equal to a subscription of that sum per mile.

I do not intend to touch upon the vexed question of the Tariff. I know that there is a diversity of opinion in respect to the protective policy. This is not the place to agitate it; but I would submit that, under present circumstances, that question cannot be fairly raised in reference to the repeal of the duty upon railroad iron. I speak on good authority, when I say such iron may be made in the United States at $60 a ton, and also that it cannot be imported into this country for less than that sum, not including the duty, in consequence of the great increase of the price of railroad iron in England within the last few months, from the great demand for the article for making roads there. Under such circumstances, the only effect of the repeal of the duty would be to prevent our own manufacturers from greatly raising the price in consequence of the monopoly of the home market.

I approach a subject still more delicate, in connection with the protective policy. I have shown that we already produce of the leading articles of food and raiment and others of considerable importance, more than can be consumed within our own limits, including other portions of the Union, and that we must depend upon the rest of the world for a market for the surplus. I have also shown that to these, in a short time, will be added the important articles of sugar, hemp and wool, and that to obtain fair remunerating prices, it is indispensable that the market shall increase with the increasing development of our resources, on the great principle that price is regulated by the relation between supply and demand.

Without an increase of the market equal to the increase of supplies, prices will fall till they cease to be remunerating, which will effectually put a stop to a farther development of our resources. But it is clear that, on a free exchange of our products with the rest of the world, depends our capacity for commanding its market, and that every barrier interposed in the shape of tax or duties must necessarily limit its market for our products to the same extent.

The position being admitted, it is to be hoped that all will concur, whatever may be the diversity of opinion respecting the Tariff, that no duty shall be imposed which is not necessary, according to the respective views of each, of the policy which the Government ought to adopt. I am of the impression that the existing Tariff throws many impediments in the way of our exchanges with the rest of the world, which, even upon the principle of protection, might be dispensed with.

There remains one other topic of deep interest to all the lower sections of this magnificent valley—I refer to the reclamation of your lands subject to annual inundation, by a system of leveeing. They comprehend a large and most valuable portion of the whole region, and are capable of sustaining a population greater than any portion of the globe of the same extent. A large portion is held by the Federal Government, and I do not doubt that it ought to contribute to leveeing them, in proportion to its interest, or terminate its proprietorship, as soon as it can be done, in favor of the States within whose limits they lie, so as to leave it to the respective States and the individual owners to construct the levees. There will be great difficulty in the former in fixing the proportion which the Federal Government and individuals ought to contribute; and I am of the impression it would be the most advisable every way for the Federal Government to take measures to terminate its proprietorship at an early period. Indeed, upon principles of general policy, I am of opinion that it ought to cease its proprietorship in land as early as it can be practically effected, in all the new States, except what may be necessary for forts, arsenals, magazines, navy yards, and other buildings. Under this impression, I introduced a bill some years since for the purpose of effecting this object, which among other things provided that the price of public lands which had been offered for sale without being entered, within a fixed period, should be gradually reduced from one dollar and a quarter to one dollar, and then to seventy-five [cents], and then to fifty, and lastly to twenty-five cents, and all that was not sold within a short period at twenty-five cents, to be surrendered to the States in which they were situated.

I have now given you my views briefly, as to the resources of the South and West; how they could be best developed, and how far the aid of the General Government might be invoked to assist in their development. And now let me add, in conclusion, you occupy a region possessing advantages above all others on the globe, of the same extent, not only for its fertility, its diversity of climate and production, but in its geographical position; lying midway between the Pacific and Atlantic Oceans, in less than one generation, should the Union continue, and I hope it may be perpetual, you will be engaged in deliberations to extend your connection with the Pacific, as you now are with the Atlantic; and will ultimately be almost as intimately connected with the one as the other. In the end, you will command the commerce of both, and this great valley become the centre of the commerce of the world, as well as that of our great Union, if we shall preserve our liberty and free popular institutions. We are about to give the first great impulse, and you will, gentlemen, I trust, set an example of moderation, harmony and unanimity, which will be followed hereafter. May the result of your deliberations be such as to accomplish not only the objects for which you have convened, but to strengthen the bonds of our Union, and to render us the greatest and most prosperous community the world ever beheld.

From Crallé, ed., *Works*, 6:273–284. Also printed in the Charleston, S.C., *Mercury*, November 28, 1845, p. 2 (from the New Orleans, La., *Bulletin*); the Columbia, S.C., *South-Carolinian*, November 28, 1845; the Mobile, Ala., *Register and Journal*, November 28, 1845, p. 2; *Niles' National Register*, vol. LXIX, no. 14 (December 6, 1845), pp. 212–213; the Baltimore, Md., *Constitution*, December 13, 1845, p. 1; the Jackson, Miss., *Southern Reformer*, December 13, 1845, p. 1; *Journal of the Proceedings of the South-Western Convention, Began and Held at the City of Memphis, on the 12th November, 1845* (Memphis, Tenn.: 1845), pp. 7–14. At least three different early and slightly variant reporters' accounts of the same speech were printed in the Memphis, Tenn., *Weekly American Eagle*, November 14, 1845, p. 3; the New Orleans, La., *Bee*, November 18, 1845, p. 1; the Mobile, Ala., *Register and Journal*, November 20, 1845, p. 2; the Natchez, Miss., *Mississippi Free Trader and Natchez Gazette*, November 20, 1845, pp. 1–2; the Charleston, S.C., *Mercury*, November 21, 1845, p. 2 (from the Memphis, Tenn., *Appeal*); the Cincinnati, Ohio, *Daily Enquirer*, November 22, 1845, p. 2; the Cincinnati, Ohio, *Daily Gazette*, November 22, 1845, p. 2; the Nashville, Tenn., *Whig*, November 22, 1845, p. 2; the Richmond, Va., *Enquirer*, November 25, 1845, p. 2; the New York, N.Y., *Herald*, November 25, 1845, p. 1; the Charleston, S.C., *Courier*, November 25, 1845, p. 2;

the Washington, D.C., *Daily Union*, vol. I, no. 178 (November 26, 1845), p. 710 (from the Memphis, Tenn., *Appeal*); the Washington, D.C., *Daily Union*, vol. I, no. 179 (November 27, 1845), p. 714 (from the Memphis, Tenn., *Enquirer*); the Greenville, S.C., *Mountaineer*, November 28, 1845, p. 1; the Springfield, Ill., *Illinois State Register*, November 28, 1845, p. 2; the Pendleton, S.C., *Messenger*, November 28, 1845, pp. 2–3; the Edgefield, S.C., *Advertiser*, December 3, 1845, p. 1; the Jackson, Miss., *Mississippian*, December 3, 1845, p. 1; the Tuscaloosa, Ala., *Independent Monitor*, December 10, 1845, p. 1; Henry G. Wheeler, *History of Congress, Biographical and Political* . . . , 2:418–425. NOTE: Crallé did not state the source for his text, which, however, agrees except in incidentals with the later and fuller newspaper texts and probably rests on Calhoun's own version. The different newspaper reports of the same speech do not offer any substantive points of difference. The Charleston *Mercury*, December 3, 1845, p. 2, commented on whether its own or the Charleston *Courier's* report of the speech was the most authentic: "We have reason to believe, the one which we published. We have the assurances of a most respectable New Orleans journal that it is entirely authentic . . . . that it is Mr. Calhoun's own report of his remarks, and that we are to look to it for the true meaning of whatever he said." There were numerous accounts of the proceedings. One concisely informative one reported of the first two days: "The Western and Southwestern Convention which was assembled at Memphis, Tennessee, on the 12th instant, was duly organized on the following day, the Hon. John C. Calhoun having been chosen to preside. He addressed the convention, in exposition of its objects, for nearly an hour. The day was passed in hearing the reports of the several committees appointed at the July convention; and a resolution was adopted allowing the States and Territories represented, including Texas, a 'perfect equality' of voting in all the important proceedings of the body." Washington, D.C., *Daily Union*, vol. I, no. 177 (November 25, 1845), p. 707.

Receipt from E[noch] B. Benson & Son, [Pendleton], 11/14. "Rec[eive]d of Mrs. R[ebecca] W[eyman Foster] Gaillard Six dollars & twenty five cents to be entered to credit of Mr. J.C. Calhoun." DS in ScU-SC, John C. Calhoun Papers.

From W[illia]m Cullom and Others

Memphis, Nov. 14, 1845

Sir, The undersigned, in behalf of the delegation of the legislature of the State of Tennessee, of the City of Nashville and Davidson County, and of the adjacent Counties; in view of the eminent rank which you have so long and so honorably held in the estimation of the American people and especially in view of your known zeal in favour of the present movement to advance the interests and develope the resources of this great portion of our confederacy now engaging so much attention in the South and West; have pleasure in the opportunity afforded them by your presence here to invite you to visit Nashville on your way home.

In tendering this invitation, which we do with sincere pleasure the undersigned feel additional gratification in the assurance that they are but giving expression to the wishes of their constituency, to whom your acceptance would not be less gratifying than to themselves individually. We have the honor to be With great respect Your ob[edien]t Serv[an]ts, Wm. Cullom, V. Sevier, J.T. Lenoir, John D. Fletcher, W[illia]m Houston, J[ohn?] A. Whiteside, Rob[er]t S. Holt, J[ames?] Overton, Alex[ander] Allison, V[ernon] K. Stevenson, James A. Porter, Anth[on]y W. Vanleer, Ephraim H. Foster, James C. Jones, Jno: Bell, Sam[uel] D. Morgan, Andrew Ewing, J.J.B. Southall, Nicholas Perkins.

LS in ScCleA; PC (dated 11/13) in the Nashville, Tenn., *Union*, December 2, 1845, p. 2. NOTE: An AEU by an unknown person reads "E.H. Foster, Saml. D. Morgan & A. Ewing (committee) called at the 'Gayoso House' to deliver this invitation, & hope Mr. Calhoun will accept this as a personal delivery." Cullom and Ewing were later to be Representatives from Tenn.; Foster was a former Senator from Tenn.; Jones was a former Governor and future Senator; Bell a former Secretary of War and future Senator.

FURTHER REMARKS AT THE SOUTHWESTERN CONVENTION

[Memphis, November 14, 1845]
[*S. Snowden Hayes, a delegate from Illinois, offered a resolution that the convention "only present to Congress a recommendation of such works as shall come within the harmonious action of both political parties, and are strictly of national character." In his discussion the delegate took issue with Calhoun's use of the term "inland sea" for the Mississippi River.*]

I wish to be very distinctly understood, that the power of the General Government to construct roads, &c., is limited to the purposes of defence of the confederated States. There is an error in the common understanding of the words "National power," and "general welfare." The words are frequently misapplied. There is no "national power," as applied to the General Government, beyond what is expressed in the Constitution. We are, in our confederation, a congregation of nations, of sovereign states; and on that feature our system depends. When you say an object is of national importance, you mean it is of Constitutional importance. If we had no constitution to bind us in one compact, there would not be what is commonly called the "general welfare." Now these things all come back on the one grand feature, that we are several nations congregated in one compact.

The General Government cannot grant appropriations for local purposes not connected with national defence. But the Mississippi River and its navigable branches are peculiarly an object within the range of their Constitutional aid. It washes several of these sovereign States—and in that view it may truly be considered as much an inland Sea as either the Chesapeake or Delaware bays.

Local appropriations, it is true, gentlemen, are always abused by what is commonly called "log rolling", and the result thereof is to be seen in the fact which I stated yesterday, that the entire value of the works thus far completed by the General Government in that manner at the expense of nearly seventeen millions of dollars, is now reduced to about a million of dollars.

I take the liberty of making these remarks, that I may not be misunderstood.

From the New Orleans, La., *Bee,* November 21, 1845, p. 1. Also printed in the Washington, D.C., *Daily Union,* vol. I, no. 179 (November 27, 1845), p. 714 (reprinted from the Memphis, Tenn., *Enquirer* of November 15, 1845). Variant in the Charleston, S.C., *Mercury,* November 21, 1845, p. 2; the Cincinnati, Ohio, *Daily Gazette,* November 22, 1845, p. 2; the Richmond, Va., *Enquirer,* November 25, 1845, p. 2 (reprinted from the Memphis, Tenn., *Appeal* of November 15, 1845). Another variant in the Charleston, S.C., *Courier,* November 21, 1845, p. 2. Another variant in the Memphis, Tenn., *Weekly American Eagle,* November 21, 1845, p. 1. NOTE: The resolution was adopted. The variant, more concise summaries of the proceedings which are cited above help clarify some points of Calhoun's discourse. The first variant reads: "Mr. Calhoun took occasion to explain: he considered the Mississippi as an Inland Sea, for purposes of commerce, to the States of this confederacy, and as such, its improvement became as much within the power of Congress, as that of the Chesapeake Bay, or any other of our inland seas or harbours. He considered the terms 'national interest,' or 'national importance' to signify properly, that for which, a specific grant of power to Congress, is contained in the Constitution. He considered this as an assemblage, or confederation of nations." The second variant reads: "Mr. Calhoun, at this point, rose from the chair, and confessed himself happy at an opportunity of making himself properly understood by all members of the Convention. He was hostile to any system of *internal improvement* to be conducted by the Government. His experience as a legislator had afforded him full opportunity to witness the powerful local interests which could be brought into operation, and the system of 'logrolling' with which it was connected. The General Government had expended 16 or 17,000,000 dollars for works, which, if thrown into the market, would not bring $1,000,000. He considered, however, the defences and fortifications of the Mississippi river in a different manner. It was a national question—*national* in the *constitutional* and *federative* sense. In no other sense could our's be considered as a national Government. It was a community of nations and not a nation." The convention proceedings of 11/14 were described in the Washington, D.C., *Daily Union*, vol. I, no. 177 (November 25, 1845), p. 707, as follows: ". . . committees were appointed to take charge of the following subjects: the military and naval resources of the South and West; the Ohio river; the western rivers; the ship canal to the lakes; the western armory; the Arkansas road; forts and defences on the Indian frontier; the western mails; the western marine hospital; reclamation of Mississippi lowlands; manufactures in the South; agriculture; a railroad connection between the Mississippi river and the South Atlantic ports; the warehousing system. Fifteen states and territories are represented by five hundred and sixty-four delegates."

From S. Snowden Hayes

Memphis, Nov. 14th/45

Sir, With very great respect and deference I venture to explain in this manner the view I wished to express this morning with reference to the power of Congress to make internal improvements. I trouble you with this communication, because, I approve to a great extent of that doctrine of construction of the U.S. Constitution which you have always advocated, and I believe that reasoning on that subject coming even from the most humble source is not without interest to you.

The general government is the creature of compact and the Constitution. As far as its action is directed towards internal interests and the interests of States, it has only powers expressly granted or *necessary* to the exercise of those expressly granted and flowing from them by inevitable inference: with reference to such action, that instrument ["must" *canceled*] should be construed *strictly*, in favor of the rights of States and individuals.

As respects foreign relations, the U.S. government is ["an" *changed to* "a"] unit, invested with full sovereignty and equal right among nations, except where the Constitution directly or by fair inference imposes a limitation. Whatever England or France or Russia may do *by the law of nations*, the U.S. general government may do. Hence Congress may construct forts, ship canals, harbor fortifications, armories &c and peaceably extend our territories to make our boundary coincident with natural ramparts, or secure the country against aggression: and in this point of view the constitution should receive a *liberal* interpretation in favor of the sovereignty of the general government.

Wherever legislation is *necessary*, and "individuals alone or individuals and State governments can legally do nothing, the general government may act"; thus it may improve great rivers which are the natural boundaries and channels of intercourse between States. A word here as to what was said of the expression "the Mississippi is a mighty inland sea and under the control of Congress as our marine coast." To this extent the writer agreed, that the Mississippi (with its branches) is a fit object for the action of Congress as far as it is the boundary ["and" *canceled*] of sovereign States and beyond their control. He objected to the expression because, though in connection with other principles laid down it might be unexceptionable, taken by itself it was liable to receive a dangerous construction, first, to ["warran" *canceled*] authorise improvements by Congress of branches of that river entirely within the territory and control of particular States, secondly, to warrant appropriations for certain river harbors, evidently not necessary for defence, under the pretence that they are ports of entry.

Then the general government cannot interfere to extend commerce within a State or between one & another. It can neither become a broker, nor a factor, nor a commercial road proprietor. Its commercial regulations are restricted to the imposition of customs and others similar. Clearly it may in its character of land proprietor sell lands to companies or individuals ["for as to others" *canceled*] for road or canal purposes as for any other, at the established price; and when the rail road or canal can evidently be used to advantage for military purposes, it may sell lands to the State, or company, for the consideration of having forever free right of way for the transportation of troops and munitions of war.

But how far as a land proprietor can the general government act to increase the value of its lands? Certainly it cannot build houses or open plantations on them. Nor can Congress do indirectly what it cannot directly. They cannot make special grants of land to individuals or companies, merely in order that they by building houses, opening farms, or making roads or canals, may cause the remainder to rise in value. Can they go further than to make lands, of little or no value, either from inundation or other cause, fit for market as wild lands, when the cost of the improvement will not exceed the amount realised from the consequent sales?

Now as to the policy of frequent applications to Congress for appropriations of doubtful necessity. Will they not tend to increase the present power of the general government, and the evident tendency towards centralism? Will they not make Congress ["the dispenser" *canceled*] the dispenser of bounty, and the States and individuals humble recipients of favor?

Will they not increase the danger of a national debt, and an extension of the present unequal taxation of the laboring and planting classes?

Will they not ultimately give birth to a mania for stock speculation, similar to that which has now thrown Europe into frenzy, and portends a terrible convulsion which will shake the financial system of the world?

And will they not pamper too much a spirit of avarice, and cause at least a partial deadening of the love of country, a forgetfulness of the duties the citizens of republics owe to themselves & mankind?

The result of these considerations is that the constitutionality and legality of each proposed movement should be settled beyond cavil, and then the utmost caution, even distrust, should be used in determining its expediency.

These views are thrown together hastily and in some disorder, and would not now be presented, had not indisposition and embarrassment prevented the writer from properly presenting them this morning. He trusts that there is no impropriety in thus addressing one whose intellect has become in a manner the property of his countrymen, and if he is mistaken he begs that the blame may be charged to his youth and inexperience, not to intentional disrespect. Your ob[e]d[ien]t servant, S. Snowden Hayes.

ALS in ScCleA; slightly variant ALS in ScCleA. NOTE: This letter was addressed to Calhoun at the Gayoso House in Memphis. Why there are two versions of the letter from Hayes among Calhoun's papers is not clear.

From DANIEL E. HUGER, [Senator from S.C.]

Savannah River, Nov[embe]r 14th 1845
My dear Sir, Your letter of the 9th of October [*not found*], gave me great pleasure, as it an[n]ounced your willingness to resume your seat in the Senate of the U. States; a measure this which I have long desired, as you know, and one which, in the opinion of millions, will contribute much to the honor and wellfare of the Country.

My feelings on this occasion are ["more" *interlined*] exalted than any which could be excited by personal considerations alone. It is true I wished to retire from public life but I would have submitted to any privations rather than desert my post incompetently occupied, when we were threatened with an unjust war for Oregon—an unequal and unjust tax for the benefit of a few, and a disgraceful abandonment of Texas, whom we had seduced into a position requiring a full and liberal performance of all our engagements with her.

Critical as our situation is and painful as it may be to every lover of our Country, I cannot but congratulate her on having a son not only able but willing to assist her in every emergency.

Accept, if you please, the assurances of my esteem & regard, Daniel E. Huger.

ALS in ScCleA.

From JAMES H. LUCAS and Others

Memphis, Nov. 14, 1845

Sir, The undersigned, Delegates from Missouri in the Memphis Convention, gratified to witness your presence in the great Valley of the Mississippi, and while yet in the midst of it, beg leave to avail themselves of the occasion to tender you a respectful invitation to visit the city of Saint Louis—a City, which rivals in its promise every other in the west, and which, we assure you, amid the bustle of its vast business, is never unmindful of the rites of hospitality, nor of the respect due to those who, by their influence, or their acts, render distinguished services to the Republic.

We will only add the expression of our confidence that the journey, if accomplished, will the more strongly confirm in your mind those ideas of the vast importance of the Mississippi Valley, and those noble sentiments relating to the condition and prospects of its population, which distinguished and commended to our approbation, your opening Address to the Convention. We have the honor to be your ob[edien]t serv[an]ts, James H. Lucas, Chairman, Tho[mas] Allen, Sec[retar]y, Geo[rge] Collier, David Chambers, James E. Yeatman, Geo[rge] W. Good, D.D. Mitchell, R. Wash, W.F. Wright, Isaac A. Hedges, H[ezekiah] P. Maulsby, G.H. Netherton, Hardage Lane, Jno. Magwin, W.M. McPheeters, L[uther] M. Kennett, J.M.

Field, J[ohn] B. Martin, A.B. Chambers, Welton O[']Bannon, Firmin A. Rozier, Jno. H. Walker, A.P. Ladew, Asa Wilgus, James Glasgow, Henry M. Shreeve, S[hadrach] Penn, Jr., G[regory] Byrne, S. Blood.

LS in ScCleA; PC in the Charleston, S.C., *Mercury,* December 9, 1845, p. 2.

From JOHN J. WINSTON and Others

Memphis, 14th Nov. 1845

Dear Sir, At a meeting of citizens of Greene Co[unty] Alabama for the purpose of appointing delegates to the convention held at this place, the said delegates were requested to invite you on your return to visit them at Eutaw, their county seat & to express to you the gratification it would afford them, without distinction of party to pay their respects to one who has so largely contributed in the councils of the nation to our national prosperity.

We feel great pleasure in tendering to you this invitation & in adding our individual assurance of esteem[,] respect & confidence. John J. Winston, W[illia]m F. Pierce, David J. Means, Richard T. Nott, Anthony Winston.

LS in ScCleA.

To JA[ME]S H. LUCAS and Others

Memphis, Nov. 15, 1845

Gentlemen—I greatly and sincerely regret, that it will not be in my power to accept the invitation which you have so kindly and acceptably tendered to me [yesterday] to visit the city of St. Louis at this time.

My engagements will compel me to return home with as little delay as possible. Were it not the case, I would be very happy to extend my tour to your already great and still rapidly growing city. I think, however, it will not be long before I shall have the pleasure of making it a visit. If nothing should intervene to prevent it, I shall, during the next summer or fall, make a tour through the upper part of the Valley of the Mississippi, when I shall make it a point to visit St. Louis. With great respect, Yours truly, J.C. Calhoun.

PC in the Charleston, S.C., *Mercury*, December 9, 1845, p. 2. Note: The Columbus, Ohio, *Ohio State Journal*, December 4, 1845. p. 2, reported that Calhoun had received a highly complimentary invitation to visit St. Louis and that he had replied that he might visit the upper Mississippi Valley next year. "The great Expunger [Thomas H. Benton]," commented the Ohio paper, "would like to expunge that arrangement. He does not like Calhoun at all."

Remarks on leaving the chair of the Memphis Convention, 11/15. "Mr. Calhoun gave notice, at the afternoon session, that, upon that adjournment, it would be necessary for him to vacate his seat as President of the Convention. It became necessary, whether the Convention continued its settings or not, for him to leave, however much he might regret it. On motion, a resolution was passed by an unanimous and enthusiastic vote, *That the Hon. John C. Calhoun, for the able, dignified and courteous manner in which he has presided over the Convention, is entitled to the highest regards and gratitude of the whole body.* Mr. Calhoun responded to the compliment with a chaste and elegant speech, which, for its kind, has, we conceive, never been surpassed." From the Charleston, S.C., *Courier*, November 24, 1845, p. 2. Variant in the Memphis, Tenn., *Weekly American Eagle*, November 21, 1845, p. 1.

From R[ICHARD] K. CRALLÉ

Lynchburg, Nov. 16th 1845

My dear Sir, Your letter written from Georgia was received in time to have replied to it while you were in Alabama; but I have deferred an answer until I could see and converse with some of your friends in this section of the State in those judgment and fidelity I reposed implicit confidence. They all differ with me in opinion, as to the main point suggested in your letter; and concur in (what appears by the public prints) the *general* wish that you should return to the Senate. Still I feel anxious about it on many accounts. If you go back you must inevitably enter into a desperate conflict with the basest and most reckless faction that ever existed in this or any other country. Their fortunes, for the future, depend upon the cast of the present, and their struggles will be as convulsive as those of drowning men.

So far as you are *personally* concerned I am still unchanged in the opinion that the step ought not to be urged upon you by your friends. You have served the Country for many years, and secured a reputation amongst friends and *enemies*, which no other ["living" *canceled*] individual possesses, or perhaps ever possessed except [George] Washington; and you can add nothing to the dignity of your character, nor to the purity of your fame by a contest with scoundrels, for such must follow your entrance into the Senate. The venal myrmydons of [Thomas H.] Benton and [Silas] Wright, and, perhaps, [Robert J.] Walker and [George M.] Dallas, will be ready to unite against you as a common enemy; when, if left to themselves, they would, most probably, devour each other. And, in such a contest, on whom could you rely for support? On the Democratic Party *as a Party?* I fear it is, as yet, too much leavened with the *spoils principle* to warrant such confidence. I distrust the leaders altogether. I am told by an intelligent gentleman just from Washington, that Mr. [James] Buchanan will vacate the [State] Department in favour of Walker. This is what I anticipated from the first; and the fact, if it occur, will indicate in what direction the patronage of the Government will be employed. If you stand alone in the Senate, with an organized Government Press against you, the services which you may be able to render the Country will not, I fear, compensate for the labours and hazards to which you may be subjected. If Walker be, as I understand he is, the master spirit of the Cabinet, can you confide in its professions in regard to the Tariff? I think not. His policy, *as to the first step,* will jump with that of Benton & Wright; and this will be to use the Tariff question as a covered mine[?] against you *personally.* I fear another McLane's Bill, which, by a *nominal* reduction, may serve to throw you again into a false position before the Country; and not until its party purpose is effected, as in 1832, will they be willing to do justice to the Anti-tariff States. The appointment of Mr. [Levi] Woodbury to the Supreme Court Bench, seems to me to be pregnant with sinister and undisclosed purposes; and may be intended to weaken you in the Senate; for the Administration is doubtless aware of the probability of your return to that body, and this may be a measure in advance to embarrass you there. In short I have no sort of confidence in the friendly dispositions of the administration. Its own weakness will be the only security for its fidelity.

But these views, I confess, may be regarded as springing rather from personal than public interests. Such, I dare say, is the light in which your friends regard them, so far as I have been able to ascertain their sentiments. All concur both in the propriety and expediency of the proposed step. Indeed, they are clamorous in their appeals; and the public press has set it down as a thing certain that you will return to the Senate. A private letter from a friend in New

York, received a day or two since, says that the public there are much gratified at the intelligence; and [Charles] Nichols (our Consul at Amsterdam) who has been with me for some ten days, informs me that the commercial community generally will cooperate with you upon the Tariff.

In this state of things, and regarding it as settled that you will be compelled to go back to the Senate, I have been looking around for some one to take the place of [William C.] Rives [as Senator from Va.], who might afford you efficient aid in the approaching contest. It appears to me that Mr. [Henry A.] Wise would be far the most eligible selection. His knowledge of men and things is far more extended and accurate than that of any other of our Virginia politicians; and his fearless independence of character will ensure him respect. I have mentioned the matter to Judge [Daniel A.] Wilson only, who cordially concurs with me; and we are determined to go down to Richmond before the day of meeting, and to prepare our friends in the General Assembly to nominate him. What think you of it? If you do not concur, write *immediately.*

You speak of the indications of the Court organ [the Washington *Union*]; and I entirely agree with you as to its inclinations, and probable future course; tho' there are some late arrangements of rather a strange nature. [Thomas] Ritchie is certainly not liked by the Benton clique, and has lately written to R. Latham of the Abingdon Banner, a warm friend of yours, to assist him in the conduct of the Union. He passed through this place about a fortnight since and called on me to talk over matters. He was on his way to Washington, & expressed the warmest interest in your favour. He is firmly persuaded that Ritchie will sustain you, as well as his sons in Richmond; and seemed to be much surprised when I expressed a doubt. I told him that he might say to Ritchie that you knew nothing of the Mercury's Correspondent, & that you felt every disposition to give the administration a cordial support. He will write to me from time to time.

Mrs. [Elizabeth Morris] C[rallé] unites with me in the kindest regards to Mrs. [Floride Colhoun] Calhoun and family. We hope yet to entertain you during the summer at *Meadowdale* our mountain home, whither we shall go early in the spring. With high regard and veneration I am truly yours, R.K. Crallé.

ALS in ScCleA.

To W[illiam] C. Anderson and Others

Steamboat Maria [at Memphis], Nov. 17, 1845
Gentlemen: Had it been in my power I would gladly have accepted your invitation, and that presented by the delegation of St. Louis to the Memphis Convention, to visit your great and growing city; but such is not the case. Engagements, which I cannot disregard, compel me to return with as little delay as possible to my residence in South Carolina, by the way of South Alabama, where my family are now waiting for me to join them. I have long desired to visit your city, and, if not unavoidably prevented, shall carry my intention into effect next summer or fall.

I feel, gentlemen, highly honored, that you should place your approbation of my public conduct on the grounds, on which you do. Time has but served to strengthen and fix immovably my conviction, that a sacred regard for the Constitution, and the maintenance of the federative character of our Government to the fullest extent, are indispensable to the preservation of our glorious Union and free popular system of government.

You do me no more than justice, in attributing to me a vigilant regard to the interests and rights of the West. I have ever regarded its great growth with admiration, and have ever been ready to promote it, as far as the Constitution would permit; in proof of which, I appeal to my public acts in the various capacities in which I have acted.

Nor, gentlemen, do you over estimate the importance of annexing Texas to the Union. Now that the measure is about to be consummated, I cheerfully leave to time and experience to decide on the importance of the acquisition, with the most perfect confidence, that their decision will be such as to leave little doubt in reference to it, as is now entertained in reference to the acquisition of Louisiana. With great respect, I am, &c. &c., John C. Calhoun.

PC (from the St. Louis, Mo., *Reporter* of unknown date) in the Springfield, Ill., *Illinois State Register*, December 5, 1845, p. 2.

To A[LBERT] G. BROWN, "Chairman, and others of committee," Jackson, Miss.

Steamboat Maria, Nov. 17, 1845

Gentlemen: It is with deep and sincere regret, that I feel myself compelled to decline the invitation you have tendered in behalf of a large meeting of your fellowcitizens, to visit the seat of government, as the guest of the state. My family are at Selma in Alabama, waiting my return. A prior invitation, which I accepted, compels me to visit Natchez on my return; and engagements of a nature I cannot postpone, will compel me to return with as little delay as possible to my residence in South Carolina.

Be assured, gentlemen, that under different circumstances, I would accept with the greatest pleasure your invitation, and that I will endeavor to seize some early opportunity to visit your seat of government, when I shall have more time and leisure to renew old acquaintance, and form new, with my fellow citizens of a state, I so greatly respect, than I could possibly have at this time. For the very kind and highly flattering terms in which you have conveyed the invitation of those, in whose behalf you act, you will please accept my sincere acknowledgement and profound gratitude. Next to the approbation of my own conscience, the approbation of my fellow citizens, regardless of party distinction, is the highest reward, in my estimation, which can be bestowed on me as a public servant. With great respect, I am, very respectfully, &c., J.C. Calhoun.

PC in the Jackson, Miss., *Southern Reformer,* November 22, 1845, p. 3.

To W[ILLIAM] CULLOM and Others

Steam Boat Maria, Nov. 17, 1845

Gentlemen: I very greatly regret that it is not in my power to accept the invitation which you have tendered me, in behalf of the delegation of the Legislature of Tennessee, of the city of Nashville, and of Davidson and the adjacent counties, to visit Nashville on my return home. My family are in South Alabama, and my engagements are such as to compel me to return with as little delay as possible to my residence in South Carolina, which will make it necessary to take the route by New Orleans.

Under different circumstances it would be very gratifying to me to accept your invitation. I have long desired to visit Nashville, and if nothing should intervene to postpone my intention, I shall certainly make it a visit during the summer and fall.

Permit me, gentlemen, to thank you for the very flattering terms in which you have tendered your invitation, and to assure you that I feel deep interest in the early completion of a railroad connection between your city and Charleston and Savannah. When completed it cannot fail to be profitable to those who may vest their capital in the work, and highly advantageous to each of the cities and their respective States. With great respect, I am, &c, J.C. Calhoun.

PC in the Nashville, Tenn., *Union*, December 2, 1845, p. 2.

From I[saac] E. Holmes, [Representative from S.C.]

Charleston, Nov. 18[t]h [18]45

My Dear Sir, Judge [Daniel E.] Huger informs me That What we all desired would be accomplish[e]d. Again you would go into the Senate. By the time you receive this letter you will have been elected, and my object in writing you is to request if possible that you be at Washington early.

It is feared that the Whigs may have a majority at the meeting of the Senate and elect [Joseph] Gales & [William W.] Seaton Printers. Mr. [John] H[e]art is very Anxious on this subject and wrote to me accordingly. When in New York the other day, The merchants expressed Their anxiety, That you should come into the Senate—in y[ou]r hands they say are the Issues of peace and War. This is a high compliment from Whigs. Mr. [Daniel] Webster also has expressed a wish that you might come into the Senate, and enforce upon the minds of the Senators y[ou]r "wise and masterly inactivity." There can be no doubt that a war spirit is abroad, and it will require a master[']s hand to keep in leash, the *"Dogs of War."*

I leave here on Monday [11/24], so as to be in Washington four or five days before Congress meets. I doubt whether we will be able to agree in Caucus upon a Public printer. The impression is that [Francis P.] Blair & Reeves [*sic;* John C. Rives] will play old [Thomas] Ritchie a trick. With great resp[ec]t Y[ou]rs truly, I.E. Holmes.

ALS in ScCleA. NOTE: This letter was addressed to Calhoun in Pendleton.

Remarks at Vicksburg, Miss., [11/18]. Calhoun arrived at the city wharf by steamboat and was greeted by a large crowd and an official committee of welcome. "After Mr. [Jefferson] D[avis] had concluded [his speech of welcome], Mr. Calhoun, in a brief speech returned his thanks to Mr. D[avis] for his approval of his public life and to the citizens of Vicksburg and the South West generally for the warm and continual manifestations of respect and kindness he had met with in his travels. He was much excited during his speech and apologized for his manner by saying that he was unable to address a promiscuous assemblage and could only speak when he had a subject before him." Calhoun mingled freely with the ladies and gentlemen and then departed. Many were reported disappointed because he stayed only a few hours, though it had been reported after his first visit going upriver a week before that he would stay a whole day. From the Vicksburg, Miss., *Daily Whig*, November 20, 1845, p. 2. [Varina Howell Davis, who was present, summarized Calhoun's remarks many years later as follows: "Mr. Calhoun made no appeals to any emotion. The duty of a citizen to the State was his theme; the reward he offered was the consciousness of having performed it faithfully." From Varina Howell Davis, *Jefferson Davis, Ex-President of the Confederate States . . . : A Memoir*, 1:212. See also the accounts in Joseph D. Howell to Margaret L. Howell, 11/21/1845, in *The Papers of Jefferson Davis*, 2:374–379; the Vicksburg, Miss., *Sentinel and Expositor*, November 25, 1845, p. 1; and H.S. Fulkerson, *Random Recollections of Early Days in Mississippi*, p. 60.]

ACCOUNT OF CALHOUN'S RETURN JOURNEY FROM MEMPHIS TO NEW ORLEANS

[New Orleans, November 21, 1845]
The steamboat Maria left Memphis early on Sunday morning last [11/16], with the Hon. John C. Calhoun and some one hundred and thirty cabin passengers. On arriving at Vicksburg, on Tuesday evening [11/18], Mr. C[alhoun] proceeded to the Prentiss House, where he was welcomed to the city by Jeff[erson] Davis, Esq. The honorable guest, after making a short response, was introduced to many of the inhabitants, and soon after returned to the boat. About 10 o'clock, on Wednesday [11/19] morning, the Maria reached Natchez. Here the boat remained some two hours, during which

time Mr. C[alhoun] was conducted to the City Hotel and received the calls of the inhabitants. Yesterday morning [11/20], about 11 o'clock, the Maria stopped at the fine plantation of the Messrs. La Branche, some twenty-five miles above this city, Captain Dunnica politely waiting long enough to allow Mr. Calhoun an opportunity of witnessing the process of sugar making, and the gentlemanly owners of the plantation affording him every facility to gratify his curiosity in relation to this branch of our State's agriculture.

During the trip to and from Memphis, the utmost respect and cordiality were every where extended to the great Southerner, and he has expressed himself highly delighted with the beautiful scenery and vast productiveness of the valley of the Mississippi. To-day [11/21] we learn that he leaves for South Carolina, and in good health.

From the New Orleans, La., *Daily Picayune*, November 21, 1845, p. 2. Also printed in the Richmond, Va., *Enquirer*, December 2, 1845, p. 1. Another account in the New York, N.Y., *Herald*, December 4, 1845, p. 2 (reprinted from the Mobile, Ala., *Herald and Tribune* of unstated date). NOTE: The New Orleans *Daily Picayune* of 11/22 reported: "Mr. Calhoun, after receiving the visits of many of our citizens yesterday, started for South Carolina, by way of Mobile, accompanied by his son, A[ndrew] P. Calhoun, Esq." Many members of the LaBranche family owned plantations in the adjacent parishes of St. John the Baptist and St. Charles west of Lake Pontchartrain.

From ARMISTEAD BURT, [Representative from S.C.]

Hamburg [S.C.,] 24 Nov. 1845

My dear Sir, I have written to my Overseer, Mr. Palmer, to let you have my carriage horses, if you send for them. I will be glad to hear, by letter addressed to me at Washington City, immediately on your return from Memphis, whether you will take them, as I shall direct that they be sent to Augusta for sale, if you decline to take them.

I am glad to see that you went to Memphis and shall look with much anxiety for the proceedings of the Convention, of which I have seen, as yet, only a meager sketch of the first days.

I have not yet received a letter from you, in answer to mine sent to Alabama, but presume I shall receive it at Washington. I shall, in the mean time, take for granted that you will go to the Senate. The necessity of your doing so, has been made apparent and imperative, by the late revelations from the Cabinet.

Martha [Calhoun Burt] and I will leave here in the morning for Washington. We are both quite well.

Our regards to Mrs. [Floride Colhoun] C[alhoun] and Miss [Martha] Cornelia [Calhoun]. Yours sincerely, Armistead Burt.

ALS in ScCleA.

Remarks at a dinner in his honor at Montgomery, Ala., 11/25. James E. Belser complimented Calhoun with a toast, hoping to see him use his talents to strengthen the bonds of the Union in the future. "In replying, only to the last part of the sentiment, Mr. Calhoun referred to the recent measures of the Memphis Convention. His address (says the Montgomery Advertiser) was listened to with much interest, from the explanations he furnished in regard to the great channels of communication which have been projected to unite in closer bonds the different sections of the Union. Mr. Calhoun concluded by offering the following toast: 'THE SYSTEM OF RAILROADS: The best means to advance the social, political, and commercial prosperity of the country.'" From the Alexandria, Va., *Alexandria Gazette and Virginia Advertiser*, December 10, 1845, p. 2. Partly printed in the New Orleans, La., *Daily Picayune*, December 2, 1845, p. 2; the New Orleans, La., *Bee*, December 4, 1845, p. 1; the Natchez, Miss., *Mississippi Free Trader and Natchez Gazette*, December 6, 1845, p. 2; the Raleigh, N.C., *North Carolina Standard*, December 10, 1845, p. 3. [According to the report carried in the Natchez paper cited above, Calhoun "entered the city [of Montgomery] unheralded—unexpected at the time," but "a public dinner was at once prepared in compliment to him, at which about a hundred gentlemen sat down."]

From F[RANCIS] W. PICKENS

Edgewood, Tuesday 26 Nov: 1845

My dear Sir, I re[ceive]d yours from Andrew[']s [Andrew Pickens Calhoun's plantation in Marengo County, Ala.], & was pleased to hear of your fine prospects in planting &c. The crop here will be very short. The late bolls did not open as was expected from the late fall. The Summer was so dry that there was not sap enough in the stalk to mature the late bolls. We had no frost to kill even pepper until the 10th of November and yet the cotton never grew at all.

As to the sale of Mr. [Thomas G.] Clemson's place I have sent Mr. [James] Vaughn to see about it, and wrote Mr. [John] Mobley & Mr. [Allen] Dozier &c—but they decline to take. Mr. Dozier says he would take it if he could sell his Big Creek place, but he cannot keep up both. I have no doubt but it can be sold. It seems to me that the price he asks exceeds what he gave, by not allowing for the credits of three years allowed him in the purchase &c. Yet I do not think it more than it is worth and will bring when known. The most efficient mode of making it known ought to be resorted to. I will mention it at Columbia, and perhaps you might advertise it, or some one in Pendleton might buy. Tho[ma]s Pickens did want a place very much. I will do any thing I can with pleasure to assist in the sale. But if it were advertised and then put up at auction upon those credits I have not the slightest doubt it would bring what you ask. I think it the best way to sell it, allways keeping some one ready not to allow it to go off under its value.

They have made without rain 102 loads of corn off of about 115 acres of land, & I think the cotton will be about 36,000 lb[s]. in seed—which is about ½ crop or more.

We were all delighted to see the enthusiasm with which you were rec[ei]v[e]d in the South West. I hope it will do good, and only wish that you could have extended your visit further to Nashville & St. Louis &c. Your Presidency of the Convention was a happy circumstance.

Col: [Franklin H.] Elmore sent me your letter in which you allude to his to Mr. [Armistead] Burt and his apprehensions "as to confusion in the State this winter." I never heard any thing of it, and had not the slightest apprehensions myself. Those who seem to be moving through the [Charleston] Mercury have no weight in the State and [there] are but very few who are more dissatisfied with power in the State than any thing at Washington. Without Elmore and the Bank they have no influence. It may be that Elmore alluded to local matters and the complaints ag[ain]st the manner in which the Bank has been used of late. Last Session the last night after midnight he and [Wade] Hampton [II] got resolutions through loaning them through the iron works $141,000 for 10 years without interest until the end of 10 years, under nominal regulations as to selling the works, & lately Elmore under these resolutions bought the works for $50,000 and the negroes for $80,000 for himself & Hampton, when they originally cost $400,000, and I hear great complaints made about that. The truth is the State is in a most miserable condition as to its finances, and New York never was more governed by the "Albany Regency" & the

"Saf[e]ty fund" than is So[uth] Ca[rolina] by the same means. Between [James] Gadsden with the R[ail] Road Company ["& his own debts" *interlined*] & Elmore & the Bank we are plunged into circumstances which will finally make a loss to the State of at least $3,800,000 certain, and things are so managed that it ["is" *interlined*] impossible to do any thing at present, so many are identified with the gains. I was only elected to fill a vacancy and this winter is my last, & I shall never run again without we have war.

I start in the morning for Columbia. I could not leave before. Very truly & sincerely, F.W. Pickens.

P.S. You speak of hiring out Mr. Clemson's negroes &c. You had better sell them as they will suffer much from being hired, & if you will sell I will buy at a fair valuation upon the same credits as offered on the land. F.W.P.

ALS in ScCleA.

Report of a committee of the S.C. Senate, [11/27]. "The committee appointed by the Senate to count the votes for U. States Senator" [in the joint balloting of the South Carolina General Assembly], report that John C. Calhoun received 135 votes [out of 139 possible]. Seventy votes being a majority, Calhoun "is therefore elected." DU in Sc-Ar, Records of the General Assembly, U.S. Relations.

From THO[MA]S G. CLEMSON

Brussels, Nov. 28th 1845

My dear Sir, Your favour of the 18th Sept. was recieved [*sic*] a few days since eit[her] by the Great Britain, Great Western or Hibernia for they all arrived within a day or two of each other. The first did not use her propellers all the distance. From some cause they were broken soon after she left the U. States and therefore had to depend on her sails. The second got on shore on our Coast and was retarded, and the last brought us news up to the 6th inst. Judging from the tenor of the American papers and those of England the Oregon question may bring difficulties of a very serious character. England has been arming for the last year; of this there is no doubt, and I have been asked frequently why it was that England was arming. Both sides are com[m]itted and I do not well see how a conflict can be avoided if the President [James K. Polk] reiterates what he stated in his inaugural, and takes the ground which is taken by the [Washington] Union, that all Oregon is ours. Sir Robert Peel & Lord Aberdeen were decided[,] as much so as the President. I have heard it intimated that Sir Rob[er]t Peel would go out of office that his place might be filled by some one, not committed and who could take a course more in accordance with the interests of the two nations which is any thing but war. Joshua Bates the partner of Barings (and father in law of Mr. [Sylvain] Van de Weyer the Belgian Minister of the Interior & formerly the Belgian Envoye to the Court of St. James) was here a few days since. He told me that he had been in Company with Lord Aberdeen who *would* talk with him upon nothing else than Oregon. Lord Aberdeen said to him that he would try to settle that question as it ought to be settled between two intel[l]igent nations. Mr. Bates thought there could be no doubt that it could be settled by making the 49° the boundary. I should judge myself that there could be little doubt upon that point. An intelligent Englishman who I saw in this city the other day, a man of some note as an author, and a writer for English papers & periodicals deprecated all idea of War, and regretted the position of the Question. He said that he thought the thing might be arranged easily. Sir Rob[er]t Peel & Lord Aberdeen had taken too high ground and all England *wanted was to be let down easily*. Be it as it may. The last steamer[']s news caused the funds in England to fall, and the funds is a pretty good Thermometer of public opinion.

I have been very much occupied lately with business between the two Governments. I concluded the Treaty of Commerce and Navigation on the 10th inst. It is now being examined by the Committee of the Chambers, and will come up before the Chambers in the course of ten days. It will meet with some opposition[,] perhaps a good deal, but it will pass and if it is ratified by the U. States Senate we shall have one of the most advantageous treatys ever made[,] not because Belgium is so large but because all Germany is behind the treaty. The 8th article makes the United States the Carriers for Belgium and if I mistake not for Germany through Ostend and Antwerp. The former port is the best in the channel. Our Treaty with the Hanse towns is becoming a dead letter so far as our shipping is concerned and the ports of Belgium are destined to take their place, for Germany, in trade with the United States. We will before long send raw cotton to Germany in much greater quantities than we are doing now. The Zoll Verein are very anxious for direct trade with the United States but so long as she thought the late treaty had a chance of passing she would not act against England to which nation Prussia is closely allied. England sends Cotton yarns to Germany to the amount of seventy millions of dollars. If the Zoll Verein would lay duties on yarns of English manufacture or Enact differential duties in favour of the United States, it would increase our trade immensely. It would make our ships the carriers of Cotton, under the treaty I have just concluded, & make a cotton market in Belgium for Germany. Belgium is now using her influence with the Zoll Verein to bring about that kind of action against the introduction of English manufactured cotton into Germany, and the Baron [Heinrich Alexander] d'Arnim told me the other day that he had come to my opinion and that he was writt[i]ng [*sic*] a pamphlet on the subject of those views. He said to me also that he had finished a Despatch to the Prussian minister of Foreign affairs [Heinrich von Bülow] which ended with these words, "The treaty with the United States should have been ratified at Carlsrhue [*sic*; Karlsruhe]." I have worked pretty hard to make those views evident, and have succeeded so far as to make the Prussian Minister here a convert to the opinions, (Baron d'Anninim [*sic*]) and he has great weight in Prussia. Heretofore the main difficulty to prohibitory duties on English yarns, came from Prussia[,] the Southern part of the Confederation being in favour of high duties. Mr. Deschamp [*sic*; Adolphe Dechamps], the Minister of Foreign affairs here I know has given instructions to their minister at Berlin to act in that line. If I do not much mistake[,] my views together with the treaty will tell largely before long in favour of the United States, and particularly with the Cotton States. It appears to me if I were in Berlin I could bring things about to our advantage. I would almost underwrite that I could make Prussia favour the United States by laying duties on English Cotton yarns. And I think I could make a treaty that would pass the United States & be immensely to our advantage. Of the advantages of the Treaty I have just concluded with Belgium you will be the judge before long. Mr. [James] Buchanan paid me the compliment ('tho long delayed) of returning me the projet with ["scarce any" *canceled and* "no" *interlined*] alterations beyond a few verbal corrections to make the sense clear. I am now negotiating a treaty of Extradition between the U.S. & Belgium, but from what Mr. Buchanan said in his last instructions he wants it signed in Washington. I do not think that fair. I shall have had the work, and he the honour. Belgium is now about entering into negotiations with our Government through me for a postal arrangement. If I have time sufficient I will very shortly perfect the alliance between this

Govt. & the United States. Belgium now admits all grain free of duty and among the number particularly mentions *Indian Corn.* What a chapter is here opened to the United States. Indian corn is admitted duty free into Belgium until June next. If the papers in the United States would but talk a little about these advantages it would send that grain here ["and" *canceled*] in such quantities as to make it so cheap that the Government of Belgium never would be able to lay duties again on that grain. Let Indian Corn be admitted free in Belgium, and England will have to give way. Cheap food insures cheap production, and who ever sells the cheapest monipolises [*sic*] the greatest foreign markets &c &c. Sir Rob[er]t Peel anticipated that the Diet of the Zoll Verein would ["prohibit" *canceled*] lay a duty on English Cotton yarns, (he understood that it would not go above 2 thalers) and in order to enable the English manufacturers to continue to sell to Germany he altered the tariff of last winter. He took off the duty on Cotton, and other articles necessary to enable the producers to sell as cheap or with as much profit to Germany as if the latter had laid a duty on Cotton yarns. Next year England[']s profits will be greater than they ever have been. But if we only use exertion we can cut the grass from under her feet. We can supply Belgium with cheap food, *Indian Corn* &c, and with this lever we can act efficiently upon England. We can send our Cotton twist to Germany or our raw Cotton without making use of England[']s agency who reaps such immense profits on her ["yarns" *canceled*] spinning our Cotton which we might do as well as she. Since I have been in Europe my eyes are a little opened. Our foreign relations are too much neglected. We blunder along, fall down & rise again[;] so rapid is our growth, that no attention is paid to questions of the greatest moment. It is Cotton & Tobacco mainly the first that vivifies the commerce of the world. Other nations, are growing rich and quarrelling for what we throw away. We ought to be more active abroad. Let us have direct trade with Germany & a market of Sixty millions of inhabitants is open to the reception & consumption of Cotton for which they are dependent upon England. Germany recieves but about 70,000 bales & pays England for spinning it. With a little exertion in a few years the linen trade would cease and Cotton would take its place, & what activity would our commerce have if we could supply this world with Indian Corn, what a revolution in the West and South.

My relations here are of the most agre[e]able kind. The Government are willing to do any thing that I ask. The Minister of foreign affairs ["tells me" *canceled*] says to me "Tell me what to do & I will

do it." The claims are now finished[;] all our claimants have recieved their certificates which will be paid at the end of 1847. My
treaty of Commerce & Navigation is signed and will be ratified.
Our commerce with Belgium is rapidly increasing. Indian Corn is
admitted duty free until June 1847. A treaty of Extradition for the
mutual surrender of fugitives from justice is far advanced, and a
postal arrangement about to be made, or shortly commenced. And
if the line of steamers should come to Antwerp it will give a greater
impulse to our trade. Belgium sends to the U.S. a minister instead of
a chargé d'Affaires. She is building a free warehouse in Antwerp.
These things should be considered, and advantage taken of them by
our Govt. I have worked hard since I have been [here] and with
success, as great as one man can have[,] and I hope the United States
will return the compliment to Belgium by sending a minister to her
Court. The advances ought to be met on our side, for the good of
the country. If they should think proper to do so & give me a shove
up the ladder it would come very opportunely for I have hard work
to make the two ends meet. The pay is not adequate to the expense
entailed on the position.

Whilst I am thus absorbed here with public business I fear that
my property is sacrificing in the United States. I really know not
what to do. If I give up this position I must seek another. I can not
live on my place[—]it will not give me a support[,] besides which I
think I can do better for my family & myself by a different course
than that of spending my life on a plantation. I know you have your
occupations and feel lo[a]th to trouble you, but what am I to do. I
wrote you a long letter giving you my views about my business some
time since. I hope you recieved it. If I knew to whom to confide my
business, or to whom to write, or in whom to have confidence you
would hear nothing more about my affairs. If my money were invested in safe bonds or interest yielding securities it would relieve
me from a world of anxiety not about myself or on my own account
but upon that of my family.

I have almost thought of asking permission to return for a couple
of months to save you the trouble of reading my letters about my
own business, but what could I do in so short a time as that the
Govt. would allow me to return home. Very little. The steamers
will now run but once a month and before I have time to recieve an
answer to this the country may be at war. So that I am forced to say
to you, in order to prevent my interests from being sacrificed, give a
little thought to my affairs and try what can be done to insure me
from loss and perhaps ruin. My family is dear to me, and I can not

help feeling a world of anxiety on their account. My position here is becoming better every day; it would be nothing on a plantation. If my funds were secure & bearing interest regularly paid my position here would give me support & I might accumulate the amount of interest that would yearly accrue from my property. If I should be mistaken in my position here, and should have overvalued my services to the country or the hold on the Govt. arrising [*sic*] from my conduct here, then the position is entirely changed. In that case it would be useless for me to strive in the line I am in and I had better return and go at something else. But again if I could hope to retain my position, and be kept in a position requiring me to work, and could hope for promotion I should be contented to continue in this service ["for a few years" *interlined*] provided my affairs or property in the U.S. could be safely transfer[r]ed to such securities as would secure me the interest & finally the capital, without troubling any one in the matter. The idea that I am obliged to trouble others or make my affairs known to any one is a source of annoyance to me, and one that I never felt as vividly. Mr. [Francis W.] Pickens has written me that I ought to do something[,] that he would do what he could, but that would not be much, that he warned me that my interests were in jeopardy &c &c but what to do I know not.

Anna [Maria Calhoun Clemson] & the children [John Calhoun Clemson and Floride Elizabeth Clemson] are well and join me in love to all the family. Your affectionate son, Thos. G. Clemson.

ALS in ScCleA; PEx (dated 11/25) in Boucher and Brooks, eds., *Correspondence*, pp. 308–309.

From Sam[ue]l A. Cartwright

Natchez, Nov: 29t[h] 1845

Dear Sir, I am truly sorry that I had not an opportunity of paying my respects to you when you were in Natchez. I was absent from town & before my return you had left. The circumstance of missing you I offer as an apology for troubling you with these hasty lines—lest it might be inferred that it arose from indifference. So far from it I was very anxious to see you & to have the pleasure of conversing with you. I take the liberty of sending you a newspaper [*not found*] containing some remarks of mine on the subject of rail roads. I would not trespass on your time so much as to ask you to peruse them, were it not that they have a bearing on a subject you have always had time to consider—the interest of the whole country, particularly the Southern States. Any suggestions of means to increase the commercial & political importance of the planting States cannot be uninteresting to you if they be such as have not attracted your attention. A rail road through the planting States to the Pacific has, however, attracted your attention, but you seem to view such a work as belonging to ["the" *interlined*] age that is coming on & not to the present. The remarks, I send you, would make it the business of the present age. The question, whether it belongs rightfully to the present or future might be worth further consideration. By waiting we get weaker. That some good may be done by the numerous rail roads now being made in South Carolina & Georgia is very clear. Some 25 years ago the Parish of Concordia [La.], opposite Natchez, was a swamp. Each proprietor began to make levees on every little lake or bayou on which his property was situated, & thereby reclaimed much of the land. At length, after an immense sum had been expended in leveeing, about ¼ of the land only was reclaimed, & it was discovered that by stopping up two large bayous, leading from the river, the whole could be reclaimed. The work was done & the effect followed. The whole Parish was reclaimed. The multiplicity of little roads now making in every direction remind me of the immense sums spent in the Parish of ConCordia in making some hundred or two levees, that the stopping up of two bayous have superceded. A road to the Pacific would be to the South what the stopping up of two large bayous was to the Parish of Concordia. The one great work will not cost as much as the more numerous little works. The great rail road would make the smaller ones of little use that were not auxillary to it. The various rail roads, running almost at random, that are now projected, will exhaust the resources of the present age to complete them. When finished they will add little or no weight or influence to the Southern States in comparison to what would be added by a rail road to the Pacific. The commerce of Asia, the islands of the Pacific & the western coast of South America if thrown into our Southern States by a rail road would do every thing for the South that could be desired. It would make the Southern States the centre of commerce, add vastly to their population, increase their wealth, & soon give back again to them their lost political power & importance.

Were the South & West to husband their resources for the great work & let the smaller ones alone, until that was completed, there is no doubt in my mind of its practicability. The rail road is a great improvement on the caravan. A line once established between the

309

Pacific & Atlantic would change the face of things entirely. One road bringing every variety of exchangeable commodities would do our South more good than a thousand roads not bringing a variety of exchangeable commodities. A great variety of exchangeable commodities is essential to commerce. There is a sameness in the production of the Southern States. Carolina & Mississippi produce the same things. An hundred roads between the two States would not add much to commerce, unless one or the other imported articles the other had not. The growth being the same, any amount of cotton may go through a southern town without adding much to its trade unless the town has something to give in exchange for the cotton. Besides no one in the South wants the cotton except the exporters. But a caravan of Asiatic goods could not pass through any one of our towns without finding purchasers—without affording a basis for commerce. The place in Georgia where all the rail roads meet will not be as much benefited by them as it would be by a single rail way bringing a variety of exchangeable commodities. Atalanta [*sic*] has no use for cotton & articles that the surrounding country produces—& hence the products of the country will not stop there to be exchanged. Columbus was seeking the prize of Asiatic commerce when he discovered America. A rail road to the Pacific will give us the prize he sought. Under whosesoever auspices such a great work shall be accomplished must, in all after time, be considered among the greatest benefactors of mankind. But I beg pardon for trespassing so long on your time with these dissultory observations. Very truly your &c, Saml. A. Cartwright.

ALS in ScCleA. NOTE: An AEU by Calhoun reads "Dr. Cartwright." Samuel Adolphus Cartwright (1793–1863) was a native of Va. and a physician in Natchez since the 1820's.

From SILAS REED

Cincinnati, Nov. 29th 1845

Dear Sir, When I left St. Louis last week it was believed by your friends there that you would probably answer their letter of invitation as soon as you reached Washington City.

Since I have seen on my journey here the strong ground taken by the [Washington] "Union," upon the Oregon question within a week or two past, I have feared that there might be some design in the movement beyound [*sic*] that of mere patriotism, or the defence of our just rights on the Pacific coast, in which Col. [Thomas H.] Benton might be acting a silent part for Ulterior purposes, and I am so anxious that you should assume the highest and strongest ground upon the same question, at all compatible with your expressed opinions and past action thereon, that I must beg to be excused for reminding you, in this manner, of the importance to you, at this crisis, of being behind no one in the position you now take upon the subject.

The almost entire population of the West will sanction the doctrines of the "Union," and are ready to sustain and defend our rights in that quarter at all hazards. I do not believe England would dare to war with us upon a question in which we would be so clearly in the right.

The importance and value of that country to us is hardly sufficiently appreciated by any of our leading statesmen, except yourself and one or two others, and very few indeed realize the deep interest felt towards it by most western people since the emigration of several thousand of our own citizens to that country within a year or two past.

I am firmly persuaded that we ought not to surrender any thing short of 54° 40′ north, unless it be to save war and we can be certain of carrying the public sentiment in favor of throwing off two or more degrees for the mere sake of a compromise for peace. Still, I should regret to feel obliged to adopt even such an alternative in a question of right.

Our laws should be extended over the whole territory this session without fail, and the year's notice, I think, should be left to the discretion of the President, as to the time when it may most safely be given.

Your future political success so much depends upon the position you now assume upon this deeply exciting question, that I trust you will excuse the liberty I have taken in expressing the anxiety I feel that you should take as high ground in the matter as you think the best interests of our common country will possibly justify.

I shall hope to see you in Washington in a few days. With great respect I remain your friend and Ob[edien]t Serv[an]t, Silas Reed.

ALS in ScCleA; PC in Boucher and Brooks, eds., *Correspondence*, pp. 309–310. NOTE: An AEU by Calhoun reads "Silas Reed[,] relates to Oregon." Reed had been Surveyor General of the U.S. General Land Office at St. Louis during 1841–1845.

DECEMBER 1–31
1845

▯

The 1st session of the 29th Congress convened on December 1, about the time Calhoun arrived home at Fort Hill from his trip to the West. He left Pendleton with Mrs. Calhoun and Cornelia on December 9, arrived in Charleston on the 16th, and left there in the Wilmington boat two days later. They reached Washington on the evening of Sunday, the 21st, and Calhoun was in his seat in the Senate the next day in time to cast a yea vote for the joint resolution admitting Texas into the Union. It had already passed the House of Representatives. The Senate vote was 31 to 13.

A number of newspaper reporters commented that he looked well and vigorous and many echoed the sentiments of the Baltimore American *(December 23, 1845, p. 2): "Mr. Calhoun's appearance here excites great interest, and particularly in reference to the Oregon Question, as much depends upon the line of policy that may be marked out by Mr. C. and his friends. The balance of power between conservative and safe action and extreme ultraism probably rests with Mr. Calhoun and his friends."*

Calhoun understood this well, as is indicated by his comments to his son-in-law the day after Christmas: "I find myself here under circumstances involving great responsibility. There is, I fear, great hazard of war with England on the subject of Oregon. The question has become greatly complicated & the country, it seems, looks to me to avert the calamity of war."

There had been speculation that Calhoun would be appointed chairman of the Committee on Foreign Relations. According to other speculation it took the combined efforts of Thomas H. Benton, Lewis Cass, and William Allen to avert this calamity (for the jingo party). Instead, Calhoun was, two weeks before he arrived, appointed chairman of the Committee on Finance. (On January 7 he asked the Senate to excuse him from this duty as his voice was not up to the long and labored explanations that would be required to present the committee's business to the Senate. The committee was placed in the safe hands, tariff-wise, of Jesse Speight of Mississippi.)

In his earlier decade in the Senate Calhoun had taken part al-

most daily in the debates, on every subject. He was evidently sav-
ing his voice now, for he took little part until December 30, when he
made his first move with a speech and resolutions designed to thwart
the war party.

◫

FLORIDE [COLHOUN] CALHOUN to Margaret M.
[Green] Calhoun, [Marengo County, Ala.]

Forthill, December 3d 1845
My dear Margaret, I am at last safely landed at home after a very
fatigueing journey, and found all well. [Martha] Cornelia [Cal-
houn], looks better than I ever saw her, she has had her hair cut
short, and it has improved her appearance much, her form is decidedly much better. She hears through the silver trumpet some
distance, and seems pleased with it. Cudy [Martha Maria Colhoun]
and herself go tomorrow evening to William Ga[i]llard[']s wedding,
the world and all are to be there. Cudy goes with us to Washington.
Eugenia [Calhoun] does not go. Mr. [Armistead] Burt, and Martha
[Calhoun Burt] have gone on.
I have been up to my eyes in business ever since I came home.
[I] was resolved not to unpack any thing but what we could not do
without, and lo and behold a Gentleman, came to stay several days
with Mr. [John C.] Calhoun, and Mrs. [Placidia Mayrant] Adams
came after dark to take tea with us, she is as queer as ever. I have
not yet seen Cousin Becky [Rebecca Weyman Foster Gaillard], but
it will not be long before she comes.
James [Edward Calhoun], and William Lowndes [Calhoun] have
gone to School [Erskine College], and are much pleased, We will
call to see them on our way down to Mr. [Thomas G.] Clemson[']s
place. Several letters have been received from Brussells[;] all have
been suffering from colds. Little Floride [Elizabeth Clemson] was
very ill, from over eating herself, but is well again. Anna [Maria
Calhoun Clemson] says she is delightfully fixed in her new house,
and has a remarkably fine cook. The children begin to speak french
fluently, their nurse speaks nothing else to them.
I have just received a long and affectionate letter from [James]
Edward [Boisseau] in answer to mine written just before I left home,
in it he says he wishes me to get what I wish in Washington, and he

will pay for it, and that I must write him for any thing I wish in New York, and he will take pleasure in get[t]ing it.

The gold pencil he sent to Mr. Calhoun is superb. Cornelia[']s dress is beautiful, he sais he would not send mine until I arrived in Washington. Is he not the kindest person in the world.

I fear it is a bad chance to send you any thing this winter as Mr. Calhoun says if he does not get Mr. Clemson's Negro[e]s, he will not send ours before fall. Francis [W. Pickens] has written Mr. Clemson, he wishes to buy his Negro[e]s, and I think he will get them.

[December] 4th[,] I am truly sorry to see by Andrew[']s, letter that the children have been so sick, hope they are entirely well by this time. Do write me immediately as you receive this letter and let me know how the children are. You must remember me affectionately to all the ladies, in the Canebrake, and say to them I shall always think of my visit to that place with pleasure. Also love to Mrs. Lyon and the young Ladies. Cornelia had a long, and interesting, letter from your sister Mary [Green], all were well and she says their winter is to be uncommonly gay. I am glad on Cudy[']s account. You must excuse this awfully written letter, as I have to write it by peacemeals constantly some one calling, and Pike bothering me about what to do next. My room is a [s]cene of confusion, all at work in it. Cousin Becky Ga[i]llard has just left me, She is in fine spirits at having married her last child so well. She fixed up all my caps beautifully. I take Nancey with me. She is delighted at the idea, her health is much better. I have fixed her up very nicely[,] gave her the dress, I thought of giving Issey, it fits her beautifully. Mrs. Pike says she never has seen a servant so handsomely clothed in every respect. I have not bought a thing for her but 2 p[ai]r of stockings to travell with. We leave tomorrow and will go as far as Anderson Courthouse, the next day to Erskin[e] College, and the third to Mr. Clemson[']s place. I cannot get any satisfaction from Mr. Calhoun about what he is going to do with respect to sending the Negro[e]s out, therefore will not be able to send you anything. He says perhaps he will send out some Negro[e]s in the fall. I told Andrew [Pickens Calhoun] by all means, to sell Issey as I am determined she shall never be about me again. Cornelia consents to having her sold. Tell Andrew to be sure to send her to Louisianna, I prefer it, particularly on account of their not being a prospect of her coming where I shall ever see her again. If she remains at the Canebrake, I never will visit it again, I have a horror of ever seeing her again, she has behaved so badly to me. I am sorry to be obliged to express my feelings so warmly, but I do so, on account of thinking that Andrew, does not intend selling her, but if he does not, he will repent it, when it is to[o] late. I must have the money I sell her for, to buy another.

Willy writes Cornelia, he is very much pleased with the school. James went there, but did not stay longer than two days, but went to his Uncle Jame[s]'s [James Edward Colhoun's] to stay with him. I will now conclude as my back, and eyes have both given out, and it is late. I will write you again when I arrive at Washington. Cornelia joins me in love to Andrew, and yourself. Kiss the children for me, and adieu for the present. your devoted mother, Floride Calhoun.

ALS in ScU-SC, John C. Calhoun Papers.

From S[HADRACH] PENN, JR.

St. Louis, Dec. 4 1845

Dear Sir, Since my return from Memphis I have ascertained that the followers of Col. [Thomas H.] Benton expect him to go the whole figure for the whole of Oregon, war or no war with England; and they also calculate that he will *head* you on that question. An impression has been produced to some extent by articles that have recently appeared in the [Washington] Union, that the Oregon question may soon be settled by negotiation, but I have not yielded to it. The whole West is firm against yielding any portion of that territory—and if England proves obstinate the Hunker anti-Annexationists will be fiery, with a view to cover their late dereliction by the smoke they will raise on the Oregon question. On this point I cannot be deceived. Benton will be even more furious than he was in discussing the Ashburton treaty. If, contrary to my expectations, an adjustment of boundary shall be agreed upon, he will assail it, even though Vancouver[']s Island and Puget's Sound should be secured to us. He will not go with you—nor will he sustain the President [James K. Polk] if he acts with you. Your policy is to ascertain what has been or may be done, and so to shape your course as not to be thrown into the back ground.

If no settlement of boundary can be satisfactorily effected, in season to prevent decisive action by Congress on the subject, I think you should move *in advance* in favor of repeating authoritatively the Monroe declaration of 1823, against farther colonization by any

European power on this continent. This may be done in such a manner, as not to commit you in detail on the Oregon question. It is necessary to be wary on this subject, as it is really the only one that I can think of, on which your adversaries can, by possibility, throw you in opposition to the popular feeling of the country.

In taking ground against farther European acquisition on this continent and in favor of the extension of free institutions, Col. Benton's former positions should be combatted gravely and sternly, as if they were propositions now before the country. In 1824, in a speech, he was for erecting a statue of the God Terminus on the highest peak of the Rocky Mountains, beyond which this country was never to pass, &c. In 1828 he was for the parallel 49, and for allowing a separate Republic to grow up in Oregon &c—a Pacific Republic as [Daniel] Webster says now. In his speech on the Ashburton treaty he was for extending the line between the English and American possessions to the Pacific—of course on the 49th parallel, and always refers to Oregon as the Valley of the Columbia, &c. The importance of Vancouver's Island and Puget's Sound seems to have wholly escaped his observation.

I am aware that I can give you no information as to Oregon or our title to it; I also know your views and feelings to be correct and patriotic; yet I apprehend there are periods when too much candor or fair dealing may be displayed, especially when one is watched and envied by men wholly destitute of principle. You have been and are now so watched, and the hope of your enemies is, that you will commit yourself at an early period of the session in favor of compromising the Oregon question on terms which Congress and the nation would reject. If we can secure Vancouver's Island and Puget's Sound, it is very probable the country would approve any reasonable adjustment in other respects; but Puget's Sound and Vancouver's Island are deemed too important, in a naval and commercial point of view, to be surrendered. This is the feeling of this quarter of the Union.

If the President should act in good faith in favor of a proper and reasonable adjustment or reduction of the tariff—if on that great question you can sustain his views—you may expect opposition from Col. Benton. He will risk the consequences of opposing the President, rather than concur with you on any great question—except the admission of Texas, which it is probable he will not *dare* to oppose, as no State in the Union is more thoroughly in favor of Texas than Missouri. I hope Mr. Polk will be true to his pledges on the tariff, but, sir, I cannot do otherwise than distrust him. Should he act fairly and correctly on this subject, I will sustain him—at least to that extent.

The action of the Memphis Convention is very generally and cordially approved, and the people expect a liberal course on the part of Congress towards the West, especially in reference to the improvement of the Mississippi and its principal tributaries. Your views, though very imperfectly reported, are generally, I may say, almost universally, approved—and, as the impression you made was as favorable as could have been desired, you must not forget the tour you are to make at the close or after the close of the present session of Congress: Baltimore, Philadelphia, New York, ["Buffalo" *canceled*] Albany, Utica, Cananda[i]gua, Rochester, Buffalo, Erie, Detroit, Cleveland, Columbus, Dayton, Cincinnati—thence through Indiana and Illinois by land to St. Louis. You should see the Rapids of the Mississippi and the Platte country on the Missouri—then you should go by water, via Shawneetown, Evansville, Smithland and Paducah to Louisville. By land from Louisville via Frankfort to Lexington, and from thence to Nashville—then through East Tenn., home. It will be a very pleasant journey, and you should accomplish it, if not for yourself, for your friends.

We received here an answer to the letter of invitation I presented to you, signed by a number of Democrats, but the answer referred to was without a signature. After perusing it, I regarded it as genuine, and therefore affixed your ["name" *canceled*] name to it. Was that right? If it was not, we have been most admirably hoaxed.

Some of the appointments here should be rejected. The Surveyor General [Silas Reed] will have charges preferred against him, and charges of swindling have already been prepared and perhaps forwarded against [Edward] Warrens, recently appointed Consul to Trieste. Our Postmaster [Samuel B. Churchill?] is also a worthless fellow, and money has been transmitted to his office that has never been received by the house to which it was directed. Besides he turned the son of Mrs. [Elizabeth Relfe] Linn out of a Clerkship and put a very inefficient man in his place. Mrs. Linn's son was first Clerk, and was very competent and efficient. Make the acquaintance of Maj. [Leonard H.] Sims of the House [from Missouri]. He can tell you much about appointments in Missouri.

I write in confidence and great haste—giving you merely crude ideas, without regard to the manner in which they are expressed. Yours Truly, S. Penn, Jr.

ALS in ScCleA. NOTE: Silas Reed was the subject of an investigation which found incompetence but not criminal intent. In 2/1846 Polk nominated John B. Wimer to replace Samuel B. Churchill as Postmaster at St. Louis.

From F[RANKLIN] H. ELMORE

Columbia, Dec[embe]r 5, 1845

My Dear Sir, I have just rec[eive]d a letter from Mr. [Robert Barnwell] Rhett who with Mr. [George] McDuffie & Mr. [Armistead] Burt had been delayed a day in Richmond, written from that place. Mr. Rhett desires me if possible to confer with you or to inform you of the state of things at Richmond in regard to yourself. What he says is so important that I write to you for fear I shall not see you.

He tells me that he & Burt have seen & conversed with some of your friends there. He mentions Mr. [William O.] Goode late a member of Congress & a Mr. Harvey [*sic*; Lewis E. Harvie] a very warm friend of yours especially with whom they conversed & they both stated that your speech at Memphis had caused your friends great concern. That Mr. ["Harvey" *canceled and* "Goode" *interlined*] had said that Resolutions on the subject would probably be introduced by Mr. Harvey—and that he sought an interview with Harvey who met him in Mr. Goode's room. He (Rhett) then conversed with them & advised against it, but Harvey said if he or someone of his party did not, the Whigs would & would force them into positions they did not wish to occupy. Against this Rhett argued & promised to write to me to induce me to see you & urge you to call & remain a day at Richmond to see ["your" *canceled*] & confer with your friends. He says that he apprehends from what these Gentlemen tell him that unless you do, you may lose many valued friends there.

This letter is written in very earnest terms & I do hope, if you have not left home, you will so arrange your movements as to stop a day in Richmond. The effect of the meagre reports of your speech here was much the same as that at Richmond, but the impression has been removed to almost its entire extent. You have doubtless seen all the proceedings. The resolution of Mr. [Frederick J.] McCarthy [in the S.C. House of Representatives] was here supposed by some to have been suggested by Rhett—but this is not so. I arrived here after the resolution was before the House & found Rhett. He

318

disapproved of McCarthy[']s resolution & told me he had advised him against offering it. And I was told the same thing by others who were in intimate relations with them. He told me he would see you the first moment he could on your arrival at Washington & have a free & full understanding of your views, until when he should reserve his decision as to what he should do.

There seemed to be a great deal of uncertainty amongst our friends here as to what to do in regard to Mr. McCarthy[']s resolution. I advised them to let it lie over for a week but Mr. McCarthy insisted on immediate action & they then postponed it to 1 Jan[uar]y. The votes were no tests of opinion. I had prepared heads for [Adam G.] Summer[']s paper [the Columbia *South-Carolinian*] of an Editorial which came out next day—and the same night[']s mail brought the speech as reported in the N[ew] O[rleans] Bulletin. Had these preceded the consideration of the Resolution I think it w[oul]d have had but very few votes in its favor. As it was many voted ag[ains]t postponement because they thought it looked like smothering debate. Several of your best friends so voted.

I wish you would come by Columbia if possible. In great haste Yo[ur]s truly, F.H. Elmore.

ALS in ScCleA.

From HENDRICK B. WRIGHT

Wilkes-Barré [Pa.,] Dec. 5th 1845

My dear Sir, I congratulate you on your return to the Senate: I congratulate the country on this important event. The times at home and abroad, seem to indicate the approach of a crisis, and one too which will carry about it matters of vast moment to the future hopes & prospects of the Republic. The talents and experience of the Union should fill the halls of legislation—and the sagacity and wisdom of the nation are demanded at Washington. The honor, and possibly the very existence of free institutions, are involved in this Congress, and every man who earnestly feels a solicitude in the great cause of popular gove[rn]ment must be glad in his heart that you are again in the Senate—the able defender, of our only sure and abiding trust, the Constitution. Invocations from profane lips may not avail; but may God in his infinite wisdom and mercy guide and protect you in the discharge of those high & important duties, which have during a long & well spent life distinguished your course of conduct.

Bel[i]eve me Sir, I speak in all candor, and totally void of the imputation of flattery, when I alledge that the country owes you as great a debt for the preservation of popular rights, as any man living or dead. Your votes, your speeches your writings—are all the property of your country, and living evidences of the unal[i]enable rights of man. Bel[i]eving all this, as I most religiously do, I cannot refrain from congratulating you on again taking your stand in the national Congress along side of the Constitution—its champion and defender.

Excuse me, my dear Sir, for the frankness of my expressions: but beleive [*sic*] me they come from a heart sincere, and they are not overwrought, as the opinion of the country sustains me: and while I despise the courtier, I can easily discriminate between such sycophancy, and the effusion of the feelings of a heart which beats in the cause of popular freedom, and which does not hesitate to speak its admiration of one of the great men of the land. I seek no favours— the tribute is a free offering. Very truly Your ob[edien]t S[ervan]t and friend, Hendrick B. Wright.

ALS in ScCleA.

From ROBERT W. GIBBES

Columbia, Dec. 6, 1845

Dear Sir, I am instructed by the State Agricultural Society of South Carolina to inform you, that at the slated meeting held on the 27th ult. you were unanimously elected the Anniversary Orator of the Society for the ensuing year.

The Society will meet on the first Monday of the session of the Legislature, and the Address is usually delivered on the following Thursday, in the Hall of the House of Representatives.

With the hope that your public and private business will allow you to comply with the wishes of the members of the Society, I am With respect Y[ou]r ob[e]d[ien]t Serv[an]t, Robert W. Gibbes, M.D., Corresponding Sec[retar]y, S[tate] A[gricultural] Society.

ALS in ScCleA. NOTE: An AEU by Calhoun reads "Informs me that I have been app[ointe]d to deliver the next anniv[ersar]y address before the Ag[ricultura]l Soc[ie]ty."

From DUFF GREEN

New York [City], 6th December 1845
Dear Sir, I regret that I will be detained here some days, because I have some facts that will be interesting to you, and which you should know before you define your present position.

I have had several interesting conversations with persons having influence on the several subdivisions of parties here, and a knowledge of the views & purposes of the Whigs is as important to you as a knowledge of the views and purposes of the administration.

I give you a few facts. You can draw your own inferences.

There have been several of [Henry] Clay's western partisans here, and among them Leslie Combs, to ascertain whether Mr. Clay can be made the candidate [of the Whig party for the Presidency in 1848]. The *New England* portion of the Whig party discouraged the proposition in the most decided manner.

The *old* leaders of the *Clay* party say that they will have no one but Clay, & that they expect there will be *three* candidates and rely on an election by the House [of Representatives]. They take the chapter of accidents.

The [Martin] Van Buren & [Thomas H.] Benton men of this State are very hostile to [William L.] *Marcy* & [Robert J.] Walker. They have no confidence in [Daniel S.] Dickinson [Senator from N.Y.] & rely on [John A.] Dix [Senator from N.Y.]. They admit that [Silas] Wright cannot be reelected Governor of this State & yet he was *their* candidate for the Presidency.

[Michael?] *Hoffman* of this City is the *present* leader. They are hostile to [Cornelius Van Wyck] Lawrence the Collector & Witmon [*sic*; Prosper M. Wetmore] the Navy agent, because their purpose is to plunder the treasury and Lawrence will not give them the control of his patronage and Witmon, *they say*, has his own favorites.

I know that Van Buren has advised them to await the course of events, and when the time comes to make themselves felt by giving their united influence in favor of the man whom their influence can elect. One of them remarked, that Dix was acting on Mr. Van Buren's advice, that he must reserve himself for the purpose of making the next President.

The [annual] message [of President James K. Polk to Congress] & the Report of the Secretary of the Treasury [Robert J. Walker] were *intended* to put you in a false position. They go for your *measures*, but they make war on you through your friends. They remove your friends and appoint your enemies. Be upon your guard: the whole weight of the administration is hostile to you. Yet you have more power than you ever had.

The manufacturers are convinced that they have more to fear from Domestic than foreign competition. They will be willing to give you aid in adjusting the tariff. They see that their best protection is a stable currency and they are disposed to aid you in adjusting the currency question. They see that there is great danger of war with England and they are prepared to strength[en] you as the advocate of peace. They see that the tendency of the present organisation of party is to band together the worst elements of both parties for the purpose of plundering the treasury, and they see that the only means of defeating that organisation is to rally a party for the preservation of peace and reforming the administration.

The weak point of the administration is the public printing, and the party subserviency. I have much to say to you on these things, and wrote that y[*ms. torn*; you m]ay hold yourself in reserve until I see you. I have the prospect of arranging my affairs so as to pay all my debts and have a large surplus left for my family. My health is good and having means I can be once more an efficient aid in a good cause. I hope to see you in a few days. Yours truly, Duff Green.

ALS in ScCleA. NOTE: This letter was addressed to Calhoun at the Senate in Washington.

From THO[MA]S H. HOLT

St. Louis, Mo., Dec[embe]r 6th 1845
Dear Sir, Your friend, Capt. H[enry] M. Shreve (late one of the Vice Presidents of the Memphis Convention) has informed me, that he requested your influence with the President of the U. States, in procuring me an appointment as Chargé d[']Affaires. Nothing could be more gratifying to me, than to have the recommendation of such a distinguished gentleman; and, if not incomp[at]ible with your duty, and feelings to aid my friends in the matter, you will place me under the most lasting obligations.

By the *unanimous recommendation* of ["the democracy of" *interlined*] our last legislature, I was presented to the President, for the appointment of U. States Attorney, for Missouri. That recommendation was endorsed by six of our congressmen and by all the democratic members from Kentucky. But the President, through the influence of Mr. [Francis P.] Blair, was induced to confer it upon Mr.

[Thomas J.] Gantt. My friends are now asking of the President, the appointment as Chargé, and I need not assure you, that your support in my behalf, will ever be remembered, with the deepest gratitude.

My friend, Col. R[ic]h[ard] M. Johnson of Ky. sent to me, while I was in Washington City last winter, a letter [*not found*] of introduction to you, which I had not the pleasure of presenting, owing to your indisposition, at the time of my visit. The letter, I have taken the liberty to enclose to you. It is from a gallant man, and a *true friend of yours.*

Like most of the young men of the west, I felt anxious to see, and know one, whose name was identified with most of the great questions which have agitated our country during this century, and to take by the hand a statesman, whose mighty mind has shed a halo over the history of his native land. This pleasure I hope yet to have.

Pardon me for having obtruded my self upon your valuable time, and believe, me with sentiments of sincere respect Very Respectfully your Friend, Thos. H. Holt.

[P.S.] Will you please confer with my friend, Senator [David R.] Atchison from this State, on the subject about which I have troubled you. H.

ALS in ScCleA. NOTE: An AEU by Calhoun reads "See Gen[era]l ["Ahison" *canceled*] A[t]chison."

From JOHN M. SIMS and Others

Philadelphia, December 6th [18]45

Dear Sir, It affords us pleasure in communicating to you on behalf of the "Young Men's Democratic Association of the City and County of Philadelphia," of your unanimous election as an Honorary Member. The object of the Association is fully expressed in the subjoined clause of the Constitution.

"The undersigned Democratic Citizens of the City and County of Philadelphia, feeling a deep sense of the importance of our Free Institutions to the World, and properly appreciating their blessings Are Resolved to protect and perpetuate them by such means as every virtuous and patriotic heart must sanction and approve. And in pursuance of this object have determined to Associate themselves together for the promotion and dissemination of those pure principles of Democracy which constitute the essential and firm foundation of our Republic, and to defeat every attempt to establish any Institution at variance with the rights of man, or the Sovereignty of the people."

The Association duly appreciating your services in the cause of Democracy, hope[s] this Act on their part may meet your approbation. We have the honor to Remain Y[ou]r Ob[edien]t Serv[an]ts, Jno. M. Sims, Chairman, Thomas B. Florence, E.C. Lambert, Jno. McKibbin[?], Th[omas] S. Fernon, Committee of Correspondence.

LS in ScCleA. NOTE: An AEU by Calhoun reads "Democratick young men[']s association of Philadelphia."

From A. P. STINSON

Memphis Convention
St. Joseph[,] Berrien Co[unty] Mich.
Dec[embe]r 6, 1845

My Dear Sir, I have Just risen from reading the Proceedings of the *Great Memphis Convention,* Over which you were Called to Preside. It is now about One year, Since I addressed you Last & though the Correspondence was Cut off by Events over which, It would Seem, nothing human Could Controll, yet Sir, you have been in all my thoughts & my *highest Aspirations have been* & Still are, to See you Stand to the *American People* as you did to the Great Convention at Memphis, *Their President.* Willingly would I (It does Seem to me), go Into Se[r]vitude as Long as *Jacob* Served for *Rachel,* If by It, I Could be *Instrumental* of accomplishing What is So desirable to me & as I have good Reason to believe ["It Is" *interlined*] to the Democr[ac]y of this Nation, your Elevation to the Executive Chair. I believe Sir, I did on a former occasion Give you to understand, that In Mich. you were the fi[r]st *Choice* of the Democr[ac]y. The Peopl[e; "here" *canceled*], Notwithstanding the *Result* & I now reiterate It—and had we *Sooner organized,* or had we *Known Our Strength,* a verry Differe[n]t Result would have been Produced. But we did not Know It, & were not Sufficiently organized to for [*sic*] Effic[i]ent & Energetic Action & hence the "Old Hunkers" Victory. Subsequent to the Presidential Election, I have seen & Conversed with *Many* Democrats In the State, who I had Supposed were Either [Martin] *Van Buren* or [Lewis] *Cass Men,* but who (to *my great astonishment*) I found were your Warm & Ardent friends, Among whom is *Hon. J[ohn] S. Chipman* M.C. of this District & whose Acquaintanc[e] Should You Return to the U.S. Senate, I beg you will make—but he is but one of Hundreds, I was no Less Disappointed[?] in. I have Sir, been totally in the *Dark* & am ["So" *interlined*] now, of your Ulterior views in this matter.

It does Seem to me that a Brighter day is Dawning upon you—& that the *Ball* is in motion, Commenced with your Journey to the *South West* & Received a momentum at *Memphis,* which cannot by human hands be stay[e]d in its Onward Progress. Never Sir, have I Seen Such Demonstrations of *Joy* Since I resided In the State, as is Every where to be *Seen* & *felt* In this Quarter growing Out of the *Memphis Convention* & your Address on taking the Chair. "A New Era (say they) is begun in the Life of *John C. Calhoun.*" The *Democr[ac]y* are in *Extasies,* while the Whigs yes Sir, the Whigs, Speake in terms of *high Commendation of your Course!*

You will Recollect that In my Letters to you, *Mr.* [Thomas G.] *Clemson* [and Robert B.] *Rhett,* or Some of your *South Carolina* friends, I advised that you travel & visit the *Eastern* & *Western States* & had you done So, I doubt not you would now have been Occupying the Chair of our worthy President [James K.] *Polk,* & Wher[e]-fore? Your Sentiments have been most grossly perverted & No one Could have more Effectually put this matter Right than your Self & this done, the *Way was Open* to you. In this Opinion I was not alone, am now not alone, but you Sir, from a Sense of duty, (& I honor your motive) declin[e]d making what might be, & would undoubtedly have been termed "an Electioneering Trip."

May I hope Sir, you will yet make the acquaintanc[e] of your Numerous friends In the *East* & "far off *West*" Shortly, & at a time when your motives cannot be *Impugned.* Come & Visit these "In Land Seas" the Great Western Lakes, towards the Improvement of which, your Convention Seemed favorable.

I am Sir, but an humble Individual of the Demo[cratic] Party, yet I will go as far as the farthest, in favoring your wishes, when made Known to me. I Regret, Extremely Regret, that my friend *Levi Woodbury* has accepted of the Judge Ship of the U.S. Court. We want[e]d him in the *Senate.* He is your friend & If I Know him, is a *warm* & *Devoted One.* I will be most happy to hear from you & to Learn your wishes So far as It is proper to Communicate them to One, with whom you have So Slight an Acqu[a]intance. Believe me Sir, *my highest aspirations for any thing Earthly is to see John Cald-*

well Calhoun In the *Presid[e]ntial Chair* & to accomplish which "I am ready to Spend & be Spent." Your friend In Weal or Woe, Always, A.P. Stinson.

P.S. Should you be in Washington—& my friends *Woodbury*[,] *Jno. Fairfield* [Senator from Maine], *R[obert] P. Dunlap* [Representative from Maine], *J.S. Chip[m]an* be there Please make my Regards acceptable to them. A.P.S.

ALS in ScCleA.

To A[NDREW] P[ICKENS] CALHOUN,
Faunsdale, Marengo County, Ala.

Fort Hill, 7th Dec[embe]r 1845
My dear Andrew, I have just received your letter & regret to learn, that there has been so much indisposition from coulds [*sic*] in your family. I hope all have recovered and are again in the enjoyment of good health.

We arrived here on the 2d Inst., & found all well, & that my business had gone on well in my absence. My crop of corn & cotton has turned out fully as well as I expected. Corn is selling currently at 75 cents. Colds have been very prevalent here, as well as with you, accompanied in many instances with fever, & followed in not a few by death. The river plantations have almost entirely escaped. The highest & healthiest places have generally suffered most.

I set out tomorrow for Washington. Your Mother [Floride Colhoun Calhoun] & [Martha] Cornelia [Calhoun] accompany me. We shall go by private conveyance to Aiken, taking Mr. [Thomas G.] Clemson's place in our route where we shall be detained a day or two. I do not expect to be in Charleston before the 15 or 16. I have written to Mr. [Franklin H.] Elmore to meet me. I do not anticipate that there will be any difficulty in making the arrangement we agreed on before we parted. I will write you from Charleston.

Since my arrival, I have looked over the foreign papers received in my absence; and I find the s[c]arcity in Europe far more general & intense than I had supposed. I see in one of them an extract from a German paper, giving a statement of the grain market on the continent, from which it would appear, that the s[c]arcity will be universal over all Europe, with very inconsiderable exception. The panick seems great in Great Britain. I think it almost certain the corn laws will, before its force, go by the board, which will be a great point gained; but I fear the price of cotton will be seriously effected. That the crop will be short, all I saw & heard on my return leave[s] little doubt. I saw but one tolerable field of cotton from James' [probably James Martin Calhoun's, Richmond, Ala.] to Montgomery, and every where it was stated that it would fall short more than a third; some said more than a half.

The friends of [Robert Barnwell] Rhett endeavoured to get up a clamour about my Memphis speech. In their haste, they went off on the first imperfect report, & made some impression, but on the appea[ra]nce of the report from the Bulletin, the whole affair died away.

I find negroes have advanced considerably in price since I left home. Mr. William Sloan thinks a good gang would sell for 350$ round, but thinks the rise will prove temporary.

Your mother & Cornelia join their love to you, Margaret [Green Calhoun] & John [C. Calhoun, Jr.]. Kiss the children for their grandparents. Your affectionate father, J.C. Calhoun.

ALS in ScU-SC, John C. Calhoun Papers.

From F[RANKLIN] H. ELMORE

Columbia, Dec[embe]r 7, 1845

My Dear Sir, I have just rec[eive]d yours tonight & find myself with only half a sheet of paper to answer you.

The Legislature adjourns on the 15th & I fear I cannot be absent that day. I will run down on the 14th to Branchville to meet you & continue down 'till I meet the Charleston train & then return. This will give us time to talk over & arrange all you may desire.

I am very much rejoiced that I shall have the opportunity to see you. I wrote to you a few days ago to Pendleton, too late I fear for my letter to have reached you.

I have just seen the President['']s [James K. Polk's] Message & rec[eive]d a letter from [Isaac E.] Holmes [Representative from S.C.]. He tells me that Mr. [George] McDuffie [Senator from S.C.] expresses himself content with it. I have not read it all. That part on the Tariff seems sound & fair enough. The Minister to Mexico is [John] Slidell of N[ew] Orleans.

I will attend to your commission. Yo[ur]s truly, F.H. Elmore.

ALS in ScCleA.

From William Aiken, Governor of S.C., Columbia, 12/8. The Senate and House of Representatives by joint ballot have elected Calhoun Senator of the U.S. to complete the term of Daniel E. Huger, resigned, which ends 3/4/1847. DS in DNA, RG 46 (U.S. Senate), Credentials, South Carolina, Calhoun.

Account of John C. Calhoun with E[noch] B. Benson & Son, Pendleton, 12/8. This document itemizes two pages of small household purchases for Fort Hill between 11/1/1844 and 12/8/1845, with a few occasional payments on account. Calhoun owed on 12/8 a balance of $241.81. DU in ScU-SC, John C. Calhoun Papers.

From MILES M. NORTON

Pickens C[ourt] H[ouse] S.C., 8th December 1845
Dear Sir, Permit me to congratuate yourself and our country, on your return to the U.S. Senate. Although you have nothing to gain by it, yet I am sure you will be gratified to be able to do all in your power for us as a nation & as a people. I write you however, to ask your assistance in behalf of our old friend Mrs. Issabella Reid, (widow of Joseph Reid Esq.) formerly of Abbeville District, but now of this District (the mother of Mr. Sam[ue]l Reid) whom you probably knew in Abbeville. You at least know the family from character, and know that they are highly respectable. About two years ago, I commenced trying to get a Pension for the old lady, and have had a great deal of trouble about it; got the Comptroller Gen-[era]l[']s certificate & copy of an Indent issued to Joseph Reid as a Lieut[enant] and the am[oun]t receipted for by George Bowie (now Maj[o]r George Bowie of Alabama) who I presume you knew very well) then proved the marriage, and now the only difficulty is to identify Mrs. Reid as the widow of the same Jos. Reid to whom the s[a]id Indent was issued. This I have attempted to prove by the old neighbors of Reid, but the office being one which gave him no title, they are, none of them that I can find, able to recollect that he "was recognized in his neighborhood as a revolutionary officer." But I have sent to Alabama and procured the affidavit of Maj[o]r Geo[rge] Bowie on the subject, and I think it is full enough to satisfy the Department on that subject, if they can be informed of the character of Maj[o]r Bowie, for intelligence and veracity. I therefore enclose herewith the affidavit, which I hope you will be so kind as to hand

over to Col. [James L.] Edwards Com[missione]r of Pensions, with the aforesaid information. I am Dear Sir, with the highest respect, Your friend & Ob[edien]t Serv[an]t, Miles M. Norton.

ALS with En in DNA, RG 15 (Veterans Administration), Revolutionary War Pension and Bounty-Land Warrant Application Files, 1800–1900, W9249 (M-804:2021, frames 838–843). NOTE: To Bowie's enclosed affidavit of 11/29/1845 is appended the following AES by Calhoun: "I do hereby certify that I am well acquainted with George Bowie Esq[ui]r[e] whose name is subscribed to the within affidavit, & that I know him to be a man of intelligence and strict veracity. I know of no one more so. J.C. Calhoun, Washington, 25th Dec[embe]r 1845." A Clerk's EU indicates that a pension certificate for Mrs. Reid was issued on 12/27/1845 and sent to Calhoun.

From F[ITZWILLIAM] BYRDSALL, "Confidential"

New York [City,] Dec[embe]r 9th 1845

Dear Sir, I beg leave to direct your attention, for a few moments, to the following quotation from the New York Courier and Enquirer of the 20th of September last, extracted and condensed from the columns of the Charleston Mercury of a prior date.

"A Mr. Byrdsall of New York, an unwavering Democrat in the Custom House, but a States Rights man, has been ejected from office, on account of *the taint of Calhounism.*"

While it was believed in this city that my removal was on account of the "taint of Calhounism," for there was no other taint, I prevented my case from appearing in the Newspapers of this city, and the "Constitution" and U.S. Journal of Washington, because I conceived it might be unpleasant to you, and could do no good; but it was not in my power to prevent the publication in the Mercury or Courier. Since then, some four or five weeks ago, I had an interview with [the Collector,] Mr. Laurence [*sic*; Cornelius Van Wyck Lawrence], and he voluntarily assured me, that my removal was accidental, that there was a supernum[er]ary Measurer in the Department, and in looking over the names of the encumbents [*sic*], he fell upon mine as one that he did not know; but that since he has had information respecting me, and found that many of his most respected friends are also mine, he has regretted my removal. [*Interpolation*: "He expressed himself similarily to the Hon. Walter Bowne formerly Mayor of the city and W(illia)m B. Maclay now M.C."] In the course of our conversation, he spoke of you in terms of the highest consideration personally and otherwise, which for an obvious reason, I should not repeat here.

As you are now a Senator of the U.S. it seems to me but an act of justice to Mr. Laurence that I should impart the facts of the case to you, notwithstanding my entire confidence that no personal—no other consideration but that of public duty, would influence your action upon Executive appointments. But as the above publication was made without my knowledge or approval, and as it may have created unpleasant feelings which should not exist, I deem it proper to correct the mis[s]tatement, assuring you at the same time, that I write this of my own volition unknown to the Collector or any of his friends. And as I believe him to be a perfectly trust worthy officer, and a man of high moral sentiments, I beg your permission to add as a citizen of this Republic, though not presuming in the least to advise, that your best friends here as well as myself would be pleased to find when his nomination is acted upon by the Senate, that you have given your vote in his favor.

Rejoicing at your return to Senate ["at this crisis in our National affaires" *interlined*] and renewing my assurances of high consideration and esteem I am Dear Sir Your ob[edien]t Ser[van]t, F. Byrdsall.

ALS in ScCleA. NOTE: An AEU by Calhoun reads "Mr. Byrdsall."

From R. L. KING

Racine [Wisc. Territory,] Dec[e]mb[er] 10, 1845
Dear Sir, As the whole Union now look to you as the one who can save us from a war with England I take the liberty of stating some facts to you concerning the feeling of the West so far as Orrigon is concerned.

The majority of the People of ["the" *interlined*] west want and desire peace, but the States of Michigan, Indiana, Illinois, and Missouri wish war for the purpose of wiping out the debts due English men of some $50,000,000 which they dare not repudiate in this age of the world. Therefore such men as [Lewis] Cass [Senator from Mich., John W.] Davis [Representative from Ind.,] and Douglass [*sic*; Stephen A. Douglas] also [John W.] Wentworth [Representatives from Ill.,] all heavy land Holders in these States are urging war when they know that the Southern and Eastern States would be ruirned by a war. But as these respective States are to pay off the debts they owe they are verry patriotic for war. I have resided West for 16 year[s] and claim to be democrat. Yours Resp[ec]t[fully,] R.L. King.

ALS in ScCleA; PC in Boucher and Brooks, eds., *Correspondence*, pp. 310–311.

Bill for *Brownson's Review*, 12/11. B.H. Greene, Boston, invoices Calhoun for $3 for Vol. 2 (1845). DU in ScU-SC, John C. Calhoun Papers.

From [THOMAS G. CLEMSON]

Brussels, Dec. 12th 1845

My dear Sir, Your letter dated Cane Brake Ala. Oct. 27th came to hand too late for me to reply by the steamer that left Liverpool on the 4th inst: & as no other steamer will leave England before the 4th of Jan: I fear tho' I shall send this by one of the packets you will not receive it before its double which I shall send you by the steamer of the 4th of Jan. Whatever arrangement I could or would be willing to make for the better or more profitable disposal of my negroes is [depen]dent on the possibility of selling my plantation. As unprofitable as that whole concern has been it would be still more so if the negroes were taken from the place. The latter would in that event be a total loss. Supposing however that Col. [Francis W.] Picken[s]'s statement of my being able to sell the place may have been found practicable[,] which by the time you receive this you will have ascertained[,] I shall proceed to remark on your letter in connection with the disposal of my negroes. When I wrote you on the sale of my place I did not foresee the event of my proposition not meeting your views or arrangements nor did I at that time entertain a thought of disposing of my negroes, a result the necessity of which has come upon me since the receipt of your letter. I confess I entertain it with reluctance even now. My determination to invest in land & negroes was made with great deliberation & at a time when the great distress caused by too much confidence in American funded investments convinced me of the greater security of landed property above all with a young & growing family from whom I might be called & to whose interests I look much more than to my own in all my arrangements. [With] these views I am certainly reluctant to give up at once all idea of possessing negro property. I say all idea for my present gang once entirely out of my power I could never expect to procure a better or even another as good, & should in that case turn my views to something else. I am nevertheless convinced that what you say is just & that I cannot retain them & this place together & since as I have written you before I cannot afford to relinquish this place at present the question arises what is to be done[,] more especially when the uncertainty of my retaining this position is taken into consideration[,] thereby rendering [more] complicated my arrangements for the future. This then is what I should prefer. You will take the entire gang of negroes as your own at a certain sum[,] paying me only the legal interest of the State of Alabama on the sum, as you propose in your letter, for three years with the agreement that after the first year I may have them back any time in the three years by giving a year[']s notice, (you only paying the interest on the sum for the time you had them which would in that case be only equivalent to a very moderate hire,) & the arrangement to be capable of a longer extension at the close of the three years with the consent of all parties. This would give you the negroes at least for two years & from the present uncertainty of my views a great probability that at the end of the three years they would belong to you while to me it would give the opportunity of looking about me a little longer before I finally decided to get rid entirely of my negroe property or in other word quitting the South which for several reasons I think the most desirable part of the Union as a residence. I cannot think the proposition an unfair one. You have the use of an unrivalled gang of negroes for two years certainly; by making payment which you yourself offered me with as I said before a prospect of retaining them as your own after the three years & should you not retain them their labour will have aided to render the purchase of others in their place more easy. I do not see either that the arrangement thereby would be made more complicated. You would give me bonds & mortgage with personal security as for a sale[,] inserting the conditions which I have specified. The interest to be paid regularly in the city of Charleston.

Let me now say something of the price you offer ($12,000) or in the event I prefer it the negroes to be valued by disinterested persons. I am too long absent from the United States to be aware of the price of negroes & am perfectly convinced you made me what you considered a fair offer in the $12,000 but I will take the liberty of making a few observations on the subject & what I think their value as I do not think you are in possession of the entire premises. In the first place the portion of my gang purchased from Mr. J[ohn] E[wing] Colhoun was purchased when the monied pressure of the United States was at its extremest point nor did I then pay the market value for them because no one would purchase for fear of the title & it was only the manner the negociation was conducted & the number I agreed to buy that induced him to give me a sheriff's sale title. Besides which all my negroes may be considered as having been paid for in cash when they were unusually low. Seven men cost me between $4 & 5,000 not one of them as low as five hundred (William the carpenter $800) though purchased for cash. Soon after the sale at Pickens C[ourt] H[ouse] the late Mr. [Fair] Kirksey offered me $450 [for] Polydore or $1600 for the four smallest boys. They are now of an age the most desirable & would command the highest price. Six months after the purchase of Spencer[,] Jack & Nim[,] the person in Charleston from whom I purchased offered me an advance of [$]100 on each. The negro man I purchased on a year[']s credit near Pendleton & afterwards resold (& he was sold for a much less sum than the others cost me[)] upwards of $600. Joe was the only infirm one in the whole gang when I purchased & he was before I left as efficient as any man I had. He is a good waggoner coachman cooper & very handy with tools & has been at work ever since I owned [him] making waggons &c with my carpenter William & consequently cannot be considered as less valuable than any I have except William & in Edgefield I was informed I could hire him (William) for $25 or $30 the month the year round. I therefore consider if I had purchased my 15 boys for *cash* in Charleston when negroes ["were" *interlined*] selling lower than they are doing now (& they are always lower in Charleston than in the country,) they would have cost me merely as field hands certainly not less than $8000 cash & considering their qualifications that sum would not have secured them. Gen. [James] Gillam offered about the same time for a carpenter (not such a one as William) $1200 or $1400 & did not get him. There is besides Jack a blacksmith & Charles a good cook &c. Bill Laurence as a hand on a plantation is invaluable (a good shoemaker & master of all kinds of work on a plantation) & when I purchased I attended many sales & do not reccollect [*sic*] of having seen a good field hand sell as low as $500. If then I am right in valuing those 15 boys at $8000 *cash* & the nine women or girls at $400 round which would make $3600 then the men & women alone [ought] to bring $12000 cash at the price negroes were selling when I purchased them without counting the 13 children & judging from the age of the youngest now more than a year old there must be now or shortly will be a considerable increase. The entire gang from last accounts however equalled 37 of which 24 are workers & with but two exceptions all as efficient as full hands & some with valuable trades & not an old person among them. I have given you this statement by no means exaggerated & not by any means to induce you to believe what is not [*ms. torn*]nt but to give you an opportunity to judge of the gang & as a reason why I think $12,000 on three years credit too small a sum. They may from my absence be a little spoiled & I suppose are but I can safely say they were an uncommonly well behaved gang while I was with them & I have heard nothing to the contrary since.

Taking another view & throwing them together as ordinary field hands. The 24 workers on your plantation in Alabama & in connection with your force there ought certainly to be able to increase your crop by 140 or 150 bales. Say the first number which at 5 cents the lb. would give $3,500 besides the other plantation work such as ditching[,] clearing &c &c which would be value added to your property. I consider any calculation based on the present price of cotton & negroes as safe. The price of both has been now low & stationary for a long time. The annexation of Texas must decrease the price of land & increase that of negroes. I do not make this statement to endeavour to show what they would be worth to you & thereby give them value by induction as you understand that as well or better than I do but merely to show you the process of reason by which I have come to the conclusion that the sum of $14,000 (fourteen thousand dollars) would be a just sum for both of us on the conditions mentioned above & which it is unnecessary here to repeat. You may be sure I have not named what I consider an exaggerated sum for I would rather you should have them than any one else if I am obliged to sell them besides my wish to make the arrangement I specify in regard to them provided my plantation could be sold.

As I do not wish to prevent the sale of my other property [*ms. mutilated; one or two words missing*] plantation grain[,] fodder &c which would be the case if you did not take my negroes or if the above proposition should not suit you. In that case I propose that you remove them to Alabama & work them as your own allowing me such hire as you may think fair until we can make some arrangement more definite & mutually agreeable & advantageous. If however I should have presented the matter to you in such a way as to make it impossible for us to agree in that case send this letter to

Mr. Pickens & beg him to value the negroes as you propose on three years credit & on the receipt of his evaluation I will decide. If after all that I have said it should appear impossible for us still to come to a decision I would beg you to speak to Mr. [James] Buchanan [Secretary of State] & consult with him on the possibility of my getting leave of absence for a few months leaving here in March or April. Anna [Maria Calhoun Clemson] & the children [John Calhoun Clemson and Floride Elizabeth Clemson] could remain here & if it suited you I would pay *half* of John's [John C. Calhoun, Jr.'s] expenses from the United States & back for him to come out & stay with Anna whilst I should be absent. I do not think Mr. Buchanan could object to my leaving here during the next summer. By that time I shall have finished all the heavy business I have on hand & during the summer season the Diplomatic corps absent themselves from Brussels. I have been hard at work since my arrival in Belgium. The claims are settled or may be considered so for all is done that can be done ["that can be done" *canceled*] until the money be finally paid which will not take place until the end of 1846 or commencement of the following year. The treaty of Commerce & Navigation is now before the Chambers & will be ratified before the end of this month &c &c and in fine every thing here now is in the best possible state & I feel happy in having participated in bringing about so perfect an understanding between the two countries. The ports of Belgium may now be considered as nearly our own & they are now open to the free introduction of *grain* of all kinds & *Flour or Meal* on the same terms.

As to the proposition you make me about my waggons mules or horses sheep &c I accept your offer. I have now but one or two remarks to make on the subject. If we should agree & you should take my negroes on the terms mentioned above I wish that there should be no possibility of our misunderstanding the agreement & with a view to avoid anything of the kind I propose Mr. Pickens (if he will do so) to act for me & that the papers should be most rigidly legal & beyond misconception as well to the security of the sums[,] principal & interest[,] as the punctuality of payment. This you must be aware I insist upon from the long experience I have of Andrew [Pickens] Calhoun's great unpunctuality & unbusinesslike habits of action which have already caused me so much trouble & have been the means of even placing me at times in a false position towards yourself. This has been indeed the great & only cause of my hesitating at all in making the arrangement we propose about my negroes. Not only the difficulties he has caused me to suffer from but their effect upon my health. I say my health for with my nervous temperament these perpetual misunderstandings & difficulties & even the uneasy anticipation of their occurrence causes me bodily as well as mental suffering the avoidance of which is becoming as necessary to me as money.

I therefore depend on you as equally interested in the welfare of both to make use of every possible means to avoid [for the] future a like state of things not as mistrusting his ultimate desire to do right but only from my experience of his disagreeable manner & unpardonable negligence to say the least in fulfilling his business engagements with myself. Supposing even the fault may have been on my side as you have often said that I misunderstood the nature of our agreement it is then the more necessary that *this* should be so scrup[ul]ously arranged that I shall not have the slightest shadow of an excuse for doing so in future & to make this more certain & to take the responsibility off Col. Pickens as much as possible let a copy of the papers be sent to me for my approval before all is finally arranged. This will make no delay or prevent your taking possession of the negroes immediately on the sale of the place. I think further delay might also be avoided by selling the cotton ginned & packed with the other articles. I saw this done at my neighbour's the late Col. Richardson's sale where it brought even more than the market price in Charleston. The great point is the securities given by whoever may purchase. Many purchase on credit that would not do so without it & I suppose this year (owing to the short crops generally) articles of all descriptions will sell higher for credit & many might be induced to pay a large credit price for cotton because it would enable them to realise immediate cash.

I have now said all that occurs to me as necessary in answer to the part of your letter which relates to the negroes. As to that part which mentions the interest on the [*ms. torn;* balanc]e[?] of your's & Andrew's debt to me[,] I am left in doubt as to your intention. Mr. [John Ewing] Bonneau has not sent me a statement of the amount of monies he has paid on your account for me & therefore I do not know how it stands precisely at this time. If I am correct in my reccollection [*sic,*] throwing out of the calculation for the moment the amount not paid on the notes which fell due before Nov. 1844[,] there remains a balance due me on those two notes of between $13,000 & $14,000 after deducting the last instalment due A[rthur] Simkins. On the first of Jan. 1845 there was due on [these?] notes

336

Capital	$17,000
Interest for same for 14 months at 7%	1,388
	18,388
Deduct payment to A. Simkins	3,000
Balance due me in Jan. 1845	15,388
Interest on last sum for one year ending 30th Dec. 1845	1,077
	16,465
From which deduct last instalment to A. Simkins	3,000
Balance due me Jan. 1846	13,465

All the notes have now come to maturity & I should [like] very much to have your statement with that of Mr. Bonneau & also wish to know whether it be your intention to pay the balance due me immediately. If so I must instruct Mr. Bonneau accordingly. If not I think Andrew & you ought to give me a bond & mortgage for the sum due me. It will prevent complications & misunderstandings. I wish to keep my affairs straight & in any event that my papers may show on their face the state of my pecuniary concerns. Besides which the notes in Mr. Bonneau's hands are no longer negociable[,] they having been paid at maturity & so far as the balance due me from you & Andrew may serve you I should much prefer (if you desire it) that you should have the use of it until such time as I shall require it. What I want is an adjustment of the accounts & the balances ascertained & specified in a proper instrument which will leave you at ease & be satisfactory to myself. I am particularly anxious that every transaction between us shall be so explicit that there shall not be the possibility of a doubt about the intention on either side. [Unsigned.]

LU (retained copy?) in ScCleA. NOTE: An AEU in Clemson's hand reads: "Letter to Mr. Calhoun about sale of place." Occasional words have been supplied in brackets where the ms. is deteriorated at its middle margin.

From AUGUSTUS MITCHELL

St. Marys [Ga.,] Dec. 12th 1845

Dear Sir, Having commenced my medical studies within the limits of your native State and there imbibing a taste for the pursuits of natural history—affiliated to its soil by marriage I take the liberty to enclose this letter [dated 9/24/1845] to you from my esteemed friend Gen. H[enry A.S.] Dearborn of Roxbury Mass. My reasons for so doing [it] is hoped will be excusable in your sight—not having the honor of your acquaintance nor the privilege of being near enough to your person to present previous letters in my possession I could ["not" *interlined*] resist the feelings which prompt me to act in this manner.

There are many things which I should wish to elucidate and impart to your generous mind but for fear of encroaching on your business and tiring your patience I will briefly state in unalloyed American language that during the period of the past seven or eight years I have been enthusiastically engaged in the pursuits of natural history especially in the departments of Ornithology and Botany, following up strictly with close investigations the designs of our Great Creator as exhibited in the structural developements of all animate beings[,] the phenomena of life[,] comparative observations on digestion[,] respiration[,] vision and motor power adhering likewise to the plan of [Baron Georges Leopold] Cuvier in comparative anatomy. My field of action has been principally limited to your State, and that of mine—the State of Maine, wherein the latter I have been engaged the past five years, struggling alone and by dint of perseverance—without the aid of any one—or competent means I collected and mounted nearly the whole of the Ornithology of Maine with numerous dissections amounting to six hundred specimens of Birds[,] Quadrupeds & skeletons. Five hundred ["of" *interlined*] them I disposed of for mere nothing—and founded ["a" *interlined*] natural history society at Portland Me. I am now engaged at this place forming another collection of the indigenous species of Florida, Georgia and South Carolina.

It is wished that it may be understood that I expect no adequate reward for my labors in a pecuniary point of view but as my means are restricted which hinders my progression I respectfully beg of you—to use your influence as a friend in procuring an appointment for me from General Government as a naturalist and collector of indigenous specimens exclusively within the limits of our United States, to be added to those specimens of the [South Seas?] exploring expedition which I have considered as a nucleus to form a National Academy of Sciences at the city of Washington. Confident that you will do everything in your ["power" *interlined*] that will tend towards the aggrandizement of our Nation—and the promotion of scientific pursuits which will develope the hidden treasures that are contained in the Great Arcanum before us. As to my pretensions to this science and qualifications beyond the letter of my friend—I will refer you to the Boston Natural history society, Prof. Simon

Greenleaf, Cambridge, Hon. Nahum Mitchell Boston, Hon. John Anderson Portland [Me.], Judge Ether Shepley president of the Portland N[atural] H[istory] Society, Chief justice [Ezekiel] Whitman of Maine, and the Hon. Albion K. Parris [of] Wash[ington] whom I presume is my friend. Also Gen. D[uncan] L. Clinch, of Georgia and Gen. [Joseph M.] Hernandez of Florida, and Prof. Samuel Dickson of Charleston S.C. and our members [of Congress] from Maine who certainly cannot deny me their friendship. Permit me to say, that where moral worth, domestic virtue and sound integrity with greatness of soul are all combined in a Statesman it is evident that the truth is becoming widely disseminated throughout our Union and men of strong partizan feelings begin to enjoy independent thoughts ascribing merit to those—where merit is due—who richly deserves a nation[']s highest honors and thus it is we look forward for more parity of thoughts and parity of feelings in exalting those that have been veterans in the councils of their country. My political knowledge is derived from the history of our country therefore I feel as an *American* and speak as an *American* and love those who maintain the perpetuation of our institutions and the liberal distribution of independent principles. With esteem I subscribe myself Your friend & Obed[ient] Serv[an]t, Augustus Mitchell.

ALS in ScCleA.

To T[homas] G. Clemson, Brussels

Cane Brake [Edgefield District, S.C.,] 13th Dec[embe]r 1845
My dear Sir, I have been so incessantly in motion, or otherwise occupied, since I wrote you from Marengo [County, Ala.] in repley [*sic*] to yours, in which you informed of your intention to sell this place, that I have not had leisure to answer your two intermediate letters.

You will have seen, that I have again been elected to the Senate, much against my inclination, but under such circumstances that I could not with propriety decline accepting. I am now on my way to Washington with Mrs. [Floride Colhoun] Calhoun & [Martha] Cornelia [Calhoun], after remaining a few days at Fort Hill on my return from Alabama. We came this way in order to attend to the contents of your letter to me, & Anna's [Anna Maria Calhoun Clemson's] to her mother, in reference to your affairs here. We found

339

all well & things going on reasonably well. The corn & cotton crop has done pretty well considering the extraordinary drought. The cotton is all gin[n]ed and packed, except about what will make 3 bales, which with that already packed, will make 34 bales of say 350 pounds. Eight I learn have been sold at 8 cents the pound. I have with the aid of old Mr. [John] Mobl[e]y estimated the corn now on hand, and make it to be about 1170 bushels. Two hundred & fifty I learn has been sold, & we estimate that 630 will be sufficient for the supply of the place until the 1st Oct[obe]r next, when the new corn will be fit for use; so that 540 bushels more may be sold. There will also be about 180 bushels of oats for sale; or, if the oats should be fed away, an increased quantity of corn to sell. The corn sold went at 75 ["cents" *interlined*] the bushel. What remains will probably bring $1 & the oats 50 cents the bushel. The cotton, I think, will command 7 round by spring. I think you may estimate the whole to yield $1600; what the expenses will be I cannot say, as they have passed through Col. [Francis W.] Picken[s]'s hand, from whom you will learn the amount. I think, however, they will be found to be moderate from what I hear. You have, I think, done well considering the year.

The weather has been bad since our arrival; so much so, as to prevent me from going round the place, & seeing the stock, except the Horses & Mules. They are in good working order. The Stables, barn & Gin house have been removed, & considerable progress made towards completing the dwelling house. William says the whole may be completed in four months, if lumber should be had. They have now got considerable on hand.

Not having yet hear[d] from you in answer to to [*sic*] my letter from Alabama, together with the lateness of the season & the impossibility of my remaining to attend to the sale of the place & the disposition of your property here generally, I have come to the conclusion, that you had better postpone your decision, as to the final disposition of your property here, for another year. I have the more readily done so, because I find since my arrival here, that the present overseer, Mr. Mobl[e]y, a nephew of your old friend, had already been engaged for next year; and also because, I think, the pressure of the times unfavourable for a sale. I hope you will approve of the decision. It will give you farther time, & experience to make up your ["final" *interlined*] decision; & should ["you" *interlined*] continue of the opinion, that it is best for you to sell, it will give leisure, during the summer & fall, to make the necessary arrangements to carry your decision into execution. Your present overseer seems to me to be ["an" *canceled*] active & attentive, & I hope will do well. In order to relieve Col. Pickens from the trouble of attending to your affairs, as far as possible, I have directed him (Mr. Mobl[e]y) to write to me, in reference to the business of the coming year, whenever he thinks your business ["should" *canceled and* "may" *interlined*] require my interposition.

["Anna" *canceled and* "Mrs. Calhoun" *interlined*] requests me to say to Anna, that she has packed up carefully ever[y] thing, & locked them ["up" *interlined*] in one of the rooms of the new house & left the keys with Mrs. Mobl[e]y, & that she will write to her fully about every thing, as soon as she arrives in Washington.

I had a very interesting tour in the West. I was received every where in a manner sufficient to gratify the feelings of any, the most illustrious for talents & ["services" *canceled*] publick services. All parties every where united without distinction, in a demonstration of respect, not exceed[ed] by that shown to Gen[era]l [Andrew] Jackson in passing through the same places, and much greater than that extended to any other citizen. I every where I [*sic*] was received as the guest of the place, & passed without expense, or charge through my tour to & from Memphis.

On my return home I found all well & that my crop, considering the severity of the drought, had yielded well. I shall have the place in fine order by the end of the coming year, when I shall commence a regular system of manuring.

Mrs. Calhoun & Cornelia join their love to you, Anna & the children [John Calhoun Clemson and Floride Elizabeth Clemson]. Your affectionate father, J.C. Calhoun.

[P.S.] The negroes all appear to be much attached to the place and were much alarmed at the idea of its being sold. They look remarkable well. There has been no death, nor birth, but the prospect of a large increase next year. JCC.

ALS in ScCleA; PEx's in Jameson, ed., *Correspondence*, p. 674. NOTE: Calhoun evidently retained this letter while awaiting an opportunity for its transmission to Europe. Almost two weeks later, in Washington on 12/26, he wrote further to Clemson on the same paper. The second portion of the letter appears below under date of 12/26.

From F[RANCIS] W. PICKENS

Senate Chamber [Columbia, S.C.,] 13th De[ce]m[be]r 1845 My dear Sir, I understand from Col. [Franklin H.] Elmore that you have written him to meet you to-morrow &c. I therefore take the opportunity to inform you that Mr. [Francis B.] Higgins of Newberry desires to purchase Mr. [Thomas G.] Clemson's place, and he is to let me know certainly if he will take it. I suppose he is now looking at it. I shall go home to-night and if he still desires to take it I will let you know.

I suppose your long experience and sagacity will enable you *now* to understand the movements in this State. Far more is under the surface than what is seen through the papers.

Letters were received here as I understand from Washington stating that your friends in Virginia at Richmond were in arms ag[ain]st you, and that resolutions were to be introduced into that Legislature in relation to the Memphis Convention. But I take it for granted this is all Humbug—and that no such resolutions will be introduced any where except in this State unless we are also to take into jurisdiction the proceedings of all conventions that may assemble on Temperance or any thing else. I did not arrive here for a week after the meeting of the Legislature, and when I came it was urged to bring resolutions into the Senate affirming "our old positions" &c. But I expressly discountenanced every thing of the kind, and no move was made in our body. There is a pretty strong organised party of active talent in the State who are dissatisfied & restless, but I take it for granted you must *now* understand how matters are. I think the same feelings have existed for four years. But so far as the people are concerned and the great mass of the country members, you never were stronger in their hearts than at present. Very truly, F.W. Pickens.

ALS in ScCleA. NOTE: This letter was addressed as to be sent "By Col: F.H. Elmore."

To "Col." JAMES ED[WARD] COLHOUN, [Abbeville District, S.C.]

Cane Brake [Edgefield District, S.C.] 14th Dec[embe]r 1845 My dear James, I enclose a letter [*not found*] to James [Edward Calhoun], which I wish you to read, & then seal & deliver to him.

I hope in deciding not to remain at Erskine [College], he acted under your advise, and not in disregard of his promise, or my authority. William [Lowndes Calhoun] informs me, that he left, because the course during the session did not admit of taking the tickets he wanted. I wished him to enter one of the classes and to proceed with it for a year in order to prepare him to enter some other college of a higher order another year. I did not think it advisable to send him this year to any such college, because he is not sufficiently prepared to enter with advantage, & because he is so perfectly thoughtless about his expenses, that I was averse to sending him ["to" *interlined*] any place, where he would have an opportunity to indulge in his thoughtless extravagance, which not only threw away money, but produced habits incompatible with his studies. I hoped, that one year at an institution placed in the woods, where there was nothing to divert his attention, would fix his habit of study, & correct his extravagance. I hope, if you should accord in these views, that you will use your influence ["with him" *interlined*] to join the institution, & take a regular course, in some one of the classes, ["the" *canceled*] at the commencement of the next session. My impression is, that it would be of great ["use" *canceled and* "service" *interlined*] to him.

He has good talents and great ambition, & all that is wanted is to give them the right direction to make him distinguished in life; while on the other hand, if they should not take the right direction now, I fear, that instead ["a" *canceled and* "of" *interlined*] a credit, he will be a discredit to the name. His greatest weakness is, that he is easily lead [*sic*] astray by bad company, into which he is too ready to fall.

I know the great interest you take in him & feel assured, that while he is with you, you will not permit his time to be unemployed or misdirected. I would be glad to have your advice fully as to what course ought to be taken with him, & to hear from you early in reference to him.

Our Alabama crop has yielded well both of cotton & corn. We had on the 30th Nov[embe]r 450 bags picked & packed & about 10 to pick & pack out, and expect to make 600 of 500 pounds each; & to have five or six thousand bushels of corn for sale. The place continues to enjoy almost perfect health.

My reception every where in my tour was of the most gratifying character. There was no distrinction [*sic*] of party, & the warmth & cordiality could not be exceeded.

I am happy to inform you, that there ["was" *canceled*] was great unanimity & Zeal in the [Memphis] Convention, in reference to our rail road system. I have no doubt of its completion in all its parts in a moderately short period. When done the union between Charleston & Savannah and the valley of the Mississippi will be of the most intimate & perfect character. I was told by the President of the Montgomery Rail road, that light goods have actually been brought already from Charleston at a cost less the ensurance [*sic*] round by water, although 130 miles of the route, between the two places, remains yet to be filled by rail road. I do not doubt the time is coming, when Charleston will be a great importing city, & the stock of the rail road to Hamburgh will be worth 200 per cent.

I have read the Message [of President James K. Polk to Congress] hastily. I fear we shall have trouble about Oregon. I cannot doubt, if the recommendation of the Message be carried out into acts, the termination will be war with England. I hope there is a good prospect to reduce the Tariff greatly. The present scarcity of provision in Europe will do much to effect it. The Message is not satisfactory in reference to it, although it is fully as good as I expected. Your sister [Floride Colhoun Calhoun] & [Martha] Cornelia [Calhoun] join their love to you. Yours affectionately, J.C. Calhoun.

ALS in ScCleA; PEx in Jameson, ed., *Correspondence*, p. 675.

From F[RANKLIN] H. ELMORE

Columbia, Dec[embe]r 14, 1845, (late at night) My Dear Sir, I was inexpressibly mortified this morning in finding myself too late at the Depot. I was misled by my watch & servant & got there only in time to find I was just left.

I would go down tomorrow, but the Legislature adjourns tomorrow night & I dare not leave at so critical a time—nor would I be certain of meeting you.

If you have not left the City, pray leave for me whatever you may wish attended to & I will try & have it done. I apprehend I know in part what your object was in seeing me & if I can serve you you have only to point out how.

It is very late at night & I have not been home, having been engaged in preparing a paper for the Senate tomorrow. Y[ou]rs truly, F.H. Elmore.

ALS in ScCleA.

From F[RANKLIN] H. ELMORE

Columbia, Dec[embe]r 16, 1845

My Dear Sir, Y[ou]rs of yesterday I rec[eive]d tonight & I very truly regret that I cannot get to Charleston before Saturday. There is a bare possibility that I may on Friday, but it is a bare possibility. Nothing but extremely urgent, indeed controlling business would detain me, but it is such as leaves me no alternative & I must stay. Several Gentlemen from distant points are now waiting here with me adjusting matters of the greatest consequence to us all & which we cannot postpone. It is not possible to close them before Thursday & probably before Friday. I therefore fix on Saturday as the earliest day I can come down.

Finding I could not come down, on Monday I wrote to you to Charleston. If there is any Bank [of the State of S.C.] matter you wish to arrange for pray send for Mr. Cha[rle]s M. Furman our Cashier & let him know as much as you deem advisable. If there be any thing more, if you will leave your wishes in a letter to me, I have hardly any doubt we can have them carried out. Mr. [John Ewing] Bonneau will I suppose be your Agent. If you prefer it, let him be the medium between us. You will in that respect, be [*one word canceled*] at no disadvantage from my absence.

I did wish very much to see you on several public questions.

Your Memphis speech has given as you have seen some uneasiness. When I reached here some days after [the start of] the Session I found it the subject of much talk & the the [*sic*] Resolution of Mr. [Frederick J.] McCarthy was before the House. I endeavored to get any action on it postponed to hear from you or for more information from the newspapers, as the reported speech was evidently not from your hand. I prepared the Editorial of Mr. [Adam G.] Summer in the [Columbia South-]Carolinian, to precede the debate— but Mr. McCarthy[']s impatience forced the action of the House. I believe he was afterwards sorry for his precipitancy.

Mr. [Robert Barnwell] Rhett wrote me urgently from Richmond to press you to go by & stop there a day. He said he found much the same anxiety there on this subject. Messrs. [William O.] Goode [former Representative from Va.] & Harvey [*sic*; Lewis E. Harvie] two devoted friends of yours he said, were particularly anxious on the subject, as they understood you to have changed your views on Int[erna]l Imp[rovemen]ts. I wrote to you immediately & directed to Pendleton to let you know this. Mr. Rhett is in Charleston probably & if so you may see him.

I have seen it stated in some of the papers that we were to have an authentic report of your remarks from yourself. I would be glad to know if either of those published have done you justice & if not if you intend publishing a true report. If you have seen the Editorial of the Carolinian, I would be glad also to learn if I put the right view of your remarks, in it.

The Oregon question presents a totally new feature by the British rejection of the 49th°. It seems to me to put them in the wrong & that it leaves us no alternative but to support the Executive firmly in all proper measures for asserting our rights. Is there no room for mediation? Can[']t France, or Russia or Holland interpose to save us from war?

Mr. [James K.] Polk has undoubtedly gained here on this question, while his Message & Mr. [Robert J.] Walker[']s [Treasury Department] report on the Tariff have added not a little to his influence on this question too.

Rhett writes me that Walker tried a compromise with the Pennsylvanians & failing in that, he fell back on principle & gave us this fair Report.

Is it not an extraordinary circumstance that you are ["made a" *interlined*] Chairman before you are Senator?

I have inclosed the Editorial I alluded to—it was prepared very hastily as the time was very short. Yours truly, F.H. Elmore.

ALS with En in ScCleA. NOTE: Elmore enclosed a clipping of "Mr. Calhoun's Memphis Speech," which had appeared in the Columbia *South-Carolinian* of 11/28. The first session of the 29th Congress had convened on 12/1, and on 12/9 the Senate had elected Calhoun Chairman of the Committee on Finance.

From [Bvt. Maj. Gen.] EDMUND P. GAINES

New Orleans, December 17th 1845

My dear Sir, I send for your perusal an editorial in the Picayune of the 16th with another of this date by which you will see the impressions of the able Editors of this paper regarding the President's [James K. Polk's] message, and the war aspect of the British Government.

Never have I been more astonished than to see what has been said upon this subject embracing *in part statesmanlike views—anticipating war at no distant day—without a single sentence urging the propriety of immediate preparation.* If it was necessary and proper in all times past—"In peace to prepare for war" the ten thousand times increased facilities which steam power affords to bring on *the war suddenly*—to render it "almighty in its birth"—and widely destructive in its commencement—surely it is far more essential now that vigorous measures of preparation should be taken when we find a powerful unprincipled nation *menacing us* than it ever has been at any former period. Although I do not consider the President's message strictly speaking a *war message*. Yet convinced as I am that England has long been resolved upon war, as soon as she finds herself prepared to send against us 150 to 200 war steamers with 200,000 seamen and 200,000 land forces—so as to enable her to send one fourth of that force to this city, one fourth to New York, and divide the residue between Boston, Philadelphia, Baltimore[,] Charleston S.C. and Pensacola and Mobile—to make a simultaneous attack on each place on one and the same day and hour—I can not but believe she will avail herself of the present occasion to take this extraordinary step as soon as she can—and withhold her declaration of war until she is prepared to *herald* it from the mouths of her improved cannon—while we have no such improved means to enable us to repel her assaults.

all men of sound wisdom known to me in the west and South, and especially all practical men of military mind look to you as the first chief in the councils of the union able to provide the requisite means of preparation. They all believe with me that in as much as this nation can never be defended in a war with England by any one *Political Party*—that the civil chiefs and fighting men of both parties will unite in every essential measure for the defence of the country. In this union of light and strenght we all feel well assured that you will take the lead—as you have hitherto taken the lead in war—and subsequently in preparing the country for war.

I regret to find that an impression has bewildered the minds of some of the best educated officers of the army that England—now that millions of her population are laboring under the apprehension of a *famine*, would be less disposed to avail herself of any plausible cause to invade this country than when in the enjoyment of plenty of food. The reverse of this supposition I believe to be true. It is evident to my mind that a man of the Duke of Wellington's experience and talent would assert to the Queen and his associates of the British Cabinet, and convince them of the truth of his assertion that, by an immediate augmentation of their land and naval forces to 500,000 men—and sending them to the United States—one fourth to this city—one fourth to the city of New York and the residue to our other principal sea Port towns, with authority to provide as best they may for their own support—the British will in this way at the least possible expense—and probably without any expense whatever, contribute to the support of two millions of such of their people as would otherwise starve.

This opinion is based upon the deeply mortifying conviction that such a British army and navy would be able to lay many of our cities under contribution, or otherwise force from our defenceless frontier inhabitants, not only an ample supply of subsistence for their own support, but money and property sufficient to pay and clothe them. This would enable the British Government to distribute the *regular supply of these forces*, thus saved, amounting to fifteen millions of rations per month, amongst their suffering mechanics and other destitute inhabitants. And I know from experience that a man *can live*, with tolerable comfort one month upon seven complete rations such as our own troops and seamen are authorised to receive. And I have reason to believe that millions of the people of England have seldom or ever enjoyed as much *good meat and bread* as a quarter of a ration per day each for a year. Give to any family *residing in the country*—even in England, Ireland or Scotland a quarter of a ration of good meat and bread per day for each member of the family during the summer and autumn, in addition to the many wild or spontaneous fruits and vegetable productions of which they always obtain a ["scanty" *interlined*] supply (but such as the members of a large army and navy can but seldom have access to,) and they will live comfortably.

For heaven's sake preserve us from the degradation and heavy pecuniary loss of our being compelled *to feed and clothe a British army and navy*. The expense would amount to near five millions of dollars per month. Give me a quarter of that sum per month with authority to call into service whatever volunteer corps may be needed, and I will insure the protection of every vital part of the Western Division. To do this effectually our first object must be by temporary works—added to our Forts, to secure our inlets, and thus compel the enemy to separate his land forces from his war steamers. We can then beat them in detail with ease and certainty. But without the means such as I have required in my letter of the 28th of June last to the Secretary of War [William L. Marcy]—of which I will tomorrow send you an extract—we must submit to outrages such as we never have dreamed of.

We may to a moral certainty anticipate an attack by any European ["power" *interlined*] no where upon our seaboard, but at or in the immediate vicinity of our sea Port towns; first—because no experienced commander would be disposed to separate his land forces from his war steamers; and secondly—European commanders—but more especially English commanders are known to be a money loving people—to say nothing about Plunder and Booty— they would seldom attempt a conquest which would give them nothing of value. I am most respectfully your friend & ob[e]d[ien]t S[ervan]t, Edmund P. Gaines.

ALS and draft ALS in ScCleA. NOTE: The draft ALS contains a postscript that reads: "We are all well. E.P.G." Gaines was at this time commander of the Western Division of the U.S. Army, which embraced all American territory west of the Appalachians except for part of the Great Lakes region.

From ROB[ER]T PATTERSON

Natchez [Miss.,] 17 December [18]45

Sir, Some days after parting from you on board the Maria, I rec[eive]d a letter from Mr. [Richard] Abbey of Yazoo County, informing me that he had anticipated my intention of sending you a package of the *Mastodon* [cotton] *Seed,* by forwarding from himself a bushel to your address.

Fearing that he may make some mistake in the shipment I shall address your son at Demopolis [Ala.] on the subject.

I rejoice that you have again gone into active service, and can assure you that such is the feeling with all men of all parties in this region—Louisiana and Mississippi. Your course at Memphis has caused some slight *carping,* but *no comment worthy notice.* The fact is, amongst the partizan editors in our two States, we are cursed with many who have no capacity save that for doing many small things in a small way.

I have not left my room since parting with you, and am now preparing to start on a trip down through the Islands probably as far as Trinidad. I have ordered the [Concordia, La.] Intelligencer addressed to you during the session at Washington. With great respect Your Ob[edien]t S[er]v[an]t, Robt. Patterson, Natchez.

ALS in ScCleA. NOTE: Patterson edited the Concordia *Intelligencer.*

From F[RANCIS] W. PICKENS

Edgewood, 20 Dec[embe]r 1845
My dear Sir, I rec[eive]d yours from Canebreak & from Charleston also enclosing a draught to Arthur Simkins for $3,000.

I have not yet heard from Mr. [Francis B.] Higgins. But of course the place will not now be sold for a year. In the mean time I entertain not the slightest doubt it can be sold.

I thought when you wrote from Ala: that you offered it certainly, but I think the course now pursued is best. I rec[eive]d a letter from Mr. [Thomas G.] Clemson but he does not allude to selling his place.

As to the message & the probabilities of war to which you allude—I do not see how any one could have done more than the President [James K. Polk] has done and I cordially approve of his sentiments, and such I know is the feeling of 99 in 100 of our people. You will recollect I wrote you this Fall fully & candidly to Ala: in relation to these questions in answer to yours, and then entertained the same sentiments before I knew what the President would do or say. I do not think war will come. It looked like it on the N[orth] Eastern Boundary and when we tried [Alexander] McLeod for the Burning of the Caroline, & England then bullied by sending near 20,000 of her best troops into Canada &c. So it was on the Texas question. She is now arming & fortifying full as much ag[ain]st France & the Continental powers as ag[ain]st us. There must be a convulsion upon the death of the King of the French [Louis Philippe], and she is preparing for that as well as for us.

I trust in God war may be avoided but I would not bend ["or" *interlined*] swerve from the direct path of independence and right one inch to preserve peace with as ["inso" *canceled*] insolent and overbearing a power as G. Britain. I wish you would send me the documents from the State Department connected with our Oregon difficulties, as I never recieve [*sic*] any thing from Washington except occasionally from [Richard F.] Simpson [Representative from S.C.]. Direct them *to Charleston* as I will spend January in that city with my family. I am going to place three of my children with Mrs. [Julia?] Du Pre and perhaps may hereafter spend my winters there in order to superintend particularly their education. I should also be very glad to hear from you there as to the probabilities of war &c.

I do hope there will be a good feeling between you & Mr. Polk and a cordial understanding, and if there is, I know it will unhorse

[Thomas H.] Benton entirely, particularly as I see [William] Allen [Senator from Ohio] is now seperated from him. There is no kindness between Benton & Polk and killing the [Washington] Globe was the first step to kill the former. There are persons at Washington, and *near you* too, who have an interest in fomenting differences between you & the President, and all sorts of tales will be made up to operate upon your mind, but their real object is no friendship to you or the President. They have been ["caugh" *canceled*] found in an unfortunate & selfish position and their struggle will be to get others into the same position with themselves.

I feel very much relieved by the President's message in relation to the Tariff—it has redeemed every pledge I ever made in this State as I knew he would. My interview with him at his own house August 1844 was full on the Tariff—the Globe, Benton, [Silas] Wright, &c &c—and he has done exactly every thing so far he ever promised. There is one member of his cabinet I had no idea would have been there. These circumstances and the course I pursued in the Legislature last Winter, & the course of certain gent[lemen] in this State (particularly [George] McDuffie), [*Marginal interpolation*: He is the only one I cared a (*ms. torn;* "fig for")] made it my duty to refuse the mission to England, which under other circumstances I would have taken with pleasure, not because I cared for that or any other office on earth, but because it might have been *my duty* to take it. Present us kindly to Cousin Floride [Colhoun Calhoun]. Very truly, F.W. Pickens.

P.S. You are mistaken if you suppose I have the proceeds of Mr. Clemson's crop. Mr. [John Ewing] Bonneau has that.

ALS in ScCleA; PEx in Boucher and Brooks, eds., *Correspondence*, p. 311.

From WILLIAM H. SMITH and Others

Philad[elphi]a, Dec[embe]r 20th 1845

Sir, The undersigned Committee of Invitation for the celebration of the ensuing anniversary of the glorious battle of New Orleans by "the personal and political friends of *George Mifflin Dallas*" take great pleasure in requesting the honor of your company at a public dinner, in the 3rd Congressional district of this State, and in the county of Philadelphia, on the 8th Jan[ua]ry next. If inconvenient to attend have the kindness to favor us with a sentiment for the oc-

351

casion. We have the honor to be, very respectfully, William H. Smith, Geo[rge] Clymer Geyer, James Martin, Lyman Ackley, Wm. Goodwin, D.K. Miller, Henry Simpson, Stewart Magee, James Sandy, Committee.

LS in ScCleA. NOTE: An AEU by Calhoun reads "Invitation to attend a dinner to be given by the friends of Mr. Dallas on the 8th Jan[uar]y."

From LEWIS CRUGER

New York [City,] Dec[embe]r 22, 1845
Dear Sir—A few days since I took the liberty to enclose you a copy of the Journal of the "First Congress of the American Colonies" [the Stamp Act Congress,] held at New York [City] in Oct[obe]r 1765. This Journal I have had republished from the old publication of Mr. [Hezekiah] Niles which appears to have been almost unknown to the Historians of our Country. I was induced to bring into notice the patriotic proceedings of these patriarchs of our Independence from the knowledge which I possessed, & the just pride that I felt, in the part taken by one of my paternal Ancestors [John Cruger of N.Y.] in this glorious Assembly of primeval patriots. This Congress is designated by Major [Alexander] Garden [Jr.] of So. Carolina in his Anecdotes of the Revolution the *"Ovum Reipublicae,"* & I am anxious to learn whether you, or any of our leading Statesmen have any knowledge of the part taken by the members ["of" *canceled and* "from" *interlined*] your respective States in its important proceedings. If you could spare a little of your precious time to give me any information on this subject you would greatly oblige Most Respectfully your ob[edien]t [servant,] Lewis Cruger.

P.S. I have not the vanity to suppose that you would remember me as a young Brother-in-law of Gov[erno]r [James] Hamilton [Jr.], at Columbia, & the humble Author of the *"Book of Nullification,"* before I removed to Louisiana to cultivate Sugar. Having last year disposed of my property there, I now pass much of my time in New York ["State" *interlined*] where my father's relatives reside. But I shall return to Louisiana to recommence planting, in the course of January.

ALS in ScCleA.

From J[OHN] TOWNSEND

St. John's Colleton [Parish]
(Edisto Island) [S.C.] Dec[embe]r 22nd [18]45

Dear Sir, An apprehension that this letter may put you to some trouble, in complying with the request which it contains, has almost prevented me from writing it at all; but the great anxiety which I feel, in common with very many ["many" *canceled*] others of the community, with which I am surrounded, has outweighed my scruples, and urged me to commit, what might be considered, an unwarrantable intrusion upon your time. At no period, since the war of 1812, has such deepseated anxiety taken possession of the minds of our citizens on the Seaboard, as that which at present, so painfully oppresses them; arising out of the extremely threatening aspect of our relations with England, on the Oregon question.

The conflicting, and apparently irreconcilable claims of the two countries, to the paltry patch of land in dispute, which neither of them really stand in need of at the present time, and both can do without, for a half century to come—and the extreme pertinacity with which Great Brittain [*sic*] rejects the moderate pretensions of our Government, and insists upon her own Claims, would seem to betoken, that there is something else besides Oregon, which actuates her, in the disposition she shows, to provoke hostilities, between the two countries. The quiet, but steady, and large military preparations, which, as we have been informed, she has been making in her N. American possessions contiguous to us, and doubtless in Bermuda, and the West Indies; the immense preparations also, which we are told she has been making in all of her Dockyards at home, (which is without a precedent, it is stated, except when Napoleon kept Europe in commotion, and threatened England with invasion); and the persevering industry which she has shewn for a long time past, in putting her most formidable Navy, (with her hundred War-Steamers) in a condition of complete efficiency—all these circumstances, and many more, with which you are doubtless better acquainted than we—are an admonition to the world, and especially to this country, that she has some great Scheme of Evil and mischief on foot, which will in due time develope itself, in some real or attempted advantage to herself; altho her path may be marked, by the calamities or desolation, of some devoted country.

And is she too good, or generous, or just, to do such a thing! What is her past History; in India; in this country; in China; now in South America; and I fear, about to be renewed again in this country? And what is her Character, as she stands before the world?—arrogant, overbearing, and insolent to all other People. In her Government, the insolvent Bankrupt at home, & desperate in her circumstances; and the swaggering Bully among the trembling Nations. In her foreign policy—selfish, grasping, reckless, and unprincipled, in every thing, in which she can promote her own interests: in her Religion, not only Pharisaical, presumptuous, exclusive, and intollerant to all other denominations of Christians—but setting up herself as the Standard of Christianity, morals, and humanity; whilst she hypocritically uses it as the cloak, to cover her ambitious designs, against other nations, in subserviency to her pecuniary, and political aggrandizement. Power, with her, is the measure of right; and she scruples not at any thing, which she may fancy, can promote her interests; satisfied, that she can always invent some plausible pretext, to justify her acts, among the troubling, or sympathizing monarchies, with which she is in intercourse.

Such being the views which we entertain, of this mighty, but unscrupulous and most dangerous Power, it naturally fills us with great anxiety, when we contemplate these formidable preparations on her part, in contrast with our own utterly defenceless condition; and reallize to ourselves the many causes of jealousy and dislike, which she has against us; the strong *interest* she has, in several points of view, to do us damage; and the strong temptation, which our present weakness and want of preparation hold out to her, to gratify her chafed, and long irritated feelings.

It is true, there are many who contend, that it is not the interest of Great Brittain to go to war with us. But this is not at all clear to my mind. Would it not be greatly to her interest, to *Cripple* this country for several years to come? which she can so easily do, at this time; with her ample means of Destruction, all in readiness, as they are, for this purpose. Could she not with such overwhelming odds, and with such good will, on her part, to do it; by a sudden irruption upon us, annihilate our Navy; destroy our commerce, with all the exports of our Agriculture; desolate our seacoast, and lay in ashes all our tide water cities; and this too, before the Government and People of this country could be awaked up to the danger; which will no doubt be her plan of tactics, as it will be her best policy? What more to her interest, than to destroy our Navy, our dockyards, our seacoast cities, and our commerce: *and so Crush* that hated Rival, who now wounds her pride by jostling her in every port, and ["by" *interlined*] contesting with ["her" *interlined*] the dominion of the Seas! What more to her interest, than to parallize us in our slave labour institutions; and thus dry up the main source of our wealth and power as a Nation: by which means also, she would establish her ascendency, in the production of Cotton in the East Indies, as she thinks, and procure that independence in obtaining the raw material for her looms, which she has been so long aiming at?

But suppose that she may design, not entirely to destroy, but only to damage greatly, the Agricultural capital of the S[outher]n States, (which latter, it is probable, would be the only result)—would it ["not" *interlined*] be greatly to her interest, under the pretext of war about Oregon, to overrun and take possession of Texas; and thus obtain by force, what she has been so desirous to accomplish by diplomacy and trickery. Once in her possession, of what infinite value to her, as a Nation, would Texas be! of more value than all of Oregon or Canada into the bargain, to the North pole. It makes her complete as an Empire. It gains her a *Cotton producing climate* and soil—which she does not now possess, in all her extended dominions, in the far or near regions of the globe, which owns [*sic*] her sway. I[t] opens to her the way to California, (which is already mortgaged, it is said, to her people) with all the intervening country—all of which (between 26° and 36° of Latitude) is a Cotton growing climate and soil.

Such an acquisition would supply her, in ample abundance, with one of the chief materials, towards her national industry and wealth; and which makes her now dependent on, and consequently, civil, to the United States. Now, all that belt of Climate and soil, so eagerly desired by her, is, or is likely to become, the exclusive inheritance of our own more fortunate Country. Great Brittain possesses none of it. Her northern possessions in Europe, and on this Continent, from 45° upwards, are too Cold: Her Southern possessions in the Indies, (East & West) are too hot and sultry; too subject to the violent extremes of droughts and rains, and she is ["there" *interlined*] devoured by insects and caterpillars.

Does it surprise any one then, that she should have desired to acquire an ascendency and control in Texas, as she lately attempted: or that she should now be willing to make the sacrafice of lesser interests, by a War with this country; in order to secure so great present and prospective advantages, as Texas and California will bring to her?

Let it not be supposed that because she is (professedly) opposed to Slavery, and as cotton cannot be cultivated successfully without slave-labour, that therefore, she does not want Texas. Her "philanthropy" can be easily forgotten, at the demand of her interests, as it was hard for her, at first, to assume (the pretence of) it. Besides, once in possession of the country, she will make a merit, of permitting and perpetuating Slavery, on the plea of respect to the private rights, of the Citizens now owning slaves there: and she will find means and apology, to multiply them, to the full extent of her wants, by importing them from Africa, or the East Indies, and calling them "Coolies"—as is now about to be done in Jamaica.

But can she keep possession of Texas, after she has overrun it? Why not. Harrass the Atlantic States by a war of five years: shut up the breadstuffs and meat provisions of the West, for the same time—impoverish the whole Country, by destroying our Commerce and Agriculture—and there will be such a cry for Peace over the Land, that with the influence of the Abolitionists, East, North, & West, Texas will be given up; or bartered for Oregon, or Canada, or some other such worthless bauble!

Pardon me, my dear Sir, for indulging in these speculations. To one like yourself, so deeply read in the designs and policy of nations, they may appear very trite and common place. I throw them out here, only as justifying me in the indulgence of ["this"(?) *canceled*] the painful anxiety I feel, and have expressed to you, at what I regard the eminently perilous condition of our country, and especially of those of us, who live upon the seacoast. All of my family; almost all the friends I have in this world; and all the property I own, will be at the mercy of the enemy, in the event of a war. And when it is considered, that, that enemy has not only the superabundant ability, and I fear the inclination, but also (what has ever been most potent with her) a very strong *interest* to bring this calamity upon us, I trust you will regard with indulgence, those feelings, which now intrude upon you, for information and advice. I apply to you, as to one, possessing information, which we are persuaded, few other men can impart: and in whose judgement and foresight, your constituents here on the Seaboard, not less than in other parts of the State, have given you repeated evidences, that they have great and merited[?] confidence.

Is it then your opinion that war with Great Brittain must grow out of this controversy about Oregon—and if it come, that it will overtake us, before our Govt. and People shall be prepared to meet it. From the aspect of parties in the Senate, how are they likely to decide on that question: and if they decide in accordance with the recommendations of the President, to claim, & exercise jurisdiction, over the *whole* territory, what is the course which things are likely to take, after that, between the two countries. I seek your opinions thro' this private channel, since considerations of publick expediency may restrain you, from giving expression to them before the publick, from your place in the Senate. I need not assure you, that I shall make no other use of them, than you may permit, or suggest, as for the good of your Constituents, who are so deeply interested, in obtaining early, and correct information, and counsel.

We feel persuaded that our Representatives will do all in their power which may be consistent with the honour and dignity of the Country, to avert from us so great a calamity, as that of war. There is but one sentiment among those with whom I have had communication on this subject—and that is—that a more causeless ground of quarrel, and for a more worthless object, never existed between two Countries, since the seige of Troy. And what a spectacle does it present, for the Wise and Benignant Ruler of Nations, to look down upon! Two great nations, boasting to be the most civilized, intelligent, and religious on the whole Earth, and upon whom rest, the hopes of Protestant Christianity, and that highest liberty which Mankind is deemed capable of attaining—these two Nations spilling each other's blood, and covering the land with dead bodies; burning each other's cities; laying waste their territories; and inflicting unspeakable misery [upon] the aged, upon women, and feeble children; destroying each other's property; fitting out armies and implements of destruction, at a cost to each, ["of" *interlined*] from sixty to a hundred millions annually—and all for what?—for a contemptible patch of country, almost out of sight, of the remotest borders of civilization; which neither nation really wants, and about which, no virtuous principle is involved, either of honour or justice; which is not larger than some of our own individual States; and whether barren or fertile, is not worth, in the best market in the world, four millions of dollars!

Surely in the eyes of all Christian men, that nation will entitle itself to the largest share of virtuous applause, which shall, in such a quarrel, make the farthest advances towards the cause of Peace. And if any scheme can be devised, by which our Government can, with dignity and grace, *make* a *present* of the territory in dispute, to G. Brittain, or any body else, it will meet with the approbation, I am persuaded, of a majority of the *People* of the U. States; so worthless is it considered by all, who have looked into the matter, since the President has brought it to their notice, in his late Message. It is judged that ["a" *interlined*] five year[']s war, will cost us more, in morals, treasures, and comforts, than Oregon will be worth, to the end of time. We have a confidence then, that our Representatives

357

will give no support to the extravagant claims set up lately by the President, to the *whole* of the territory; but will be satisfied with an adjustment of the difficulty upon the basis of the compromise offered by former administrations; or even with less.

But should you from the advantageous point of observation which you occupy, and which no one knows so well how to make good use of as yourself, perceive indications on the part of G. Brittain, (in refusing all reasonable terms) to pick a quarrel with this Country and provoke us to a fight, to satisfy old grudges; or if the rabid West make such extravagant demands, that from this blameworthy cause on our part, war is likely to follow; then, my Dear Sir, in either case, it will be only necessary for you to put yourself in our situation on the Seaboard, to feel, how exceedingly important it will be to us, to receive the very earliest intelligence of these indications in order that we may prepare ourselves for the danger which may be approaching, and be ready to meet ["it" *interlined*], in a manner, befitting us, as Men.

With the celerity and certainty, which Steam imparts to the modern movements of Navies, and invading armies, twenty days can convey our Enemy from their dock-yards to our shores; a time, unhappily much too short, to wake up our People, and enable them to occupy their stations. For that policy will be the wisest, safest, best in every way; and that resistance the most effectual, which will begin the dispute at the *Water's edge*; and which will not suffer our soil to be polluted even by their foot-prints.

But this I shall despair of; except we can have the benefit of such (**the earliest**) intelligence and warning, (which can proceed only from great watchfulness, & a far-seeing sagacity), and such energy of preparation, (which I fear, our Govt. is incapable of)—that our Citizens may be stirred up, and prepared, perhaps months in advance. What priceless advantages we shall lose, if, instead of contesting with them the *landing*, we suffer them, by our apathy or tardiness, to choose, and fortify their positions—if, instead of measuring our strenghth with them, whilst under the fatigue and exhaustion of their voyage, we suffer them first to nourish, comfort and recruit themselves, out of our own resourses [*sic*]—if instead of our having possession of the country, and being the entrenched Defenders of it, and they the unsheltered assailants, we allow them to preoccupy and take from us all these advantages, which ought properly to have belonged to us.

May the wisdom, moderation, and prudence of our Rulers, avert from us the threatened Evil: But should a War be unavoidable, may they, by their forecast and energy, enable us to make it more fatal to our enemy, than it may, otherwise, become to ourselves. We have the confidence, that you, at least, will use every effort which becomes your station, to accomplish for us these desirable objects. I am Dear Sir, with sentiments most respectful, your ob[e-dien]t S[er]v[an]t, J. Townsend.

ALS in ScCleA.

From W[illia]m W. J. Kelly

House of Representatives
Tallahassee, 23d Dec: 1845

Sir, The enclosed communication, which was enclosed to Maj: W[il-lia]m H. Chase our delegate in the Memphis Convention, did not come into the possession of that Gentleman, until his return to Pensacola, owing to some irregularity in the Mail by which it was sent. That gentleman has very kindly sent it to me that I may as Chairman of the Committee of Invitation forward it to you, evidencing Sir, the lively interest which the Citizens of Pensacola felt in the course which you have pursued in the great and important measures of our Common Country. I have the honor to be very Respectfully, Y[ou]r Ob[edient] S[er]v[an]t, Wm. W.J. Kelly.

[Enclosure]
W[illia]m W.J. Kelly and Others to J.C. Calhoun

Pensacola, 8th Nov: 1845

Sir, The undersigned have been appointed to the distinguished position of being the medium through which the citizens of Pensacola and its vicinity, may communicate to you an Invitation to visit them, should it be convenient after you have done with the duties which shall have devolved upon you in Convention. In tendering this invitation to you Sir, your fellow citizens are not only actuated by their admiration for your private worth and excellencies—the great and distinguished Services which you have rendered as a Statesman to our common Country; or that you may come amongst them and mingle those Social relations which cement the ties of friendship—but that they may also pay individual tribute to those virtues which adorn the private walks of life, while they shed additional luster around the noble works of the Statesman! !

Wishing you the fine fullness of health, and that we may realize our sincere desire to see you in our midst, We have the honor to be

Very Respectfully Y[ou]r Ob[edien]t S[er]v[an]ts, Wm. W.J. Kelly, chairman, Walker Anderson, James H. Campbell, Wm. McVay, E.E. Simpson, Chas. W. Jordan, Robt. W. Mitchell, J. Saville[?], Geo. G. Paterson & John Hunt, Com[mittee] of Invitation.

ALS with En in ScCleA.

From FRANCIS WHARTON

Philadelphia, Dec. 24, 1845

My dear Sir, When I had the pleasure of waiting on you at Washington, last February, you mentioned to me Mr. [George W.] Woodward, as the man whom you preferred for the vacant U.S. [Supreme Court] Judgeship. I think you were the first person who brought forward his name in connection with that high office; and I well recollect the surprise with which he received from me the intimation I threw out that you had looked upon him as a man ["for" *canceled and "to" interlined*] whom Judge [Bushrod?] Washington's seat might fall. Since then things have changed, and Mr. Woodward's name is before the Senate. My long and very intimate personal intercourse with him enables me to speak truly of his character & views; and I can only repeat now what I mentioned to you before. The great charge made against him in the Democratic Caucus last winter was, to use Mr. [Thomas?] Ross'[s] language, that *he was a Calhoun man.* He is a strong personal advocate of your views—free trade, anti-Dorr, and strict construction. Nobody ever attempted to touch his character—it is purity itself. The only cause of his want of popularity with the masses is [*one or two words canceled and "the" interlined*] stern purity of his manners and demeanour; but in point of real ability and energy there are few men in the country equal to him. I do not dwell on the subject, as I have not only addressed you previously in relation to it, but have had the honour of an interchange of views with you. I need only say he is a States right's man at heart; and I have reason to say so, for we have been in active correspondence with him for two years for the promotion of views which we have all held so dear.

You have been always so kind in your expressions of interest in my prosperity that I know it will not be taking to[o] much of your time for me to mention that under Mr. [Francis R.] Shunk's administration [as Governor] I have received the post of prosecuting attorney for Philadelphia. It is one not only lucrative but honourable, and paves the way for higher professional advancement. Truly yours, Francis Wharton.

[P.S.] Your friends are gaining great ground, both here and in N.Y., especially in the latter city. The Memphis address did wonders. I hope Oregon will come up right. The President[']s [James K. Polk's] views have made a deep impression.

One of the booksellers here talks of republishing your speeches with historical notes, & I have had some conversation with him on the subject. I may address you again, if you think the matter worthy of consideration.

ALS in ScCleA. NOTE: Polk's nomination of George W. Woodward to the Supreme Court was rejected by the Senate.

From H[ENRY] WHEATON, [U.S. Minister to Prussia]

Berlin, 24 Dec. 1845

My dear Sir, As it has been stated in the newspapers that you would probably resume your seat in the Senate, I beg leave to call your attention to a subject in which the public interests, as well as what is due to yourself & me as public servants, are deeply concerned. I have always considered that great injustice was done me in taking off the injunction of secrecy from the proceedings of the Senate, so far as respected the *Report* of the Committee of Foreign Affairs upon the Zollverein treaty, whilst the injunction was continued as to ["the" *canceled*] my Despatches of the 10, & 25 March, 1844, accompanying the Treaty, & which would have anticipated & met, with more or less conclusiveness, the arguments urged by the Committee against the ratification. So long as there were any reasons connected with the public good for with[h]olding these documents from the People, I should have been perfectly willing to have submitted to any personal inconvenience that might have followed. But now that the Zollverein states have declared that they are not willing to wait any longer the deliberations of the Senate upon the Treaty, I see no possible inconvenience in publishing the correspondence relating to it. I have therefore to request that you will have the goodness to call for it in the Senate, & have it printed & published.

In order to have a complete view of the subject, it is necessary to go back to the origin of the negotiation in the conferences at Stuttgard [*sic*] in 1842, ["wh" *canceled*] the despatches relating to which, you will perceive are intimately connected with *our* Tariff question. I have therefore prepared the enclosed list of the Papers which I conceive to be indispensably necessary—not *extracts* merely, but the *entire* Despatches with all their *Enclosures.* I have not omitted even my Despatch of the 25 March, 1844, although it has already been communicated confidentially to the Senate; as it ought to be printed in connexion with the other Documents, especially as I presume few Copies will be found of the former impression. I have carefully read over all the Papers, & can answer for it that there is nothing in them, the publication of which can prejudice the public interests. The unanswerable argument contained in your Despatch of the 28 June, 1844, will amply supply ["in" *canceled and* "any defects in" *interlined*] the views I had taken by anticipation of the constitutional difficulty raised by the Committee of the Senate.

The Zollverein states are not disposed, at present, to revive the negotiation on the basis of the former Treaty, as they expect to obtain, in the revision of our Tariff by Congress, reductions in favour of their manufactures, without ["giving" *canceled*] conceding any ["redu" *canceled*] equivalent reductions in favour of our agricultural staples; & should this be ["the" *interlined*] result of the deliberations of Congress, it will be seen that a golden opportunity has been lost, in not obtaining such equivalents for reductions, which we shall have been compelled to make gratuitously in order to get rid of an exaggerated Tariff.

We have not yet received the President's [James K. Polk's] message at the opening of Congress, but I shall look ["f" *canceled*] with intense interest for the result of your deliberations on the present state of our relations with G[reat] Britain, respecting which I have no other information than what is contained in the Newspapers. But so far as I am able to judge from the means of information which are equally open to the whole world, I still continue to think that "the wise & masterly delay" referred to in your Speech on the Ashburton treaty, continues still to be our true policy in respect to the Oregon question. But as I do not know how far the position of that question may have been changed by what has passed between the two Governments during the negotiations of the two last years, this opinion is, of course, subject to such qualifications as may result from the Paper, which will doubtless be communicated to Congress. I am, my dear Sir, ever, truly your obliged friend, H. Wheaton.

ALS in ScCleA; variant PC in Jameson, ed., *Correspondence,* pp. 1063–1065.

From ——

New York [City,] Decem[ber] 24th 1845
Dear Sir, At this momenteous crisis, at this period when our peaceful and happy Country is pregnant with serious and uncertain consequences as to the future[;] When the ambitions and corrupt passions of some of the leading men of our country are called into action and the nation is threatened with a sad and desolating war, For what! Merely that these, would be Statesmen, may attain popularity, knowing well, that the conflict should it come, will not fall upon them, neither will they have to bear the burden and heat of the day, regardless alike of the hearth's made desolate, and the mourning of widows and lamentation of orphan's, and the almost innumerable train of evils resulting from sanguinary warfare, which they themselves, have brought upon the people, I say at this momenteous period, a million eye's are turned towards the master spirit of the south, a million ear's are listening with breathless attention, to hear the course which *He* will pursue, who in days past recommended "a wise and masterly inactivity" in reference to the vexed [Oregon] question, now pending, in the councils of the nation. If such an one should be made an instrument of averting the dire calamity which seem's to threaten us, not only a million of his countrymen would cherish his memory, but I trust in the calm moments of the people a whole nation will delight to exalt the man who himself joys in a nation's welfare. His name shall not go down to posterity as a political sycophant, but pure and unsullied, a true philanthropist and bright ornament in his country's annals. He also will have the conscious feeling of having exerted himself, for a nation's weal, to avert a nation's woes. The sentiments of many who can in some degree appreciate the talent's and influence of South Carolina's favoured Son. [Unsigned.]

ALU in ScCleA. Note: An AEU by Calhoun reads "Anonymous." The handwriting of this letter is perhaps feminine.

From Geo[rge] D. Phillips

Clark[e]sville, Habersham County [Ga.,] Dec[embe]r 25th 1845
Dear Sir, No event could have given the Democracy of Geo[rgia] more satisfaction, than your return to the Senate of the U.S.: but they at the same time, regret that your consent should have been

coupled with any conditions relative to any future position. This however was a matter for your own decission, and the newspaper version we have of the condition, may not be true.

Thinking men of all parties must agree, that the present crisis in our national affairs, requires the highest order of statesmanship, united with prudence & firmness. Our title to Oregon may be, not only the best extant, but perfect, but to assert and maintain that right by the sword at this time, may not be our best policy. Can we do it with our present Navy; & would we of the S[outh] not be hazarding too much. If we must fight, to which I am nothing loath, had we not better get ready first. John Bull will give us no child[']s play, now he is at peace with all Christendom, and against the cotton growing States all his energies will be directed.

We are looking with great anxiety for the closing scene of Annexation, & expected the constitution of Texas would have been acted upon, *at least,* during the second week of the session. I passed the greater part of last winter in Texas, and witnessed the efforts made by several talented gentlemen to arouse the masses on the question of annexation; and think the advocates of that great measure both here & there, more indebted to Gen[era]l [Thomas J.] Rusk for its consummation, than to any other one beyond the Sabine, he is a bold, talented, energetic man, and I am sure you would be pleased to see him in the Senate from the new State. In a late letter I received f[r]om him on the Subject, "he says It was not my good fortune in early life, to have the benefit of even an academick education and by the side of such men as Calhoun, [Henry] Clay & [Daniel] Webster, I should contrast badly." Notwithstanding his disinclination to engage in political life, I have no doubt but he will be elected to the Senate, and for the following reasons would be glad, you would (if you think it proper, and prudent, to do so) express some wish to him on the subject. He is a sincere admirer, & devoted friend of yours now & for many years past. He is I think, the most popular man in Texas & must retain a firm hold on the affections of the people, from his military services & other causes. His influence will not be confined to Texas proper, but to the other States when formed. His feelings are as they should be, truly American—in other words Southern. There will be no non slave holding States in Texas. Now you may have coupled your consent to return to the Senate, with the condition that your friends should never use your name in connexion with a higher office. Not one of your friends in twenty thousand signed the bond—& may protest against the condition—publick feeling & the state of the country may even wrest the decision of that question out of your hands & should they do so I would have Texas & Carolina move together. As to Georgia, she can never have rank or position until the Simon Smoothes die off.

I know you would be more profitably engaged than reading a hasty letter from me, but I could not resist the desire I felt to let you know how much your mountain friends in Geo[rgia] are gratified at your return to the Senate & none more so than your H[u]mb[le] S[er]v[an]t, Geo. D. Phillips.

ALS in ScCleA.

To T[homas] G. Clemson, Brussels

Washington, 26th Dec[embe]r 1845
We arrived here on the 20th Inst. and found your letter of Nov[embe]r 28th & Anna's of the 5th of the same month, and were much gratified to learn that you were all well & ["that you" *interlined*] had succeeded so well in negotiating a treaty & acquiring the respect & confidence of the Government to which you are accredited.

I find myself here under circumstances involving great responsibility. There is, I fear, great hazard of ["great responsibility" *canceled*] of [*sic*] war with England on the subject of Oregon. The question has become greatly complicated & the country, it seems, looks to me to avert the calamity of war. I shall not hesitate to ["meet" *canceled*] do my duty, be the responsibility what it may. If the peace of the country can be saved it shall be, if it can be by my exertions. The great point, as things now stand, is to prevent the adoption of the Resolution to give notice to terminate the Convention of joint occupancy. If that can be effected, & Great Britain should not become the aggressive party, time will be gained, when I hope the difference may be settled. If the Resolution should pass, I fear there will be no hope of maintaining peace.

We are all well & in comfortable quarters for the session. Mrs. [Floride Colhoun] Calhoun & [Martha] Cornelia [Calhoun] unite their love to you & Anna. Kiss the children for their Grandfather. Truly, J.C.C.

ALI in ScCleA; PEx in Jameson, ed., *Correspondence*, pp. 674–675. NOTE: This letter was written on the same paper as, and as a continuation of, Calhoun's letter to Clemson of 12/13.

365

From FERNANDO WOOD

New York [City,] Dec[embe]r 26 1845

Dear Sir, Enclosed I send a slip from the Journal of Commerce of this city. The two articles marked contain the sentiments of a very large majority of our business men. We feel much alarmed by the ill-timed and imprudent course of [Lewis] Cass [Senator from Mich.] and [William] Allen [Senator from Ohio]. We can see no necessity for forcing the country into a position from which there is no retreat and which makes *war* inevitable. We say do us justice on the Tariff question and England[']s ministry cannot be sustained by her people in hostilities on account of Oregon. Her people will think that the interests of the Hudson[']s Bay Comp[an]y are not paramount to those of her starving populace.

I need not add, all eyes are turned on you! Twenty times a day I am asked "What course will the great Calhoun take on the Oregon question?"

Politicans of all parties look to your sagacity—experience and far seeing wisdom to stand between the great interests of the country, and the Hotspurs who in a spirit of demagougism [*sic*] would destroy us as they ["have themselves" *interlined*].

We know that even popular sentiment cannot drive you from a position which in your heart you deem to be correct—and we also know that in your estimation the loud declamation of adventurers is not to be heeded when the calm, silent opinion of the indus-tr[ious?] and producing classes is antagonist to them.

My dear Sir as a friend allow me to recommend that in your course on this great and at present excitable question that [*sic*] you let the impetuous patriots who are bidding for the war party have "their say" for be assured "they have their day" *now*!

Moderation—*silence* and caution on your part will in a few months, when peaceful relations are restored and public sentiment sees its present folly, place you on higher ground than any living man can attain in this country. Excuse me when I add that J.C. Calhoun needs but to stand still and as sure as the day comes, so sure will '49 see him where his deserts long since should have placed him—*viz.* the chief magistrate of the confederacy. Your course in 1812 established fully your reputation as an advocate for war, when good cause called for it. No man can or does doubt your patriotism. It needs therefore no endorsement, or reitteration [*sic*].

The great speech [of 1/31/1843] on this Oregon question in

which "masterly inactivity" was recommended lives in our hearts and is our position.

Hoping you will excuse the liberty which an old and sincere friend thus takes, and believing it a duty to express my views freely and frankly on this important subject I remain, As ever Truly Yours &:, Fernando Wood.

ALS in ScCleA; PC in Jameson, ed., *Correspondence*, pp. 1065–1067.

Affidavit for Margaret Carlile, 12/27. "I hereby certify, Mr. Francis Carlile was well known to me in the early period of my life, when I resided in Abbevill[e] District South Carolina, & that I often heard my father and many others speak of him, as a brave officer & soldier in the war of the revolution, and never heard any one doubt of his being so." Calhoun's statement is appended to a letter by James L. Edwards, Commissioner of the Pension Office, dated one day earlier and addressed to R[euben] Chapman, [Representative from Ala.]. Both documents concern the Revolutionary pension application of Francis Carlile's widow, Margaret Carlile. ADS in DNA, RG 15 (Veterans Administration), Revolutionary War Pension and Bounty-Land Warrant Application Files, 1800–1900, W10576 (M-804:470, frames 407–408).

From J[OEL] R. POINSETT

White house, PeeDee
Georgetown, So. Ca.
December 27th 1845

My dear Sir, As it appears to me, that in the present aspect of our affairs with Great Britain, the only alternatives that remain are to maintain our rights by arms or to submit them to the decision of some friendly power; and perceiving that the latter is repudiated by our friends on the ground that the monarchs of Europe are prejudiced against us and will not deal fairly with us I have thought it might be in the interest of peace to intimate my belief, that the court of Russia might be safely trusted with the settlement of this question. The Emperor Alexander [I] frequently spoke to me on this subject. He advocated our claim to the 54° and proposed to enter into a treaty of mutual guarantee of the possessions of Russia and the United States to that limit.

These proposals I submitted to Mr. [James] Madison and Mr. [James] Monroe; but our possessions on the North west coast did not excite much interest, at that period. It is true they were made prior to the treaties concluded with Russia by the United States & Great Britain which secured those possessions to the former; but the policy of that power is unvarying and no doubt the views entertained by that government at that ["period" *changed to* "time"] are recorded in their college of foreign affairs and would govern it's decision. I have the honor to remain very respectfully Your ob[edien]t Serv[an]t, J.R. Poinsett.

ALS in ScCleA; variant PC in Jameson, ed., *Correspondence*, p. 1067.

Remarks on the Vice-President's power to appoint a substitute to preside over the Senate, 12/27. Vice-President [George M. Dallas] had left a letter asking that Ambrose H. Sevier of Ark. preside over the Senate for this day. Some Senators contended this was in keeping with the rules, others moved the election of a President Pro Tem. "Mr. Calhoun did not clearly recollect any similar case. The Secretary [of the Senate, Asbury Dickins] had been long here, and he (Mr. C.) would be glad to hear from him if there was any precedent." Later in the discussion, "Mr. Calhoun said that the rule of the Senate gave the Vice President the power to appoint a substitute. If there was any doubt, it was because the gentleman was not in the District [of Columbia]. He may be out of the city. Believing, however, that the rule contemplated that he may appoint a substitute for one day, he could not vote for the motion" to elect a President Pro Tem. From *Congressional Globe*, 29th Cong., 1st Sess., p. 96. Variant in the Washington, D.C., *Daily Union*, vol. I, no. 204 (December 27, 1845), p. 814.

Remarks on Oregon, 12/27. David R. Atchison of Missouri introduced resolutions to organize and defend Oregon as a U.S. Territory. "Mr. Calhoun stated that these resolutions were of great importance and required great deliberation. The Senate was now thin; and he would suggest to the Senator from Missouri to postpone their consideration until some day which might be fixed after the holydays." Later Calhoun "expressed a wish that the resolutions and the joint resolution of the Senator from Ohio [William Allen] for terminating the joint occupancy should be considered at the same time." (After further discussion, Atchison's resolutions were referred to the Committee on Foreign Relations.) From *Congressional Globe*, 29th Cong., 1st Sess., pp. 96–97. Variants in the Richmond,

Va., *Enquirer*, December 30, 1845, p. 3; the Washington, D.C., *Daily Union*, vol. I, no. 204 (December 27, 1845), p. 814; the Alexandria, D.C., *Gazette and Virginia Advertiser*, December 30, 1845, p. 2; the New Orleans, La., *Daily Picayune*, January 7, 1846, p. 2.

From FRANCIS WHARTON

Phil[adelphi]a, Dec. 27, 1845

My dear Sir, I wrote to you very hastily on Thursday [*sic*; 12/24, a Wednesday] on the subject of Mr. [George W.] Woodward[']s appointment [to the U.S. Supreme Court]. Since then, I learn that the object of attack is to be his supposed nativism. At the time of the Senatorial election [in 1844 in which Woodward was the defeated Democratic candidate] he addressed a letter to Mr. Hollingshead, one of the native delegation, in answer to enquiries which were then made of him as to his probable course on the naturalization question. He gave me, at the time, the letter, with the liberty to use it if necessary. I beg leave to deposit ["a copy of" *interlined*] it [*not found*] in your hands, as it may enable you to settle what may be a vexed question. Truly yours, Francis Wharton.

ALS in ScCleA. NOTE: An AEU by Calhoun reads "Relates to the app[ointmen]t of Judge Woodward."

To HENDRICK B. WRIGHT, [Wilkes-Barre, Pa.]

Washington, 28th Dec[embe]r 1845

My dear Sir, I could not read your very friendly & complementary [*sic*] letter of congratulation on my taking my seat again in the Senate, without the emotions, which the kind expressions you have been pleased to use, are calculated to excite, when coming from a friend. Indeed, the interest which seems to be so widely felt on the occasion, indicates a confidence in my integrity & patr[i]otism among my fellow citizens, that has made a deep & solemn impression on my mind. I feel to the full the responsibility under which it places me. I may not be able to meet the expectation of the country, but of one thing my friends may be assured, that no consideration, personal to myself, shall deter me from doing my duty. If peace can be honorably preserved, no efforts shall be wanting on my part to preserve it;

but if not, none shall be ["wanting" *interlined*] to carry the country through the mighty struggle, which must ensue. I shall know & regard nothing but my duty. With great respect yours truly, J.C. Calhoun.

ALS in Eugene S. Farley Library, Wilkes College, Wilkes-Barre, Pa. NOTE: An AEU by Wright reads "J.C. Calhoun Dec. 28, 1845, P[olitical?] Answ[ere]d."

From CH[ARLES] AUG[USTU]S DAVIS

New York [City,] 29 Dec[embe]r 1845
My D[ea]r Sir, I cannot express to you in language stronger than the fact would author[i]ze—the real gratification felt here and in all this quarter at your return to the Senate. And now let come what may I for one feel that we shall be kept on the right track and start right at any rate.

To make use of a familiar Rail road expression—it is very important to have good "switch tenders" otherwise the train might get on the wrong track and either "smash" or "be smash[e]d" or "back out"—either of which is not agre[e]able to passengers.

The fact of it being known here to day that you see nothing to alter your *original views* in regard to the Oregon Question—and which at the time I recollect met here entire approbation—has given great confidence to our security market and arrested its downward tendency. And were it not for other matters bearing on the money market irrespective entirely of Oregon & like subjects—we sh[oul]d see rates indicating an almost entire restoration of confidence. A considerable am[oun]t of State debt falling due at this period and paid off—will be remitted to Europe where it is own[e]d. But for threatened troubles it w[oul]d seek *reinvestments* ["here in U.S." *interlined*] in roads & other enterprizes. Capital is a timid character—and will starve itself and let its best neighbour starve too—if it is not free from alarm.

What has alarm[e]d me a little at the present time was the *possibility* that the manufacturing and mining interest might in the event of seeing a disposition to lessen their Profits (real or expected) by a reduction of the *protective feature* of the Tariff—incline to join in the War Cry—regarding "a maritime obstruction" about as good a tariff as they c[oul]d desire. Hence I was inclined to hope that for the present the moderation of the Tariff w[oul]d be confin[e]d to that feature which I regard no sound mind can object to—and that

370

is to do away with all *protective* duties on articles which being manufactured here under protective duties have become *Exports*—for then
it shows clearly that no further protection sh[oul]d be ask[e]d as
our manufacturers are able to compete abroad with their rivals where
our "protective duties" do not reach—and sh[oul]d be better able to
do so at home. Otherwise a protective duty is a downright monopoly and compells our own consumers to pay higher prices and profit
than the consumers in distant markets pay for the same articles.
This is the case now in respect to *Cotton goods* which are largely
exported & sh[oul]d no longer be *protected.* I am glad to see that
the Rail road system meets in you a hearty advocate—but it will drag
heavily under a duty of $25 p[e]r Ton whilst our Iron makers can't
furnish Iron enough for that special work (in addition to other demands[?]) to make a road of twenty miles in one year.

The least that Congress could do w[oul]d be to admit foreign
Iron free of duty for Rail roads which had begun before the law
was changed. For some of these roads are now like a House begun
under one contract & before the roof was on an "Ex Post facto" Law
as it were arrested its progress and leaves owner and contractor in
the condition of the House itself "ruinously exposed." With great
respect and high personal regard I am very truly Y[ou]r friend &
Ob[edien]t Ser[vant], Ch: Augs. Davis.

ALS in ScCleA.

From G[eorge] Bancroft, [Secretary of the Navy], 12/30. "In
reply to your letter of to day [*not found*] I have the honor to inform
you, that young Mr. [Wilson] Gunnegle was some time since appointed to the grade of Midshipmen." FC in DNA, RG 45 (Naval
Records), Miscellaneous Letters Sent by the Secretary of the Navy,
1798–1886, 35:467 (M-209:13).

REMARKS AND RESOLUTIONS ON OREGON

[In the Senate, December 30, 1845]
[*Edward A. Hannegan of Ind. introduced resolutions affirming that
all of the Oregon territory was the property of the U.S.; that "there
exists no power in this Government" to transfer any part of it to a
foreign power; and that the "surrender of any portion of the Territory" would be an "abandonment" of the "honor, character, and the
best interests of the American people." Hannegan moved that the*

371

Senate fix a day for the consideration of his resolutions. He withdrew his motion temporarily at the request of]

Mr. Calhoun, who stated that, without any design to oppose the motion, he was desirous to make a few remarks preliminary to offering certain resolutions which he had prepared, and which he proposed to submit as an amendment to the resolutions of the Senator from Indiana. Although he could not consent to give his support to the resolutions now under consideration he was glad that they had been brought forward. Whatever objections might be urged against them they were at least direct, open, and manly in their character. They denied in direct terms the authority of this Government to make a treaty by which any portion of the territory lying between latitudes 42° and 54°40′ should be transferred to any foreign Power, and denounced, as he understood them, by implication the proposition which had already been made by the President of the United States to settle the existing difficulty by adopting the parallel of the 49th degree of latitude. If, therefore, it shall appear that a majority of the Senate sustain these resolutions it will be clear that the question can only be settled by force of arms; and that no peace, should war be commenced between the two countries, can ever be obtained but by our dictation at the cannon's mouth. To vote on these resolutions, therefore, will draw a broad line which cannot be misunderstood between those members of the Senate who desire to settle the question by a resort to arms and those who are disposed to continue the pacific course of negotiation.

He was for a pacific course of procedure, for an adjustment of the question, if possible, by negotiation; and with these views and impressions he had prepared a set of resolutions directly opposite in their character to those of the Senator from Indiana, which he desired to submit with a request that they should be printed as an amendment to those resolutions. He would take this occasion to state what would be his course: he was for peace so long as peace can be preserved without a surrender of our national honor; for continued negotiation so long as there may be a possibility of an adjustment by negotiation; and if after every effort to preserve peace between the two countries shall have been exhausted war must ensue he desired that we should occupy a position in which the *onus* of a war would be thrown from our shoulders and be cast upon Great Britain.

He desired to express his approval of the course of the Administration in making under all the circumstances an offer to adopt the 49th degree as a boundary line. It was his sincere wish to continue to coöperate with the Executive. The Executive desires peace, and it was his wish to preserve peace so long as it can be honorably preserved. Whenever it shall be found that no effort which we can consistently with the honor and interests of the country interpose will avert the evil and that war must come[,] he would never be found in a position antagonistic to that which every honorable man must occupy. Even although the war should be the result of our own improper course[,] still when it shall appear that it cannot be averted he would stand by his country; but if war should come it will be no common war. While he would give every support to his country he would hold those responsible by whose rashness it had been provoked.

Whenever these propositions came up for discussion he hoped that they would be discussed in a becoming spirit and in the calmest manner; and if when its true grounds are clearly seen and understood we come to the conclusion that we can avoid war [he hoped] that we shall by our course invite a continuance of our peaceful relations; while, on the other hand, should we decide that a rupture of those peaceful relations is unavoidable, that we shall make wise and prompt preparation and enter into the contest with the united vigor and energy most likely to insure a successful issue.

He would conclude by offering the following resolutions as an amendment to the resolutions of the Senator from Indiana:

Strike out all after the word "resolved" and insert:

That the President of the United States has the power, by and with the advice and consent of the Senate, to make treaties, provided two thirds of the Senate present concur.

Resolved, That the power of making treaties embraces that of settling and fixing boundaries between the Territories and possessions of the United States and those of other Powers in cases of conflicting claims between them in reference to the same.

Resolved, That however clear their claims may be in their opinion to the country included within the parallels of 42° and 54°40′ north latitude, and extending from the Rocky mountains to the Pacific ocean, known as the Territory of Oregon, there now exists, and have long existed, conflicting claims to the possession of the same between them and Great Britain, the adjustment of which has been frequently the subject of negotiation between the respective Governments.

Resolved, therefore, That the President of the United States has rightfully the power under the Constitution, by and with the advice and consent of the Senate, provided that two thirds of the members present concur, to adjust by treaty the claims of the two countries to the said Territory by fixing a boundary between their respective possessions.

Resolved, That the President of the United States in renewing the offer in the spirit of peace and compromise, to establish the forty-ninth degree of north latitude as a line between the possessions of the two countries to the said Territory did not "abandon the honor, the character, or the best interests of the American people," or exceed the power vested in him by the Constitution to make treaties.

[*Hannegan said that there could be no objection to Calhoun's first two resolutions, but that the rest came into conflict with his own. He denied that he had any intention, directly or by implication, to censure the President.*]

Mr. Calhoun explained. He did not accuse the Senator of censuring the President. He had merely said that by implication they cast a censure on the President because he was willing to surrender a portion of the Territory of Oregon; but stated that such would be the effect of the resolutions.

[*Hannegan again denied that he intended any censure of the President. He continued at some length, contrasting the warlike attitude of some "peculiar friends of Texas" with their hesitancy on the question of Oregon. In his opinion, "Texas and Oregon were born the same instant" and nursed in the same cradle of the Democratic party.*]

Mr. Calhoun said he merely rose to allude to a single remark which applied to himself personally. The Senator from Indiana had endeavored to draw a contrast between his course upon the Texas question and his course upon this. The views which governed me upon that question govern me also upon this. I pursued in reference to Texas what I conceived to be the best course. If I acted boldly and promptly on that occasion it was because boldness and promptness were necessary to success. It was the golden opportunity; and one year's delay would have lost Texas to us forever. If I am for more deliberate measures on this occasion it is not because I am not a friend of Oregon. On the contrary, Oregon has no better friend than myself; there is no one who would venture more to save it. But it is asked why I do not pursue the same course of action as in regard to Texas. If the gentleman will refer to my remarks in 1843 he will find that the views which governed me then are the same with those which govern me now. I believe that precipitancy will lose you Oregon forever; no, not forever; but it will lose you Oregon in the first struggle, and then it will require another struggle hereafter when we become stronger to regain it.

I will not go into this question now; I am prepared when it comes up for discussion to show, if argument can show, that the principle involved in these resolutions so far from gaining Oregon will for the present lose every inch of that Territory; and it is on that account as much from the fear of losing Oregon as from the desire of avoiding war that I have proposed amendments to the Senator's resolutions. It is for this reason that I am opposed to the resolutions. Sir, if my advice had been pursued we should never have been involved in this controversy at all. I now act under circumstances not produced by myself, and I will do the best I can to save the Territory of Oregon, which I hold as valuable as the Senator from Indiana himself can do. If you institute a comparison between Oregon and Texas I would say that the former is as valuable to us as the latter, and I would as manfully defend it. If the Senator and myself disagree we disagree only as to the means of securing Oregon and not as to its importance. Sir, I intended to say nothing about censuring the President; I simply said that by implication a censure would be conveyed. I do not suppose that the Senator intends to reflect upon the President; but there can be no difference as far as the principle involved in this question is concerned between the circumstances when the proposition for a division at the forty-ninth parallel was made and now. It was as sensible then to make the offer as it would be now.

[*William H. Haywood, Jr., of N.C. was opposed to both Hannegan's and Calhoun's resolutions. He did not wish either to censure or to laud the President prior to negotiations. He wished to table the whole subject.*]

Mr. Calhoun disclaimed any intention of lauding the President; nor did he accuse the gentleman from Indiana of any intention to censure him. He had only said he approved the course of the President in offering the forty-ninth parallel. It was very certain, however, that the sense of the Senate when taken upon the original resolutions and the amendments would show very clearly the views entertained with reference to the settlement of the Oregon difficulty. Those who agreed with the honorable mover of the original resolutions would reject all further negotiations; those on the opposite side would be disposed to continue the negotiations. That was the whole amount of the matter; and his sole reason for moving the amendments was that the sense of the Senate might be fully taken.

[*A long discussion ensued among several Senators, during which*

Hannegan once more at length attacked what he regarded as the contrast of Calhoun's precipitancy in regard to Texas and his "wise and masterly inactivity" in regard to Oregon. This expression by Calhoun (in 1843) Hannegan claimed had "ruined Oregon." He suggested that Calhoun had designs on "some territory further south."]

Mr. Calhoun explained to show that he was no greater friend to the acquisition of territory in the South than in the North. Every Senator was perfectly acquainted with his sentiments relative to Cuba. While he was a member of Mr. Monroe's Cabinet he had always opposed any effort to disturb the possession of Cuba by Spain; he had ever since been opposed to it, and he would be the last man to make such a movement, believing that in its present state it is in the position which is best for all parties. Whenever the proper time came and the subject was brought up for discussion he expected to be able to show beyond all doubt that the same principle which governed him on the Texas question governed also his course in reference to Oregon. He was as much in favor of Oregon as the Senator from Indiana, and the only difference between them related to the mode by which the same object might be obtained.

He wished to make one or two remarks on what had fallen from the Senator from Delaware [John M. Clayton]. He could assure the Senator that he was as much averse to forcing the discussion as the Senator himself could be. But he thought the Senator was wrong in supposing this was an exercise of advisory power which should not be discussed openly. It was a question as to boundary; one on which we should not leave a doubt on the public mind. On this floor and in the face of the world we are called upon to pronounce our yea or nay, now that the question has been started here, or there may arise in the public mind a presumption that no treaty will be ratified here which does not conform to the particular views thrown out on one side of the Senate. The propositions which he had submitted by way of amendment were clearly not advisory in their character; therefore, although adverse to premature discussion, in order that no doubt should be left on the mind of the Executive now or hereafter as to his constitutional right of negotiating for territory[,] he desired a decision of the question. He thought this was still the more necessary because there was an evident tendency in the country to the opinions expressed by the Senator from Indiana, the effect of which might be to involve us in great difficulty. The resolutions which he had offered only assert that the President in offering to the British Government a settlement on the basis of the 49th parallel did not in any degree compromise the honor, dignity, or best interests of the country, and that it was a proper exercise of the powers confided to him by the Constitution. He hoped that a majority of the Senate would acquiesce in the propriety of settling this question by negotiation.

[*William Allen of Ohio thought the Senate ought to let the Executive act and not engage in "discussion upon barren propositions." Allen said further: "It was, therefore, with regret he heard from the authoritative lips of the preëminent Senator from South Carolina—for he would not stop at the term eminent in consideration of his acknowledged standing in the country—that any proposition introduced into that body might have the effect to divide the body in such a way as to make it appear that there were men there or anywhere in the country who desired war for the sake of war." Those who wished for all of Oregon were not to be considered "lovers of war" because they were ready to defend their country. He deplored the raising of "an artificial war-cry" that emanated from "the banks" and "the eastern States."*]

Mr. Calhoun was resolved that his sentiments should not be distorted. He made no war-cry. He said if the question could not be settled by treaty it may be settled by war. He would ask was there nothing in the resolutions of the Senator from Indiana (Mr. Hannegan) which if adopted would deny the power to settle the question by treaty? He denied the war-cry that was thus raised. He had done his duty manfully upon this and upon many other questions in which he had been concerned; and he would do his duty in relation to the peace of the country. He would meet the discussion in relation to the resolutions, and if they could not settle the question by treaty he was in favor of giving the twelve months' notice to maintain their rights; but if they did not settle the question by treaty he would go for the resolution of the Senator from Ohio (Mr. Allen) in relation to the twelve months' notice, and if that did not do he would go prepared to do his duty.

[*Debate continued at length between Hannegan and Haywood. Finally, the Senate adopted Hannegan's motion to lay his resolutions on the table "to be taken up hereafter."*]

From *Congressional Globe,* 29th Cong., 1st Sess., pp. 109–112. Variant reports in the Washington, D.C., *Daily Union,* vol. I, no. 206 (December 30, 1845), p. 822; the Washington, D.C., *Daily National Intelligencer,* December 31, 1845, pp. 1–2, and January 2, 1846, p. 1; the Alexandria, Va., *Gazette and Virginia Advertiser,* January 1, 1846, p. 2; the New York, N.Y., *Herald,* January 1, 1846, p. 3; the Philadelphia, Pa., *United States Gazette,* January 1 and 3, 1846, p. 1; the Richmond, Va., *Enquirer*, January 2, 1846, p. 1; the Charleston, S.C., *Mercury*, January 3 and 6, 1846, p. 2; the Charleston, S.C., *Courier*, January 3, 1846, p. 2; the Cincinnati, Ohio, *Daily Enquirer*, January 6, 1846, p. 2; the Pendleton, S.C., *Messenger*, January 9, 1846, pp. 2–3; the Greenville, S.C., *Mountaineer*, January 9, 1846, p. 4; the New Orleans, La., *Daily Picayune*, January 10, 1846, p. 2; the Natchez, Miss., *Mississippi Free Trader and Natchez Gazette*, January 15, 1846, p. 1; the Jackson, Miss., *Mississippian*, January 21, 1846, p. 2; the London, England, *Times*, February 4, 1846, p. 6. CC of resolutions in DNA, RG 46 (U.S. Senate), Territorial Papers, 29th Cong., 1st Sess., Oregon; PC of resolutions in *Senate Journal*, 29th Cong., 1st Sess., pp. 78–79; *Congressional Globe*, 29th Cong., 1st Sess., p. 351, and Appendix, p. 45.

From WILLIAM SLOAN

Pendleton, So[uth] Ca[rolina]
Dec[embe]r 30th 1845

Dear Sir, I have just returned from Dilonega [*sic*; Dahlonega, Ga.]. I was not able to see either of the Mr. Millners as they ware on a visit to their former residinces. On enquiry at the mint I was told there was no gold on deposit in your name; neither have they left an agent. I called on Mr. [Robert H.?] Moore who I was told could probably give me ["more" *canceled and* "some" *interlined*] information about them[.] He stated that they would be back by the 15th Jan[uar]y, that he was under the impression that they ware mining with tolerable Success, on all of your Lotts[,] that they spoke of some recent discovery on the Pounding mill branch below the shut-in.

The mint will receive a draft about the 1st Ja[nuar]y for his[?] current expenses. I authorised Mr. [William] Grisham the Clerk, and an old acquaintance to receive your tolls, from Mr. Millners, and forward me a draft for the amount, which I shall expect to receive, in the month of January, and shall so inform Mr. [Enoch B.] Benson[.]

I was assured while in Dilonega that there was a moovement by the Whigs of the State to reorganise on State right principals [*sic*], and nominate you for the Presidincy.

I consider [James F.] Cooper as an unfit person for the Presid[e]ncy of the Mint[.] He is a man of great levity of character, and bad moralls. He has established a dram shop in Dilonega as I understand he says for political purposes, and says he was advised to do so by [Representative Howell] Cobb & [Senator Walter T.] Colquitt. He is also in the habit of playing at games of hazard, which

378

in my opinion ought to be a fatal objection, to an officer having control, of publick and individual funds.

My feelings are indignant that an officer of this gover[n]ment should condicend to establish a dram shop, and the apology, that it was done for political purposes makes it still worse[.] I should like to see a change in the Presid[e]ncy and think that Do[cto]r [Joseph J.] Singleton, would be a suitable person for the place[.]

If I can be of any assistance to you during your absence, you may command my services[.] Very respectfully Your Ob[edien]t Servant, William Sloan.

ALS in ScU-SC, John C. Calhoun Papers.

From STEPHEN SMITH

Bodega[,] Upper California, Dec[embe]r 30th 1845

Dear Sir, In compliance with my promise I embrace this opportunity to lay before you in brief the results of the few observations which I have been able to make since my return here, respecting the natural resources and elements of prosperity of this Country. After all my detention and troubles in Mexico I arrived here on the 7th of August and found all things in my Establishment to my perfect satisfaction; and after making such arrangements as were necessary at this place, I proceeded to the Pueblo de los Angeles for the purpose of instituting an examination respecting the richness of the Gold Placer existing near that place. This examination occupied me something more than two months, and resulted in showing the gold washing not to be so good and profitable as I anticipated. There is gold dust to be found over a large tract of country in the vicinity of the Angeles, and also as I am informed, in many other parts of the Coast; and in some spots of small extent, it has been found *very rich*; so that some of the operatives made great wages for a short time in washing and fan[n]ing out the gold dust, and the statements of these few have made a great nois[e] in the Country; while many others have worked equally hard for months together and found nothing; or, in some cases, barely made a living. There can be no doubt however, that there is a[n] immense quantity of gold and other rich metals in the Country; for, in searching after some spots that might be rich enough in gold to pay well for *washing*; I have found various silver, gold and copper *mines*, which appear to be *very rich*, and are so situated as to be easily worked. As I have no means of essaying them here, I have sent samples of the ores to the City of Mexico to ascertain their value, and am now waiting the results. I have found in several places an abundant supply of rich iron ore, which, so far as I can judge appears to contain a large percentage of silver, and some of the veins are near the Sea Shore. I have also discovered a rich antimonial ore, which probably also contains plenty of silver; and the best indications of extensive bituminous coal mines exist here in all directions. Lead and quicksilver also, undoubtedly exist in the Country in abundance. They have already commenced working a rich copper mine within a mile of a good ship harbour on this Coast, and I have no doubt that many others could be found in that vicinity. We only want the Flag of the U.S. and a good lot of Yanke[e]s, and you would soon see the immense natural riches of the Country developed and her commerce in a flourishing condition. To see that Flag planted here would be most acceptable to the sons of Uncle Sam, and by no means repugnant to the native population. This, like the general government of Mexico is *very unstable* and the property of foreigners cannot by any means be considered secure. We hope and trust that on this account as also to protect the trade and the interests of our citizens residing here with their property, at least one American ship of war will be kept cruising on the Coast.

The soil of the Coast is rich and fertile, and with this climate of almost perpetual summer, it affords *immense advantages* for *grazing* and agriculture. The Cultivation of the grape is fast increasing and the this years crop is uncommonly fine. The licor and wine manufactured from the grape grown here will soon compete in quality with the best European, and may become an article of export. A few have commenced the Cotton planting, which has been found to yield uncommonly well.

From the accounts from Mexico we have been expecting a war between the U.S. and that republic, but from so long delay, we now begin to think it will blow over with a paper war.

Since my return to this Country my Steam Mills have gone on well and are now in full operation. The emigrants who left the U.S. last spring have arrived on this frontier to the number, as is reported of nearly one thousand.

For the best of reasons, as we are here within the power of the Mexican Government, you will please to Consider this letter strictly private and Confidential. I have Dear Sir the distinguished honor to remain Yours most truly and respectfully, Stephen Smith.

LS in ScCleA; PC in Jameson, ed., *Correspondence*, pp. 1067–1069. NOTE: An AEU by Calhoun reads "Mr. Smith of California."

To HENRIETTA F[RANCES] WHITNEY,
New Haven, Conn.

Senate Chamber, 30th Dec[embe]r 1845
My dear Madam, No one appreciates more highly the services rendered by your deceased husband [Eli Whitney] to the South & the whole Union ["than I do" *interlined*], but I am bound in candour to say, that I cannot encourage you to make application to Congress for remuneration for his services. As high as they are, I am of the impression, that Congress would not make any allowance. Indeed its power to do so under the Constitution may be well questioned. With great respect I am & &, J.C. Calhoun.

ALS in CtY, Sterling Library, Eli Whitney Papers.

From P[ATRICK] G. BUCHAN

Rochester N.Y., 31 Dec. 1845
My Dear Sir, I am perhaps taking an unwarrantable liberty in requesting a personal favor at your hands, considering that I have not the honor of a personal acquaintance with you & you may think I am presuming as a mere political friend, tho' one of your warmest political friends, in requesting you to interest yourself in my own private matters. Still, presuming on your kindness I have ventured to address you & ask your aid in reference to myself. But I ask not of course that you should do any thing for me by asking any favor in any quarter where your position should require you to stand aloof from all such intercession if such be your position.

I have seen today for the first time in the papers brought by today[']s mail that an act has been passed extending the laws of the U.S. over Texas, erecting the State into one judicial district & providing for the appo[intmen]t of a district Judge with a salary of $2000. I see also that the first term is to be held in Feb[ruar]y. For that office I wish to become a candidate & had I any idea that the bill would have passed so rapidly I would have applied before. I am afraid now it is too late. I may however be in time. I have just written a letter to the President [James K. Polk] on the subject requesting him to inform me if he has yet made any selection. If in time I will forward the strongest testimonials from our leading political friends here. I do not wish of course to be at that trouble if

I am already too late. I have been in the practice of the law here for the last 12 years & now hold the office of first (presiding) Judge of the Court of common pleas for this county & city which office I have held for the last two years.

You are aware that I was somewhat instrumental in giving an impulse to the Annexation question in the north here at a time when many of our party shrunk from the responsibility & that the effect of the somewhat celebrated meeting we had here in the very earliest stage of the agitation of that question had a strong tendency to lead the democracy here into a warm support of that measure.

Independent however of any political claims I can produce evidence satisfactory I believe of my fitness for the office, which I will do if I am in time as a candidate.

I write now of course in great haste & have only time respectfully to ask you if not inconsistent with any position which you hold in reference to the Executive to speak to him on my behalf or at least if he has not selected a candidate to ask him to suspend the selection until I can forward him satisfactory testimonials in my behalf.

I have been anxious for some years to change my residence to the South or South west & the appointment sought would be one congenial with my habits & pursuits & in a country where I would like to fix my residence.

Excuse the liberty I have taken & believe me to be with the highest respect & esteem, Yours very Sincerely, P.G. Buchan.

ALS in ScCleA. NOTE: An AEU by Calhoun reads "Mr. Buchan, desires a Judgeship in Texas."

From F[ITZWILLIAM] BYRDSALL

New York [City,] Dec[embe]r 31st 1845

Dear Sir, I cannot express the gratification I have derived from what I consider your truly patriotic exertions, in relation to the Oregon question, since your arrival in Washington. While I am one of those who go for the whole of that Region, because I beleive [*sic*] our claim is better founded than that of Great Britain, yet I, as a citizen of the U. States, desire no more territory than our rights clearly demand, and as yet, I see no necessity of ["precipating" *canceled and* "precipitating" *interlined*] two great Nations, if not all Christendom into war, before either our National rights or National honor require such a serious step to be taken. Your exertions to postpone the action of those whose personal ambition excites an infatuated desire for political capital, and who are anxious to appear before the people not only as patriots, but as champions of National honor, are properly appreciated by the majority of the people amongst whom the intelligence, patriotism and public virtue of the country exist as principles, and not as excitements. It seems almost talismanic, that in a few days, you have spread a feeling of confidence and peace over the Union, where previously there was every appearance, that the administration and Congress were involving the Oregon question between this country and England in such inextricable difficulties, as would cut off honorable negociation, and leave no other alternative but war, to involve the Nation in debt, destroy human life and property and subject the people to a high oppressive tariff.

War is the game of Kings and nobles—of monarchies and aristocracies. Peaceful annexation, not conquest is the natural Democratic policy. Our political Institutions will do more for us in this way, than armies and navies.

I learn with surprise the nomination of [George W.] Woodward to fill the vacancy in the U.S. Judiciary. He was in 1841 one of the worst partizans of the irrational principle of nativism, and advocated in the State convention of Pen[n]sylvania, the exclusion of all naturalized citizens from the right of suffrage in that State, who arrived in this country after the 4th July 1841. A man of his abilities with such prejudices, is unfit for the Judicial office and when considered in connection with the horrid scenes which took place in Philadelphia, his rejection by the Senate is due to him as a just retribution, as well as to the spirit of the age and our Institutions of Government. It is stated here, that he was nominated for the purpose of appeasing the [George M.] Dallas portion of the Democracy of Pen[n]sylvania. In our city here the offices of the U.S. have equally divided between the Van Burenites and the friends of Sec[retar]y [of War, William L.] Marcy as follows:

> V[an] B[uren]
> [Benjamin F.] Butler[,] District Attorney.
> [Michael] Hoffman[,] Naval officer.
> [Elijah] Purdy[,] Surveyor.
> Marcy
> Laurence [*sic*; Cornelius Van Wyck Lawrence,] Collector.
> [Robert H.] Morris[,] Post master.
> [Prosper M.] Wetmore[,] Navy Agent.

[Ely] Moore—[U.S.] Marshall—R[ichard] M. Johnson or neutral.

So much for cliqueism. The friends of State Rights—free trade and low duties, have had some havoc done amongst them officially, but the President patronizes their principles and measures, and that is their share of Executive patronage.

I can congratulate ["you" *interlined*] on the increase of your popularity amongst the people, with whom at no former time of your life were you so highly appreciated as now. For myself, I am as I was in the dark days of the Force Bill, your sincere friend on the ground of political principles and personal esteem, and as such have the honor to be your Ob[edien]t Ser[van]t, F. Byrdsall.

ALS in ScCleA.

From WHITEMARSH B. SEABROOK

Edisto Island, Dec. 31 '45
Dear Sir, Dr. [Robert W.] Gibbes, the Corresponding Sec[retary], has no doubt long since informed you that, at the late meeting of the State Agri[cultural] Soc[iety], you were unanimously chosen their Orator for December, '46. I hope, my dear Sir, that you will readily accede to our request, and thereby furnish further evidence of your disposition at all times and under all circumstances to promote the best interests of the State. To attain the end for which the Society was established, we need not only the moral aid, but the active practical efforts of our prominent men. I have laboured zealously in the cause of agricultural ["improvement" *interlined*] for the better part of my life, yet I have been able to effect so little that I am almost in despair. I earnestly entreat you therefore to come to our assistance, and contribute your mite on the altar of the public good. On the occasion of our next anniversary, it is expected, that delegates from several State Agricultural Societies will be present.

I request your opinion as to the probability of war. Is it possible that the matter in dispute ["between" *interlined*] the U.S. and ["England" *canceled*] G[reat] B[ritain] cannot be settled by negotiation? This is not my opinion, nor, as far as I can judge, is it the belief of the reflecting portion of either country. What course will the U.S. adopt at the expiration of the twelve month's notice? Send a fleet to Oregon to be seized by the enemy, or an army to perish in the wilderness? Last night I re-perused your speech of '43—I was glad to be reminded that you then viewed grants of land to settlers as casus belli. Every lover of peace is looking to your movements with intense interest. Shortly I presume your views on the absorbing question of the day will be unfolded.

Will the Compromise be restored? If not, will there be any material reduction of the Tariff? Respectfully yours, Whitemarsh B. Seabrook.

ALS in ScCleA.

[Varina Howell Davis's correspondence with Calhoun, 1845–1850.] In her biography of her husband, Jefferson Davis, Varina Howell Davis described her first meeting with and subsequent correspondence with Calhoun. She was first introduced to Calhoun at Vicksburg, Miss., on 11/18/1845 as Calhoun returned from the Memphis Convention. The two exchanged letters until Calhoun's death in 1850. Mrs. Davis stated that Calhoun's letters to her were "written as though to an intellectual equal. It was one of the sources of his power over the youth of the country that he assumed nothing except a universal, honest, co-intelligence between him and the world, and his conversation with a girl was on the same subjects as with a statesman." She also mentioned the fate of Calhoun's letters to her. "His letters were all lost during the war; but it was I and not posterity that sustained the misfortune, for his handwriting, though it looked neat, was almost indecipherable. I once sent him back his letter to read for me, and he responded, 'I know what I think on this subject, but cannot decipher what I wrote.'" From [Varina Howell Davis,] *Jefferson Davis, Ex-President of the Confederate States of America, A Memoir by his Wife* (New York: Belford Company, Publishers, 1890), 1:213–214.

From "A Looker on in Venice"

[*Ca.* late 1845?]

The writer of this, no matter for his name, is now as he has been for the last 20 years your sincere well wisher, and with an ardent desire that the time would come, when he [*one or two words canceled*] might stand forth your supporter for the Executive office; He has mourned over that unfortunate combination of circumstances which have held your claims in check since the affair of Mrs. [Peggy] Eaton in '29 which the Jesuit Mr. [Martin] Van Buren made use of to embroil you with Gen. [Andrew] Jackson. Your talents, experience, and eminent public services would place your claims to the Presidential Office in the first rank were the question referred to judicious and impartial men—but alas! for our Country a very different tribunal decides at the present day upon claims to political advancement, and we have before our eyes from day to day a melancholy proof of that fact.

In conversation not long since with a Gentleman in Washington City he spoke of names as probable candidates for the next Presidential term—yours was omitted, to which I called his attention, remarking your preeminent qualifications for the Office, and just claims greatly in advance of any he had mentioned. He replied—That is true Sir, and I would at once give my support to Mr. Calhoun for that station in preference to any man now living; I yield to no man in respect and attachment to Mr. Calhoun, and was there a prospect of success, I should not hesitate an instant in the course I would pursue; But Sir the time has gone by when any man of Mr. Calhoun[']s great intellectual attainments, matured experience, and above all—his decisive firm character to hope for elevation to the Presidential Office; He would indeed, *be President*—and that is unsuited to the objects and present organization of our politicians. Rely on it Sir, there exists at this time in the U. States a party, powerful—strictly united—well organised—who would oppose any man of Mr. Calhoun[']s character for the Presidency; they are of those who desire to possess and exert, "an influence behind the Throne greater than the Throne itself" and hence a second rate, or a third rate man in that Office would ["be" *interlined*] more agreeable to their views, because they might hope to control him. A man at the head of the Govern[men]t with mind to comprehend, intelligence and experience to direct, sagacity to perceive, and firmness to carry out the system of policy demanded by great national interests—is not a man for that party, and therefore Mr. Calhoun is not the man. Their President must be the mere stalking horse of the party, to be moulded to suit their will—and especially to bestow office according to the taste or wants of the party—and if need be—to become the scape Goat, and to bear whether to the mountain or the plain, the Sin of every folly the Government may commit—he must "take the responsibility" nolens volens whilst the managers remain intact.

Such is the melancholy picture held up to my view by one whose judgement, intelligence, and general intercourse with the active politicians of the present day, gives weight to his opinions, and many of the measures and appointments of the Administration shew forth most clearly the correctness of them—Appointments and efforts to appoint, that are doing their work with the great Democratic party of the U. States, however satisfactory they may be to the clique from whence they originated.

I am cheered however in the belief that a prospect has unexpectedly opened to you, pregnant of great good, and letting us see where you may take a position at once, formidable to your enemies, and at the same time made useful to yourself and the country. No doubt is now entertained of the Whigs having a majority in the next House of Representatives. You hold the balance in the Senate, and the lever of legislative Action must graduate and incline as you place the weight—your friends settle the question on whatever side they vote. Hence your position in Congress during the ensuing two Sessions is a more important one than has been occupied by any individual for 20 years—is more important than the position Mr. [Henry] Clay held in Feb[ruar]y 1825, for he governed but a single question. Your friends, (myself at least as one of them) feel confident that you will use your power for better purposes and more judiciously than did Mr. Clay. And it is my most fervent wish and hope, that circumstances may enable you so to use it, as to place you before the people in 1848 in that attitude, which the true and great interests of our Country call upon you to occupy, and which every patriot with brains enough for reflection will rejoice to see.

That you are not a favorite with the Administration is well understood; That the head of that Administration, mingles some fear with his antipathy, I have evidence to satisfy me. Why you should be an object of his dislike is not easily explained—his *declared* opinions being identical with your own on the three great questions of the day— Slavery—the Tariff—and Texas. Still he is no *friend* to use the mildest term. Can it be that he has imbibed some of the prejudices indulged against you, by the great Architect of *his fortunes?* Or that his favorite Statesman, and General par excellence, has transfused into his mind a portion of *that Love* which he bears you. Strange that this man should have gained such a hold on the confidence of the Chief Magistrate. A man whose diseased and restless ambition, goaded onwards by a vanity that knows no limit to its aspirations, and would crush or remove from its path whatsoever or whosoever appeared to obstruct its bold career—that he should exert such an influence is astonishing to everyone—not excepting his own Cabinet. Who should (without any extraordinary merit to justify the proceeding) desire to have clothed him with a power never before thought of in our Government, "Thane, Cawdor, Glamis all" Civil and Military—Generalissimo and Envoy Extraordinary, with no check upon the exercise of the powers with which he was invested—but that eventual Constitutional check to the Treaty making power residing in the Senate—Hudibrass eulogises one decked in a similar investiture,

"Mighty he was at both of these
And styled of war as well as peace"

defeated however in his great purpose, the ladder by which he looked to climb into that office, so long the cherished object of his hopes and his ambition—the Idol at whose shrine he had so long and so devoutly worshipped—to have the ladder so suddenly removed from under him—his views traversed—the veil torn aside, he stood forth like the prophet of Khorapan, exposed, defeated, the victim of ill weaved "vaulting ambition that o'erleaps itself" left to the only resource for venting the concentrated venom of a heart dark as Grebus, and unrelenting as the Grave—he will write a book.

My views are just, honorable and patriotic, they are such as I may avow before the world, and yet for the present I choose to preserve my incognito. A South Carolinian by birth, habits and Education, I now reside in a different State, where when the time arrives I may render you service. Should events transpire as I hope and trust they will, you shall know me, not only by my works, but in the flesh bodily—at the present time be satisfied in knowing me as, A looker on in Venice.

ALS (pseudonym) in ScCleA. NOTE: This letter is addressed to Calhoun at Greenville, S.C., and has no dateline or postmark.

From R[EBECCA] P[OWERS] TILLINGHAST

Paris [late 1845?]

Sir, As nothing can possibly be said, that might seem suitably to apologize for the great liberty here taken, I will only add, that I am mainly led to venture on this step, by the perfectness & extent of publick confidence, you possess, & by the unqualified sentiments of esteem & respect ever expressed toward you, by the honored person, whom I have had the unmitigated grief to survive. Well knowing, that the whole aim, of all your Sacrifices & efforts as a Statesman, have had for their sole object, the honor, & the well being of our Common Country, I am sure that you will not reject even from the humblest source, any suggestion that is founded on truth, & made under an irres[is]tibly deep conviction of its importance. In coming abroad, & passing through England, to the Continent it has unexpectedly Continually fallen in my way, to hear the affairs of America freely discussed, & with these was always in some way blended surprize & regret that the ambassador to Berlin, the Hon[orable Mr. [Henry] Wheaton, should resign, or that the nation should be deprived at such a moment! of such an officer & that by their own consent—A Scholar acquainted in the fullest manner, with the languages, the literature, history & politicks, of the whole of Europe—profoundly versed in the Science of government, & international law—wise, simple, honorable, firm, clear sighted holding always his high position as an American citizen, uninfluenced, respected & regarded by all ranks. Such is his name & character abroad & ["this is" *canceled*] reflects back upon his country with no little advantage. If this person should be *recalled*, after having given his choicest days, to the publick service, & in rearing a delicate family in foreign nations, spent perhaps his whole patrimony, it would seem a case for even history to note down as a national injustice. All this, Sir I know will be better thought in your own mind than by me, but there is another point & one which first gave me Courage to write, namely—the importance under such circumstances to himself, & his interesting family of being early delivered from the perplexity of suspense. May I dare then to ask of you, one word in reply addressed to Mrs. J.L. Tillinghast at Mr. Samuel Chace[,] Blodgets-Take[?] Street[,] Liverpool ["England" *interlined*] giving me the seeming probabilities, with regard to the reappointment of Mr. W[heaton] to his former post, or to any other place in which his distinguished talents & services can still promote the honor & advancement of his Country.

Having long had the honor of being slightly known to Mrs. Calhoun, & taking always a lively interest in persons, & things connected with your native State, which was once my home, I endeavour to find encouragement that the freedom here used will not be received without kindness. With unfeigned respect, R.P. Tillinghast, Paris.

ALS in ScCleA. NOTE: The writer of this letter was the widow of Joseph L. Tillinghast who had been Representative from R.I. during 1837–1843.

JANUARY 1-31
1846

◫

The 1st session of the 29th Congress continued. "Mr. Calhoun and family have removed to the St. Charles a few doors below the United States Hotel. The St. Charles is a new and elegant establishment on the European plan, under the modern northern style." So reported the Calhouns' hometown newspaper, quoting the Washington correspondent of the Charleston Courier (Pendleton, S.C., Messenger, January 9, 1846, p. 2).

Calhoun kept up his efforts to block precipitate Congressional action on giving notice to Great Britain of termination of joint occupancy of the vast Oregon territory. On January 14 he attacked the disingenuous policy of the ultra-expansionists: either prepare for war or prepare for compromise; don't pretend that John Bull can be bullied into peaceful submission. On January 26 he found it necessary to avow that what was coming to be called the Monroe Doctrine was not an excuse for a bellicose position on Oregon. He had, after all, been a member of the Cabinet which had vetted the doctrine. His bitter old Cabinet mate John Quincy Adams, now serving in the House from Massachusetts, did not agree, and was generally disgracing himself by demanding the sending of troops to Oregon. Adams, of course, saw war in the North as a way of breaking the South. His fellow abolitionist Joshua R. Giddings of Ohio joined in the war cry.

Calhoun's stand for peace was having effect. Not only the public speeches but also the meetings between anti-war Democrats and Whig members in which he was playing a leading role, as well as his good offices between the British Minister Pakenham and Secretary of State Buchanan who were now talking again. He wrote on January 29, in regard to his efforts: "Thus far, the effect has been a very considerable abatement of the war fever, both in Congress & the Country." This was not his opinion alone. Louis McLane, the American Minister in London, wrote Calhoun long and frequent letters about the situation. He evidently valued Calhoun's opinion as much or more than he did those of the President and Secretary of State.

The newspapers were full of Calhoun's praises, as was his correspondence from all over the Union. Wrote one Kentuckian on January 15: "You form an item of our Moral Capital as a people."

〖〗

From C[ornelius] C. Baldwin

Balcony Falls, Rockbridge Co[unty]
Va., Jan. 1st, 1846

Dear Sir: I would be greatly indebted to you for a copy of your correspondence with the British Minister in relation to Oregon, & also for copies of the official votes of Mr. [Daniel] Webster & Mr. [James] Buchanan on the same subject. I wish to investigate our *title* to Oregon, about which I have at present but very little accurate information. Assuming our title to be good, I heartily approve of the President's position on that subject, because I am satisfied that the only effect of it will be to arrest the serious attention of both countries, & prepare the way for a speedy & amicable & favourable adjustment of the controversy. I have not thought for a moment that there was the slightest ground to apprehend a hostile collision between G[reat] Britain & the U.S. about their conflicting claims to Oregon, or rather to the small portion of it actually in controversy between them. But perhaps I am wrong.

I would also thank you for copies of any speeches you may make in Congress, & of any interesting documents printed by the Senate for the information of the country.

About a year ago I had the honor to drop you a note, tendering my poor services to the government, if you had at your disposal, as Secretary of State, any *vacant* office in which I could be useful. As I never heard from you in reply I presumed that you had nothing at your command, & long since dismissed the subject entirely from my mind, without the least disappointment or chagrin at the unsuccessful result of the—perhaps, *presumptious*—application. I am now zealously & quite successfully engaged in cultivating & improving my little farm, & I am sure I am far happier in the quiet scenes of rural & domestic life, than I would be amidst all the splendor of the American metropolis. I have such an utter abhorrence of the whole tribe of vulgar & mercenary office-seekers that I regret having written to you, least you should suspect *me* of belonging to that predatory horde; which, thank God, *I do not.*

My intimate acquaintance, some years ago, with our new Senator, Judge [Isaac S.] Pennybacker, enables me to assure you that he is an ardent admirer & friend of yours—a fact I communicate with great pleasure in the hope that it may prepare the way for cordial personal relations between you. The Judge is not a very brilliant orator or a very profound statesman, but he is quite respectable. His mind is rather subtle than ["acute(,) bold &" *interlined*] comprehensive, & hence, I incline to think, he is better qualified for the bench than the Senate Chamber. I was sorry to see that he had mounted his legs almost as soon as he had entered the Senate—that he had tried his wings almost before he was fairly hatched—but I suppose he was actuated either by the promptings of patriotism, or by a very excusable desire to let the American people know who I.S. Pennybacker was—an inquiry which had been extensively & anxiously agitated. But how I run on. With great respect, C.C. Baldwin.

ALS in ScCleA.

From D[ixon] H. Lewis, *"Private"*

Capitol Hill, Jan. 1st 1846

My D[ea]r Sir, I have just seen [James A.] Black of your State, who sympathises more with the *war* feeling of the west, than any other Southern man. Black has just been among the extreme war men, & he says they are willing to forego *"notice"* & submit awhile to the joint occupation, if they could be assured that they might be allowed to pass their several Bills, to protect American Emigrants in Oregon, to the extent, that G. Britain has protected her own subjects—and if they could be further assured, that instead of pressing on them a Treaty for the 49th we would go in honestly & in good faith, for getting the whole or at least the desirable parts, including the Harbours on the Pacific. I told Black I thought such was in truth *your policy*, that you attached much more importance to the country, than I thought it deserved, & I believed your whole course was a sincere effort to get by peace[a]ble means & by time, what you could not hope to get by precipitation & war. He said he should see you in the morning about it & would also see the President [James K. Polk]. I told him it would be very desirable to see you both together if he could so arrange it—& to have [David R.] Atchison [Senator from Mo.] or some other of the coolest of the war men present at the interview. This suggestion struck him. Look out for him, & the proposition, & if you have time, say in *ten words* on paper, what you think of it. Y[ou]r friend, D.H. Lewis.

ALS in ScCleA. NOTE: This letter was addressed to Calhoun at the "U. States Senate, *By Jacob.*"

From L OUIS M CLANE, [U.S. Minister to Great Britain]

London, Jan. 2, 1845 [*sic*; 1846]

My dear Sir, The enclosed letter from Mr. [James] Wilson, the able conductor of the Oeconomist, and the well known author of some valuable [*one word altered to* "treatises"(?)] upon the corn laws, and free trade generally, I venture to enclose to you; and to ask the additional favor of being permitted to present Mr. [Alexander] Mackay to you.

You will no doubt find him sufficiently intelligent to give you very interesting information upon a subject at present so engrossing on both sides of the water; and it has not occurred to me that there could be any objection to afford you an opportunity of affording him such salutary advice as may best promote the interests of both countries. I remain, my dear Sir, with Sentiments of the highest esteem, Louis McLane.

[Enclosure]

James Wilson to Louis McLane, "American Embassy"

15 Hertford St. May Fair, Jan[uar]y 2, 1846

My dear Sir: Mr. Mackay, the gent[lema]n of whom I spoke to you yesterday goes out to Washington by the present packet for the purpose of devoting his attention to the discussions on the Tariff in Congress; and of furnishing such reports as will keep us best informed on the progress of that question, in order that we may judge what measures or means we can use on this side to aid the efforts of those in America who in Common with ourselves are above all things ["so" *canceled*] desireous to see a perfectly free and unrestricted intercourse between the United States and this Country, as the best and most effective means of develloping the resources of ["t"(?) *canceled*] each, and of uniting the two greatest countries in the world, by ["one" *canceled and* "the" *interlined*] surest[?] bonds of mutual and reciprocal advantages and good offices.

I will feel greatly obliged if you will give him a letter to some gentleman at Washington who can give him good advice as to the best means he can use to accomplish the object in view. I am my dear Sir Yours very truly, James Wilson.

ALS with En in ScCleA. NOTE: James Wilson (1805–1860), a British politician, economist, and free trade advocate, was the founder and editor of *The Economist*. Alexander Mackay (1808–1852) was a Scottish journalist and author of *The Western World; Or, Travels in the United States in 1846–47*, a three-volume work published in London in 1849.

From CHA[RLE]S H. POND

Milford (Con[n].) Jan[uar]y 2d 1846
Dear Sir, With a vast many others I rejoice to see you again in public life. I was sadly disappointed that you was not one of President [James K.] Polk's cabinet; for as far as I could see I thought that you would be invited as a matter of course. And I know not why you was not invited, *only,* on the ground that the President's cabinet was to contain no prominent candidate for the *"succession."* If he has fully carried out this plan, so be it—time will show. But be this as it may, I thought that you deserved an invitation & I think so still. Other counsels, however, prevailed. My motto is—never dispair!

And now your friends are divided somewhat on the point whether you should have remained at home or come to the Senate. Some say that when Gen[era]l [Andrew] Jackson knew that he was a candidate he left the Senate & went into private life. But circumstances alter cases. The successful General whose reputation was chiefly military & whose views on subjects could be as well expressed by friendly committees as by himself might go to his farm & repose on his laurels. But a man who is full of the elements of eminent statesmanship & possesses a brilliant & controlling eloquence may safely appear "in propria persona."

In a retrospect of many years I do not remember an instance where a man has returned to public life in more favorable circumstances than yourself. Your name & fame spread over our country; Texas, whose entrance into the union was mainly prepared by you, has come in by acclamation & the resulting benefits will be felt in all this region; & the state of the Oregon question is such that your course will decide whether we are to have peace or war. With thousands of others I rejoice to see by your "Resolutions" that your voice is still for peace—an honorable peace of course—& that this vexed question, as soon as practicable, will be settled on terms which will preserve the rights & dignity of our country; or ["that" *interlined*] it will be honorably postponed. You know whether this subject can be soon finished; or whether by a "wise & masterly" policy it will take such a course as to have a controlling influence for two or three years to come. You know that Texas made the present President. Cannot Oregon & California mainly make the next? I have attentively read what you said on offering your amendment to Mr. [Edward A.] Hannegan's "Resolutions" & I expect to read many more of your sayings when the subject is again discussed. It is plain that the Western members are enthusiantic [*sic*] on that matter & will talk long & loud about it, to their own popularity & to the gratification of their constituents. And whoever undervalues Oregon, or consents that England shall have any more of it than can be kept & peace maintained, will be no great favorite in the West. Our rights must be maintained & the West will be heard: yet it is very evident to my mind that we & England should not go to war for Oregon. But as it is the great question of the day it should be treated with much circumspection.

When the Tariff is to be modified I hope that you will so speak as to make it evident that you oppose direct taxation; favor a tariff mode of raising revenue; are opposed to horizontal duties; & favor discrimination towards American industry within the revenue standard. I believe that your real views about a tariff are misunderstood in New England & the middle States, & misrepresented to your injury. Justice to your views of a tariff requires that your position be frankly stated. Do not all *now* agree that revenue is to be raised by a tariff; & that agriculture & commerce are to be cared for as ["well" *interlined*] as manufactures? Then why not say so distinctly? Nothing but plain truth from your own lips is wanted to place this matter just right. This would work a good change.

While you are smiling at my crude suggestions, I pray you to award me kind & good intentions, & believe that I have a lively interest in your prosperity. And what can any one do more than to do all he can under existing circumstances?

As there are some of the ablest whig champions in the Senate the State right democratic republican phalanx will expect a great deal from you.

Were it one day earlier I should certainly, wish a "happy New Year" to you & yours.

I should like to have your views on matters & things & the prospect before us. I remain, dear Sir, very truly Your old friend, Chas. H. Pond.

ALS in ScCleA. NOTE: An AEU by Calhoun reads "Mr. Pond. Approves my course on Oregon."

From J[OHN] S. SKINNER

New-York City Hotel, 2 Jan[uar]y 1846
My dear Sir, I may call it a sense of duty to you, as well as of common patriotism, that impels me to say, that in a course of observation of public men and measures, neither brief nor listless—I have never known any act of public servants, in a great emergency, to be more widely or *gratefully* approved, than ["the" *altered to* "your"] stand, and that of your associates, on *the Oregon question.*

You are not to judge of public sentiment alone by what may be said in the papers, more especially ["of" *altered to* "in"] mere *party* papers—the current of approbation runs deep & quietly, while, at all times, those who are for *war,* and for all its chances of preferment and plunder; will ever be *noisy.* But rely on it Sir the mass of all who are most worthy of heed and of influence rejoice whether in town or country, Merchant or Farmers, that in view of your duty you should have deemed it imperative to throw, at all hazards, the weight of your opinion and character *into the scale of peace.* Pursuing your policy, we have everything to gain—certain accumulation of all the elements of wealth & power & moral influence while the most fertile imagination has not yet realised the certain evils—and yet less the *uncertain issues of war.* Save us then my dear Sir, you and your friends, from that dire calamity—let us go on, and grow on, prospering and to prosper—free alike from that ["arrogant" *altered to* "arrogance"] which is so apt to be the concomitant of power, and from ["that" *altered to* "all"] stain of *real* dishonor, which destroys the sense of self respect at the same time that it invites aggression, and you will deserve and receive the benedictions of all *true* patriots now and hereafter. Excuse me I pray you for this freedom. I need not say more. I could not say less. I took my pen, only that you might learn, from at least one friend honestly and frankly that the course of yourself & those who act with you has been, so far, hailed with joyous approval by this community.

Driven by an despotic exercise of power, [*asterisk*: "when it was known that I had retrenched the expenses of a single Bureau more than $150,000 in four years"; "which" *altered to* "such" *and* "as" *interlined*] the Framers of the Constitution vainly imagined would be followed by Impeachment—to seek my bread here among strangers—I find it by devoting all my time ["in a manner most congenial to my feelings" *interlined*] to the management of a journal dedicated to that great interest of the country which is most plunder'd in peace, and suffers most in war—And I should be basely derelict to my duty, if I did not raise my feeble voice against precipitating a state of things which can only benefit the unproductive[,] the idle and the profligate. I rejoice to learn thro a common friend that you have ["were" *canceled and* "been" *interlined*] appointed to deliver the next annual address to the South Carolina Agricultural Society & hope it will not be deemed amiss that I should thereupon congratulate the Planting interest, in the columns of the *Farmers Library.* Your friend & ob[edien]t Ser[vant,] J.S. Skinner.

ALS in ScCleA. NOTE: Skinner (1788–1851) had previously been the publisher of *The American Farmer* and *The American Turf Register and Sporting Magazine* at Baltimore. Recently he had been removed by Polk from his post as an Assistant Postmaster General of the U.S.

From B[ARTHOLOMEW] R. CARROLL

Columbia, Jan. 3d, [18]46

Dear Sir, When I last had the honor of a correspondence with you, it was on a subject personal to myself. The kind interest you then evinced in my behalf, has made me your debtor ever since. You may have perceived, that a year ago, I became part proprietor and editor of the [Columbia] South Carolinian; and that instead of leaving the State, as I contemplated when I wrote to you, I have cast my anchor on our beloved soil. If your time has permitted you to read our paper I trust its tone has satisfied you. Our task however has been one of no little difficulty. In most instances, we have been compelled to make up our minds and express ourselves upon ["highly important questions" *interlined*], almost in the dark. In a word we have been compelled to speak for our party in Washington, in many cases very much at venture. Nor have we had at home, any rudder by which to guide ourselves. However safely we may have floated along heretofore, it is our impression that there are dangers ahead, and we ought to be apprised of them. In a word that we should know what sails to unfurl, and for what harbors to make. Our politics it is needless to say, have been in the same school with your own—after your teachings have we followed. Nor have we had cause to differ with you except in a single instance[,] viz[.,] that of giving the election of electors to the people. With great reluctance we have expressed our editorial dissent from ["you;" *interlined*] as much because we had previously committed ourselves on the subject, as because, we have not been convinced by your late exposition on the subject.

Individually I have not been able to give my hearty assent to your views in relation to the improvement of the Mississippi &c. I still think that the States thereupon bordering, could procure the assent of Congress to ["unite" *canceled*] their union for the purpose contemplated; and the great trade and wealth and population of that section of country only proves its great ability to render such union profitable and desireable. This however is only my individual opinion. You will perceive that our editorial, assented to your views, *in toto*. For this you are indebted to the convictions of my coeditor Col. [Adam G.] Summer. I express to you my individual dissent, not that the policy involved in your plan is not excellent; (perhaps the very best which wisdom could invent) but because, I believe it stretches the ligatures of the constitution too much. I am doubtful and doubting and wish to be convinced. Without conviction I can neither write with strength nor beauty[?].

It is because I know you love honesty and frankness, that I have ventured to trespass so much upon your time. Upon all other questions, then, other than those indicated above, we agree with you most cordially; nor would we have you for a moment believe that a difference on those points could separate us from your support. You have been too long tried, to leave us to doubt, that in following you we could either go wrong, or see the nation retarded in its career of grateness [*sic*] and happiness. May we rely then upon your confidence in us; and beg that at your earliest convenience; (and indeed, whenever you deem it necessary, [)] you would mark out such a map for our direction, as may at least show us some of the way, it is prudent for us to travel. You will at once appreciate the obligation, under which you will place us when we assure you we are absolutely in want of such an index. By informing us from time to time what is going on at Washington—When to wait events—and when to take stand in advance of them, you will do us an essential service, which you shall never find us backward to repay in any manner you may indicate. Pardon the liberty of this letter; and believe me Honored Sir Y[ou]r very ob[edien]t ser[van]t &c &c, B.R. Carroll.

P.S. Inclosed I send you two editorials I penned last summer. As you may not have met with them, in looking over other papers of more interest than ours; and as some of your friends have complimented the articles as a very just appreciation of some of the points of your character, You will pardon my vanity in thinking you may take pleasure in reading them.

ALS in ScCleA.

From P. Gwinner

Philad[elphi]a, Jan[uar]y 3d 1846

Dear Sir, On my return to the City after an absence of ten days, I found quite a sensation on the Subject of your position in the Senate in relation to Oregon, & I am gratified to say, ["that" *interlined*] your views have met the approbation of the honest, intelligent & Patriotic of all parties. The grogshop politicians with a few demagogies brawl[?] out for the whole of Oregon or none. The [Daily] Keystone ["K" *canceled*] paper under the Control of Mr. [George M.] Dallas & his friends this morning denounce your course. I send you the paper of this morning. The [James] Buchanan papers have not yet come out. I did expect the first attack from that quarter, as they are exceedingly sensative on meeting with what they consider a rival to their idol, in public estimation. I nevever [*sic*] witness to sudden a change [*sic*] in ["part"(?) *canceled*] the public mind after the receipt of your Resolutions, which had the effect to dissipate all apprehensions of war, which Gen[era]l Gass['s] [that is, Lewis Cass's] (as he is called) war speech produced. There is quite a sensation on the Subject of the Confirmations. [George W.] Woodward is no doubt one of Buchanan[']s men, so are all with one exception appointed to office here. [John] Davis the Surveyor & his Deputy [John W.] Forney, [Postmaster George F.] Lehman, [Henry] Welch all rece[ive]d their appointments as I very [much] believe through the Corrupt influence of Buchanan. ["His" *altered to* "The"] Collector [Henry Horn] has appointed the exclusive friends of Mr. Dallas, which has caused quite a bad feeling in the Democratic ranks in the City & County. I have a high regard for Mr. Dallas & am upon Social terms with him—but do not believe he can ever reach the height of his ambition. If the whole of the nominations could be defeated, it would prost[r]ate Buchanan, ["who" *canceled*] or at least break up his organization, in this section of the State. He has purchased every eight by ten in the interior, by subscribing ["for" *altered to* "to"] them, & franking dockuments to the editors, he has even neutralised the Enquirer here ["with Sever" *canceled*] as well as several other Whig papers in this State. I sent you several papers to Fort Hill during the Summer, which I presume you have received. Dr. [Joel B.] Sutherland [former Representative from Pa.] this morning said he expects to go on to Washington in a few days. He desires me to accompany him, which I will do in case I can make my arrangements. Excuse this hasty scrawl & believe me very Respectfully your h[um]ble S[er]v[an]t, P. Gwinner.

ALS in ScCleA.

From DANIEL T. JENKS

Philadelphia, January 3rd 1845 [*sic*; 1846] My Dear Sir, Haveing for a long time, admired your public and private character and haveing very recently, been if possible still more delighted, with your Senitorial course upon the subject of Oregon, I thought I could not allow the opportunity of expressing my sentiments in relation to you, to pass by without sending this line of my approbation.

It may not be important to have the sanction of an individual like myself—But still I can assure you that I am a Democrat of the old Jefferson school, who have never wavoured in my political career. You may be asscribed by some carping and snarling *Editors, of a little penny press,* of little or no standing in the community, but you may rely upon it, that the great body of the people, warmly applaud your course. I thought, proper to say thus much, because a public man, especially one distinguished like yourself, ought to be thanked both publicly and privately, for noble acts of patriotism. Respectfully I remain Yours truly, Daniel T. Jenks.

P.S. Pleas[e] excuse me, for the freedom of addressing you, being an entire stranger in person. D.T.J.

ALS in ScCleA. NOTE: An AEU by Calhoun reads "Mr. Jenks approbates my course in reference to Oregon."

From Jos[eph] W. Lesesne

Mobile, January 3d 1845 [*sic*; 1846]

Dear Sir, I received a letter yesterday from our friend Mr. [Franklin H.] Elmore and write you at his request. I think he is right in esteeming the Message [of President James K. Polk to Congress] as a universally popular document; and I think no man can help feeling that for the position assumed on the subject of the Tariff Mr. Polk deserves infinite credit. It is the first time that any President has dared to put this question upon principle and to commit his own and the fate of his administration to a bold and manly denunciation of the "Protective system" properly so called.

With regard to Oregon, I think the feeling of the more discreet part of the community, is that the temper of the Message and of the Correspondence is not free from exception; but you know that in such conjunctures there is a generous and patriotic feeling more than sufficient to apologise for an occasional error or loss of temper. The discussion in Congress, and particularly [Lewis] Cass' speech has I think struck every one as most injudicious and got up in wretched taste; and I have, as I think, all sober minded men have, misgivings that the Negotiation has not been conducted on our side in that high minded and dignified spirit demanded by the Christian standard of an age that abhors war and loves peace. Still the universal feeling is to sustain the president, and I do not believe that any movement looking to less than the 49th degree & the exclusive navigation of the Columbia [River] would receive any popular countenance.

Would not Great Brittain [*sic*] accept the proposition, nay surrender the whole of Oregon, for a Treaty admitting her manufactures at low rates of duty for 25 years. I told Mr. Elmore that I thought the course of events had placed you and Mr. [Daniel] Webster in a favorable position towards each other and towards the Country for thinking of such a measure, and that perhaps the Negotiation might be renewed on such a ["ground"(?) *canceled and* "basis" *interlined*]—but this is merely a stray thought and doubtless every thing that could give a peaceful turn to the matter has long since occurred to you. I think however the ["enlightened" *interlined*] spirit of the times requires that the intercourse of nations should be settled upon liberal terms in which each admits the blessings of an interchange of commodities as nearly approaching to entire freedom as possible. Such a measure between Brittain and the United States would be the proudest monument of modern times. It would render Peace between the two Countries perpetual, and as an example would do much to preserve the peace of the world. Certainly New England would greatly prefer to have her Industry regulated by some permanent measure of this kind which would place it above the contingencies that must always attend partial legislation.

No one here desires War, and no one believes, with one or two exceptions, that war will occur. Poeple [*sic*] generally think that it would be a disgrace to both countries to go to war upon such a theme—and that the time has gone by when the point of honor is likely to embroil Christian states who have so much at stake as the two nations in question. This I find is the feeling of the intelligent merchants, but I think it is indulged to an unreasonable degree, for really I do not see how England can accept of our proposition without a clear "back out:" and I do not think the Duke of Wellington is the man to put his country in a position to suffer a taunt of this kind.

I need not tell you, my dear Sir, that in the course which Mr. Elmore indicates as that which you have marked out for yourself, you will receive from your friends here the same cordial, firm and enthusiastic support, they have ever been ready to yield you. We know no half way measures here and leave every thing to your judgement and patriotism, resting in the confident assurance, that it will, as it always has done, look far forwards and lead us rightly on. Unfortunately, we have no paper likely to give us much aid, in any contingency. "The Register" is incurably "Old hunker"—and though Mr. [Thaddeus] Sanford does not feel unkindly his coadjutor [Samuel F. Wilson] does, and his silence is all that we could even hope for. If things take a turn that seem imperiously to demand it we must try to revive "the Tribune"; but if we do we must receive pecuniary aid from some other quarter than Alabama. While you were on your visit to the West I got a good many useful things in Sanford's paper, but recently Wilson the real Editor has returned and I can do nothing more in this way. Should events make it proper that you should support the administration warmly, I presume, even among the Hunkers you will receive for the time praise enough— but you know the Genus and how little dependence is to be placed in them.

Our friend Mr. [John A.] Campbell thinks that the Oregon negotiation has been managed in bad temper and bad judgement on our side. I suspect so too, but this is certainly not the general feeling. We shall always be glad to hear from you and I repeat *in any emergency* you may rely upon us as second to none who call themselves your friends. For all within our power and ability you may depend upon us. Very truly your friend & ser[van]t, Jos. W. Lesesne.

ALS in ScCleA.

From L[OUIS] McLANE, [U.S. Minister to Great Britain]

London, 3 January 1845 [*sic*; 1846]

My dear Sir, With my sincere congratulation upon your return to the Public Councils at a crisis so full of interest, I venture, in such confidence as my position imposes and as I doubt not you will properly appreciate, to add some observations upon a topic not second in importance to any you will be called to deal with.

By the present Steamer I send you three impressions of the "*Times*" newspaper, for the sake of the articles concerning our relations with this Country. The "*Times*," though not favorable to the Premier [Sir Robert Peel], and the Ministry generally, is supposed to be on better terms with the Foreign Office, and, if not enjoying its confidence, certainly not disposed to embarrass its policy; and it may not be too much, therefore, to regard the *leading article* in the paper of *today*, ["as" *altered to* "in"] some sort, as a feeler.

I need not tell you that the recent proceedings at Washington, the ["manly, patriotic" *interlined*] attitude assumed by the Message, and the support it will doubtless receive from Congress place our affairs with G[reat] B[ritain] in a crisis, requiring the best sense and the best temper to manage. Events, to me altogether unexpected, have left me little else to do ["here" *interlined*] than to preserve a good Disposition and keep down a bad temper on this side, and I have not been altogether unsuccessful in the discharge of this duty. The government here ["were" *altered to* "was"] prepared for [*one word canceled*] quite as strong a paper as the message, ["and that paper" *canceled and* "which" *interlined*] with the documents accompanying it have not only inspired a higher respect for our Statesmen, but have [*one word canceled and* "served" *interlined*] to enlighten the public here as to our title, to repress a warlike disposition, and encourage the hope of ultimate peace. If we, on our side, reasonably use this advantage we may preserve the peace of the world, without any sacrifice of honor. I believe too the Ministry are prepared for the carrying out by Congress of the recommendations in the Message, and will not consider that, unless they be exceeded or something should arise in some other quarter, as inconsistent with ["the" *canceled*] existing Treaties, or as increasing present difficulties. Indeed Lord Aberdeen ["freely said" *altered to* "frankly admitted"] as ["much as" *canceled*] much; and said that it might be of an advantage in bringing the affair to a definite form, & that during the year which would be allowed for terminating the joint occupation, he entertained a strong hope, that some means would be found of avoiding ultimate difficulty.

He was disappointed and mortified at the rejection by Mr. Packenham [*sic*; Richard Pakenham], without sending it here, of the proposition directed by the President, and I have reason to know that Mr. Packenham's [*one word canceled*] conduct in this respect, has been entirely disapproved. If, as was expected, he had sent the proposition to his government, before finally disposing ["of" *interlined*] it, I have great reason to believe that, if it had not been accepted, it would have led to some modifications which, under the then aspect of the affair, might have been satisfactory to our government. Indeed, if the President had not withdrawn it, Lord Aberdeen, I have very little doubt, would have censured Mr. Packenham for his course, and proceeded to deal with it as though it had not been rejected at Washington.

Although better prepared for war than they have ever been at any antecedent period, this government is, I am persuaded, sincerely desirous of ["mak(?) maintaining" *canceled*] peace, and, short of the point of honor, will make great concessions to maintain it. One of their difficulties, is in agreeing now, especially after the message, to offering, without any modification, what they have rejected before, and another is, that the obligation of makeing some adequate provision for the rights of the Hudson's Bay Company is pressed upon them more pertinaciously than ever. Indeed, they contend, and not without ["some" *interlined*] force, that even if the title should be conceded to be in the United States to the 49th or any other parallel, any partition of the territory, after so long a joint occupancy, could only be made on the basis of some regard to interests which had grown up under the joint occupation. And so well persuaded am I of the magnitude which this consideration has acquired, that if I had been dealing with the subject with more latitude I would have treated it as an important element; & so I think it will have to be treated, sooner or later.

It is very certain, I think, that this government has determined, ["fo" *canceled and* "in" *interlined*] the present ["to propose" *canceled*] state of the negotiation, if I may so speak, to propose *arbitration*, and that an offer will no doubt have actually been made before you receive this letter. Their ultimate course will materially depend upon the manner in which this offer is received. I have always supposed that arbitration would ["be" *interlined*] the most difficult ["and unpopular" *interlined*] mode our government could adopt; and have uniformly discouraged a repetition of the offer. I doubt, after all I have said, if Lord A[berdeen] can have the remotest hope that the offer *will* be accepted; and I rather think that a principal object in making it is to provide the means of escape from the dilemma in which Mr. Packenham's conduct has placed them, and of standing better before the world, if a rupture should, unhappily prove unavoidable. If the offer of arbitration should be rejected upon the ground on which *you* declined it, which Lord A[berdeen] considers as pacific, to wit, that the question is susceptible of ["adjustment by" *interlined*] negotiation, they will then proceed to offer new propositions, &, in that way, reopen the negotiation. If it be rejected on other grounds, and in a way to forbid a further attempt at negotiation by this government, they almost say as much that, they could only view that course as evidence of a determination upon the part of the U.S. to lead to hostilities, and act accordingly. ["How, they have not intimated." *interlined*] Of course, my communications with the Department of State upon all these heads have been more in detail than I could pretend to go into here.

Since the rejection of the proposition by Mr. Packenham my situation here has been both critical and delicate. ["I could neither invite nor encourage a resumption of the negotiation." *interlined*] If I had been left entirely unrestricted, I could informally have acted with some efficiency, and, without committing *any* one, ["have" *interlined*] not only ["materially" *interlined*] strengthened the position of my own government, but ["have" *canceled*] acquired by no means an uncertain knowledge of the terms upon which this government would be willing ultimately to settle. My relations with the present Ministry, and especially with Lord Aberdeen, combined with the manly sincerity and straightforwardness ["of" *canceled and* "and" *interlined*] love of peace of that Minister, would have made this not difficult. I am obliged ["perhaps erroneously" *interlined*] to consider my situation too restricted and too delicate, ["however," *interlined*] for the attempt; and it is also quite natural that the great inequality between me ["acting" *interlined*] altogether ["unofficially," *canceled and then interlined*] and the Foreign Secretary who *could* not if he *would* assume that character, should prevent me, in the present posture of the affair, from rendering any very efficient service, or from obtaining any very satisfactory information.

With such means of information as I possess, however, I ["ha" *canceled*] entertain a strong conviction that the question might have been, and may yet be settled upon the *basis* of the 49th parallel, or, perhaps, upon a more northern line. ["The" *canceled and* "Such" *interlined*] modifications, however, as would ["probably" *interlined*] ensure the whole of Quadra's Island to G[reat] B[ritain], and, to the Hudson's Bay Co[mpan]y, a continuance of their present advantages for some fifteen or twenty years, might be insisted upon & expected. The extension of the 49th parallel to the Straits of Fuca, & thence by the middle of those straits to the ocean would, I have little doubt, accomplish the fact; and the right of navigating the Columbia River in parts in which it is navigable for a further length of time would I rather imagine accomplish the other; and these I think are the elements which will be of the greatest importance in the future attempts at settlement. You will, of course, understand my purpose to be to give information to a statesman who may be called to exert so great an agency in the final adjustment of this question, not to urge at present, at least, any view of my own. For I am not one who would advise any ["unreasonable concession." *interlined*] I suppose it ["but" *canceled and* "not" *interlined*] improbable that in the event of the negotiation being resumed during the session of Congress, the President may consult the Senate before finally acting upon such proposition as may be made to him; and, certainly, the whole subject will be before that body in its Legislative capacity upon the measures to carry out the recommendations of the message.

In the first case, I suppose it will be quite appropriate, if the Senate desire any modification of the new offer, to express ["its" *canceled and* "their" *interlined*] opinion and even to give their advice as to the basis upon which the negotiation should be resumed; and, in carrying out the President's recommendations, it would appear to me to be altogether wise & respectful, to advise that, in the interval before the expiration of the notice, it would be expedient to negotiate for a partition of the Territory upon such basis, and with such ["modification" *canceled*] modifications as in the opinion of the Senate would, ["under all the circumstances of the case," *interlined*] be consistent with ["the" *interlined*] honor and rights of the country. ["I believe" *canceled*] If the Senate should adopt the ["recomat"(?) *canceled*] recommendation of the President by a strong majority, thereby evincing their confidence not only in his administration but in the justice of our demand and of our cause, and their determination if need be to sustain them by the force of a united government and People, and ["if," *interlined*] at the same time, ["they should" *interlined*] announce their desire ["for a" *canceled*] to ["approve a" *interlined*] compromise ["upon" *canceled*] of our claim upon the basis of a reasonable partition, and recommend ["that" *interlined*] an attempt should be made for that purpose, ["I believe it would" *canceled and* "might it not" *interlined*] ensure a safe, expedient and honorable adjustment of the question?

I do not believe the commercial and manufacturing interests ["here" *interlined*] would allow their government to force a war for more than the 49th parallel, with some reasonable ["modifications" *canceled and* "protection" *interlined*] to the British interests which have grown up under the joint occupancy. The gradual & daily strengthening of the cause of free trade is materially adding to the influences of the commercial and manufacturing interests; and it is altogether probable that the belief that a relaxation of the corn laws will add to the trade between the two Countries, and unite the agricultural with the planting interest in the U.S. in favor of peace and free trade generally, will not be without its effect in producing an early modification of those laws. If we act wisely, therefore, we may yet get the 49th parallel, with fewer modifications than were embraced in some of our previous offers, and not likely to be injurious to us; and thereby not only preserve[?] the peace of the world, but effect the opening of the English ports to American grain, and lay the foundation for our own glorious Country ["for" *canceled and* "of" *interlined*] a career of happiness & prosperity greater than any man now living can estimate.

More than the 49th I have not the least reason to believe would be conceded; perhaps not that, without some such modification, or indemnities as I have intimated would be yielded; but ["that" *canceled*] a concession of the *whole territory* after so long a joint occupation, and the offers we have to[o] often made heretofore, and without indemnitys or consideration of any kind, I am compelled to regard as altogether impossible.

I have written you a very hasty letter, Sir, and have, perhaps, ventured upon a liberty I ought not to have taken. If so, I must rely upon the motives of my conduct, and your knowledge of my confidence in you and my estimate of your character to excuse me. I am not ignorant of my country's rights and should be inexcusable if I did not thoroughly comprehend them in regard to the Oregon Territory, or if I could be capable of dealing lightly with them.

I must say, at the same time, that I have always regarded the question, from my earliest knowledge of it, as one of equitable partition, and requiring some concession even on our side; and I have never been able to consider the point or the advantage of insisting upon the whole, ["of" *interlined*] sufficient importance to justify the long and wasting war to which that course would too surely lead. If I understand the position occupied by the President ["& Sec. of State," *interlined*] it is not inconsistent with these views, and if they should also prevail with those who may now have a share in the preliminary management of the affair, I mean the Senate, I cannot doubt that peace may be preserved, and our national rights & honor maintained. I am also quite certain that any American Statesman who may have an agency in bringing about these results will greatly strengthen his claims to the respect & confidence of his Countrymen.

I scarcely know what to say of the general affairs here. The resignation of the Peel ministry, the abortive attempt of Lord John Russell to form another and the restoration of the old have all passed as sudden and unexpected, and as unaccountably as phantasmagoria. All are ["wondering" *canceled and then interlined*], and all endeavouring, but in vain, to penetrate the mystery of these extraordinary movements. It seems to be generally supposed that the leading men of both the great parties are favorable to a total repeal or ["a" *interlined*] very material modification of the corn laws, and that the recent ministerial crises have been produced by some contemplated policies in regard to this subject. And yet the return of Sir Robert Peel and his colleagues, with so few changes, to power, and the mystery ["in" *interlined*] which he still permits his motives, and intentions to be shrouded, ["is" *canceled and* "are" *interlined*] well calculated to baffle conjecture. The most plausible solution appears to be that, Sir Robert Peel and at least many of his colleagues, having come to the conclusion that the time had arrived for a repeal or material alteration of the corn laws, were nevertheless unwilling to propose so great & radical a change in opposition to the policy, and supporters upon whom they came into power; that they, therefore, determined to resign, affording to the opposition the opportunity of composing a Ministry and repealing the laws if in their power, and intending, if ["these" *altered to* "they"] should fail, to return again themselves, and as a new government comeing in upon different principles and less ["restricted"(?) *canceled*] restricted, to propose the same measures which they could not have done under their former organization. The measures they may propose, however, even upon this supposition, are very conjectural, and I rather think in a great degree undecided even in their own minds. It will not surprise me if they should be greatly dependent upon the manifestations of public opinion now going on in various parts of the Kingdom; and that could these become sufficiently unequivocal the Ministers themselves will not decide how far to go. Of one thing you may be certain that the doom of the corn law restrictions is already sealed. Not only are the notions of free trade, progressive, and daily acquiring new strength, but the *popular influences* which are seeking to demolish the unequal advantages possessed by the landed interest, ["in other words, the *'landed aristocracy'* " *interlined*] have already become too powerful to be successfully resisted, and those who see and are compelled to acknowledge the imminent danger of their old citadel, begin already to fear much less the ["overthrow with which" *canceled*] capitulation if not the overthrow which surely awaits them, than the *influences* which are to bring it about. The voluntary subscription in one day of £60,000, and in another of £12,000 more in the town of Manchester alone, in behalf of the objects of "the [Anti-Corn-Law] League" affords the best evidence of the inesti[ma]ble determination of those who are resolved upon breaking down the "Land Monopoly."

Is it not a lesson that we should begin by times to unshackle the industry of our glorious country; so that we may never have to create such serious shocks & subject so much injury to any great interest in ["temporarily" *canceled and* "removing the" *interlined*] obstructions ["we had interposed to" *interlined*] the universal laws of trade? I will add the confession that I am not without some sins to atone for on this head; & might regret that I am not in a situation to make my atonement more publicly. I did my [*sic;* "share" *canceled and* "had some share in atoning" *interlined*] in [*one illegible word*], however, and may ["be" *interlined*] well consoled that the remainder is now, the part, in your hands.

With an apol[og]y for this long & I fear illegible letter, I beg to assure you My dear Sir—of the high respect & regard with which I am, &c &, L. McLane.

ALS in ScCleA; PEx in Boucher and Brooks, eds., *Correspondence*, pp. 311–315.

From JAMES TALLMADGE

New York [City,] 3 Jan[uar]y 1846

Sir, I see it stated from the letter writers, that Mr. Calhoun has *ruined* himself, by his course, on the *Oregon* question. Permit me to say; a very opposit[e] opinion prevails in New York. The course you have pursued, commands universal commendation here—however it may be at Washington. Be assured, D[ea]r Sir—that Mr. Calhoun, can rely on New York, for its approbation, of his high & dignified course—guided by principle, instead of Party. There is here, but one voice of approbation. Very Respectfully Your &c &c, James Tallmadge.

ALS in ScCleA. NOTE: Calhoun's AEU reads, "Gen[era]l Tal[l]ma[d]ge." Tallmadge had been brigadier general of N.Y. militia during the War of 1812, Representative from N.Y., and Lieutenant Governor. He was at this time president of the governing council of New York University.

From R[OBERT] F. W. ALLSTON

Georgetown So. Ca., 5th Jan[uar]y 1846

Dear Sir, In compliance with the Resolution of a public meeting of the citizens of Georgetown and the vicinage, on the 4th of November last; and in fullfilment of my duty as chairman of that meeting (having already communicated a copy to Mr. [Alexander D.] Sims of the House) I have the honor to transmit to you herewith certain Resolutions relating to the Tariff of 1842 and a Ware-Housing system, and to request that the same may be laid before the Senate of the U.S. at such time as you in your discretion shall think proper.

I beg you will accept my sincere wishes for your continued health & progress. With sentiments of the highest respect I have the Honor to be your ob[edien]t serv[an]t, R.F.W. Allston.

[Enclosure]

Whereas it is always desirable that those intrusted with the public interest should be informed of the public wants, And that those who represent the people should from time to time be made aware of the sentiments and opinions of the people, *And whereas* the approaching Session of a new Congress seems to afford a fitting occasion for a declaration on our part of our wants and wishes, and a representation of our grievances. And whereas there is a settled conviction among us, that our prosperity as a people is surely impaired, by an unconstitutional, unwise, unequal, unjust, and impolitic system of fiscal exactions by which commerce is driven from its natural channels, and industry chained and fettered, and shorn of its natural vigor, *Be it therefore Resolved* that we regard the tariff of 1842 as a gross violation of the Compromise which was understood as a settlement of the Revenue System of the Country.

Resolved that we look with some confidence to the 29th Congress, that it will, repeal that odious act, redress our wrongs, strike the fetters from our industry, and vindicate the Constitution.

Resolved that the Prohibitory System as practised by the General Government for the last twenty five years has been and is a grievous burthen upon the great body of the people for the sole benefit of a hand full of wealthy capitalists.

Resolved that we should regard warehousing dutiable commodities as a mitigation of the evils inseparable from the practice of a cruel aggravation of burthens in themselves intolerable and has a direct tendency to destroy commerce, save in a few favoured spots where large capital exists, Thus practically annulling one of the beneficent provisions of the Constitution, whereby it is ordained that no preference shall be given by any regulation of commerce or revenue to the ports of one State over those of another.

Resolved that we should regard warehousing dutiable commodities as a mitigation of the evils inseparable from the practice of raising the whole revenue through the Custom House. And it would result in this good among others, that when taxed we would be able to discover to what extent we are taxed. A Boon that should not in charity be withheld by those who impose taxation as a blessing, from those who groan under it as a curse.

Resolved that our Delegation in Congress be requested to use their best efforts to reduce all duties to the revenue standard, and to endeavour to engraft upon any bill that may be adopted on the subject, the plan of Warehousing in Public Stores, whereby duties may be exigible only where taxed commodities are from time to time withdrawn for sale or actual consumption. A measure that recommends itself to us by many considerations, and by none more than its entire conformity to that spirit of plain dealing which should distinguish the Legislation of a free people.

Resolved that one of our Senators be requested to lay the foregoing preamble and Resolutions before the ["U" *canceled*] Senate of the United States and that our immediate Representative be requested to bring them to the notice of the House of Representatives in Congress. R.F.W. Allston, Chairman. W[illiam] S. Croft, Secretary.

ALS with En in DNA, RG 46 (U.S. Senate), 29A-G5.1. NOTE: This letter with the enclosed resolutions was presented by Calhoun to the Senate on 1/12 and referred to the Committee on Finance.

From J[AMES] M[ARTIN] CALHOUN

Richmond [Ala.], Jan. 5, 1846

Dear Uncle, I drop you a hasty line to draw from you something in relation to your health and I hope most sincerely you may be able to say to me that it is good & that you have gotten clear of that Cough in relation to which I have felt great uneasiness.

We have all been in good health till last night when Sally [Susan Wilkinson Pickens Calhoun?] had some Fever[?]. I hope the indisposition is however slight. I was over at John[']s [that is, John Alfred Calhoun's] during Christmas found & left all well. They greatly regretted that you were not able to go by. He has a house full of fine[,] hearty children. I took Sarah [Louisa Calhoun] with me where she now is. We are all in deep anxiety about our relations with England. [James K.] Polk[']s message is very generally approved by all parties except as to the giving of Notice to terminate the joint occupancy which is generally tho't to be bad policy.

I hope you will take care of yourself and keep clear of all excitement exposure and fatigue. Lead a quiet old gentleman[']s life & let fatigue duty be performed by younger constitutions. I hope too Aunt [Floride Colhoun Calhoun] is with you. Have you tried Smoking? How does it agree with you?

If at perfect leisure I should like much to hear from you. If Aunt is with you beg her to write also for I know she will be more full in relation to your health than you will be yourself. Give me a word as to the probable issue of the Orregon & Tariff questions.

Our affectionate Love to all with you & I remain very Affectionately yours &c, J.M. Calhoun.

P.S. How is [Martha] Cornelia [Calhoun]? Is she with you?

ALS in ScCleA.

From N[ATHAN] RANNEY

Saint Louis, Jan[uar]y 5, 1846

Dear Sir, I hope you will scrutenise [*sic*] the nominations made by Mr. [James K.] Polk for Missouri—for they are nearly all made from the [Thomas H.] Benton faction, from that portion of the party who said openly here that the object of getting Texas into to [*sic*] the Union was to produce disunion, and Mr. Polk since succe[e]ding by the generous and efficient aid of the Annexation democrats he has turned to be their enemy, and has taken the dictum of Col. Benton for his favors in our State. One only of our men in St. Louis has received an office and that a small one—J.A. Hedge, Surveyor of the Port, is that one. Jno. M. Wimer nomine[e] to the Post office could not get the 10th of the the [*sic*] democratic votes of the City for the office—and the man nominated a Consul to Trieste Edward Warrens could not be trusted in St. Louis for any thing out of sight.

You do not recollect me of course but I saw you some times on the floor of the Senate when My Fatherinlaw Jno. Shackford was Serg[ean]t at Arms. I refer you as to my standing at home for the last 26 years to Judge [David R.] Atchison—and for any thing *confidential* to our Representative Maj. L[eonard] H. Sims. I hope you will do all in your power to prevent a War with our ancient enemy. I do not think the *Lord* has ["pourred" *altered to* "poured"] blessings upon us like a river, and made us great and powerful for the purpose of making us a scourge in the end to every Christian land. I have fought and bled in one war with England and am ready at all times to obey the calls of my Country—but war is an evil I greatly dread. As to Oregon I think the 49th degree might with safety be settled upon provided England now offers it. The President will undoubtedly be sustained by the democratic party generally in settleing upon this basis. With great respect yours truly, N. Ranney.

ALS in ScCleA. NOTE: An AEU by Calhoun reads: "Mr. Shackford."

From S[IMEON] DeWITT BLOODGOOD

New York [City,] Jan[uar]y 6, 1845 [*sic*; 1846]

D[ea]r Sir, I enclose you a paper of which I am the Editor, & in which I have taken occasion to defend your present position. I differ with you on the subject of the tariff, but I can not but admire the fearlessness which you display in advocating what you deem to be right.

Certain of your friends are fearful of your personal popularity by your course, but they are utterly mistaken. I have in a previous number said as much more in your support. If your relations are those of friendship with Gov. [William L.] Marcy as I doubt not they are you may if you choose learn who is the champion that steps forward in your behalf.

I send you the [New York] Daily Globe also of to day to shew, what the rabid & radical press say of you. That paper receives the patronage of the Government. It would be far better to give Mr. [Levi D.] Slamm an office, than to leave him at the head of a Press, which will embarrass the administration, & the judicious portion of the U.S. Senate. In haste Very truly Y[ou]r ob[edien]t, S. DeWitt Bloodgood.

ALS in ScCleA. NOTE: Bloodgood (1799–1866) was a merchant, journalist, and author.

From H[ENRY] W. CONNER

Charleston, Jan[uar]y 6, 1846

My dear Sir, Your letter of the 28th [December; *not found*] to Mr. [Ker] Boyce (now absent) & myself came to hand yesterday & we feel extremely obliged for the information so kindly rendered us.

I will write Gen[era]l [George] McDuffie, Mr. [James A.] Black [Senator and Representative from S.C., respectively] & others of my acquaintance from other States. I will to day also write a friend in Georgia who has the ear of the Senator from that State & will adopt the course you suggest in writing to them for it expresses my own & the sentiment of the whole country.

Col. [Franklin H.] Elmore will write Mr. [Dixon H.] Lewis [Senator from Ala.] no doubt.

Your friends have often had occasion to congratulate themselves & the country upon the influence you have exerted in the affairs of the nation in ["the" *canceled*] times of difficulty & danger ["heretofore" *interlined*] but your recent stand in the Senate as expressed in your resolutions [of 12/30 for adjustment of the Oregon controversy] has in the estimation of the whole people surpassed all other acts of your life. I was at Charlotte No. Ca. when your resolutions were

414

rec[eive]d & the confidence & security they produced in the minds of the people there & all the way along the road was magical. The belief is almost universal that you possess the moral power & will be successful in the exertion of it to the preservation of an honourable peace. Should it prove otherwise however & peace be not practical upon honourable terms, the assurance is equally strong that you will accept peace upon no other terms & you may depend upon the nation as one man standing up to the death in defence of the country.

We hope most sincerely that your efforts will be successful altho we can readily perceive the difficulties which you have to encounter & if there be any possible way in which your friends here could atall [*sic*] be made useful or available to you there is not one of us but you may command to the utmost extent of our power. Very Truly y[ou]rs &C, H.W. Conner.

[P.S.] We beg to thank you for your kind attention & Mrs. [Floride Colhoun] Calhoun[']s to Mrs. [Care Courtney] Talman my sister in law on her way North.

ALS in ScCleA; variant PEx in Boucher and Brooks, eds., *Correspondence*, p. 315.

From H[UGH] McLEOD

Galveston, January 6th 1846

Sir, Major [William H.] Chase of the Engineer Corps informed me in conversation last evening that you had learned from Mr. [Josiah] Gregg, that there was a practicable wagon road from the ["upper" *interlined*] Valley of the Rio Grande (Rio Bravo del Norte) to the Pacific Coast—and that you considered the fact very important, & desired minute information respecting it.

Knowing the value of your time, I should not intrude this note, did I not believe that it may be of service. Capt. W[illia]m G. Dryden—a Kentuckian who has resided for many years in New Mexico—Chihuahua & California, is now in Texas, & furnished ["me" *interlined*] a rude map & geographical sketch of ["the" *canceled*] Northern Mexico from the Rio Grande to the western Coast, which I sent to a friend in New York. In a few days he may pass here again & I will get another & forward to yourself. In his sketch he says that a traffic is annually carried on in wagons from the little ["Indian" *interlined*] Town of Abeca, on the West Side of the Rio Grande & below Santa Fe, to the Port of Guayamos [*sic*] and other points on the Pacific. He states that the route is easy & unobstructed, as is proved by the fact that the Mexican Cart—the most cumbersome of vehicles, (the wheels being solid masses, what we call *truck* wheels) is used in that trade. I think he made the distance 800 miles, & remember that in conversation he spoke of it, as short in comparison with the Oregon route, inasmuch as the coast converges rapidly to the Southward. He spoke of it, as the natural route to the pacific, because it had the advantage of ["being" *interlined*] the *shortest* & *easiest*, and as he expressed it, of removing Independence from Missouri to the rocky mountains—placing the real starting point, at the half way ground, in an abundant Valley, (that of Santa Fe), where provision is cheaper than in any of our States, for it has no market—& still further, he said the climate would permit this route to be travelled throughout the year, which is not the case with ["the" *interlined*] upper one, thro' the South pass. I am Sir with high respect Y[ou]r ob[edien]t Servant, H. McLeod.

ALS in ScCleA. NOTE: An AEU by Calhoun reads "Mr. McLeod, relates to the passage from St. Fe to the Pacifick." McLeod (1814–1862) was a native of N.Y., a graduate of the U.S. Military Academy, and had been a brigadier general in the Texas Republic army and one of the Texan prisoners in the Castle of Perote who had been freed by U.S. intervention. He subsequently died in Confederate service.

From R. E. MERRILL

North Conway, N.H., Jan[uar]y 6th 1846
D[ea]r Sir, Being an ardent admirer of your political principles & character, and of late an open and zealous advocate of your nomination to the Presidential chair, I should think it a treasure to possess your *Autograph*, a name that is destined to shine in after ages with such brilliancy. I am well aware of the aversion which some public men have to giving their names to such purposes; but I am so desirous to obtain yours, that I take the liberty of suggesting the propriety of sending it as a private letter subject to postage. To a request so reasonable I sincerely hope you will have no objection to complying. With great respect, Your ob[edien]t Serv[an]t, R.E. Merrill.

ALS in ScCleA.

From JOHN STROHECKER and Others

Charleston, January 6th 1846

Respected Sir, The Inclose[d] Petition in behalf of myself & others Interested in the claim of the Fire and Marine Insurance of Charleston against the British Government, we respectfully request of you the favour of presenting it to the *Senate* and to advocate our claim for Justice and that protection which as Citizens of the United States, we are Intitled to. If our Government denies us this—to whom are we to apply for that relief which all Governments extends to its Citizens[?] Many of us are poor & in distress. As this case is well known to you we consider it useless on our part to urge any thing further than what is contained in our Petition. I am with Esteem your ob[edien]t Se[rvan]t, John Strohecker and others.

[Enclosure]

John Strohecker and Others to the Senate

January 6th 1846

The Petition of John Strohecker & others respectively sheweth they met with losses by the Fire and Marine Insurance Company of Charleston So. Ca. The Inability of payment by the Company was occasioned by their loss of Insurance on the Schooner Enterprize bound from the District of Columbia to Charleston So. Ca. and forced by stress of weather into Bermuda where the [slave] Property was forcibly seized and detained by the Local Authority of the Island in 1835[.] Many of your Petitioners are Widows and Orphans in needy Circumstances by whom the loss is severely felt[.] They Respectfully apply to your Honorable Body for the repayment of the amount which they were compelled by a suit at Law to pay the Insured amounting with Interest to $38,001 Dollars, your Petitioners consider the granting their request but an act of Justice to which they are Intitled to from their Government, the British Gover[n]ment having refused to make compensation. They naturally look to your Honourable Body for payment of their loss, your Petitioners could enlarge on the Injury to the Coasting trade and other Evils that will result from such Acts of the British Gover[n]ment, but they forbear & confidentially apply for that protection which all Governments give to their Citizens or Subjects. John Strohecker and Others.

ALS with En in DNA, RG 46 (U.S. Senate), 29A-G6.1. NOTE: Calhoun presented this petition to the Senate on 1/20 when it was referred to the Committee on Foreign Affairs. On 7/1 that Committee reported adversely on the petition; their report was agreed to by the Senate on 7/2.

From ROBERT WALSH, [U.S. Consul]

Paris, Jan[uar]y 6: 1846

My Dear Sir, It is only a few days since we learned here, with certainty, that you were to be again in the Senate. This will prove, I doubt not, a Signal benefit for the country. Your language and spirit at the Memphis Convention are excellent preliminaries to your return to the national councils. I shall attend to your acc[ou]nts[?] with double and the most lively interest. In case you should desire any information, publications, or any thing else, from this meridian, you know whom you can command. From the period that you left the Department of State, much has come within my observation, and entered by either my eyes or ears, that I could have wished to communicate to a Secretary. You see that all I wrote to you concerning the *Entente Cordiale* is fully verified. The Committee of the delegates of the French West Indies are eager to have the Report which Mr. [John] Hogan (said to have [been] deputed by you to Hayti & Cuba) has made or will make. I venture to request a copy.

My chief purpose at present is to ask your friendly attention to the within extract from an epistle which I lately addressed to Mr. Secretary [of the Treasury, Robert J.] Walker. As Consul I am your work; I have done all that circumstances admitted: my representation to the Secretary is short of the truth. You can understand the whole case. With cordial respect your faithful Serv[an]t, Robert Walsh.

[Enclosure]

"My appointment to this Consulate was the spontaneous act of Mr. Tyler and Mr. Calhoun. Its situation was so bad that I took some days to deliberate and I should have declined it, if, upon examination, I had not deemed it susceptible of improvement and various usefulness. I gave it at once a proper location; supplied it with books of which it was altogether destitute; and incurred other expenses more or less onerous. I undertook it at the beginning of October 1844; it required comprehensive studies in commercial and international law; and it soon became a sort of bureau of statistics to which the French public functionaries and particularly members of the Chambers often resorted. Throughout the winter, much of my time was given (gratuitously of course) to enquirers, of the respectable classes, whose object was emigration or the purchase of property in the United States. My American feelings prompted me, also, to furnish materials for the defense of our country and of the new administration, to the journals and to Deputies who published speeches and pamphlets.

Appearances—independently of Office-business—demanded a clerk; whose salary could not be less than four hundred dollars per annum, the rent of the proper rooms in which business is transacted amounts to three hundred and twenty dollars per annum. The postage of the letters addressed to the Consul himself or to his care, forms a heavy charge; pecuniary assistance cannot be denied to Americans whom irregularities or casualties have involved in distress. Hitherto, the Consulship has not supported me; but I have supported the Consulship, by literary labors and legal opinions. The winter before the last, the Agency of Claims, & salary of two thousand dollars, attached to the office, was abolished by Congress. The law precludes any reimbursement for 'house or office rent, books, stationery or other ordinary expenses of office.' But the Consulate of London is provided by act of Congress with a salary of two thousand dollars and another annual sum of two thousand eight hundred dollars for 'clerk hire, office rent and other expenses of office,' at the same time that the fees received there are much more considerable, and the cost of living suitably, not greater, than in this capital. The number of Americans to be hospitably treated is always larger here. It could be shown, moreover, that the Consulate of Paris is capable of being made quite as important at least, for American interests; it is indispensable with reference to the acknowledgment of deeds, the verification of Invoices, the execution of powers of attorney, and other documents relating [to] concerns of property, marriage, inheritance and so forth—in the United States. It is particularly valuable as an entrepot of knowledge for our countrymen, the French public, and the multitude of continental visitors to this Metropolis. What I would desire under all circumstances, is not a general fixed Salary, but simply such an allowance by Congress, as would cover the expenses of office-rent, clerk-hire, and the other objects of the provision for the London Consulate. A thousand dollars might suffice, per annum. It is a matter of equity, too, that the allowance should date from October of last year. Pardon the foregoing details. The liberality of your spirit and your sense of Justice will cause them to be tolerated, and will promote my purpose."

ALS with En in ScCleA.

From J[AMES] EDWARD COLHOUN, "(Confidential)"

Millwood [Abbeville District, S.C.] Jan[uar]y 7/46
My Dear Sir, I have just returned from Hamburg [S.C.]; had James
[Edward Calhoun] with me. Before I left home, your letter from
the Cane Brake [in Ala.] was rec[eive]d. James was present when
I opened the letter & therefore, I have *not* read the one you enclosed
to him. I can readily imagine his proneness to idle expense; hence,
the more need to let him rusticate here. I am fearful he cannot sufficiently control his inclination, as to branches of study, & that he
will not be guided by my advice; & I discover in him the obstinacy
of his race. Write to him, immediately, & urge him to embrace this
the best opportunity he can ever have for acquirement of Languages.
English he may pursue anywhere.

I wrote you just before I left home, expressing my regret that
you return to the Senate. While down I heard much that increased
that regret. [Robert Barnwell] Rhett drew [Frederick J.] McCarthy's Resolutions, went to Charleston to go on [to Washington]
with [George] McDuffie to poison his mind, wrote from Richmond
to [Franklin H.] Elmore, that your Virginia friends had given you
up & would introduce Resolutions disapproving the doctrines of
your Memphis Speech. Five blanks were thrown against you [in
your election as Senator by the South Carolina General Assembly],
& many would not vote at all. [Joel R.] Poinsett was in Columbia
chuckling at your acceptance. Simultaneously, [William C.] Preston
elected President ["of the College" *interlined*]! an empty pretender,
traitor to the State & false to you. You see then, your obligation to
remain is slight, indeed. You can get off handsomely, by giving out,
that only your official connection with the Oregon & Texas negociations have carried you back, & that you peremptorily decline at the
end of the Session; before, if possible.

The curious malice of [President James K.] Polk is profound &
incurable. I have it direct, that before leaving Nashville he was
strongly urged to continue you in office. He took it in ill part. When
Gen. [Robert] Armstrong took leave of [Andrew] Jackson, on his
death bed, the latter solemnly charged him to say to Polk that ["it"
canceled] you were the only man, who could satisfactorily settle the
Oregon ["question" *interlined*]. Gen. A[rmstrong] on his arrival, in
Washington, offered to go to Pendleton, in person, to invite your return to the State Department. The offer was badly received. Major
[Andrew J.] Donelson asserts most positively that it was the Nash-

ville more than the N. York influence that caused Jackson's hostility to you. He & [Samuel J.] Hays, both, say warmly, that they feel bound to seek every opportunity to make atonement for the injustice done you by their Uncle. This summer, [James] Buchanan had the indelicacy to urge on [James] Gadsden, as your friend, with the utmost anxiety, that you should be sent back to the Senate, shorn of all pretensions to the Presidency. [George] Bancroft, to the same effect. Will you so humble yourself to your enemies, & mortify & disappoint your friends?

For the hundredth time, & more solemnly, than ever, I warn you to beware of [Armistead] Burt & Elmore. Affectionately, J. Edward Colhoun.

[P.S.] I did not dissuade James from remaining at Erskine College; I was cautious too, not to let drop a single word to influence him. I confess, that when I carried Willie [William Lowndes Calhoun] there, the Institution did not make favorable impression on me. True I liked the simplicity of manner, in the Faculty. But the Simplicity of the Seceder is not that of the Moravian.

ALS in ScU-SC, John C. Calhoun Papers.

From J[OHN] J. FLOURNOY

Farm, nigh, Athens [Ga.], Jan[uar]y 7th 1846
My Honor'd Sir: A Deaf citizen now *would* address you. I saw you, (only at one time,) years past when Dr. [Alonzo] Church Pres[i]-d[en]t of F[ranklin] College at Athens in its Chapel, (commencement just concluded), told me you were "Mr. Calhoun," but I did not distinctly understand him, or I would have taken your hand. It was when I borrow[e]d his Baccelaurate [*sic*]. I hope you recollect.

I do tremble at the present situation of our Republick. In proportion, I rejoice to see you hold out the Olive branch. Still the spirit evinced by our President and people, does not augur well. Nor is there one trace in History, as regards past and fallen Democracies, in which War had not been the undoing of them.

Our Freedom is like the gamester's money, safe in Peace, but in war put out at stakes, and repeatedly risked. And as the most expert player looses at times, so might Liberty have a sunset in blood! no matter what the original *incentives* to the conflict. Our own Revolution tells man that war does not begin and end on one subject. It branches out into diversified ramifications. Thus, if [George] Washington waged war for our Rights, it extended to Europe; and through perverted or miscomprehended principles of Freedom, attacked Religion, set in motion a Guillotine, derided La Fayette who or whose clan fanned the embers, and broke out into the bloody and atrocious campaigns of Bonaparte, and finally, like the last war recurred to our shores! It was the *head* and *tail* to us, of that eventful Drama.

I fear the injury [Andrew] Jackson and his men did to the British from behind *ramparts* at New Orleans is too indelibly rankling in the bosoms of ["Britans" *canceled*] Britons, to be easily forgiven. That Empire now seek secretly to pay us in coin. They, before we can do any thing would fill Oregon with forts, and barricade Mountain and River, and our presumption in marching up to them would be repaid in New Orleans currency! Can nothing short satisfy Britain? I fear not; possibly better men on both sides, might restrain the War dogs by compromising the difficulty.

Packenham [*sic*; Richard Pakenham] was not the man to have been sent over here to negotiate where war was ["apparently" *interlined*] inevitable. His Kinsman fell at Orleans! Human nature in him unfits him for the part of an Ashburton! Why then did the English privy council suggest and the Crown of that Monarchy send him? I cannot say. Whether from unconscious folly, or conscious ingenuity at bringing about a tight and apparently irreconcileable job!

Our Secretary of State [James Buchanan] *must* know this, and be in a mood to handle Packenham like magnanimity over rabid decision: or he would certainly have matters more complicated—being as I said unfitted by the uncontrol[l]able passions of morbid nature. *His Uncle,* etc. . . .

Wars tho' now and then they subserve freedom, oftener fixes on countries a heavy despotism. In our case the progress from Republicity to Monarchy, or a series of monarchies, may be but the easy graduation of this country to its punishment, for forgetting the Great Creator who commanded that none commit murder! and whose Son our Saviour enjoined that greatest degree of forbearance[,] Non resistance! If we do not intend obedience to such ["a" *interlined*] dread Sovereign! to the letter and spirit of His injunction, let us at least not go a step beyond ordinary prudence and become criminal by the provocation of a war, useless and inglorious. The consequence will extend more widely than its confinement to our borders, or the present feelings of our people! If we be victorious, a Military spirit would be engendered which scorning the tedious quiet of another peace, may serve the dangerous designs of Traitors in fomenting military expeditions at home or abroad, and finally have the scenes at Rome of Marius and Sylla, and Caesar and Pompey, to fall upon our dissevering Union perhaps with identical results. If we be defeated the disastrous result would be fatal! Our Republic having hither to prevailed by sea and Land, our people, leaders and led, are proud of her destiny; and while appropriating her Glory to themselves, feel a reverence for her Institutions, which is a sort of shield to the States and Confederation, forbidding the assaults of Demagogues, or the aims of overt treason, such as denoted Aaron Burr's—but in failure, our golden glory departed, our Union dishonored, our congress and Executive humiliated—so surely would the respect of the people for the Government as now constituted, dwindle imperceptibly into contempt, and on the slightest pretense broke out into a flame of dissension and disunion! The General authority then must be despotic to hold them in check—but unavailing this check, over so vast a space, and certain only this Despotism over ["the" *canceled*] such of the original thirteen and countermivous [*sic*] tributaries, as may be after long pending civil contests consolidated. Our present Constitution scattered to the four winds!

Congress would therefore pause, be satisfied with a vast Texas—Let the British cement consiliation with us on the opposite banks of the Columbia. Look to Heaven, worship God and His Christ—be peaceable—for very existence in the *long run!*—contract with the English harmonious regards—then might our Liberty free from the horrors of unfor[e]seen dissensions, last to our children's children for many generations—perhaps for ever: Our country be still spotless and honored in the hearts of our people—and what is valuable, the friendship of England and the world at large, may from us under Divine beneficiance, be inherited by our Posterity. I am Honored Sir, humbly, Your friend and obed[ien]t Servant, J.J. Flournoy.

ALS in ScCleA.

Remarks on asking to be excused from the chairmanship of the Committee on Finance, 1/7. "Mr. Calhoun rose to ask a similar favor [to that of Arthur P. Bagby, who had requested to be excused from the chairmanship of the Committee on Claims], and said that in his absence, and before he took his seat in the Senate at the present session, he had been appointed chairman of the Committee on Finance. He would be very glad indeed to render all the service he could, to the best of his ability; but there were several reasons for his declining the acceptance of the station. One, however, would be sufficient. The business of the committee was extensive, and would require a great deal of explanation, as well as argument, in the defence of the measures presented. In all probability it would be beyond the power of his voice to undertake the duty. He had for many years been subject to hoarseness, and, after addressing the Senate, it always continued for several days; and this would incapacitate him. Under these circumstances, without assigning any other reason, he hoped he would be excused. He would add one fact: when formerly a member of this body, he was excused for the reason now assigned; and he trusted that he would be now." (The Senate granted Calhoun's request.) From the Washington, D.C., *Daily Union,* vol. I, no. 213 (January 7, 1846), p. 846. Variants in the Washington, D.C., *Daily National Intelligencer,* January 8, 1846, p. 2; the New York, N.Y., *Herald,* January 9, 1846, p. 4; the Charleston, S.C., *Mercury,* January 12, 1846, p. 2; the Greenville, S.C., *Mountaineer,* January 16, 1846, p. 4; *Congressional Globe,* 29th Cong., 1st Sess., p. 153.

Remarks on a military appropriation bill, 1/7. Thomas H. Benton was explaining and supporting a $100,000 extraordinary appropriation for defences in the north and northwest. "Mr. Calhoun suggested to the Senator a modification, that $3,000 be appropriated to defray the expenses of each military station or defense; and not exceeding $2,000 compensation to the Indian tribes who may possess or own the grounds on which each work may be erected. This will be better than appropriating a round sum for the whole." Benton said the amendment was "very good" and was acceptable. From *Congressional Globe,* 29th Cong., 1st Sess., p. 153. Also printed in the Washington, D.C., *Daily Union,* vol. I, no. 213 (January 7, 1846), p. 846. Variant in the Washington, D.C., *Daily National Intelligencer,* January 8, 1846, p. 2.

From DAVID CRAIGHEAD

Nashville, 8 Jan[uar]y 1846

D[ea]r Sir, On the probability of a war with England I have of course no information except such as may be gleaned from the contradictory publications of the day; yet I hope I will not be thought impertinent in offering a few observations on a subject which is so interesting to every citizen.

It is manifest that a great majority of the American ["people" *interlined*] is favorably disposed towards the administration; and unite in the determination to support it in a war if that last arbiter is resorted to. The unanimity of this sentiment however ought not to be mistaken for a com[m]on consent in favor of a war waged upon points of special pleading in diplomacy, or for remote or trifling interests. Many of those who are vociferous for a deffinite line to be agreed to upon the instant in an unknown not to say imaginary region would upon the first shock of war complain that there was no proportion between the sacrifice and the object for which it was made. Even now many moderate men[,] firm friends of the administration are at a loss to know what has recently occurred that renders war necessary. The british government denies our boundary; they have allways denied it. There is therefore no more cause for war on that account now than existed when we entered into and when we renewed the treaty with them for joint oc[c]upation. There is still space enough for the enterprising of both nations, and probably will be space enough for many generations. The british government has neither attempted nor threatened to impede our settlement of the country. Their only offense is that they do not agree to our lattitude[,] ours that we can not abandon it in argument. If we are to have a war then it will not be because either nation has done or meditated an injury to the other; but because neither is able to convince the other in the argument of a question which is of no present practical importance to either of them. If the discussion could be deferred until the dessission [*sic*] of it becomes necessary the difficulty might possibly disappear. If not it would then be time enough perhaps to fight.

If all this should appear otherwise to the gods and if this debate must end in carnage I would call your attention for a few moments to the Mississippi river which you have happily christen[e]d an inland sea. This appellation at all times apt is peculiarly so when the an[n]ual floods prevail. The dark current as you know rises within a few inches of the top of the mud embankment which confines it. The surface of the river is then on a line with the upper rooms of the cottages within these defenses. Often in despite of the vigilance of the entire population by night and by day; the insidious crawfish drills his minute tunnel and delluges large regions of country.

A[t] this stage of water a few hostile war Steamships asscending from the Balize to Batton Rouge which they could accomplish in three or four days, and breaking the levee at a few points on their way would leave behind them a litteral dead sea. The City of New Orleans and the entire sugar coast with all the beauty and all the booty so gallantly defended by our [Andrew] Jackson against the troops of Wellington would fall an easy prey to the unfettered current nor in my opinion could all the land forces of the nation if assembled on the spot defend the country or escape themselves from inevitable destruction. This is a new danger and is one of the consequences of the improvements of the age And if war be threat[e]ned I submit that measures should be promptly taken to provide new and adequate defences against this new mode of attack.

I am neither alarmed nor an alarmist. ["but" *canceled*] My interest, my position and my duty all direct my attention to the great river when war is mentioned; and as the eye and the hope, and the confidence, of the entire west rest upon you there is not another to whom I could so properly offer my observations on a subject so important to them.

This will I hope be my sufficient appology for oc[c]upying your time with so long a letter. Most sincerely and respectfully Your ob[edien]t Ser[vant,] David Craighead.

ALS in ScCleA.

From E. G. McGinnis

Louisville [Ky.,] Jan[uar]y 8 1846
Dear Sir, Tho' I am a whig & a stranger to you, I think it my duty to say that I feel grateful, for your efforts to preserve the *peace* of this country. I would not have peace at the sacrifice of national Honor, nor would I have war, without first placing England in the wrong. That she does not desire to be thus placed, I feel almost certain; so that if war comes, the fault will be ours, and of all the errors committed by the government, since its foundation, none has been so great as this will be. Could you hear the praise the whigs bestow on you, for your efforts to prevent an unnecessary war, I think, you would be gratified. ["Should" *canceled*] Whether you succeed or not in preventing war between this count[r]y and Eng-

land your course on this subject will deserve the lasting gratitude of this nation and shall have mine. Yours, E.G. McGinnis.

ALS in ScCleA. NOTE: An AEU by Calhoun reads "McGinnis, relates to my course in reference to the Oregon Question."

To President [JAMES K. POLK]

[Washington] 8th Jan[uar]y 1846
Dear Sir, I am informed, that James Webb Esq[ui]r[e] of Texas has been recommended to you for the place of [U.S. District] Judge [in Texas]. I have not the pleasure of being acquainted with him, but from information, on which I place entire confidence, I feel myself justified in adding my recommendation in his favour, as one every way qualified in point of intellect, character, standing & legal acquirements to fill the place with honor to himself & advantage to the Country. With this impression I shall feel much gratified should he receive the appointment. With great respect I am & &c, J.C. Calhoun.

ALS in DNA, RG 59 (State Department), Letters of Application and Recommendation during the Administrations of James K. Polk, Zachary Taylor, and Millard Fillmore, 1845–1853, Webb (M-873:92, frames 458–459). NOTE: Webb did not receive the appointment.

Remarks on a monument to George Washington, 1/8. Under consideration was a joint resolution from the House of Representatives authorizing the erection of a monument by the National Monument Association. There was a motion to refer the matter to the Committee on the District of Columbia rather than pass it directly to a third reading. "Mr. Calhoun said he hoped the resolution would be referred. If he understood the terms of the resolution, it provided for the erection of a monument by an association of individuals. He knew of no association, nor was an association known to the Senate, to whom such a work ought to be entrusted. He hoped that whenever a monument to George Washington should be erected that it would be done by the Congress of the United States, and not by any association of individuals." After much further discussion, "Mr. Calhoun said he now understood that the resolution was not intended to involve Congress in any expense; he therefore had no desire to insist upon its reference to a committee." From the Washington, D.C., *Daily National Intelligencer,* January 9, 1846, p. 1. Also printed in the Alexandria, Va., *Gazette and Virginia Advertiser,* January 12, 1846, p. 2. Variants in the Washington, D.C., *Daily Union,* vol. I, no. 214 (January 8, 1846), p. 849; the New York, N.Y., *Herald,* January 10, 1846, p. 4; *Congressional Globe,* 29th Cong., 1st Sess., pp. 160–161.

Remarks on a bill to pay debts owed by the U.S. to Texas when it was independent, 1/8. Calhoun made barely reported remarks in support of a payment of $55,975 to Texas in compensation for two claims that the Texas Republic had had against the U.S., one for seizure of arms by a party of U.S. Dragoons and the other for a seizure of goods from a Texas customs house by citizens of the U.S. From *Congressional Globe,* 29th Cong., 1st Sess., p. 162. Variant in the Washington, D.C., *Daily Union,* vol. I, no. 214 (January 8, 1846), p. 849.

Remarks in the Senate, 1/8. The Committee on Foreign Relations Chairman William Allen presented a motion instructing the Secretary of the Senate to acquire maps, globes, and atlases for the use of the Committee. "Mr. Calhoun suggested that there was no necessity of going to the expense of a globe. There was an excellent thirteen inch globe, as good as could be produced, in the State Department, which could be had by the committee." From the New York, N.Y., *Herald,* January 10, 1846, p. 4.

From ALEX[ANDE]R JONES

New York [City,] Jan[uar]y 9th 1846

My Dear Sir, I will respectfully call your attention to the [New York] Journal of Commerce of this, date, which places Mr. Preston King [Representative from N.Y.] in an unenviable position.

I am happy to inform you that your course in the senate, has received the approbation and applause of all men in this community whose good opinion is worth having.

You have gained an immense number of freins [*sic*], among, the virtuous, intelligent, and substantial classes ["of" *canceled and* "in" *interlined*] this section of country. And after all, it is their support and favourable ["opinions" *altered to* "opinion"] which ["which" *canceled*] stand the ["best" *canceled and* "best tests and" *interlined*] endure the longest, ["as" *canceled*]. It is the approbation of the good, of men of probity, integrity and means, which must confer the greatest satisfaction, upon those conscious of their own rectitude of conduct.

To every discerning man, it is as clear as noon day, we ["loose" *canceled and* "lose" *interlined*] Oregon, if, we go to war. Those who ["can" *interlined*] command the approaches by sea on the North West coast, will maintain possession of Oregon. In a contest with England, no one doubts, who, reflects upon the subject, that, she would, shut us out by sea.

When, I was in England, in 1840 & '41—Two fine English steamers were built by a company, and despatched to the Pacific; the first, which, ever appeared in those seas.

One was called the *Chili* and the other the *Peru.* They doubled cape Horn—and since their arrival on the coast, they have been profitably employed in transporting passengers and goods between the cities on the west coast of South America, having succeeded in breaking ["up" *canceled*] up sailing packet, passenger vessels, employed in the same trade by citizens of the United States. I went on board of these Steamers to examine them, before they sailed from London and found them, equal in size and equipment to the largest and best of the Cunard Steamers. Their business has been found so profitable, that, 2, or 3 others have been recently built and sent out to engage in the same service.

Now, supposing, a war to ensue, what an immense advantage would these English Steamers, in the Pacific, give the enemy? Suppose, a fleet ["in their servi" *canceled*] to blockade the North West Coast, under British commanders, who could at *all seasons of the year* ["could" *interlined*] have access to Oregon, supply their Garrisons with munitions of war, provisions &C—while we could have no access to the country except across the Rocky Mountains and that in *summer,* and through, an uncultivated country inhabited by savages, of over 2000 miles of travel?! In such a position of things, it ["is easy to see" *canceled and* "would it not be" *interlined and then canceled*], how important ["a part" *interlined*] the English Steamers in the Pacific, ["would be" *canceled and* "could act," *interlined*] in cooperation ["of" *canceled and* "with" *interlined*] the fleet, in conveying despatches, troops ["and" *canceled*] provisions &C.

How much sooner could the English deliver their despatches to their fleet off the mouth of Columbia River than we could?

Their lines of West India Steamers are now run to Vera Cruz. They have only [to] change them to Chargrés [*sic*; Chagrés, on the Isthmus of Panama], from whence, their despatches could be carried accross the country to the Pacific, where one of their steamers would be ready to receive them, and proceed at once up the coast to the fleet! And, were more vessels or troops wanted from China, or India, it would only be necessary to despatch one of these steamers, across the Pacific with orders for the same, to obtain them in comparatively a brief period of time. And pray, how, would we ["in" *canceled and* "reach the country" *interlined*] under such circumstances? By ["sea" *canceled and then interlined*] it would be impossible. By land, it could only be done in summer, and that in a Journey of from one to two months! !

Suppose we have 20,000 troops in Oregon, when the winter sets in, and the Rocky mountains with vast tracts of country ["on either side" *interlined*] become covered with impassible snows; cutting off all intercourse with, and prospect of succour from the states[?] Would it not be easy, for the English to select that period for making a conquest of the entire country? Making our troops prisoners of war, and fortifying their own troops in our Garrisons, and turning our own Guns against us? ! !

A man who expects to secure Oregon, to the United States by waging a war for it, is *either a madman or a fool.*

Can it be possible, that, any sane man can look upon physical force on our part as sufficient to defend that country against ["England" *interlined*]?

Those who clamor for a war, therefore, are wrecklessly [*sic*] playing a game, ["as" *canceled*] such as they think will advance the pretensions of ambitious aspirants ["to" *canceled*] for the Presidency in 1848—believing they can thus act, without, enhancing the dangers of war—or, if such motives do not govern them, they cannot be considered otherwise, ["than" *interlined*] as *Lunatics,* or *natural fools.* All I have said is familiar to you, and to all who have the sense to look at the question in a *common sense, and common honesty light.*

I have occasionally felt inclined to drop you a note; but I am but a poor and humble man; and from your recent movements, uncertain where a letter would find you.

While my poor life last[s], you can always depend upon my steadfast and unalterable esteem, friendship and support, ["and" *interlined*] however, humble it ["wil" *canceled*] may be, it will not be the *less sincere.*

I have received nothing from the administration, still I believe as you will no doubt agree, [it] is best; to support the President in all the just measures of his administration.

Wishing that ["you may" *interlined*] long live in the enjoyment of good health, and be long spared to your country and friends. I have the Honor to Remain as Every [*sic*], Your Sincere friend & Ob[edien]t Serv[an]t, Alexr. Jones.

(P.S.) If your public and other duties should give you leisure, I shall be happy at any time to hear from you.

ALS in ScCleA.

From F[RANKLIN] H. ELMORE

Charleston, Jan[uar]y 10, 1846

My dear Sir, I have just ret[urne]d to the City after a week[']s absence on business by which I was very much occupied. I re[ceive]d just before I left y[ou]rs of the 28 ult[im]o [*not found*] which had been delayed some days. I had no time to write to any body before I left. Staying one night at Columbia I wrote to [Dixon H.] Lewis. By a letter I received on my return, written a few days after yours, I found he was very safe. I saw Mr. Summers [*sic*; Adam G. Summer] Ed[ito]r of the [Columbia South-]Carolinian & put him in full possession of your views & the necessity of supporting them. I had already written to my Brother [William A. Elmore] at N[ew] O[rleans] & to [Joseph W.] LeSesne & [John A.] Campbell at Mobile & to D[avid] C. Campbell Editor of the Federal Union at Milledgeville [Ga.]. I see in his paper of the 6th he supports further negotiation—from the others I have not heard.

Your resolutions are universally approved here—& in the State. I hope you will carry them triumphantly. They will be hard to get over. The effort in the House I suppose was to forestal[l] you. It gives uneasiness here & we are all in the greatest anxiety to learn something of the real state of things. I have never seen this community more anxious. Can you in any way relieve our suspense? Will your resolutions pass? And what is the prospect of adjustment?

Lewis writes me that you have had an idea of some modified notice, to extend the notice to 49° & leave from that to 54° 40′ under the joint occupation. How would that work? Would England submit to it? And will it content the Western men?

I would be very glad to have our anxieties relieved by you if you can do it. Y[ou]rs truly, F.H. Elmore.

P.S. I write to [George] McDuffie tonight. I saw [Ker] Boyce today & he promised to write too.

ALS in ScCleA.

From ELLWOOD FISHER

Cincinnati, 1 Mo[nth] 10, 1846

My dear Friend, Having but a moment to write before leaving Columbus, on the night of the 8th, I wrote thee but a line to announce the position that was taken by the [Ohio Democratic] Convention concerning Oregon. The adoption of [Edward A.] Hannegan[']s resolutions by that body was to some extent accidental—but not on that account the less ominous and significant. The Committee on Resolutions was chiefly engaged on the currency question, and was so much delayed by discussing that, as to delay their report, until late in the afternoon, and until sent for by order of the Convention. The gentleman who proposed the Hannegan resolutions to the Committee did so as he afterwards assured me, in haste, and without having examined the question. They were opposed in Committee by two members, one of them John B. Weller—both of whom I had previously conversed with on the subject. But there was no time for discussing them in Committee.

I arrived at Columbus but one day before the Convention met. I found much more excitement on the currency than on the Oregon question, though there was excitement in relation to that. The disposition to give notice was unanimous, and rested almost entirely on three grounds. 1. The assumed certainty of our title to the whole. 2. The improbability of War. 3. The willingness for war. These were the general opinions: but few had examined the title. The condition of the currency question added to this untowardness of the Oregon. The [Lewis] Cass men, favourable to Banks and distrusted by the party were loud for Oregon and War, in order to sink the currency and their treachery in relation to it. The [Martin] V[an] Buren men being in advance of the Cass on the currency and in popular confidence were disposed to risk nothing by moderation on Oregon. I went at once to our immediate friends—they all thought opposition hopeless, and even fatal to any body that might attempt it—against giving notice, for terminating the joint occupation. They even thought it vain and hazardous to oppose any thing that might come from the War party. I then determined to make the effort alone, not with the expectation or even hope of success, but from a sense of duty. In order however to secure every chance of success I determined to take advantage of the peculiar state of the Currency question. The Cass men were averse to the hard money position; so were some of the V[an] Buren men. Most of the latter however were in favour of taking general and abstract grounds in favour of a metallic currency. Our friends were in favour of recommending as in the Carthage resolutions specific measures for effecting the expulsion of paper. I therefore agreed with [William M.] Corry, that the report of the Resolution Committee should be by him met immediately on being read with an amendment recommending the collection of the revenue of the *State* in Gold and silver, which he was to support in a speech. This I knew ["was" *canceled*] should be followed by the opposition of all that class of men who having hitherto supported banks and lost the ["public" *canceled*] confidence of the party, would aim to regain favour by the display of devotion to Oregon and War. And I intended after they had been heard to reply and demoralize them, on that subject by exposing the policy they had uniformly pursued in relation to it; and thus shorn of confidence, they would have but little weight in advocating war. Circumstances were unfavourable to the execution of this plan. The Convention was large and tumultuous. The forenoon of the eight[h] was occupied in organization, and this done, we adjourned to 3 P.M. But the Com[mittee] on Resolutions were not ready to report and some time was spent in details and in general declamation. 'Twas past four when the Com[mittee] reported. And the great mass desired to leave town the next morning—[David] Tod having been nominated by acclamation in the beginning of the afternoon session. When the resolutions were reported, and began with those of Hannegan on Oregon, I thought myself fortunate, as their extravagance and absurdity could be easily shown. I was prepared with the following.

Resolved, that the settlement of ["the" *canceled*] Oregon and the extension of our institutions to the Pacific is a glorious result of the sublime policy which originally colonized the Atlantic coast, and has successively won for us the territories of Louisiana, Florida and Texas. America has conquered more by Peace than any other modern power has achieved by War, and with far more honor. In the settlement of the Oregon controversy we hope that honor and peace may still continue united.

On ["the" *interlined*] reading of the Com[mittee] report a motion was made for its *adoption* at once. This was ["amended" *canceled*] followed by Corry[']s motion to amend by recommending the immediate collection of the ["State" *interlined*] Revenue in Gold and Silver as an addition to one of the reported resolutions which was in favour generally of returning to a metallic currency. Corry supported his motion in a brief and able speech, and was followed in opposition by [Edwin M.] Stanton. The previous question was then moved, but lost. I replied to Stanton, and succeeded in a few moments in securing the attention of the house which at first was disorderly. It was now late, and it was apparent that to have time for discussion we must adjourn til next day. I gave way to a motion for that purpose. But pending that motion a clamour arose among all that class that was anxious to return home immediately, for an adjournment sine die. And on being told that ["there was" *canceled*] nothing further was to be done if the report ["was" *altered to* "were"] adopted they determined by clamouring for "adjournment" and "question" to prevent all other proceedings whatever. In this of course they were aided by all whose views were met by the Resolutions, and they prevailed.

After the adjournment, when it was too late, a reaction commenced. The Resolutions ["on Oregon" *interlined*] were denounced by Corry and myself as worthy of bandits and pirates—of men who deriding treaties would shoot the bearer of a flag of truce. And were deprecated by some, defended by none, not even as I remarked by him who offered them in Committee. But so it was by a curious contalenation [*sic*; concatenation] of accidents the thing was done. It is a curious and admonitory illustration of party action. ["A war movement" *canceled.*] The Oregon movement did not originate with the people, as in fact, no movement ever does. It was begun by [Thomas H.] Benton on his own account to secure Western favour. It was handed over to Van Buren in '43 to countervail Texas although V[an] B[uren] had opposed Benton[']s original agitation of it in the Senate by a vote to lay the bill on the table. It is seized from its ["offen"(?) *canceled*] susceptibility of a military excitement by the Cass men to supplant the V[an] B[uren] or [Silas] Wright [Jr.] men and the latter not to be underdone join loudly in the clamour, until the Whigs fearing that votes may be lost to them also join in the ignoble strife. As yet however even Ohio is not all mad on this subject, but she may become so. And I ardently indulge the hope that the absurd position assumed at Columbus will precipitate a separation of the war and peace party, whilst the latter is yet so greatly superior in strength.   On one account I wanted to discuss the question at Columbus.   I wanted to visit with the contempt it deserved ["the charge" *interlined*] that the South wanted to give up the territory North of 49 in order to weaken the North!   I wanted to remind all the modern swaggerers for Western rights, of their long abject and pusillanimous submission to and even support of protection, leaving the South for years to ["support" *canceled and* "maintain" *interlined*] that contest alone.   With greatest regard, Ellwood Fisher.

ALS in ScCleA; variant PC in Boucher and Brooks, eds., *Correspondence*, pp. 316–318.

From J[AMES] H. HAMMOND

Silver Bluff [Barnwell District, S.C.] 10 Jan. 1846
My Dear Sir, I can scarcely express the gratification I feel at the course you have pursued in reference to Oregon, & the apparent effect of it.   Though I could not doubt your views of the matter or that you would in due time express them firmly, it really seemed to me at this distance that the tide of popular feeling was running so furiously in favour of the "whole of Oregon" as to render timely interposition ["ho"(?) *canceled*] almost hopeless, & that even you might deem the sacrafice [*sic*] useless to attempt to stem ["it" *interlined*].   Your boldness, has taken all by surprise, filled your friends & the true friends of the country with extacy [*sic*], dismayed your enemies & the madmen who to promote themselves were rushing into this absurd yet terrific contest, & completely overwhelmed the *quidnuncs*.   Whatever may be the ultimate result, I doubt if any act of your life ["will" *canceled and* "has" *interlined*] elevated you more in the estimation of ["the" *interlined*] best men of the country among all parties, or will add more to ["y(ou)r" *interlined*] reputation with posterity.   The sentiments it has called forth, prove I think fully that after all there is among all those in the U.S. who would have to bear the brunt of it & I have no doubt with the vast ["majority" *canceled and* "proportion" *interlined*] of our ["people" *interlined*], the utmost horror of war.   Fools like [Edward A.] Hannegan—popularity hunters like [Lewis] Cass & [William] Allen— base conspirators against every ["thing" *interlined*] good like [Thomas H.] Benton, were rushing us headlong into a war about the merest phantom ["of" *interlined*] national honor & the most ["abs" *canceled*]

ridiculous pretence of national interest, that demagogues & desperadoes ever yet set up to justify it. I have no doubt the case is precisely the same in England. And that four fifths of the *intelligence* of both countries ["if" *canceled*] would be willing to relinquish Oregon altogether to the bears, the Blackfeet Indians or their worthy compatriots the refugees from both nations who have fled to it. Under such circumstances it would be horrible to go to war. Yet such is the complication of the matter that I do not by any means feel easy. Before the message [to Congress from President James K. Polk] I really apprehended war this spring. That I thought might postpone it a year. Your movement gives me a hope of peace. If you can get England to accept the 49th degree after having so often & unceremoniously rejected it, our Country will have achieved her greatest victory since the acknowledgement of our independence—fruitless it is true—but glorious considering what England is. If in addition she repeals her Corn Laws, & with the aid of peace & this repeal, you can bring down our Tariff, ["or"(?) *canceled*] our triumph will be complete & all the glory of it will I trust & do not doubt enure to you—the substantial benefits of these last measures to *every body* on both sides of the Atlantic. But can you get England to accede to the 49th degree? On that all evidently depends, for obviously that is the utmost concession that our people can now be brought to. I presume you must have hopes of it, from the efforts attributed to you to bring about a renewal of negociations. Is there any thing that any body can do in these parts to strengthen ["you" *interlined*] a hair[']s weight in this attempt? I would do any thing short of taking a trip to Oregon to be of the least service in the cause. I say this to show my *animus*. I can see no way in ["which" *interlined*] So. Ca. or any individual here can do more than has been done to back you.

If we can secure peace the juncture ["for pushing for(?) the" *canceled*] seems the most favourable of any that has occurred in my time for pushing free trade principles & fixing them on a foundation to secure their complete & speedy triumph. The discussions in England aided by the famine, those President[']s & [Secretary of the Treasury Robert J.] Walker[']s able & sound official communications in which they appear to aim to steal your very arrows from you, ["are" *canceled*] must produce powerful effects amounting to the creation of a simultaneous & profound crisis in both countries. The intrusion of this foolish quarrel about a miserable spot of bare & remote territory, which after all that has been said of it is not now & in my opinion *never can be* of as much consequence to either nation as the obscurest port on any Atlantic Coast, at this imminent juncture looks really like a visitation of Divine displeasure. That it may be averted is my sincere prayer.

I receive now a days no letters or documents from Washington. An ex-politician & particularly an ex-governor is you know an object of universal contempt. I do not complain of what is the universal fate & my occupations are such that I seldom think of it, never am annoyed by it. I know the value of your time & the constant intrusions on it. If you could drop me a line when some dull speech gives you moments [of] leisure I should be glad to know anything you may feel at liberty to communicate on the topics which at this moment affect us all so deeply.

The excessively cold & wet weather have interfered with our winter's operations in farming almost as much as the summer's drought did then. This is all the news of our region. Very sincerely yours, J.H. Hammond.

ALS in ScCleA.

From W[ILLIAM] A. ELMORE

New Orleans, January 11th 1846

Dear Sir, The mail which reached us two days since, brought, the resolutions introduced by yourself and Mr. [Edward A.] Hannegan into the Senate, on the subject of Oregon; with the remarks made by different Senators thereon. In reference to the resolutions, and the course of policy, you intend to pursue, on this subject, as indicated by your remarks, I have heard but one opinion expressed, & that opinion sustains you throughout. All say, that you are right: and I believe that the whole country would be perfectly willing to entrust the settlement of this vexed question entirely to you. *All parties unite in their approbation.* The truth is, the impression produced by the conduct of Gen[era]l [Lewis] Cass, Mr. [William] Allen & others, from the west, was, that they were rapidly hurrying the Government into a false position, from which it would be almost impossible to extricate ["it" *interlined*] without a resort to arms; and that they were to derive advantage from that state of things.

In the main, whig and democrat approve the views of the message in reference to our foreign relations; and if the honor or interest of the country, can only be maintained by war, why then we are ready to go into it. But war, is to be the last alternative. We are still willing to compromise; and take the 49th paral[l]el of latitude. Entertaining these views, we rejoice, that you have taken your stand; and that the result must be favorable. We all agree with you that the *President* [James K. Polk] should if possible ["settle" *interlined*] the question; and that the action of Congress, should not be hurried—but all things should be done deliberately.

I am sure, that ["the" *interlined*] people in every quarter of the Union, as well as in New Orleans, will sustain your policy in reference ["to Oregon" *interlined*] and that it will triumph. You may depend upon New Orleans. Yours truly & in haste, W.A. Elmore.

ALS in ScCleA. NOTE: Calhoun's AEU reads: "Mr. Elmore of N. Orleans."

From A[ARON?] LOPEZ

Mobile Ala., Jan[uar]y 12, 1846

D[ea]r Sir, I desire to place my youngest Son at West Point when he has attained his 16th year, which will be in Jan[uar]y 1847. For this purpose I applied in Ap[ri]l 1844 thro' the Hon[ora]b[le] W[illiam] R. King late Senator from this State, and the Hon[ora]b[le] I[saac] E. Holmes from our own Native State. By these gentlemen his name was duly enrolled to which Effect I rec[eive]d an acknowledg[e]m[en]t from the [War] Departm[en]t. All the requisitions were complied with, by stating his size, age & qualifications. I also according to the regulations, *renewed the application in April 1845.* Our present Representative in the U.S. Senate, the Hon[ora]b[le] Ed[mund] S. Dargan has kindly undertaken to superintend the Claim, but from his last letter, I feel some apprehension, and I have therefore taken this liberty to solicit your Cooperation, & have so advised Judge Dargan by this same mail.

I would not trespass upon your time, at a period like this when so much depends [upon] your guardianship of the public safety and the public honour, but I am extremely solicitous of success for many reasons, none greater than the benefit it will confer on me. With a large family, & newly settled here, I am anxious to effect any means to lessen my expences, and in this step I am consulting the cherished wishes of my Son. I have sent to Judge Dargan a Certificate from his teacher, by which you may ["per" *altered to* "decide"] on the youth's qualifications.

You are aware that the mere recording an applicant's name is far from assurance of Success, but I think your influence would consummate the deed, and if any apology were required, I find it in the fact of being a South Carolinian, and an active participant in the stirring days of State Interposition. I am d[ea]r Sir with profound respect Y[ou]r ob[edient] S[ervan]t, A. Lopez, M.D.

P.S. I do not know under ordinary circumstances whether a commission can be anticipated, but if at all practicable, I place every reliance on your ability to effect it. My object is to place the success of my application beyond a contingency, knowing by experience that many circumstances of personal presence & influence frustrate the arrangements of those having the superior claim.

ALS in ScCleA. NOTE: An AEU by Calhoun reads "Dr. Lopez, relates to a Cadet[']s warrant for his son."

Remarks on postponing the Oregon resolutions, 1/12. Under consideration was a motion to postpone until 2/10. "Mr. Calhoun rose and said, that as regarded himself personally, it was a matter of entire indifference to what day the question should be postponed. If any Senator desired to delay the consideration of this or any other grave question for the purpose of deliberation or any other cause, he would be unwilling to make any opposition. But in voting for the most distant day, as he now should, he desired it to be understood that he was influenced solely by a desire to accommodate other Senators round him." From *Congressional Globe*, 29th Cong., 1st Sess., p. 183. Variants in the Washington, D.C., *Daily Union*, vol. I, no. 217 (January 12, 1846), p. 862; the Washington, D.C., *Daily National Intelligencer*, January 13, 1846, p. 2; the Alexandria, Va., *Gazette and Virginia Advertiser*, January 13, 1846, p. 3; the New York, N.Y., *Herald*, January 14, 1846, p. 4; the Charleston, S.C., *Mercury*, January 16, 1846, p. 2; the Charleston, S.C., *Courier*, January 16, 1846, p. 2; the New Orleans, La., *Daily Picayune*, January 22, 1846, p. 1.

From JAMES WISHART

St. Clairsville [Ohio,] Jan[uar]y 12th 45 [*sic*; 1846]

My Dear Sir, You are, I perceive, again in the Senate, in the midst of stir[r]ing events. On the eve of my departure with my family for St. Louis as my future residence I address you to request, that should you favor me with any documents any time after the 1st of Feb[ruar]y you will address them to me there. When in that city a short time before the Memphis convention, your friends informed me that the delegates were instructed to invite you to visit that place, and that if you did so, you would meet with such a reception as no other man had. Hitherto I have been opposed to the practice of some distinguished men of both parties traversing the country. You have abstained from this course, but I believe the time has passed for a perseverance in that course. There is surely nothing in your present position which forbids a personal survey of this great vall[e]y. Great in its natural resources, but weak in its intellectual and moral developements.

The administration of [James K.] Polk has, I confess, in many things greatly disappointed me. Intellectually he falls far below the estimate I placed upon him, and though I am disposed to give him credit ["for" *interlined*] his course on the Texas question, the tariff and the sub treasury, there is little else to which I can give an unqualified approval. His appointments throughout the west are such ["that" *canceled and* "as" *interlined*] the veriest hunker of the north or west would not dare to make. Almost in mass they are, protective tariffites, anti Texas, Oregon warhawks.

From what I see and hear the impression is strong that a compromise on the 49th degree of north latitude with G[reat] B[ritain] on the Oregon question, will be as unpopular in the west, as a war for all north of that paral[l]el would at this time be unwise and impolitic. Although I see strong efforts making to turn your "masterly inactivity" into ridicule, I hope it is the policy that will yet prevail. It is supposed that Col. [Thomas H.] Benton will not agree to fight England yet on this question, and some of his greatest admirers are cursing him in advance.

As the views I presented to Mr. [Richard K.] Cralle last winter met with no answer or response, I infer a difference of opinion in the premises. I have the honor to be respectfully your sincer[e] friend, James Wishart.

ALS in ScCleA; PC in Boucher and Brooks, eds., Correspondence, *pp. 318–319.*

From R[ICHARD] ABBEY

Yazoo City [Miss.,] Jan[uar]y 14, 1846

Dear Sir, I have the pleasure of acknowle[d]ging the rec[eip]t of your favor of the 24[th] ult[im]o. When in N[ew] Orleans a few weeks since I requested my friends to send a sack of the Mastodon

Cotton Seed to some friend of yours at Charleston for you; which I presume they did. But I will now put up a sack myself, somewhat select, and forward as directed by you.

The Mastodon Cotton, in ["the" *canceled*] the most intel[l]igent commercial and agricultural circles, has acquired a reputation beyond any thing I had anticipated, some intimation of which you may have seen from the prints of this quarter. So far as I learn, it is the unhesitating opinion of those best informed, that it much supercedes all other varieties in this country except the Sea Island, and that also, to a very considerable extent. I regard it *a great Southern improvement.* With sentiments of the highest regard, Your Ob[edient] Serv[an]t &c, R. Abbey.

ALS in ScCleA. NOTE: An AEU by Calhoun reads "Mr. Ab[b]ey[,] relates to the Mastodon Cotton Seed." A planter and Methodist minister in Miss., Richard Abbey later became the financial secretary of the Southern Methodist Publishing House in Nashville, Tenn.

From B[EN]J[AMI]N H. BREWSTER

1 Sansom Street, Philad[elphi]a
14 Jan[uar]y [18]46

Respected Sir, Permit me to congratulate you on your return to the Senate. The whole nation now looks anxiously to that body for the adoption of those wise and prudent measures which must arrest a rash and furious course of misguided policy which will embroil the country in a war. You Sir stand foremost among the leading spirits of the land to whose custody is confided not only the peace of our people but perhaps of Christendom.

It has been my intention for some time to write a few words to you; but each successive day brought with it, its pressing duties, and when they were over I felt but poorly fitted to express even the simplest forms of common courtesy.

You would not now be troubled with this letter, if I were not anxious from a sense of duty to press upon you my views upon two subjects that will professionally and politically and personally affect me.

Your body will have before it the nomination of Mr. [George W.] Woodward for the office of Judge of the Supreme Court of the United States. I do not hesitate to say to you that he is wholly disqualified for the place. His nomination should not ever have been made. He is an obscure and unsound man. His professional attainments are few and his views are narrow. He has not one of the qualities that should characterize a lawyer for that high post. The whole bar—I mean the men of standing and learning are shocked with it, and openly express their wonder that any influence should have ever been used to advance him to a place for which he is so unsuited both by education and nature. He is a man [of] some cleverness but of very little experience and still less learning. No one I am certain would ever venture to propose him as Chief Justice of Pennsylvania! How much the less then is he fit to be a Justice of the Supreme Court! I have said this to you from a sense of duty and from no other motive. If the President had selected a man like John Fox who is a lawyer[,] a scholar and a gentleman, he would have chosen a man whose appointment would [have] reflected credit on the Executive and given dignity to the post.

Mr. H[enr]y Horn will be before you for collector of the Customs. This is the worst *political* appointment Mr. Polk has made. Mr. Horn was at Baltimore denouncing and dragooning the Penn-[sylvani]a delegation for [Martin] Van Buren. He set his crew upon me when I returned and openly in his Hickory Club denounced me and those who voted for the 2/3 rule as Miscreants and traitors. The harmony of the party will be disturbed if he is allowed to exercise authority and denounce the active and zealous supporters of Republican principles who are not associated with his petty clique of office hunting politicians. He is of that School of which you once spoke to me—The school of combinations—The Aaron Burr and Martin Van Buren School!

If the men who revolutionized the party at Baltimore are to be respected and not put under the bann let this bad[,] proscriptive and violent man be rejected. I am ever with respect, B[en]j[ami]n H. Brewster.

ALS in ScCleA. Note: Brewster was at this time a lawyer and minor Democratic politician. He later became a Republican and Attorney General of the U.S. under President Chester A. Arthur.

REMARKS ON WILLIAM ALLEN'S RESOLUTION IN REGARD TO EUROPEAN INTERFERENCE IN THE AMERICAS

[In the Senate, January 14, 1846]

[*William Allen of Ohio asked leave to introduce a joint resolution which strongly denounced "recent manifestations of a disposition by certain Powers of Europe to interfere in the political arrangements" of America, and asserted that this interference "would justify, the prompt resistance of the United States."*]

Mr. Calhoun expressed a hope that a resolution which appeared to be of great importance would not be introduced without the question of leave being first decided. He trusted that it would not be taken for granted. He did not himself comprehend the full import of the resolution; and he believed there were not five Senators who did. He called for the reading.

[*There was further discussion, and the Chair stated that the question was on leave to introduce.*]

Mr. Calhoun said that every Senator must be aware, in the present situation of the country, that this resolution called on the Senate to make a declaration which called for the most solemn deliberation. It would be matter for serious consideration, if this resolution was introduced and acted on, how far we are disposed to give effect to this declaration. No man could view with stronger feelings of indignation than he did the improper interference of the European Powers with the nations of this continent. And he would take this occasion to say that, as far as his information went, the interference of France and England with the concerns of the Government of Buenos Ayres was an outrage, high-handed in its character, and without precedent in the history of nations. But the great question presented by this resolution was, whether we should take under our guardianship the whole family of American States, and pledge ourselves to extend to them our protection against all foreign aggression. Had we arrived at that state of maturity when we could wisely and effectually do so? Was this to be the understood and settled policy of our Government? If so, it would become necessary for us to pursue a different course from that we have heretofore adopted. The entire energies of the country must be concentrated and put forth to enable us to carry out this policy, if we intend that our declaration shall mean anything. He regretted that, at this moment, such a question should be urged on the Senate. He was fearful that, in the eyes of the world, it would have the effect of injuring our character for wisdom and moderation, and of still further perplexing other questions which were now pending. The President had, in his message to Congress, made the same announcement as is made by this resolution. Why should we not, for the present, be satisfied with this announcement? He knew that the views thrown out by Mr. [James] Monroe, on this subject, did not meet with the approval of some wise heads in this country. He [Calhoun] was then comparatively young in experience, and they were approved by him; but he had understood that negotiators who were then abroad complained that it had produced an unfavorable effect on certain claims which were awaiting adjustment. Certainly, no practical benefit had resulted from the declaration, as it had been followed by no action on the part of our Government. In a great crisis, like the present, he was afraid that we were disposed to act without that solemn deliberation and forethought which the exigencies of the times required of us. We appear to have reached a point at which two roads branch off before us, the one leading to the right, and the other to the left, and fatal may be the consequences if, instead of a wise and well considered selection of our course, we hastily and rashly choose the path of error and danger. On the measures of this session may depend the destiny of our country. He was for solemn deliberation even on the question of receiving such a resolution as this. He regretted that the chairman on Foreign Relations had introduced it, as he would prefer to leave the matter where the President had placed it. He hoped, therefore, that the Senator from Ohio would not urge the introduction of his resolution at this time.

[*Allen spoke at length.*]

Mr. Calhoun remarked that the manner in which the resolution was introduced struck him as extraordinary. Notwithstanding the Senator from Ohio was the chairman of the Committee on Foreign Relations, to which that part of the President's Message had been referred, he had introduced, as he (Mr. C[alhoun]) understood, the resolution on his own authority, without consultation with the other members on the subject referred.

Mr. Allen said it was his own proposition.

Mr. Calhoun observed that there was no precedent to be found, and he questioned whether the resolution was not entirely out of order. Had other members of the committee been consulted? Had the Senator from Michigan, (Mr. [Lewis] Cass,) the oldest member of the committee, and whose long experience in our foreign affairs entitled his opinions to respect? Had his gallant friend from Arkansas, (Mr. [Ambrose H.] Sevier,) or any other member? No. The resolution was introduced on the authority of the chairman of the committee, as he had just acknowledged, without consulting a single member. He (Mr. Allen) had taken up a part of the Annual Message on his own authority, and that, too, comprising one of the greatest subjects in the Message. If this course were proper, why not take up every other subject in the same manner? If there were no other reasons why we should not give leave for the introduction of the resolution, this of itself would be sufficient. The chairman had asserted that twenty-one years had elapsed since Mr. Monroe had announced a similar opinion; and that it had settled the opinion of the American people with reference to it. Why, then, was this resolution introduced, unless it was designed to produce effect on other questions? For himself he intended to speak without disguise. He knew the bearing the resolution was designed to have, and he well knew where he stood on the questions involved. He had taken his stand on the questions intended to be affected. He was for peace, if it could be honorably preserved; and he would not be forced to countenance any measure which would render more difficult an honorable adjustment between the two countries on the Oregon question.

He was against the resolution, unless Senators were prepared to go on and meet all contingencies which might result. If so, we would be compelled to take this stand: put forth all our strength, become a great military Government, and take measures to repel all foreign interference with the affairs of this continent. With great deference to the Senator from Ohio, if he was really in earnest in his desire to carry into effect the principle involved in his resolution, instead of introducing it in a general form, he ought to introduce one calling on the Government at once to interfere in behalf of Buenos Ayres, to be prepared to take that Republic under our protection, and repel the interference of France in her concerns. It was the part of wisdom to select wise ends in a wise manner. No wise man, with a full understanding of the subject, would pledge himself, by declaration, to do that which was beyond the power of execution, and without mature reflection as to the consequences. There would be no dignity in it. True dignity consists in making no declaration which we are not prepared to maintain. If we make the declaration, we ought to be prepared to carry it into effect against all opposition. He was directly opposed to granting leave to introduce the resolution; and before he resumed his seat, he would ask for the yeas and nays.

[*After brief further discussion, the Senate adopted, 28 to 23, a non-debatable motion to table the motion for leave to introduce the resolution.*]

From *Congressional Globe,* 29th Cong., 1st Sess., pp. 197–198. Variant reports in the Washington, D.C., *Daily Union,* vol. I, no. 219 (January 14, 1846), p. 870; the Washington, D.C., *Daily National Intelligencer,* January 15, 1846, p. 2; the Alexandria, Va., *Gazette and Virginia Advertiser,* January 15, 1846, p. 3; the Richmond, Va., *Enquirer,* January 16, 1846, p. 2; the New York, N.Y., *Herald,* January 16, 1846, p. 4; the Philadelphia, Pa., *United States Gazette,* January 16, 1846, p. 1; the Charleston, S.C., *Mercury,* January 19, 1846, p. 2; the Pendleton, S.C., *Messenger,* January 23, 1846, p. 2; the New Orleans, La., *Bee,* January 23, 1846, p. 1; the New Orleans, La., *Daily Picayune,* January 23, 1846, p. 1; the London, England, *Times,* February 4, 1846, p. 5.

Remarks on parliamentary order, 1/14. John J. Crittenden of Ky. asked leave to introduce resolutions on Oregon, to be considered on 2/10 with other resolutions on the subject. The Chair stated that the request required unanimous consent. "Mr. Calhoun merely made a suggestion on the question of order. He considered the parliamentary rule as established, that when a question was in the possession of the House, no other proposition on the same subject could be received until that was disposed of; and that the only way a similar proposition could be brought up was in the form of an amendment to the original measure. This rule had been departed from, he knew, in the other House, and to a certain extent in this, to the great inconvenience of the proceedings of each. He would suggest to the Senator, in lieu of introducing this resolution as an independent measure, to give notice that when the resolutions from the Committee on Foreign Relations shall come up, he will move his resolution as an amendment." Later, Calhoun remarked that he "made no objection, but had merely suggested the parliamentary course." From *Congressional Globe,* 29th Cong., 1st Sess., p. 198. Also printed in the Washington, D.C., *Daily Union,* vol. I, no. 219 (January 14, 1846), p. 870. Variants in the Washington, D.C., *Daily National Intelligencer,* January 15, 1846, p. 2; the Richmond, Va., *Enquirer,* January 16, 1846, p. 2; the New York, N.Y., *Herald,* January 16, 1846, p. 4.

From L[EWIS] L. ALLEN

St. Louis Mo., Jan. 15/46
Dear Sir, You will I trust excuse an humble individual in addressing
an Illustrious Senator who by his statesmanlike conduct[,] ardent
devotion to his country and patr[i]otism won for himself a wreath
of imperishable fame, and enduring honour. Will you permit me to
say although I have never had the honour of a personal acquaintance,
yet it has always afforded me the most profound pleasure in reading
your truly eloquent, learned & tallented [speeches] on all the subjects which have claimed your attention. My most ardent prayers
with your many friends is that your valuable life may be preserved
for many years to our Nation and to the world. Will you be so obliging as to send me your speeches[,] Congressional documents &c.
from time to time and thereby very much oblige your Ob[e]d[ien]t
Serv[an]t, with the most profound regard Very Respectfully, L.L.
Allen.

N.B. Please direct to the address of Rev. L.L. Allen[,] St. Louis
Mo.

ALS in ScCleA.

From W[ILLIA]M P. DUVAL

Tallahassee [Fla.,] Jan[uar]y 15th 1846
My dear Sir, It is a fortunate event for our country that you are again
a Senator, and most opportune, was your appearance in that body,
just in time to check, intemperate action, as indicated (not by the
resolutions of Mr. [Lewis] Cass) by his speech, which went far
beyond them. His remarks were artfully designed, to give himself
(not his country) some signal advantage. I think he has signally
failed with the nation, whatever success he may command in the
Senate. Young and ardent Senators, seemed to have catched the
Senator's warspirit dusted over (as the fire was with ashes) as is
evinced by the several speakers on the same side, followed by the
imprudent, & hasty resolutions of the Senator from Ohio [William
Allen]. I am delighted with your amendment to the intemperate
resolutions offered by Mr. [Edward A.] Han[n]egan. ["They" *canceled*] It ["are" *canceled and* "is" *interlined*] drawn with great force,
and with statesmanlike ability, and so clear, as to command the ap-

447

proval of every sound minded man in the nation. Your amendment is admirably designed to draw the sting alike from Gen[era]l Cass[']s remarks, and Mr. Han[n]egan[']s resolutions.

It would be most unwise to close the door to all negociation between Great Brittain and the United States on the Oregon controversy. What though Great Brittain has thrice rejected our offer of the 49° north [latitude] as our boundary, will that justify war, if she should yet accept our proposition? It may be said that our offer has been withdrawn, admit it; does it therefore follow no proposition will be made by that government, or that our offer heretofore declined—may not on further consideration be accepted. Suppose the latter should be now proposed to us. Are we such Don Quixottes as to fight a shaddow of a windmill, for nothing more substantial, than a false notion of national honor. Can ["exist(?) to" *canceled and* "a mear shade" *interlined*] produce a war? Your course is approved in this State by every thinking patriot, and I am greatly mistaken, in the good sense of Congress, if your wise & enlarged views on this important measure, ["is" *canceled and* "are" *interlined*] not sustained.

I have taken my stand at this point and a new paper is now speaking the doctrin[e]s, that should govern the action of the South. I trust the *Southern Journal* will be conducted with ability, firmness, and moderation. Hundreds, if not thousands of the Whig party in this State, are so dessignated by certain men of our own party—who from mere selfishness, and poor ambition, would sacrifice the best men in our State, who they fear will be too prominent for them. We have already felt a shock from this reckless course, that is likely to react with effect in favour of the Whigs. So much disgust has thus be[en] occasioned in our own ranks—that ["if" *canceled and* "it" *interlined*] will not surprise me, if our next General Assembly should have a majority of Whigs. This we are now endeavoring to counteract, and we hope to succeed. If the election, for representative from this State should be sent back to the people, it is my intention to become a candidate, and at any rate our election for member to Congress will take place next October, as after the 4th of March 1847 we would be without a member untill October following. I do not wish this intention communi[c]ated to either of our Senators because I know [James D.] Westcott [Jr.] cannot be trusted, and because I am the last man in Florida, he would be willing to see in Congress. I have believed Mr. [David] Levy [Yulee] was your friend and left to himself, would like to act with your friends but certainly since his election with Westcott, he has held no communication, with any of your friends as far as I can learn and I have taken some pains to assertain this fact. I am fearfull he wants moral courage, and his having Westcott elected with him, when I knew he disliked him, and when he was fully apprised he had always denounced you, and your friends, seemed strange to me. It has greatly impaired Mr. Levy[']s standing with the people, and I do not believe if he was now a candidate for Congress, he could come within 1000 votes of the poll he received in May last. He and Westcott will go down together, if Mr. Levy follows his counsels. It is the policy of our friends here to treat the great portion of the Whigs kindly, for many of them are as sound democrats of the 1798 school as can be found in any State. You must understand a Florida democrat, is one who has mixed himself up with all the local questions, that were agitated under our territorial government. The broad and great principles of the democracy, had little to do with ["true" *canceled and* "Florida" *interlined*] democracy—hence many of our best men are branded as *Whigs*, either because they were in favour of sustain[in]g ["it" *canceled and* "some" *interlined*] local system, or corporation in existence at the time. Our object should be to unite all the sound men of either party, to *proscribe none* who wish to unite in the Southern policy.

These views will govern me, because they ["are" *interlined*] just and prudent. I never fear responsibi[li]ty where I know I am right. I want to see how our Senators will act on your amendment to Han-[n]egan[']s resolutions. I will venture to say that Westcott will be with you, for he is alarmed, at the fate that is certain to attend him, should he go counter, to the wishes of the people of this State, who are decidedly in favour of your course. But don[']t trust the man, for a moment, however much he may appear to act with you. I tell you I know the man, and if ever you should be induced to confide in him, remember what I now say—he will *betray you* when ever it may suit his views. Such has been his course through life, not one man that ever trusted him, but will acknowledge the same. Gov[erno]r [John] Branch and all his friends will join us, and they can do much in Middle Florida. We shall have Gov[erno]r [William D.] Mosel[e]y heart, and hand with us—and it is gratifying to me to say, you have not a truer, or warmer friend in Florida. I am sure any documents, or speeches you may send him, would be greatly valued by him. I wish you to transmit to me such documents, or other state papers, as should be published here in our Southern journal. I do not look for any from either Mr. Levy or his col[l]eague. I will see that every thing you deem proper to give for publication shall be printed for the people of Florida.

You would not like perhaps to be considered as directing the course of the journal, and it is for this reason I request that I may act.

I would rather be in the next Congress, than in the Senate. The only representative in the popular branch if a sound practical man, can have more influence, and effect more for the Southern democracy, than both of our Senators. I do not desire a seat in Congress with the wish to continue, for if I am elected to the next Congress, I should retire at the end of its term. I am too poor to remain in Congress. Whatever you may communicate to me in confidence, no other shall see or know—such communications may sometimes be necessary to guide the course of our friends—and if so, will be used so, as not to commit you, for any view or opinion thus given. We have never, had a paper in this State that was the advocate of the Southern doctrines. The Floridian published here is Westcott[']s paper, and speaks *his doctrin[e]s*, not for the party, but himself. Our object is to compell that paper to follow our lead and it will be compelled to do so or it [will] sink if it does [not] pursue the right track. We will make no war on it, but treat it with respect, for my policy as before stated is to conciliate and strengthen our Southern phalanx. Let all join our cohort and march in order, and the victory will be owers [*sic*].

Gov[erno]r Moseley has appointed [former] Gove[rno]r Branch and myself commissioners on the part of this State, to ["meet and" *canceled*] adjust the boundary between Florida & Georgia—we are not yet notified who the Georgia commissioners are. It is a long line to run, but we shall see many people, and shall take care to become acquainted with them. I think I shall be soon master of their wishes & opinions on many political topicks. With sincere respect and esteem your friend, Wm. P. Duval.

ALS in ScCleA. NOTE: Duval was a former Representative from Ky. and Governor of Fla. Territory. He did not achieve his intention to become Representative from Fla.

From NATHAN GAITHER

Columbia (Ky.), Jan[uar]y 15th 1846
Dear Sir, Many years ago I promised you a notice from the West. I have occasionally performed my promise and the the [*sic*] gloom

that shrouded us from the Mantle of the idol of our forest country [Henry Clay] gave me nothing very hopeful to say to you.

Our sky is now brighter—and even Kentucky will in a few years resume her proud stand as in '98 with the democracy of the Union. We hail your return to the Senate as an earnest of the onward & upward course of democracy, but we do regret the condition upon which you resumed your station. You form an item of our Moral Capital as a people & we must have an executive head. Our choice ["as" interlined] an ag[g]regate must be unrestricted & your condition will only relate to your State, not the Union. The most excellent Message of the President with his Secretaries [sic; of the Treasury, Robert J.] Walker[']s report on the finance has worked like a charm upon the people and the Whig nonsense of high duties making cheap articles is fast passing off. The free trade doctrine in the sense use[d] by democrats is taking deep and abiding hold on their minds. Agriculture and commerce unshackled is what they want.

If States have grown wrinkled with age & her people not having the nerve to remove for more room; let them hurdle [sic] in their work houses & create My Lords of Capital & Knights of the spindle, but don't tax others & deprive them of the proffits of their honest industry. I now fear little from consolidation but yet fear much from the power of capital. The issue is fairly made up between labor & capital. Labor wishes nothing but her fair proffits. Capital wants infinitely more in her purse and in political ["power" interlined]. It is a fearful enemy but I believe we can meet her successfully and equal rights & priviledges will prevail. The consum[m]ation of the Annexation [of] Texas is hailed by comparatively all in Kentucky and I hope our legislature will speak in a voice to let the lone star know altho she was not heard in your Senate she nevertheless hails her admission as cordially as any other State. We desire no war, but if it must come about Oregon let it come[;] we would rather not tho.

In by gone times some of my friends thought I yielded my judgement from fear to [Andrew] Jackson[']s procla[ma]tion. Injustice was done me. I condemned that unfortunate Government paper & my vote on the force bill ought to have shielded me from even suspicion for if I pride myself upon any vote while in Congress it is that vote. The power of Mr. [Henry] Clay ultimately overwhelmed in this country but did not subdue me. I have battled for our Cause under all circumstances for the Cause itself & shall continue to do so.

My friends upon the election of [James K.] Polk without my

451

knowledge presented my name to him for office. When informed of it I protested against it but they would not consent to withdraw their claim. The President & myself were together in the Bank struggle & they were sanguine of success in their application. I know the press upon the President and have had no feeling about the matter until lat[t]erly. I do not wish the kind opinion of the democracy of (Ky.) lessened towards me. Their failure will make them believe that they had overrated me. If I could [have] discharged the duties of half Mission abroad to my country, I would be willing or if it can be better done. *Well.* Respectfully, Nathan Gaither.

ALS in ScCleA. NOTE: Gaither had been a Representative from Ky. during 1829–1833.

To JOHN [S.] LORTON, Pendleton, S.C.

Washington, 15th Jan[uar]y 1846

My dear Sir, I enclose you a check for $180 on New York, which I hope will answer your purpose. I could not get one on Charleston.

The question of peace or war is very doubtful. Its fate depends on the Senate. As yet, the indications there are not unfavourable. I trust that its wisdom & firmness will prove suffi[ci]ent to avert so direful a c[a]lamity as war would prove in reference to such a question & in the present state of things. With great respect yours truly, J.C. Calhoun.

[P.S.] Please acknowledge the rec[ei]pt of the draft.

ALS owned by Fort Hill Mansion, Clemson, S.C.

To ANDREW PICKENS CALHOUN [in Ala.]

Washington, 16th Jan[uar]y 1846

My dear Andrew, I am happy to hear by your's [*sic*] of the 2d Inst., that all were well.

Considering the weather, you have, indeed, done well to get out 500 bales at the date of your letter. Since then, the weather has been here good for the season of the year; mild with but little rain. I hope it has been equally so with you, & that good progress has been made in gathering cotton. You say nothing of the corn crop. I hope that is all gathered.

I agree with you, that we must increase our force. It is the most efficient means, that can be adopted to meet our engagements. By increasing we might raise our cotton crop to nearly 1000 bales without purchasing an additional acre of land, which at 6 cents would give us a clear income of $14,000. But I would think it unadvisable to enlarge our crop beyond, what could be ["done" *canceled and* "well cultivated" *interlined*] with due regard to the good condition & efficiency of our hands, in the meane time; & I hope in proposing to plant enough of cotton this year to increase our crop to 700 bags, you will not go beyond that point.

The next steamer will arrive probably in the next 4 days, &, I trust, that you will be prepared to take advantage of the market, should there be a rise. I think, if you can sell at 7½ round it would be well, in the present uncertain state of our relations with Great Britain. If we could be assured of peace, I would not take 8 cents. The cry of famine has nearly ceased, and the impression is, that the crops of S.C. & Georgia will fall short full one half.

The question of peace & war is still very uncertain. Every thing will depend on the Senate, and the course of Whigs in the body. From present indications notice [of termination of joint British-U.S. occupation of Oregon], in some form, will be given. If it should be in the unqualified form reported by the committees of Foreign relations of the two Houses, I would regard war almost certain. I hope, that it may be qualified by making it a condition to offer the 49th [parallel of north latitude], as the basis of a compromise, or even a reference to arbitration, if nothing better can be done.

My position is one full of responsibility. I shall meet it by a fearless discharge of duty. Thus far, I have not been unsuccessful, although badly sustained by the Whigs in my first move; I refer to the amendment I offered to [Edward A.] Hannegan's resolutions. Had they not opposed taking a vote on them, the real war party would have been seperated from the others, & left in a lean majority [*sic*] of less than a dozen. They acted better in reference to [William] Allen[']s notice for leave to introduce his joint resolution to take the whole continent under our guardianship, which enabled me to acheive [*sic*] a decided victory. While I am not sanguine, I do not despair of ["combining" *canceled and* "obtaining" *interlined*] the control, & preserving peace, by combining in all my movements the highest discretion with the ["highest" *canceled and* "greatest" *interlined*] boldness & promptitude. I have with me the wise, & the patriotick of all parties; and shall be supported by the almost united voice of Virginia & S.C. with the most talent[ed] portion of the South,

& the convictions of my own mind. No one can realize the disasters, which would follow the war, should there be one. I fear neither our liberty nor Constitution would survive.

I enjoy very good general health, but suffer much from colds, accompanied by a cough, but without any bad symptoms, such as pain, or pressure on the chest, or fever, or night sweating. ["It seems" *altered to* "They seem"] to be confined to my throat & head. All the rest are well & join their love to you, Margaret [Green Calhoun] & ["children" *canceled*] John [C. Calhoun, Jr.] & the children. Your affectionate father, J.C. Calhoun.

ALS in ScU-SC, John C. Calhoun Papers; PEx in Jameson, ed., *Correspondence*, p. 677.

To Ja[me]s Ed[ward] Colhoun, [Abbeville District, S.C.]

Washington, 16th Jan[uar]y 1846
My dear James, I have received your two letters of the 26th Dec[embe]r & 7th Jan[uar]y, & will write to James [Edward Calhoun] in conformity with your request, in reference to his studies. He has good talents & only wants them to be well directed & applied to acquire distinction. I do hope you will acquire a sufficient control over him to fix the habit of ["study" *canceled and* "attention" *interlined*] & systematick application to his studies, and also of due economy in his expenditures.

I see in the portions of your two letters, which refer to myself strong evidence of that abiding friendship & deep solicitude in relation to all that concerns ["me" *interlined*], which you have ever manifested towards me. But you must permit me to say, that I do not think you have attributed to their true cause, the motives, which induced me to accept my appointment to the Senate, or properly estimated the, effects, which it is like to have personally.

You seem to think, that I yielded to the solicitations of a few persons, who were not my real friends, & that I came under pledges to renounce all pretensions to the Presidency. Neither is the case. The pressure on me to accept came from all parts of the Union, & every party, urging me, as I regarded the peace & safety of the country, not to decline, if the place should be offered to me. But as strong as the pressure was, I would not have yielded, ["in" *canceled*]

454

my aversion to return to publick ["life" *interlined*] again, had I not a deep conviction, that there was great danger of a war, the end and the consequences of which no man can see; & that I might, by possibility do something, to avert so great a c[a]lamity. I could not but see the danger & responsibility I would have to run in encountering the strong current in favour of war, which had been created by the folly or weakness of the administration; but I would have been unworthy of the high place, in which my friends ["desired" *altered to* "desire"] to place ["me" *interlined*], had I yield[ed] to such considerations. Such are the circumstances under which I accepted ["the place" *interlined*] & the motives which induced me to accept. I did so with a full knowledge of the ["whole" *canceled and* "consequences" *interlined*], reluctantly & only from a sense of duty; but without any pledge, such as that you allude to, or of any kind whatever; and let me add, without any one ever suggesting ["such" *canceled*] the policy or propriety of such a pledge, except Col. [Francis W.] Pickens. This I mention, however, in strict confidence. I have never ["mentioned it" *interlined*] to any one else. I attributed it in him to error of judgement. Nothing could induce ["me" *interlined*] to give such a pledge; not from any desire I have to fill that high office, but from what I regard the indelicacy & impropriety of such an avowal on the part of any individual.

As to my course here, & the effects it may have on me, I am guided solely, by the views, I entertain of the best means of preserving peace consistently with the honor & interest of the country, without regarding the management & intrigues of administration, or opposition, or any of the cliques, into which they are broken, or what effect my course may have on my future prospects. To defeat the war, ["in my opinion," *interlined*] is to gain every thing, & to fail to defeat it is to lose all. It would leave us of the South little worth having. I regard it as quite uncertain, whether it can be defeated or not. The only hope is in the Senate. It may be there, if the Whigs should be united & act the part of patriots. I fear they will not. We are, indeed, in a strange state. The party desiring peace constitute a great majority both in Congress & the Union, & neither our Executive, nor that of Great Britian [*sic*] desire war, & yet things have been so managed, on our part, that it is difficult to avoid it, calamitous as it must prove to us.

We are all well, ["except" *canceled and* "with the exception of" *interlined*] colds. I am laboring under a severe one, accompanied by a bad cough, but without any other bad symptoms. Cuddy [that is, our niece, Martha Maria Colhoun] is much delighted & enjoys herself much. She has made a very favourable impression, & is indeed a fine girl.

All join their love to you & James. Yours affectionately, J.C. Calhoun.

ALS in ScCleA; PEx in Jameson, ed., *Correspondence*, pp. 675–677.

From F[RANKLIN] H. ELMORE

Charleston, Jan[uar]y 16, 1846

My Dear Sir, I have today rec[eive]d the accompanying letter from my friend D.C. Campbell who edits the [Milledgeville, Ga.,] Federal Union. It explains his position so correctly that I think it best to show it to you. I had written to him shortly after receiving the letter you left for me in Charleston on your way to Washington. In both the last papers are short editorials covering your position with cautious but I think judicious remarks. They may not seem bold enough, yet I think they are more telling in that region for that reason, as they will not alarm the ultras of the party before they are indoctrinated.

It seems to me that you will do a good service by attending to Campbell. It will please & encourage him in tendencies which are as you see already strong & will become controlling.

I also send you a letter of [Joseph W.] LeSesne of Mobile, by which you will see that all are on the alert there. Would it not be well for you to show some attention to the Editor of the Mobile Register? His name I do not know. You will see that LeSesne says he was a good deal warmed to you when you were in Mobile.

From my Brother [William A. Elmore] in N[ew] Orleans I have not heard since I wrote him about y[ou]r move.

The recent vote in the Senate postponing the consideration of [William] Allen[']s resolutions to 10 Feb[ruar]y against his opposition, & by so decisive a vote, has given us more hopes that the Senate will sustain you than we had before. It has given very great pleasure here—and I hope our auguries will not be disappointed.

I have urged those who could influence Mr. [George] McDuffie to write to him. I don[']t know if they have. [James] Hamilton [Jr.] is here & promised me to do so. [Ker] Boyce also promised. Hamilton promised also to write to [Walter T.] Colquitt [Senator from Ga.], who I can[']t think can be in the least danger of being wrong. Yours truly, F.H. Elmore.

[Enclosure]

D[avid] C. Campbell to F.H. Elmore, Charleston, S.C.

Milledgeville [Ga.,] Jan[uar]y 14th 1846

Dear Elmore, Your kind favor of the 24th ult. would have received an immediate reply, but about the time of its receipt, I was called to Macon & there detained more than a week, in effecting the final settlement with the purchasers of the Monroe Rail Road. The N. York Company, aided by your citizen Ker Boyce, who has taken some $50,000 stock, are now going on with the Road & will have it finished to the junction with the State Road by the 1st of June.

I thank you for your friendly suggestions in reference to Mr. Calhoun. His speech last year, made me a convert to his views on the Oregon question. They are those adopted by the Whigs of this State, and they are sustained by the more intelligent and moderate of our own ranks. We have however a large class of the Young Democracy, who contend that the Party is bound by the Baltimore resolutions, that the whole party must act as a unit, and that as our allies of the North and West stood manfully by us on the Texas question, it would be base and treacherous to desert them in the issue for Oregon. My position is a peculiar one. My paper, is the only one of the party at this place and is regarded as its organ throughout the State. To maintain its influence & secure the objects which I wish accomplished, demand great caution. I heartily approve every step Mr. Calhoun has taken, and shall have no hesitation in sustaining his measures so far as they have been developed. Indeed such is my confidence in his prudence & foresight, that I regard his movements, as carrying with them at least *prima facie* evidence, that they are right. You may be assured, he shall receive from me all the justice, it is in my power to render, consistently with my relations to ["the" interlined] Democracy of the State & of the Union. I will publish in my next paper, [William L.] Yancey's speech on the Oregon question, which I ["take" canceled] regard as an exponent of Mr. Calhoun's views. In this way, the best impression can be made upon the public mind.

The Democratic Delegates in Congress from this State are all warm friends of Mr. Calhoun, with perhaps the exception of [Howell] Cobb, I am in correspondence with most of them, and fully advised of their views.

The Legislature had adjourned when your favor was received.

Gen. [William B.] Wofford will be here in February when I will show him your views upon the subject of the Augusta Bridge.

It will afford me pleasure to hear from you at all times. Yours truly, D.C. Campbell.

[Enclosure]

Jos[eph] W. Lesesne to F.H. Elmore, President of the
    Bank of the State of S.C., Charleston

Mobile, January 2d 1845 [*sic*; 1846]
My Dear Sir, Your letter of the [*blank space*] reached me to day and I hasten after having shown it to [John A.] Campbell and several of our other confidential friends ["hasten" *canceled*] to answer it. I coincide entirely with the sentiments you express with regard to the message. I think it is one of the ablest and boldest documents that ever issued from the Executive Department. It is the first instance in which a president has had the independence to put the Tariff question upon principle. This feature alone is enough to immortalize both the President and the Message. For myself I confess ["on this score" *interlined*] my profound homage for the man and the measure—and he must behave hereafter very badly to induce any good man of our way of thinking to feel or act towards him otherwise than kindly and respectfully.

The Declaration in the Inaugural about Oregon was silly and wrong in the Extreme, ["yet" *canceled and* "and" *interlined*] the temper of the message and still more of the correspondence and conduct of the negotiation is subject I think to just exception. [James] Buchanan['s] last letter altho' well reasoned is not statesmanlike, lacks coolness and dignity, and I fear this entire subject has been handled in a braggart and bullying disposition on our side. This is Campbell's feeling—although I think the Democrats generally approve warmly all that Polk[']s administration have done, or said, on the subject, barring the indiscreet declaration of the Inaugural. But no one here desires war, and I think I stand alone in the belief that there is real danger of a war. Certainly it would be madness to ["spill embroil the country on such theme(?)" *canceled*] embroil the two countries on account of such a dispute. But we can not and perhaps ought not to recede from the last proposition (the 49 degree). But how Great Britain can accept it and yield the navigation of the Columbia I can not see. It will be a clear case of "back out," and after being bullied and cheated by our people as she has been, will she ["incur the disgrace which taunts she is likely to receive on this score(?)" *canceled*] consent to eat her own oft repeated words on this subject; if not we must get ready to fight.

With regard, however, to the main point of your letter—I need not tell you that Mr. Calhoun will receive the same Cordial support from his friends here that they have ever been ready to yield him: and the course on the Oregon question which ["you say" *interlined*] he ["seems to have" *canceled and* "has" *interlined*] marked out for himself is precisely that which has already prefigured itself in the minds of his friends. If we are really ["to l(?)" *canceled*] in danger of a war, the country looks to him ["to pre" *canceled*] 1st to do all within his great powers to preserve peace, and 2dly if we are to fight to get us at it in an honorable way.

The discussion in Congress on the subject has struck every one as an indiscreet affair and got up in wretchedly bad taste. Particularly [Lewis] Cass' speech, which has nothing but its correct English and passable Rhetoric to redeem ["it" *changed to* "its"; "from appea(?)" *canceled*] manifest demagogue spirit. Mr. Calhoun[']s great office in this business will be, I think, chasten this spirit and infuse dignity temper and decorum into the conduct of the administration. [Thomas H.] Benton's and [William] Allen's prominence are not favorable.

I agree with you, that ["his" *canceled and* "Mr. Calhoun's" *interlined*] crisis is at hand. During the present year the die will be cast which decides his fate so far as the Presidency is concerned. But he ought ["to" *interlined*], as I have no doubt he will, act without reference to this. ["And a war would, whatever credit he might acquire by it, destroy his prospects for the Presidency" *canceled.*] Would not Great Brittain give up the whole of Oregon for a commercial treaty with us, letting in her manufactures at reduced rates for Twenty five years? And is not this, after all, the true mode, (in an age like ours, all of whose tendencies and interests are peace and commerce) of settling ["the" *canceled and* "this question as well as the future terms of" *interlined*] intercourse of ["the two" *interlined*] nations? Such a treaty would be the noblest monument of modern times. It would render peace between England and ourselves perpetual, and do much, as an example, to secure the peace of the world, ["while it would present Republican Institutions in a new aspect" *canceled*]. It appears to me that the difficulty about Oregon presents a favorable ["time" *canceled*] juncture to press such a measure; and that *Mr. Calhoun and Mr.* [Daniel] *Webster* by the course of events are placed in position towards each other and towards the country which they might use to infinite advantage in this respect; and that in this way both questions (the Tariff and Oregon) might be permanently settled. ["This is merely a trifling thought of my own" *can-*

celed.] The same number of words never before conveyed so much meaning as those of Lord Aberdeen when he said that "the views of G[reat] B[ritain] are purely Commercial." They deserve to be studied as a volume; for they ["unlock furnish the key to unlock every mea(?) explain" *canceled and* "explain not only her conduct in the Texas business, but" *interlined*] every measure of the foreign department of the Brittish Government. It is not ["Territory" *canceled*] land but markets and customs that she desires and to get these she will sacrifice almost every other consideration.

I regret to say that we have no political organ here likely to render Mr. Calhoun much aid. The "Register" you know is incurably "old hunker." It is impossible to galvanize the dead carcase of that wretched concern. While Mr. Calhoun was here [Thaddeus] Sanford (the proprietor) could not help feeling some portion of the general enthusiasm, and I got some useful things in the paper—but he has relapsed again into his original state of torpor and suspicion. If things take the course you indicate we must try to revive the Tribune unless we can get controll of the "Register" which would be preferable. But unfortunately we are poor and although we might start a paper again it could not be sustained without pecuniary means which are not within our reach in this State. Could you help us in Carolina? For the present I think (and our friends concur in the opinion) we ought to say nothing betraying a disposition to run Mr. Calhoun for the next Presidency ["but" *interlined*] let events bring him forward. *The movement ought to come from the West,* if possible, and those who signalized themselves in the contest with [Martin] Van Buren ought to keep carefully in the back ground at the outset at least, or "Old Hunkerism" will inevitably imagine that its corns are in danger of being tread upon, and so to our great detriment kick and cry out before they are hurt.

I am compelled to write in great haste, and thus to send you a very ill looking and I fear unsatisfactory letter. Very truly yours &c, Jos. W. Lesesne.

P.S. If you make any use of this pray read, and do not hand it to any one.

LS with Ens in ScCleA.

From J[OHN] H. HOWARD

Columbus Georgia, Jan[uar]y 16th [18]46

Hon[ora]bl[e] John C. Calhoun. While I thoroughly oppose your views in relation to the Miss[iss]ippi being an inland sea and the appropriations which would follow, if such a construction should generally obtain, I concur with you most cordially upon what I suppose to be your policy in regard to Oregon. It is *peace* (& *honorable* peace only of course) which I would maintain between the two governments if I could. Much is said now about the honor of the nation. I would preserve it most scrupulously, but I cannot conceive how it is forfeited or even endangered by pursuing such a course as will enable the British govt. to accept terms which she has heretofore rejected. The nation was not considered dishonored by offering the 49th and the circumstance of the British govt. having rejected that offer does not necessarily demand of us to insist upon all or lose our honor. If it was right to offer it, it is still right to receive it. And it is for those who approved of that offer to prove why it was *then right*, & *now wrong* to settle upon the same terms. I confess that I have not fully investigated the claims of the two parties and do not profess to understand their relative rights ["of the parties" *canceled*] as governed strictly by the laws of nations, but have predicated my opinion upon what I believe to be our policy in the present exigency, taking it for granted that the U.S. was not dishonored by offering to define the 49th as her boundary. The question now upon which there seems to attach the greatest importance is the *notice* to terminate the joint occupancy. If this would either prevent negotiation, or be looked upon by the British govt. as a menace, I do not believe that the true policy of the country would justify it. If such would be the effect of giving the notice, it would be impolitic & harsh, as we believe, that the matter could be settled by negotiation if no firebrand is thrown in the way.

It is to be deplored that party influences are mixed up with these important questions. Many gentlemen of much patriotism, think it incumbent upon them to support *all* the recommendations of the President [James K. Polk] or ["of" *canceled and* "they will be" *interlined;* "subjecting" *changed to* "subjected" *and* "themselves" *canceled*] to the charge of refusing to support the administration. I consider Mr. Polk[']s [first annual] message [to Congress] one of the best I ever read, but it is the privilege of a freeman, and the *duty* of Senators, while they may heartily approve of allmost all his views, still to be independant enough to differ with him (especially if they be of his own party) upon an isolated point, if the true policy of the country in their judgement demands that difference. I may be mistaken, but I do think, that the *final* adjustment of this Oregon question is *hurried* upon us before the nation is ready, or before there is any real pressing necessity for terminating it. I wish the Senate to stand up for the honor of the nation, and sooner than it shall be tarnished, I am an advocate for war, yes *war* with all its disastrous and distressing consequences, but I do not believe a temperate prudent course in the settlement of this question can subject us to the imputation of cowardice, or crouching to British power. No matter how much boasting men may disregard consequences, yet it is sound philosophy (where our honor is not implicated) to look at consequences and weigh them well, and the responsibility of our representations should warn them of the effects which a rash and imprudent act might bring upon their constituents. War would to us be a great calamity and benefit *no part or section of the country*. The West could sell us nothing for we should not be able to buy any thing; moreover if the culture of cotton was abandoned, we should raise vastly more than a supply of provisions, and if the West had the monopoly of supply (which she would not expect) of the whole army it would not equal the present outlet for her provisions. Mr. Polk has recommended the modification of the Tariff. War will not only defeat this measure for the present but for a great number of years, and I should not be surprized if it ["did not" *canceled*] entailed upon us all the evils of the paper system, which I look upon as disastrous to the real interests of the country as the war itself. I am truly yours &C, J.H. Howard.

P.S. It is to be regretted that your prominent position furnishes good cause for many to oppose whatever policy you may bring forward. Your resolutions support the administration fully, but if you oppose the notice, that moment the followers of mere *party*, denounce you as *opposing* the administration and courting the whigs. I am fully sensible of your delicate position, but you have the advantage upon this question. Your policy is the same as it has been for years. They can[']t charge you with any inconsistency. You may rest assured that although the influence of party feeling may give in a little while a very different tone to public sentiment; yet at *present* most thinking men of both parties are ["in this quarter" *interlined*] with you, and desire that such a course should be given to the Oregon question as shall *avoid war*, provided of course *peace* can be maintained upon honorable terms. I cannot venture to advise you, although I would take that liberty if I thought, I could either benefit you or the country; but I would suggest the propriety of their [*sic*] being *no* opposition to the notice if it cannot be prevented, but to vote for it and couple with it something which would deprive it of all its menacing character, so as to renew negotiations upon the subject. Suppose instead of one year[']s notice you make it two or three and ["in" *canceled and* "at" *interlined*] the same time invite negotiation to settle the matter. You know this, that right or wrong the war cry becomes popular, and the war party soon claims to itself exclusive patriotism, and I do not wish you to place yourself in a position that you would be deprived of influence. Your friend, J.H. Howard.

["Please remember" *canceled.*] My best respects to Mr. [George] McDuffie and say to him I wish him improving health. Please make my respects also to the *Alabama* Senator Dixon H. Lewis, & to my friend Judge [Walter T.] Colquitt [Senator from Ga.].

ALS in ScCleA; PEx's in Boucher and Brooks, eds., *Correspondence*, pp. 319–320.

To H[ENRY] W. CONNER, [Charleston]

Washington, 17th Jan[uar]y 1846

My dear Sir, The question of peace, or war still remains in a state of great uncertainty. I am of the impression, that the war fever is abating, & that there is a decided majority in the Senate against hasty & rash measures. But I do not think the prospect is strong for defeating notice in the Senate; although, I hope, if that cannot be done, it will be connected with some provision, that will reopen the negotiation and thereby counteract its otherwise almost certain tendency to involve us in war.

From present indications, the prospect is, that the abolition party will go for war, under the lead of [John Quincy] Adams [Representative from Mass.] & [Joshua R.] Giddings [Representative from O.], with the avowed view of abolishing slavery; and it is to be feared, that both parties at the North will court them to get their aid in elections. Already the Whig convention in Connecticut, convened to nominate State officers, have offered them the right hand of fellowship on the Oregon & Tariff questions. This of itself ought to openen [*sic*] the eyes of the South to what they may expect, if war should ensue, and to unite every portion of it on the side of peace, if it can be honorably preserved. Those who doubted before, as to our true policy ought to doubt no longer, after seeing our most deadly enemy openly take the side it does. It seems to me, that our papers are not suff[ici]ently active in calling the attention of the South to the disclosures, which we daily have of the course which this vile party intends to take, & the motives which they openly avow for taking it. They ought to call on the South to unite & defeat them by taking the opposite course. Yours truly & scincerely [*sic*,] J.C. Calhoun.

ALS in ScC; photostat (of ALS) in DLC, Henry Workman Conner Papers.

From W[illia]m S. Hastie

Newyork [City,] Jan[uar]y 17, 1846

Dear Sir, I not only congratulate you, but the country upon the position you have taken on the Oregon question.

Amongst all classes of men that I have come in contact with in this State, there is but one opinion upon the subject, and that opinion clearly sustains you in every position you have taken on this question, indeed since the speech of Mr. [John Quincy] Adams the war fever, so far as the Democratic party is concerned has entirely subsided.

Gen[era]l [Lewis] Cass'[s] peace offering in the shape of a ship canal around the falls of Niagara will not help him, you may depend that the people, the rank and file, have placed their seal upon every man who is endeavouring to force the Country into a war.

Fifteen years silence upon this question would have enabled the western States to pay their debts.

I shall pass through Washington in a few days on my way to Pendleton and will endeavour to do myself the honour of calling on you. With great respect &c &c, Wm. S. Hastie.

ALS in ScCleA.

From Louis McLane

London, Jan. 17, 1846

My dear Sir, By the Massach[u]setts which sails tomorrow may arrive earlier than the steamer of the 4th In[stan]t I send you some newspapers which may interest you both as it regards our relations with G[reat] B[ritain] and the movements for & against the Corn law monopoly.

The former have reached a crisis requiring all the good sense and courage—I mean moral courage that the statesmen on both sides of the water can bring to their management. I understand the position of the President [James K. Polk] to be pacific—such as will warrant a compromise of the Oregon question upon terms honorable to both nations, and if an offer of that kind be made to him by G[reat] B[ritain] or the negotiation be resumed by the Senate in a way not only not to censure but to strengthen his own course, he would not be unwilling for the sake of peace to assent to terms mutually satisfactory to both governments. I sincerely hope he will not be driven from this high ground by any extravagance from any quarter whatever. Unless the offer of arbitration made at Washington has been rejected in terms to make it impossible in this Gov[ernment] to renew the negotiation by a farther proposition, it would not be difficult in my opinion to lead to a proposition that might be made satisfactory. As I stated to you in my former letter, however, the inequality between my position here, and that of Lord Aberdeen as to impose too much restraint upon him to allow him to be very communicative, and certainly unless I had some reason to know what would be likely to be satisfactory at home, I could not venture, however informally to lead the way to an offer.

If I could form a tolerable conjecture of what would be accepted at home I would not be unwilling to incur any responsibility not in compatible with the honor of a gentleman nor inconsistent with my country's honor to lead to an offer which he might accept; and I feel unshaken in the conviction that such terms as I hinted in my former letter might be had. At present and up to this time my duties, since Mr. Packenham[']s [*sic*; Richard Pakenham's] rejection of our proposition, have consisted mainly in moderating the demands and expectations of their government, in predisposing them to reasonable adjustment, and to preparing them for what was to take place in the U.S. with the Executive and in Congress, so as to prevent the consequences of an bad temper on both sides. Unless the sentiments of "General" [Lewis] Cass, and the principles of Mr. [Stephen A.] Douglas's Bill find more favor with Congress & the Country than I think they will these impressions & disposiations will I have every reason to believe be permanent.

The Times Newspaper of today, which I send you, contains some

465

temperate strictures upon the recent news, and the present state of affairs. The reference at the close of the leading article, to the rejection of the offer of arbitration would seem to imply that the writer was not without access to official authority. In this view, and from the fact that it reiterates the offer of Mr. [Albert] Gal[l]atin as the proper basis of compromise, it is quite significant. In my former letter I referred to the palpable misapprehension of Mr. Gal[l]atin's proposition, though this may not weaken the force of the article as a feeler. That which appear[s] to me most important to a settlement is to afford this government a pretence for taking less now than they have heretofore demanded, in order to see what it deems the point of honor, and to enable them to discharge, what they consider their obligation to the rights & interests of the Hudson's Bay Company. Now would it not be easy so to conduct the negotiation as to do both? Would it be unreasonable to do so? Must it not have been ["in the contemplation of" *canceled and* "contemplated by the" *interlined*] Treaties of 1818 & 1828 that interests would grow up on both sides during the joint occupation that when the time arrived for partition would require in some way or other to be considered? And is it possible that after such occupancy for nearly thirty years one party can expect entirely to ["exclude"(?) *canceled*] expel the other without any provision whatever for those interests, without a fight? They seem here to set a great value upon the navigation of the Columbia—perhaps because they have heretofore made it a point, perhaps because they really believe it important as a way to market for the Hudsons Bay Company. They would probably accept of the right of continuing the passing by the Company for a term of years, and of the free navigation of the river during the same period. Or might not the occasion be taken to secure the free navigation of the St. Lawrence, by giving that of the Columbia? You have no doubt already considered the real nature or value of the concession of the *free navigation* of such rivers *in the present state* of the trade & commerce of the world—when are they done[?] between friendly nations—and according to the spirit of all the commercial treaties of the present age?

However, Sir, I am very sensible that I have no right to take so many liberties with your time, as my hurried letters must do. Nevertheless you will I hope excuse the trouble I give you, and use my communications with the discretion be coming my situation. No one I am certain[?] will[?; have] more sincere pleasure if by them I have given you the least information calculated to assist your efforts in preserving the peace and promoting the glory of our Country. I remain, my dear Sir, very faithfully your ob[edient] S[er]v[an]t, Louis McLane.

ALS in ScCleA.

From ISAIAH RYNDERS

New York [City,] 17th Jan. 1846
Respected Sir, I understand that Several Gentlemen from our City have Called upon you and Have Said to you that your Friends in this City Have been very much disappointed with your Course in Relation to Oregon. This is Partially True and undoubtedly you must Have foreseen such a Result but Permit me to Assure you that you Still Have many ["unshak" *canceled*] warm Friends in this City who have an abiding Confidence in your Political Sagacity and Experience and above all in your unshaken Firmness[,] Integrity and Love of country. Although we beleive [*sic*] our Title to Oregon Clear and Indisputable and that If Necessity Requires it we would most willingly defend it with our Lives. Yet we think that Peaceable adjustments of all National disputes Preferable to War if Practicable without Injury to the Interests or Honor of our Country. Such are the motives upon [which] we beleive you Acted in Relation to the Oregon Question and in Such Position we are willing to Sustain you and I have no doubt that before one year Rolls Round you will Have gained instead of Losing Friends. I may be mistaken but such are my Present Convictions. I again Repeat War to the Knife before we Suffer Indignity or Reproach to be Cast upon our Nation but Peace if Honorable and Pacific adjustment Can be made. I am with great Respect your Humble Ser[van]t, Isaiah Rynders.

ALS in ScCleA. NOTE: Rynders was leader of the Empire Club, an Irish street gang, and a Tammany politician.

From LEWIS SHANKS

Memphis [Tenn.,] January 19th 1846
Dear Sir, Having so lately visited our city, & confer[r]ed with so many of the citizens of the west, & indeed observed for yourself the

actual condition of a portion of the southwest, so far as it could be seen by a hasty trip on our great highway, you will not be surprised, at being called on, to throw the weight of your influen[c]e, in your present station in the scale, in favor of those Just claims of the south & west, that have been so much neglected.

The universal desire to see him, who had been so long & prominently identified with the history of our country, manifested by the crowds that assembled at every point, and especially at Memphis on your arrival, was but the honest & voluntary award of distinction to talent & public services; which was still farther exhibited, in a more intel[l]igent & flattering way, by the unanimity with which you were called to preside over the Convention.

As you were induced to take the responsibility of presiding over a body, representing so extensive a range of public interest, & feeling, against the opinion and wishes of your S.C. friends, I feel great pleasure in being able to assure ["you" *interlined*], that all subsequent developements prove, that your course has not only been such as to promote the prominent interests of the West & south; but to point to you, by general consent, as a most efficient & influencial agent, & representative of those interests.

You will please consider the allusion to these facts, as being designed to shew, that the people of the west have felt the want of a statesman, combining a knowledge of their condition, wants & claims, with the disposition & boldness ["to press them" *interlined*], & at the same time the influence to secure their success. The scale of numerical strength is now turning in favor of the west & south; & the next apportionment of representation will give a decided preponderance.

Before inviting ["to" *canceled*] your attention to a few subjects of western interest, I must be excused for alluding to one, that is now interesting the whole country. Strictly partizan politicians, or those governed more by impulse than wisdom, may expect, what they may feel, & exhibit as national honor & patriotism, will be calmly applauded & sustained by the people at large; but in this they are often mistaken.

Whatever may be the opinions & feelings of the people of the northwestern States & ter[r]itories in this region of country, your course on the Oregon question has so far given, I think I can say, universal satisfaction.

You will see the importance and necessity of Marine Hospitals on the Miss. River, from your knowledge of the immense number of persons necessary to carry on the trade of the west, in the various kinds of craft used.

There was no subject presented to the Convention on which there was more unanimity than this. Memphis has been receiving some aid from the State, which is likely to be withdrawn entirely, which will throw upon the Corporation the necessity of contributing from $5 to $10,000 annually to relieve sick paupers here, from every part of the world, invited by the public works & the peculiarly prominent position of this point.

The importance of the immediate establishment of a Marine Hospital here by the general government, you will perceive without troubling you with farther details of its necessity.

The Legislature of Ten[n]. has passed a Memorial to Congress, asking the relinquishment of the small amount of Public Lands in the Western district of Ten[n]. for purposes of education & designating $40,000 of the proceeds [of sales of the lands], to the College at Jackson—sixty miles from Memphis.

We hope if this relinquishment is made that a part of the proceeds will be given by Congress to the University of Memphis, recently chartered, & just started under favorable auspices. I have written to Hon. F[rederick] P. Stanton [Representative from Tenn.] on these subjects, whom we hope you will aid.

With the hope that you will not regard this as an unwarrantable intrusion upon your time &c, & that your time will permit you to give it some attention. I am sir very respectfully, Lewis Shanks.

ALS in ScCleA. NOTE: An AEU by Calhoun reads "Shanks of Memphis."

From THO[MA]S P. SPIERIN

So. Ca.[,] Abbeville C[our]t House
19 Jan[uar]y 1846

D[ea]r Sir, I have undertaken to aid Mrs. Elizabeth Gillam, widow of Rob[er]t Gillam, and mother of Gen[era]l Ja[me]s Gillam, to obtain a pension under the Act of Congress passed in 1838, and the principal objection is ["want of" *interlined*] proof of her marriage previous to January 1794. Is there any circumstance within your recollection, to proof [*sic*] the fact of marriage in this case. Mr. [James L.] Edwards the Commissioner of pensions, will shew you the Declaration of Mrs. Gillam, corroborated in part by the Testimony of Col. Z[achariah S.] Brooks of Edgefield, and the testimony of Hugh O'Neall of Newbury [*sic*], accompanied by the Certificate of Judge [John Belton] O'Neall. It would be a great favor conferred upon this relict of [a] worthy revolutionary soldier, to give your aid, in her [a]pplication, for a pension, as I am informed she is your relative, & that you are well acquainted with her, & her family. Yours Very Respectfully, Thos. P. Spierin.

ALS in DNA, RG 15 (Veterans Administration), Revolutionary War Pension and Bounty-Land Warrant Application Files, W8848 (M-804:1073, frames 107–110). NOTE: An AEU by Calhoun reads, "Relates to Mrs. G."

From A. P. STINSON

St. Joseph[,] Berrien Co[unty] Michigan
January 19th 1846

My dear Sir, Soon after the receipt of the doings of the "*Memphis Convention*," over which you Presided, I addressed a Note to you at "*Fort Hill South Carolina*" & subsequently at *Washington*, whether they reached you or not, I am not Advised. Since your *position* has been *defined* on the "Oregon question" there has been much said ["by" *canceled and* "in" *interlined*] the Papers & By ["the" *interlined*] people on Both Sides of that question & your Course has alternat[e]ly been *Lauded* & *Conde*[m]*ned*[?]. You are aware Sir, that from the *Position* taken by the *President* [James K. Polk] in his *Message*, the Correspondence between *Messrs.* [*James*] *Buchanan* & [*Richard*] *Packingham* [*sic*], that the masses had *formed* & *expressed opinions*, based on what they supposed was to be the course of Policy, to be persued by the *Administration*. Our Party going for "*The whole or none of Oregon*" & our *opponents* for a *Compromise* on the *49 Paral*[*l*]*el*. Since your Course has been defined based on your *Ressolutions*, a different state of things exist. Many who heretofore were boisterous for the "*whole or none*" are "*taken all aback*" & *Concede* that *Mr. Calhoun*[']*s* course of Policy is Right & will best subserve the Interest of the Country! Never Sir, have I seen so *sudden a Change*, on an *Important question*, as has been Produced within the Last few days among the *Intelligent* of the *Democratic* Party. The *Democratic Press*, In our State however, Still Cling to the Doctrine of the "*whole or none*" & this more perhaps to be *Con-*

sistent. But the *People*, the *more considerate of them*, seem to *have undergone an entire Change*, Little Less *Sudden*, than the Conversion of *St. Paul*, & quite as unexpected by them as Him!

This may be accounted for from the fact, that they are *quite willing* to see Gov. [Lewis] *Cass "floored"* in the Senate & Nation. His Course Relative to *appointments* in this State, has *Lost the State to him Now & forever It is believed!* The course he took in procu[r]ing the appointment of C[*harles*] G. *Hammond Collector of Detroit* was most *unauspicious* & has Called Down on him *Denunciations*, the *Length* & *breadth* of our State, & Caused a *Denunciatory Ressolution to be passed by our State Convention!*

Col. Daniel Munger, was the *Choice* of the Democr[ac]y, ten to one over *Hammond*, but *Gen. Cass* being a man *filling an Important Station* & Knowing *Hammond* was a man who he could *use* to *subserve his ulterior purposes*, had Influence eno[u]gh to procure the Nomination. But whether he will have Enough to Secure a *Confirmation, Remains to be seen*. If he has & Does, It will prove a *blow* to the Democr[ac]y which If they survive It, will be a Long time before they will Recover, Is my Prediction. That you may *Know something of the feeling* In Our State, I send you an *Editorial Article* taken from the *Kalamazoo Gazette*, a *Leading Democratic Journal of Michigan*. This article Sir, *contains* the *Sentiments* of the Democr[ac]y of this State & of *your friends Particularly.*

If Sir, you will send me your *Speech* on the *"Oregon question"* when made, I will be much oblidged. Your *Remarks* in the *incipient stages* I have seen in the Papers thus far. I Regret that our friend [Levi] Woodbury is not now in the Senate to *"Lead off"* in New England on that question. Mr. [Benning W.] *Jenness* [Senator from N.H.] who takes his place, is a *younger* & *less experienced man*, but one who is *Democratic* & will (I think) *Do Right*. I have Known Mr. J[enness] for many years, while I Resided In N.H. He is a *worthy man* & to Whom, If you meet him, please make my regards acceptable. I have written him, Immediat[e]ly on Seeing he was on the *Committee* of *Finance with you*. Allow me Sir, to say a *Crisis* in your History is at Hand. What the Result of your *Present course* may be, time alone can Determine. I think It will work for good. I have Just Rec[eive]d Gov. *Silas Wright*[']s *Message* to *the N.Y. Legislature*, & If I understand him, He is with you in Opinion & If so, *your policy* will *obtain*. [*Marginal notation:* "Herewith I send also Gov. Wright(')s Message."] That done, *It Requ[i]res not the Ken of Prophecy* to foretel[l] what will follow. You will perceive I am *ardent* in my *temper[a]ment* & in my *attachments*. So It is, so

It always has been & will be I assume. As Ever Yours Truly, A.P. Stinson.

P.S. The *frank* manner with which I have ever addres[s]ed you, will readily suggest that they were Intended for your *eye alone* & so I desire you to Consider them. A.P.S.

ALS in ScCleA.

From [Lt.] P[ATRICK] CALHOUN

St. Charles Hotel
New Orleans, Jan. 20th 1846

Dear Father, I see by the papers that there is a probability of one or two new Regiments being added to the Army; as promotion is what I look forward to as long as I remain in the service, it is of course my great desire to get it. There can [be] it appears to me no great difficulty in my getting the appointment of Captain in any new Regiment which may be raised. This appointment would enable me to get higher ones in case of war. I would be greatly pleased should it meet your approbation, if you would yourself or through some of your friends, forward my wishes. I do not of course desire or look forward to, any thing less than a Captaincy—and, there can be no earthly reason why it should be refused. My present appointment is one that suits me, but it is uncertain, and my wish is to get a more stabl[e] one.

I write this from my bed to which I have been confined for more than twenty days—I am in hopes that I shall be able to leave my room in the course of a week. I[t] was my desire to write you at great length but finding my position an awkw[ar]d one to write in I must finish. On my recovery I will write again.

My love to all. Your affectionate son, P. Calhoun.

ALS in ScU-SC, John C. Calhoun Papers.

From GEO[RGE] W. TAYLOR

Philadelphia, N.E. cor[ner] Broad & Spruce
First month 20th 1846

Dear Friend, Having for many years felt my mind drawn towards thee with particular interest, and for several months past, increasingly so, though entirely unknown to thee, I cannot well resist longer the constraint I feel laid upon me; to address thee privately on a subject highly interesting to our beloved country at this time, and intimately connected with the future welfare of the countless millions who are yet to call the United States, their father-land. As a friend to peace, I have been well pleased with thy advocacy of pacific measures in regard to the Oregon question and greatly regret that it should have been brought up at this time so prominently for discussion & decision; believing with thyself that if it had been let alone for a few years, the rapid settlement of the territory by our citizens, would have rendered an amicable adjustment of the difficulty with Great Britain comparatively easy. I have had no doubts on the question of title, for several years; and by the new light which has been shed upon it of latter time, by thyself and our friend [James] Buchanan, I am more confirmed in the conviction that the whole of Oregon belongs of right as well as by fitness to the United States. If no rash steps are taken, I think the time is not distant when the British Government will see the propriety of yielding her claim so far as to admit of an adjustment of the boundary such as the Government of the United States may not hesitate to agree to.

I would now, with no overweening confidence in my own judgment, nor pretensions of any special light on the subject, but with great diffidence, venture to ask thy attention to a few enquiries or remarks, in relation to the great question of difficulty to this otherwise happy nation, which stares us constantly in the face.

In what way can the descendants of Africa so unhappily situated among us, both for them and for us, be disposed of, so as to guarantee to the next and future generations, a reasonable prospect of deliverance from the growing difficulties, inseparable from their present relation to the white population, who in the ordering of Providence, are the masters of the country. I have never considered it my place to unite with the abolition or anti-slavery societies of the North, to agitate and press this subject on our brethren of the South, who from position or whatever causes, are more heavily burdened with this trouble than we are; but, a native of Pennsylvania, and a member of ["the" *interlined*] religious society of Friends, I have from childhood had but one opinion upon the relationship and condition of this unfortunate and degraded class of mankind. I do think there is something required at the hands of our Statesmen of the acting generation, at least preparatory to some energetic effort being made to relieve our great Republic from this enormous clog which alone seems to hang in the way and render doubtful our continued progress to unrivalled prosperity.

Whether the condition of the coloured population can be so changed as to admit of their dwelling in our midst, consistently with the good of both races; or whether means should be sought to provide for the African an ample dwelling place in the land of his ancestors, or in the West India islands, or in some other congenial clime, may well claim the serious enquiry of statesmen and philanthropists.

For many months, thy honoured name has recurred to me again and again, with the conviction, that from thy favourable position and wide-spread influence, those well-known talents and acquirements, which Divine Providence has dispensed to thee, particularly qualify thee to originate and promote a plan for the deliverance of our country from this appalling & intolerable yoke.

The consciousness of having been instrumental in effecting so great a good, which, pardon me for suggesting as probably within thy power, would be thy sure and lasting reward—to say not, that thou would receive the blessing of ages to come.

Excuse me, I mean not to flatter; but, I am persuaded that there is no other man in the United States, who in all respects is so well qualified, and so favourably circumstanced, for such an undertaking as thou art. Permit then, a humble citizen to ask thy calm reflection upon this question. I trust thou art a professor of the Holy Religion of Jesus Christ, and therefore not a stranger to the language of prayer, nor unmindful of the promptings of the spirit of the Redeemer. I would then, commend thee to this unfailing source of wisdom and guidance, needful both in the origination and carrying forward of every good work, and there leave the subject with thee at present. Believe me sincerely & respectfully thy friend, Geo. W. Taylor.

ALS in ScCleA.

From M[ARIA] D[ALLAS] CAMPBELL

Phila[delphia,] Jan[ua]ry 21st 1846
349 Chestnut St:

My dear friend, I am anxious to visit Washington at the moment most likely to interest me, in the debates in the Senate, and as *you* know best whose lucid views, *I* best like, to listen to, & be improved by, I have thought you would not be sorry to find an opportunity to oblige me, by specifying at what moment you thought I had better make my visit—and although I am most ready to unite in your sentiment of "masterly inactivity," yet I should not desire to find *you* inactive, when I visit the Capitol.

When I parted from you in March, I had very little idea, that either you, or myself, should desire to be in Washington this winter. That you have changed your mind & views so frankly expressed to me at that time, may easily account for my infirmity of purpose, but why you have done so, you have yet to explain to me. In my humble opinion, you *are where you ever should be*, directing for your country's good, the Councils of the nation, & curbing those rash spirits, which would recklessly drive us into ruin. Let me hear from you, when I shall come on, for I feel the deepest interest in these momentous questions. Believe me now as ever truly & faithfully y[ou]r friend, M:D: Campbell.

[P.S.] If you can, do give me some of your opinions on our present position. I have little or no confidence in our helmsmen. Energy, sagacity, & firmness all are wanting.

ALS in ScCleA. NOTE: The writer was the sister of Vice-President George M. Dallas. Calhoun's AEU reads: "Mrs. Campbell."

From H[ENRY] A. S. DEARBORN

Hawthorn Cottage
Roxbury, Mas[sachuset]ts, Jan[uar]y 21, 1846

Dear Sir, Last autumn, I took the liberty of giving to Doctor [Augustus] Mitchel[l] of Maine, a letter of introduction to you, as a gentleman most worthy of your ever ready & kind attentions to the meritorious. This day I received a letter from him, dated at St. Mary[']s [Georgia], in which he informs me, that he has daily made excursions, in pursuit of of [sic] subjects, in the natural history of that region, & has already collected many. He intends to extend his researches into Florida.

I have written to Gen[era]l [Duncan L.] Clinch & Mr. Evans, asking them to use their good offices, to enable the National Institute to avail itself of the services of Doctor Mitchell, & thus enlarge the bounds of his explorations, for the benefit of the whole country; & well knowing that your patriotic & expansive views are extended far beyond the "Dark Dorndaniel" [*sic*; Dardanelles?] of political strife, & include those of infinitely more consequence, in the grand domain of *Science*[,] *Letters* & the *Arts*, I have no doubt, but that you will also do what is possible, amidst the tempest of the times, for the accomplishment of objects of such *perennial* importance; & much can you achieve.

[Oliver] Cromwell said, in one of this speeches to the House of Commons, ["or rather the Parliament of one House" *interlined*] when Protector, that "he did not pretend to much concern with rhetoricians, nor with what they used to deal in—*Words*. That his business was to speak *Things*." So it is your wont to talk of *things*; for you properly appreciate that all-conquering verb *To Do*. There have been, in all ages & nations, innumerable men, who wasted their lives, in uttering resultless words; but *Did* nothing & could *Do* nothing; because they had not that mighty *creative* attribute of intellect, so rare in the human race—no *conception* of *achievement*; no *power* to *project* & *execute*. The route of Hercules was known by his *tracks*, & men of capacious minds *perform deeds* which cause their names to be enrolled among the Immortals of Earth.

Every advance of man & of nations has been the result of one mind. Whatever there is in history, that stands out in bold relief, one man accomplished. Combined minds never have done any thing, great. Alone, with his own energy, genius & talent, has man acted, who has acted in a manner to excite admiration. One effort of *one man* is of more potent influence, than of combined millions. Thence it is that ever & anon a truly great man appears to guide the destinies of a nation, or make an onward stride in Science or Art. A Sully, or a Chatham—a Watt, or a Fulton—a Newton or La Place—a Phidias, or a Powers—a Titian or an Alston, merit & receive the praise & gratitude of all succeeding generations; so that in after days, well may it be said, "there were giants in the land." Such giants are the *heralds* & *apostles* of *truth*, & of *mighty deeds*. They go forth indomitable for they bear the flaming sword of omnipotent genius.

Our government has done but little for the advancement of Science & the Arts; but I hope the time has come, when this vast Republic of twenty millions of freemen, will take its position in the front rank of civilization, by the adoption of all such measures, as will promote the interests & glory of the nation. But our greatest men must *introduce* them, & *establish* them, & thus become worthy companions in *fame*, as they will have been in *actions*, for the *great remembered* of all past ages.

Ignorance can not do more than follow, & therefore a few really great men in ["the" *interlined*] Parliament of England & the American Congress *Do* all that is *Done*, honorable to the country; & therefore it is, that I repose confidence in the men of *intelligence*, who have the *ability* to *propose* & *perform great deeds*. The *talking, voting, busy nothinganians*, who annually go up to London & Washington are like the rank & file of an army—of no consequence, unless there are capable Leaders, to conduct ["them" *interlined*] in the march to victory, & renown. With sentiments of the highest respect, your most ob[edien]t S[ervan]t, H.A.S. Dearborn.

ALS in ScCleA.

Remarks during debate on the Naval appropriations bill, 1/21. There was an extended discussion in which Edward A. Hannegan and William Allen played a prominent part. Calhoun said: "Whatever might be the opinion of the chairman of the Committee on Foreign Relations (Mr. Allen,) the bill before them had an intimate connexion with the other questions now pending [Oregon]. He had heard the debate with great reluctance, and differed much with the gentleman from Ohio in his views of the matter. He had, however, heard with pleasure the Senator from Indiana, (Mr. Hannegan,) say that he was for peace. I am (said Mr. Calhoun) for peace; for peace on honorable conditions. The question has been reduced to that, and I hope to see it still more narrowed. I was happy also to hear from the chairman of the committee that a 'masterly inactivity' would not lead to war, but that the course he (Mr. Allen) recommended might lead to war." From *Congressional Globe*, 29th Cong., 1st Sess., p. 228. Also printed in the Washington, D.C., *Daily Union*, vol. I, no. 225 (January 21, 1846), p. 894. Variants in the Richmond, Va., *Enquirer*, January 23, 1846, p. 2; the Alexandria, Va., *Gazette and Virginia Advertiser*, January 23, 1846, p. 2; the New York, N.Y., *Herald*, January 24, 1846, p. 4; the Charleston, S.C., *Mercury*, January 28, 1846, p. 2; the Charleston, S.C., *Courier*, January 26, 1846, p. 2; the Pendleton, S.C., *Messenger*, February 6, 1846, p. 1.

From JAMES GADSDEN

Charleston S.C., Jan[ua]r[y] 22d 1846

My Dear Sir, Accompanying you have a memorial I was requested to prepare from the Memphis Convention. It has been delayed from my not knowing untill very recently that it was expected I sh[oul]d draw it up. Perhaps its presentation had better come from some No[rth] Western Senator. You will use your pleasure however in this. I would draw your attention to my remarks on the improvement of the Mississippi and the reclaiming of the Public lands. The two objects on which there was some disagreement in the Convention as to the powers of the General Government. I had none myself as to practical results; all I apprehended was that the subject was so large it might lead to extravagant expenditures on abortive efforts & experiments, which previous scientific examinations might check. The abuse of the exercise of power is what we are to guard against. I think I have shewn that there is a connection between the improvement of the Mississippi Bed, and the reclaiming the swamps. Let me hear your opinion on this subject.

What think you of a Commission for examination and Report before there is any action? This might prevent extravagance without results. [*One or two words canceled.*] If such a project sh[oul]d be carried I should be pleased to be pleased to be [*sic*] at the head. I think I could connect with that position, and more agreeable to my *tastes* and bent of mind, a Supervision over all the Rail Roads we have projected. Something like an inspector General, with a view to produce harmony of action making all the parts play in with each other.

My present position is too confining & laborious—To[o] much in detail to attend to and which so absorbs my time & weakens or rather benumbs my intellect that I cannot meet my Western friends, now in fine spirits; with the spirit I sh[oul]d desire. I am laboring hard night & day, and the Memphis convention on Rail Roads have [*sic*] not been without fruit. The movements in Tennessee, Mississippi & Alabama are all ominous of zeal & success. Pittiful [*sic*] narrow minded Savannah has alone imposed a temporary objection[?]. But it will be broken down. Now if I could be removed from my present place, or only hold the relation to the Carolina Road I would hold to others as Inspector General of all, connected with a similar Place from Congress to examine the Mississippi and the Public Lands, I would be willing to close my public career on the consummation of these Great Works. You can see whether my memorial has any effect [or] makes any impression & perhaps suggests to some one from the West the necessity of such an office. Indeed it is due me from a Body who 22 years ago, deprived me of a commission assimilated in some degree to it, & which would have afforded me the opportunity of presenting views in accordance to these on the Great Projects I wish to see carried out. Yours truly, James Gadsden.

[P.S.] I congratulate you on the pause you have produced in the Senate on the aggitating [*sic*] subject. Perhaps my memorial may divert some of these excited men from Oregon to the Mississippi swamps, certainly more fertile than all Oregon. [Dixon H.] Lewis['s] & Levy'[s] now Eulee's [*sic*; David Levy Yulee] vote on [William] Allen[']s Resolution astonishes every one. We had some distrust in Florida of [James D.] Westcott [Jr.], but Levy was confided in. He will hear from his friends.

[Enclosure]

"Memorial From the Memphis Convention to The Honorable
    The Senate of the U.S. of America"

Charleston S.C., Jan[uar]y 22 [18]46

To the Honorable the Senate and House of Representatives in
    Congress assembled[:]

The undersigned a Committee appointed to memorialize the Congress of the U. States on the various topics embraced in Resolutions passed at the Memphis Convention most respectfully represent— That at a convention held at the City of Memphis in the State of Tennessee on 12th November 1845, There were 583 Representatives assembled from the States of Pennsylvania, Virginia, North & So[uth] Carolina, Florida, Alabama, Louisiana, Texas, Mississippi, Tennessee, Arkansas, Missouri, Kentucky, Illinois, Indianna, Ohio and Iowa—That the object of the meeting was to confer on the important, agricultural, commercial, social and political relations of the South Western States and of the Valley of the Mississippi with the other portions of the American Republic; and to consult on the measures necessary to advance and protect these Relations as interests in common to the whole Union. At an early period of the meeting it was decided, and with great unanimity that no Questions should be entertained, on which the action of the General Government was to be invoked, which involved any *political differences of opinion as to the powers of the General Government*: and in conformity with this Resolve, a General Committee appointed to supervise the proceedings, presented the following Resolutions as extracted from the Documents and Reports of the different Committees on the respective subjects submitted to their consideration

1st. Resolved, That the Report of the various Committees presented to the Convention be printed, together with such documents accompanying them as the Committee appointed to supervise the printing of the proceedings of the Convention shall deem necessary.

2d. Resolved[,] That safe communication between the Gulf of Mexico and the interior, afforded by the navigation of the Mississippi and Ohio rivers and their principal tributaries is indispensable to the defence of the country in time of war and essential also to its commerce.

3d. Resolved. That the improvement and preservation of the navigation of those great rivers, are objects as strictly national as any other preparation for the defence of the Country, and that such improvements are deemed by this Convention impracticable by the States, or individual enterprise and call for the appropriations of money for the same by the General Government.

4th. Resolved. That the deepening of the mouth of the Mississippi, so as to pass Ships of the largest class, cost what it may, is a work worthy of the nation, and will greatly promote the general prosperity.

5th. Resolved. That, if the policy of reinforcing our navy with war Steamers be adopted, the Western waters are proper sources of supply, as they abound in iron, the best material for their construction, and in lead and Copper[,] important materials for munitions of war; provisions also being cheap, and the skill requisite for their construction and navigation being ample in this region, which already posses[s]es the largest Steam commercial marine in the world.

6th. Resolved. That the project of connecting the Mississippi river with the lakes of the North, by a ship canal, and thus with the Atlantic Ocean is a measure worthy of the enlightened consideration of Congress.

7th. Resolved. That the intercourse between the Gulf of Mexico and the Atlantic coast ought to be preserved unimpaired, and ample military and naval defence and additional lighthouses and beacons should be established along the coast of the Gulf of Mexico, at the most eligible points.

8th. Resolved. That the Gulf and Lake coasts are greater in extent than the Atlantic Seaboard; that the interests to be defended in One quarter are quite as important and altogether as national as those in the other; and that the expenditures required for the proper defence of the Gulf and lakes will fall far short of what has been as freely voted for the coast defence of the Atlantic.

9th. Resolved[.] That Congress should establish a national armoury and foundry at some point on the Western waters, at as early a period as practicable.

10th. Resolved. That the marine hospital on the Western and Southern Waters, the construction of which has been commenced or authorised by Congress, ought to be prosecuted to completion with the least practicable delay.

11th. Resolved[.] That the mail service of the West and South requires great improvement in speed and regularity and particularly on the western waters. That measures ought to be taken for the prompt extension by Government of the Magnetic telegraph into or through the Vall[e]y of the Mississippi.

12th. Resolved. That millions of acres of the public domain lying on the Mississippi River and its tributaries, now worthless for purposes of cultivation might be reclaimed by throwing up embankments, so as to prevent overflow; and that this convention recommends such measures as may be deemed expedient to accomplish that object, by grant of said lands or an appropriation of money.

13th. Resolved. That Rail Roads and communications from the Valley of the Mississippi to the South Atlantic ports, in giving great facilities to trade, greater despatches in travelling, and in developing new sources of wealth, are, in all their salutary influences on the commercial, social, and political relations, strongly urged upon the consideration and patriotism of the people of the West; and they are the more recommended as works within the power of private enterprise to construct, as affording profitable investment of Capital.

14th. Resolved[.] That in order that the earliest opportunity may be afforded for private individuals and enterprise to direct their capital and energies to the Completion of the important roads projected, the Convention recommend to the delegations present, to appoint Committees charged with the duty of prompt and early applications to their respective legislatures for Charters to construct such roads as may pass through their States; and to ask such aid and patronage from said States as they in their discretion, may deem proper and necessary to aid in the construction of the Works.

15th. Resolved. That as many of the roads projected may pass through the public domain, this Convention would respectfully urge upon the consideration of Congress, the equity of granting the right of way and alternate sections, in aid of the work so situated—such grant, in the opinion of this convention being no more than a fair compensation paid by the proprietor for the enhanced value imparted to the section of land retained by the Government.

16th. Resolved. That efficient steps should be taken by the General Government to move and prevent the recurrence of the obstacles in the Mississippi opposite the City of St. Louis, so that the harbor there may at all times be accessible, as objects of public utility and of a national character and entirely beyond the ability of Missouri to accomplish.

17th. Resolved by this Convention that it is expedient that Congress should make an appropriation of money for the purpose of completing a military road from the West Bank of the Mississippi (opposite Memphis) through the swamps to the highlands in Arkansas, in the direction of the various military posts on the Western frontier.

18th. Resolved. That a dry dock and convenient arrangement for the repairs and refitting of Government Vessels should be established at some suitable point on the Gulf of Mexico.

19th. Resolved. That the President appoint a Committee of five members of this convention to memorialize Congress on the various topics embraced in the foregoing resolutions.

20th. Resolved. That the President appoint a Committee of five members of this convention to address our common constituents on the same subjects.

Your Memorialists therefore approach Your Honorable Body with the more confidence as they believe there is nothing recommended in the foregoing Resolutions which may not claim the legitimate action of Congress, and no new project submitted not worthy of the enlightened consideration of that Honorable Body. The safe and certain communication between the Gulf of Mexico and the Interior States of the West; the improvement and preservation of the navigation of the Mississippi and Ohio Rivers, on which now border Ten States, and Two Territories; the connection of the Northern Lakes with the Mississippi and Atlantic by a Ship Canal; and the keeping open the mouths of the Mississippi, so as to be accessible at all times to the largest class of vessels—The fortifying of the Gulf and Lake coast, and the erection of additional Beacons and Light Houses—the increase of our naval marine; the establishment of naval Depots, Arsenals, Dry Docks, Armories, Foundries and Marine Hospitals—the reclaiming a large portion of the Public Domain now in swamp—the ceding the right of way and alternate sections to Rail Roads passing through the public lands—and the ensuring greater certainty and despatch to mail conveyances, whether of Steam or Magnetic power—are objects not within the jurisdiction of a single State to control; *but common in their benefits to the whole Union* and within the powers of the General Government. Without however speculating on the ceded or reserved rights of the States, Your Committee feel confident that, under the *Commercial jurisdiction* of the General Government, and under the obligations to provide *for the general defence,* and as a *Proprietor* of the public domain, there is no power claimed in the resolutions enumerated which may not be legitimately exercised by the Congress of the U. States. If there be any doubts entertained as to the jurisdiction of the Mississippi River—which has for years been exercised in the establishment of Port of Entries; in the erection of Light houses and in the supervision of Steamers and Ton[n]age duty imposed on them—it is resolved by the fact, that if the power of preserving its navigation unimpaired, and of keeping open the communication between establishments of its own creation is not in the General Government, it is to be found no where—for no one State or Territory can claim or perform what belongs *to*, and requires the joint action of the many; and the free and uninterrupted navigation of which is indispensable whether for the purpose of general trade or means of general defence.

Relying therefore on the Legitimate powers of the Congress of the U. States, The Committee in behalf of the States bordering on the Mississippi and Northern Lakes and of the Gulf of Mexico, represented at the Memphis Convention, do most earnestly urge on the grave consideration of Your Hon[ora]b[l]e Body, the early and efficient exercise of your powers on all the objects enumerated in the resolutions and which in the opinion of the people of the West have not hitherto commanded that attention which their importance would seem to claim from Your legislation.

The Valley of the Mississippi is no longer a Territory or a Frontier. It has now become the "Bone and Sinew["]: the center of the Union standing midway between those States on the Atlantic which first gave life and impulse to our free and liberal institutions and those which under the silent but Certain influences of those institutions are destined to form new stars to the very borders of the Pacific, in the American Constellation. In the rapid progress of improvement the valley now numbers 10 Sovereign and independent States, who have become parties to the compact of the old thirteen; and contains Ten Millions of inhabitants; with an internal and export trade, transcending all other parts of like extent, and population in the World and very nearly equal to the entire Export and import trade of the U. States—not one tenth of its resources either in agricultural, commercial, manufacturing or mineral wealth has as yet been developed—it is difficult for the most sanguine to estimate or rightly appreciate the destinies yet in store for this favoured land of promise—it has however but one natural outlet to the highway of nations, but one common channel on which must float to market the annual productive industry of its enterprising and increasing population. This concentration of all its trade; of all its external and internal communications, on but one common avenue, renders it the still more important, and necessary that the navigation of that highway for all public purposes should be preserved unimpaired and its mouths kept unobstructed by the annual alluvial deposites brought down by the descending currents of its tributary streams. Your memorialists are bewildered by the mere speculation of what would be the terrible consequences to the Commercial, Social and political relations of these United States if like the Nile (an event not at all impossible) the Mississippi should be closed to the *ingress* and *egress* of foreign shipping. That river is as important to States on the Atlantic as is the Atlantic to the communities bordering on the River. They are both highways of commerce, and in all their relations to the States of the Union exercising an influence so *common* in their benefits to ["the" *interlined*] whole, as to demand, as Your memorialist[s] believe it will, the Supervision and protection of the General Representatives in Congress. The United States of America may for the present be divided into three Grand Sections. *First* The States bordering on the Atlantic. *Second* those bordering on the Northern Lakes—and *Third* those on the Gulf of Mexico and what may be considered an arm of that Gulf, the Mississippi. The Legislation of Congress has with a vigilant eye and a liberal hand fulfilled all its obligations to the first section. Hundreds of thousands of Dollars have been expended on the preliminary work of a coast survey; to ascertain with accuracy, its Longitudes and Latitudes, and to lay down with ["precaution" *canceled and* "precision" *interlined*] its head lands and its shoals. Light Houses attract notice at every entrance, and Beacons on every prominent point, indicate the shoals on the coast which endanger navigation. So illuminated is the Atlantic Horrizon by these commercial stars, that the navigator scarcely has passed one on his sterne, but another casts its light on his bow. Its harbors from St. Croix to Cape Florida, have been examined, surveyed and resurveyed, some of them improved, and all of them fortified. A system of military and naval preparations for defence has long been perfected, and in that section is in rapid progress of completion. The Annual Appropriations show the large sums which have been applied in the building of naval stations, Dry Docks[,] marine Hospitals, in the furnishing of the materials of war[,] in the erecting of arsenals and armories, and in the Casting of cannon. Under likewise the powers of the Post-Office Department a system has been organized, by which intelligence by mails and the Magnetic Telegraph is extended to every village, Town, and City in the Atlantic with all the certainty and speed practicable.

On the Lake Border the admonitions of the Late war and its frontier relation to a foreign power has early attracted attention to the improvement of its harbors, in the erecting of Light Houses and in the military and naval preparations in progress of completion; and although much is yet left unaccomplished in that important section, Your Memorialist[s] feel assured that it will continue to claim the impartial legislation of Congress.

In behalf of the last and by no means the least important section of the Union, whether we estimate in the Comparison, its population, its productive industry, the Capabilities of its soils, its varied agricultural and animal productions, its manufacturing powers, and its inexhaustible mineral resources—In behalf of this vast Valley of the Mississippi, and of the Gulf of Mexico, now extending from the Capes of Florida to the Rio del Norte; of this center assemblage of Independent Nations; of this midLand body of the American Eagle: whose eastern and western wings are now expanding from the Atlantic to the Pacific; Your Memorialists ask no more than an *equitable* and *just proportional* legislation for their *common interests* and *protection* within the legitimate powers of the General Government: which has been and is still annually claiming the consideration and action of Your Hon[ora]b[l]e Body on the Atlantic and Lake sections. They ask, not as a boon: but in *justice* and for *common good* That the Rivers Mississippi and Ohio be kept open, and their navigation as far as practicable be preserved unimpaired at all times to the Gulf; believing as they have been sustained by the unanimous voice of the Memphis convention, that those Rivers, but in a vastly greater and more imposing degree, bear the same military and commercial relations to the Gulf of Mexico, as does the Chesapeake to the Atlantic. It is the Right and strong arm of the Mexican Gulf: as essential to its defence in time of war, as it is important to its commerce in the more pacific days of peace. But for the facilities which the Mississippi afforded for the transportation of the personal [*sic*] and material of war: the triumphs of 8th Jan[uar]y would probably have never been achieved; and the Delta of Orleans would have fallen an easy victim into the hands of the Invader. The angry floods however of that mighty stream, at the hour of danger, came to the rescue of [Andrew] Jackson, and inundated the plains of menaced Orleans; with stout hearts, and strong arms in the hour of need; as it now does its Leveé with the rich productions which nourish and animate its trade. In its Commercial as well as its Military relations to the Gulf Frontier, the Mississippi claims the consideration of Congress—and to that Hon[ora]b[l]e Body Your Memorialists are instructed to appeal for the appropriations which on examination, may be found necessary, to preserve unimpaired the navigation of the Mississippi, and of the Gulf and for those military and naval preparations in Peace, which may be essential in time of War. Under the first division are included Light-Houses, Fortifications, Arsenals and a National Armory and Foundry. In but few of the harbors of the Gulf are there at present any fortifications; many of them still remain exposed, while in others the works are incomplete, and most of those finished destitute of armament. The Key of the Gulf, at Key West & The Tortugas still remains unoccupied; and altho' examined and reported upon many Years since most favourably by a Board of Both Military and Naval Engineers, as the *point* which not only commands the Entrance, but would exercise a powerful control over that whole inland sea; the appropriations have as yet been limited to a sum scarcely adequate to prepare the ground for a foundation. While on the subject Your Memorialists may be permitted to advert to the fact, that no part of the world affords greater facilities for the construction of works of Defence as do the Keys of Florida. The most important and costly material, the stone, may be quarried on the spot, and of a quality for durability such as has stood the test of ages in the impregnable fortifications at Havannah. As natural appendages to these fortifications in the Gulf, Your Memorialists ask for armories, arsenals and founderies on the Western Waters, and in this appeal they are sustained by the consideration, that munitions of war should be held in deposite at the most eligible point nearest where they may be required for use, and by the fact that no part of the Union can furnish better locations for such establishments, where the materials, the labor, and the skill can all be commanded on the spot, and applied with the greatest economy. The mineral wealth of the West is not unknown; most of the materials now used in the Eastern armories; particularly Iron, lead and copper, are drawn from the Mississippi valley, manufactured, and returned in a new form for use at the place from whence first removed.

One of the Resolutions relates to a national Foundery and Your Memorialists have been directed to impress this object particularly on the notice of Your Hon[ora]b[l]e Body, as such an establishment though often recommended has not hitherto met the sanction of Congress. Our Cannon are cast by contract; The Arm which of all others (as it endangers the life of those who use it, as well as of those against whom directed) should require the lights of science, and vigilant inspection in preparing the material for casting. Whatever may have been the past fidelity with which contractors have fulfilled their obligations, the melancholy catastrophe on board the

Princeton, inculcates a lesson, that the Cannon, like the arms, on which the U. States rely for success in war, Should be fabricated in Establishments under the sole direction and government of competent, scientific, and responsible Officers of the Army. In the Naval Defences of the Gulf, the Resolutions of the Convention enumerate, the construction of War Steamers, the establishment of marine Hospitals, and of Dry-Docks. These are all appendages of Naval preparations for defence, and the same ["agreements" *canceled and* "arguments" *interlined*] which enforce the propriety of the construction of Armories & Founderies, on the Western Waters, apply with equal force to those vessels of War, and establishments connected with the Naval system. If Iron Steamers for purposes of war, should become the policy of our Government, the Western Country, in the material, skill, and economy of labor at hand, all furnish the elements by which they may be cheapest constructed, and the consideration which should induce their construction in the West. Marine Hospitals are so essentially a part of the Naval system, that the neglect of these establishments on the Western Waters, for the comfort and relief of the Sailors, under all the exposure, hazards, and sufferings of his adventurous profession, is more a matter of surprise, than of complaint. Your Memorialist[s] therefore believe that it is only necessary to advert to the fact to claim for these establishments, Your earliest action. Dry-Docks, for examination & repair in the Gulf of Mexico, would seem to be an indispensable part of a Navy-Yard.

The Mexican Gulf, is isolated, and the intricacies of the navigation by the Florida Capes, and Reefs, add both to the hazard, and the time, necessary, to accomplish a voyage to the Atlantic Ports. The Naval force therefore operating in the Gulf, may often be embarrassed for the want of the means of supply, and refitting at Yards near at hand. A Recent occurrence, and at a crittical [*sic*] moment, furnished the strongest argument in favor of the policy suggested. The Potomac, the flag Ship of the Com[m]odore, though direct from a dock on the Atlantic[,] was found defective on her arrival in the Gulf. Though every expedient, which ingenuity could devise at the Pensacola yard, was resorted to, her leaks could neither be discovered [n]or remedied. One day in Dock, would have sufficed for examination and a few more in addition, repaired her for Service. But the want of a Dock compelled the Com[m]odore to send her North, and her condition required an escort. Thus at a Critical period the flag Ship and her consort, were withdrawn from a Fleet, then engaged on a most important enterprise, in which the cooperation of these two vessels might have been indispensable to success.

On the Mail facilities to which one of the resolutions relate[s], Your Memorialist[s] do not deem it necessary to enlarge, as the able Head of the Post Office Department [Cave Johnson] is from the West, and cannot be indifferent to the necessity of promptness and dispatch of the Mail, or to the wants of that growing and rapidly improving section, where Towns, villages and communities, all requiring mail facilities, rise like magic, and have confidence that the General Government will extend, to them the same dispatch, and certainty in transmitting mail intelligence, whether by Steam, Horse, or Magnetic power which is afforded to other parts of the Union.

The Resolutions which relate to the removal of the obstacles in the Mississippi River at St. Louis, and for an appropriation for completing the Military Road (opposite Memphis) to the High Lands in Arkansas, ["were not embodied among those presented by" *canceled and* "were objected to by many of the members of" *interlined*] the General Committee, ["as they had doubts whether the objects embraced did not come" *canceled and* "and convention as" *interlined*] in conflict with the rule of entertaining no question which involved a difference of opinion on the powers of the Gen[era]l Government. They were however ["presented by the Representatives of the sections interested, and" *canceled*; "after after some" *interlined and then canceled*; "after some discussion" *interlined*] passed by a majority of the Convention. Your Memorialists therefore in presenting these among the other objects claiming Your patronage, are bound to state the fact, that those who dissented from the majority of the Convention, may not be considered as committed as to the legitimate ["power" *interlined*] to whom application for the remedy asked should be made. The obstructions in the River at St. Louis alluded to are truly alarming to that enterprising and populous city. They are threatened with the possibility of their loosing [*sic*] their position on the river and of being transformed from a Seaport to an Inland Town; and the subject of remedy merits, as we have no doubt it will receive, the consideration of Your Hon[or-a]b[l]e Body as to the extent to which relief can be extended.

The Road through the Swamp to the High-Lands of Arkansas, was deemed of sufficient military importance, many years ago to command the action of Government; It was surveyed, located, and in part finished by appropriations made by Congress. The recommendations in favor of the public importance of the Road not only remain in full force, but are stronger under the influences of the present day, now that the tide of emigration at full flood is setting

West; and the great width, and impassable character of the Mississippi swamp, presents such insuperable obstacles elsewhere, to a communication with the high lands in the Interior.

The 6th Resolution is on the project "of connecting the Mississippi River with the lakes of the North by a Ship Canal and thus with the Atlantic Ocean," and is presented as a measure worthy "the enlightened consideration of Congress"—As a mere speculative improvement, within the limits of a single State, simply to open a new channel between other natural outlets of commerce, this project could claim probably, no action from Your Hon[ora]b[l]e Body. As a Ship Canal (if practicable) connecting the Northern lakes by the Mississippi with the Gulf of Mexico, it may however under the powers of the General Government to provide for the General Defence merit "the enlightened consideration of Congress." The frontiers of the Lakes and Gulf, are now disconnected. They are in opposite directions and at the extreme points of the Union, and the Naval forces intended for the defence of either must be local: prepared for that specific object. By no means could they now be made to combine or cooperate together. If the Mississippi however could be made navigable at all seasons for War Steamers, and a communication of like capacity could be opened between that River, and Northern Lakes, it must be apparent to Your Honorable Body that the project might be made to contribute most essentially to the security of the Country in time of war, not merely in the great dispatch secured, but in the greater economy in the application of the means to the End. It would enable our fleets to circumnavigate ¾ of the Circle of the Union. It would enable one fleet to act on two frontiers or two fleets to combine and cooperate whether in the Gulf or Lakes wherever danger called. The practicability of the project established by scientific examination and survey; and its policy as a means of protection would merit grave consideration. The Resolutions relating to the reclaiming of the Swamps of the Mississippi, and to the patronage of the General Government in behalf of Rail Roads, come within the powers and jurisdiction of Congress as a land proprietor. It is well known that the Mississippi in its downward course to the Gulf, inundates in its annual floods an immense domain on both of its banks. Uncontroulable when the mountain elevations are discharging their accumulated waters; a boundless and agitated sea is presented; alarming even to those who have not in their improvements encroached on the Low lands. The settlements of the Emigrants, and the labor of Years have often been destroyed in a night; and during this period of flood all intercourse between the highlands East and West is cut off. At no point on the Mississippi are bluffs on one side met by corresponding head-lands on the other, and thus it is only during the period of low waters, can any intercourse between the hither and thither sides of the Mississippi be maintained—these swamps however, thus formed from alluvions of the River, are among the most fertile lands of the West; and like those of the Nile derive fresh vigor and fertility from every inundation. If they could be rendered safe from these overflowings, they would be the Garden spot of the U. States: and contribute more to the Wealth, and subsistence of man than any portion of similar extent in the world. Most of the Lands are owned by the U. States. Private enterprise can not improve them; and no project of reclamation can be carried but by the combined operation of all concerned. The motive and consideration to reclaim them, is founded in the fact of the enhanced value which will be imparted. The Lands in their present condition are worthless; *reclaimed they would be of inestimable value*; and Your memorialist[s] present ["present" *canceled*] therefore to Your Hon[ora]b[l]e Body as worthy of consideration of appropriating a part, or some other plan which in Your wisdom would seem more appropriate and practicable, by which these swamps may be reclaimed for cultivation, and Government indemnified for the portion surrendered in the enhanced value of the part retained.

Intimately connected with this subject is the improvement of the Navigation of the Mississippi. The science of the Engineer has been bewildered on the subject of the improvement of Rivers. Those free from Rock and which like the Mississippi course through alluvial formations inundating its banks, depositing and making the very soils through which they cut, are uncontrol[l]able and most difficult of improvement. A Great Engine[e]r in England when substituting a Canal for a River is known to have exclaimed in explanation "That Rivers were made to feed Canals." The Expenditures on the Mississippi thus far, if reports are to be credited have produced no results corresponding to the vast sums appropriated—where the Channel has been straightened at one point, it has been lengthened at another and obstructions or deposites in one bend have only been transferred in their removal to another. Sawyers and planters have in one season been reduced in number, to be replaced the succeeding One. The only fact clearly established: and it is one to which attention should be particularly directed as bearing with peculiar influence on the proposition submitted: is that where the Banks of the Mississippi has been levied [*sic*] and prevented from inundating the

Swamps, the Spring rises are scarcely perceptible, and the surplus waters are discharged by *deepening the bed*. Its currents no longer able to rise and expand over a wider surface, they have to deepen the bed to furnish vent for the waters to be discharged. This is particularly the characteristic of the River below Natchez: the highest point of continued embankments; the River from thence to its mouth is comparatively uninter[r]upted, and presents few or no sand bars obstructing its navigation. Opposite New-Orleans its depth is very great; and as the City authorities encroach on the river, it either deepens its bed, or cuts from the opposite shore. The reclaiming therefore the swamps and confining the River to its bed, will deepen it and do more to preserve unimpaired the navigation of the Mississippi than all the projects which have hitherto been devised or acted on for its improvement. The suggestion however is worthy of examination and it is the stronger recommended as it may accomplish a great object at comparatively little cost. The swamps of the Mississippi now worthless, and made so by the inundations of that River, may be made by their own reclamation, the instruments of improving the Navigation of that stream.

The last Resolution on the subject of Rail Roads invokes no aid from Your Hon[ora]b[l]e Body, but such as a Proprietor of the Public Land it may be for the interest of Gover[n]ment to grant; and which would in all similar instances be cheerfully ceeded [*sic*] by private individuals through whose domain a Rail Road might pass. The Projects which received the favourable consideration of the Convention were Roads passing at Right angles to the natural outlets or avenues of Trade; crossing the Ridges and mountains and intersecting interior districts, remote from navigation and hitherto from their secluded situation of little value. They develope therefore new sources of agricultural and mineral wealth, and bring into more intimate commercial and political relations the West with the South Atlantic Border; hitherto estranged from each other by the interposition of mountain elevations. These Roads are in the direction from the Seaports of So[uth] Carolina and Georgia, *First* in a Northwestern direction to Nashville on the Cumberland—*Second* to Memphis on the Mississippi; *Third* by Montgomery to Vicksburg, Grand Gulf, and Natchez—*Fourth* from Montgomery to Pensacola, Mobile and New Orleans. Though these Roads in their incipient conception are made to terminate on the Gulf of Mexico, and the Mississippi, they must and will advance with the onward population west and find no *Terminii short of the Pacific*.

Sections of these Roads, many of them have been commenced,

some finished, others in progress. They are all within the powers of the States and Territories through which they pass to construct, and all present sufficient objects for private enterprise to embark on. Your Memorialist[s] therefore in behalf of the Memphis convention do not ask of Your Honorable Body pecuniary appropriations in aid of these undertakings, but simply that You will by a general Law, grant the right of way, and the alternate sections to those Roads which pass throughout the Public domain; and they ask this with the more confidence, as from the interior position of the Country through which these roads will course, they will bring into notice Lands now of little value and will in the appreciation of the sections retained, more than remunerate Gover[n]ment for the sections surrendered. Were Your Memorialist[s] however authorised by the Convention, they might transcend the limits of their application for public patronage, by showing that there is more than a common interest in all the Commercial, social, political and moral influences which these Rail Ways are destined to exercise on the whole U. States. Steam has in its application to machinery and navigation, revolutionized the World; and in its last application in the Locomotive on land it has achieved its greatest triumph. The antiquated notion, that Republics could not cover space, and were only adapted to communities limited in territory and population—The morbid sensibility of Patriots now no more and the sickening apprehensions of living Statesmen, that our confederation of nations would be weakened by expansion, or break down by the ponderous power of its own weight, have all been dissipated by the Developments of Steam on Rail Ways. By the magical flights of the Locomotive, and the Magnetic influence of the Telegraph, distant worlds have been brought into close communion, space has been an[n]ihilated, Rivers leaped, and mountain elevations been subdued. The most remote communities have been narrowed into neighbourhoods, and Boston and Charleston by continuous Rail Ways, have as to time been brought nearer to the Capitol at Washington, than are many of the contiguous counties of Maryland and Virginia. These Roads then extending with our population, following in close succession the Emigrant[']s track to the West, making him feel that he has not seperated from his kindred and friends, will prove the surest guarantees of that Union, which a common Origin, common sympathies and common Institutions gave rise to, and fidelity to which can alone perpetuate.

All of which is Respectfully Submitted by Y[ou]r Ob[e]d[ien]t Ser[van]t, James Gadsden of So[uth] Carolina, Chairman, and in behalf of Committee[:] J[ames] Guthrie of Kentuckey [*sic*], R[oger] Barton of Mississippi, Leroy Pope of Tennessee, J[ames H.] Luca[s] of Missouri.

ALS in ScCleA; En (a 21-pp. ms. in unknown hand) in DNA, RG 46 (U.S. Senate), 29A-G25; PC of En in Senate Document No. 410, 29th Cong., 1st Sess., pp. 27–36; PC of En in Crallé, ed., *Works*, 5:293–311. NOTE: Calhoun presented the memorial to the Senate on 2/3. It formed the subject of the report of a select committee on 6/26. Guthrie and Lucas were active entrepreneurs of Louisville and St. Louis, respectively. Nineteen of the twenty resolutions in the enclosure are printed in *Journal of the Proceedings of the South-Western Convention Began and Held at the City of Memphis, on the 12th November, 1845* (Memphis, Tenn.: 1845), pp. 25–27.

J[ohn] C. Calhoun and Others to President [JAMES K. POLK]

Senate Chamber, 22 Jan[uar]y [18]46

Sir, Permit us most respectfully to recommend to your Excellency, an application made by the Friends of Mr. Jerome Napoleon Bonaparte Jun[io]r of the City of Baltimore, for a cadetship at West Point.

From information upon which we are certain we can implicitly rely, we have no doubt of the Excellence of his habits & of his capacity, & that he would do credit to the Academy.

We hope therefore that your Excellency will find it consistent with what may be due to other applications of the same sort, to gratify the one to which we refer. Very resp[ectfull]y y[ou]r ob[e]d[ien]t Serv[an]ts, J.C. Calhoun, J[ames] A. Pearce, Reverdy Johnson [Senators from Md.], William F. Giles [Representative from Md.], and Geo[rge] McDuffie [Senator from S.C.].

LS (in Johnson's hand) in DNA, RG 94 (Adjutant General's Office), Application Papers of Cadets, 1805–1866, 1845, 301 (M-688:159, frames 428–430). NOTE: Jerome Napoleon Bonaparte (1830–1893), son of Jerome Napoleon and Susan Williams Bonaparte, graduated from the U.S. Military Academy in 1852 and served two years in the U.S. Army before joining the French Army during the reign of his cousin Emperor Napoleon III, where he served with distinction and rose to the rank of Lieutenant Colonel before resigning his commission at the fall of the Empire, when he returned to the U.S.

Remarks in clarification, 1/22. William Allen objected to Calhoun's statement the previous day that Allen's course would lead to war. Calhoun said that he had said Allen's course "might" lead to

war, not that it "would." From *Congressional Globe*, 29th Cong.,
1st Sess., p. 232. Also printed in the Washington, D.C., *Daily Union*,
vol. I, no. 226 (January 22, 1846), p. 898.

To J[AMES] H. HAMMOND, [Barnwell District, S.C.]

Washington, 23d Jan[uar]y 1846

My dear Sir, Your warm & cordial approbation of my course, in
reference to the Oregon question, is highly acceptable to me. It is
one full of responsibility & difficulties, but under a high sense of
duty to the country & its institutions, I shall tread it boldly, without
regard to consequences to myself personally. Whether I shall be
able to succeed in averting pending calamities time only can decide.
The odds are greatly against me. The South, most unfortunately, is
devided. The whigs are timid, jealous & distracted, & many who act
with me have but little resolution, while those extreme men; those
who go *for all or none*; that is for war, are bold and decided. But
the worst of all is, that the administration, while it professes to desire peace & express great confidence that it can be preserved, go for
unqualified notice—a measure, which under circumstances must almost certainly lead to war. If it should not lead to compromise,
such certainly will be the result; & that it will not, we have the President's [James K. Polk's] own declaration, that there is no hope of a
satisfactory compromise.

But as bad as this state of things is, I do not dispair. I cannot
doubt, but that there is an overwhelming majority in both countries
opposed to war. They are yet quiet, because they do not fully
realize the danger; but as it approaches they will be roused, & utter
a voice that will ["I hope" *interlined*] be respected. I also believe,
that those charged with conducting our affairs, have been looking
more to popularity, than duty, & have been acting under the impression, that they could at pleasure avert the calamity to which they
have exposed the country; but when they find their mistake, will be
glad to seek the aid of the moderate to save themselves. Under this
joint influence of both causes, I hope, if we of the peace party should
not be able to prevent notice, we shall be able to amend the resolution for giving it, so as to reopen the negotiation on the basis of the
49th parallel, or to authorise a reference to adjust the conflicting
claims of the two countries.

In the meane time the change of ministry in England must have a strong bearing on the question, & I am of the impression a salutary one on the whole; but as we shall have in the course of a few days much fuller information, than we now ["have" *interlined*] I forbear to speculate on the subject. I shall send you the first spare copy of the Pres[iden]t[']s Message with all the documents, which I may get from the printers. It is the only one of any importance, which has been printed.

You ask me what you can do to aid in maintaining the great cause of peace. You can do much. Few men wield a better pen than you do. If you can get admission into the columns of the [Augusta] Constitutionalist, or any other democratick paper in Georgia, you might do much to rouse publick attention in that State to the dangerous condition in which the country is placed & especially the South. The abolitionists are all for war, with the avowed intention of crushing us & our institutions, headed by [John Quincy] Adams & [Joshua R.] Giddings. Truly, J.C. Calhoun.

ALS in DLC, James Henry Hammond Papers, vol. 12; PC in Jameson, ed., *Correspondence*, pp. 678–679.

From J OHN S. L ORTON

Pendleton, January 23d 1846

Dear Sir, I received your favour of the 15th instant enclosing a check on the National Bank of New York for One hundred & Eighty Dollars, which I have placed to the credit of your account, for which you will please accept my thanks. We have had a very severe winter here so far, which will I fear make provissions very scarce and high-priced. Very Respectfully Yours &c, John S. Lorton.

ALS in ScU-SC, John C. Calhoun Papers. NOTE: An AEU by Calhoun reads "John Lorton[,] acknowledges a draft."

From W[ILLIA]M PINKNEY STARKE

Paris, Jan. 23d 1846

Dear Sir, Although a private letter may perhaps intrude upon your public engagements at this moment, I cannot yet better manifest my sense of your kindness to me while in Washington & of your very flattering request to write to you, than by giving as concisely as possible a sketch of my travels since my last letter.

My tour comprised Italy, Egypt, Nubia, Palestine, Turkey, a part of Asia Minor, Greece, Austria & some of the smaller German States, and I have but recently concluded it. In many respects Egypt was to me the most interesting of all the count[r]ies I visited. It was there that I ["first" *interlined*] became acquainted with the Mohammedan religion—its forms, dogmas, the character of the Civil & penal legislation founded on it, the Eastern institution of Polygamy & its effects upon individual & national character. Nor in its physical character, vegetation & manner of cultivation was it less striking. I beheld a river presenting the anomaly, of increasing in size as you ascend it; a valley of great and exhaustless fertility, protected from the sands of deserts which threaten it on either side, by mountains of sandstone, limestone and (in Nubia) of granite. I found this valley strewn with stupendous monuments of Art, bearing testimony to the wealth & greatness of an early race, and by its wonderful fertility still supporting in comfort a vast ["& robust" *canceled*] population.

The extent of arable land is given at three & a half millions of acres—of cultivated land, at perhaps the half of this amount and yet under a most oppressive Government, the population is set down at between three and four millions. Ancient writers speak of of [*sic*] a population of more than three times as great and Appian tells us of the treasures of Ptolemy Philadelphus amounting in an age when the precious metals were comparatively scarce to more than 740,000 talents or to near 900 millions of dollars. The regular army of Mehemet Ali consists of 130,000 men & amounts ["in all," *canceled*] with the irregulars, national guards, workmen in arsenals &c—to about 275,000. His 32 vessels of war carry 1600 men and there are immense public establishments for education, civil & military. A country of so small extent that can ["support" *canceled and* "maintain" *interlined*] such an enormous military force, and which amidst all the obstructions to trade by exorbitant duties, bad communications, want of harbours, long quarantines, extortions on part of Government rendering property insecure & deterring industry: ["I say" *canceled*] can show a sum total of exports & imports amounting to 20 millions of dollars; I say that a country which can afford to make such enormous sacrifices ["and" *canceled*] for a series of years and yet manifest increasing wealth & power should possess ["a soil" *in-*

terlined] of amazing fertility. It would doubtless strike one coming from the naturally weak & worn-out soils of Europe as unexampled in this respect, but to one fresh from the primeval forests of the ["old" *canceled*] new World the surprise would be not at the comparative fertility of the soil, but at its *power when fully developed* by ["population" *canceled*] *labour.* An American will recognize in the Egyptian valley the alluvial ["soil" *interlined*] of our Southern rivers and the strength of the vegetation when compared with that of many parts of his own country will seem by no means astonishing. He will naturally be prone to draw ["a" *interlined*] comparison between ["it &" *canceled*] the valley of the Nile & that of the Mississippi and I know of nothing which will more strongly impress him with the resources of his own country. For many months of the year the Nile is not navigable for boats of a greater tonnage than ["the size of" *canceled*] our small Savannah [and] Petersburg boats and though tolerably large about the cataracts, the river by filtration through a porous soil, ["evapation" *altered to* "evaporation"] by being spread ["out" *interlined*] in numberless canals under a ["bur" *canceled*] warm sun, loses such an amount of its waters, that not being repaid by rains or contributory streams, it diminishes to such an extent as to present very considerable obstacles to navigation near its mouth.

Considering the equality in soil & climate of the Mississippi valley, its immeasurable superiority in point of extent, power of navigation, character of population, political institutions, Art & science pertaining to Arts and reflecting on the wealth & population of Ancient Egypt and on the sacrifices which Modern Egypt can submit to; one is almost frightened at the anticipation of the future destiny of a country of which this valley forms by no means the ["whole" *canceled*] whole.

I made it a part of my business while in Egypt to collect seeds of trees, plants & vegetables. This I was induced to do from the similarity in some respects, as to climate & soil & from the thought that a crowded ["agricultural" *interlined*] population would be naturally forced into the cultivation of the most productive & nutritious plants. Besides, of the few Southerners who have visited that remote country, it might not perhaps have occurred to any one to go ["troub" *canceled*] to the trouble & expense of making such a collection. Should I succeed in introducing into my country or State a new plant ["of importance" *interlined*] my trip will have been of some practical utility; if not, no harm will have been done ["in the attempt" *interlined*] or disgrace incurred, in the failure.

The Egyptians are a large, well-formed race, but ignorant & cowardly. They live in mud huts which it would be a compliment to compare with our negro cabins. In point of intelligence they are on a par with our slaves & in comfort far below them.

Passing into Palestine, I made the Scriptures my particular study and my belief in their truth was greatly strengthened. The admirable coincidences of the topography & physical appearance of the country, its productions & the manners & customs of even the present inhabitants, with that given in the Bible affords certainly a presumption in favour of the ["general narrative" *canceled*] truth of the general narrative, which can only be weakened ["or destroyed" *canceled*] by opposing the conflicting testimony of Authentic History, or by showing some manifest contradiction in the narrative itself, neither of which is the case.

Over & above these things there was a particular argument which struck me with great force & which can ["prop" *canceled*] only be properly appreciated by one who has seen the country. I refer to the admirable adaptation of the Promised Land to the purposes for which we are told it was designed, viz: to contain a people whose end was to hand down amidst universal idolatry the knowledge of the true God. Washed on the west by a Sea without harbours, bounded on the South & East by vast deserts & on the north by the lofty chain of Libanus with hardly a pass, and intersected by a thousand mountain chains & peaks, no country ever was less calculated for ["com" *and* "extended" *and one other word canceled*] commerce or intercourse with ["com" *canceled*] neighbours enjoying ["a worship in" *canceled and* "religions" *interlined*] less exacting & more alluring in their worship. It is upon this ground & ["on" *interlined*] the exhausted condition of the soil that I found my objection to the common belief of the actual return of the Jews to the Holy Land. This people are notoriously a race of brokers, bankers & merchants. Besides the apparent allusions in Scripture to this circumstance ["have reference" *canceled*] are in my opinion entirely ["allegorical or" *canceled*] Spiritual.

You may depend upon ["it that" *canceled*] the assertion I have before made that the French are looking to the possession of Syria. The Turks are unable to hold the country and it is the jealousy of the Great Powers that ["pr" *canceled*] alone preserves it. The French have Algiers—the possession of the Italian ports[,] those of Corfu, Alexandria & Beirout would make of the Mediterranean, a French lake & ["thus" *interlined*] carry out the idea of Napoleon. A war between England & the United States, would in my opinion be the signal for a partition of the East. There are in that part of the world three sects of religion independent of the Mohammedan or ruling religion: the Greek, Maronite & Druse. The first sect is under the protection of Russia who annually scatters immense sums among them in the way of presents to churches; the second is protected by France & the third is somewhat more particularly under the care of Turkey. The Greeks not of Syria & Asia Minor but even those of European Turkey ["are" *canceled*] receive these presents from Russia. What a miserable spectacle does the last mentioned country present? Divided by sects, some of which are powerful and wealthy and others under the open protection of such disinterested neighbours as Russia & Austria, the only safety for Turkey is ["in" *interlined*] the jealousy of foreign Powers & the disunion of internal sects. She is no longer inhabited by those hardy warriors ["of Kurdistan" *canceled*] who swept down from the mountains of Kurdistan & overthrew with so much ease the Empire of Constantine. Their faith is dailing [*sic*] giving way before the advance of Western civilization & power and the institution of Polygamy has long been preparing them for the final crisis. Besides this institution I consider that the other main cause of weakness among the Oriental nations is their long settlement in the same countries. An emigrating bustling people are always "caeteris paribus" superior to one stationary. Motion of body gives activity to ["th" *canceled*] both the mental & physical parts of man. Besides emigrants are the most adventurous & vigorous portion of a nation. It is this that gives to Europe originally her superiority over Asia and which will give to our own country the superiority over all.

The Greeks (to judge from busts & Statues) are ["probably" *interlined*] less changed in appearance as they certainly are in character & language from ["their ancestors than" *interlined*] any other people with whom they may be compared in these respects. They are the same *brave, enthusiastic, shrewd & lying* race as of yore. What a choice possession to a nation is the memory of her great men, the deeds and sayings of a noble ancestry. The spirit of Demosthenes and Leonidas breathed upon the dry bones of a lost race and straight way they rose up covered with flesh and [dis]tinct[?] with life.

Greece however can ["only" *canceled*] no longer expect ["an" *canceled*] to occupy anything more than a very secondary station among the European powers. The day of city-states has passed away & that of agricultural states begun.

Italy ["was(?) to me" *canceled*] is to all a country of great interest and I ["fondly" *interlined*] lingered in a land which with the Sword[,] the crosier or the easel ["had" *altered to* "has"] ruled the world for more than two thousand years.

Austria is apparently well-governed, the country is well-cultivated and beautiful and the people, contented and happy.

France is the most warlike nation of the age. Her people are infinitely better off than before their revolution. But in some respects they are altered in character for the worse: the French of all people are the most rude and impolite.

My travels and observations abroad have only served to impress me with a profounder ["love &" *interlined*] respect for my country and her institutions and with perhaps too great a contempt for those of the old world. We have no vast metropolis to give laws to a whole country; an agricultural people cannot easily be corrupted. As long as we are a simple, hardy race and our women are virtuous, so long will God be with us. The hand of Providence in laying out a great country over which has been scattered with profusion all the elements of Beauty & Sublimity—in preventing its settlement before the noblest of all races had reached a certain point in the scale of freedom—in finally causing its settlement in States, whereby has been introduced the diffusive principle in Republican Governments—are things too evident not to ["call for" *canceled*] excite the liveliest feelings of gratitude in the hearts of all lovers of their country.

Upon the whole I am glad that I have [been] able to travel abroad. The pleasures of actual travel are perhaps more than counter balanced by its fatigues and exposure. The novelty which is so pleasing on first entering a country different in physical appearance from any previously seen or in the manners & customs of its inhabitants soon wears away & nothing is left to amuse or interest, but very occasional incidents of travel or the sights of spots illustrated by memorable events or marked by works of art. Afterwards however the memory not only of ["these" *altered to* "the"] pleasant incidents but even of this very fatigue & expense becomes a source of gratification and when to this be added the consciousness of having under gone a sort of practical education & of having accumulated a store of correct information, the great and increasing satisfaction of one who has properly travelled can readily be conceived.

I am now in Paris pursuing the study of the French language and literature and taking a farewell of my classical studies before beginning that of the Law. My main object however is to train my mind in the rules of a formal Logic by which I mean the just appreciation of language & the force of argument. It is to this latter class of studies that I am most inclined & it is in them that I find my progress to be most rapid.

The analysis of the masterly arguments of Mr. Calhoun & Mr. [George] Mc Duffie on the principles of our Government & on the great questions of public policy arising under our Constitution ["are" *altered to* "is"] a source of great delight to me. A small degree more of foresight on the part of the founders of [the] Constitution might have placed certain important questions beyond all doubt and dispute; but when we consider the vast activity of mind that has been produced by the discussion of them, the omission can hardly be regretted. The time now rapidly approaching when I shall have to assume the responsibilities of an American citizen, I have ["been" *interlined*] busily preparing myself to ["meet &" *interlined*] fulfil them in a proper manner. As an humble seeker after truth I have not confined my researches to only one side of the great questions before the people of ["I" *canceled*] my country. I have examined with all my attention the arguments of Messrs. [Henry] Clay & [Daniel] Webster. I will admit that personal and sectional prejudice may have had, ["despite me," *canceled*] some influence in deciding me. Mr. Webster I consider to have been through life consciously advocating a wrong policy—Mr. Clay honestly pursuing the same course. Neither of them therefore can be fairly entitled to [the] epithet of a truly great mind, which consists not merely in the power of discovering the true, but in an irresistible attraction towards towards [*sic*] it—an incapacity to resist its force. The one is a great party leader and orator—the other a great *lawyer*, nothing ["more" *interlined*]. A second generation is beginning to pronounce judgment on these matters & Mr. Calhoun need not fear its decision.

Hoping very soon to have the pleasure of seeing Mr. Calhoun I beg to acknowledge myself with the greatest respect His Ob[e]d[i-e]nt & Humbl[e] Serv[an]t, Wm. Pinkney Starke.

ALS in ScCleA.

From [Nathaniel] B[everley] Tucker

Williamsburg [Va.,] Jan. 23, 1846
My dear Sir, The death of Mr. [James] Hoban [Jr.] and a letter from my young friend Mr. A[rchibald] C. Peachy of Georgetown, who

wishes to succeed him [as U.S. Attorney for the District of Columbia], lead me to bear my testimony, at his request, to some points in his character, of which I ought to be able to speak more confidently than any other person. He was my pupil [at the College of William and Mary] in the Study of Law municipal and political. Of his acquirements I had the best means of judging. Of his opinions, I have the most intimate knowledge. It is of the last he wishes me to speak to you.

He is a State's Right man, and a strict constructionist of "the most straitest sect." He is a free trade man of the school of President [Thomas R.] Dew; and he is all this, not merely because he is a southern man in all his principles[,] feelings & habits, but because he understands these subjects perfectly, and is fully prepared to give a reason for his faith. If I had occasion to choose a successor to Mr. Dew (and we have had to think seriously of this) I should choose him. If I had to nominate a successor to myself, to uphold the Doctrines known as *Virginian*, on the subject of the Constitution, I should nominate him. No man understands them better, no man believes them more confidently, and few men are better qualified to maintain and expound them.

I am not called on to speak of more than this. That he is a gentleman in his bearing, all who see him must know. That he is a gentleman in his principles and habits all who know him will testify. That his habits are sober[,] studious and businesslike none, who will sound the depths of his acquirements, can doubt.

I cannot close this letter without begging you to accept my thanks for the efforts you are making to save the Country from the ruin which threatens it from the presumption of men whose proper place is between the handles of the plough, but who affect to lead in great affairs. When the *mind* of a country does not govern, its doom is sealed. Other men, however enlightened, are sold to party. You alone are free to stand forth as the representative of the *Mind of the Country*. It is a noble constituency, unrepresented unless by you. Is there any thing in the gift of man worthy to be compared with the honour of filling this otherwise vacant post?

You once did me the honour to write to me occasionally. I lost it (I will not say by my own fault), but by circumstances which neither could control. May I hope to be restored to it? There are men great by position, whose disproportion to the places they occupy does but show their littleness. There are men great by talent—but dwarfed by business. Of none of ["them" *canceled*] these would

502

I condescend to ask this. With very high respect I remain Your obed[ien]t Serv[an]t, B. Tucker.

ALS in ScCleA. Note: An AEU by Calhoun reads "Prof[esso]r Tucker."

From ANNA [MARIA CALHOUN] CLEMSON

Brussels, [*mutilation*; January?] 24th 1846

My dear father, A few days ago we received mother's [Floride Calhoun Calhoun's], & sister's [Martha Cornelia Calhoun's], letters to me, & yours to Mr. [Thomas G.] Clemson, (for you never write *me* now a days,) telling us of your safe arrival in Washington, which gratified me much, & makes me almost feel as tho' you were nearer to me, since we hear so much more regularly when you are there, than when in Carolina. The account you give of the way things are going at the Canebrake gratified us much, especially what mother says of the health, & contentment, of the negroes. I often feel quite unhappy, lest they should be neglected, or ill used, being left so entirely in charge of an overseer. I feel much better contented about my things, since mother has seen what state they are in, & left them in the new house, & am much obliged to her for the trouble she took about it.

Since I wrote last, I have been really ill. I was confined to the house more than two weeks, & to my room more than a week, & even now am obliged to be very careful. I had a violent cold, which fell in my head, ears, & teeth, & nearly set me crazy, & affected the nerves of one eye, & indeed the entire side of the face, so much, that I became alarmed lest it should end in tic douloureux. I am however well again, tho' still obliged to be cautious in going out, especially at night, which is the more unfortunate, as this is the season of gaiety here, & tho' we get off all we can, yet, strange as [it] may seem, we are *forced* to go out, for an invitation here is quite a serious affair, not to be lightly refused. Mr. Clemson also is not well. He is complaining of his liver, & one thing & another, & his spirits are not good, &, within a few days, he also has a dreadful cold. This is the more surprising, as the winter so far, tho' wet & disagreeable, with much high wind, has been even warm, in comparison with the last. We have not had one hard freeze, indeed scarcely ice at night, & tho' it has snowed once or twice, the snow has not remained on the ground but a few days. This is a great comfort to the poor, for had the winter been as severe as the last, in addition to the want of food, their state, bad at the best, would have been awful. They talk of slavery. I never saw in all my life at the South, the amount of suffering & misery that one sees here in one month, & so I tell all who mention the subject to me. I say, "make your working classes in Europe, as happy as our slaves, & then come back to me, & we *will talk* about the abolition of slavery." I wish mother could have six months trial of the mean[n]ess, debased condition, & utter want of truth, & honesty, among the servants of this country; she would be sick of white servants for life. I don[']t know what I should do without Basil, who tho' careless, & negro like, is faithful, & honest, & really a treasure to me.

The children grow, & prosper, wondrously, &, without the imputation of a mother's vanity, are really much more than commonly intelligent. Floride [Elizabeth Clemson] has my memory, & learns very rapidly, but [John] Calhoun [Clemson] is the most original fellow you ever heard talk & is much better company, & has more powers of [*ms. torn; one word missing*], & observation, than one half the town people one meets with. His remark[*ms. torn; words missing*] almost startle me. He sings very well, & has given all [the] indications of a talent for drawing, & what is better still, is as hearty & strong as possible. How I wish you & mother could see them, as they are playing round me at present. I asked Calhoun what I should tell you, & his grandmama. "Tell them I love them, & send them *my compliments*," said he without a moment[']s hesitation. Floride says "I have nothing to tell them, but give them a kiss." I give you these little messages, not as anything remarkable, but as being verbatim, they may give you pleasure, as messages from the little rogues.

We are all here on the lookout for news from America, & indeed the question of war, or no war, occupies the attention of every one. I am very peaceably inclined, being [on] the wrong side of the water for war, which would interrupt the arrival of my letters, & I do hope the matter may be arranged without loss of ground on our side yet, but if we must have war there is one comfort, we can stand it better than England, & if England now gives way, she must ever hereafter stand second best, which is a punishment she richly deserves for her arrogance, & presumption. A Mr. Hyde, (an American,) quite a sensible person, just from England, says the war fever is very high, & the most active preparations making in every department for it. The King [Leopold I] said to me the other day, apropos to the Oregon question, "but you will get your country out of all shape with these numerous additions." "Oh no[,"] said I, ["]if you will

look on the map, you will see we are only trying to make it *square.*"
He laughed heartily.

Things in Belgium are very quiet just at present, but I understand the french ambassador has [*ms. torn; one or two words illegible*] out that our [treaty?] with Belgium, will be to the advantage of ourselves, Belgium, & Prussia, but wo[e]fully against the interests of France ["*& England*" *interlined*] & is quite put out, that he did not discover it soon enough to prevent it. Mr. Clemson is over head & ears in business. The increased trade with the United States, renders the Consular business at Antwerp more heavy, & of course more frequent difficulties arise, & since our hopeful consul there, Mr. [Francis J.] Grund, (who is a disgrace to the country in every way,) chooses to absent himself entirely from his post, & has finally gone, with his family, to spend the winter in France, the whole matter falls on Mr. C[lemson], who without receiving the fees, is virtually consul. The consular agent not liking of course to assume any responsibility, more especially as he is a Belgian, & this added to the business of the legation, gives Mr. C[lemson] enough to do, & me plenty of my old business of copying, as I am secretary of legation. I think they might give me the salary, for I am sure I need it, as it is just all we can do to keep from running in debt, altho' this winter we do not even keep a carriage, but only hire one when necessary, & it is to this I partly attribute my dreadful cold.

We had to breakfast with us the other day, the Mr. [John Arthur] Roebuck whose name you so often see in the debates of Parliament in England. He is one of the most sensible & *liberal* englishmen I ever heard speak. He was struck the moment he saw your likeness with its resemblance to Lord Lyndhurst, & said "that I suppose is Mrs. Clemson[']s father, as I have always heard he resembled Lord Lyndhurst." He is anxious for peace & says he will do all he can to preserve it.

Mr. C[lemson] joins me in love to mother, sister & yourself. I will answer mother[']s letter soon & sister['s] next. Your [devote]d daughter, Anna Clemson.

ALS in ScCleA. NOTE: John Singleton Copley, Baron Lyndhurst (1772–1863) was the son of the American painter John Singleton Copley and was Lord Chancellor of England.

From EUSTIS PRESCOTT

New Orleans, 24th Jan[ua]ry 1846

My Dear Sir, Important events have been crowded upon us since we had the pleasure of conversing upon the prominent topic of the day. I say crowded *upon* us, as I conceive the motion and speech of Gen-[era]l [Lewis] Cass [Senator from Mich.] to have created the war feeling in the people, and blinded them—not only to the effect, but the origin & motive of the movement. Commerce is prostrate, the Merchant dare not commence an operation—the terminus of which should extend beyond thirty days, stocks will be thrown back upon us from England, and Cotton—which is now low enough, will I fear meet another decline, particularly as the stock in Liverpool is near one million of bales. And in this perilous position of the country, the members of the House of Representatives are indulging in exciting speeches made for *home*. It is indeed humiliating that at such a crisis so many demagogues should have obtained seats in that body, but if their conduct should open the eyes of the people—some good may be attained.

With pride and satisfaction I have witnessed the decided stand you my Dear Sir have taken in opposition to this war-cry, and premature action, particularly as it is dangerous to your popularity with the mass—but proves to all who think, or whose opinions are of any value, that you never think of self—when the interests of your country are in your estimation jeopardized.

Altho I believe that a majority of the people of Louis[ian]a approve the course you have taken, yet there are a multitude of both parties who shout for *all* of Oregon—heedless alike of reason or consequences.

In all the speeches made on *Oregon*, I have never seen a fair examination of the British title to the country north of 49°. I believe that it is fully as good—if not better than ours, and in a settlement now we must relinquish it, while the delay so strongly enforced by you would eventually have given us the whole territory. I trust that on 10th Febr[uar]y you will let the country clearly understand that your policy would secure 54—while Messrs. [William] Allen[,] Cass &Ca's course is certain to deprive us of it.

Had Congress commenced with the passage of a law to extend the jurisdiction of the U.S. over our own people in Oregon, provided for their protection in passing into the territory, and then authorised the President to give notice to England—when he deemed it judicious, we should have had no excitement on the subject.

As I believe the war-cry to proceed from a desire for large appropriations, fat contracts &c &c I trust the gentlemen will now turn their eyes southward and demand them for the speedy punishment of Mexico—here is legitimate action, a nation that has heaped injury upon insult, and yet expects forbearance for her weakness. I trust her last act—a deliberate insult to an American Minister [John Slidell] will not go unpunished. We ought to take possession of Matamoros, establish Forts on the Rio Grande, occupy California, and bombard or blockade Vera Cruz, this is the only course to compel Mexico to respect us. To do this 100,000 men may be had in a month from the valley of the Mississ[ippi] and more if required.

I have written your son Andrew [Pickens Calhoun] several times in relation to our Cotton market—which continues to be the best either in the U.S. or Europe.

Your son the Capt[ai]n [Patrick Calhoun] has been ["quite" *canceled*] ill, but I am pleased to say is now quite recovered, looks however thin and must be cautious of his health.

Judge [Isaac] Johnson of Feliciana is elected Governor by a large majority, a Democratic majority in both houses, many of your friends were candidates, and all elected, a Senator will be chosen this winter to succeed Mr. [Alexander] Barrow. The contest has been conducted with spirit but without rancor—the people of Louisiana are "a law and order party" universally.

I send you a [New Orleans] Picayune containing I think some correct views as to the course of Mexico. I consider [Mariano] Paredes a mere tool of [Juan N.] Almonte—who is the most sagacious man in that country.

The "Commercial Times" a strictly commercial journal having a large circulation contained lately a very judicious notice of your course in the Senate, you probably see the paper in Washington.

If the late news of the formation of a Whig Ministry in England is confirmed, I shall look anxiously for a free trade movement of more value to us than the possession of all Oregon.

I hope it will encourage our free trade friends in the house [of Representatives] to early action on the tariff—a settlement of the question the country are determined to have—be it a tariff of 10[,] 20 or 30% let it only be permanent, and we can accom[m]odate ourselves to it.

It is strange that in advocating [Asa] Whitney[']s scheme of a R. Road to Oregon—even some southern men overlook the direct and easy route to St. Francisco thro Texas—nature appears to have marked the line and so far as known no extraordinary difficulty presents itself on any part of the route. Who will direct public attention this way[?] I hope some one who has talent and information enough to demonstrate it clearly. Col[o]n[el James] Gadsden might do it.

If a bill to establish the "Warehouse system" should ever reach the Senate I trust my Dear Sir you will examine its details, they ought to be very simple—indeed our whole revenue system is entirely too complicated—a vast deal of unnecessary machinery which ought to be reformed. Very sincerely and respectfully yours, Eustis Prescott.

[Marginal P.S.] I perceive that our Collector has not yet been confirmed. I hope that he will not—for public, not private reasons. He is not competent—*entre nous.*

ALS in ScCleA. NOTE: The P.S. apparently refers to Denis Prieur who was nominated by Polk to be Collector of Customs at New Orleans on 12/29/1845 and confirmed by the Senate on 2/24/1846.

From JAMES B. REYNOLDS, [former Representative from Tenn.]

Clarksville (Tenn.), January 24, 1846

My dear Sir, I now regret that I did not attend the Memphis Convention. I have seen the time, that I should have went that distance to have seen you and heard you talk, but a broken down politician ["and put down," *interlined*] without reason, has many curious notions to contend with. Besides, I saw no practicle good, to result from such a meeting, excepting becoming acquainted with one a nother, which I admit in ["a" *interlined*] Republican point of view is great and salutary.

I pray God, that you may be successful in aiding to ward off war. I thank you for the noble stand you have taken for the good of mankind. May you be quite triumphant, and that you and Mr. [Daniel] Webster & other worthies may yet be hailed as the Sav[i]ours of their beloved land.

I think it is strange, that ["our" *interlined*] friend Jose [that is, Joseph Gales, Jr.], of the Intelligencer, should be so much alarmed, from the debate in the house [of Representatives], respecting Oregon. It is the finest theme in the world, to let off the steam, maiden speeches, & speeches for ["Bunckom" *canceled*] Buncomb. And I am glad, the debate on the same subject has been postponed ["in the Senate" *interlined*]. All that has been said, or to say in that

Chamber will have completely evaporated before you commence. I cannot think that my old friend Gales ["is" *interlined*] in his dotage. I esteem him the greatest Editor, and the National Intelligencer the best news paper in the world. I trust he will make no such weak retractions on this subject again.

It seems to me, that it is almost impossible for two such nations to go to war on the subject of Oregon, or any other topick, that may be honourably negotiated at this enlightened period of the world. Let us be still and quiet, and the stream of emigration flow on towards the Pacific, and my words for it ["in a very few years," *interlined*] we can have any parallel we desire without one drop of blood being shed. I would not even give notice to Britain, to put an end to the joint convention.

Put no obstacles in the way, of the hardy sons of America going to Oregon, and they will very soon dispose of all Conventions but their own. But why anticipate your speech. I hope you will enclose it to me.

I have a nother suggestion to make. When all this smoke and talk about war is over I wish you could start the subject, and that is, that ["the" *interlined*] two governments would employ their Navies, in bringing over the *Excess* of the population in Sweet[?] Ireland, and land them at the mouth of Columbia [River], and then appoint *me the Governor for four years,* and ["I" *interlined*] would present you, with the *most growing, prosperous and happy people on the Globe!* Please to submit this idea to friend Webster. I must here close lest I become too idle and troublesome, &c. I remain very Truly your old friend, James B. Reynolds.

[P.S.] Please to renew & present my kind respects to Mrs. Calhoun, Patrick and the other Children. By the Bye, they are all men & women now.

ALS in ScCleA. NOTE: Reynolds was a native of Ireland and had been Representative from Tenn. during 1815–1817 and 1823–1825.

From ELIZABETH A.R. LINN

St. Louis, Jan[uar]y 25, 1846

My Dear Cousin, I fear from the great number of letters, that have been lost, between this place, and Washington City, this Winter, that the letter which I addressed, to you, signed by a number of Ladys in this City, has also miscarried. It is true, that it did not contain, any thing of importance but I did wish you, to know, with, what enthusiastic delight, we hailed your return, to the U.S. Senate, as a happy Omen, for the prosperity, of our Country. We felt, that your luminous mind, and most exalted moral integrity, would be a *Polar Star*, to guide our President safely through, any Political Storms that might arise, to disturb the happiness, of our Nation. I am very anxious for you, to visit Missouri, where you have, so many devoted Friends who long to see you. It gives me great pleasure to hear frequently from my kind Brother, Doctor [James H.] Relfe [Representative from Mo.], that you & your interesting family enjoy good health. Has dear Mrs. [Anna Maria Calhoun] Clemson, yet returned to the United States? I hope that Mr. [Thomas G.] Clemson, & herself with their little family have fine health.

Mr. Ferdinand Kennett, a Gentleman, of great worth, & influence, from this City, is now, in Washington City, on a visit. He is one, of the most devoted admirers, that you can possibly have, and has the greatest anxiety, to see you, a pleasure, that Dr. Relfe will give him, by introducing him, to you. I will be much gratifyed, (should you have the leisure,) if you would have some conversation with Mr. Kennett. My Children unite with me, in many, respectful, & kindly regards, to you & Mrs. Calhoun. With affectionate sentiments, of the highest Esteem, I am, most truely your Friend, Elizabeth A.R. Linn.

ALS in ScCleA. NOTE: Lacking a postmark, this letter was probably hand delivered by Kennett.

From F[ITZ]W[ILLIAM] BYRDSALL

New York [City,] Jan[uar]y 26th 1846

Dear Sir, I congratulate you on the fact that your course of policy on the Oregon question has been triumphantly and almost immediately vindicated by events. The civil commotions in Mexico, the change out and in again of the Peel & Wellington administration of Great Britain, and other lesser circumstances, if they do not indicate that your course was dictated by a prophetic foresight, they certainly prove that you could not have moved more wisely had you known those events beforehand.

The war movements of [Lewis] Cass, [John Quincy] Adams, [Joshua R.] Giddings, [Edward A.] Hannegan, [William] Allen & Co. so full of patriotic fire and enthusiasm, produced for a brief space of time a correspondent feeling here, and a course dictated by a more enlarged patriotism, was charged to considerations only for the Southern States, regardless of the rest of the Union. On the corners of the streets I was greeted with the question in all directions, ["]well, what do you think of Mr. Calhoun now?" Sometimes I had several antagonists at once, declaring "we must have the whole of Oregon— no foreign nation shall interfere in the concerns of the Western world"—and "if Mr. Calhoun opposes giving the notice he will be politically dead."

All this is changed—acknowledgments are made of your being right, of your statesmanship &c. No man ever occupied a more eclipsing position in this nation than yourself at the present juncture. But the belief has long been impressed upon my ["mind" *interlined*] that so much prejudice has been instilled amongst the people in some parts of the Union, by the politicians of a Certain Dynasty since 1832, that voluntary justice will not be rendered to you. It is only rendered when extorted by actions so self evidently worthy that they cannot be misrepresented.

To embroil ourselves with Great Britain before we have established amicable relations with Mexico, would be national insanity. Mexico would be induced by Great Britain to be her ally in the contest, and British officers amongst mexican soldiers would teach them the art of destructive warfare. We want California—we want all Mexico in our confederacy, for we *need* the isthmus that connects the northern with the Southern America, that we may construct a ship canal or ship Railway between the two great Oceans, by which we can controll the greatest commerce of the world. What is the whole of Oregon compared to these great objects? By peace with Mexico we can acquire them all—By war we gain nothing at best but glory, while England might annex Mexico to her empire.

Never since the Revolutionary war has there existed such extreme necessity for peace between us and Great Britain as at present, because war can subserve none of our great present or prospective interests, but on the contrary would endanger them all. Peace—peace with Mexico first upon a firm basis, and the "notice" afterwards to Great Britain if you please.

When American Senators make speeches to Bunkum, I regret that they have not more regard for principles and less for political capital.

If the war paroxysm be not quite over here—it is considerably abated. Yours with highest consideration, F.W. Byrdsall.

ALS in ScCleA; PC in Boucher and Brooks, eds., *Correspondence*, pp. 320–321.

From T[homas] R. Dew

[Williamsburg, Va.] Jan[uar]y 26, 1846
D[ea]r Sir, I understand that A[rchibald] C. Peachy Esq[ui]r[e] an attorney in the Dist[rict] of Col[umbia] is a candidate for the Dist[rict] Attorneyship, lately made vacant by the death of Mr. [James] Hoban [Jr.]. I take great pleasure in stating to you, that Mr. P[eachy] was educated in this Institution. I lived for many years in his father[']s family, & consequently I can speak from the most intimate knowledge of the man. He is a gentleman of the highest order of intellect, & one of the most thoroughly ["educated" *interlined*] I am acquainted with. He has taken the Degree of A.M. in this institution, & is one of the most successful students who has ever passed through the College. I have no doubt he is destined to distinction in his profession. If you can with propriety aid him in his present design, it will confer an additional obligation on D[ea]r Sir, Y[ou]r ob[edien]t s[er]v[an]t, T.R. Dew, Pres[iden]t, W[illia]m & Mary Col[lege].

ALS in ScCleA. NOTE: Peachy apparently did not receive the appointment solicited.

From James Kelly

New York [City,] Jan[uar]y 26 1846
My Dear Sir, I take the liberty of addressing you at this time, from the fact of my being one of your Constituents in South Carolina on your entrie into public life. Having then the fullest faith in your young love of Country—your patriotism & your policy—I have watched at times—with great anxiety—the efforts made by the unscrupulous & unprincipled politicians against you—especially ever since the bublication [*sic*] of that most *odious* of Federal Documents—I *mean* [Andrew] Jackson[']s Proclamation. I shall never forget the party Clamour which was raised in this section against *yourself* in particular & your *friends* in general. But Sir, "*Thank God,*" Truth, & the Justice of your Cause have produced a mighty change—even in this State—once the great political Erena in which you were denounced by the Demagouges [*sic*]—as so dangerous to the perpetuity of the Union—(& much other garbage of the Kind). I am indeed gratified [*one word canceled*] to see many, who wer[e] among the most violent of your defamers—now the loudest mouthes

in your praise—indeed the great mass of the people, mechanics, & merchants, are anxiously looking to you as the Saviour of the Country—in this intricate crisis of affairs.

I have grown old, since I left the South & of course I am somewhat gar[r]ulous—& your official duties forbid me trespas[s]ing upon your time—Yet I am anxious to say a word or two in this letter with regard to my Nephew James Kelly. I feel as if I ow[e] it to him—& it may be the last time I may have the power of addressing you, my health, & age, rendering my probation here very uncertain. My Brother Barnard Kelly, was killed at the Battle of Lundy's Lane[,] his son James, who you may remember from an interview he had with you in Washington on the Subject of uniting your friends with those of Mr. [John] Tyler's previous to the Election of Delegates to the Baltimore Convention. He visited the Capital & saw Mr. Tyler & told him honestly, there was no chance to elect a single Delegate to that Convention. But if he would consent to a union of his friends with Mr. Calhoun's that a portion of the Delegates from this State could be elected in your favour. *Tyler* would not consent to the proposition, & my nephew had an interview with you that Evening, & I know that he much regret[t]ed the difference then existing in Congress between your friends, & those of Mr. Tyler.

You may remember I wrote to you some years since asking your influence with the Navy Department in favour of my Nephew, for the appoint[men]t of Purser. In your reply which I have now before me—you regret that your relations with the administration (*Jackson*) forbid your placing yourself under any obligations, but you added, that if hereafter it should be in your power, it would afford you pleasure *&c &c*. My Nephew is at this time one of the Weighers attached to the New York Custom House. I told him I was going to write to you, & he forbid me troubling you with any personal matters, that no true friend of yours would attempt to embarrass your mind with extraneous subjects at this time. My only excuse is, that I am under great [o]bligation to him[,] He having ministered to my comforts for the last 10 years. When I left South Carolina in 1815, if I had retired from business I would have had a Competency. But I have been unfortunate. Circumstances beyound my control, has placed me at the age of 80 years entirely dependant upon my *Nephew*, ["for" *interlined*] whom I now ask ["you" *canceled*] that you will—should an oc[c]asion present itself, lend ["him" *canceled*] the influence of your official position, to promote ["him" *interlined*] in any way you may deem best. ["calculated" *canceled*.]

As a man, he is upright, & honest to a fault & I will venture to say *no one* in this Section is more truly desirous for your suc[c]ess, than he, & I know that he has ["as" *canceled*] many friends among the people ["as" *altered to* "to"] sustain him. He is *President* of one of the largest Associations in the U.S. called the Hibernian Benevolent Society—all of whom are, & have for a long time been with you.

With my best wishes for your health & hap[p]iness together, with the Success of your policy Believe me Your Obedi[en]t Serv[an]t, James Kelly, No. 91 North Moore St.

ALS in ScCleA.

REMARKS IN DEBATE ON OREGON WITH WILLIAM ALLEN AND LEWIS CASS

[In the Senate, January 26, 1846]
[*Under discussion was William Allen's request for leave to introduce resolutions against European interference in the Americas, which he had first raised on 1/14. Several Senators, including Lewis Cass, discussed the matter of whether defence appropriations were needed. Calhoun questioned whether the substance of the resolutions should be debated when the question was on leave to introduce. Allen spoke at length, decrying Calhoun for what he considered a personal attack on him earlier. Allen rejected Calhoun's statement that he had acted improperly in submitting his resolutions without consultation with the Committee on Foreign Relations, of which he was chairman. He pointed to Calhoun's Senate resolutions of March 1840 as an instance of resolutions introduced that interfered with existing negotiations.*]

Mr. Calhoun said: Mr. President, I trust I have too much self respect, and too great a regard for the gravity of the subject-matter under discussion, to follow the example set by the Senator from Ohio, in giving this discussion a personal direction. I had not the slightest intention of wounding the feelings of the Senator in stating what I did. He himself had stated, in his remarks to which I replied, that he had introduced this resolution on his own responsibility; and yet he takes great offence in my simply stating in detail what he had expressed in general terms, by saying that he had not consulted the Senator from Michigan, (Mr. Cass,) and the Senator from Arkansas, (Mr. [Ambrose H.] Sevier,) or any other member of the committee. I made no insinuation, but simply stated the fact. I never make them. What I say, I say openly and directly; and mean neither more nor less than what I do say.

Having thus noticed the remarks of the Senator having a personal bearing, I shall now proceed to notice the other portions of his remarks. I shall be very brief.

The Senator, in the first place, has utterly failed in his elaborate researches to find a single precedent to justify the course he has taken on this occasion; not one of his precedents afford an example of a chairman of a committee, to which a specific subject-matter is committed, moving for leave to introduce a bill or resolution, on his own responsibility, on the subject-matter referred to him. That is his case; and, as he has found no example of the kind in his careful search, I hazard little in presuming that none such exist. On the occasion to which he referred, I intimated that I considered his resolution out of order; but I then intimated, and now boldly assert, that it was clearly a violation of a plain parliamentary rule, that, whenever any specific matter is referred to a committee, it is for the time withdrawn from the Senate, and cannot be made a subject for action by the Senate while it is so withdrawn. Not expecting this point to come up, I have not turned to the rule referred to; but it can be easily found, I presume, in the Manual, if any one chooses to refer to it.

The Senator from Ohio, without directly denying the rule, has undertaken to point out several examples, not warranted, as he alleges, by the rule. The first of these was the resolution of the Senator from Indiana, (Mr. [Edward A.] Hannegan,) introduced at the present session, in reference to Oregon, and the amendments which I offered to his resolution. The Senate will remember that the object of the resolution was to deny the right of this Government to settle by treaty the boundary between the United States and Great Britain in reference to Oregon. Now, the President [James K. Polk], in his message, said not one word on the subject of the right of the United States to settle the boundary; and, of course, in referring the part of his message to the Committee on Foreign Relations to settle the boundary in reference to Oregon, the right in question formed no part of the subject referred to that committee, and, of course, fails to sustain the grounds assumed by the Senator. It also follows, of course, that if the original resolution itself does not furnish a precedent in support of the Senator, neither does my amendment furnish one.

The next precedent relied upon is the case of the brig Enterprise, in reference to which I moved three resolutions [in 3/1840]. Most of the Senators present will remember that that was a case where an American vessel had been stranded at the Bahama Islands, and in reference to which the local authorities had acted in a manner wholly inconsistent with the laws of nations. Why the Senator has selected the resolutions offered in that case as a precedent to justify his course, I am wholly at a loss to understand. The President had made no allusion to the case in his annual message, nor had the subject been referred to any committee. It was a clear case of a movement upon a subject not before the Senate in any shape, nor referred to any of its committees.

But the Senator asserts, by way of justifying his resolution, that my resolutions were of a more general character, comprehending all times and places, and of universal application. He overlooks the fact which distinguishes them from his: that, as general as they were, they affirmed simply the general law of nations which was violated in the particular case: a law so well known and admitted as to receive the unanimous vote of the Senate. I doubt whether the Senator will be as fortunate with his resolutions.

His next precedent is the case of a resolution moved by Mr. Mallory [*sic*; Rollin C. Mallary], when a member of the House of Representatives [in 12/1823]. That was a case of a call for information on the Executive Department in reference to the grounds on which the declaration of Mr. [James] Monroe, referred to by the Senator from Michigan, (Mr. Cass,) was made. The Senator did not undertake to show in what manner that could constitute a precedent to justify his course. Admitting the part of the message alluded to had been referred to the appropriate committee, it is obvious that a call for information in reference to it is wholly different to introducing a resolution on the subject-matter referred to, and cannot justify the course pursued by the Senator on this occasion.

As to the last precedent cited by the Senator, he has not stated in sufficient detail the facts of the case to authorize me to state whether it was embraced in the parliamentary rule in question or not. Nor do I recollect whether the message [in 1824] of the President [James Monroe] referred to the insurrection of the Greeks against the power of the Sultan; or, if it did, whether that portion of the message had been referred to the appropriate committee when the Senator from Massachusetts [Daniel Webster], then a member of the House of Representatives, introduced his resolution: if not, the precedent would not cover the case. But, even suppose it should prove to be a precedent in point, (which I by no means believe,) it should be considered but an accidental and solitary departure from a well-established parliamentary rule.

Having dispatched the Senator's precedents, and shown that they do not justify his course on this occasion, I shall next proceed to make a few observations on the remarks made by the Senator from Michigan. The Senator undertakes to vindicate this resolution by the declarations made by Mr. Monroe in his annual message at the commencement of the session of 1823–'4. The cases are not analogous. However general the terms in which the declaration of Mr. Monroe was couched against the interference of the European Powers in the affairs of this continent, they had at the time a practical bearing in reference to an anticipated interference. I do not remember whether the diplomatic correspondence of that period has ever been published. A friend informed me last evening it had been. But, be that as it may, I presume, after so great a lapse of time, it would not be considered any violation of confidence to state the circumstances which led to that declaration.

We all remember the holy alliance established between the five principal continental Powers after the overthrow of Bonaparte. England declined to become a member, although she acted for the most part in concert with it. This powerful combination of sovereigns, established for the purpose of upholding monarchical power, and for repressing the establishment of democratical institutions, contemplated at the time an interference with the affairs of South America, in order to restore the dominion of Spain over her revolted provinces. Our Executive received an intimation—Mr. [George] Canning was then at the head of the British Ministry, a man of great sagacity and talent—of the intention of the allied sovereigns, and intimated that, if our Government would support the British, it would discountenance and take a stand against such an interference. The declaration of the message was the response before the world to this intimation, instead of being a mere general declaration, without any practical bearing, and signifying nothing.

With the declaration referred to there was another and a broader one against European nations colonizing on this continent, particularly referred to by the Senator from Michigan in his remarks, and on which he specially relies to vindicate this resolution. As to it, the then Secretary of State, (Mr. [John Quincy] Adams,) and now a member of the other House, claims, I understand, the paternity. My impression is, that he is fairly entitled to it. I have no recollection that it formed any part of the Cabinet deliberation, when the response made to Mr. Canning's intimation was under deliberation.

I will not speak with confidence, as the events are long past, but my impression is that it never was a subject of deliberation in the Cabinet at any time.

When the distinguished individual referred to came to be elevated from the State Department to the Presidency, he did not forget his paternal relation to it. It was one of the leading measures recommended in his first annual message to Congress, to be carried out through the Panama convention, which was so much distinguished in the political history of the day. And surely, if the principle upon which this resolution rests be correct—if all attempts at colonization or interference on the part of the European Powers are to be resisted, it would be far more rational to do it by concert, like that of the Panama convention, than to undertake it single-handed, as proposed by this resolution.

This recommendation, so far from meeting with the approbation of the Republican party of that day, united them against the then Administration. The opposition to it, on the nomination of members to represent us in the convention, led to one of the most animated discussions ever witnessed in this Chamber. It continued for many weeks, and, before it terminated, the Administration fell prostrate, never to rise again.

The Senator from Michigan has thought proper to attribute the opposition to this resolution to deference to Great Britain and other European Powers. He makes a wide mistake. It is to be attributed to a deference not to them, but to ourselves—a deference to that good sense which would teach us not to make declarations which we cannot perform, or to rely upon them to defend us against the encroachments or injustice of others.

Notwithstanding all that has been said by the Senator from Michigan, I am not capable of perceiving a single advantage likely to result from the adoption of this resolution. I would ask him what practical benefit can we possibly expect to derive from it under present circumstances? Will it facilitate the adjustment of the difference between us and Great Britain, or tend in any way to prevent a collision with that Power, which he and all profess a desire to avoid if it can honorably be averted? Or, if collision must ensue, would it tend to attract the sympathy and co-operation of other European Powers in our support? Or would it prevent the five great Powers, who he says have the regulation of the balance of power, and for whom he seems to have so much dread, from attempting to carry the principle of regulating the balance of power to this continent? Will declarations, will mere words, have any such potent effect? No. If we intend to oppose their interference, we must adopt a far different course; we must act, and not talk; we must build navies, arm and equip them; raise powerful armies, and a great revenue from internal and external taxes, and put forth the whole of our strength to make any effectual resistance. Instead of good, will not the adoption of this resolution be followed by the very reverse effects? Will it not throw embarrassments in the way of an adjustment of our conflicting interests with England, and increase the hazard of war instead of the prospect of peace? Will it not alienate and excite the jealousy of all the European nations against us, instead of eliciting their sympathies and support? Will it not combine the five great Powers more strongly together, and unite them in carrying out the balance of power in reference to this continent which the Senator so much dreads? Viewed in every light, instead of good, nothing but unqualified evil can flow from it. Under this impression, I resisted it when the resolution was first introduced, and under the same spirit I resist it now.

[*Allen spoke again at length.*]

Mr. Calhoun. The Senator supposes that I would have transferred the whole power on this subject to the committee. It is hardly necessary to reply to that. Committees are but the creatures of the Senate. As to Texas, Mr. President, as far as I had any share in the management of that particular question, I can only say that that declaration of Mr. Monroe had not the weight of that piece of paper; and if a thousand such declarations, in even stronger terms, had been made and passed the Senate, they would not have had that weight. Declarations, sir, are easily made. The affairs of nations are not controlled by mere declarations. If a declaration of opinion were sufficient to change the whole course of events, no nation would be more prompt than we. But we must meet interference in our affairs in another way: we must meet it as it was met in the case of Texas—decidedly, boldly, and practically. We must meet each particular case by itself, and according to its own merits, always taking care to assert our rights whenever it is necessary to assert them. As to general abstract declarations of that kind, I would not give a farthing for a thousand of them. They do more harm than good, or rather no good at all, but a great deal of harm. While up I wish to allude to some remarks of the Senator from Michigan. He seems to think that the news by the last steamer was as belligerent as he could have anticipated.

[*Cass remarked that he did not regard "the late news to be such as to warrant any change in our defensive policy."*]

Mr. Calhoun proceeded. Such an opinion, coming from such a quarter, and having the weight which it must have, may make it advisable that I should state mine, as I entirely differ from the Senator. I have read with attention the papers received [from Great Britain] by the late arrival, as far as they refer to the relations between the two countries, and I am of opinion that the information is very favorable to the peaceful settlement of the difficulties between the two countries. I regard the restoration of Sir Robert Peel to the head of the Ministry, with the increased power and influence it must give him, as highly favorable. I cannot doubt that he is sincerely desirous of preserving peace; nor can I doubt that such is the feeling of the people of England at large—such certainly is the tone of the English press, without a single exception, as far as I have seen. I do not except the [London] "Times." The short paragraph read by the Senator from Michigan might, taken by itself, seem to justify the conclusion to which he has come; but, taken in connexion with all which has appeared in that paper in reference to the Oregon question, a very different conclusion must be drawn. Instead of regarding Canning's line as the ultimate concession of Great Britain, it very distinctly refers to the 49th parallel, as offered by Mr. [Albert] Gallatin, as the basis of the settlement of the difficulties of the two countries.

But while the tone and spirit of the press exhibits this peaceful character, we are not left to doubt that Great Britain holds that she has rights in Oregon to be protected; and that if we undertake to assert our exclusive right to the whole, the result must be an appeal to arms.

On the whole, my conviction is now strong—much stronger than it was—that the question may be honorably settled by negotiation. If it should not be settled, I fear much of the responsibility will rest upon us. With this favorable prospect before us I cannot but regard the agitation of the subject now under consideration as any thing but [un]wise. The tone of moderation with which the whole British press has received the President's message, appears to me to set a proper example for us; if followed, we might, I think, look forward to a favorable and honorable settlement of this vexed and dangerous question at no distant day.

[*Several other Senators spoke.*]

Mr. Calhoun remarked that his expression with respect to the point of order was, that if any resolution were offered embracing subject-matter already in the hands of a committee, it was unparliamentary. And as to the proposition itself, it was not to be supposed that, because Senators might vote against its introduction, they would not be disposed to resist the interference of European Powers in matters in which the United States were directly concerned; but it would be simply because they did not choose to involve this Government in any general declarations, which they might not, in all cases, be prepared to carry out. Those who voted against the proposition he would undertake to say, would be as ready to meet any such interference on the part of European Powers, so far as their capacity went, as the gentleman from Ohio himself. But this was a matter concerning which there was great diversity of opinion in the Democratic party at the time of the Panama debate. It then occasioned a dissolution of the [John Quincy Adams] Administration; one Administration was turned out, and another came in on that very question.

[*The Senate then voted 26 to 21 to grant leave for the introduction of Allen's resolutions, which were referred to the Committee on Foreign Relations and ordered to be printed.*]

From the Washington, D.C., *Daily National Intelligencer,* January 29, 1846, pp. 2–3. Variant in *Congressional Globe,* 29th Cong., 1st Sess., pp. 242–248; the Washington, D.C., *Daily Union,* vol. I, no. 229 (January 26, 1846), pp. 910–911; the Alexandria, Va., *Gazette and Virginia Advertiser,* January 29, 1846, p. 2. Other variants in the New York, N.Y., *Herald,* January 28, 1846, p. 3; the Philadelphia, Pa., *United States Gazette,* January 28, 1846, p. 1; the Richmond, Va., *Enquirer,* January 31, 1846, p. 4; the Charleston, S.C., *Mercury,* January 31, 1846, p. 2; the Charleston, S.C., *Courier,* January 31, 1846, p. 2; the London, England, *Times,* February 16, 1846, p. 5. NOTE: In 1958 there was reported to be in the possession of a private collector an 11-pp. ms. of Calhoun's speech, corresponding to the *National Intelligencer* version transcribed above, in an unidentified hand, with emendations by Calhoun. If such a ms. is extant, it would be the only contemporary ms. from Calhoun's hand of a Senate speech.

To "Messrs. [JOSEPH] GALES [JR.] & [WILLIAM W.] SEATON"

[January 26, 1846?]

D[ea]r Sir, The report of the Union is so imperfect, that nothing short of rewriting ["them" *canceled and* "it" *interlined*] can correct its errors. I have not time to do so at present; but, if you could aid me by furnishing ["me with" *interlined*] one of your stenographers, or one who writes rapidly, I will endeavour to dictate, what I said during, the sitting of the Senate to day, in one of the Committee Rooms. With great respect, J.C.C.

ALI in NNPM. NOTE: This note, undated by the writer, can be dated only by an endorsement, apparently by the recipient, that reads January 27, 1846. It was addressed to Gales & Seaton "or in their absence The Foreman of" the National Intelligencer office. The letter has been dated 1/26 on the assumption that it may have been written late on 1/26, in reference to Calhoun's remarks of that day in the Senate, and delivered the next day. See the note to the remarks of 1/26 immediately above. It is possible that the ms. mentioned in that note was produced by Calhoun and a *National Intelligencer* stenographer.

From H[ENRY] WHEATON

Berlin, 26 Jan. 1846

My dear Sir, I had the pleasure to write you on the 24 Dec. suggesting the expediency of your calling for the correspondence respecting the Zollverein treaty in order that it may be *published*, & that justice may be done us respecting the motives & grounds on which that negotiation proceeded.

I have seen with the greatest satisfaction the manly stand taken by you in the Senate in favour of an honorable arrangement of our disputes with G. Britain respecting the Oregon territory. If we escape, as I trust we shall, the calamities of an unnecessary war, the most ["enligh" *canceled*] enlightened & virtuous portion of your Countrymen will certainly attribute it mainly to your patriotic exertions. No official station to which you could be raised by the suffrages of your fellow citizens would give you a higher place in their affections, or enable you to render a greater service to the Country.

I think it due to the friendship with which you have so long honored me to state *confidentially* that having received some time since an intimation ["that t" *canceled*] from Mr. [James] Buchanan [Secretary of State] that the President [James K. Polk] had determined to send a new Minister to Berlin in the course of the present Session of the Senate, which ["determination" *interlined*] was communicated to me in such a way as left me no other alternative but to ask for my recall, I have accordingly done so, & expect to receive it in the month of April. I cannot help thinking that if I had been supported *in the proper quarter*, the President would not have taken this step. But whether it is now too late for him to retrace it, I do not know; or whether he would be disposed to do so, if he knew that I was a *friend of yours*. But I thought it right to let you know that although I have nothing to complain of as to the *manner* in which this measure was adopted & intimated to me, yet it will be attended with very great personal inconvenience, without any adequate correspondent advantage, that I can perceive, to the public or the party. Mr. Buchanan states to me that it has been taken in pursuance of a supposed rule limiting all foreign missions to the term of four years. The best proof that no such rule exists, or at least that cases of peculiar aptitudes for the diplomatic service have been considered as exceptions to it, will be found in the fact of my having been employed in this mission more than twice that length of time, [*one word or partial word canceled*] during which it is admitted that I have performed my duties "with distinguished zeal & ability" to make use of Mr. B[uchanan]'s own words. But what I have to complain of is, that ["*the*" *canceled*] I had not sooner been informed that it ["*is*" *canceled*] was meant to apply this asserted rule to my case. Had this been done, as it might have been immediately on the formation of the present Administration, I should have received the appointment of Professor of Law in the University of Cambridge [Mass., that is, Harvard University] vacant by the death of Judge [Joseph] Story. But as my friends could not learn on enquiry at Washington that there was any intention of recalling me, they were not able to answer for my accepting the vacant chair at Cambridge, & as there was a necessity for filling it almost immediately it was impossible to wait until my determination could be known.

Under these circumstances I should be very glad to learn whether the President may not perhaps still be disposed to avail the public of my Diplomatic Services in some other mission. I understand that both the missions to Paris & London will be vacated in the course of the present year, in which case an opportunity would be afforded for that purpose. I write to no other person but you on the subject, because I know that it is only through your powerful interposition that I can hope still to continue in my present line of employment.

Apologizing for troubling you so often on my personal concerns, I remain ever, my dear Sir, truly your obliged friend, H. Wheaton.

P.S. My address is care U. States legation London.

ALS in ScCleA; PC in Jameson, ed., *Correspondence*, pp. 1069–1071.

From J[osé] M. Caminero

Santo Domingo City, January 27th/46

Honourable Sir, I hasten to express my great exultation on being informed by the late public papers of the U.S. that you are now seating in Senate, and congratulate myself of such aid & assistence to the Dominican question in Congress.

Though to date I have not been favoured of any letter from J[ohn] Hogan I have been informed that his report has been presented to the Executive [James K. Polk] & that a complete success is to be hoped about the recognition by the Government of the U.S. of our national independence, that on which I rely with more confidence by your interposal as a Senator.

Our progress in consum[m]ating & consolidating our liberty & in repressing Haytian negroe's usurpations & attacks are daily advancing: About the middle of December last they sent five armed vessels to blockade Porto Plata on the North part of the Island, but on the night of the 21st, by a gale of wind, three of their ablest vessels ran ashore within three miles of the town & windward of said place; by our efforts we have been able to save one entire & undamaged as also the salvage of the other two composed of all their armaments & equipments & &; we have also secured the Haytian Admiral, Cadet Antoine, officers & crew made prisoners & forming a number 170, & by the Haytian papers we were apprised here of the wreck of another of their vessels near Cape Hayti.

By this series of ill luck of the Haytians & by the increase of our naval forces we are positively superior by sea, having actually eleven well armed vessels amongst which a fine corvette carrying 20 Paksem [*sic*; Paixhan] guns & two 24 pounders on pivots as also a small brig. As for land, no ag[g]ression has taken place since our late victory at Bellair, on the river Massacre, where more than three hundred blacks were killed.

I cannot do otherwise but urge a speedy determination of the recognition of our national independence, as any further delay may be prejudicial to our cause, fearing as I am surely entitled, an intrigue between France & Spain, as it is evident that the first is highly interested to the possession of the Isthmus & Bay of Samana; but I am highly satisfied to say that in our Republic there is not at present a single person of patriotic feeling that has a simpathy nor thinks any thing of France so as to urge any encouragement to the possession of the object of their desire. In my opinion our recognition would be a great step to the annexation in all points so interesting to the U.S. I therefore think that the Dominican question as a matter of fact, cannot suffer any opposition nor delay, that of which I entirely rely upon the simpathetic feeling you have manifested to our cause.

I shall request to be so kind as to give me all possible information by all opportunities of the state & progress of our national question, ad[d]ressing your communications through Messrs. Aymar & Co. of New York that of which I shall feel highly grateful to you. I remain Honourable Sir Your Most Obedient Servant, Dor. J.M. Caminero.

ALS in ScCleA; PC in Boucher and Brooks, eds., *Correspondence*, pp. 321–322.

To [JAMES L. EDWARDS, Commissioner of Pensions]

Senate Chamber, 27th Jan[uar]y 1846

Mrs. [Elizabeth] Gilliam [*sic*], the widow of Robert Gilliam, is an Aunt of mine. I have no knowledge of her marriage, but as far back as I can recollect, which extends back beyond 1794, she was called & regard[ed] as the wife of Mr. Gilliam, and [I] have not the least doubt, that she was lawfully married to him before 1794. If a more particular statement should be required, I will call & see the declarations refer[r]ed to in the above letter. J.C. Calhoun.

ALS in DNA, RG 15 (Veterans Administration), Revolutionary War Pension and Bounty-Land Warrant Application Files, W8848 (M-804:1073, frames 107–110). NOTE: Calhoun added this statement at the bottom of the letter to himself from Thomas P. Spierin dated 1/19. In the same file there is an ALS from James A. Black, Columbia, S.C., to the Commissioner of Pensions dated 11/9/1854; it states: "Mr. Calhoun[,] knowing the [Gillam] family well[,] told the then Comm[issione]r of Pensions [James L. Edwards] that the Claim should be passed as he was aware of merits of the claim upon the reputation of her husband or from knowing the parties who testified in her behalf, I suppose." Other documents in the same file indicate that a certificate of pension was issued on 1/30/1846 and was sent to Calhoun.

From SAMUEL GALLOWAY

Lawtonville S.C., Jan[uar]y 27th 1846

Dear Sir, Presuming upon your benevolence and public spirit, I have ventured to trouble you for an opinion respecting my proposed publication. Seeing the sorrowful effects of human legislation upon property, I was led to examine the ["laws" *altered to* "law"] of property, and found it reducible to a single principle. I am a Presbyterian clergyman of a finished education, and have given several years to philosophic occupations, and this is the first of a series of works which I intend to publish. This *introduction* ["sent to you" *interlined*], though I have since made some corrections, will give you a specimen of my style and philosophy. You need not return ["the" *interlined*] copy sent you as I have the corrected one. This part, of necessity, is somewhat dry, while the body of the ["work" *interlined*] is adorned with variety, with historic and classic allusions. Mental elaborations are always inducted with physical elaborations. I give you a brief syllabus.

II. *Materials* and physical laws are all Divine gratuities. Chemical and mechanic laws, their cooperation. Equilibriums. The adaptation of the globe for laboring, and for commercial intercourse.

III. *Elaborator* is man, composed of body and mind, a perceptible individuality. Body and mind are employed in every elaboration. Man's bodily structure, chemical constitution, senses, memory, intellection, sense of beauty, and power of language, suited for laboring in society.

IV. *Wants* of this compounded nature are many and increase with his facilities of satisfying them. The wants of his senses, of literature, of the fine arts.

V. Man works upon existing materials, forming arts, and sciences, Instanced in agriculture, Literature, Architecture, statuary and painting.

VI. Consumption destroys the pleasing effects of the inhering labor. Some consumptions rapid other[s] slow. Some consumptions are intermedial, others final. Consumptions in literature and science react upon labor.

VII. *Taste* exhibits diversities in food, dress, architecture, literature. This gives a rich variety in elaborated commodities.

VIII. *Varieties* in the human race fits them for laboring in society and ["f" *canceled*] causes pleasing appearance in the world. Negroes suited for servants in hot countries. Man is happiest in his proper calling.

IX. *Divisions* are territorial as minerals, vegitation, and animals are located to physical latitudes. Men elaborate different parts of the same commodity in distant locations.

X. Mensuration arises from competition in buyers and vendors. This mensuration, from numerous mental averages, is very exact. The quantity and price fluxionary, and in inverse proportions.

XI. Surplusage arises from the superiority of locations.

XII. *Distribution* arises from the fluxion of commodities to the highest market. Food is prolonged during the season, and given out to places as wanted. The progress of commerce.

XIII. [*"Maximums"* altered to *"Maximum"*] of elaborations arises from working and trading with perfect freedom. Men produce most when following their genius, and on laboring on the materials with which nature has furnished them to the best advantage. If you would be willing to look at the whole work, when I have finished it, I will send you the whole manuscript. Several literary gentlemen who have seen portions of my manuscript, have all united in thinking it just such a work as the present times [*"demands"* altered to *"demand"*]. I would like to have the judgement of one of your discernment and experience, as I intend to publish on my own responsibility. I intend [*"it"* interlined] to be a work making the science perfect, never to be superceded. The next work will be on *finance*, carrying out *labor* in that department. The third work will be *morals* on the same principle. The fourth will be *government* and *jurisprudence* on the same principle. These sciences are reducible, as far as property enters into them, as certain as astronomy. Yours, Samuel Galloway.

ALS with En in ScCleA. NOTE: Galloway enclosed a turgidly-written, ten-page manuscript entitled "Industrial Science[,] Inductions," in which he applied his notions of scientific principles to economics. Galloway published a book on this subject, *Ergonomy; Or, Industrial Science*, in 1853.

From A[BBOTT] H. BRISBANE

Albany Georgia, 28th Jan[uar]y 1846
My dear Mr. Calhoun, you got me an appointment to West Point when a boy—you advised my employment in Florida under Gen[era]l [Simon] Bernard, in 1826; in 1836 you urged me to apply my professional skill as Engineer in the developement of the resources of the State of Georgia, in as far as she held the avenues to the west & southwest; and now, in 1846, I crave a farther interposition on your part, as you will see in the sequel.

Since 1836, I have been diligently employed in effecting all for the object that brought me to Georgia, that my energy & ability could accomplish. As far as the passage across the Aleghanies [*sic*] to the waters of the Tennessee [River], by the "Western & Atlantic Rail road" is concerned, success has attended our efforts; for the State of

Georgia has determined, although slowly, to complete that great work. With regard to the *Cotton* road to the Alabama River from the Ocmulgee [River]—the favorite of Gen[era]l Bernard, and his substitute for the passage of the Southern Peninsula by any other route or means of transit short of a ship channel; we have been less fortunate. The first link of this thoroughfare, is comprised between the Rivers Ocmulgee & Flint; the first an Atlantic water, the latter a Gulf. This I essayed in concert with the late Bishop [John] England of Charleston on a plan of independent stock labor; the proviso being, that the planter of the South Western portion of Georgia, should provide the support. As far as the labor went, we succeeded nobly; but the distresses attendant on the culture of cotton in our new section of country, and a thousand other lesser evils, cut us off from our supplies; and although we have graded 76 miles of road (the entire distance from one river to the other), and laid the superstructure on 40 miles of it, the work was compelled to be suspended. I had heard you say that all the improvements that eventuated upon the waters of the Atlantic, south of Charleston, would accrue to her trade, and from the inland facilities that connect her with all the rivers of the South; this first stimulated me to this enterprise. I know too, that the greater the exports of *Cotton* from our Atlantic seabo[a]rd, the greater our chances for an independent commerce. As soon then as I found that Georgia would open the *demand* market of the Great West upon us by the State road to the Tennessee, I saw the greater importance of the greater export of cotton.

But what is individual conviction or effort, when there are contracted policies and limited means always in opposition. For five years have I exerted every nerve, and yet the Cotton road—the Gulf road—the road that Gen[era]l Bernard pointed out as the *Southern work* to be opened in Conjunction with the Cumberland road *north*, under the old Federal system of improvement, is left unfinished for want of a few thousands [of dollars]. Now I state these things as important in a commercial point of view; and under the consideration of our national warfare's being happily confined by you all to peac[e]able operations; but should this not prove the case, and we be forced to defend the southern country against the aggression of England; then in a hundred fold does our need for the road from the Atlantic waters to those of the Gulf increase. But you are already conversant with all this; my object for writing you, is to keep you advised of the state of our work—the parties to whom it belongs—its cost so far—and the amount that it would require to complete it; leaving it to your own judgement as to the best method of forwarding its operations pending a war with England. I wish to submit the entire matter to you, as though you were the party most interested; and thus be directed in all things by you. I have already said that most of my prominent moves have been under your suggestion and agency; [I] wish this, the most important of them to be equally so.

But to the statement; and *1st* the state of the rail-road. 76 miles have been graded and 40 miles laid; but the time that has elapsed since the superstructure [was built], will have caused more or less decay. *2nd*—the work is owned by the laborers principally in the shape of shares issued to them for work—say ¾ of it; the rest by individuals residing in the neighborhood of the road, who bought shares through the provisions furnished by them. *3rd*—the cost of the work so far, has been $200,000—covering outlays, debts and all contingencies—and *4th* the amount required to complete it in six months would be $100,000 more; this taking up the debts above stated as a part of the future cost, or some $30,000 dollars. I say that I leave it entirely to you to advise the best plan for having this work put into operation, should your mind settle down upon the conviction that war must come: Either that *dispose* of the work to the Federal Government—*obtain a loan* from the War Department for its completion—mortgaging it for the $100,000 borrowed, or any other idea that may suggest itself to your mind; the necessary steps to be taken while Congress is in session, that the means may be provided. My dear Mr. Calhoun, this is an object worthy of your attention.

My next object for writing you, is to beg you remember that if war come, I am a protegê of yours én militaire; and must request you see that I find favor with the President as a good officer. I refer you to Gen[era]l [Winfield] Scott, under whom I served in Florida for three months, by the appointment as Volunteer ["of" *changed to* "and"] Gov[erno]r [George] McDuffie, a Col. commanding there, and since Brigadier Gen[era]l Successor to Gen[era]l [James] Hamilton [Jr.] of the Charleston Brigade, which I commanded for some time. My familiar acquaintance with the *Southern Coast*, will render my ability to command in this unenviable neighborhood, where West India negroes will campaign it, a matter of consideration with the President. But like the former case I leave it to you to act as though I were a stranger, and you only wanted some one whom you could rely upon to serve your country. With sentiments of sincerest reg[ar]d I subscribe my self your Ob[edient] Ser[van]t, A.H. Brisbane.

P.S. I would have you write me at your earliest convenience on these subjects directing to Albany[,] Baker County Georgia; & if you think there is need for my personal attendance—the chances being in favor of some[?] action on the premises, I will place[?] myself at your disposal.

ALS in ScCleA.

From ROBERT B. CAMPBELL

U.S. Consulate Havana
Jan[uar]y 28th 1846

My dear Sir, I have taken the liberty of sending by the U.S. Sch[oo-ne]r Flirt a small box of segars, small and pressed and esteemed here by smokers, which I beg you will accept as a trifling testimony of the regard of an old friend and acquaintance who has received so many kindnesses and favors at y[ou]r hands & who hopes yet to see the day when the people of the United States laying aside the trammels of Caucus dictation will confer on your talents, patriotism, and purity, the reward you have so long and eminently deserved, a reward for y[ou]rself, scarcely worth acceptance, but all important to your country[']s welfare. I know y[ou]r time too valuable and too much occupied to permit me to trespass upon it, and therefore cut short much I would like to say. Y[our]s Mo[st] truly & sincerely, Robert B. Campbell.

ALS in ScCleA. NOTE: An AEU by Calhoun reads: "Gen[era]l Campbell[.] Sends a box of segars."

From [JAMES L. EDWARDS, Commissioner]

Pension Office, January 28, 1846

Dear Sir, In consequence of the note which you appended to Mr. [Thomas P.] Spierin's letter in the case of Mrs. Elizabeth Gillam, I send herewith her declaration under the act of July 7, 1838. By those regulations a detailed statement of the service is necessary. In some cases, however, they cannot be made. Our usual course is, when claims are presented for service in the South-Carolina militia, to ask for the Comptroller's certificate as to the amount of the indent issued for the service, and to regulate the pension accordingly. In this case the Comptroller's certificate has not been furnished. The Dept. would be justified in allowing for eighteen months service in this case, however, if you would certify as to the credibility of the witnesses. The evidence as to the time of the marriage is perfectly satisfactory.

The pension granted to widows for Revolutionary service is a pro rata allowance; and hence it is important for each claimant to show at least two years service to obtain the maximum ["rate of" *interlined*] allowance. I have the honor to be with great regard Your ob[edien]t Ser[vant].

FC in DNA, RG 15 (Veterans Administration), Letters Sent by the Commissioner of the Pension Office, 1800–1866.

To Mrs. LETITIA [PRESTON] FLOYD, [Abingdon, Va.?]

Washington, 28th Jan[uar]y 1846
My dear Madam, I regret very greatly, that it has not been in my power to save your Nephew, Maj[o]r John G. Floyd. I called on the President [James K. Polk] in his behalf, but found the case already decided, under the pressure, as he told me, of the united voice of the Illinois delegation.

I deeply lament the fact. It is the fruit of the abominable policy, that the spoils belong to the victors, which is corrupting the whole community & eroding the Government to the core.

I am happy to hear, that the health of Mr. [John W.] Johnston [your son-in-law] is partially restored.

I know not that I can do any thing effectual to preserve the peace of [our] country, or to arrest the downward course of the government; but my friends may rest assured, that whatever my duty may call me to do shall be done fearless of all consequences personal to myself.

With best wishes for the continuance of your health, & the prolongation of your days, I am yours truly & sincerely, J.C. Calhoun.

ALS in DLC, George Frederick Holmes Papers, vol. 1. NOTE: The addressee of this letter was the widow of Governor John Floyd of Va. John G. Floyd was removed by Polk from his post as Superintendent of Lead Mines on the Upper Mississippi, apparently because his too zealous concern for the interests of the government had antagonized the local operators.

To T[homas] G. Clemson

Washington, 29th Jan[uar]y 1846
My dear Sir, We have been very much disappointed in not hearing from you, or Anna [Maria Calhoun Clemson] by the last steamer, which I attribute to some accidental failure, as I learned at the State Department yesterday, they had not heard from you, nor received your duplicate of the treaty, though Mr. [Charles] Serruy's [*sic*; Belgian Minister to the U.S.] had received his.

The steamer, which takes this, will take letters to Anna from her mother [Floride Colhoun Calhoun] & [Martha] Cornelia [Calhoun], which will give all the domestick & social news, & which will leave me nothing to communicate, but the political.

You will have seen by previous conveyance, that I have taken my ["stand" *interlined*] on the side of peace, with what success time only can decide. Thus far, the effect has been a very considerable abatement of the war fever, both in Congress & the Country. The arrival by the last steamer has contribute[d] farther to abate it, as the news is considered very favourable. Indeed, it is so much so, that there ought to be, in my opinion, no hesitancy on the part of our Executive to take immediate steps to terminate the controversy. I hold it almost certain from the contents of the English papers & from what I learn through other channels, that the British Government is prepared to adjust the difference by agreeing to the 49th parallel as ["the basis of" *interlined*] the boundary, while I am quite certain, that an adjustment on that basis would be acceptable to a large majority of the country & Congress. And yet, I fear, that it is still uncertain, whether we shall be able to avert the opposite termination; ["by" *canceled*] an appeal to Arms. I fear that there is a state of uncertainty & hesitancy on the part of Mr. [James K.] Polk & his Cabinet. I have no doubt, but that they are sincerely desireous of peace, & see that peace cannot be preserved, without a compromise, but dread taking any step to compromise, in consequence of the unfortunate declaration of the inaugural, that our tittle [*sic*] to the whole was clear & unquestionable. That, with the course of the organ & other party presses, has created an ardennt [*sic*] party in the Western States, which go ag[ai]nst all compromise; & it is the dread of so large & decided a party, which causes the hesitancy. That party goes ardently for notice, forthwith & unqualified, under the belief, that it will prevent all compromise, while the administra[tion] urge notice as the most certain means of producing compromise & securing peace. Their joint influence, I fear, will be be [*sic*] sufficiently strong to carry it through both Houses; but, I hope, we may be able to qualify it, by making it a condition, that when the notice is given, that it shall be accompanied with the offer of the 49th as the basis on which to adjust the difference; or, if that should fail, a reference of the question to arbitrators. Without some such condition, I fear notice will lead to an appeal to arms, for I doubt whether, if the British Government should offer the 49th, it would be accepted by our Executive, unless Congress should express an opinion, which would make it ["their" *canceled and* "his" *interlined*] duty; in so awarked [*sic*; awkward] a condition is Mr. Polk placed in reference to this delicate subject.

In the mean time our relations with Mexico have again become very delicate, which may involve us in a war with her. If it should, I greatly fear that a war would follow almost as a matter of course with England about Oregon. England would not willing[ly] stand by and see us overrun Mexico; and if she should feel it for her interest to side with Mexico, she will decline an adjust[ment] about Oregon. I took this view of the subject, while charged with the negotiations, & was anxious to avoid such a result. For that purpose, I was desireous of settling the Oregon question as speedily as possible, when I saw there would be no difficulty in settling our difference with Mexico.

[William] Allen's resolution ag[ai]nst the colonization of this continent by European powers, which was laid on the table in the first instance on my motion, has been taken up & referred to his Committee. It would indicate, that there had been a change of opinion on the part of the Senate in reference to it, but such is not the fact. It will be rejeected [*sic*] by a decided vote when reported back.

I hope you all continue to enjoy good health & the children [John Calhoun Clemson and Floride Elizabeth Clemson] to grow & improve finely. I hope also you have got my letters written at Alabama & since my return.

All join in love to you & Anna, & the children. Kiss them for Grandfather. Your affectionate father, J.C. Calhoun.

ALS in ScCleA; variant PC in Jameson, ed., *Correspondence*, pp. 679–681.

From A. P. Stinson

St. Joseph[,] Berrien Co[unty] Michigan
Jan. 29, 1846

My dear Sir, It has well been said that "Self Preservation is the first Law of ["our" *canceled*] natures." The Longer I Live, & I have Lived more than two S[c]ore years & ten, the more have I become *satisfied* of the Propriety of the *adage*. And in the History of No man Is this adage been less attended to, than In that of *John Caldwell Calhoun*. Your Country *first* & your self *Last*, seems to me to have been the axiom with you. Not so with with [*sic*] Others. The time has come, nay Sir, It Long since came, when It was (as I believe) *your Duty* to *your Self* & the Country that you take a *Stand*, & Never till *now* have I seen any manifestations of that Disposition, "*Self Preservation.*" Heretofore It has been in the Bentonian Principle "Every thing for the Cau[s]e, Nothing for Men." When Sir, I have *Seen* & *heard* of the *Havoc* made of *your friends*, because they were *your friends*, In various Offices In the Gov[ern]ment during the Past Year, & Particularly in the *Custom House Departments* at *Detroit, Boston, Philadelphia* & *Portsmouth N.H.* It is has *pained me*. Why is It, I have Involuntarily asked my self that ["a"(?) *canceled*] Democrats must be Pros[cr]ibed because they ["had" *interlined*] favored, or favor ["Now" *interlined*] Mr. Calhoun! I see the *Cause*. I see a *Determined disposition* by the "Old Hunkers" to "Head you Off" & Hence; they have Determined to prosc[r]ibe any & Every one who *Dared* Advocate your Claims!

By the Boston Mass., & Portsmouth N.H. Papers, as also by *Numer[ou]s Letters* rec[eiv]ed from friends Living there, I have become *fully satisfied* of the *Hostility of Ex Gov.* [Marcus] *Morton*, Collector of Boston, & *Mr.* [Augustus] *Jenkins* of Portsmouth N.H. to you & your friends & Hence It is, they have been *unceremoniously Removed* to make way for the more *pliant tools of "Old Hunkerism"* & so In *Detroit. C[harles] G. Hammond* the Coll[ector] has so far as I have seen or Known *Studiously avoided* appointing or *Recommending any* who was *Suspected* of favoring "*Calhounism.*" Is this Sir, to be *tolerated*! Has not the time Come, fully arrived, when not only your friends but your self Even, Should take a *firm*, a *Decided Stand*! Can you or your friends, with these facts Staring you in the face, & you can but see them, *consent* to the *Confirmation* of Such Men, as *C.G. Hammond, Marcus Morton,* Augustus Jenkins & all! I hope not—Let men be Selected, Impartial men, who have such a *vast amount* of *Patronage* at their bestowal, that all alike may Share the Beneficen[c]e of the Gov[ern]ment. This is Right is proper In my Humble Opinion. That Your friends, have been *Singled* out for *Pros[cr]iption* Is Every where to be Seen. Not that the President [James K. Polk] is *privy* to It. I would not for a moment Indulge such an opinion, but that those he has vested with a Little *brief Authority* In *Subordinate Offices* has *acted up* to It, to *the verry Letter* I *Know full well*. Why Sir, In the Pitiful Little Office I hold under the Gov[ern]ment I have been *threat[e]ned* & *menaced* in various ways, solely because I was, what is termed, "a Calhoun man" & because I have not "day or night Shun[n]ed to Declare It." Nor will I, though I kn[o]w I should be Removed tomorrow on account of It. I am a "Freeman"! I thank my *God I am* & Live, yet, in a free Country. I Sir, after Seeing you had been at *Memphis*, wrote you at *"Fort Hill S.C."* & Subsequently at *Washington*, but have no answer, or token of their Reception. I fear they may have been *Intercepted*. I fear there is an Espoinage [*sic*] in Our Office Here—Still remote ["as we are" *interlined*] from any other, have concluded to put this in *Our Office*. I wrote *Mr.* [Robert Barnwell] *Rhett*, & sent a Copy of a Letter from Washington of Jan. 3d taken from the *N.H. Gazette* of Portsm[ou]th which I like. I have no hopes Sir, of your Receiving A *Nomination* in '48 by a *National Convention*. No Sir, not Even though 3 fourths of the Demo[cra]cy of the Count[r]y were for you! The *"Wire workers*[,]" the *"Cliques*[,]" manage these matters & as Neither you or friends, will *de[s]cend* to *"Manageme[n]t"* In the *"Primary meetings"* ["and" *canceled*] hence It is the "Vox Populi" Is *Stifled*. That your friends will at the Proper time announce the Name of *John C. Calhoun* as an *Independent Candidate*, as the *People[']s Candidate* for the *Preside[n]cy* in '48 Is now generally Conceded, & If a *Hearty Response*, does not follow, I confess there is naught in the "Signs of the times." I feel that ["I" *interlined*] should apologize to you Sir, for So Oft obtruding my self upon your Notice. The only apology is, I desire in my *Inmost Soul* to be of Some Little Service to a man who for the fi[r]st time I saw in '36 & Since which, I have been, though Humble, a Devoted & sincere friend. As Ever Yours Truly, A.P. Stinson.

P.S. If you see my friend *Judge* [Levi] *Woodbury*, please make my regards acceptable. A.P.S.

[P.S.] Of all the *Deputy Collectors* & *Inspectors* on these Lakes, within the District of Detroit, Mr. C.G. Hammond[']s Collection

District, I have to find the *first Person in Office* who is not of the "Old Hunker" Stamp & Consequently Opposed to you! ! ! Stinson.

ALS in ScCleA.

From ——

Baltimore, 1 Mo[nth; that is, January] 29, 1846

In perusing the enclosed remarks I was struck with the noble[,] magnanimous and true Christian conduct of Lord Gray [*sic*; Henry George, Lord Grey], and thy late acts in the Senate of the U. States, which will command the admiration and approbation of the wise and good of all nations. There appears in this noble and disinterested conduct, more than the mere wisdom of man; it shews the finger and guidance of him who knoweth all things and is indeed the guide and Protector of all who put their trust in him; and may thou ever be lead and governed by this *unerring* light and sperit, which enlighteneth every man that cometh into the world is the sincere desire of an observer of the actions of men.

ALU with En in ScCleA. NOTE: The anonymous writer of this letter, probably a Quaker, enclosed a newspaper article entitled "Lord Grey and Mr. Calhoun." The article, clipped from an unknown newspaper that had reprinted it from the New York *Courier*, praised Grey and Calhoun for sacrificing their personal interests as well as party considerations in order to maintain peace between Great Britain and the U.S.

From M [ARIA] D [ALLAS] C [AMPBELL]

Chestnut St. No. 349 [Philadelphia]

Saturday Jan[ua]ry 30th [1846?]

My good & old friend, I wrote you a letter a week since, to which I am sure, unless you are unwilling I should presume upon your friendship by any call upon it, you would not have found it troublesome to reply to[.] It was merely an enquiry as to whether you thought I should hear an interesting debate in the Senate, & as you know *best*, those whom I liked *best* to hear, I begged a line from you, to tell me *when* I should time my visit[.] I am suspicious that my letter may not have reached you, & only trouble you this time, to be assured of that fact[.] If it has—& you have found it intrusive, forgive me in remembrance of our former friendship & be assured the error shall never be repeated. Very truly y[ou]rs, M:D:C:

ALI in ScCleA. NOTE: This letter has been assigned to the year 1846 because of its apparent relationship to Mrs. Campbell's letter of 1/22/1846 to Calhoun above—despite the fact that 1/30 did not fall on a Saturday in 1846 but on a Friday.

From THO[MA]S G. CLEMSON

Brussels, January [30?, 1846]
My dear Sir, By the Acadia which has just arrived we received your letter dated Cane Brake[,] So[uth] Carolina[,] 13th Dec. and finished at Washington under date of the 26th inst. [*sic*; 12/26]. Your trip to Memphis and the manner you were received by all parties must have been highly gratifying to you. It seldom happens that one man receives such marked honours as have fallen to your lot. It is the highest praise & the greatest of recompenses. I hope that your going to the West will do good by uniting the South, without which little can be effected to advance their prosperity which certainly stands in need of amelioration. My position here has given me abundant proof of how much the South looses [*sic*]. In the eyes of Europe among all intel[l]igent classes, the importance of the whole country is based upon the great staples Cotton & tobacco, without which we should be insignificant. Those two articles vivify the commerce of the world, have enriched England (particularly cotton) and the truth of it is our power over this continent depends on those two articles. The treaty which I have concluded with Belgium will eventual[l]y be of great service to our shipping & to the Southern States for I have laboured hard here to make it apparent that the interests of Belgium & the Zollverein are to have direct trade with the Cotton States. My views on these subjects have created some considerable stir here & in Germany, & if the Zollverein will put on a high enough tariff upon English twists the consumption of Cotton will increase amazingly. That this will be done eventually I have no doubt. And if the United States Govern[men]t understood her interest on this subject the increased consumption of Cotton would be rapidly increased. Baron [Heinrich Alexander] d'Arnim the late Prussian Minister at this court (who is now in Berlin & who is to go to Paris as minister if not retained as minister of Foreign affairs in Berlin) is a complete convert to my views on that question & I feel

confident that if I was in Berlin I could change the action of Prussia & the Zollverein in our favour. The Zollverein receive Cotton twists to the amount of seventy millions of Prussian dollars from England, and only receive about seventy thousand bales of Cotton whilst England receives one million six hundred thousand bales. So soon as our treaty is in action (that with Belgium) our ships will do the carringing [*sic*] trade, which has been done heretofore by the vessels of the Hanse towns under the unfavourable treaty we have with those ports. England now supplies the whole of Germany nearly and her sixty millions of people with cotton of her manufactures and not only Germany but nearly all the Continent. If the ports of Germany could be closed to England[']s manufactures, do not suppose it would lessen her consumption, not atall. It would only make her a commission merchant more to sell our cotton, & her manufactures for she could not afford to turn her manufacturers to other pursuits. Depend upon it these views are founded & we ought to be active. I will underwrite for it that if our interests are properly managed in Berlin ["Cotton" *canceled*] the consumption of Cotton would soon surpass the production.

I am very much obliged to you for your visit to my place [in Edgefield District] & the details you give me concerning my interests. I acquiesce in the decision you have come to in not selling my place. So far as my feelings are concerned I should much prefer holding the place and negroes but whether in doing so I should be consulting my interests perhaps it may admit of a doubt. I agree with you that the time was too short for a sale & think you have acted wisely. I do not desire to trouble any one with my business. I would prefer a sacrifice to doing so, and that was one reason why I desired its sale. I wrote you as soon as I could after receiving your letter but steamers now during the winter leave but once a month which prevented your receiving my answer as soon as I would have desired. We were very much gratified to hear that negroes were all well and appear so well satisfied.

Mr. [Napoleon Alcindor] Beaulieu the new minister resident from Belgium leaves Liverpool in the next steamer. He carries out a small package for old Mr. & Mrs. Mowbley [*sic*; John and Lucretia Simkins Mobley] and addressed to your care, which you will be good enough to send to them by the first safe opportunity. I hope the Government will return the compliment & give me the same grade & increased pay, for that of Chargé is not sufficient in Brussels where the expenses are nearly as great as in London or Paris. I shall have been here this summer nearly two years, and by the month of August will have gotten through all my extra funds, and another outfit would not come amiss. When I last saw Mr. [Henry] Wheaton he told me that he had done all that he could do in Berlin and was then anxious to go to Vienna. If there was a chance for promotion I would rather go to Berlin than any place because I think I could advance my country[']s interests and do myself credit. Besides which it is a very laudable ambition for one to desire [*several words canceled and* "promotion" *interlined*] and the pay being larger I should have more room. I am told that Mr. [Washington] Irving has asked to be recalled from Madrid. I should even prefer that position to this if I could not procure that at Berlin. I write you these views more to express my feelings than with a hope that you can aid me in getting a step higher, as I know in your position that is difficult for you to do. I stand as well here as I can desire and my only objection to the place is the inadequacy of the salary for the position I am obliged to maintain. Tho I feel that I am doing all that I can do & have done all that was possible for the good of my country yet I feel curious & should be pleased if you could ascertain from Mr. [James] Buchanan how he is pleased with the manner I fulfil my duties & whether my despatches give him satisfaction as a man has no idea of his own efforts. Of course I do not wish you to ask the question of Mr. Buchanan in my name but as from yourself.

In 1844, 48 American vessels entered Belgium with a Tonnage of 18,245. In 1845, 81 vessels came to Antwerp alone with a tonnage of 32,684. So that the commerce has nearly doubled in one year, and it [is] evident that the business will now increase most rapidly & if steam boats come here from the United States the business will be very heavy on this Legation. Already I have as much to do as I can well attend to, for [Francis J.] Grund the Consul [at Antwerp] is always absent & I have much of his business to look after. The fact of it is our consulate system is rotten to the heart and wants remodelling, and a good deal might be said of our Diplomatic business.

The weather thus far here in Belgium has been exceedingly mild[,] little or no snow, little or no ice but much rain and high winds. A few days since we had a violent thunder storm accompanied with vivid lightning. In some of the late gales much damage was done to shipping and many lives were lost on this coast and that of England. It is fortunate that the winter is not severe, for had it been the suffering among the poor would have been greater, ["and" *canceled*] it is already bad enough.

The Acadia's arrival brought the doings in the United States on the subject of Oregon. I will here remark, that the message of the President [James K. Polk] might have been equally firm without awakening the jealousies and giving food for crimination & recrimination, of which there was enough without his repeating Mr. [James] Monroe[']s decision upon all the North American continent. We talk too much about ad[d]ition of territory & Levy's [that is, David Levy Yulee's] resolution in the Senate was wrong and could effect no good. If there is likelihood or probability of a war with England we ought to prepare for it without so much talk. I suppose that there can be very little doubt but that England is arming & making great preparations, yet we hear little about ["about" *canceled*] them. The position which the President has assumed in his message has unfortunately created a feeling on this side of the Atlantic, that England must go to war for her honour, or supremacy. If she does not she must hereafter act a second part to the United States. I beleive [*sic*] to a certain extent that such is the feeling in Great Britain, but independant of that our relations with the continent of Europe makes England fear that we are becoming too important for her interests, and a war with the United States would cripple us in that respect and aid her. At all events after a war with us her position would be bettered and ours less strong. Since writing the above we have received accounts of the opening of Parliament, and the English views on the message and the Oregon question. I understood before the arrival of that information, that [Sir Henry Floyd?] the brother in law of Sir Rob[er]t Peel who lives in Brussels remarked that there would be no war, "for the United States would loose nothing, whereas England had too much at stake" to risk a war with the United States.

What a singular season we have sure enough. We have scarce had any frost here, whilst the French soldiers in Africa have suffered much from cold and many of them perished.

Mr. [Philippe] Bourson the editor of the Moniteur (the official paper of this country) remarked to me the other day that he had gained more information from the study of your speeches (I loaned him the copy I have) than from any work he had ever read, and that the solution of many questions treated here found a solution in a phrase in your speeches. He also remarked that your speeches were infinitely superior to any thing of the kind on this side of the Atlantic. He is now writing some articles on the Tariff, Free trade, Finances, &c which will be principally taken from your efforts. He says that since he has seen your work it is absolutely essential that he should have a copy of it for his library. If you desired I think

I could have your speeches republished in England and if you will send me copys of any other of your efforts you have made since the publication of the volume that you would desire to see published, I will go to England & see whether publishers would not print them on their account. My impression is they would be happy to do so. If you have an extra copy you might send me a copy for the purpose through the State Department.

To return to the Oregon question I heard some time since an Englishman (a resident of this place and a contributor to English papers) say that that [*sic*] all England wanted was to be let down easy. Mr. Rowbuck [*sic*; John Arthur Roebuck,] a member of Parliament and very intelligent man[,] was here a week or two since & he said to me that there was not an intelligent Englishman that cared one cent about Oregon, but they could not be bullied out of it, & he believed that England would be happy to exchange Oregon for any other even nominal advantage. If there be any speeches made of note & published by their authors in Pamph[l]et form, please send me a copy of such. We are now all very well & in the midst of the winter gaieties. Anna [Maria Calhoun Clemson] writes by this Packet & joins in sending much love to all that are with you. Your affectionate son, Thos. G. Clemson.

N.B. I send you a copy of some certificates of an agricultural discovery that is making some noise. I think the seed are steeped in a salt of ammonia before planting. I have seen some of the results & they are really surprising. T.G.C.

ALS in ScCleA. NOTE: This letter, dated only "January," has been assigned to 1846 from internal evidence and has been assigned a tentative date of January 30 on the assumption that it may be the letter of "yesterday" referred to in Clemson's letter of 1/31/1846 below.

From W. T. SANDERS

Pottsville [Pa.,] Jan[uar]y 30, 1846

D[ea]r Sir, Permit me to congratulate you upon the success you have met with since your return to the Senate. Your course in relation to "Oregon" meets the hearty approbation of every Good Citizen in this part of Penn[sylvani]a. Your course in the Senate has ever been that of a great man, possessed of Gigantic intellect, and your fame shall be handed down to posterity, and be rever[e]d by other Generations as one of America's highest, ablest sons.

Your friends here are only wa[i]ting the opportunity of proving by their works, in elevating you to the presidential Chair, what they now profess, and God Grant we may soon have that high priviledge. I hope Sir, you will excuse the liberty I have taken in addressing you, as we are strangers personally, but believe me Sir, ["you" *canceled*] I know you well, you are, and have been my moddle in politics ever since I could read, and so long as you pursue the high course you now occupy, I shall hope to follow. I should be glad to hear from you occasionally, by letter, or Pub[lic] Doc[uments]. Very Truly Your Humble Ser[van]t, W.T. Sanders.

ALS in ScCleA.

From CLEMENT C. BIDDLE

Philadelphia, 31st January 1846
My dear sir, Understanding that the name of Mr. Peter G. Washington is now before the Senate for confirmation as Auditor of the General Post Office, I feel called upon as one of his friends and well wishers to give my testimony in his behalf.

I have known Mr. Washington for twenty years, and during that period have had much correspondence and have transacted business, with him. I do not believe, without any disparagement to other heads of bureaus, that the Government has in its service a more able and faithful accountant, or one better qualified to discharge, with satisfaction to the public, the important duties assigned to his office. Mr. Washington married one of the daughters of the late general [William] Macpherson of Philadelphia, and I am the trustee of his wife's estate here. Another sister was married to my most intimate, and most valued, friend, the late Philip H. Nicklin, and the brother in law of Vice Pres[iden]t [George M.] Dallas. Mr. Nicklin & myself were always considered as among the most active, & I may add steady, friends of South Carolina, in her struggle for the maintenance of her, and our, just rights, and were always called the "Philad[elphi]a Nullifiers." Mr. Washington always has been a democrat, and, I believe, of the best and soundest school; at all events of that school of equal rights, and State rights, which it is my happiness to belong, and to place you at the head. I feel, therefore, deeply interested for his success on every account.

I gave the Rev. Mr. Spencer of the Church of England an introduction to you. I hope he had the pleasure to see you.

The news from England is cheering. I now think the Corn Laws must go; & the Oregon question be quietly settled. Ever with the highest regard & esteem faithfully yours, Clement C. Biddle.

ALS in ScCleA.

From Tho[ma]s G. Clemson

Brussels, Jan[uar]y 31st 1846

My dear Sir, Since writing you yesterday we have received Sir Rob[er]t Peel[']s momentous speech on the reductions proposed in the tariff. I send you a copy of the [London] Times which contains that speech. I also send you a copy of the last Economist[,] the most respectable free trade journal in the World, & if you should desire I will send you all the numbers as they appear. The Oregon question has given way to the alterations in the English tariff. I hope you will have been successful in your efforts to stay action on the Oregon question. It has given you a very prominent position on that question on this side of the water. Anna [Maria Calhoun Clemson] sends her love to all & hopes you will come to England to settle the matter, & I think if you were to do so that you would be entirely successful. Your affectionate son, Thos. G. Clemson.

P.S. If you have a leisure moment to write Messrs. [J.B.] Crockett & [D.C.] Briggs[,] my attorneys at St. Louis[,] I would be much obliged to you for I should like to know what they have done with the mine La Motte case. I have written them on the subject but can get no answer.

ALS in ScCleA.

From J[ohn] D. Gardiner

Sag-Harbor [N.Y.,] Jan. 31st 1846

My Dear Sir, Be assured I am happy to find you again in the councils of the nation; and more especially at the present crisis of our public affairs. Nothing gives us more quiet and confidence in a storm at sea, than to know that the ship is under the guidance of wisdom and experience.

In the political as in the natural world, there are times when clouds rise and dangers threaten. The present seems to be one of those seasons.

The question of Oregon appears to take a deep hold of the public mind, and to produce no little excitement throughout the Country.

A sort of war-panic has been produced by the premature and injudicious agitation of this question in the present Congress. The speeches and resolutions introduced into the Senate, by [Lewis] Cass, [William] Allen, [Edward A.] Hannegan and others of a like belligerent spirit, have served to create considerable alarm, in many minds, in this part of the Land. War with England, our ancient and inveterate foe, is the chief topic of conversation at all times and in all places. The course pursued, in the Senate, by these gentlemen, is very unpopular in this quarter, with all parties. And whatever may have been their motives, their course is almost universally condemned. The direct tendency, if not the design of their movements, is to bring on a war between this Country and great Britain—A war deprecated so much by all, and considered entirely unne[ce]ssary, either to the preservation of national rights, interests or honor.

The subject of the controversy is too remote, and, at the present time, of to[o] little importance, to rouse the spirit, and call into action, the energies & and [sic] resources of the nation, in a war for its defence. A war under such circumstances could hardly fail to be unpopular. To carry on a war, successfully with such a power as England requires popular una[ni]mity. There must be union in councils and concert in action. In order to produce this, in such a government as ours, there must ["be" *interlined*] known and acknowledge[d] generally, something at stake of great national importance; in which all feel a deep interest; something, in the public estimation, paramount to all the evils unavoidably connected with national warfare.

But no such interest, is felt by the people as a body, I believe, in the Oregon controversy, as would lead them to take up arms, with a view to effect its settlement. They prefer ["a more" *canceled*] a more cheap, expeditious, honorable, and just mode of action for the accomplishment of this object, viz, further negotiation on the subject. There is nothing, it appears to me, to forbid this course on the part of either government. It is certainly, the most pacific and reasonable course, and one which seems to be desired by both Nations, so far as I am able to learn. Why then should not this course be at once taken, and negotiation resumed? Should this be done, in a friendly and conciliatory spirit, there can be little or no doubt, in my mind, that it would be connected with the happiest results to both Nations; and the existing dispute terminated in an amicable and satisfactory adjustment.

In the present stage of the controversy, and until further means are used, and have utterly failed; war should not be so much as named or thought of by either government. There is nothing in nature of the dispute that requires hasty or precipitate action. Due time should be taken for mature councils. Nothing will be lost by moderation on the part of the government. There are in Congress, I perceive with regret, some firey spirits, who seem very desirous of urging the Country to extremities, and of plunging the two Nations into a war. These must, by all means, be checked in their inconsiderate folly or madness. In the view of the Country there is no necessity for the manifestation of such a spirit. It works evil and evil only. It is uncalled for under present circumstances, and deserves to be rebuked by all sober, thinking men. At present the people have no sympathy for those who cherish or indulge it.

They are for moderation, for the use of conciliatory measures, until it shall be clearly seen by the whole civilized world, that they are of no effect. When this is done, and all are convinced of their entire inefficacy, then it will do much better to talk about the Ultima Ratio Regium.

Then every true American will cheerfully put his shoulders to the wheel, in the support of the government, when thus driven to extremities by the wrongs and encroachments of a wicked and arbitrary power. This appears to me to be the true policy of our government, and the one which promises the best results. I may be mistaken.

On this ground, I perceive, with great pleasure, you have taken your stand, with your accustomed boldness and independence. It is the right ground. It is popular ground, and you will be sustained by the voice of the nation, without distinction of party. In this crisis of public affiars, you have, I must say, nobly planted your foot upon the rock; and breasted the torrent. The position, which you have so fearlessly taken, meets with an almost universal approval. And to cheer you on, permit me to observe, that in the whole course of your public life, your long political career, never have you taken a stand, on any national question, to which all eyes are turned with deeper interest, or ["more" *interlined*] anxious solicitude, than the one which you at present occupy. I trust in God, you will be enabled to hold it, with firmness, against the waves of turbulence & faction that may break around it. Peace is our policy; and every thing should be sacrificed in its support except our rights and ["indepence" *altered to* "independence"]. The cup of conciliation and forbearance should be drained to the dregs, before the sword is drawn and the match is lighted. You and I, my Dear Friend, have passed through one war, and witnessed its fruits; and for slight causes, we cannot wish to see our country involved in another. If it be possible let there be peace in our day. All that can be gained by the strife of arms, can be more honorably attained by pacific measures. It is far more honorable to settle disputes by the voice of reason, than by the thunder of Cannon; and if justice cannot be obtained by the one, it is very uncertain whether it can be secured by the other.

By this I do [not] mean that our Country is, at all times, to yield a tame submission to the haughty dictates, and all grasping power of Old England, or any other nation on earth. I am the last man who would consent to do this. I would not have the government terrified by threats, or intimidated by power. No Sir, I would have the Country, conscious of her independence & strength, stand up boldly and fearlessly in the defence of every "clear & unquestionable right["] at all and every hazard. Any appeals to our fears, come from what quarter they ["may" *interlined*; "is" *canceled and* "are" *interlined*] to be indignantly spurned. At the same time I would urge her to listen to every appeal to her reason, magnanimity and sense of justice; and to resort to every honorable means to prevent open hostilities with any nation on the globe. I love peace but I love right better. And when all pacific means have failed to secure our rights, and we are left to the dire alternative of either of abandoning them to the enemy, or maintain[in]g them by force, then we are justified by the first law of nature, in waging war in their defence. But it does not appear to me, that, in ["the" *interlined*] Oregon dispute, our Country is yet brought to this sad dilemma. The olive branch still waves; and it gives me ["pleasure" *interlined*] to believe that you will do every thing in your power to preserve it safe & unsoiled. The nation is now looking to you and your coadjutors with great confidence & hope, as the Ajax Talemon [*sic*] of popular peace & popular rights. But I beg pardon for thus trespassing upon your time & patience.

I am in good health, and in the enjoyment of every other blessing the world can give. My family is well, and my children are all about me, comfortable & happy. Please to let me hear from you, when you can find leisure, with your views of peace or war. Any communication which you may make will be thankfully received by your old friend & Class mate, who never thinks of you, but with the pleasing associations of youthful days & of College life. With my fervent prayers for your happiness & prosperity, I remain your steadfast & unalterable friend, J.D. Gardiner.

P.S. D[ea]r Sir, Your Resolutions on the Oregon question introduced into the Senate were of the right stamp, and were read with pleasure. The doctrine which they contain is constitutional and unanswerable, in my view. They ought to be adopted and carried out.

ALS in ScCleA.

From [ALEXANDER] MACKAY

Fuller's Hotel, Washington
Jan. 31st 1846

Mr. Mackay will wait upon Mr. Calhoun, either immediately, or at any time & place, which Mr. Calhoun may please to appoint.

ALU in ScCleA. NOTE: In his book, *The Western World; Or, Travels in the United States in 1846–47*, 2 vols. (London: Richard Bentley, 1849), 1:191, Mackay described Calhoun as follows: "Foremost of those who do honour to their country by the pre-eminence of their talents, the purity of their intentions, and the lustre of their social qualities is John C. Calhoun, one of the senators for South Carolina. It was my privilege frequently to enjoy the society of this gifted and distinguished personage, who, by the charms of his conversation, as well as by his affable demeanour, excites the admiration of all who approach him, whether old or young, friend or adversary." On 2:190, describing the Senate, Mackay wrote: "Mr. Calhoun, . . . although far advanced in life, still possessing all the perseverance and much of the vigour which characterised his early career."

FEBRUARY 1-28
1846

▣

The 1st session of the 29th Congress continued. On February 3 Calhoun presented to the Senate a memorial to Congress prepared by James Gadsden, head of a committee appointed by the Memphis Convention the previous fall. Calhoun was appointed chairman of a select committee on the matter (which would report in June).

Calhoun rose to speak very little until near the end of the month, when he re-entered the fray on Oregon. This was in part, as he wrote his son-in-law, because "I was suffering under a bad cold, accompanied by a severe cough. It continued so long that I began to get uneasy." But also because, as Calhoun said in the same letter: "I have not, as yet, taken part on the question of notice now before the Senate; but shall before it terminates. I have waited developements. The Whigs are uncertain allies, & I have to act with caution."

On the very same day, long before he could have received Calhoun's letter, the prospective recipient, Thomas Clemson, wrote Calhoun from Europe: "The position which you have taken on ... Oregon has given you a most prominent position on this side of the Atlantic. The papers in England as well as on the Continent have been filled with your name, and if you were in England there is no doubt but that you could arrange the matter with the greatest ease."

A few days before, Duff Green wrote Calhoun from the North, where he was now engaged in multifarious business ventures, some well-considered advice. Green found Calhoun's position to be, in many respects, very strong, and he advised how it could be made stronger. He reminded Calhoun of what practical men knew to be the failing in his conduct: "Not having mingled with the masses as I have done you cannot understand or appreciate the effect which studied misrepresentation of your views and position ... has on the public opinion of the North."

▣

From [Maj. Gen.] EDMUND P. GAINES

[New Orleans, La., February 1, 1846]
My dear Sir, My *Plan* here refer[r]ed to has been submitted to the secretary of war [William L. Marcy], who I trust will lay it before Congress, and solicit an appropriation for the purpose of enabling me to construct the work. Give me authority to employ *four* thousand labourers with two hundred mechanics—(and I would as soon have able bodied *black men,* to the number of two thousand, with an *overseer* to every fifty blacks, as any other description of labourers). I will have the *chevaux defrize* ready for service in a few weeks. This would give to the people of this city and this State a very high degree of confidence in our ability in the event of war to render this city secure—*perfectly secure.* And the principle here relied on is strictly applicable to almost every sea Port of any considerable value in the United States. New York [City] and more especially Philadelphia, Baltimore, Savannah and Mobile and Pensacola may all be to a great extent secured by my new fashioned *chevaux defrize,* aided by Floating Batteries—with our present Forts. Of this last mentioned means of defence we have none that can possibly arrest the movement of a Fleet of war Steamers, without the help of either fixed or Floating obstructions. Of these it is evident that such Floating obstructions as I here recommend are the most simple, economical, and by far the most formidable. Boston, Mass., and Charleston, S.C. will probably derive less benefit from these Floating obstructions than any other of our sea Port towns. I am convinced however that these vital points of approach may be greatly strengthened by this new fashioned *chevaux defrize.*

In war, as in most other branches of science, it is of great importance at once to discover the *vital principle of action.* I think I have made this discovery in showing what no military man of experience will doubt—that *if we can by any means force the approaching foe to seperate his army from his war steamers—and leave the latter seventy, or even ten or fifteen miles from our great sea Port Towns, we shall assuredly take or destroy his Army*—who at all former periods suffered much by the moral effect of such seperation; but now that the mind of every soldier is filled with the impression that of all the means of assault ever invented or devised war steamers are *the most invincible*—seperate the soldier thus impressed from the Fleet with which he has been rapidly wafted across the Atlantic in the hope of being sustained in Battle by this supposed *invincible arm of Royal service,* and he is thus taken by surprize, and stript of more

549

than half the spirit of enterprize with which he had long *revelled in visions of triumph*. Under these circumstances—thus torn from his most reliable means of triumph and of safety, he is prepared upon the first moment of firm resistance to yield to inevitable panic, and throw down his arms before he is half beaten. In this view of the subject I know well that I here do justice to a very large portion of the men usually found in the ranks of every army hitherto known to me. And although many true hearted officers and private soldiers would soar above the weakness of such a Panic, yet I doubt whether one officer in ten, or one private soldier in a hundred in any British army would be found free of this weakness.

Who then can doubt the immense importance of our being everywhere prepared to force the invader to seperate his army from his war steamers? I am with great respect your friend, Edmund P. Gaines.

[Printed Enclosure]

Circular (Confidential.)

Head Quarters, Western Division
[New Orleans] January 14th, 1846

Sir—The various, strange and contradictory views which prevail regarding *war*, in the new aspect which steam power, applied to *Rail Roads and vessels of every description*, has given to the subject, as well as the requisite means of preparing for the protection of this city and other important sections of the sea-board and national frontier, suggest the propriety of the remarks which follow:

1. No European power will ever dare to attack this city without *War steamers to co-operate with their Land forces*. If I am correct in this opinion—and I will gladly pledge my life and all I am worth upon its correctness—our first duty doubtless is to *Lock up* the Navigation of the River at Forts Jackson and St. Philip. This I am sure can be done by preparing the Forts for action, and adding thereto the works which I have proposed at that all important Point. We shall thus compel the invading foe to separate his Army from his Naval forces, leaving the latter below Forts Jackson and St. Philip—seventy miles distant from New Orleans—and we can then meet and beat his army at any place in his march between the above named Forts and the English Turn or this city.

2. In order to make assurance doubly sure I propose to Lock up the navigation of the river at or near the English Turn, so that if by any accident our first mentioned barrier at and near Fort Jackson should fail, we will present another, and in some respects a more powerful barrier at or near the English Turn. A barrier in approach-

ing which the resistance and losses sustained by the Enemy in passing the works below will contribute to lessen his means of assault and thus increase our chances of success in repelling him. And even should we succeed in forcing his war steamers to remain below the English Turn, I shall consider New Orleans safe, as we can by prompt movements take or destroy his Land forces between the city and the English Turn.

3. Until we can be sure of forcing the proposed separation of the Enemy's Land forces from his war steamers, we should not permit ourselves to waste a dollar, nor a day's labor upon any such scheme as a fort upon Ship Island, the Dry Tortugas, or at any other place *but upon the deep passes* immediately in the vicinity of our great Sea-Port Towns—our vital Points of approach. These *must be* secured. Then and not until then can we prudently think about other projects disconnected with the immediate security of the vital Points of defence. We should construct no Forts but upon sites which the enemy will be *compelled* to come in contact with, in his immediate operations against our principal Sea-Port Towns. When these are rendered impregnable, we may then go to work at the *Dry Tortugas*—at *Ship Island*, and at *fifty other places upon the Sea-board and Northern frontier*—even upon Lake Superior to build Forts and a Ship Canal to protect the *trade* of that Lake carried on "*in a Brig and Schooner*"—a trade which Major General [Winfield] Scott in his annual report of December 1844, represents as being an important trade!

4. With the most perfect confidence in the patriotism and civil capacity of many of the advocates of a Fort on Ship Island, and a Ship Canal from the Mississippi River near this city into Lake Pontchartrain, I should entreat them not to touch the awfully delicate and doubtful subject of such a canal. Such a work might jeopard the safety of this great city itself by turning the whole of the water of the Mississippi River into this Lake and Lake Borgne—convert these Lakes into one great "trembling Prairie;" and ultimately prepare them for an extensive succession of beautiful Sugar Plantations. We cannot safely take any liberty with this mighty Inland Sea, other than quietly to clear out of its present channel all snags and other obstructions—improve in this way its great navigable facilities, and enjoy the increased and rapidly increasing blessings of its navigation thus improved. If we do this carefully and constantly we shall, I am sure, be able thus to confine the water of this River to its present bed—forever. I recommend no *obstructions* whatever *to be placed in the bed of the River.* I would not even risk an Anchor upon the

bottom of the bed of this river if it could be avoided, nor otherwise than, for mere temporary purposes. Floating obstructions aided by long chain cables secured upon the mainland under *the Guns of our Forts* or *Floating Batteries*, are the only kind of obstructions I have ever recommended upon this River.

5. All obstructions are useless or worse than useless excepting those placed *under the Guns* of such of our Forts, Mortello Towers or Floating Batteries as we can certainly defend. If a thousand large merchant ships laden with Granite were sunk in the shoal waters upon what is called the *Bar* of each of the Passes embracing the *mouths* or *outlets* of the Mississippi river, and left unprotected by the Guns of our Forts or Floating Batteries, they would not obstruct for many hours the navigation of the river. They would doubtless have the effect of producing one of the two results which follow: First—they would force the mighty current of this great river to break out of its present bed and force open one or more *new outlets* into the sea, probably much deeper passes than any we have had for a century—or, secondly—the enemy could very soon contrive means to *grapple* (*with their iron hooks or anchors and chain cables,*) and remove as many of these sunken ships as would effectually open to them a ship channel deep enough for their largest war steamers. This can easily be accomplished by the aid of steam power. For example: Fasten to each of the sunken ships two or four strong iron cables, and apply to each cable one or more *towboats* with engines of the greatest power, and thus drag the sunken ships down the stream into deep water, which is within a few chains of the bar. Fifty of these sunken ships thus dragged through the soft mud and sand composing the bar, would speedily deepen the channel to any desirable extent. We have no means of baffling the enemy in such an enterprize, but to go to work without delay and build the *floating obstructions* which I have recommended immediately above Forts Jackson and St. Philip; with similar works at or near the English Turn. By which works, we can, in a few days, lock up the navigation of the river at both places—as we should in the first instance be compelled to rely upon temporary works, until permanent ones can be constructed, they would be very soon completed by having as many mechanics and laborers as could be employed in their construction. But in answer to all the sophistry hitherto expressed and published as to the opinion that the enemy will not be able to bring into the river any of their *large war steamers*—I reply that, we ought to know European commanders well enough to be convinced that they will bring no ship of war to the mouth of the Mississippi river,

but such as *they know, as well as we know, how to get into the river.*
6. In respect to the published memoir of our talented engineer
Major [William H.] Chase, I take much pleasure in saying that most
of his views are such as I have for nearly a quarter of a century past
considered sound and praiseworthy; and which I should urge as
essential to the national defence provided we had secured our most
vital and most vulnerable *Sea-Port Towns.* I would then gladly
go with this gallant Engineer to the Dry Tortugas, and after rendering them as impregnable as Gibraltar—if possible—I would, in the
event of a war with England, most willingly accompany him to any
and every vulnerable British province in the West Indies, and in
lower and upper Canada; and having disposed of them, I would even
go with him in "carrying the war into Africa"—and into Asia, and
finally into Old England, and there retaliate upon the *Capitol of
Great Britain,* and pay the degenerate sons of our old English friends
and relations whatever balance may be due for every outrage we
shall have suffered at their hands. All the Rail Roads and every
Floating Battery I have ever recommended, were designed by me to
lay the foundation of the only possible system of defence that can
ever enable us to take and maintain the attitude of *proud defiance*—
which Major Chase has assumed, but in which we must fail—signally
fail—without first rendering our own *Havens* and *Homesteads invulnerable in war.* Since steam power enables us to do so, in ap-
plying it as we should to Rail Roads leading from the central and
Western States to our principal Sea-Port Towns—whereby the dis-
posable volunteer forces of the centre and West will fly in two days
to the succour of their exposed city friends and thus speedily punish
the invader, terminate the war of invasion, and protect the interior
commerce of the nation upon the proposed Rail Roads; while our
extra Floating Batteries—all readily convertible into *war steamers
for sea service*—by the simple process of taking leave of the Land
Service in our harbor defences, and entering upon the equally appropriate, and to their accomplished naval commanders more desirable theatre of action upon the broad ocean; upon which they may
doubtless accomplish much of the essential and glorious service suggested by Major Chase—by convincing our enemies and our neighbors everywhere that we are not only determined to protect—but
able to protect our own Sea-Port Towns, and extend protection to
our commerce in every sea, and in every quarter of the Globe; to
do right ourselves and to admonish our *neighbors to do right;* and
moreover to convince them that *we will submit to nothing that is
wrong.* But to hold forth the language of *proud defiance* while we

have no adequate means of repelling any such sudden invasion as we have good reason to anticipate, is, to say the least, unavailing—and something worse than useless; because it tends to deceive the good people of the sea-board, most exposed to the first shock of war, by amusing them with theories and hopes of protection which we have no certain means soon to realize.

7. In the event of my being assured that war shall have been commenced, or that it will be very soon commenced by England, I propose instantly to concentrate at Forts Jackson and St. Philip such force, with mechanics and laborers, and such steamers and other vessels, together with as much timber and other materials as will enable me speedily to render that section of our river defence as strong as our limited time and means will permit.

The *chevaux de frize* which I propose will consist of two wings—one to be constructed on each bank of the river above Forts Jackson and St. Philip—each to consist of a large cylinder from 9 to 11 feet in diameter and near 1700 feet in length—to be constructed of hewn white oak, cedar and cypress timber nearly two feet square, and from 24 to 48 feet long; these timbers to be dressed, and fastened together by strong iron bolts. The interior of the cylinder to receive, as the work progresses, cylindrical *iron tanks* made of boiler iron, 20 feet long and 5 feet diameter, and hermetically sealed against the possibility of receiving water to give buoyancy to each wing of the *chevaux de frize*. When the two wings are thus completed on shore, they will be launched and each wing secured with three large chain cables—each cable to pass from a *capstan* placed in a *mortello tower* or *redoubt*, some 60 or 80 yards from the bank of the river. The lower part of each wing to be permanently secured at or near the edge of the water. The upper part of each wing of the chevaux de frize to be occasionally fastened by chain cables to a *Floating Battery* propelled by steam engines of great power, but so fastened as to be disengaged and reattached at pleasure and within a few minutes. Each wing to be so secured with chain cables as to ennable us in ten minutes time to bring the upper ends of each wing of the chevaux de frize together, in the middle of the river, where they will rest against each other, be firmly clamped together and sustained not only by the six chain cables here referred to, but by the two Floating Batteries which will be held ready for action, and on the approach of the enemy will co-operate with the forts and mortello towers in a *quadruple* cross-fire upon the enemy's war steamers as they approach the *chevaux de frize*. In the absence of the enemy however, each wing of the chevaux de frize will be kept afloat in the edge of the water near the river bank of each shore, so that the navigation of the river may remain open always in the absence of the enemy. It is intended that a few inches more than half the cylinder of each wing of the *chevaux de frize will be habitually under water.* This will secure the work, shielded with bar iron, as it must be, from suffering any material injury from the enemy's cannon shot and shells, as they can strike the cylinder only at an angle of less than 20°, they will *ricochet* or glance off without ever penetrating the vital part of the cylinder.

The plan will show the manner in which the lower side of each wing of the chevaux de frize is to be armed with massy spears or spikes of iron sufficient to cripple any vessel that may have the temerity to run against them. (See my plan hereunto annexed marked A.C.) Six Floating Batteries of a large class propelled by steam engines of great power and armed with the best of cannon will be held ready for action, as a reserve—three near each bank of the river—to participate in the immediate defence of the place—or, in the event of the enemy being able to pass our works at this place, to ascend the river, taking care to keep up an efficient retreating fire thus vigorously disputing every inch of the way—and then to aid in his final destruction at the English Turn. [Signed,] Edmund P. Gaines.

Postscript. Examine these papers attentively, I pray you, dear Sir, and if you approve their contents, signify your approbation by such *action* upon the subject as may, in your judgment, be necessary and proper to enable us *in peace to prepare for war.* But should you disapprove the whole or any part of my views, do me the favor to apprise me of your objections. In this way you will not fail to contribute, perhaps very materially, to the interests of the service. It may be matter of very little consequence to you to learn that I have often publicly and officially declared that I have long been willing and anxious to embrace as a brother any officer[,] soldier or citizen of the United States who would sustain my system of national defence, *or who would himself present to the War Department another and a better system.*

We have much to learn in everything connected with the subject of *war* in its present and approaching aspect, changed as the *art* has been by the application of steam-power to *ships of war* and to *Railroads.*

In war, as in surgery and some other sciences, it is of the utmost importance in preparing for active operations, to save life by cutting off a diseased limb, or to protect the country by destroying the invading foe, that we should at once discover *the vital point of action*, as well as *the vital principle of action*. I am sure I have long since made this discovery *in the science of war as it is*, (*not as it was fifty years ago*,) in showing that *if we can by any possible means compel the approaching foe to separate his army from his war steamers, and leave the latter seventy or twenth-five* [*sic*], *or even ten miles distant from our seaport towns, we shall assuredly take or destroy his land forces.*

The armies of England have often suffered much by the moral effect of being unexpectedly separated from their ships of war. If this was the case near this city in the winter 1814 and '15, and at many other times and places, when ships of war were propelled only by wind and sails, how must it be now, that the mind of every soldier is filled with the impression that of all the means of assault ever invented or devised *war steamers are the most potent and invincible*? With this impression, should the aspiring or vainglorious soldier be unexpectedly separated from the fleet with which he has been rapidly wafted across the Atlantic, and long buoyed up with the confident hope of being sustained in battle by this supposed *all-invincible arm of Royal Service, he is taken by surprise, he is at once stript of more than half the prowess with which he had long revelled in delightful visions of triumph over the despised people of his vengeance.* Under these circumstances, thus torn from his most reliable means of *victory*, of *safety* and of *comfort*—(all his hopes of good eating, good drinking, quiet smoking and good rest being left on board the transports with the fleet)—he is in this way fully prepared upon the first moment of a sharp conflict to yield to that inevitable panic which falls to the lot of the *unready*, and to all men when *taken by surprise*. They will often, in this way, be willing to throw down their arms before they are half beaten. Who then can doubt the immense importance of our being every where prepared to force the invader to separate, at a good distance, from us, his army from his war steamers. [Initialed,] E.P.G.

ALS with Ens in ScCleA. NOTE: Gaines wrote his letter upon the back of one copy of the printed circular and enclosed another copy with an added, printed postscript. The circular was "Addressed to the Commanders of Departments[,] Regiments and Military Posts in the Western Division." The text herein transcribed is that containing the postscript. An AEU by Calhoun reads "Gen[era]l Gain[e]s." Gaines' undated letter bears a postmark February 1 and from context is from the year 1846.

From SAM[UE]L M. WILLIAMS

Galveston [Tex.,] February 1st 1846

Sir, I am fully sensible of the annoyance you must experience from applicants for office in the gift of the Gen[era]l Govt. (and their friends) where the approval of a nomination is a province of the Senate. Nevertheless, I feel myself impelled to intrude upon you, and even at this distant period to avail myself of a fact, to you certainly forgotten, that in Decem[be]r 1818 when you was Secretary of the War Department, Mr. [David] Henshaw of Boston did me the honor of introducing me to you—a fact I would not now mention but for the great interest I feel in the appointment of Judge for the District of Texas.

I have been in this Country 24 years, was the Companion and partner of the late Stephen F. Austin and know well and fully the history of Texas, and of course can duly appreciate the importance to the inhabitants of the Country that the office of District Judge should be filled by a person who unites with moral worth, extensive legal knowledge.

It is generally believed here that from among the numerous applicants to the President, three gentlemen are the most prominent, Judge [James] Webb, Judge Burnett [*sic*; David G. Burnet] & Mr. [John C.] Watrous. Judge Webb is esteemed here a good lawyer, Judge Burnett is not so esteemed, and Mr. Watrous has always been esteemed here as the most able Lawyer of Texas.

You are no doubt fully aware of the local party spirit which has prevailed in Texas, and it has been the misfortune of both Judge Webb & Judge Burnett to have figured largely on the weakest side— whereas Mr. Watrous has had no connection with either party and cannot be objected to by either. It is a fact Sir that every day devellops that Gen[era]l [Samuel] Houston is the most important figure in Texas in spite of every thing that his op[p]onents may urge against him, and although I have not had any communication with him on this subject, and do not know his opinions, I do not hesitate to say that he would never aid either of the two first gentlemen named, for they have been bitter oponents of his. Besides which I am fully satisfied that the appointment of Mr. Watrous as District Judge would prove universally satisfactory in Texas.

I have taken upon myself to place this subject before you without being apprised of your feelings and opinions, except that you are anxious to promote the best interests of Texas, beyond which you could not have any interest, and that your position is not to be influenced by any political considerations of this community.

Should the subject matter of this letter rest any time on your memory, and you should see Col. John Darrington he will assure you that I have no personal views to subserve the opinions I have given. I am Sir with much respect y[ou]r Ob[edien]t S[ervan]t, Saml. M. Williams.

ALS in TxU, Thomas Jefferson Rusk Papers.

From W[ILLIA]M GRASON, [former Governor of Maryland]

[Queens Town, Md.] February 2, 1846

Dear Sir, Though your course would not be influenced by public excitement, yet I suppose you are not indifferent to public opinion, and that it may not be uninteresting to you ["to" *interlined*] know your efforts for the preservation of peace are properly appreciated by the great body of the people. It is to inform you of their sentiments, so far as I have been able to ascertain them, that I take the liberty of troubling you with this letter.

Previously to the session of congress, I was twice in Baltimore; and once after the appearance of [James K. Polk] the president[']s message and the correspondence with the British government. I had opportunities of conversing with the citizens of Baltimore, and with persons from every part of the State, and had already ascertained the views of the people of my own neighbourhood. Before the meeting of congress, I heard not a single individual express the opinion that we ought to go to war for the *whole* of Oregon. On the contrary, it seemed to be the wish of every one that the dispute should be settled in a spirit of mutual compromise and concession; and this disposition was strenghthened [*sic*] by the impression, that the territory in *dispute* was of little value to the United States. I was surprised at this uniformity of opinion, because the articles in the [Washington] Union were evidently intended to prepare the public for the assertion of our claim to its utmost limits. The message and correspondence produced a slight change; but, *after* their publication, I conversed with only two men in Baltimore who were advocates of war in preference to a compromise; and one of them took the philosophical ground that nations became enervated by a long continuance of peace. While the desire for an amicable settlement remained, I regretted to find, that many persons expected greater concessions from Great Britain on account of the failure of her crops, and the agitations existing in her own dominions. They contended that no ministry would wage war with this country for any part of Oregon, while the British people were in absolute want of our breadstuffs and cotton. The Union had frequently thrown out intimations of this kind, as if we could extort concessions from the embarrassments of the British government. It was forgotten that the consumers of any product suffer less from a stinted supply, than the producers do from the want of a market; and that in the event of a war, the places, whence these articles were exported, could be blockaded, or not, at the discretion of our enemy. A war would diminish the supply, and enhance the price, of cotton in England, but it would produce the same effect in the rest of Europe, and the British manufacturers would have every market except the United States. Our Eastern manufacturers would derive but little benefit from the reduced price of raw cotton at home, because the coarse cottons, which are now sent to other countries, would be captured at sea, or forced back upon an oversupplied home market.

With respect to the title to Oregon, there appears to be a great impression that Mr. [James] Buchanan[']s reply to Mr. Packenham [sic; Richard Pakenham, British Minister to the U.S.] has settled it in our favour, because his arguments were not answered by the latter. But this impression was as strong before the correspondence was published. Our countrymen think it a proof of patriotism to claim every thing than [sic] can be disputed. The president considered our title clear and unquestionable before the correspondence had thrown a ["new" interlined] light upon the subject; and with regard to the N.E. boundary, all of our people, whether they had examined the subject, or not, pronounced the English claims to be totally unfounded. There was an attempt to raise an excitement upon that question, but the Ashburton treaty gave satisfaction every where, because it settled a controversy which was continually threatening us with war. There is no war excitement now, though the English and French papers, and Mr. [Albert] Gallatin, suppose that the president and a portion of congress are influenced by popular feeling to take higher grounds than are consistent with an amicable settlement of the dispute. Instead of this being the case, the excitement began in Washington and became weaker as it spread to a distance. Of course the sentiments of the administration are repeated by orators, town meetings, and the press, whose object is to recommend themselves to the favour of the administration. They have some influence in forming public opinion by professing to respond to it; and, in this instance, they are assisted in propagating furious doctrines by the president and those who are supposed to be acquainted with his views. The president could have had no such intention, but his inaugural speech, his message, and the articles in the official paper, have furnished the grounds of agitation. The Union, at the very time when the proposition was made to take the 49th degree for the dividing line, was preparing the party to assert our claims to the whole territory. Party leaders were consequently led to contend for the whole of Oregon or none; and having committed themselves, they do not like to recede from their position; especially as the president has withdrawn the proposition, and declared that he only made it in deference to the course of his predecessors. In this respect, they are perhaps as much misled by the message, as they were by the articles in the Union. If the president considered it his duty to follow the course of previous administrations, he is as much bound by that authority now, as when he made the offer, because its recent rejection could have no more effect in releasing ["him" *interlined*] from the obligation, than its previous rejection when made by his predecessors. In deference to the same authority, he ought to have offered the priviledge [*sic*] of navigating the Columbia river, which will be conceded in practice, whatever may be the conditions of an adjustment. Without being able to form a more correct opinion, I have regretted that the proposition was withdrawn. I think it ought to have been suffered to stand as a record and proof of our consistency and moderation. Mr. [Thomas] Ritchie [editor of the Washington *Union*] would have then found it an easier task to rally the people in support of the government. He calls upon the democratic party to unite now, but leaves them in the dark, whether they are required to sustain Mr. Polk[']s rejected proposition, or to contend for more than we have declared, before the whole world, we ["we" *canceled*] were willing to take. It is said that the president is for peace, but that it must be on honourable terms. Can it be considered honourable to claim ["now" *canceled*] more now than we claimed last summer, or to refuse terms which we were then willing to take? If we cannot agree, would it be dishonourable to submit the question to the Emperor of Russia, or some other impartial arbitrator? Some would object to such a reference, on the ground that we could not expect justice from a monarch; but there does not appear to be much wisdom or liberality, in assuming a position of hostility to other governments because they are different from our own.

I have said a great deal more than I had a right to say, to one who understands all these subjects so much better than myself. My only excuse is, that I wished you to know that the people feel no hostile excitement, but a deep and serious ["anxiety" *canceled*] apprehension, that the half way measures of congress may lead to an unnecessary war; and that they are not indifferent spectators of your exertions for the preservation of peace. With Sincere Respect Your Obedient Servant, Wm. Grason.

ALS in ScCleA. Note: An AEU by Calhoun reads "Mr. Grayson [*sic*]."

Memorial of the executor of Thomas Cooper, presented by Calhoun to the Senate on 2/2. In this document, dated at Charleston, S.C., December 1845, Dr. M[ardici] H. DeLeon, sole executor of Thomas Cooper, requests Congress to repay the fine, with interest, levied against Cooper in 1800 for violation of the Sedition Act. This is claimed on the grounds of justice and "to vindicate the rights of the American people." The claim has been submitted several times previously, referred to committees, and favorably reported on, but no action taken. (The petition was referred to the Committee on the Judiciary, which on 3/18 reported a bill which was never acted on.) DS in DNA, RG 46 (U.S. Senate), 29A-G8.

Petition of Peter Von Schmidt, presented by Calhoun to the Senate on 2/2. The petitioner asks for compensation for a model of a "pneumatic dry-dock, constructed under the direction of the Secretary of State, for the use of the China mission." The matter was referred to the Committee on Claims. (The committee subsequently reported a bill for Von Schmidt's relief, which passed the Senate but was not acted on by the House of Representatives.) Abs in *Senate Journal*, 29th Cong., 1st Sess., p. 125; Abs in *Congressional Globe*, 29th Cong., 1st Sess., p. 290.

REMARKS ON THE DEBT DUE TO TEXAS

[In the Senate, February 2, 1846]

[Under consideration was a bill to compensate Texas for claims against the U.S. dating from before annexation, arising out of border incidents: the seizure by Capt. Philip St. George Cooke of the U.S. Army of the arms of a Texan force he believed to be in U.S. territory,

and a raid by certain citizens of Ark. on a Texas customs collector on
the Red River.]

Mr. Calhoun rose to say a very few words on the question. As
to the claim for the arms, there could hardly be any difference of
opinion. No further evidence was wanted on that point. The
United States had got possession of the arms and ought to pay for
them. With respect to the seizure of goods no one could doubt that
a great outrage had been suffered by Texas. It was not the inconsiderable case of an individual passing over the line, but it was that
of a considerable force of armed men—amounting, he believed, to
forty or fifty men, passing over in a violent and a lawless manner,
seizing the custom-house officer, tying him, and taking the goods out
of the stores. He had looked into the case with some attention when
it had come before him in an official capacity [while Secretary of
State]. There were authorities on both sides, but he had given the
most weight to those which favored the weaker party. But to put
that out of the question a great wrong had been done to Texas, and
how was it to be redressed but in the mode proposed? It was to be
borne in mind that the line between Texas and the United States
when the former was an independent republic, was very long, passing through woods and prairies, and frequently forming ground of
controversy likely to lead to collision. The present was only one of
several cases of a like character; and had it not been for the equivocal position of Texas, there would have been a treaty embracing a
settlement of this boundary line. As it was, why refuse to settle the
matter now in the manner proposed by the bill?

From the Washington, D.C., *Daily Union*, vol. I, no. 235 (February 2, 1846), p.
930. Variant in the Washington, D.C., *Daily National Intelligencer*, February
3, 1846, p. 3; *Congressional Globe*, 29th Cong., 1st Sess., p. 291.

To [NATHANIEL] B[EVERLEY] TUCKER,
Prof[esso]r, [College of William and Mary,
Williamsburg, Va.]

Washington, 2d Feb: 1846
My dear Sir, I regret, that yours & Pres[iden]t [Thomas R.] Dew's
letter[s] in favour of Mr. [Archibald C.] Peachy came too late. The
place was filled before I received them. Had they been received in
time, I would, with pleasure, ["have" *interlined*] brought [h]is name

to the notice of the President [James K. Polk]. I have a very favourable opinion of the principles & intellect of Mr. Peachy.

I am much gratified, with your approbation of my course in reference to the Oregon question; and am happy to inform you, that the war fever is abating & the prospect of peace bright[en]ing. The worst indication at present is, the state of things in Mexico. There is a very intimate connection between the Oregon & Mexican questions; so much so, that a war in reference to one would almost certainly involve a war about the other. Yours Truly, J.C. Calhoun.

[P.S.] I will thank you to present my respects to Pres[iden]t Dew. J.C.C.

ALS in ViW, Tucker-Coleman Papers.

From W[ILLIAM] H. BARNWELL

Charleston, Feb. 3d 1846

My dear Sir, The Sermon, which I herewith send, and which you will see, I have taken the liberty of dedicating to yourself, was preached at a time, when war with England seemed to be not only expected, but by too many, desired. The instrumentality which you had in averting it led me, ["to" *canceled*] when the discourse was published at the request of some that heard it, to dedicate it to you. Let me express the hope that by the Gracious Providence of God, you may be led not only to do much good, and prevent much evil in your political course but to enjoy that Peace of God, which passeth all understanding, and which the World can neither give, nor take away. Sincerely Your friend & servant, W.H. Barnwell.

ALS in ScCleA. NOTE: Barnwell's sermon was entitled *"Prayer for National Peace." A Sermon delivered in St. Peter's Church, Charleston, on the 4th day of January, 1846* (Charleston: 1846).

From JOHN S. COGDELL

Charleston So. Ca., 3d Feb[ruar]y 1846

My dear Sir, I write from my Chamber, where I have been confined near thirteen weeks. I feel assured as a member of the same State, this my communication, will be re[ceive]d and respected by you,

3 February 1846

even tho' we may not agree in the matter to be submitted to you. I hold it a doctrine sound in our country, that every *Citizen*, was at liberty to contribute his views on every subject—respectfully tendered, in w[hic]h he might benefit his country. With these views—some little time ere I was taken to my bed—I wrote to the President—saying that I had a suggestion or two, which I w[oul]d respectfully lay before him in relation to the Finances of our Government if he w[oul]d permit me the liberty to do so & they were founded on experience, but I have never been honored with a line, from Mr. [James K.] Polk.

You Sir, are chairman of the Finance Committee, or was so made ere you took your place in the Senate. I will say to you therefore all I have thought and done on the subject of finance. You will remember, that for some years past, nay before the first bill respecting the Sub Treasury was passed—I had been honored by the Stockholders of the Bank of So[uth] C[arolin]a as their President. When the bill now referred to ["wh" *canceled*] was under discussion, I took the liberty of writing to Mr. [Joel R.] Poinsett then in the Cabinet—to use his efforts to prevent the *issue* of the Sub-Trea[sur]y notes, bearing In[teres]t—that they were contemplated as a circulating medium & that the grant of interest w[oul]d embarrass their passing from hand to hand—requiring a calculation by each holder & receiver— that they ought to go as Bank bills—and be so drawn, payable at given Sub-Trea[sur]y Stations—or Banks selected as the case may [be], with the understanding that at such B[an]k or Station, they c[oul]d command specie if wanted—that I foresaw, if they were issued payable with In[teres]t—we w[oul]d never hear of a single bill, in circulation—that they w[oul]d be all taken up by the B[an]ks and held till matured—and then demand their redemption—*and this proved to be the case.* There were at our Bank daily applications by Travellers and Mercantile Men desirous of making remittances—aye & many offering a premium—but they were not in circulation. At a subsequent period when I saw some move in Congress to issue new Sub-Treasury Paper I wrote again to Mr. Poinsett, to remind him of what had occurred, & beg[g]ed he would avail himself of the experience of the past—and let the Government prove their confidence in themselves. 'Tis true they essayed unsuccessfully at first with their 6 per C[en]t Stock, & some of it came to our City & c[oul]d not be sold—but ere it was returned to the North it took a start & has since shown that there is an abiding confidence in the resources of the Government & her issues.

Now Sir it does appear to me a circulating medium under Gov-

564

ernment authority without In[teres]t say like Bank paper, is a desideratum. It is wanted to subserve all the purposes of domestic Exchange. It would diminish a source of revenue to Brokers, who prey upon the vitals of necessity—and when B[an]ks can no longer draw to accom[m]odate their customers—that class step in & compel the Banks to surrender their specie. All these harrassments would be soon dissipated in the easy circulation of your Trea[sur]y Notes as Bank paper. Now there w[oul]d be nothing more easy—than to keep a supply of specie at all the Sub Treas[ur]y posts or the Banks employed to redeem such of the Treasury Notes *made payable at either of those places*, because, the dues paid in daily, in the current papers of the place is immediately convertible into specie, but I have no doubt ["but" *canceled*]—but that a full confidence in your Sub Trea[sur]y Notes w[oul]d make them pass so freely that to take specie away for them, w[oul]d seldom if ever occur.

It w[oul]d not be hazzarding much to say they w[oul]d soon be used for foreign Exchange—remember—there c[oul]d be no repudiating on the part of Congress while we were a Government & this w[oul]d surround all your issues with foreign & domestic confidence & you w[oul]d at length find you had acquired the so long looked for circulating medium.

These thoughts—as you take them up—I am sure will find more in your own Mind of improvement ["in" *altered to* "if"] there be in them propriety & if not, the sooner destroy the whole scheme. I omitted to state that to insure Mr. Polk[']s audience I stated to him, I was not seeking an appointment—& my mind has undergone no change in that determination—by a confinement to a sick room so long. Suffer me to congratulate my Country & our State individually that you are again found, in your distinguished seat in Senate & may all eventuate in an honorable Peace. Y[ou]rs with great Respect, John S. Cogdell.

ALS in ScCleA.

From J[AMES] H. HAMMOND

Silver Bluff, 3 Feb. 1846

My Dear Sir, I have lost no time in complying with your suggestion in your letter of the 23rd ult. I wrote two articles under the signature of "Phocion" & sent them up to the [Augusta, Ga.] Constitutionalist yesterday. The Editor [James Gardner] is a particular friend of mine & I entertain hopes they will be admitted tho' he has been so indiscreet lately as to express the opinion that notice should be given on the ground that the excitement in both countries required a settlement of the [Oregon] question. I carefully avoided noticing this reason for notice in hopes of securing admission to my articles. If they are not published this week I will go up & see about it. There are so many points on which this question may be considered & all in favour of peace that I scarcely knew which to touch. I thought however that the *pressing* question was as to giving notice & took that up endeavouring first to show that it would almost certainly lead to war & next that neither our honor nor our interests required it, condensing as much as I could with a view to popular effect & only touching on a few prominent points. My main view however was to produce an effect on the Georgia delegation, not by my reasoning when I know that they hear & will hear so much better at Washington, but to show them that the matter is understood in Georgia & how it is viewed. If the Editor as I have requested, keeps the secret & the articles can pass for Georgia opinion it may do some good ["at" *canceled*] in that way at Washington. If these articles are published I will see the Editor & endeavour to get out others taking a wider range. Besides urging the evils to arise to us in the South in every point of view ["from war" *interlined*], I should not hesitate, if permitted, to differ from all of you so far ["as" *interlined*] to say that our title to all of Oregon ["was" *canceled*] is very far from being "clear & unquestionable" & that the British have claims almost as good as ours, certainly demanding our respect. In fact neither party has a *"Title"* in my opinion to a foot more than they can *get & keep*. But I do not propose to ["take" *canceled*] impair the effect of a full view of known facts & clear consequences, by urging extreme speculative ["views" *canceled and* "opinion" *interlined*]. I do not however believe that Oregon is now or ever will be worth a risk & would cheerfully barter the whole of our claim for the single port of San Francisco. An important topic however, & one now up for consideration & decision, is how far we are to extend this mania for annexation. While I wish, & believe it will happen that *our institutions* will prevail over the whole continent, I am very far from concurring in the utopian idea of incorporating it all under one Government. I would as soon think of *annexing* not only Ireland, but half the old continent for instance as Oregon. Bombay itself is nearer to us in point of fact than this Territory. I think the time is at hand for discussing this topic thoroughly, but would prefer that it should be done without connecting it with any exciting question of Foreign Relations. You see the necessity for it not only from the Oregon matter but from [William] Allen[']s absurd resolutions. I am very glad [John M.] Clayton [Senator from Del.] suggested the Panama question in relation to them. If you pin that on them I think Allen will be demolished & [James K.] Polk too. The fact is that both of them & [Lewis] Cass too seem to me to be demented—doubtless made so by the goadings of reckless ambition. If I thought that any thing like a majority of the U.S. thought like these men I should be in utter despair not only of our institutions but of every thing like free Government on earth. If they are not speedily overwhelmed by the indignation of of [*sic*] a people coming up to a calm & common sense ["of" *canceled*] view of the matter after their first emotions of illusive patriotism have subsided, I give up republicanism, all faith in self government & go for as free a monarchy as can be organized. If these men succeed in their wild, reckless, & world disturbing schemes a few years will reduce us to the condition of Mexico with annual revolutions & bloody military rulers. I cannot permit myself to doubt that you will put down Allen[']s resolutions & I believe the achievement will redound to your credit equally with your great stand for peace.

You will perceive, if "Phocion" reaches you[,] that I have carefully avoided naming you. The time for that has not yet come. We must reserve all that until ["the" *canceled*] you have won the victory or suffered a defeat which will be the next most glorious thing in such a cause to victory. I must mention however that your old friends in Georgia are I think rejoicing in the opportunity of rallying to you again. I heard of [William C.] Dawson's saying the other day that the Georgia whigs would stand by you hereafter. And leaving out [John M.] Berrien, the whig Party of Georgia is far better than the democratic. It has been led off by Berrien into a disgraceful career. But they are itching to drop him & come back to old principles & friends again. A few men acting with the Democrats are noble fellows, but the great mass of that party ["(in Geo[rgia])" *interlined*] is utterly despicable in every point of view.

I wish I could entertain strong hopes of Peace. The breaking up of Lord John's [that is, Lord John Russell] administration on the ground of Palmerston's war propensity is a very favourable symptom & the compromise proposed by the "Times" looks like peace. But our Democrats I fear will give up the free navigation of Columbia & as to getting of the St. Lawrence in lieu of it, I imagine England would sooner surrender all Oregon. I am sorry it has been suggested & I fear it will complicate the question. The catastrophe of L[or]d John seems favourable to the repeal of the Corn Laws. If they fall in ten years—without a resort to civil war—they must fall under [Sir Robert] Peel's blows. If as the London Examiner says Wellington is with Peel, they must very soon go by the board.

Should—contrary to all our hopes—the notice I [*sic*] pass, I trust you will take an early occasion to propose vigorous measures of prepation for war. It will be the proper finale to your course on this question. Of course you will not bind yourself to support every wiled [*sic*] scheme for expending money for warlike purposes. But an enlarged, judicious, & vigorous system of war measures ought I think to be digested & the execution of it commenced as early as practicable. But I do not mean to advise *you*. I merely state what I should be happy [to] see done *by you*. Very sincerely yours, J.H. Hammond.

ALS in ScCleA.

From LOUIS MCLANE

London, Feb. 3, 1846

My dear Sir, I send you by the present steamer a few newspapers containing the Exposition of Sir Robert Peel of his comprehensive scheme of free trade. It will speak for itself, & needs no comment from me. It will be violently resisted, and may possibly lead to a dissolution of Parliament; though the general impression appears to be that it will pass both houses at the present session. It will not surprise me, whether it succeed or fail to see a change of ministry at no distant day; nor do I believe that a whig ministry would be particularly unfavorable to us, especially if Lord John Russell should be at the head of it. You may infer from his observations and those of Sir Robert Peel in the House of Commons, that if Mr. Packenham [*sic*; Richard Pakenham] had sent our proposition home, a slight modification of it would have made it acceptable here. However, ["my purpose" *canceled*] I need *here* add nothing to what I have already said upon this head: only that I am more than ever persuaded that the adoption by Congress of the recommendations in the message will not be regarded here as warlike, and will do no harm. On the contrary it might do great good; whereas a refusal by Congress to sustain the President [James K. Polk] would have a mischeivous tendency. There will be a year after the notice to settle the question, and unless one side be *bent* on war that *cannot* be difficult. Believe me to be Dear Sir, very Truly y[ou]rs, Louis McLane.

ALS in ScCleA; PC in Boucher and Brooks, eds., *Correspondence*, pp. 323–324.

REMARKS ON PRESENTING THE MEMPHIS MEMORIAL

[In the Senate, February 3, 1846]

Mr. Calhoun rose to present the memorial of the Memphis convention. The document was, he remarked, drawn up with great ability, and presented a full view of the important subjects which occupied the deliberations of the convention. In presenting the memorial, he would take the opportunity to state that there were some of its recommendations which did not come within his view of the provisions of the constitution; and there were others based on grounds in which he could not agree. But in the great point of the memorial, he entirely concurred. He moved that it be printed for the use of the Senate, and referred to a select committee of five.

From the Washington, D.C., *Daily Union*, vol. I, no. 236 (February 3, 1846), p. 934. Slightly variant report in *Congressional Globe*, 29th Cong., 1st Sess., p. 297. Variant reports in the New York, N.Y., *Herald*, February 5, 1846, p. 3; the New York, N.Y., *Evening Post*, February 6, 1846, p. 1; the Charleston, S.C., *Courier*, February 7, 1846, p. 2; the Pendleton, S.C., *Messenger*, February 13, 1846, p. 2. NOTE: The Senate agreed to Calhoun's motion to print and to refer to a select committee without discussion. A committee was appointed consisting of Calhoun, David R. Atchison of Missouri, James Semple of Ill., Joseph W. Chalmers of Miss., and Alexander Barrow of La. (The Committee reported on 6/26/1846.) On the same day as the Senate presentation, Isaac E. Holmes of S.C. attempted to present the Memphis memorial in the House of Representatives. This inaugurated contentious proceedings which spilled over into much of the next day's session. Motions that the document be read and that it be printed were defeated by close recorded votes. Ultimately the memorial was referred to the Committee on Military Affairs.

From JOS[EPH] J. SINGLETON

Dahlonega Ga., 3th Feb. 1846

My Dear Sir, Your excellent friend & neighbor Mr. William Sloan, informed me not long since at my home, that you were very successful in your farming operations in Alabama. To hear of your success any where, or in any undertaking, I hope you will believe me, when I tell you, it has always afforded me pleasure save one short period of my life, and that was during the discussions of the doctrines of State Rights. Need I say to you, that I was ignorant of the orriginal principles of our government, at the time you and your friends were endeavoring to sustain them. I was not alone ignorant, as you well know. It has so turned out however, that the discussions of those very doctrines in your noble State, has "opened the eyes of the blind" and caused the ["desponding" *interlined*] Patriots to stand erect in defense of the only doctrines which will bear them out, when all others will fail. At the head of which nothing could afford me more pleasure than to see the *one* who has been so conspicuous in their defence, standing at the Helm steering our political Bark for the Haven of our national perpetuity.

I have digressed from the orriginal purport of this letter, which was not intended at its commencement. Your friend Mr. Sloan also informed me, that you spoke of increasing your slave force in your planting interest; if you are so disposed, permit me to offer you for sale some 30 or 40 in families, on time, or for cash. I prefer the lat[t]er. Be pleased sir, to write me whatever your disposition may be in relation to this increase of your Negro property, and should it be your determination to increase it, I will then give you the ages & sex of the above numbers, when you can make me an offer for them, or I will make you one. I have the hon[or] Sir to be your friend &C., Jos. J. Singleton.

ALS in ScCleA. NOTE: This letter was postmarked in Dahlonega on 2/8.

To L[ITTLETON] W. TAZEWELL, Norfolk, Va.

Senate Chamber, 3d Feb. 1846
My dear Sir, This will be delivered to you by Dr. [Frederick] Hollick, to whom I take pleasure in introducing you.

Dr. Hollick has devoted much of his attention to Anatomy. You will find him very intelligent and exceedingly well informed on the subject, which he has made the especial object of his study.

His immediate object in visiting Norfolk is to satisfy himself, by enquiry & investigation, whether there is any foundation in fact, for an opinion, which is becoming more or less prevalent, that after several consequetive [*sic*] crosses between the European & negro race, say at the fourth, the female becomes barren.

The subject is one of no small curiosity & interest; & the Doctor has selected Norfolk, as a place favourable to enquiry & investigation, from the fact, that the two races have longer coexisted in the same region ["there" *interlined*] than in any other portion of the Union. Yours truly & sincerely, J.C. Calhoun.

ALS in DLC, John C. Calhoun Papers. NOTE: Hollick (1818–1900) subsequently became a noted obstetrician and the author of an extremely popular *Marriage Manual* published in 1850. He published also *An Inquiry into the Rights, Duties, and Destinies, of the Different Varieties of the Human Race, with a View to a Proper Consideration of the Subjects of Slavery, Abolition, Amalgamation, and Aboriginal Rights* (New York: W.B. and T. Smith, 1843).

From GEO[RGE] R. C. FLOYD

Milwaukee, Feb. 4th 1846

My dear Sir, A rumor has reached me in the last three days that I am to be removed from office [as Secretary of the Wisc. Territory]. And that I am a defa[u]lter to the Government. This charge is false. I received $34,525 dollars from the Treasury Department to pay the expences of the Legislature of 43 & 44, and 44 & 45 and have accounted to the department for $32,625 dollars and have vouchers on hand for $3,300, three thousand three hundred dollars. I last May received $13,749 dollars to pay the arrea[ra]ge claims which had accrued prior to 1842. I received written instructions at the time how to pay the same. These arrea[ra]ge claims were scattered from St. Louis to New York. I have not paid all of them but I have paid [those] that have been presented. And I received $1,200 dollars by order of the department from Collier and Pettis [of St. Louis] which I acknowledged to the department. Now there has not been one man in the entire Territory as far as I know who has complained of me as an officer. Is it just that I should be charged with defalcation under such circumstances[?] I feel exceedingly indigna[n]t at such treatment and I shall make the man or men whome soever they be accountable to me for such slanders. I cannot however think for one moment that the President [James K. Polk] would remove me or any one without a charge and if charged with not haveing fulfilled the duties of his office that he should be heard in vindication of his conduct. I have never received any intimation what ever from any quarter that I had not performed my duties honestly and promptly. But alas I am sorry to say that honesty doese not receive its dues in these days. I have never hesitated here or ["at" *interlined and then canceled*] any where now or at any time ["to express" *interlined*] my decided parciality for you as the man of all others in this union the best qualified ["from" *canceled*] to fill the office of President of the U.S. for on account of your virtues and abillite. If these opinions have had any affect prejudicial to me with the powers that be I care not. I entertain them from a full conviction of trouth, and being a free man (though a federal office holder) I will express them be the consequences what they may to me. I ["shall" *canceled*] will be under many obligation[s] to you if you will see the Presiden[t] as soone as convenient, and state the facts of the case ["and" *canceled*] for I should like to heare the charges and make my defence. I have written you [a] long letter but I hope you will excuse it. I could not however say less feeling as ["as" *canceled*] I do that if any charges have been made against me that that they are false and unjust. I hold my honor above all things in this world. It I will defend and protect lett the cost be what it may to me. I should be much pleased to receive any documents that you would think worth sending me. I am sir with the highest regard your friend, Geo. R.C. Floyd.

ALS in ScCleA. Note: Floyd was a member of the John Floyd family of western Va. He was removed from office.

From Jos[eph] W. Lesesne

Mobile, February 4th 1846

Dear Sir: I take the liberty of writing you on a subject on which you had some conversation with our friends on your late visit to Mobile. An opportunity is now offered us of purchasing the [Mobile] Register under very favorable circumstances, and I write to learn whether we can look for any pecuniary aid in the purchase ["to Caroli" *canceled*] to any quarter out of the State, and whether you or any of our friends in Washington or Charleston can suggest any one who could be depended on to take charge of the Editorial department. This latter is our greatest difficulty. We believe that with the aid of a few hundred Dollars out of the State the purchase can be made, but we have no one here willing to do, what we regard as indispensible viz. [*one word canceled*] surrender himself entirely to the business of conducting the Editorial Department. Our friends who have been in the habit of writing—Mr. [John A.] Campbell[,] myself and others, are willing to do as much as we can in this way, and no doubt contributions from this source would do something for the paper. But still, an able man ought to be at the head of it—one who would attract the confidence and respect of the public by his character as a man and talents as a writer. Is there none such in Washington[?]

The paper can be purchased for between 10 and 12 thousand Dollars on long time and we could, we think raise three thousand Dollars in cash, which we would be willing to give to any able man, appropriating it to the first payment. The rest we would expect him to pay. A few years ago this same establishment sold for 30 thousand Dollars; and I have no doubt that it would at 12 thousand Dollars pay for itself in five years and at the same time yield the owner from 3 thousand to $3500 income annually. Its advantages from long standing and a large commercial patronage are great: and I am serious in the belief that placed in the hands of an able and practical man under the circumstances we propose, it would be a handsome fortune to him.

I need not say a word to you on the importance of our having an organ here. The influence of Alabama properly directed would be very great. Hitherto the moral power of the State has been in hands wholly unfit to wield it. The State has acquired little or no character. Its abundant talent has been useless to it. The present time, too, is most auspicious for making a movement to give our party the advantages which fortune seems to offer it. There is a growing feeling in our favor with Democrats and Whigs—and all that we require is to be in a situation to watch events and use them with judgement. The Register does us all the harm it can, and although this, from the loss of all character on the part of its conductors is not much, yet it must if it remain in their hands, always be a serious obstacle in the way of any active movement, on our part.

I sincerely wish some young man of known character and talents could be found in whom we could place entire confidence, ["for the Editorship of this paper," *interlined*] and it does appear to me that if our friends at Washington would look about them they could send us such a one. I think what we offer is very handsome. It would place the person taking the task upon himself, for a year or two, beyond all pecuniary difficulty. It would enable him to devote to the extinguishment of the balance due for the paper, for that time, the entire income of the establishment, and if he is a single man and of economical habits $700 would be ample for his support. Under these circumstances I can not see how the enterprise could fail.

If, my dear Sir, I do not take an unwarranted liberty in thus addressing you, it would be very gratifying to us to hear your views on this subject, if not directly—then through Col. [Franklin H.] Elmore or some other friend, who is in the habit of attending to these details. I fear I am presuming on your good nature in troubling you with them.

May I take the liberty [*two words canceled and* "to express my" *interlined*] profound admiration for your course in the Senate, and to say that I have not met a single man of any party who has not expressed a similar feeling. There is no war party here, and the news from England, has only tended to show the justness of your views, by satisfying every one that nothing but prudence and dignity is required to enable us to disentangle the Oregon question with honor to both countries and with decided advantage to our own.

Mr. [William] Allen's course has excited a feeling of general distrust and disgust. When all the inflam[m]able materials for speech making shall have been consumed in Congress the advocates of a pacific and dignified course of policy will ["occupy" *canceled*] appear in their true character to the public. Mr. Andrew [Pickens] Calhoun left here yesterday afternoon, in excellent health and spirits, and with the determination to hold on to his cotton for a time. Some Eight thousand bales have been sold since the last advices [*three or four words canceled*]. Ordinary 6¼ @ 6¾. Mid & good Mid. 7 @ 7¾; mid fair to fair 7⅞ to 8½; Fair to G & F 8⅝ @ 9¼—these are the quotations of this morning Feb[ruar]y 5th/46. Very truly & respectfully your f[rien]d & Ser[van]t, Jos. W. Lesesne.

ALS in ScCleA.

From V[ERNON] K. STEVENSON

Nashville Tennessee, Feb[ruar]y ["15th" *altered to* "5th"(?)] 1846
Dear Sir, In giving you the products in agriculture & manufactures for middle Tennessee in refference to our R. Road to Chatenooga & there to connect with the great ["works of" *canceled and* "R. Road System" *interlined*] of Georgia & South Carolina I reserved to the present moment the pleasure of speaking of the importance to Charleston[,] Savan[n]a[h,] Augusta & Nashville & more particularly to the stockholders in all of the ["Georgia & South Carolina" *interlined*] Rail roads of the vast mines of different kinds of coal lying in the bluffs & in many places for miles hanging over the con-

templated line of R.R. commencing a few miles west of Chatenooga & continuing for near fifty miles towards Nashville & allways so situated as to the R.R. line that a short inclined plane would deliver it in the cars without any [*one word and "for" canceled and "labour" interlined*], the coal allways being from six to Ten hundred feet above the line of the R. Road[,] this coal projecting as it does from the edge of the mountain presents [*"very" canceled and "so" interlined*] little difficulty in quarrying that the [*sic*] I understood when there the last summer that the price was ½ cent p[e]r bushel but we will say one cent & the owner[?] one cent making two cents the price of coal ready for shipment on the R.R. then say the R. Road could afford, (which she certainly could do having a vast business beside to do) to carry coles [*sic*] as cheap as the Redding Road in Pennsylvania carries it (she having to go back empty having nothing to carry but coal one way) which is 1 cent a ton p[e]r mile which would be a dollar a ton p[e]r 100 miles[,] the ton being thirty bushels & the cost of raising [*"or quarrying" interlined*] & delivering the coal to the rail road being two cents & car[r]iage 3⅓ three & one third cents would be five & one third cents delivered at Nashville one hundred miles from the nearest mines. It could at the same rate be delivered at Atlanta in Georgia 140 miles from the nearest mines to that place at six & an half cents p[e]r bushel & at Augusta Ga. 310 miles from the mines for 12½ cents p[e]r bushel at Charleston 446 miles from the mines at a fraction under seventeen cents p[e]r bushel. I am aware that this rate could not be afforded upon as light built R. Roads as those of S. Carolina but for the fact that the coal would ondly [*sic*] be carried to fill out loads & at an idle season of the year just as the South Carolina road from Hamburgh now brings cordwood to Charleston & that the Redding road is enabled to make money at this low rate mainly by carrying immens[e] loads on her heavy iron & allways having plenty [*"to" interlined*] do which would in all probability be the case with these roads soon for with our immense products of middle Tennessee & the great abundance of this coal & the superior quality of the greater part of it for parlor use as well as manufacturing it being highly Bituminous & at the same time producing no dust & a very [*"sp" canceled*] small quantity of white ashes. We could not fail to furnish these Rail roads with plenty to do to say nothing of the vast number of passengers from the valley of the Miss. traveling to the north & back that would find this the most certain & greatly the quickest rout[e] even from St. Louis to N. York.

If [*"my memory serves me" canceled*] I am not mistaken in the last report of the business of the Redding Rail way which I saw they stated that even at the low rate 1 cent p[e]r ton p[e]r mile 54/100ths of the am[oun]t rec[eive]d was clear money or that 46 p[e]r cent of it ondly was consumed in expenses the balance going to dividends.

This coal Region through which it is contemplated to run the Nashville & Chatenooga R. Road also abounds in the richest Iron ore which lies in some places allmost in contact with the coal which with such facilities as afforded by this—long lines of R. Road would induce the manufacture of iron to a great extent in this vicinity where there is now none made though higher up the Tennessee River in east Tennessee pig metal is made in such abundance that it is not uncommon to hear of sales of it at 12 to 14 dollars p[e]r Ton when ["the same" *canceled*] it commands forty dollars readily at Boston.

With Iron, cole, Limestone & lumber in such abundance as they are known to be upon this rout[e] as above stated for near fifty miles & in many places altogether is it not fair to suppose that there will be immense Iron work erected if this Road is Built & that they will also contribute largely to the carrying of this R. Road[,] provisions also being cheaper than any where in the union.

I have taken great paines to learn fully as to the cost of carrying goods from N. York to Nashville Tenn[esse]e or to the mouth of the Ohio[,] the centre of the Miss. Valley & find that the average price at present paid from N. York to Nashville by N. Orleans including every charge[,] Insurance &[c] is $2.89 cents p[e]r 100 lbs. of average ["Dry" *interlined*] goods from N. York to Nashville by Pittsburgh from March until June inclusive is including as above $2.96 cents p[e]r 100 lbs. By the [Great] Lakes & Cincinatti the same or rather higher at the same seasons & by both ways from July 1st until 1st March the average prices either by Pittsburgh or Cincinatti the price depends so much upon the ga[u]ge of water in the Ohio &C that you can not approach anything like regularity as it reaches from $3.00 to 12.00 p[e]r 100 lbs. but is usually from three to six dollars and to the mouth of the Ohio the cost would be probably 20 cents p[e]r 100 lbs. less at all seasons on an average than to Nashville[;] this would be fully as much as ["it" *canceled and* "the difference" *interlined*] would amount to. The cost including insurance ["& car(r)iage" *interlined*] from N. York to Charleston or Savan[n]ah & R. Road carriage to Nashville will be from 1.75 to 2.00 per 100 lbs. and can as the Chief Engineer of the Georgia R.R. and Banking Co. advises me, be ["considerably" *interlined*] reduced and still be profitable as this is much higher than they will cha[r]ge upon other freight[,] they expecting to make their profits chiefly from this kind of freight. Insurance from N. York to Nashville by N. Orleans is 2¼ p[e]r cent & by the other rout[e] 1¼ to 1½ p[e]r cent[;] by Charleston it is but ½ to ¾ p[e]r cent.

I should have written sooner but I learned soon after receiving your last letter that our report would not be ready before the 20th of this month and as I could not readily find lots of goods that come round bringing their distinct charges of every kind and as these make so large an item in the cost of transportation from the North to Nashville I determined to be fully informed if possible before writing which I have succeeded in.

I have also gone far enough in testing our citizens to be certain that our city corporation will take half a million of dollars of the stock of the R. Road & have every assurance that we can get half or more probably of the whole amount of stock taken in Tenn[esse]e in work on the Road lines as money.

After looking over this please write to me and if there is any further information wanting relative to our products[,] manufactures[,] carriages or any thing concerning us ["please" *canceled*] I will advise you immediately.

I feel every assurance that we will build the R. Road immediately and I have sent to Ky. a charter which if they grant we will also lock & dam the Cumberland to the Ohio River & this eternal com[m]unication beteunt [*sic*] Charleston & the Mississippi River below the freezing point. Truely, V.K. Stevenson.

ALS in ScCleA. NOTE: Stevenson was a successful Nashville merchant who had probably come originally from Ky. In 1846 he became an "agent" for the Nashville & Chattanooga Railroad, of which he was president during 1848–1860. He was disgraced during the Civil War, being accused of profiteering and abandoning his responsibilities in the Confederate defense of Nashville in 1862 by escaping in a private train. He apparently was unable to return to Nashville after the war and lived in New York City.

From KER BOYCE

Charleston, Feb[ruar]y 6, 1846

My dear Sir, I feel it due to to [*sic*] you to write you oc[c]asion[al]ly, when ever theare is any thing which might add to your present or future prospects. I hope and feel that the Oregon Question is now, to be settled, by boath countreys, on proper terms and that the proper reduction on the Tariff of 42, will with the opening of the ports of England ["of the" *canceled*] free to our corn, will [*sic*] compleatly unite boath countrys, by the inter[e]st of Free trade so as to make our trade so mutual as to prevent any thing that could be got up to cover a warr betwe[e]n the two Countreys. Now, My Dear Sir, at present you occ[u]py a a [*sic*] station which, is some what delicate ["and" *canceled*] in the Oregon. You should not, be drawn in to opposition, to Mr. [James K.] Polk, on that Question so as to place yourself hostile, to him or his administration, for the Question on the Oregon [will] pass off as I believe in 12 months, but the Main Question is the Tariff, and on that, depends peace heare after, and as [you] know some of our prominent men are opposed to Mr. Polk, and would like above all things that a split should be made betwe[e]n, you and him in order to cover theare retreat, and unless you can be got in that prosission [*sic*], they will be left in the back ground. I feel it my duty, as a friend to Warn you not to be allowed to be placed[?] where you are to be injured and do a[n] injury to your futer prospects and possibly defeat the Tariff, which is all in all with us in the South. You have been injured by, some of your pretended friends before and I think it high time you would not allow, them to put you in, a wrong possistion. This I give, you as a friend[,] one that, have nothing, to ask, but the welfare of the Countrey, and that wellfare I think depends on you, being President of the U. States, While I know some of the leading men, think other wise. You must excuse the liberty which I heare take to offer you advice, but Sir I know you are a Confiding Man, and thearefore, is eas[il]y dec[e]ived by those who are designing, who look to prosission [*sic*], which they can never gain only by your popularity in South Carolina, and as I know many a wise man may be put on his g[u]ard by one that does not pretend, to great knowledge or Profecy. Thearefore a word to the wise is soficient. Your most sinsare friend & obedient Serv[an]t, Ker Boyce.

ALS in ScCleA.

From F[rancis] W. Pickens

Charleston, 6 Feb[ruar]y 1846

My dear Sir, I never rec[eive]d yours [*not found*] until yesterday. It went to Edgefield, then to Savannah and then here.

Of course I cannot judge of matters as well as you do who are in possession of all the grounds. Besides your exper[i]ence and sagacity are vastly superior to any thing I can pretend to. But there is one thing that strikes me as strange, and that is that England should make war upon us because we chose to give a notice provided and contemplated by treaty stipulation. Now for a man to believe that we have no right to the country either north or south of 49°—and that it is impolitic to own it, and therefore for him to be opposed to the notice is quite natural. If I believed that the U.S. had a clear right to, at least, all below 49° I could not see how it would ["produce war" *canceled*] be just cause of war to give the notice especially as it was provided for by treaty. If England made it a pretext for war then she could do so on any thing else just as well. If I believed we had a clear & just right I could not be deter[r]ed from the assertion of that right by any apprehension of war. The truth is that I never believed there would be war, and you allude to my writing you on that point, and I think the news from England proves that there was no serious danger. I see, from yours, you anticipated a different reception to the President's [James K. Polk's] message from that [which] it met with. I have no idea that England can risk a war with us in the present state of Europe & particularly considering the peculiar state of things in France. But of course I need not dwell upon these points as I know you are in a situation to attach no importance to them from me.

However I will say that I think the greatest of all present questions is the Tariff, and I hope the Oregon question will be but temporary and all will pass off in less than a year, while the real question is the tariff. And what I dread is that the divisions on the Oregon question will be seen on the Tariff, and that you will be so far seperated from Mr. Polk that there will be no harmony or consultation on the Tariff. And this is what the whigs are working for. A portion of the Democrats desire a rupture between you & Polk; at the head of this interest is [Thomas H.] Benton and a *few* in *the South*. The whigs desire this so as to preserve the Tariff, with them, the greatest of all questions. If they can use the Oregon question so as to accomplish this object they will succeed. Whatever professions of friendship they may make towards you they never will aid in giving you power. There are many thousands of whigs in private, South as well as North, who feel admiration and express it towards you, but that party are managed entirely by a few politicians who hate you more than any man in this Union, and when the time comes to act they will move *their whole party ag[ain]st you certainly*. It may be that my views are influenced by my over estimating the importance to the country & the reform of the Gov[ernment of] your being President &c, and my consequent fears on that subject. I had once expected (as I wrote you to Ala.) that you would be certainly called out with great unanimity the next time, if you were unconnected with the active & bitter politics of the passing day. And I now fear exactly what I anticipated by your entering eagerly & warmly into the exciting topics presented & made up by politicians. You will pardon me if I utter my sentiments to you more candidly than you may be accustomed to, by those who flatter you and urge you into positions to cover & protect them in any weak situation that they may have fallen into either at Washington or at home. As I have nothing to care for or to hope for I can write as a candid friend. And of course what I say must be only as a distant observer, for I have not recieved [sic] a single letter from any one at Washington except yourself.

I have been on a visit to Savannah and only returned a few days since. It is a beautiful and very hospitable city with great elegance and luxury. I visited the rice lands of that river and found them superior to any thing I had concieved [sic] of. It is undoubtedly the most perfect system of agriculture in the world. The Rice planters are realizing immense incomes. A friend of mine Col: [John Elliott?] Ward makes this year $360 clear to every hand that hoes. He gave $250 cash for rice lands adjoining him—his income this year is $96,000. And $300 to the hand is common. Rice lands, part of Gen[era]l Hamilton's [James Hamilton, Jr.'s] land, sold here a few weeks since at outcry for $136 per acre. Negroes average all round large gangs $425. The demand for the lower part of this State & Georgia is greater than La: or Texas. I saw planters in Savannah from Early county [Ga.] who made this year 10 bags of cotton per hand. We have had a very cold winter—so much so that the orange trees were injured very much. I learn that it has been much colder in Edgefield. I suppose you see cotton has gone down very low. I think the cause temporary, for the crop will not exceed 2 millions of bags. I have just ship[p]ed 336 bags of mine to Liverpool yesterday, to take the spring market and to get the advantage of the war fever, which I suppose will be fomented, to enable the [Robert] Peel ministry to sustain itself and call for supplies.

I enclose with this Arthur's [Arthur Simkins's] receipt. As soon as my family are well (the infant being sick) I shall return home. I hope to be there by the 10th. I have 3 of my children here at school & have been devoting myself to their improvement, as their prosperity is all I care for now. Present us kindly to Cousin Floride [Colhoun Calhoun]. Very truly, F.W. Pickens.

ALS in ScCleA; PEx in Boucher and Brooks, eds., *Correspondence*, p. 324.

To "The President" [JAMES K. POLK]

6th Feb. 1846

Dear Sir, I understand, that a change is contemplated in the Pourtegal Mission. If such should be the fact, I hope you will find it compatible with your sense of duty to confer the appointment on Mr. [Francis] Markoe of the State Department. He is one of the few names I left with you last spring, when I left the Department of State. I know him well, & cannot doubt, that he would fill the office with honor to himself & country. I take much interest in his success. With great respect I am yours truly, J.C. Calhoun.

ALS in DLC, James K. Polk Papers (Presidential Papers Microfilm, Polk Papers, roll 44). NOTE: Markoe was the son-in-law of Calhoun's deceased friend Virgil Maxcy and had been head of the Consular Bureau of the State Department for some time.

To LEWIS SHANKS, [Memphis]

Senate Chamber, 6th Feb. 1846

My dear Sir, I am much gratified to learn, that my course in reference to Oregon, meets with the approbation of my fellow citizens in your region of the country; and am happy to say, that the war fever is abating and the prospect of peace bright[en]ing. But the danger is not yet over. Our foreign relations are in a very entangled condition. It will require much good sense & skill to disentangle them.

I have received & presented the memorial prepared by the Committee in reference to the subjects embraced by the resolutions adopted by the [Memphis] Convention; & had it refer[r]ed to a special Committee. The members are judiciously selected, and will be, I have no doubt, well inclined to carry out all the leading views of the Convention.

I will, with pleasure, give my attention to the two subjects to which you refer, with my disposition to favour the wishes of your citizens. With great respect I am & &, J.C. Calhoun.

ALS in ScU-SC, John C. Calhoun Papers; transcript in DLC, Carnegie Institution of Washington Transcript Collection.

From D[ANIEL] M. FORNEY

[Hayneville, Ala.] Feb[ruar]y 7, 1846
Dear Sir, The present time is one of uncommon interest to the American people. The indications you have given afforded many of your old friends pleasure. I claim to number myself one of those. In times past when I could not implicitedly follow you, I always was ready to give you the most unbounded confiden[ce] of honesty of purpose. And believing it right & proper that I should express those feelings that I now entertain, and that I have not done so before, perhaps upon equal necessity, (I allude to the time when a separation took place between you and Gen[era]l [Andrew] Jackson) I can plead no excuse but perhaps a too great a sensitiveness to man worship. I say to you, go on, in the singleness of purpose and the time will come, when justice will be done to you, in your political career. The times seem entirely out of joint, and may an over ruling providen[ce] constrain all for the best. Your friend, D.M. Forney.

ALS in ScCleA. NOTE: Forney had been Representative from N.C. during 1815–1818 and had moved to Ala. in 1834.

From J[OHN] S. BARBOUR

Catalpa [Va.,] Feb[ruar]y 10th 1846
My Dear Sir, It is in the power of your friends in Virginia to controul the elections in the Spring.

I do not think that the Whigs have the slightest wish or purpose at present to abandon their Candidate & support any one else. It is the delusive hope at the bottom of Pandora[']s box which leads them away from what they might accomplish in retribution for the evils they have let loose upon the world.

In my intercourse & correspondence I find that they mean to nail their colours to the mast. Their aim is to the triumph of party & leave patriotism *in the lurch*.

This era of intrigues & corruption, is filled with supple & dextrous men, who mean to deceive whilst they are most fair in the view. I am very desirous that the individual who is our present Gov[erno]r [William Smith] shou[l]d remain in his late political associations. I hope & believe that he will do so. Others think he will not—& they draw their auguries from his own words.

If the peace of the Country is broken by war with England, the

Whigs will inevitably be in the ascendent in all the Atlantic States. There is no spirit for war or war measures in all that I can see or hear. In Richmond the Legislative voice (if for war) does not speak the voice of the people at home. I am told that there candidates & supplicants for federal office in our Senate & House of Delegates [are numerous enough?] to give the President [James K. Polk] a corporal[']s *squad* on every question.

This will be the case as long as your Government pays the high salaries for petty duties which are now given to the most inferiour minds & abilities. Why shou[l]d not the Govt. wages of labour be graduated by the prices paid for like labour by individuals?

As long as you give these high bounties for venal[i]ty its existence is certain & destiny—patriotism is ["a" *interlined and* "an" *canceled*] trade, & Government a job.

Hence the purer part in the political Sanhedrin have been deceived & always will be deceived. They throw their power into the contest & are betrayed the moment it is over:

> "There is no anguish like the hour
> Whatever else befall us,
> When those, the heart hath raised to power;
> Asserts it, *but to gall us.*"

As soon as my family distresses will allow, I shall visit Alabama. I wish Mr. [Dixon H.] Lewis [Senator from Ala.] w[oul]d give me the name of some Lawyer in Greene County to whom I may confide business of some magnitude. I can however write him myself without troubling you with it.

Our bar & Court are expressing some anxiety for the decisions of the Supreme Court which are proposed to be published. They say that as the decisions of that Court make law, their publication is as necessary as that of the Acts of Congress.

The deeper interest with the Bar doubtless is in the Cheapened price of the books. A friend of yours asked me to mention the subject to you and I have fulfilled his request, & added the motive that probably influences the request. This last is however my conjecture.

If Mrs. [Floride Colhoun] Calhoun & the young Ladies with her cou'd make us a visit, it w[oul]d give my wife [Elizabeth A. Byrne Barbour] great pleasure to see them & the relaxation from City enjoyments might be agre[e]able to them. With all Respect, y[our]s Sincerely & Truly, J.S. Barbour.

ALS in ScCleA.

From H[ENRY] W[HEATON]

London, Feb. 10, 1846

My dear Sir, When I last wrote you I did not expect to have occasion to address you from here. But having no business on hand, I left Berlin a few days since to make a visit to my family at Paris, intending to return to my post very soon, *there* to await the arrival of my successor [as U.S. Minister to Prussia, Andrew J. Donelson] who is expected in the latter part of April.

Since I have been here I have availed myself of frequent opportunities of intercourse with leading personages, of all parties & in various positions, to ascertain the prevailing impressions with regard to our differences with this Country, & I have been very happy to find even a more conciliatory & pacific spirit prevailing than I expected to perceive. I believe the subject is beginning to be understood in all its bearings, & that neither the Govt. nor the People are disposed to push matters to extremeties [*sic*] unless it should be ["made" *interlined*] necessary by some provocation on our part, & I do not believe that the passage of a joint resolution authorizing the President [James K. Polk] to notify the expiration of the Oregon Convention would be considered as a measure of hostility. Indeed it appears to be very important to the Success of the negotiations that we should not appear to be a *divided* Nation, & in my conversations I have always let it be distinctly understood that we shall *all* stand upon the parallel of 49 as the boundary most just, equitable, & convenient for the partition of the Country—without admitting ["to them" *interlined*] the possibility even of some *modification* of this basis of adjustment although some such appears to be desired here. Still it is universally regretted that Mr. [Richard] P[akenha]m should have so peremptiroly [*sic*] rejected that proposition, & the difficulty now seems to be how to correct this error. Our rejection of their [*partial word canceled*] counter proposition for a reference will not, I fear, help us in public opinion here; but it will do no harm if the ["Gov" *canceled*] two Governments will set about in earnest to treat the question as one of *boundary* to be settled between them, so as to divide the territory fairly with a view to all the circumstances of ports, navigation, &c. & to the maintenance of peace on the frontier thus established.

Much mischief has been produced here by the intemperate language used in Congress respecting this Country, which even our friends do not consider as warranted by the occasion. I believe the Govt. may be induced to yield the 49th parallel, as the basis of boundary with some modifications, but I think they will require ["at least" *interlined*] the *temporary* navigation of the ["Oregon river or" *canceled*] Columbia river. The interests existing north of the river are not considered here as important, but it is deemed a point of honour to maintain them, & that the navigation of the river for a term of years is necessary ["un" *canceled*] for that purpose until the fur trade ceases to exist. In short this is one of the modifications of the President's propositions which I think would be desireable to ["render" *canceled*] them ["in order" *interlined*] to render the concession more palatable to the Nation. I repeat that there is a sincere desire for peace with us, & no exag[g]erated notion of the [*a few words canceled*] value of the Country to them; but a strong determination not to yield to threats, & a strong feeling of their tremendous power of annoying us. Indeed *they* would also be a united nation, if war should be the result of a rejection ["of"(?) *canceled*] on our part of what the civilized world would consider as fair terms of compromise. The great movement which is going on here in favour of the principles of free trade, it is hoped ["that" *canceled*] will have a favorable effect in encouraging a pacific feeling with us. It opens the prospect of our being hereafter more useful to each other than we have ever yet been, & I hope will induce ["our"(?) *canceled*] both Nations to reflect how much more good ["than" *canceled*] they can do each other in peace, than they can inflict of evil in war—if indeed there were any comparison in the choice of these so far as the true interests of nations are ["consid" *canceled*] concerned. I have great pleasure ["of" *canceled*] in assuring you that your efforts as a *mediator* ["between" *canceled*] are duly appreciated here, whilst it is well known that you are the last man who would yield any thing in which the rights & honour of our Country were concerned.

It is not doubted that Sir R[obert] Peel's propositions will be carried in the Commons by such a majority as will render their rejection by the Lords utterly impossible. Truly yours, H.W.

ALI in ScCleA; PC in Jameson, ed., *Correspondence*, pp. 1071–1073.

To Mrs. P[LACIDIA MAYRANT] ADAMS, Pendleton, S.C.

Senate Chamber, 12th Feb: 1846

My dear Madam, I am of the impression, that you ought by no means to go into bank under existing circumstances. The proceeds of the sales of the Michigan lands will soon ["be" *interlined*] available, as the sale was ordered for the 14th Inst.; and I requested the proceeds to be placed to my credit in some bank in New York, which will place it under my immediate control. Besides, I should think it far better to sell the bank stock of the estate than to go into bank. It gives a low rate of interest, while the note in bank, should you go into the bank, would be bearing an interest of nearly 7 percent. The difference would be so much income lost to the estate, which can illy bear it. Mr. [John Ewing] Bonneau told me that he did think there was much prospect, that the price of the bank stock would rise. I would, then, advise you by all means to sell the stock, rather than go into bank, should the proceeds of the ["proceeds of the" *interlined and then canceled*] sales of the land not be ["able" *canceled*] available in time to meet your demand for funds. I should think they will certainly be available early in March. Yours truly, J.C. Calhoun.

ALS owned by Mr. Holbrook Campbell.

From W I L L I A M   S L O A N

Pendleton, Feb. 12th 1846

Dear Sir, Not hearing aneything from Mr. [William?] Grisham in January on the subject of the late gold due you, I wrote him the first of this month, an answer to which has just come to hand[.] He says "Your letter of the 5th came to hand to day and hasten to reply[.] I have conferred with E.J.C. Millner[,] the only one of them now up and he says there is some rent due from others to Mr. Calhoun and that he has not been able as yet to get it[;] did not state how much, that he had none now nor did he owe any on his own account, but that he expected soon to be operating on Mr. C[alhoun's] mine & would pay soon as aney amount could be due worthy of depositing."

This statement is so very different from what I ["was" *canceled*] expected from a conversation with Mr. [Robert H.?] Moore an intimate friend of Mr. Millners, who I called on in the absence of the Mr. Millners, for information about your mining interest, that I have thought propper to advise you immediately. Very respectfully Your Ob[edien]t Servant, William Sloan.

ALS in NcD, John C. Calhoun Papers.

From E[NOCH] B. BENSON

Pendleton, February 13, 1846

D[ea]r Sir, I am verry sorry to trouble you on the subject of money matters, as you have enough to do without attending to little things of that sort. You recollect when you was leaving Pendleton I mentioned to you that Mrs. [Placidia Mayrant] Adams had disappointed me verry much[,] that I had advanced money & lifted a note for her & that I held other notes on her in all amounting to about $350 which she promised I should certainly rece[i]ve last October & that the money was coming from Mr. Calhoun[.] You told me I should have it in the month of January—the middle of February has come & no money yet. If not paid by the 1st of next month I must take legal steps to collect it.

Your own a/c of about $250 and your a/c to the Factory of about $80 is not paid as you expected by rents of Gold Mine. Mr. William Sloan informed me this day I need not depend on getting any thing from that Quarter. Next month I shall be in great need of money & hope you can pay us. Respectfully yours, E.B. Benson.

ALS in ScU-SC, John C. Calhoun Papers.

To F[RANKLIN] H. ELMORE, [Charleston]

Washington, 13th Feb: 1846

My dear Sir, I take much pleasure in making you acquainted with Mr. V[ernon] K. Stevenson, who will deliver you this.

He is a citizen of Nashville of great respectability & much influence. He has taken a very active & prominent part in forwarding the plan of extending the rail road from Chat[t]anooga to Nashville & visits Charleston in connection with its prosecution.

I regard the extension of vast importance to both cities and am decidedly of the impression, that there is not a link in the whole chain of our system of internal ["improvements" *interlined*] more important. It will, when completed, effect a great revolution in the commerce between the Atlantick & the valley of the Mississippi.

Thus thinking, I do hope Charleston will enter Zealously into the support of the projected plan of uniting by rail road ["of" *canceled*] the two cities. Yours truly, J.C. Calhoun.

ALS in ScU-SC, John C. Calhoun Papers.

From P[ETER] H[AGNER]

[Washington] 13 Feb: [18]46
Sir, I have the honor to return herewith the two letters of James Murdaugh Esq. left by you with me this morning. They seek information in relation ["in relation" *canceled*] to the Rev[olutionar]y Services of Dr. James Martin & Dr. Hugh Martin. Upon an examination of the Rev[olutionar]y records in this office, there is found in an original receipt book of the So. Ca. Line, a receipt as follows,

"Army Comrs. Office[,] Charleston So. Carolina, 28 July '85 Received of John Pierce Esq. Comr. of Army accots. by the hands of George Reid Asst. Comr. Three Certificates dated the 1st March ult[im]o on Interest the 23 April 1783 No. 92 220 B for 600

" " 21 C — 600

" 22 H — 793⅚₀

$1,993⅚₀ dol[lar]s

amounting to Nineteen hundred & ninety three Dollars ⅚₀ in full for balance of pay & commutation due by the United States to Doctor James Martin Surgeon of the 3 Regt. of this State. by order, James Kennedy."

From this Dr. James Martin is shown to have been fully settled with. In relation to Hugh Martin, I find his name entered on a book called "Depreciation of the Pennsylvania Line" as being of that Line as a Surgeon in 1780. He has been fully settled with in that capacity, & has received his commutation. With great respect Y[ou]r mo[st] ob[edient] Se[rvan]t, P.H., [Third] Aud.

FC in DNA, RG 217 (General Accounting Office), Third Auditor: Congressional Letterbooks, 9:59–60.

From JOSEPH WALKER

Charleston, Feb[ruar]y 13th 1846
Dear Sir, I have taken the liberty of addressing you, at the suggestion of Col. F[ranklin] H. Elmore, who has authorised me to use his name with you in reference to Publishing a Series of Pamphlets in defence of our Southern Institutions, which are now so much assailed by Northern & British Abolitionist[s]. Col. Elmore and several other Gentlemen of our State wish me to Publish a series of Pamphlets for *general* distribution, particularly at the north, to try and counteract

in some measure the efforts of the abolitionist by placing in the hands of the well meaning people of the north, documents which will place the Insti[tu]tions of the South in their true position, and at the same time to furnish them with arguments against the abolitionist, which now they are much in want off.

Our purpose is to publish all the leading articles that have been written upon the subject, viz. Prof[essor Thomas R.] Dew[']s Essay, Judge [William] Harper[']s Memoir, [James H.] Hammond[']s Letters, [William Gilmore] Simms['s] answer to Miss [Harriet] Martineau, [Samuel A.] Cartwright[']s Letters, [William J.] Grayson[']s Review of Hammond, [Richard] Fuller &c &, Dr. Fuller[']s Letter, Your Letter to Mr. [William R.] King, (which a copy of I have, having printed it for distribution last Fall) and your Reply to a resolution of House of Rep[resentatives] offered by John Q[uincy] Adams, requesting an alteration & correction of the last census of the United States in reference to negroes. This last document we have not, and would be very much obliged to you if you would furnish us with a copy of it and all the information connected with it which we think was printed. We would be very happy also [to] hear any suggestions that you may make in relation to our project & would [be] glad of information that you can furnish us with. Please address either to myself or to Col. F.H. Elmore.

I hope that I am not tresspassing too much on your time and attention, & trust that my object will be sufficient excuse & with much Respect I Remain Yours Truly, Joseph Walker.

ALS in ScCleA. NOTE: An AEU by Calhoun reads "Mr. Walker[,] wishes my reply to the case of the House on the errors of the last cencus." Joseph Walker (died 1873) was a New Yorker who had lived in Charleston many years and was, with his brother John C. Walker, perhaps the leading publisher in the city.

From ASA BACON

Litchfield Con[necticut], Feb[ruar]y 14th 1846

Dear Sir, Your course, relative to the Oregon, has received the unqualifield [*sic*] approbation of the good & the wise men of this nation—and of this World. Persevere, and by the blessing of God upon your efforts, our country may yet be saved. Very respectfully your Obed[ient] Ser[van]t, Asa Bacon.

ALS in ScCleA.

From AARON CLARK

New York [City,] Feb[ruar]y 14th 1846
D[ea]r Sir, I presume I am not the first person who has addressed
you previous to an introduction. And I ask your forgiveness for
trespassing too unceremoniously upon your time and *privilege*. But
my young daughter has a friend residing in Virginia to whom she
has directed the enclosed harmless "Valentine." Kiss K—— is a relative of Mr. [Henry A.?] Wise. She is exceedingly desirous to obtain
your autograph—and I have undertaken the task of asking Mr. Calhoun to condescend so much as to place his name as a frank on the
enclosed letter and allow it to be dropped into the post office with
his own. If this request be improper you will of course pardon me
for making it—& in a few weeks my daughter & myself will be in
Wash[ington] & hope to have the honor of asking your forgiveness
["for" *canceled*]. I have the favor to be known *here* as one who has
been Mayor of *New York*. Ever, with the most profound respect
Y[ou]r most H[umb]l[e] S[ervan]t, Aaron Clark.
P.S. Allow me to thank you as I do from the bottom of my heart
for your noble efforts to preserve the peace of our beloved Country.
A.C.

ALS in ScCleA.

From R[ICHARD] K. CRALLÉ

Lynchburg [Va.,] Feb[ruar]y 15th 1846
My dear Sir: It was my purpose to have visited Richmond some
weeks ago; and I delayed writing under the expectation of seeing
your friends in the Legislature, and sounding their feelings[,] opinions and future plans of operation. Engagements of an imperious
character have, however, defeated my wishes, and I write merely to
inform you of the state of public sentiment in this immediate section.
From what I see in the public papers I fear that the anticipations
expressed to you in my letter of November last, are fully realized, at
least so far as the Oregon question is concerned. You will not only
not be sustained, but denounced by the Administration Party proper
in both Houses. You must, of course, be thrown with the Whigs; a
position of no little delicacy and embarrassment. Still I do not see
how you could well have avoided it. Knowing the fixed principles

upon which you would act, I would not doubt but that the first step of your opponents would be to throw you into a false position; though I did not expect Gen[era]l [Lewis] Cass would have been foremost in the movement. I suppose there was an understanding between him and the President, and that the recommendations of the Message as to the notice, were designed to arm him against you; as your views on the subject must have been well known to Polk. But *cui bono?* Is this movement to result in favour of Cass only? Will [Silas] Wright postpone his pretensions? Such seem to be the indications at present. I supposed they would coalesce against you in the first instance of course; but will there be not some jar between them in the sequel?

I take it for granted the notice will pass the Senate by a small majority. What will be the result? Will the negotiations be renewed? If not may we not anticipate a speedy collision with G. Britain? These are questions of engrossing interest throughout this section of the State. The Administration stand only upon the assurance that the measure will *prevent* war. Should the opposite result be probable, it would have but little support. Few even go so far in its defence. Your course is approved by a vast majority of the People; and must, I think, add to your strength in the State—more especially if the subject should assume a more threatening aspect after the notice has passed.

It seems to me in the present attitude of affairs, having been forced by the Administration into a *quasi* opposition with the Whigs, I should not much regard the future consequences. Your principles and duty required you to occupy your present position, and I see no reason why, *without committing yourself to them,* you should not secure the advantages it may offer. It is madness again to trust to any one of the school of Polk. None of the *Clique* can ever be trusted again. We must be in stern opposition to them *forever* hereafter. The Whigs will not, I think, attempt to succeed on any one of their Party. A new Candidate must be started, who can carry a portion of the Republican Party, and at the same time secure their support. Already the leaders hereabouts point to you as the man; and many who have been heretofore hostile, now proclaim their readiness to enlist for the war in your favour. This, I apprehend, will be the final result of present movements. The political gamblers of the Party will never consent for you to remain where you can check them in their system of plunder and corruption. A separate organization of your friends is absolutely necessary; and through [James A.] Seddon, [Robert M.T.] Hunter and Baley [*sic*; Thomas H. Bayly] much might be effected before the adjournment of the Legislature.

These are the views which present themselves to me here—though I am as you may suppose in profound ignorance of the state of public matters at Washington.

What is the state of the Press in the Metropolis? Mr. Cawthorn [*sic*; Richard Cawthon] the former Editor of the [Lynchburg Republican] Paper here is anxious to establish one in Washington. He is the best practical manager I know, and devotedly your friend. He has some means, and would only need an Editor. He is ready at a minute's warning, if your friends should deem it advisable.

Pray inform me what is the disposition of [Dixon H.] Lewis. I see he voted against you some weeks ago. Is he estranged from you? I wrote him[?] two months since, but have received no reply.

When you can command leisure, pray drop me a few lines to let me know if I can render any service. My *nights* are my own here, and I could devote them to some use, if I knew exactly the state of affairs.

We have not heard whether Mrs. C[alhoun] is with you. Should she be be pleased to present to her our kindest and most affectionate regards. Mrs. [Elizabeth Morris] Crallé also desires to be respectfully and cordially remembered to you. Mary is at school in the Country. Very truly and gratefully yours, R.K. Crallé.

ALS in ScCleA.

From MARCUS MORTON, [former Governor of Mass.]

Boston, Feb[ruar]y 16, 1846

Dear Sir, Without my consent and against my wishes I was appointed Collector of this port. I at first determined that I would not accept the office. But the importunities of my friends including almost all of the most respectable democrats in the State who seemed to think I owed it to the party, and that my refusal would ["be" *interlined*] a great injury to the party did much to overcome my first determination. Then, the personal request of the President [James K. Polk] being added, induced me to accept.

I had twice before refused the same office and I assure you I deeply regret that I did not now follow the dictates of my own Judgement. The business is not at all to my taste and in any event I will not long remain in it.

I may be allowed to say that my appointment was most favourably received, by the whole community. And were the question of my confirmation submitted to all the people of the State, or to the democratic portion of them, or to the whig portion of them—or to ["all" *interlined*] the businessmen—or to the democratic portion of them, or to the whig portion of them, I ["should" *interlined*] have no fear of the result under the "*two thirds*" or even a three quarters' rule.

An opposition however to my appointment has been got up but I am confident I don[']t say too much when I say that it owes its origin entirely to disappointed office seekers—either men who have been removed from office or disappointed in their applications. It ["are" *canceled and* "is" *interlined*] not unexpected to me that this opposition is carried to Washington and that efforts are being made by artful and indefatigable men to induce the Senate to reject my nomination. Now however unpleasant the office may be to me, I assure you a rejection would be a source of deep mortification to me. I have taken no steps to induce the Senate to make a favourable decision. I have no wish to do so. My only wish is that they should obtain the truth. I have no correspondent in Washington. I have written only two or three letters to any members of Congress during the Session. I hear objections are made against me, but what they ["are" *interlined*] I know very little except what I get from that most uncertain source[,] letter writers for papers. I therefore presume I have very little ["correct information" *interlined*] of what occurs in relation to myself.

It is said that very strong efforts have been made to induce yourself and your Southern Friends to vote against me. I know not how much truth there may be in the report. But our excellent friend Col. Peirce [Franklin Pierce] of N. Hampshire attached so much importance to it that he advised me to address you on the subject. In obedience to his advice ["that" *canceled*] I now take the liberty to submit these remarks to your consideration. I may have been misled by the reports; but it is reported that I have been charged with *Abolitionism, Nativeism,* and *prejudice against yourself and your friends.*

Abolitionism

I should be glad to have my Southern friends understand my true position on this subject, and I would willingly abide their Judgement. I admit in the outset that I am *opposed* (if you please) *decidedly opposed to slavery*. But I deny most emphatically that in any way I ever did any thing to aid or encourage the abolition party or the doctrine of abolition. I have ever opposed any interference with the domestic regulations and laws of the slave-holding States. They alone are responsible for their principles and conduct as we are for ours. As a private citizen; as a professional man, and as a judicial and executive officer, I have exerted myself to secure to our Southern brethren a full and fair execution of the laws, in relation to their slave property. While I was at the Bar, a Virginian undertook to reclaim his ["property" *canceled*] slave under the U.S. laws. But he was resisted, indicted for assault & Battery on the Slave and thrown into prison. No member of this Bar would appear for him. I went forward, at the hazard and loss of business and reputation, procured bail for him and with the aid of my young partner carried his case through the courts and sustained the law against passion and prejudice. The decission [*sic*] may be seen in the 2d [volume] of Pickering[']s Rep[orts] Com[monweal]th v. Griffith.

I have for a long time been before the public in a situation which exposed me to many calls which I was under the necessity of answering; and I have written ["numerous" *interlined*] letters, perhaps a hundred on this subject yet my op[p]onents have found only two, and these ["private" *interlined*] ones, which they thought would tend to support the charge. If they had produced the others[,] especially those written with more care for more public occasions, they would have shewn that I always opposed the organization and movements of the Abolition party and all interference with the municipal affairs of the Southern and all other States. If they will refer to my official acts they will find in them evidence not to support but to refute the charge. When I was Governor in 1840 and 1843 the two parties seemed to run a race for the favour of the Abolitionists, who held the balance of power in the State; and passed several very high-toned abolition and anti-Texas resolves, some of them unanimously. These, notwithstanding the strongest importunities of some of our leading democrats I refused to approve. And now, some of the men who blamed me for not signing them, try to involve me because at the request of the Legislature, I forwarded them to their destination—or rather the Secretary did under ["a usage &" *interlined*] an implied authority from me.

In relation to the two private letters refer[r]ed to, only extracts are published. Whether these are correct copies, I have no means of Judging. I do not mean to be understood that I think there are any material alterations. But the parts omitted would shew ["the occasions on which they were written and" *interlined*] that they were private and confidential. The one to [John G.] Whittier was written in answer to one received long before and to which an answer had been promised. I had ["made" *interlined*] repeated efforts to convince the more honest Abolitionists that their measures defeated the very object they had in view. I desired to try that argument with Whittier, who is a talented and I believe a very honest man.

The letter [of *ca.* 11/1837] to [Morton] Eddy was written in very great haste and very late in the night. It was expressly asked in confidence and written in confidence. Had I deemed it possible that it could ever be published I should have taken care to use ["very" *canceled*] different language. You will at once perceive the difference between hasty unguarded expressions used to a confidential friend and language prepared to be seen by everybody. You are doubtless aware that the Eddy letter was published in violation of the strictest confidence, & an express promise.

It may have been stated that I signed the resolve to appoint commissioners to Charlestown and N. Orleans and ["a" *interlined*] law to authorize marriages between whites & blacks. If so I can only say it is *false.*

I defy any man to produce any proof that I am an Abolitionist or ever favoured the Abolitionists. There is not a prominent man in Massachusitts [*sic*] against ["whom" *interlined*] stronger evidence cannot be produced. I have been misunderstood as well as misrepresented; and a strong desire to set myself right has carried me quite too far in these remarks. Yet had I time I might add many more circumstances in refutation of this charge. But ["I" *interlined*] trust I have said enough. I close with the assumption that no patriotic Southern man will be influenced in his vote upon a man because he is *opposed* to slavery and no Northern man will ["be" *interlined*] influenced against a man because he is in *favour* of slavery.

Nativeism

No more unfounded charge can be brought against me than this. From the days of the Alien law to the present I have always been an advocate for the Naturalization law and the rights of foreigners— and especially [Roman] catholics. I have heard that some quotations from a letter of mine, have been circulated with a view to raise an impression that I am unfavourable to the catholics. It is wholly untrue. I never was influenced against any man on account of his religion[,] catholic or protestant. Few if any men ever went farther in favour of religious liberty and perfect equality of religious denominations. I might in proof ["refer" *interlined*] to many of my printed opinions while on the bench.

I was called upon to reccommend [*sic*] a man for a Post-Master in North Bridgewater. There were two candidates. One I suppose a protestant supported by nearly all the democratic citizens of the town and by the County Committee. The other of whom I knew nothing was represented to me by respectable men to be an unfit person. They said he was extremely unpopular and as causes of this said that he was a chatholic [*sic*] and a political trimmer. I knew the Inhabitants of the town were very calvinistic and could but infer that they would be very averse to have a catholic Postmaster, as the Gentlemen stated to me. I supposed the aversion of the people to the man whether founded on prejudice or reason, formed some objection to his appointment. I therefore repeated to the Post-Master what had been told me[,] not as facts known to me—but as what ["had" *interlined*] been *said* to me. A reference to my practice will test my opinion in this matter. There are in the Boston Custom House *five* or six catholics, which they will admit is their full proportion. In my removals I have not displaced a single catholic. Strong objections were made to one but in my investigation of the subject, I assure you he fared none the worse for being a catholic. It was my intention not [to] let the man[']s religious faith have any influence; but if it had any it was ["not" *interlined*] unfavourable to the Catholic.

It has been the policy of certain office seekers, who were removed by me or who imagine that their chance of getting office will be increased by my rejection, to represent that I have been influenced by our late presidential predilections. Those who circulate this story don[']t believe it and I know it to be untrue. A reference to facts will show its falsity. I have removed *eight* or *ten* officers who called themselves *democrats*. Every one was for what I deemed *good cause*. It was either because he was unfaithful or incompetent or of objectionable moral character. In removals or appointments I never enquired into any man[']s Presidential preferences; and did not know them except in a very few cases. In my removals I happened to discharge every [Martin] Van Buren man in the office. And in my appointments I happened to include a portion of the friends of all the different candidates. Untill this charge I did ["not" *interlined*] know the preferences of one third of the men in office[.] But I have since requested one or two Gentlemen to make enquiries;

and they inform me ["that" *interlined*] of the men holding office under me, a *large majority* were and are *Calhoun men.*

In my official ["course" *interlined*] I have been on the most friendly terms with my predecessor [Lemuel Williams, Jr.] and have to a great extent ["been" *canceled*] followed his advice, especially in reference to removals—and those who have made the greatest complaint and are now the most active against ["me" *interlined*] were removed by ["my" *canceled*] his advice and from information communicated by him.

I suppose many things have been or may be fabricated of which I never shall have knowledge. I know how indefatigable and unscrupulous my opponents are. But I cannot excuse myself in going any farther. I will therefore close by renewing to you the sincere assurance of the high respect & consideration of Your Obedient Servant, Marcus Morton.

ALS in Vi, Robert M.T. Hunter Papers; PC in Charles Henry Ambler, ed., *Correspondence of Robert M.T. Hunter,* pp. 79–83. NOTE: Morton's appointment was confirmed by the Senate on 5/28/1846 by a vote of 28 to 11.

From AARON H. PALMER

New York [City], February 16th 1846

Sir, I beg to acquaint you that having conducted a foreign agency in this city during the last 15 years for the purpose of making known in foreign countries, the superior skill of our mechanics, manufacturers and machinists in some of the most prominent branches of American Industry, particularly in the construction of steam vessels, steam engines and machinery, generally; and to solicit orders in such business, I have been at great labor and expence in issuing and transmitting throughout the West India Islands, Mexico, Central America, all South America, Egypt, Turkey, Russia, Asia, Africa, Australia, Oceania &c. upwards of 140,000 large circulars in 4 languages, relating thereto, and of which about 14,000 contained a series of lithographed drawings of steamers, with estimates *pro forma* of the cost of construction and outfit thereof, in this port. This has been the means of eliciting a great variety of orders for many objects of our Industry—including a large order from the Pasha of Egypt, and for several steamers that have been constructed here for foreign accounts.

With the circulars addressed by me to Independent Eastern Sovereigns, Sultans, &c. I have generally sent the latest American Almanac[s], Maps and statistics of the United States, Publications of the American Institute, Agricultural Periodicals, and files of the latest New York Newspapers and Prices current; with the addition, to the Japanese Government, of the Constitution and Bulletins of the National Institute, for the Presidents of the Imperial Colleges of Jeddo and Miako; and samples of cotton and Tobacco seeds &c. This general distribution of these circulars ["had" *altered to* "has"] led to an extensive correspondence with most of those countries, and a desire has been manifested on different occasions, by several of the High Authorities thereof, to open commercial relations, and form Treaties with the United States.

In 1838 I submitted to my late friend John Forsyth, when Sec[retar]y of State, a letter in Arabic, I had then recently received from the Sultan of the Comoro Islands, in which he expressed a desire to make a Treaty with the U.S. as he had done with the English. Mr. Forsyth, to my surprise, did not know of the existence and situation of those Islands, until I pointed them out to him on a map, in the Dept. of State, and explained to him that they are 5 in number, inhabited by an intelligent and hospitable race of Arabs, carrying on considerable traffic with Madagascar, the east coasts of Africa and Arabia, are much frequented by American and English vessels for trade, and by our whale ships for refreshments; he promised to lay the Sultan's letter, of which I gave him a brief translation, before the President; but I regret to state that no further action was had thereon by our Govt. The Sultan is since dead, and his son Abdullah has succeeded to the sovereignty of those Islands. The natives style themselves the Hingoorna Tribes; Johanna their capital. I take leave to annex herewith, for your information, a literal translation of the Sultan's letter.

From such correspondence, the publications of the American and Foreign Missionaries, the documents and communications of the Royal Economic Society of the Philip[p]ine Islands, Manila, of which I have the honor of being corresponding Member for the U.S. and which has voted me a Gold medal, and other valuable Testimonials for my services; and from the leading Journals of the British Possessions and Establishment in India, China & Australia, which have been regularly sent to me for several years past, I have been enabled to collect a mass of valuable statistics, and important information relative to the movements and progress of civilization, trade and commerce, in the Eastern Hemisphere, which I am now desirous of placing at the disposition of our Government, and making profitably available to the commerce and Industry of the country, by a special Mission to the East, for that purpose.

With respect to Japan, I have obtained with great care and research, at official sources in Holland, personally, in 1839, the Journals and Reports of the latest Dutch Resident and Mission to Jeddo, and from other reliable accounts and narratives, a variety of interesting facts and particulars, attesting the superior intelligence, civilisation and refinement of that remarkable people, above all the surrounding Asiatic Nations. The Japanese Govt. takes great interest in the progress of science, and political movements in Europe, and maintains a Board of competent linguists at Nanjasaki [that is, Nagasaki], thoroughly versed in the principal European languages, to translate and publish in their own Japanese Encyclopedias and Periodicals, the latest discoveries in Science, and improvements in the Arts, together with notices of important political events, which they derive from the Dutch Journals, for the information of their people; and the President of the Imperial College at Jedd[o], is reported ["to" interlined] be well versed in the Mathematics and Astronomy. The people evince an increasing desire for more extended intercourse with foreign nations; whilst the Govt. has gradually relaxed its arbitrary and rigid restrictions on their trade and intercourse with the Dutch and Chinese, since the English war with China, and the opening of the Privileged ports of the latter, by Treaty stipulations with England[,] France & the U.S.

In this auspicious state of things I have been encouraged to renew my efforts to open a correspondence with the Governor of Nanjasaki, and the Ziogoon, or First Governor of the Empire, at Jeddo; and on ten different occasions, by the favor of my friend Chevalier [Jean Corneille] Gevers, the Chargé d'Affaires of the Netherlands, at Washington, via Batavia, per[?] privileged Dutch ships in the Japanese Trade, and through my correspondents in Manila, and China, by privileged Chinese Junks trading regularly from Ningpo to Nanjasaki, I have forwarded some, with the superscriptions in English and Chinese, containing respectively the enclosures, as above mentioned; and have recently received advices that several of those voluminous missives had safely reached their destination, and been formally received.

In addition to the privileges of commercial intercourse with Nanjasaki, the only port at which the Dutch and Chinese are permitted to trade with that country, it would be very desireable for our Government to obtain permission for the numerous ["American" *interlined*] whale ships employed in the lucrative sperm Fishery on the coasts of Japan to enter any of the ports and harbors of the Japanese Archipelago for repairs, or refreshments, and for hospitality and succor, in case of shipwreck.

In respect to Cochin China, I have reason to believe that the present Emperor is more favorably disposed toward foreigners than his immediate predecessor, the late despotic and tyrannic Ming-Ming [that is, Minh-Mang], who declined receiving our Envoy Mr. [Edmund] Roberts in 1833; and that Government, it is to be hoped, will ere long, see the policy and expediency of imitating the ["Chinese" *canceled and* "recent" *interlined*] example of China. Borneo, Celebes, and the other independent islands of the Indian Archipelago, and Papua, offer an immense field for the profitable extension of American trade and commerce in those seas, where, it ought to be one of the objects of the proposed Mission, to select some suitable port, as a mart and rendezvous for our Traders, and whalers. The English and Dutch are making great efforts to control and monopolise the trade with the natives of those Islands, the former having lately obtained from the Sultan of Borneo proper, a cession of the Island of Laboan [that is, Labuan], lying adjacent to Borneo, abounding in coal, and which they intend to establish as a mart for trade, and obtain for [it] a line of English steamers to ply between India and China.

About 2 years since I received highly encouraging accounts from Burmah, that Tharrawaddy the King, had framed and put up several of my circulars in his Palace at Amarapoora, & was desirous of procuring one or more steamers from this ["country" *canceled*] city, and make a Treaty with the U.S. By recent advices from that country I learn that he has been deposed on account of his insanity, and one of his legitimate sons, a minor, proclaimed King, under the Regency of Prince Mokkou[?], uncle to the late King. The prince is distinguished for his love and patronage of science, and was about 3 years ago upon my recommendation, elected a corresponding member of the National Institute. With Prince Y. Momfanoi, half brother to [Rama III,] the King of Siam, also an enlightened and enterprising Prince, speaking and writing our language exactly, I am in frequent correspondence, having likewise recommended him as a corresponding Member of the N.I. and sent him his document in 1842.

Under these circumstances, deeming the subject of sufficient importance to merit the serious consideration of our Government, on the 31st ult. I addressed a letter to the President containing some of the particulars as above, and took the liberty of submitting to him the expediency of sending a Commissioner with Plenipotentiary powers, similar to the Mission of Mr. Roberts to Siam &c. and of Mr. [Caleb] Cushing to China, in a Sloop of War, to open intercourse and make commercial Treaties with the Independent Sovereigns, Sultans &c. of the undermentioned Islands and maritime nations of the East, with which the U.S. may not hitherto have made any Treaties, viz: The Sultan of the Comoro Islands; Queen of Madagascar; Schah of Persia; King or Regency of Burmah; Emperor of Cochin China; Sultans and Rajahs of Borneo, Celebes, and other principal Islands of the Indian Archipelago; and the Emperor of Japan.

The mission to consist of a Commissioner, or Envoy, Chief Sec-[retar]y of Legation, to be fully empowered to act in the event of the death, or other impediment of the Commissioner, Private Sec[retar]y and a limited number of attachés; including a Physician, who ought to be a skilful Naturalist and Botanist, with a suitable collection of American seeds &c. for distribution and exchange, and to make collections of minerals, seeds, plants &c. of the countries to be visited, to be provided, moreover, with suitable presents, such as Maps, and statistics of the U.S. and specimens of American products, manufactures and industry, to be selected for the occasion and adapted to the wants or trade of these nations, respectively. To proceed successively to Johanna; Thannannarivo [that is, Tananarive, Madagascar]; Teheran, from Bassorah or Bashir[?] on the Persian Gulf; Rangoon and Amarapoora; Hué, the principal ports of Borneo, Celebes, and other Islands of the Indian Archipelago; and Nanjasaki and Jeddo; touching in the course of the ["voyage" *canceled*] expedition, at Zanzibar, Mocha, Muscat, the Pepper ports of Sumatra, Batavia, Singapore, Ban[g]kok, Manila, Canton, Hong Kong, Amoy, Fou-Chow-Fou, Ningpo, Shang-Hai, and the Loo Choo Islands; and generally to protect American interests in those remote seas and countries, and open new markets for the trade and commerce of our enterprising Merchants and Navigators; returning by the way of Oregon, California &c.

As a Mission of this character would naturally excite the rivalry and jealousy of other nations ["having colonial possessions or establishments in the East" *interlined*] especially the English and Dutch; it would perhaps be desirable, for obvious reasons, to fit out and expedite it as quietly as possible; the Commissioner to use due diligence and despatch, and conduct the respective negociations with as little parade and ostentation as may be required for the successful accomplishment thereof.

I have also addressed letters of the present tone to [James Buchanan and George Bancroft] the Secretaries of State and of the Navy, Gen[era]l [Lewis] Cass, Mr. [Daniel] Webster and other friends in the senate, soliciting their influence and co-operation in the furtherance of the Mission, and of my claims to be placed at the head of it, whenever authorised by our Government; and would now try respectfully to bespeak your Patronage in favor of it; thinking that the attention I have so long devoted to the subject, my known untiring energy, activity, rigid temperance, and business habits, practical knowledge of several foreign languages, together with some slight pretensions to Oriental Scholarship, would have due weight with the President and senate in making and confirming the appointment. I have the honor to be With great respect, Sir, Your Most Ob[edien]t Ser[van]t, Aaron H. Palmer.

[Appended] Translation:

To the American city of New York: For the beloved Sheikh Aaron H. Palmer, No. 49 Wall St. May Allah be his Guide! Amen! Badooh[?]!

By the Grace of the Most High:

To the dearest[?], the most glorious, the most generous Sheikh Aaron H. Palmer, the honored, the exalted, the magnificent, the contented. May Allah the Most High, be his Guide! Amen! Now after offering the honor and protection from the Hingoorna[?] city and its inhabitants, this is what I tell thee. Thy noble letter arrived and we read it. Thy friends understood its contents. May Allah reward thee well! Thou sayest in thy letter that thou desirest selling and buying in our land, and that thou wishest for friendship with us. Thou art welcome. We thank thee and accept thy offer. Thou didst tell us that we should advise thee of any thing that we should need from thee. Again we thank thee and inform thee that thou mayest send to us a person on thy part that shall dwell in the Hingoorna country. In order that thy business may be complete a Bazaar of the merchants, and every thing that there is in the country shall be made ready on our part, if it please God. Whatever shall be wanted in these regions shall be paid for on delivery.

I and all my Hingoorna Tribes request that thou unite us with the American Tribes, in friendship and good fellowship like as we are united with the English, and we will serve you all as we serve them. Now we have conceived here a great desire for the American Tribes. Tell them to send us their letters, or a Man of War Ship on their part, and we will bind ourselves by a binding Treaty. Now the thing we need and desire from thee are sealed letters of advice for our assurance, and in order that thou mayest know that this letter is from us, we stamp it with our seal. We request that thou send us all kinds of linnen goods, and cottons, both white and brown, and fine stripes[?]; and all kinds of woollen cloths; and ten bedsteads and sixty chairs; all kinds of Glass; lamps, large and small, and some for placing on the table; and fine silk handkerchiefs. This is what we tell thee. Now salutation and prosperity be with thee forever!

Dated the 10th of the month Drot Hugeh[?], 1252[?], (corresponding to about 10th March 1837). From thy friend the Sultan the Sublime, son of the Sultan Abdullah the Sublime, Shirazy.

ALS in ScCleA. NOTE: An AEU by Calhoun reads "Mr. Palmer. Relates to ["th" *canceled*] a mission to the east."

From CHARLES ANTHONY

Arnoldton[,] Campbell County Va.
17 February 1846

Dear Sir, Altho an entire stranger to you I take the liberty to address this note to you to inform how much your friends are pleased with your course on the Oregon controversy. You are gaining the good opinion of those who were before politically op[p]osed to you. I have not seen a single man that does not disapprove of the President[']s [James K. Polk's] course and that it will lead to war. They believe he is influenced by those who are aiming at the next Presidency and don[']t regard the distress and ruin it will bring on the Country. A war with England would nearly ruin Virginia as she would have no market for her Tobacco. It would not bring one dollar per Hundred. I knew my Father in the time of the last war with England to exchange a h[ogs]h[ea]d of good Tobacco for one sack of salt and had to give three dollars to boot. Such would be the effect of a war at this time. It would enrich the northern manufacturers at the expense of the Southern States. It is very astonishing that Southern members should be in favor of any measure that John Q[uincy] Adams and [Joshua R.] Giddings should approve of, that of itself should make them disapprove of giving the notice. The people in this section of the Union look upon you as the only man whose weight of character and influence, can avert the calamity of war from our beloved country; and they look with confidence to your doing all that man can do to effect it. With great Respect yours Truly, Charles Anthony.

ALS in ScCleA; PC in Boucher and Brooks, eds., *Correspondence*, p. 325.

From J[OHN] S. BARBOUR

Catalpa [Va.,] Feb[ruar]y 17th 1846

My dear Sir, I was not from my house until yesterday. Nor was there a very large assemblage of the people but I heard no dissenting voice from Whig or Republican to the course of the Virginia delegation in Congress. I mean a majority of the delegation on the question of notice [on Oregon].

I heard from both parties the strongest approbation of your course thus far.

I hope that we shall be released from the evils of war & that the national Honour will be maintained & preserved without tarnish.

The "point of honour" as [John] Randolph once said to you in my presence, (& he quoted [Charles J.] Fox as his authority for it) should never be surrendered. On this Nootka Sound question [Edmund] Burke [in "1791" *interlined*] said in the British Parliament, "He hoped the amicable adjustment of this matter would not be incompatible with the National Honour. *As we ought never to go to war for a profitable wrong, so too we ought never to go to war for an unprofitable right.*" "He trusted therefore that that [*sic*] the intended armament wou'd be considered as a measure ["not" *interlined*] to terminate the war happily, but carry on the negotiation vigorously." "He had seen three wars & we were gainers by neither." "Our abilities & resources were great, but a Country manifested her magnanimity most clearly, when her moderation was proportionate to her power." These were the words of Edmund Burke ["on this identical topick with Spain" *interlined*] & if our power be equal to the boast of every minatory Bobbadil [*sic*] & every ragged lazzaroni, we might draw counsel from the wisdom of that great conservative politician whose voice was always on the [*one word or partial word canceled*] side of that "Liberty, which is security from wrong."

I hear direct from Richmond, that the ultra's of the *Ochlocracy* go for notice & for war. The Gov[erno]r ([William] Smith) is with them. The party is feeble & powerless for any other good or ill, than their capacity to change front on the field in the face of the enemy &

diminish our strength by defection from principle with ["out" *inter-lined*] cohesion with the Whigs.

The motive avowed is that [Robert M.T.] Hunter & [Lewis E.] Harvie will not join in the mischievous purposes of the worst of the party, who make politicks a trade & are faithful only as long as they are fed.

You need not doubt this intelligence. My son had it from the lips of *"Extra"* [that is, Governor "Extra Billy" Smith] last Friday, who affects to have discovered a plot to elect Hunter next winter to the Senate & to his exclusion, by a combination of all the Whigs & the *Anti Extra* democrats.

I throw this out to you that you may be guarded. When Lathem[?] told me of this (in effect) weeks past; I gave it credence. Smith[']s explanation made me pause, but this recent declaration, when all the guards which distrust plants round evil avowals were away, he spoke & declared as I write you.

The State is perfectly safe—Sound to its core, and will do its duty *malgré* all treachery & perfidy.

I write you because you ought to know the public sentiment. *Preserve the point of Honour* ["*at all hazards,*" *interlined*] and preserve the national peace ["*if you can*" *interlined*]. That is the sentiment of Va. & ["it" *interlined*] rides over every other. With perfect Respect, in great haste, Y[ou]rs Sincerely, J.S. Barbour.

ALS in ScCleA.

From JOHN C. CALHOUN CARROLL

Cincinnati, Feb[ruar]y 17, 1846

Dear Sir, I presume to direct this document and matter to your Honor, humbly hoping that thereby I may not place myself in an offensive position before you. You Dear Sir had a warm friend in the person of my Father, now deceased, and I was named and Christened after you. In the matter of this Pension I feel for the Old Revolutionary Hero [Thomas Auten] who is truly an object of public Charity. I do all I have done for him truly gratis.

I published a Dem[ocratic] Newsjournal in City of Natchez Miss. in 1840, The Natchez Political Herald, and last year I publish[ed] &c. the "Marietta Democrat" in Washington Co[unty] Ohio. I studied the Civil Law in the City of N. Orleans. I am well acquainted with the Hon. William Allen and Isaac Parrish of Ohio now in the Congress of the United States also with all the Mississippi Delegation, Jacob Thompson &c. I chose to submit this to your honor in preference to any other. Hon. J.J. Ferran [*sic*; James J. Faran,] Rep[resentative] from our City here is a worthy Gentleman indeed but I would rather have your Honor's attention. I had the pleasure of hearing your address at the "Memphis Convention."

With all due respect and high esteem for your virtue & glorious reputation in our Western Country I remain your most obedient Servant at Command, John C. Calhoun Carroll.

ALS in ScCleA. Note: An AEI by Calhoun reads "J.C.C. Carroll. Relates to a Pension. Attended to & directions given from the Pension office how to proceed. J.C.C."

From ——

Chester County Penn[sylvani]a, Feb[ruar]y 18th 1846
Sir, Permit me to take the liberty of addressing you on a subject of much importance to this Country at the present time & is about being brought before Congress shortly viz. the tariff Question. Although I have not a personal acquaintance with you I have conversed with those who have & your fame as a statesman has perhaps far outtraveled your person. However If I should ever travel to Washington I shall endeavour to get an introduction to you. Some of my young acquaintance have visited the Capital. But I never have ["yet" *canceled*] been there. The first point I shall make on the question above alluded to is that it ["is" *interlined*] incorrect to tax one part of the community for the bennifit of the other part for such in effect is the tarriff of 1842[;] it enriches one part at the expence of the other which I contend is contrary to our form of government & is anti republican. I will briefly state some facts that came under my own immediate observation. When I was at Philadelphia I wished to purchase some New Market muslin by the piece say from 30 to 40 yards in each piece. It could not be obtained for less than 10 C[en]ts p[e]r yard & I understand it is now 11 C[en]ts still advancing. Eighteen months ago the same article was offered to me at 7 & 7½ C[en]ts making a rise of 33 percent on the same Article. Now Sir I am a practical agriculturist & could not understand why the price was so enhanced when I saw by the newspapers that the raw material had fallen to wit Cotton. We should think [it] very singular

if flour advanced to 7 Dollars p[e]r barrell & wheat from which it is made was to fall to 90 Cents p[e]r bushel. I should begin to think something was wrong. This led me to examine into the cause & it resulted in the tariff. Clothing is indispencebly necessary for all classes of Society & the coarser article for the poorest of them[;] therefore the fall of raw material & the rise of manufactured one is certainly a tax on the consumer for the bennefet of a few for it is caused by the tariff & the consumer has to pay the duty eventually in every case ["it" *canceled*] & it amounts [*ms. torn*] indirect tax. Iron is the same & the agriculturist [*ms. torn*] dispense with that for ploughs, Harrows, Carts, waggons [*ms. torn.*] Now Sir why should one portion of citizens be protected in their business by the government at the expence of the other[?] It ought not to be so & I think it is certainly very wrong except the government was greatly in debt or had not sufficient means to car[r]y it on. But such is not fact for the government loans a much above par. Why Sir some of the manufacturing Co. are declaring from 12 to 40 per Cent ["p(e)r annum" *interlined*] on the capital invested after fully defraying all expences & then laying by a large surplus fund to meet incidental expences & some of our individual manufacturers boast that they have made 40,000 forty thousand Dollars nett proffit in one year. Why Sir It would take fifty farms where I live to am[oun]t to that nett proffitt. We ware told during the president[i]al campaign in 1844 if H[enry] Clay was elected grain would go up & the people would get two Dollars p[e]r day & roast bieff for dinner. But thank God he did not succeed. If It had have been so we should have another national Bank & the country flooded with paper currency as the old one did to the ruin of thousands of orphans & widdows as was the case with the Last Bank with a capital of [*ms. torn*] wasted away to nothing. Keep the currency sound & a Judicious tariff & we have nothing to fear, no fluctuations & panicks & business would be steady. The contractions & expansions of Banks makes things very unsteady. If we must have paper currency let us have one that the government shall be accountable for the its [*sic*] redemption. As to the tariff of 1842 it was got up without proper discrimination & certainly ought to be modified & I Hope Peresident [James K.] Polk will be firm & endeavour to car[r]y out his views expressed in his message. Why Sir thousands of Dollars were expended by the manufacturing interest in publishing pamphlets to prevent the election of J.K. Polk & persons employed to circulate them through the country & those they believed would not take them they were th[r]own into their yard at night to endeavour to get them to read them. Why the campaign of

1844 for the president was carried on entirely different from any thing I had seen before except 1840 & that was not equal to the Last. Large teams of Horses were decorated with ribbons[,] the waggons covered by a canopy & factory girls employed to sing political songs against the present president & also [e]mployed to get all the young men to vote against him they [*ms. torn*] any influence with why this is carrying the point a [*ms. torn*] length to be shure to car[r]y an election. But to the point in question. It has been asserted by the manufacturers that competition will keep down the prices. Now Sir that was asserted as long ago as 1817 but it is not the fact nor never will be. The manufactu[r]ers are combined togather & meet at Philad[elphia] twice a week to regulate prices where there is a regular correspondence kept up all over the union where they exist & the prices are regulated accordingly & it is well assertained what weight of cotton or wool it takes to make a yard of cloth & it is well assertained what the English can send it in for & pay the duty & as it is an article indispencebly necessary for clothing & must be got they will put it up just a shade lower than ["than" *canceled*] it can be imported for into this country & there it will be kept. It is all folly to think a man will sell his goods Lower than the market price even though he should get a great price. A farmer will not sell his butter at Philad[elphia] market for 15 C[en]ts p[e]r lb. when the market will afford him to get 25 C[en]ts. It is not consistant with trade. Another reason why it will not soon be lower is the surpluss if any there should be is shipped to South America to get it out of the market even though it should not afford any proffit after deducting freight &c. But rely on the return cargo for proffit. The tariff will keep up the price here & exporting surpluss will keep the demand steady & Prices can be sustained which prices will afford a very large proffit indeed & make princely fortunes for them out of the earnings of others for wages have not advanced at the factorys (view Pittsburgh not Long since). The only thing that keeps down the exchange in this Country is the produce of the South viz. Cotton[,] rice[,] tobacco & Indigo are nearly all the p[r]oduce we can export except Solely[?] flour & corn meal on which prices would not have been enhanced except for foreign demand as the president said in his message. Now I should like all to live & get along comfortably. We ought & must have a tariff. But give us such a one as will operate on all equally as near as can be done & not one that will take out of the pocket of one & put it into the pocket of the other part of the community. I have much more to say on the subject But as I have filled the sheet it will suffice at present & I intend to call & see you if I should be [*ms. torn*] to see Washington this winter which I shoul[d; *ms. torn*] to see. Resp[ec]t[full]y yours &c a [*ms. torn*] administration & [*ms. torn*] Ag[*ms. torn.*]

ALU in ScCleA. Note: An AEU by Calhoun reads "Anonymous."

From J[ohn] S. Barbour

Catalpa [Va.,] Feb[ruar]y 19th 1846

My Dear Sir, The language of Mr. [William] Allen of Ohio in menace & reproach to England is more offensive than like terms of disparagement which Bonaparte used in 1803 & which provoked an immediate declaration of war. Bonaparte said, "Government asserts with just pride that England single-handed is unable to cope with France." (Carey & Harts edition of [Louis-Adolphe] Thiers Napoleon (Consulate & Empire) No. 4 in pamphlet page 490.) And the translator & Editor says that it was known ["that" *canceled*] this declaration "England cou'd not cope with France," "revolted every English heart" & "from that moment the declaration of war was inevitable."

How worse in taste & judgement is Mr. Allen[']s denunciation "that England 'dare not go to war[']." It is a reproof for her weakness & an insult to her courage.

How did this man get to the Chair of the Foreign Committee? Is God in his wrath to blight us with his curses? Or are we to show the providence of *Luck*, by showing with how little wisdom our Country may be successfully Governed?!! Formerly the wise men came from the East—are all God[']s providences to be reversed, in favour, *or in wo[e] to us?*

Was this appointment the act of the party in the Senate, or the single maneuvre of Mr. [George M.] Dallas?

Judge [Richard H.] Field asked my son whether I had written you of the publication & distribution of the decisions of the Supreme Court.

I know nothing of the subject, and write only what is suggested by others who are your friends. "*De minimis* ["non" *canceled and then interlined*] *curat* [*lex*]" [the law takes no account of trifles] might induce me to forbear this little thing, but it is said the State of Georgia has taken it up, in the vote of its Legislature.

I have neither thought nor feeling but what I write you on it.

I never saw the wheat crop so unpromising.

Do you know anything of the "South down Sheep"? I have the Bakewell; but I am told to day that the South down are offered in New York, Delaware & Phil[adelphi]a.

As they send ["notices of all" *interlined*] all [*sic*] such matters to distinguished Congressmen, if you receive any thing on this point of "South down Sheep," I w[oul]d be glad to know, & w[oul]d gladly purchased [*sic*] a *Ram* & three or four ewes.

If it is thrown in your way (or you can point me the way), by anything before you, I will be obliged to you. All agricultural ["pursuits" *canceled*] pursuits are profitless with us. Grasing [*sic*] of sheep yields a profit on poor lands & the "South down" mutton sells ["highe" *canceled*] highest in the market, as I learn.

Having written you so recently I am reluctant to add to the penalty of reading a longer letter. With all Respect, Y[ou]rs Sincerely, J.S. Barbour.

ALS in ScCleA. NOTE: This letter was addressed to Calhoun in Washington "via Fred[eric]ksb[ur]g mail" and was postmarked in Culpeper on 2/22.

From ROB[ER]T HUDDELL

Philad[elphi]a, February 19, 1846

Sir, I have taken the liberty of addressing you to know if it is your intention of permitting your friends to use your name as a Candidate for the Presidency of the U. States at the next Presidential election. It might be presumption on my part to say, that you can have no idea of the numerous admirers and friends you have amongst the commercial community, who are willing and ready to rally under the "Free Trade" banner hoisted by you. Do not think it impertinent in my addressing you on this subject. Any answer that I may receive shall be strictly confidential.

I would suggest for your consideration when the Tariff Bill comes before Congress, to offer as an amendment to the duty on Sugar—Sugars coming from Porto Rico to pay 5 per c[en]t more than those from St. Croix and Brazil—Sugars from Cuba to pay 7½ per c[en]t more than those from Porto Rico. This will in a measure allay any hostile feelings of Southern planters and [be] an act of justice to the Agricultural States.

I have had it in contemplation for some days past to have written the Hon: Sec[retar]y of the Treasury [Robert J. Walker] on this subject, but as I have stated my views to you, will decline it. I will be pleased to have a copy of the "Tariff Bill" as soon as reported to Congress and will make comments on it, should you desire it. I have the honor to be your ob[edien]t Se[r]v[an]t, Robt. Huddell.

ALS in ScCleA.

To FERNANDO KENNETT, [St. Louis]

Washington, 21st Feb. 1846

My dear Sir, This will be delivered to you by [my] son J.C. Calhoun Ju[nio]r, who I informed you would visit St. Louis this spring with the view of joining some company gowing [*sic*] to the Rockey mountains for his health. From all I can learn, I have concluded that he had better make Fort Bent his head quarters, from which he could join some one of the companies in their hunting excursions into the Rockey mountains. But, it is possible, when he arrives at St. Louis, he may hear of some other arrangement which may be thought to be preferable.

Whatever attention you may show him, while he is at St. Louis, or aid or advice you may afford him towards accomplishing the object of his visit, will place me under lasting obligation. With respect yours truly, J.C. Calhoun.

ALS in MoSHi, Western Travel Papers. NOTE: Bent's Fort was on the Arkansas River in what became Colorado.

To JOS[EPH] H. [*sic*; W.] LESESNE, [Mobile]

Washington, 21st Feb. 1846

My dear Sir, I am much gratified to learn, that our friends contemplate the purchase of the [Mobile] Register, & sincerely hope they may succeed. I am of the impression, that nothing but a good paper in Mobile is wanting to give to them that influence & control in the State, to which they are so well entittled by their intelligence & worth.

I consulted with [Dixon H.] Lewis in relation to the portion of your letter which refers to an editor. We could think of none well qualified, who would agree to take charge of the paper, except Mr. [William L.] Yancey of your delegation. We have shown him your letter & conversed with him on the subject. He sees its importance, and authorized me to say, that he would agree to take the paper on the terms you state, provided he could be assured, that it would give an income of $4000 the first year. Should you think so, write him on the subject. His standing in the State would give him great advantages over any other who could possibly be had.

His loss would be very sensibly felt in Congress. There is no man of the same age of equal standing. If his pecuniary means were more ample, where he now is would be his proper place; but as it is, no one could blame him, if he should retire.

The news by the Cambria is highly important, as you will see. It may be said, almost with certainty, that it puts an end to the hazard of war for the present, while it will do much to ensure the triumph of free trade, & thereby prevent almost the possibility of war between the two countries hereafter. Yours truly, J.C. Calhoun.

Transcript in NcU, Joseph W. Lesesne Papers.

From EDWARD J. BLACK, [former Representative from Ga.]

Scriven County Georgia, Feb[ruar]y 22nd 1846

My dear Sir—I have been watching, from my retirement, the scenes of the American Senate, in which you have been so prominent and influential. In common with your friends in this section of the State I was extremely solicitous for your personal and political success, and not a little anxious about the position you would assume upon some of the more important collatteral questions springing out of the great Oregon controversy. I am highly gratified to be enabled to say to you that your friends entirely approve the course you have pursued, and are proud of the triumphant manner in which you have sustained yourself. I have just returned from Savannah, and the sentiment there in your favour was very decided. Many of the thorough-going whigs, even, in that City, are openly calling themselves "Calhoun men," and the mass of the Democrats avow "*Calhounism*"; a sort of faith which, but a few years since, was denounced by some of the old [Martin] Van Buren leaders as a wild and dangerous heresy, while by others it was silently avoided, as they would gunpowder that might, from the power and efficacy of its materiel, explode to the great detriment of its adherents. In common with yourself your early and constant friends partook of the cold favour which these errors of the public mind begot, and you may well immagin how ardently we feel for yourself and our cause, now that these glimpses of sunshine are harbingers of a brighter and better day. We fully agree with you in your views of principle, policy, and expediency relative to the Oregon question, and do not hesitate to say that you are perfectly right in your opposition to the unadvised and premature war-cry so unnecessarily raised by certain red hot democrats in Congress. I know of no man in Georgia who does not sustain the offer on the part of our government of the 49th degree—and all are agreed, with you, that at least an other effort at negociation should be made before we resort to the *ultima ratio regum*. For myself, I regard one of the greatest curses of war at this Juncture to be the postponement, perhaps indefinitely, of the settlement of the Tariff question; which with us at the South is the great question which absorbs all others, and in the adjustment of it we look to you more than to any other man for aid and assistance. I have recently consulted with a great many of our friends in Georgia ["recently" *canceled*] upon the subject of the next Presidency, and this is what we agree in; namely, that you are our first, and last choice—indeed, that ["we" *canceled*] you are our only choice. That is our determination; and on my part I think you know me well enough to believe that it cannot be shaken. In relation to that preference we do not consult you. It is useless—for other than yourself I have no predilection. But we are anxious to ask your advice as to the *time when* a firm and decided movement ought to be made in your favour. Not a movement deferential to the opinions of others, but one that openly proclaims us the friends of those who go for you, and the opponents of those who go against you. I believe the present to be the proper and oppertune time for your peculiar friends in Georgia to take this uncompromising stand. For we shall have not only the whigs, but some of our own people to bring to terms—and with certain democrats in this State that can only be done by convincing ["them" *interlined*] in ["in" *canceled*] advance that their only hope of success is in coming to us. Between us—perhaps there is a Senator at Washington [John Macpherson Berrien] who it may be necessary to convince in this way. But I do not wish to injure our prospects by a premature movement. And it is to solicit your view as to when it would be advisable to make this demonstration, that I now trouble you with this letter; for the stand *will* be taken—peremptorily, and decidedly—*when* is the only doubt, on our minds. If you deem it proper to confer with your true and unwavering friends upon the subject, let me hear from you, and your communication shall be confidential, if you please, as this is. I would have written you before, but I knew that your time must be very much engrossed, and I feared to multiply your labours of correspondence. Believe me, as Ever, Yours very truly, Edward J. Black.

N.B. I have just conversed with a very intelligent friend from the so[uth] western part of Georgia who confirms every thing I have said of your growing favour with the people of this State. His name is Asa D. Smart, Bainbridge, Decatur Co[unty] Geo[rgia]. Send him a Document occasionally, as he is your friend, and originally from So. Carolina. E.J. Black.

ALS in ScCleA; PC in Boucher and Brooks, eds., *Correspondence*, pp. 325–327.

From DUFF GREEN

Trenton [N.J.,] 22nd Feb[ruar]y 1846
My dear Sir, Excuse me for making a few suggestions on points personal to yourself and which it is important for you to treat of in the debate on the resolutions for notice.

The partisans of [Henry] Clay & [Lewis] Cass are laboring to creat[e] an impression that you are sectional—not national; and that your support of the annexation of Texas is inconsistent with your present course as to Oregon and attribute it to a desire to keep up a "balance of power" between the slave holding and non slaveholding States.

It is important to show that the idea of such a balance of power is preposterous, that the slave holding States are now and ever must be in a minority, that the South stand on the defensive and that the attacks come from both parties at the north, who, knowing that the South are and ever must be in a minority agitate the question because the tendency of that agitation is to create a sectional northern party organised on the basis of placing the government in the hands of *northern* men.

Your course in relation to Oregon is the same now that it has been heretofore. It is the only course that can secure to us the whole of Oregon.

You were *then* for immediate annexation of Texas because that was the only course to obtain the whole or any part of Texas and because the acquisition of Texas was an important step in securing our rights in Oregon.

You are *now* for "masterly inactivity" in relation to Oregon, because that is the only means of obtaining the whole of Oregon & in this connection I would meet and denounce in the most solemn and decided manner the imputation that you have been influenced by any jealousy of the growth or political preponderance of the north as such.

So far from restricting the territory out of which free States are to be made your policy would enlarge that territory. This is now the most important part of the whole subject.

If notice is given now that notice will find the English in undisputed possession of all the country north of the Columbia [River]. How are they to be dispossessed? By force? If so it is war. By negociation? If so will notice strengthen our claim or place the question in a shape more favorable to us? It cannot be denied that so far the negociation and the discussion have been so conducted on the part of England as to throw upon us the *onus* in case of war, and ["at" *interlined*] the same time to place England in a position that she cannot well be the first to resort to hostile measures.

If we give notice England will take measures to prevent settlement north of the Columbia and thus limit our possession to the south. Whereas if we do not give the notice we can take measures to colonise as far north as 54 40 if we desire it, and in a few years possess the whole country without giving cause for war. If we give notice we must abandon all north of 49°, if not all north of the Columbia unless we enforce our claim by war. Whereas without notice we can acquire the whole country up to 54° 40.

This aspect of the question enables you to meet the imputation of "punic faith" which much as you may despise the charge is now the hope of your political enemies. Silence that *charge* for *charge* it is, and you obtain a triumph for yourself & for the country which will have a permanent influence for good. You have never occupied a more enviable position. The eyes of the world are upon you, the hopes of the country rest on you. Millions are prepared to speak your praise—meet this slander and you give an argument to the friends of the Constitution every where that will for a long time silence or overwhelm the abolition movement, for this charge is but the political aspect which that question has assumed and should be so treated.

Again the slave holding influence cannot be increased by bringing ["in" *interlined*] new slaveholding States—that influence depends upon the numerical increase of the slaves themselves and not upon the acquisition of new territory.

Again, If there were but 9 instead of 14 slave holding States the Jealousy of the majority would cease. Now political agitators assert that the[re] is a *minority* holding *equal* political influence and they make war on a system which gives an equality of power to a minority—get rid of this idea of a "balance of power" by showing that no such balance exists and you take from these agitators the foundation on which their agitation rests.

Not having mingled with the masses as I have done you cannot understand or appreciate the effect which the studied misrepresentation of your views and position in relation to this subject has on the public opinion of the North.

At this moment the great body of the people sympathise with you on the Oregon question and the most important results will follow the proper use of the present occasion, for your speech will find its way into every news paper and be read by almost every man in the country capable of reading it. What is more to the point they will be in a state of mind to be favorably impressed by what you say. All that has been said by others prepares the way for you to take this view of the subject and upon your doing so, in my opinion very much depends your standing and influence with the country.

I would call your attention to the remarks of the London Times which you will find in the [New York] Herald of the 21st (yesterday) in which they say that war with the United States will be popular in England, and there is much force and truth in the statement of the reasons for it.

It is said that the notice will not be considered by England as a cause of war or offence. It is even said that England is willing that the notice should be given.

The notice if given strengthens the position of England. It leaves her in possession of all north of the Columbia and compels us to become the aggressor. If we do become the aggressor, after what has transpired in Parliament and the offer of arbitration we will be divided and England united. The consequence will be that we must lose the country north of the Columbia.

Excuse these suggestions. They may have no merit but it is the part of friendship to make them. Yours truly, Duff Green.

ALS in ScCleA; PC in Jameson, ed., *Correspondence*, pp. 1073–1076.

From PATRICK HENRY

Madison County Mississippi, Feb. 22nd 1846

My Dear Sir: The shameful correspondence on the part of our govt: in which the peaceful propositions of the British govt: was rejected, has just been received, and I do not exaggerate the state of public feeling when I state, that it has filled all hearts with apprehension, and alarm, and indignation. I have conversed freely with men of all parties, and I frankly declare, that the *maddest* portion of them are *startled* at the rejection of the overtures of Peace. This is going farther, than even they had bargained for. Tho' loud in their braggart professions, they did not for a moment doubt, but that pacific measures would yet prevail.

The whigs, of whom I am an humble member, look with consolation and hope to the great conservative body, the U.S. Senate, and in particular to you, who have already won the proud appellation, of the great conservator. They, in common with all the South, with a few mad cap exceptions, regard you as the hope of the country, as the only man who can avert the awful catastrophe of a causeless war. Your self sacrificing course, so far as mere party & its behests go, has won for you friends by the thousand—aye, hundreds of thousands. The country will remember such services, rendered in the time of peril, & will take pride in elevating you to the highest pinnacle of fame. I mention this not as inducement to your high prosecution of the course you have chalked out for your self—but as the mere expression of my feelings, & I hope they may be prophetic. If war were necessary or just, none would more loudly call for it than the whigs of the South, but when it is neither, when we can get all we have hitherto claimed without that last & dire resort, it ["is" interlined] wickedness & folly to bring it upon our country. If our claim be so clear, where the objection to submitting it to arbitration, when we can arrange the whole mode & manner of reference? It was the madness of the moon to have rejected it. It will cause the republican principle, which is founded on principles of immutable justice & right, to suffer in the estimation of the civilized world. It places us in the wrong before our friends every where, & will lose us the sympathy & kind feeling of the good & free in spirit ["every where" canceled]. It will not and cannot come to good, and I hope the Senate will *instruct* the imbelice [*sic*] who holds the reins of our once intellectual govt: in the paths of peace, for the sake of the country, and for the sake of proving, that ["that" canceled] those who bear sway, have no right to attempt to build their greatness on their country[']s ruin.

Pardon these remarks, but I felt as tho' I were addressing my own representative. Mr. [Jesse] S[peight, Senator] from our State, has acted nobly with you, & I hope he will stand firmly by you. Again I beg of you to pardon the frankness with which I have spoken. With great respect, y[ou]r friend, Patrick Henry.

ALS in ScCleA.

From ROB[ER]T M. MCLANE

Ba[l]t[imore,] Feb[ruar]y 22, 1846

Dear Sir, I have this morning letters from my Father [Louis McLane] to the 3d Jan[uar]y, and he writes with so much anxiety in regard to our action in Congress on the subject of the Oregon, that I can not refrain from addressing a few suggestions to you, although his letter leaves me to understand that he would write you himself.

He deems it very necessary that the "notice" and also the other recommendations of the message should be sustained, without reserve or qualification, but in a spirit of dignified[,] peaceful and honorable resolution to settle the controversy within the year. With this result accomplished, he does not doubt that the British government, will make such propositions as we may and *will* accept for he seems to have measured exactly the character and force of the war spirit in Congress and does not anticipate much mischief from it. They are beginning to understand us so well in England, that our Co[n]gressional Explosions do no more harm abroad than at home. The extraordinary news in the commercial politics of England seem to have eclipsed the Oregon question, as indeed it well ought to do, both here & there, for I can not doubt, that old England once on[?] the way, ["that" *canceled*] we will be relieved from the task of resisting that School of American statesmen, who have so long struggled to fasten upon us the restrictive system, which they loved for no better reason than that it formed part of the English constitution. Left to battle only with the *"protectionists proper"* on this side of the water, I do not believe the friends of commercial freedom will ever again be in a minority. My Father thinks Sir Robert Peel will carry his scheme in this ["present" *interlined*] parliament, although great doubts are entertained of his success. The struggle will be violent, & should he be driven to a dissolution of Parliament, the chances would be against him. The gold of the aristocracy would be freely showered upon the English constituency.

Our own resolution to shake off the like shackles, operates powerfully to sustain the new movement in England. It is truly wonderful that this principle so long despised and rejected in England, should have burst into such glorious action at the very moment when we are in condition to march hand in hand with our old mother in a work so fruitful of prosperity & plenty to our people. With great respect Your ob[edien]t Ser[van]t, Robt. M. McLane.

ALS in ScCleA.

From Ch[arles] Aug[ustus] Davis, "Private"

Newyork [City,] 23 feb. 1846

My D[ea]r Sir, I take the liberty of inclosing for your perusal a letter [*not found*] from ["R(igh)t Hon(ora)ble" *interlined*] Edward Ellice, a member of Parliament, which contains some remarks about our affairs. Mr. Ellice is an intimate friend of Lord John Russel[l] and sits between him and Lord Palmerston on the opposition side of the House. You may recollect him as a member of the Cabinet under Lord Grey[']s adm[inistration]. He is a warm friend of our Country. You see he takes your views in some respect regarding Oregon. Please after perusal and at y[ou]r convenience return it to me. He does not write the most legible hand but he is a man of strong good sense. His opinion in regard to current & coming Events may be relied on. You will please confine his letter to your own Eye. I am with profound respect Y[ou]r Ob[edien]t Ser[vant] & friend, Ch. Aug. Davis.

ALS in ScCleA.

From P. Gwinner

Philad[elphi]a, Feb[ruar]y 23rd/46

Dear Sir, I cannot resist the pleasure of congratulating you on the late news received from England. Its effect upon this community has already been felt, which is perceptable in the countenance of every business ["man" *interlined*] we meet. I have been told by numerous intelligent men of business, that "the news is of more importance to this country & its future prosperity than any ever received, since the recognition of our independance by England,["] and what is equally gratifying to your friends is, that we owe the result to your foresight and Patriotism in being the cause of such happy effects. Your opponents now concede the point. The war spirits now hang their heads. They must resort to some other means to create political capital to promote the cause of ["those" *changed to* "their"; "several friends" *interlined*] who ["severally"(?) *canceled*] aspire to the succession. The introduction of Corn, Buckwheat, Beef[,] Hides[,] Bacon[,] meat[,] Pork &c free of duty, will be important to the agraculturalists in Penn[sylvania] who will see the propriety of abandoning their protective notions, heretofore so pertinaciously adhered to, & meet England on terms of reciprosity.

The moment I heard of your ["intention to" *interlined*] return to the Senate, I repeated to friend & foe, that you held [James K.] Polk[']s Administration in the hollow of your hand, and that he could not carry any measure adverse to your policy, believing that the whigs would fall into your views on every great ["national" *interlined*] question which might occur save the tariff.

As regards our Collector, my views of policy contained in my former letters are still unchanged, although I have no sympathy for him, but I think his comfirmation would (unless we could have one of your friends appointed, which can scarcely be expected,) ["would" *canceled*] operate beneficially in our future operations in this State. Gov. [David R.] Porter[,] R[obert] Tyler with other prominent politicians are about making a movement for the purpose of defeating [Francis R.] Shunk, of which I gave you a hint in a former letter. I was invited to meet them, which I declined. Many of your ["heretofore" *interlined*] prominent friends seem now disposed to do you justice. Some of whom you little suspect, had given you the Cold Shoulder until very recently. In haste truly [your] friend & h[um]ble Serv[an]t, P. Gwinner.

ALS in ScCleA; PEx in Boucher and Brooks, eds., *Correspondence,* p. 327. NOTE: On 12/29/1845, Polk had sent the Senate the nomination of Henry Horn to be Collector at Philadelphia. The nomination was refused confirmation on 5/25/1846 by a vote of 21 to 25. A few days after that rejection, Polk again nominated Horn to the office, and a month later the Senate rejected the nomination again by an even larger margin.

From J[OHN] C. C. CARROLL

Cincinnati, Feb[ruar]y 24, 1846

Dear Sir, I take the liberty of troubling you with these lines. Some two weeks ago I addressed to your Honor papers in the Pension case of "Thomas Auten" a Revolutionary ["soldier" *interlined*] and now I would respectfully call your kind attention to them and you will ever oblige. I am about starting a News-journal in this City but as you are aware the Party that I belong to (Democratic) are to a dangerous extent divided on the Currency question, part of them *for* a Metallic Currency and part *not* for it, causes it to present a very unpleasant prospect. My *private* opinion is that William Bibb, the Whig Candidate for Gov. (a practicing Lawyer of this City occasionally) will be elected. A large majority of the People of Ohio are for the "Oregon notice" as they quaintly call it. Our winter here has and is unusually long and severe this year. Probably it would be presumption in me to ask you to drop me a line. With high regard and esteem I would respectfully subscribe myself Your most devoted and obedient Servant in all humble duties at Command, J.C.C. Carroll.

ALS in ScCleA.

To T[HOMAS] G. CLEMSON, [Brussels]

Washington, 25th Feb: 1846

My dear Sir, I received yours and Anna's [Anna Maria Calhoun Clemson's] by the Cambria, and we are all happy to learn that Anna has recovered from her indisposition, & that you & the children [John Calhoun Clemson and Floride Elizabeth Clemson] were well. They must, indeed, be growing finely & improving much from her account of them, after making full allowance for the partiality of a mother. I have a great desire to see them.

I think, I wrote you, that I was suffering under a bad cold, accompanied by a severe cough. It continued so long, that I began to get uneasy; but am now in a great measure recovered. My general health continued good during the whole time. I will not, however, dwell on what may be called personal & domestick news, as Mrs. [Floride Colhoun] Calhoun has written Anna by the steamer, & has no doubt filled her ["letter" *interlined*] well, with all of that discription. Her letter was entrusted to Mr. Swit[?], a Belgian ["gentleman, who returns by the Steamer" *interlined*]. I informed you in my last, that we had not heard from you by the Britan[n]ia, that your duplicate of the treaty had not been received at the Department. It turned out, that the letters from you & Anna, had been overlooked in the Department, & that Mr. [James] Buchanan was mistaken, when he informed me, that your duplicate had not been received, as I afterwards learned by Mr. [Francis] Markoe. The letters were received when it was too late to write by the Britan[n]ia. I fear my letter made you very uneasy about them.

I will submit your proposition about your negroes to Andrew [Pickens Calhoun], before I give an answer. Your proposal is based on fair & equitable principles. As soon, as ["soon" *interlined*; *sic*] I hear from him, I will write to you & inform you what we will do, when you can determine what you will do. Negroes have risen considerably in consequence of the high price of rice & sugar. I hope it may prove permanent. If we should agree to take them, we would expect to allow you the fair average price at the time.

The price of cotton is still low; but I cannot doubt, it will rise, as the crop is certainly short by 200 or 300 ["hundred thousand" *interlined*; *sic*] bales. We have not yet sold. Our crop yielded about equal to our calculation.

I have not heard from your place; from which I infer, that all is going on well, as I informed the overseer and old Mr. Mowbley [*sic*; John Mobley] not to write, so long as things were doing well, & no advance needed from me. I will forward the package you refer to, as soon as the new Minister arrives, & I have received it. The ["complemt" *canceled and* "compliment" *interlined*] of the Belgian Government, I hope with you, will be returned; but I apprehend, that nothing will be done, or can be, until we shall dispense with Charges, by substituting resident ministers in their place. My impression is, that the change is desirable; but I fear Mr. Buchanan has not nerve enough to recommend it. I would of course be rejoiced to see you transferred to Berlin, should [Henry] Wheaton be to St. Petersburgh, as he ought to be. You would be, I doubt not, of service there, but I can give you no reason to expect such good luck. I do not think Mr. [James K.] Polk much disposed to favour my friends, though I do not think him hostile. The first opportunity I have, I will ascertain from Mr. Buchanan, how he is pleased with the manner you perform your duty, as you desire. Markoe thinks very highly of it.

Things here are in the same state of uncertainty, that they were, when I last wrote. It is now certain, that there is a decided majority in Congress & the country opposed to war, & in favour of a compromise on the 49th [parallel]; and, if we may judge from Sir R[obert] Peel['s] disapproval of Mr. [Richard] Pakenham's rejection of our offer, he is ready to compromise on the basis of that ["latitude" *canceled and* "line" *interlined*]. And yet, I fear, that the question of peace & war is still uncertain. The parties seem, as if they cannot get together. It is understood, that our government, or rather Executive, will not make the first move towards the renewal of negotiation, & it is to be feared, that the English Governm[en]t has gone as far as it can until ours makes another. In ["meane time" *interlined*] the vital interests of both ["are in danger of being" *interlined*] sacraficed on a mere question of etiquette.

I concur in the views you express in reference to the management of the questions belonging to our foreign relations. It has been such, as to entangle our relations with England, at a critical moment, when they ought to have been on the best footing, & to offend all Europe, when we had the greatest need of conciliating the continental powers.

I have not, as yet, taken part on the question of notice now before the Senate; but shall before it terminates. I have waited developements. The Whigs are uncertain allies, & I have to act with caution.

This is the last day for the steamer & it is now nearly 12 oclock at night, & I must stop.

Say to Anna, I shall next write to her, & would have done so by this, had it not been for ["my excess" *canceled and* "the pressure" *interlined*] of engagements. I am compelled to see company almost incessantly, which, with my correspondence & senatorial duties, leave me no leisure. My love to her & kiss to the children. Tell them how much I wish to see them, and that their Grandfarther [*sic*] is delighted to hear that they are such fine & good children. Your affectionate father, J.C. Calhoun.

ALS in ScCleA; slightly variant PC in Jameson, ed., *Correspondence*, pp. 681–683.

From Tho[ma]s G. Clemson

Brussels, February 25th 1846

My dear Sir, We were very much surprised to learn by your letter of the 29th of ["February" *canceled*] January that my Despatches which were destined to leave Liverpool in the steamer of the 4th of January had not arrived in Washington when you wrote. I can not imagine the cause of the failure or delay, and the manner in which you express yourself leaves me in doubt whether you allude to the arrival of the original copy of the Treaty, for you say that you had learned at the Department on the day previous to the date of your letter, that they had not heard from me, nor received my duplicate of the Treaty, though Mr. [Charles] Serruys had received his. The original copy (that in manuscript which was signed by the minister of Foreign affairs & myself on the 10th of Nov.) was sent by private conveyance to London, and its receipt acknowledged by Mr. McLean [sic; Louis McLane] when he informed me that he had committed it to the care of Prof[essor Samuel F.B.] Morse who left Liverpool on the steamer of the 4th of December. The Despatch which contained the news of the ratifications of the Treaty here by the chambers and many documents accompanying, left here also by private conveyance and was delivered into the hands of John Miller (the Despatch agent) in ample time to go by the steamer that left Liverpool on the 4th of January. No one could be more attentive or careful than myself & I hope that I am exonerated from all blame. I have nothing to do but to attend to business[,] not having money enough either to travel or engage in constant amusement. My business is almost the sole occupation I have. Indeed so far as I am concerned, I care for neither what are called amusements or pass times [sic]. I have seen and had all I care for and much prefer the occupation that arise from my position. If my Despatches are not received at the Department with more regularity, than those sent by the Department to me it is by no means surprising that there should have been delay. As to those sent me, letters have come from the Department by the way of Naples or Bremen and as to Newspapers though a subscriber to the [Charleston] Mercury I have long since ceased to receive that paper, and but an occasional number of the [Washington] Union comes to me but always so much after the news that all interest is lost. I regret the non arrival of the Package, but as it was a very large one can not suppose it has been lost. It contained besides very important documents to the Government many letters, among which a long one to yourself on business &c. I think that the Department of State should acknowledge the receipt of every Despatch. Instead of our Despatches passing through the English foreign office or the hands of a foreigner as is John Miller (tho I believe him to be a very correct man) our Consuls should be charged with the receipt or forwarding of all parcels between Washington and the different Legations, but in that case more care should be exercised in appointing to such offices honourable men and responsible Americans. Such is not the case with all such officers. There for instance is that notorious character Francis J. Grund[,] U.S. Consul at Antwerp. He is a national disgrace to us & his conduct since he has been in Europe has been most exceptionable. He is never at Antwerp and for the last two months has been in France or Lord knows where, but since his arrival in Europe he has not lived any two months in Antwerp. ["It"(?) *canceled.*] His functions are ["filled" *canceled*] performed by a Belgian. The intentions of the Government are not fullfilled by such conduct. He got every thing into such a mess in Antwerp that he was obliged to show himself there as little as possible. He had open quarrels at public tables in which knives were used. Letters of complaint have been addressed to me about him, so that I am glad that he is absent from the country. I understand that he is covertly abusing me in his letters to the United States and for the honour of the country should be put out of office. The salary from fees amounts to between two & three thousand dollars & is daily on the increase and would command the attention of some worthy person.

We had a visit the other day from Mr. [Henry] Wheaton [U.S. Minister to Prussia], who passed through here on his way to London. From all that I can learn and all that he told me I conclude that he has been notified to resign. He said to me that he would return this summer. I presume his successor has been appointed. Mr. Wheaton is doubtless an able man in some respects but I doubt if he be efficient in business matters. Certainly his projet of a treaty with the United States & the Zollverein did not contain much evidence of advantage to the United States. I am convinced that much might be done in Germany to advance the interests of the United States and particularly to increase direct trade between those powers & the Southern States. England takes one million six hundred thousand bales of Cotton whilst Germany receives but seventy thousand and pays England annually seventy millions of Prussian dollars for twists. Under the treaty which I made with Belgium Antwerp is become de facto a part of the Zollverein and by management & tact I believe the Zollverein could be made to place a high duty on twists in which event a trade would spring up directly between the South & the Zollverein through Belgium[,] the principle [*sic*] articles of which would be our Cotton and Tobacco, and carried in our ships. Since I first stated these views here and to [Heinrich Alexander, Baron von Arnim] the Prussian minister formerly at this court, now in Berlin, they have been making quite a noise in Germany & the Baron d'Arnim has written a pamphlet on the subject which has created the greatest sensation throughout Germany. The Zollverein Diet which was to have met in Berlin in January has not been convened. That meeting has been postponed until the result of Sir Rob[er]t Peel[']s measures shall be known. For if those measures should succeed in England the duty which they would have placed on English twists would not answer the same ends they would have done when the cost of production was less.

The fact of it is we have been misrepresented in most instances abroad and if we have advanced it has been in spite of obstacles, and the comparitive insufficiency of our agents abroad. It is to me a matter of the greatest surprise that the U. States should continue to send agents abroad who want the means of exchange or in other words who can not talk for my experience tells me that it is indispensable that one should speak the modern languages and at least the French with fluency. I have been here long enough to know what our agents are doing and how they are considered. I have just received a newspaper[,] The Transcript & Ledger[,] published in Phila-[delphia]. The paper of the 30th of January contains a long letter from Grund dated Brussels Dec. 18th abusing the treaty which I concluded and containing misrepresentations which he knew were unfounded. Every body knows here that the treaty was & is considered as far more advantageous to the U. States than to Belgium & Mr. Deschamps [*sic*; Adolphe Dechamps] stated to me that if he had ["had" *interlined*] the making of the treaty that I would not have obtained the advantages I did. A senator said in committee to him that he ought to be put in judgement for signing such a treaty. I do not believe it possible to make another treaty at this time as favourable & I obtained all that I could do. Mr. Grund knows or ought to know that Belgium is differently situated from either the Hanse Towns or Sweeden [*sic*] and that Belgium has few or no ships and that she can neither build or sail vessels as cheaply as ourselves and that a reciprocity treaty such a one as I made is entirely to our advantage. I do not think the administration should permit an official to act as Grund is doing in writing against a public measure of the kind.

It is impossible for me to know what effect my course & dooings[?] has had in the United States. Mrs. [Floride Colhoun] Calhoun mentions in her letter just received by Anna [Maria Calhoun Clemson] "that every thing was uncertain in Washington and that perhaps I would be desirous of returning shortly." Now I do not know that this was meant and written understandingly but should be pleased to know from you on the subject. I repeat if I had the offer of the income or the place I would choose the former, but do not desire to relinquish the salary, as small relatively as it is, without having something more lucrative to depend upon than my little property in the United States. We can live here by close shaving and that is all and in the mean time whatever is produced from my money and property in the United States goes to swell the capital for the maintenance of my family and their well being after I shall ["cease" *interlined*] to exist.

Belgium is very anxious to secure a line of steamers direct from the United States to Antwerp, and with a view to bring the thing about, they sent to the United States through me the Projet of a postal treaty which they are desirous of concluding. If it be the intention of the U. States to direct a line of steam boats to Antwerp & to make a postal convention with this Government[,] there is no doubt that many more advantages could be obtained by our Government previous to the establishment of the line than afterwards, and I feel convinced that no reasonable demand could be made on the part of our Government that would not be acceeded [*sic*] to by Belgium to secure such a line.

The President [James K. Polk] by repeating Mr. [James] Monroe[']s suggestion against the colonization of the American continent has done injury. It was a kind of gratuitous provocation thrown against all the monarchies of this continent. We had difficulties enough without increasing the bad feeling that already exists against us.

The position which you have taken on that question and on the Oregon has given you a most prominent position on this side of the Atlantic. The papers in England as well as on the continent have been filled with your name, and if you were in England there is no doubt but that you could arrange the matter with the greatest ease. I believe that Lord Aberdeen feels desirous of arranging the matter, and if he knew precisely what proposition they could make [that] would be accepted, such a proposition would be made. I am informed that Mr. McLean has no instructions to act in the matter, and of course can do nothing. I regret to hear by a letter just received from London that he is still ill & confined to his bed. The same letter repeats a rumour that Mr. [William R.] King [U.S. Minister to France] will leave Paris & take Mr. Buchanan[']s place in the State department, but I suppose such is hardly the case.

The British Gove[rnmen]t are now entirely absorbed with the changes proposed by Sir Rob[er]t Peel. I send you some numbers of the Times & Economist which contain the debates &c relative to these momentous measures. You will thus see the two speeches made by Sir Rob[er]t Peel. There is also an editorial on you in one of the numbers I send you. It is supposed that so soon as these measures are passed Sir Rob[er]t will retire. It is said that he suffers a great deal from over exertion and is obliged to have recourse to cupping to sustain himself. The place of prime Minister of England is a most onerous position and it would not be surprising if he was desirous of retiring.

Your position in the United States & through[ou]t the world is certainly most elevated, but in looking back I can not say that it has not been equally commanding at different periods. When the news of the doings in England will have reached you it will if possible give you increased strength. If your friends in the South let it be perfectly understood that you will be sustained to the exclusion of all others you will be elected to the Presidency in '48, but I look upon that as essential. All the maneuvering that men in the South are capable of will amount to nothing. They will be beaten at that game [*two words changed to* "as sure"] as they undertake it. The few that act in the South want position & place & throw it upon principle whilst those in the North go for bread[?]. They live by politics and never play the loosing [*sic*] game. Success to them is nothing without it brings place or position.

The weather is as delightful as possible. The trees are putting forth leaves and every thing is putting on an aspect of spring. The month of March may be cold and destroy the prospect of an early spring & the fruit. This past winter can scarce be called a winter. We have had but little ice & scarce a sign of snow ["but its character" *canceled*]. There never was a more variable climate.

We are all well, and Anna as well as the children [John Calhoun Clemson and Floride Elizabeth Clemson] join me in sending a great deal of love to yourself & all the family. Your affectionate son, Thos. G. Clemson.

ALS in ScCleA.

From ELLWOOD FISHER, "private and confidential"

National [Hotel?, Washington] 2 Mo[nth] 25, 1846
My dear friend, Soon after we separated this morning I met Gov[erno]r [Thomas] Corwin [Senator from Ohio] at the residence of Dr.

[Frederick] May where I had called to take leave of a friend. Conversation commenced between us about Oregon, and as we left together we exchanged all the information we possessed, as I think on the subject. He told me the whigs had held a caucus this morning, (that is the whig Senators to the number of about twenty). That if a proposition to day was submitted to the Senate from the Brittish minister [Richard Pakenham] by the President [James K. Polk] for a treaty on 49, it would be rejected by an overwhelming vote—even the Yankee whig Senators voting against it. Although if the President were to make the treaty himself on that ground, it would have the sanction of probably every Senator except four or five—the [Lewis] Cass-[William] Allen set. He says the whig senators who would vote against the proposition if submitted in advance by the President, are actuated by the belief ["that" *interlined*] the President would avail himself indeed of the Senatorial sanction to make the treaty—but would afterwards use the course of the Senate as a reproach against those who voted for that plan of adjustment. He intimated that the whig Senators complained of thee for not continuing to act so as to promote negociation—for not acting in favour of postponing this discussion in the Senate, recently. I replied that thy friends had for some time regarded the course of the whig Senators as unreliable—had suspected them of a disposition to either thwart thee, or to aim at some course different from thine, in order either to exempt themselves from the imputation of being led, on this question by thee, or for the purpose of preventing thee as the most prominent among democrats from gaining that credit throughout the country that would result from a pacific adjustment of the dispute. I said that if thee now pressed the question to a decision in the Senate, it must be because thee supposed recent events peculiarly favourable to a prompt settlement. And I adverted to the danger of permitting it to pass over another year stating the facts I communicated to thee this morning.

He said there *were* two or three whig Senators actuated by a desire to prevent thee from taking the lead in ["such" *canceled*] the matter—but intimated that was not the sentiment of others.

I told him on leaving, that I would ["communicate" *canceled*] confer with thee on the subject. And not usually finding thee at this time of day, have written. Thee will perceive that this view of the whigs may determine their vote on a proposition to qualify the notice—urging also as Corwin himself suggested that it would embarrass the negotiation.

Would it not be better for thee to have another interview with the President—and have a positive understanding? With greatest regard thy friend, Ellwood Fisher.

P.S. I believe Gov. Corwin will co-operate in good faith in all movements to promote peace.

ALS in ScCleA.

From MIRABEAU B. LAMAR

Austin, Texas, 25th Febr[uar]y 1846

Dear Sir, I beg leave to present to you, my highly esteemed friend James Webb Esq[ui]r[e], for some years past a resident of Texas. The name of Judge Webb, as you are apprized by my former letters, has been presented by his friends to the President of the United States [James K. Polk], in reference to the District Judgeship of Texas; and I again beg leave to reiterate to you, that there is no man in the State whose appointment to that office would give such universal satisfaction to the community and the Bar as his would. His course as an independent politician, and his firmness in openly advocating men and measures which did not meet the approbation of the two late administrations of this Government, brought down upon him the hostility of a few—very few—prominent men connected with those Administrations; and possibly his appointment to office may be opposed by them; but I assure you that such opposition would meet with but little countenance in this State; and so far as the public voice could be heard in a matter of this sort, it would be rebuked by an overwhelming popular opinion. Judge Webb's friends have already presented to the President in his behalf, the recommendation of at least four fifths of the members of the late Convention, for this office; and those who did not sign it, I am assured, were only prevented from doing so by having given recommendations to others before they were aware that the Judge would accept the Office. He is now prepared to lay before the President the recommendation of almost the entire Legislature of the State now in Session, and of every member of the Bar now at, or who have lately visited the seat of Government.

I have been a little surprised to learn that the name of Judge [John] Hemphill has been, and is urged by his friends in reference to this appointment. The Judge has repeatedly and openly declared that he is not an applicant for the office—that he has authorized no one to use his name in reference to it, and that he would not accept it if tendered to him. He has been seeking here, the appointment of Chief Justice of the Supreme Court of the State, and has so far succeeded in his efforts, as to get the nomination from the Governor [J. Pinckney Henderson] for it, which nomination is now pending before the Senate. I cannot imagine, therefore, that the presentation of his name will produce any embarrassment with the President in making the appointment [of Webb], he (Hemphill) having on all occasions avowed that it was without his authority or wish. May I again solicit your interposition in this matter. By securing for Judge Webb this appointment, you will confer a lasting obligation on those who I know to be your *true* friends in Texas. I have the honor to be With great respect Your friend & serv[an]t, Mirabeau B. Lamar.

ALS in DNA, RG 59 (State Department), Letters of Application and Recommendation during the Administrations of James K. Polk, Zachary Taylor, and Millard Fillmore, 1845–1853, James Webb (M-873:92, frames 476–478). NOTE: An AEU by Calhoun reads "Gen[era]l Lamar recommending Mr. Webb."

REMARKS ON THE PROCEEDINGS IN REGARD TO OREGON

[In the Senate, February 25, 1846]

[*The Senate began deliberation on the resolutions of William Allen to give notice to Great Britain of termination of the joint occupancy of Oregon, along with the "amendments," that is, substitute resolutions, that had been offered by Calhoun, Edward A. Hannegan, and John J. Crittenden, and a proposed joint resolution on the same subject from the House of Representatives. A discussion ensued, and after awhile William L. Dayton of N.J., a Whig, moved that the matter be postponed, arguing that it had already consumed too much of the Senate's time and there was other business waiting.*]

Mr. Calhoun. I hope the motion will not prevail. If there is no senator who wishes to address the body, I would suggest the propriety of proceeding to vote on the amendments. I suppose the discussion has been sufficiently ample to enable every senator to make up his mind. There will be considerable advantage in adopting the course which I now suggest, for then we shall see the precise question before us; and the members who wish to speak can apply their remarks directly to that question in the shape which it may then take.

I hope this course will be taken. The Senate is now full, and I trust will proceed forthwith to vote, if no senator feels disposed to address the Senate.

[*There was further discussion among a number of Senators, during which Walter T. Colquitt of Ga. offered still another substitute.*]

Mr. Calhoun. If the subject be postponed till to-morrow, I hope it will be with the understanding that the vote will be taken upon it, so that the subject may assume some definite and direct form.

[*Both Crittenden and Allen criticized Calhoun's urging of a vote and argued the need for more extended debate on the whole matter before any votes were taken.*]

Mr. Calhoun. I made the remark under the supposition that no senator was prepared to go on at present. If there are senators anxious to speak, they will have an opportunity to do so when the question assumes its final form. I, for one, intend then to offer some remarks. And if no senator be prepared to go on to-morrow, then I propose that we proceed to vote, as it is to be presumed that senators have made up their minds on the amendments at least. I have been remaining silent in order to see what final form the question would take, and then intend to express my views.

[*Allen objected to voting on the "amendments."*]

Mr. Calhoun. The senator from Ohio has not stated what is the usual form—I may say the parliamentary form—in cases of this kind. The first question is upon the amendments, and the form is to discuss the amendments themselves, and after the whole has been amended, and assumed the final form, then the discussion proceeds on it. We have departed from the parliamentary rules; and our course has not been such as to facilitate debate. The course we have taken gives an indefinite character to the discussion; and I appeal to the Senate whether, in the present instance, one-fourth—ay, one-twentieth of what has been said, has been upon the question at issue? I ask whether the senator himself (Mr. Allen) said more than a few words upon the real question? The discussion has related to the question of title, and every one but that before the Senate. Now, I hope that after every senator has been heard, we will take it up in parliamentary form—pass upon the amendments—reduce the question to some definite form, and then all who wish can enter on its discussion.

[*Shortly after, the Senate went into executive session and then adjourned.*]

From the Washington, D.C., *Daily Union*, vol. I, no. 255 (February 25, 1846), p. 1002. Variant report in the Washington, D.C., *Daily National Intelligencer*, February 26, 1846, p. 2; *Congressional Globe*, 29th Cong., 1st Sess., pp. 425–

426; Benton, *Abridgment of Debates*, 15:394–395 (part). Other variants in the New York, N.Y., *Herald*, February 27, 1846, p. 3; the Charleston, S.C., *Mercury*, March 2, 1846, p. 2; the Charleston, S.C., *Courier*, March 2, 1846, p. 2.

From JAMES [EDWARD CALHOUN]

Millwood [Abbeville District, S.C.,] Feb[r]uary 26th 1846

Dear father, The length of time elapsing between the mailing of your letters and the reception of mine, may be the means of your questioning my willingness to communicate; Although I am consoled in the supposition that should you be uneasy from any interruption in our correspondence, the irregular deposits of the mails in our office will at least command some consideration. I have been induced to mention this from noticing the post mark upon your letter, which indicates that it has been more than a month in reaching me.

I have been much consoled in the approbation with which my statement and motives for prefer[r]ing this place to Erskine has been received, and I trust I will not be considered presumptuous when I mention, that my progress has been more steady and satisfactory than in any previous portion of my life. I am much indebted to uncle James [Edward Colhoun] for the interest he takes in instructing me; Although his information is multifarious it is exceedingly correct, and so reliable have I proved it to be, especially in history, as to almost supersede the necessity of investigation through more difficult mediums.

For your kind attention to my University [of Va.] expenses and Littels periodical, I take this occasion of thanking you. I shall adopt your recommendation concerning the most profitable method of acquiring information, differing as widely as it may from that of many who have attempted to advise a course of English reading. I am partial to yours for it not only furnishes an expedient of improving and sy[s]tematising one[']s application, but is even a sure and steady mode of collecting information; its advantages over the plan selected by some of pursuing without restraint one[']s inclination is very great, in as much as the inducement of selecting is much stronger.

Your reserving a place in your letter for political matters has met with my entire approbation; I greatly desire you would make it a perminent subject for a portion of your letters should your engrossing business permit your doing so; notwithstanding I read the papers as regularly as we receive them, yet the source is not in every instance an authentic one, and it is for this reason principally that I need corroborative testimony, and your sound views to aid me in this important branch of information.

A few days since I received a long and interesting letter from Johny [*sic*; John C. Calhoun, Jr.], through whom I was gratified to hear that all were quite well at the Cane break [in Ala.] with the exception of slight colds; he as I through another source ["had been informed," *interlined*] had suffered somewhat from the effects a cold had upon his caugh [*sic*] and appetite, but was much better when he wrote. The weather has been unusually cold in the Cane-break Johny informs me, which he feels more sensibly than at the North. I presume however that it is owing more to the frequent and sudden changes than to any extremity of temperature.

Some one was saying the other day, probably Col. [Francis W.] Pickens, that you were anxious to dispose of Mr. [Thomas G.] Clemson[']s plantation. Should such actually be your intention, you will no doubt be pleased to receive the information I have recently become possessed of on the authority of Uncle James, that it can be sold for $13,500. Uncle James tells me Col. [Francis W.] Pickens is his informant, but as Col. Pickens's inaccuracy has been frequently observed in such matters, and the five hundred dollars seeming to imply that an offer had either been made or would be made to that effect, it would perhaps be your most direct mode to write Col. P[ickens] on the subject.

I returned a few days since from Pendleton, where I had been remaining a short time during Uncle James's absence, and as my visit was for the most part spent in walking over the plantation with Mr. Fredericks, I shall appropriate the remnant of my sheet to the agreeable and interesting information that has been collected there. I found all well but Daniel, whoes [*sic*] indisposition consisted in a very slight cold, from which he had nearly recovered before I left with the aid of but one dose of medicine.

Mr. Fredericks which is characteristic of him, had much to tell and show me. I was indeed much gratified to notice him acting in such strict conformity with your directions, which he seemed to take peculiar interest in citing to me. The day before I returned Mr. [John B.] Sitton handed me a letter for Fredericks, which I read to him and told him you expected a speedy answer and much local news, which he promised to give in his answer the next day—Sunday. His, or rather, your improvements and new arrangements, and his execution, I think have greatly enhanced the value of the place; in a very short time with the present culture the the [*sic*] washed hillsides before the negroe-houses, and between the dwelling house and the barn, will I think be reclaimed; the small grain planted in thoes [*sic*] as well as in other fields looks unusually well notwithstanding the cold weather [by which] it was generally supposed partially injured.

The affairs of the plantation I think have been well conducted during your absence; the cow house and smokehouse have been some time since finished, since which time the hands have been employed in clearing and ditching the new ground with the exception of the plough force, who have been kept steadily engaged in breaking up the fields. I need not mention more than this as Fredericks letter I presume has long since reached you.

I was surprised to find that a good many papers were regularly deposited in the office at Pendleton for you, mostly Western; however the [Charleston] Mercury and some foreign papers were among the number. I took the liberty of telling Mr. Sitton not to forward the Western papers or the Mercury until I could hear from you, knowing [*one word canceled*] that you had a more certain and direct means of receiving their content at the same time authorising Mr. Sharp to take them out until Mr. Sitton should receive further orders from me. I should like the Mercury directed from Charleston to this office should you be willing to spare it and dropping a few lines to the editor to that effect.

Uncle James joins me in love to all. Your affectionate son, James.

ALS in ScCleA.

From [JAMES L. EDWARDS, Commissioner]

Pension Office, Feb. 26, 1846

Sir, The declaration of Mr. Thomas ["Austin" *canceled and* "Auten" *interlined*], in relation to his claim to a pension under the act of the 7th June 1832, has been examined and filed. We have no evidence in any of the public offices here of his having served during the revolution. If he served so long as he has stated, there will doubtless be found ample proof of his service in the office of the Secretary of State at Trenton. The claimant has not set forth his service according to the regu[la]tions of the Dept. It will be indispensably necessary that he should state particularly the terms of service in the militia of New Jersey. I enclose a printed sheet for his guidance. I would advise him to write to C[harles] G. McChesney Esq[ui]r[e]

Secretary of State at Trenton for proof of his Service. We would send for such proof, if we ["had any" *canceled*] could appropriate any portion of our contingent fund to the purpose of paying office fees in such cases. I have to be [James L. Edwards.]

[P.S.] Mr. [John C.C.] Carroll's letter is herewith returned.

FC in DNA, RG 15 (Veterans Administration), Letters Sent, 1800–1866. NOTE: An endorsement reads "Ohio Index[,] act '32[,] No. 37187."

FURTHER REMARKS ON THE OREGON PROCEEDINGS

[In the Senate, February 26, 1846]

[Sidney Breese of Ill., an administration supporter, offered another substitute set of resolutions, directly authorizing the President to serve notice on Great Britain of the termination of joint occupancy. There was debate among half a dozen Senators.]

Mr. Calhoun rose and said, it is very obvious that the great question involved in this matter is this: Can the controversy between us and Great Britain be settled by negotiation and compromise? or is it to be settled by an assertion of our right to the entire territory, and an appeal to arms? Whatever doubts have heretofore existed upon this point, there can be none after the declaration of to-day, that this is the real question involved. A question of greater moment never has been presented in Congress from the days of the Revolution to the present. Sir, I hold it eminently desirable that the Senate should make an expression of their opinion upon this important matter. I cannot believe that there is a single Senator who has not made up his mind upon it, or who can hesitate to respond yea or nay, when the question is put in the form of an amendment to the resolution. Sir, I hold it important that they should respond. It is necessary to know the sense of this body, in order to guide our future legislation. If we mean to maintain our title by force of arms, let us begin, let us lay aside all other things; and let me say, if gentlemen do not begin with the necessary measures before involving the country in a war, you are most likely to be discomfited; and foremost among those important measures are those relating to your finances. Sir, I hold it to be desirable to guide the business men of the country. They know not what to do, nor have they known for the last three months. The property of thousands has been periled, and millions upon millions have been lost. Sir, there ought to be an end to this state of excitement. With due deference to the Executive, and without intending the slightest disrespect, I must say I greatly regret that it has been left in the state of uncertainty it has. Sir, I deem it to be important, and I speak without hesitation on this point, that it should be passed this very day; because, whatever our decision is, it is desirable, in my opinion, that it should reach the other side of the Atlantic as speedily as possible.

Sir, I believed from the beginning of the session that the great question of peace and war depended upon this body—upon your gravity, your wisdom, and your patriotism; and I trust that such a response will be given *this very day* as will quiet the fears of millions on both sides of the Atlantic. Sir, I entertain the most courteous feelings towards the Senator from Illinois [Breese], and I would indulge him with the time he requires, if I could consistently with my duty. And let me say to the Senator that a slight difference in mere phraseology can be of little consequence, so far as great questions are concerned, as it is not proposed, I presume, to go further than to try the sense of the Senate upon this amendment at this time, and hereafter he will have an opportunity to express his views to whatever extent he wishes.

[*There was further extended debate, during which Lewis Cass of Mich. accused Calhoun of invading the role of the President and of acting in "bad taste" since what he proposed would be ineffectual with the British.*]

Mr. Calhoun, interposing, said he hoped the honorable Senator would allow him to observe that he had narrowed down the proposition, and omitted the very point which he had made, viz. that the business of the country would be materially injured by the continuance of uncertainty in relation to this great question. He was not the negotiator, and what conditions might be proposed by England he was not prepared to say; but since he was upon his feet, he would make a single remark. From the beginning it had been his impression, whether that impression were right or wrong, that the Government of Great Britain would never take a definitive position until there had been action on the part of Congress; and he thought it was of the utmost importance that the question should be speedily settled.

From *Congressional Globe*, 29th Cong., 1st Sess., pp. 435–436. Also printed in the Washington, D.C., *Daily National Intelligencer*, February 27, 1846, p. 2; the Baltimore, Md., *American & Commercial Daily Advertiser*, February 28, 1846, p. 2; Benton, *Abridgment of Debates*, 15:400, 402. Variants in the Washington,

D.C., *Daily Union*, vol. I, no. 256 (February 26, 1846), pp. 1006–1007; the New York, N.Y., *Herald*, February 28, 1846, p. 2; the Philadelphia, Pa., *United States Gazette*, February 28, 1846, p. 1; the Charleston, S.C., *Mercury*, March 2, 1846, p. 2; the Pendleton, S.C., *Messenger*, March 13, 1846, p. 2; the London, England, *Times*, March 16, 1846, p. 5.

From A. P. STINSON

St. Joseph [Mich.,] Feb. 26, 1846

My Dear Sir, Your esteemed favor of the 13th Instant has been Received & Read, with no ordinary Interest & satisfaction. I perceive that you are fully apprised *How*, & by *what means* the wires have been pulled, that a few "Political Jug[g]lers" Have ["managed" *interlined*] & will If not put Down, Continue to man[a]ge Our Elections. We want ["Sir," *interlined*] an *Independent Press* in Every *State* & *Territory* of the *Union*, to *show up*, & *Hold up*, to the Indignation & Just Execration of the *People*, these "*Jug[g]lers*" who work the wires. While the *Press*, oft called the "Pal[l]adium of our Liberties" is *subsidized*—controlled by "*Cliques*," thereby subverting the Principles of Republicanism, we can hope for Little Else than, that the old course will be persued, that a few *Aspiring Demagogues* will *Rule*. Like your self I have become *Disgusted*, with *Caucus Nominations* as of Late Conducted. The People, who have all to do at the Polls, Have nought to do in the Primary meetings. Every thing is "Cut and Dryd" made ready to their Hands, & they are *Required* to *support* the *man* or *men*, whom the "Central Cliques" select! Much Sir, as I deprecate Whiggery, there is Little to Choose between It, & "Modern Democracy." I am, & Ever have been a Strong & unflinching Advocate for the *People*[']*s* Rights, for the "Vox Populi" & hence It ["is" *canceled*] has Pained me to see, how *Little Regard* is paid them & How tamely they have submitted to It. I believe the time has fully Come, when tis the duty of Every *Freeman*, to take a Stand, a Bold Stand & thus put down, or ["keep" *interlined*] in abeyance, those *Aspirants* for Power & Place Irrespective of qualification [or] merit. If this be not Done, the People will themselves be put, & kept, in a State of vassalage. How, in what manner, & by whom this great work of *Reform* is to be accomplished, I know not. But that a beggining should be made I believe, by first Letting the *People* know *how* & by *whom* they have been Gull[e]d. In Relation to *Rejections* of Executive appointments I agree with you there is *Danger* In Rejecting many, of Its being deemed *Prosc[r]iptive*—But that there are those who Richly merit a Rejection at the Hands of the U.S. Senate—there Can be No Doubt, In my mind—[Marcus] *Morton* of Boston, [Augustus] *Jenkins* of Portsmouth [N.H.], & [Charles G.] *Hammond* of Detroit, should be made to "walk the Plank" as they Cause your friends under them to do.

Such men for Collectors of the Revenue, should Like Angels['] visits be "few & far between." If Sir, *you*, or any one of your friends whom I may *know as such*, will advise me of what is to be done, & How to be done, when & where to Do It—I am ready, & more than willing to do all that in me lies, to further your wishes. Yours is as *sacred* as in your own keeping, and had you not noted "This is for your self," I should have known from Its *tenor* was so Intended & should have so treated It. As I hold a *small office* under Government, which may be wrested from me If my position was known at Washington, you may consider this as for your self. In Michigan as well as In the *East* I am known & Recognized as a *Calhoun Man*. I Can have a Little Influence in some Papers in the *West* & *East* & If any thing is sent me, Can get It inserted & will write my self so soon as I Learn what[']s to be done. I desire that you send me your Speech on the "*Oregon Question*" soon as convenient & believe me truly & sinc[ere]ly Y[ou]r friend, A.P. Stinson.

[P.S.] As others, who aspire to the *Chief Magistracy* are *filling* the *Country*, with their *Speeches* & "*Rub Dae*" [sic], addressed under *their own Franks*, to various Individuals, with a view of Enlisting their sympathies & Cooperation, in their behalf, & knowing as I do, the *Influence such things have*, I suggest, whether It is not *Indispensable*, at Least *fit* & *Proper*, that you do the Same, If not for the Same purpose at Least to "*take the wind out of their Sails*"?

I have Recently witnessed the *Effects* of this Course on Some in this County, who have been *Silenced* in this way, while others have become *Clamerous Advocates* of a Man, who heretofore they were not in favor of! Such Sir, is "Poor Human Nature" & we have to take men as we find them. If this meets your views, I Recommend that you Send to

#Hon. E[paphroditus] Ransom,* Kalamazoo Mich.
I[saac] W. Willard, Esq.* Paw Paw "
Gen[era]l I[saac] E. Crary,* Marshall "
Hon. F[lavius] J. Littlejohn,* Allegan "
James Sullivan Esq.,* Cassopolis "
H.P. Yale, E[s]q.,* Grand Rapids "

William Hale E[s]q.,* Detroit
Abiel Silver E[s]q.,* Marshall
Stephen Baker E[s]q.
Benja[min] F. Fish Esq.*
Hon. C[alvin] Britain
John Wittenmyer
Dr. L.S. Lillibridge*
Tho[ma]s Conger Esq.

⎫
⎬ St. Joseph, Mich.
⎭

Col. S.W.B. Chester*
James Brown Esq.
Lucius Hoit Esq.

⎫
⎬ Niles, Mich.
⎭

Hon. John Groves, Buchanan, Mich.

[*Marginal Interpolation:*] All with this mark * are, or have been your *warm supporters.*

+William H. Sullivan, Esq.* Milwaukee Wisconsin

+ Mr. *Sullivan* is my Son in Law, is Proprietotor [*sic*] of the Milwaukee Courier, the Leading Demo[cratic] Paper in that Territory— & is a *Calhoun man.* #Hon. E. Ransom is our *Chief Justice*, is your warm friend & will be our next U.S. Senator by *ac[c]lamation*—& were he now there & Called to vote on the Nomination of Ch[arle]s G. Hammond as Col[lector] of Detroit would say No—Col. David Munger If Left to the People would get 10 to 1 over Hammond & yet H[ammond] has had the tact[?] to get the Nomination. A.P.S.

ALS in ScCleA.

From Tho[ma]s G. Clemson

Brussels, Feb[ruar]y 27th 1846

My dear Sir, Tho I have written you before I take the liberty of inclosing you an extract which was cut from the Transcript & Ledger published in Philadelphia on the 30th of January and written by Francis J. Grund from this city on the 18th of December. This attack implicates Mr. [James] Buchanan at least as much as myself notwithstanding the shallow pretence that his occupations and position in Washington makes [*sic*] him incompetent to judge of a treaty founded on the broad commercial regulations of the world. No one is more aware than myself of the idleness of a defence against or refutation of the arguments of a professed letter writer whose want of principle makes him a proper caterer to the tastes of all classes. But it is considering Francis J. Grund as an official of the United States Government and therefore giving an air of importance to his calumnious imputations that induces me to notice them. Had he made any tangible statement I should have treated the matter differently. Still I can not pass unnoticed this emanation of a petty personal spite against me arrising [*sic*], as I understand from his statement to others, from my never having consulted him as commercial agent of the United States when the treaty was being negotiated. Had I been so silly as to have done so on any grounds I might as well have published the matter to the world at once[,] for his mania for making newspaper paragraphs is so great that in the abscence [*sic*] of facts he draws upon his imagination for them. Such conduct is clearly unworthy of one whose official station gives an air of truth to his statements and asseverations and who makes use of his position to throw into disrepute an important act of the administration. When these scurillous publications of this official come back to this country they have a bad effect upon our relations. Such has been the result of some of his articles written from Antwerp to Augsburg Gazette and against Belgian interests.

There may have been many such letters written and from what I know of his conduct in Brussels and his language held to others here I should be surprised if there was not. I only know of this one having been published in the United States through the kindness of a friend who being here at the time the treaty was under consideration and knowing the circumstances, was indignant as any honest man would have been, at such base conduct. I am sorry to occupy your time with such a small affair but I think the circumstances of the case make it necessary that you may ["not only" *interlined*] be aware of Grund[']s conduct, but that you may know from whom & how such attacks emanate.

I have always refrained from discussing Mr. Grund[']s conduct in my Despatches, tho [he is] far from being what I, or any American would approve, both from delicacy & because I had no one particular instance supported by proof of his neglect, & incompetency for the office & which I considered sufficient ground for official complaint. Instead of his advancing the interests of the United States by attention to business and exemplary conduct, he has been almost constantly absent from Antwerp, leaving the duties to be filled by myself and a clerk & when there, he has been engaged in disgraceful broils & fights, at public tables, & has so incensed the population of that city that I doubt much whether he could return: indeed I have

641

been assured of the fact by the most respectable residents of that city. From the date of the letter it was written just previous to his departure from Brussels for France, where he has been for upwards of two months and I doubt if he ever returns. But that is no reason why he should not date letters from Brussels or any other locality that suited his purpose. He has openly endeavoured to injure me & my acts in Belgium and now has taken up his pen to deal insidious attacks against me. Why no one knows unless as I mentioned above from the pique which he expressed at not being consulted as *commercial agent* about the treaty. Do not think I have had any difficulty with him. On the contrary he was always received & treated by me with the greatest politeness & even kindness as an accredited officer of my Government tho I disliked the man and all I knew of him & it was not untill he had been openly abusing me & using every means in his power to lower me in the estimation of others for two or three months[,] all the while partaking of my hospitality & making use of my good offices & displaying when in my presence not only politeness & deference but servility, that I was made aware of his baseness, by a friend who was indignant at his double dealing. Even when I knew of it, he was too dirty to quarrel with & tho I said to those who I know repeated it to him that if Mr. Grund considered himself ag[g]rieved by me he had only to come as a gentleman and make it known[,] still I never mentioned the subject to him & to the last moment treated him with civillity [*sic*]. I cannot but feel indignant at his unfounded enmity against me & hurt that I am placed by my position so much in the power of such a man & at the mercy of his unprincipled statements[,] for so few Americans come to Brussels & of those none are writers that he is the only one from whom the public can form an opinion of me.

This is hard when I feel that I have laboured diligently ever since I have been here to advance the interests & reputation of my country (& I may say without vanity, I hope since there is no one to do me justice with much success) not only in Belgium but in Germany & England[,] to both of which countries my central position here gave me access. You can imagine when I know this and am congratulated on all sides for having made so notoriously favourable a treaty for my country that the opposition to it on that very ground was bitter in the extreme, which no one knew better than Mr. Grund[,] that I should loose [*sic*] all credit in my own country through a man who is so notorious a liar that in conversation his statements are never beleived [*sic*].

You may perhaps think I have dwelt too much on this subject

but it is one on which I confess I feel deeply & I wished to put you in possession of the whole ground that you might know what to think of his letters when you saw them & to explain the matter should it be spoken of. I wrote Mr. Buchanan a confidential letter on the subject of Mr. G[rund']s conduct as consul but he is so much occupied that I do not like to trouble him again. You may use your judgement in showing him this letter. I confess I think it would be to the advantage of our country to be disembar[r]assed of such a miserable creature. Your very affectionate son, Thos. G. Clemson.

[Enclosed clipping]

A Treaty has been signed at Brussels with the United States. It professes to be one of Commerce and Navigation; but I have examined carefully the sixteen paragraphs it contains, and which were published in all the papers, without finding one conducive to an increased demand for our great staples. Not a single tariff stipulation is made in it, though Belgium was *last year* on the point of establishing a *tobacco Regie*, which would have stopped our tobacco trade to Antwerp. The thing was proposed by the Belgian minister of finance, and may be proposed again. Why we should be so particularly anxious to form reciprocal treaties of *navigation* with the small maritime States of Europe, enabling their vessels to come and share even our vast coasting trade, has always been incomprehensible to me. It seems as if we wanted to challenge competition, and to create it where it does not exist. All these treaties with the smaller powers tie our hands when we come to treat with the large ones. It is not the United States who were most anxious to make a treaty with Belgium, but, as the Belgian Secretary of Foreign Affairs very properly remarked, in his note to the Chambers, Belgium who wanted a treaty with the United States, as the only means (these are his own words) of obtaining *freights for Belgian vessels* to America.

Belgium, in her treaties with France and the German Zollverein, has made numerous tariff stipulations—the treaty which Mr. [Henry] Wheaton concluded in Berlin contained a provision favorable to our tobacco planters; but our present treaty with Belgium contains no such clause, though there is no doubt under heaven that the friendly disposition of the Belgian government and the circumstances in which she is placed, would have made her disposed to insert one. Perhaps it is not yet to[o] late. It is not for the American Secretary of State at Washington, occupied as he is with the arrangement of the most important questions which involve peace or war, and which affect the permanent prosperity of the country, to examine all the small details of our foreign intercourse; it is for our "Diplomates" abroad to obtain the necessary *commercial* information before they engage the faith of the country.

ALS with En in ScCleA.

From BARNARD E. BEE

Austin Texas, Feb[ruar]y 28th 1846

My dear Sir, My estimable friend Judge [James] Webb thinks of visiting Washington and I cannot consent to his doing so without a letter to you.

It would be superfluous at this day to speak of Judge Webb[']s merits—for the high office he hopes, to attain at the seat of Govt. You have long known my estimate of this Gentleman—no less—than the very first man that has visited the Country since my arrival here in 1836.

Allow me to introduce him—and I am very sure you will soon discover that I have't not [*sic*] and could not overestimate him. I am with great esteem very respectfully Yours, Barnard E. Bee.

ALS in DNA, RG 59 (State Department), Letters of Application and Recommendation during the Administrations of James K. Polk, Zachary Taylor, and Millard Fillmore, 1845–1853, James Webb (M-873:92, frames 479–480). NOTE: An AEU by Calhoun reads "Mr. Bee recommending Mr. Webb."

From ABNER S. LIPSCOMB

Austin City, Texas [*ca*. February 28, 1846]

My Dear Sir, I wrote to you a few days ago presenting, the claims of Judge [James] Webb for the appointment of United States District Judge for Texas, but, least [*sic*], you may not have received my letter I again, take the liberty to call your attention to the subject.

I have known Judge W[ebb], for a long time both as a lawyer, and in the private Relations of life, And I can say with truth, that it is no disparagement, to any man, in Texas, when I declaim, that he is in every way better qualified for that office, than any other man in the State and I know, this to be the opinion of the profession in general. He has had opportunities, to become familiar, with, the principles, and the practice, prevailing in that Court, not enjoyed by any other man. As a District Judge at Key West he gave general satisfaction, to the governm[en]t, and to the profession. It being a matter of great interest to us I must beg the favour of your assistance in procuring for him, the appointment. Judge [John] Hemphill has been nominated, to the Supreme Court of this State, and on yesterday I had a conversation with him, on the subject, of his name, being used, as an applicant, for the District Judgeship. He assured me, that it was without his Knowledge and Consent, and that he did not wish it, prefer[r]ing, a seat on the Supreme Court Bench of the State; and in the same conversation, said that it would require much, time for any man in the State to make himself as well qualified for, the office as Judge Webb.

Please pardon, the liberty I have taken with you and believe me, Respectfully your old friend, Abner S. Lipscomb.

ALS in DNA, RG 59 (State Department), Letters of Application and Recommendation during the Administrations of James K. Polk, Zachary Taylor, and Millard Fillmore, 1845–1853, James Webb (M-873:92, frames 417–419). NOTE: An AEU by Calhoun reads "Mr. Lipscomb recommending Mr. Webb." Abner S. Lipscomb (1789–1856), a native of Abbeville District, S.C., and an early acquaintance of Calhoun, was a prominent lawyer and jurist in Ala. and Texas; he served as a Justice of the Texas Supreme Court from 1846 until his death. John Hemphill (1803–1862), also a native of S.C., moved to Texas in 1838. He was Chief Justice of the Texas Supreme Court from 1846 until 1858.

To ———, 2/28. Calhoun discusses the chances of his correspondent obtaining for a friend an appointment to the Military Academy at West Point. "The act of Congress allows one cadet to each Election District & ten to be appointed by the President at large. The appointment of the one allowed to the Congressional District depends on the Representative in Congress. If his support can not be had, the only chance is to obtain one of the ten allowed the President. For them the applications are so numerous & the pressure to obtain them so great, that the chance of each applicant is very slim." This manuscript is described as being an ALS of two pages in the quarto size, datelined in Washington. Abs in *The Autograph Album: a Magazine for Autograph Collectors* (published by Thomas F. Madigan, New York City), vol. I, no. 2 (October, 1933), p. 29; and in other catalogs of the same dealer; Abs in Catalogue 97 [1943] of the Carnegie Book Shop of New York City, p. 31, item 673.

From Louis McLane

[London, late February?, 1846]
My dear Sir, The feebleness of my health, and the pressure of my other engagements are such as to lea[v]e me only a moment before closing the mail to call your attention to the news papers, and to acknowledge your last letter. I assure you without entering into any argument that we have seriously suffered from the course taken in regard to the [Oregon] notice. The delay itself is mischievous; & the negotiation will not be renewed until Congress have finally acted upon the notice.

By the next steamer I will write you more at length. Meantime I may say that I do not think the error in our negotiation consisted so much in withdrawing the proposition, as in shutting the door to an openning afterwards from this side. If arbitration had been rejected so as to hold out hope it would have repaired the error. I believe the offer was made in the expectation that the terms of the answer would encourage a resumption of the negotiation. Of this you will see full proof in the two letters from Lord A[berdeen] to Mr. Packenham [*sic*; Richard Pakenham], & now published in the [London] Chronicle which I send you.

Of all this I apprised Mr. B[uchanan] long before his answer, and yet he answered as if he were really afraid that the negotiation would be resumed.

Now we must wait for your action. When we hear what that is, we will get on; and then you will have the real struggle in the Senate. I write now chiefly to call your attention to these letters in the *Chronicle*, and to the really weak point in the negotiation on our side. The withdrawal of the proposition gave the P[resident] *strength* at *home*; it did him no harm here; for in point of fact between withdrawing a proposition after it ["was" *canceled and* "has been" *interlined*] rejected, and *protesting* that it should never be used as committing the party making it, (["as is" *canceled*] the ["usa" *canceled*] usual mode, & done by both[?] gov[ernments] in 1826–7) there is no great difference. But by withdrawing it—and refusing to give any encouragement to opening the negotiation, and afterwards sending the whole matter to Congress, completely closed the door to any attempt here, at least until very recently. However, I believe if you pass the notice, we will be able to begin again. But of one thing you may be sure; if there be a change of ministry, nothing will be done by the Whig ministry; & if it continue in power until the year expire, I shall regard a rupture as inevitable. I pray you to excuse this hasty letter; & believe me most truly Y[ou]r friend & Servant, Louis McLane.

ALS in ScCleA; PC in Boucher and Brooks, eds., *Correspondence*, pp. 322–323.
NOTE: This dateless letter has been assigned a tentative date from the content.

MARCH 1-31
1846

▥

The 1st session of the 29th Congress continued. At the end of the month the membership of the Senate was augmented by the arrival of two Senators from the new State of Texas—Sam Houston, Calhoun's old enemy, and Thomas Jefferson Rusk, who had been born in Calhoun's neighborhood and had received Calhoun's encouragement as a youth.

The great event of a busy month occurred on March 16. Calhoun addressed the Senate on the Oregon question. It was one of the most critical, most brilliant and moving, and most heralded speeches he had made—perhaps the most important since the 1833 Compromise. Crowds had to be turned away from the Capitol because there was no room, and when he had finished his plea for peace and good sense, a murmur of approval went through the galleries.

The reaction of the New York editor Parke Godwin was only typical: "Your speech in favour of Peace, as honourable in its sentiments, to your heart, as the masterly policy it discloses is to your head, has produced a fine and profound impression . . . with thinking and humane men of all classes.   Every word of it should be, not fram'd in letters of gold, but written on the hearts of the people, which is far better."

Calhoun was pleased, but too experienced and too old to be unduly flattered. He had accomplished for the time what he had intended, but he knew the Union was by no means out of the troubles that threatened in the northwest and the southwest of the continent. It is not known whether he agreed with Duff Green or not when Green wrote: "You . . . are placed at the head of the great movement of the age. . . . For the first time in your life you fill your true position."

▥

From HENRY C. CAREY

Philad[elphia,] March 2/46

Dear Sir, Can you find time, amidst the numerous claims on your attention, to read a short letter from an old advocate of free trade, whose views of the policy now to be pursued differ from those of most persons of his own side of the question?

Both sides are *ultra*, and therefore, as I think, both are wrong. Mr. Laurence [*sic*; Abbott Lawrence?] believes that every body should be permanently protected against all foreign competition. Mr. [Robert J.] Walker would at once abolish a system under which vast interests have arisen. The great maxim for a reformer is, as I think, *festina lente*, and it is to the want of regard for that maxim that so many reformers owe their failure to accomplish their objects. Make your reforms such as to insure the assent of a great majority of the people, and then they are safe from re-action, whereas if they can command but lean majorities the danger of reaction is great. Let them, as far as possible, be unfelt as to any injurious effects resulting from them, and they will go forward gradually, peacefully, and certainly, *preparing the way for further reform*. No man goes further in his belief of the advantage of permitting the free employment of capital and labour than I do, and I think I should be found to go even further than yourself, but I would go forward, step by step, so as to insure success, and give permanence to the system that was to be established. Had the Compromise bill been made to extend over a period of 20 years, instead of 10, the question of tariff would never have been heard of again, mixing itself up with questions of territory, and other political disputes. It would then have been carried over the whole period of prostration arising out of the "reforms" of the Currency, to accomplish which the people were urged to make banks, and banks were urged to extend their loans—and they would not afterwards have had occasion to see that ruin came in company with relaxation of restrictions on trade—nor would they have been led to believe, as unfortunately they have been, that the one was a necessary consequence of the other. Had it been so extended—and I have been told that you were willing that it should be—the state of opinion upon this great question would now be widely different from what it now is. Can we not now profit by past experience, and accomplish a reform that will be permanent? I think it may be done, with infinite advantage to the manufacturers themselves, as well as to that of all other interests, and therefore trouble you with this letter.

The change from our system of specific duties and minimums, even to what would be deemed a high advalorem rate of duty, would be a great one, but it might be made without much, if any, disturbance—but to go down at once to a mere revenue duty would be so serious as possibly to lead to another change of public opinion such as we have so recently seen to take place. The danger of this may be avoided by taking time—and all the time that would be required would be as nothing compared with the immensely beneficial effect that would result from carrying the measure by such a majority as would satisfy all parties that the system was permanently established. In 1832, ten years were thought a long time, but how rapidly did it pass! It is as nothing in the life of a nation, and it is for a nation that you have now to establish rules of action. The main thing that is to be desired is to see that our course is in the right direction, and that every day, and every step, will bring us nearer to the desired port.

The main difficulty under a protective system is that men are constantly induced to go ahead of the existing protection, in hopes of more being given, and the further you go, the greater is the outcry for further advance. Such was the case in this country from 1816 to 1828, and so it has been in France & Germany to the present time. The first great step towards freedom of trade, was with us, as it has yet to be in France, to let it be understood that the maximum point had been reached, and that those who could not prosper under the existing system must quit, as nothing more was to be expected. That was done in 1832, and had the currency been let alone, the year 1842 would have found the whole country prospering under the new system.

Much has been done in the time that has elapsed, but not enough, owing to the disturbances through which we have passed, to enable you to carry out advantageously the plan now proposed, yet a little more time will do all that you could desire. Whether we reach the true revenue point in 1846–1852, or 1856–is as nothing compared with the absolute certainty that it will soon be reached, and that when it shall be so, we shall have no further changes to look for. A change now from minimums & specific duties to forty per cent. with a provision for gradual reduction until it should fall to 25 per cent. would be a great advance upon our present system, but it is one that would make but little difficulty, if any, with the manufacturers, while it would, as I believe, carry with it the great majority of the nation. Experience proves to every man exposed to foreign competition that each year places him on a better footing for maintaining that competition, and that there are few that would fear it under a duty of 25 per cent, eight years hence.

We have striking evidence of the effect of a very little time in the Coal & Iron trades of this State. The former commenced but about 20 years since. Ten years ago the price of a ton of coal was from six to eight dollars, and it was a poor business at that. Now, it is from three to four dollars, and the competition between the numerous rail road & canal companies, each striving to improve the means of transportation, promises yet further reduction—reduction that will go on as rapidly under domestic competition as if our ports were open for the admission of coal free of duty—for it is impossible that under any circumstances greater exertion should be made than is done at present. Until it was established that Iron could be made with Anthracite Coal, we had no fuel for the purpose, in the Eastern part of the Union, except Charcoal, with which the process cannot be cheaply conducted. Now, furnaces rise in every direction, and the product already exceeds half a million of tons, with every reason to believe that it will soon reach a million, and that the price will be quite as low, if not lower, than that of England.

Had the bill reported two years since been such as I now suggest, it would then, most probably, have been carried, and we might now be entering upon the second year of reduction, and the certainty that a permanent system was established would have carried manufactures to a higher point than they have now reached. If you fail now, two years more may be lost, and manufactures will not advance with the rapidity that they would otherwise do, because of the state of uncertainty that will exist. At the end of that time you may be found still endeavouring to do what you would almost have accomplished, had your measure of 1844 been such as I have suggested. Forty per cent in 1844, with a reduction of one half of the difference between that and twenty five per cent. w[oul]d give in 1848, 32½ per cent, or not greatly more than Mr. Walker's bill would now give. I say 25 per cent. because that rate on the Invoice, would not differ greatly from the 20 per cent. on the home valuation proposed in 1832. Under such a system of gradual reduction, I feel persuaded that 1854, the time at which 25 per cent would be reached, would find us fully prepared to go down gradually—say at one per cent per annum to 15 per cent.

The tendency of this country is to free trade, if the advocates of free trade will only permit it to develope itself gradually, & not force it. Nothing can prevent our attaining it but want of patience on the part of its friends.

The question ought to be settled now, and permanently settled and there is no man but yourself that can do it. It is the only one that stands between you and a large portion of the people of the North, and if it were fairly out of the way, I firmly believe that there is no man who could so readily command the support of a majority of the nation as yourself.

Excuse me for trespassing on your time with a much longer letter than I contemplated when I began, & believe me Yours very truly & respectfully, Henry C. Carey.

ALS in ScCleA. NOTE: An AEU by Calhoun reads "Mr. Carey[,] relates to Tariff."

From JOHN FORBES

Nacogdoches [Texas,] March 2nd 1846

Sir, One whose name is probably forgotten but whom, during your Vice Presidency, you frequently honored with your Correspondence, whilst he was a resident of Cincinnati Ohio takes the liberty (which he hopes you will pardon) of again addressing a letter to you by his friend General Tho[ma]s J. Rusk.

For the last Eleven Years I have resided in Texas, and during our Struggle against Mexican Misrule, and for National Independance I, as well as most Texians were impressed with a deep sense of our obligations to you, for the support and Countenance you rendered us during that eventful period, and now that we are happily annexed to the Confederacy, we look forward with confidence to your further support and that you will have the interests and welfare of our young State in view and fondly hope that your influence will be always extended in its favour and that with your helping hand it will pass quickly through the period of its leading strings, to manhood, and vie with the older States of the Union in prosperity. The Election of Gen[era]l Thomas J. Rusk and Gen[era]l Sam Houston to represent Texas in the Senate of the United States have given great & general satisfaction. Gen[era]l Rusk stands deservedly high in the estimation of his fellow Citizens throughout the State and you will find in him, Sir, a worthy and able Coadjutor, in carrying out that policy and those wise measures of yours, which tend, so materially to the well being, and prosperity of the Union and the maintainance of its honor and dignity.

I look upon this, as one of the most critical periods in the History of our Country whether for good, or evil. At no time did we need more than at the present, in our National Councils men who have an eye single to its true interests, and courage to maintain it. Such I trust and beleive you will find Gen[era]l Rusk to be. I hail his election to the Senate as a fortunate event at this juncture, as strengthening as it will be of the hands of those, whose only object is, their Country[']s honor & prosperity.

We are awaiting with great anxiety to learn the determination of our Executive upon the Oregon Question. The settlement of that vexed matter, upon amicable and honorable terms with England is very much to be desired. If a war should unhappily ensue (which may the Almighty avert) Texas would be from its position greatly exposed, and if I mistake not would become the Battle field of the South. But come what may, Texas will be *no* laggard in defending our soil from aggression. Its Watch Word, would be, in such an event, God and our Right.

But I sincerely hope Sir, that the Counsel of those Senators who advocate conciliatory measures will prevail, and that peace and good will, will continue uninterrupted between two nations, so strongly connected by the ties of interest & Kindred. Praying for such a happy result I remain Sir Your Ob[edien]t Serv[an]t, John Forbes.

ALS in ScCleA. NOTE: Calhoun had in fact known Rusk when he was a youth at Pendleton, S.C., and by tradition had assisted Rusk's education.

From W[illia]m F. Gordon, [former Representative from Va.]

Albemarle [County,] Va., March 3d 1846
Dear Sir, Permit me to make you acquainted with Mr. George W. Carr of this County & State. He visits Washington in pursuit of a commission in the army. He is a gentleman of education & standing among us, & I have no doubt would ["would" *canceled*] do honor to the service.

Mr. Carr is the great nephew of Mr. [Thomas] Jefferson, & his grand father [Peter] Carr, is a name illustrious in *our* annals. He is the son [of] Colo[nel] Samuel Carr of this County, a gentleman of great worth & estimation. He is I think a worthy stem of his stock, & is moreover so thoroughly *State Rights*, in his political opinions that I am sure even a military life will never make him forget them.

We are all looking with intense anxiety to our relations with England. If war can be honorably avoided, & the mutual commercial policy of this & that Country can be carried, the South & all America, indeed the commercial world will be the debtors of the great men, in either nation, who have contributed to results so grand, & so beneficent. On our part we can have no hesitation in pointing to the man who has most constantly & clearly advocated & advanced the great Doctrine of free Trade. With sentiments of sincere regard I am Dear Sir y[ou]r friend & S[ervan]t, Wm. F. Gordon.

ALS in DNA, RG 107 (Secretary of War), Personnel Papers, 1838–1912: Applications for Appointment, no. 7. NOTE: Carr was appointed a 2nd Lt. of Infantry on 2/23/1847.

To James K. Polk, [3/3]. Calhoun appended an undated statement to a letter to Polk from 11 of the 15 members of the U.S. House of Representatives from Va., who were recommending George W. Carr for a commission "in one of the regiments of Dragoons expected to be authorised during the present session of Congress." Calhoun wrote: "I am not personally acquainted with the applicant; but from the recommendation of one of the first men of the State [William F. Gordon], who resides in his neighbourhood and is intimately acquainted with him & his family, I do not doubt that he is well qualified for the place for which he applies." AES on LS in DNA, RG 107 (Secretary of War), Miscellaneous Application Files, George W. Carr.

From LOUIS MCLANE

London, 3 March 1846

My dear Sir, Although I am too enfeebled, from a severe illness, to go into much detail, I continue my correspondence, in ["the" *interlined*] same confidence as heretofore.

I am afraid the state of the Oregon question is more critical. It is unfortunate, I think, that so much opposition should have been made to the notice recommended by the President [James K. Polk], or that more should have been attempted than, while ["giving" *canceled and* "authorizing" *interlined*] the notice, to recommend an adjustment upon an honorable basis. If the notice, as recommended, had been promptly authorized, it could have done no harm. The manner in which it has been treated, on both sides, in Congress only could make its effect doubtful. Here, it would not have been regarded as ["an" *changed to* "a"] hostile measure: and while at home it would have deprived those who appear to be bent on an ultra course of much aliment they will now have to get up an excitement in & out of Congress, it would have enabled our government to have presented united Councils and an undivided front ["to" *canceled*] abroad. A year would remain, after notice, for negotiation, and even a longer period might be calculated upon; since if at the end of the year, negotiations should be pending, unless one government should commit some violent or offensive act, we would have been in no worse situation than in 1818. I think there is reason to apprehend that divided councils at home, if they do not encourage more extravagant demands from this government, will at least encourage delay, and lead to a waste of time which must be ultimately fatal. I yet hope that these consequences may be avoided.

I am afraid too that this government has been encouraged, ["from" *canceled*] by advices from the U.S. to believe that, although the President has twice rejected proposals to arbitration, ["he" *canceled*] yet, rather than lead to war, that mode of settlement will be ultimately adopted by our government, in some form or other. The immediate effect of all this has been to suspend, for the present, any further proposition of compromise; and believing as I do that arbitration under any circumstances is utterly hopeless, I deeply lament that attempts should have been made to mislead this gov[ernment] upon so vital a point.

I ["have very little doubt" *canceled and* "am sure that there is the best ground to apprehend now," *interlined*] that this government ["might" *canceled and* "will not" *interlined*] be brought to propose or assent to a ["better" *interlined*] partition ["than" *interlined*] by a line on the 49th parallel to the strait of Fuca, thence down the middle of the strait to the Pacific, with the right of free navigation of the Columbia, & some protection of the present agricultural settlements of British subjects north of the Columbia & south of the 49th parallel. ["I am not without hope even(?) yet" *canceled and* "It is probable" *interlined*] that the navigation of the Columbia for 10 or 15 years ["would" *canceled and* "might" *interlined*] be acceptable; and I am quite sure that if it turn out that the river is not navigable at the intersection of the 49th parallel, the right of using it ["for any period" *interlined*] would not be insisted upon.

If the article in the Times of the 3rd Jan. ["(which I sent you)" *interlined*] ever meant any thing, there is certainly at present no intention to renew ["or assent to" *interlined*] Mr. [Albert] Gal[l]atin's proposition of 1826–7, and I have reason to know that this government will, under no circumstances, consent to negotiate for the free navigation of the St. Lawrence, in connection with the Columbia. I have apprehended that the President is absolutely committed in his message against the concession of the navigation of the Columbia; and if so and he extends his commitment to exclude the privileges even for a few years, the case may be regarded as well nigh hopeless.

I am ardently desirous of peace, if it can be honorably preserved, and am not unwilling to make the concessions ["already" *canceled*] indicated, ["in my former letters;" *interlined*] but it is not to be disguised that our cause has been weakened abroad by our divisions at home, by the public writers—especially in the North American Review & some of the newspapers, and by private letter writers, depreciating and attempting to refute our claims, and holding out encouragement to believe that the Executive will be deserted, and, ["that" *canceled*] what is called, the War Party will ultimately find no countenance.

If there be a determination not to authorize the notice according to the President's recommendation, would it not be advisable to declare immediately that the Senate would not advise arbitration; and that, unless within a given, and a brief, period, partition upon a reasonable basis (defining it) should ["not" *canceled*] be agreed to, then notice should be given?

It is only to be expected that as long as there is a hope here (and it is ["I assure you," *interlined*] encouraged from very respectable quarters) that arbitration will be ultimately assented to, or that there will be a division between the Executive and a majority of the Senate, there will be no great desire to do any thing, ["and" *interlined*] it may encourage demands which it is impossible we could agree to. I offer these suggestions to your own reflection; being very sure, however, that having made up our minds for the ["sake of" *interlined*; "preservation of" *changed to* "preserving"] peace to assent to ["a" *interlined*] reasonable basis of partition, we will be most apt to effect even that by union and spirit. If ground be afforded to calculate upon our divisions, we shall not only lose what we ought justly to have, but, instead of preserving peace, we will too surely lead to war.

I send you some newspapers containing Sir Robert Peel's last great speech; and you will ["by" *canceled and* "see from" *interlined*] the general news, the triumph which, upon the recent division in the house, has crowned his exertions. The success of the measure in the Lords is very confidently anticipated, without a dissolution. There are, to be sure, many speculations as to the continuance of "a ministry without a party" after it is all over; and many think the day is not distant when by a union between the "Protectionists," & the Whigs now supporting the present measure, it will be overthrown. I do not fully concur in this anticipation. Sir R. Peel is a statesman of too much ability and has too broad a foundation in public confidence to be easily overthrown. He has besides, the cordial support of the house, and will even increase his strength by the advance of the popular principle. He may be temporarily embarrassed, but his ultimate triumph, like that of "free trade" I regard as certain. I am afraid I have already wearied you, especially as I am compelled by the condition of my health to write so carelessly, and in so desultory a manner.

I bring my letter to a close, therefore, with the assurance of my sincere esteem & regard, Louis McLane.

ALS in ScCleA; PC in Jameson, ed., *Correspondence*, pp. 1076–1079.

From Ch[arles] Aug[ustus] Davis

New York [City,] 4 March 1846

My D[ea]r Sir, The public mind here continues exceedingly restive and in a state of uncertainty in regard to matters which involve a fear of hostilities. As an evidence of this there never has been known so large an amount of money on deposit in our various sound banks as at present. The owners of capital seem afraid to put it into action—but "call it home," like workmen from the field—when the weather is such that no work can be done profitably—or to use another illustration—business is now like a ship "hove to" whilst the fog is so thick the pilot dare not steer his way—but wait till he can see ahead a little clearer.

Pending this state of things there must be sad injury inflicted somewhere. Some interests must be suffering severely—and all interests must directly or indirectly be injured. It is said that *Catholic Countries* are left behind *Protestant Countries*—by reason of the greater number of Holy days of the former. I fear if this be so—we shall, so long, as present state of things exist feel the influence seriously—for we have a great many days (so far as profitable labor goes)—entirely "holy".

During this state of things we are not without *reports* and we

have to day some agre[e]able reports in which I see your name mention[e]d as striving to bring about an honorable adjustment of pending difficulties. I am happy amid the gloom to see our people turning with entire confidence to the belief that your views on this
question are altogether secure and safe—and all that I can say to
such, is that those views are more or less of value to the nation so far
as we the people incline to recognize your influence on those who
are to be acted upon by them—for after all, this seems to me to be the
question in point. No man[']s opinions and views can be of use to
the Country or people unless they give open evidence of recognition
and this feeling I am quite sure is taking greater & greater hold of
the people—the evidence of which—only requires a suitable occasion
to be made manifest. There never was in my judgment a more suitable occasion for such men as yourself to make a short northern visit.
You know the South and S[outh] West—but I don[']t think you know
the North and North East—at any rate I sh[oul]d like the latter to
know you. A whole generation has gone by since you were last
here—and a new one has taken their place. Our *people* want to *see*
more of those men who at present occupy stations of the deepest interest to their national and individual welfare. I think also a short
trip w[oul]d do you good—a little relaxation does no harm. You
work too hard—and here I think is the leading difference between
our statesmen of eminence—and those of Europe. Ours are compel[le]d comparatively to do all their own work—theirs have a super-
abunda[n]ce of well paid assistance. See that great speech for example with all its *details*—which Sir Rob[er]t Peel makes. ⁷⁄₁₀ if not
⁹⁹⁄₁₀₀ of it all, furnish'd at his hand by the first grade of ability. Our
statesmen w[oul]d be constrain'd to seek it all up themselves. No
wonder therefore our men are worn to the bone, whilst theirs look
fat & healthy and have plenty of time for both City & Country relaxation & yet by the world are supposed to be great *workers*. With
great regard Y[ou]r friend & Ob[edien]t S[ervan]t, Ch: Aug. Davis.

ALS in ScCleA.

From J[AMES] HAMILTON, [JR.]

Houston Texas, March 4th 1846
My Dear Sir, This will be handed you, by my friend James Webb
Esq[ui]r[e], formerly Sec[retar]y of State of this Republic in which,
he was most advantageously known, & distinguished, and before ["as"

interlined] the highly esteem[e]d & confided in, Judge of the District Court of Florida.

Judge Webb is a most sound & excellent Lawyer, a gentleman of unblemished integrity, and great private worth.

I will esteem it, My Dear Sir[,] a special favor, confer[r]ed on myself, if you can with President [James K.] Polk, aid him, in the procurement of the office of District Judge, for this State. Judge Webb, I ought to add, has at all times, been in the most cordial sympathy with our State [of S.C.], & her public Men, and has been amidst, calumny & injustice, among the warmest and most efficient of my supporters. I remain My Dear Sir with esteem most respectfully & faithfully Your friend & ob[edien]t Ser[van]t, J. Hamilton.

ALS in DNA, RG 59 (State Department), Letters of Application and Recommendation during the Administrations of James K. Polk, Zachary Taylor, and Millard Fillmore, 1845–1853, James Webb (M-873:92, frames 484–486). NOTE: An AEU by Calhoun reads "Gen[era]l Hamilton recommending Mr. Webb."

From J[AMES] HAMILTON, [JR.], "(Private)"

Houston, March 4[t]h 1846

My Dear Sir, I enclose you [the] within Letter in behalf of two Gentlemen who are warmly & influentially your friends in this Country. I will be happy if you can back it influentially as they are *Gentlemen* really of character[,] Talent & cultivation. [Samuel] Houston['s] influence will be of course exerted to get his Creatures into every office large or small in this Country.

I have designed my Dear Sir for a long long time long time [*sic*] to write you but a variety of circumstances have prevented my doing so resulting from rapid moves & intense occupation. I have not the less been a most anxious observer in relation to the high position you have occupied before the Country which has entirely reconciled me to the risks of your senatorial position in reference to the ulterior views of your friends.

I have not been inactive & feel satisfied that the whole South can be united in one solid Phalanx for you comprehending both Tennessee & Arkinsaw [*sic*,] Baltimore Convention or no Baltimore Convention—All Oregon or none of it.

Today I leave this for Austin the Seat of Government on very large business with the Legislature of Texas, and will be in Washington City early in May.

Until you hear from me from Austin (*confidentially*, which it will have to be, from Houston['s] morbid & insane jealousy of me) keep off all action on the public Debt of Texas or her public Lands as I think the Legislature of Texas will in all this month submit a *projet* on both subjects to the U.S. Govt. [*partial word canceled*] satisfactory to the public Creditors, beneficial to Texas & preeminently so to the U.S.

I shall be detained on business more than a month at Washington and I hope to know your friends and to guage [*sic*] the zeal with which they intend to bring you out as the antica[u]cus candidate and as the anti office holders nominee.

Pray with my kind regards to [George] McDuffie & the rest of our [S.C.] delegation say to the former that I will write him from Austin. I remain My Dear Sir, with sincere esteem faithfully & resp[ectfull]y Yours, J. Hamilton.

P.S. I am sure you will be pleased to learn, that I have every prospect, of having my claims on this Govt., placed on a satisfactory basis.

I forgot to inform you that every leading Democrat in Louisiana is your friend with Gov. [Isaac] Johnson at their head & a host of Whigs.

I have not said a word about war because really the Governments of both Countries would be subjects for a Lunatic Assylum if they could fight about an object so infinitely worthless as Oregon.

Be so good as to direct to me to the care of Dick & Hill [in] N. Orleans where I will meet your Letter.

ALS in ScCleA.

From J[OHN] H. VAN EVRIE

Rochester N.Y., 4th March 1846

Sir, Although personally an entire stranger to *you* I have taken the liberty of addressing you on a subject of deep and profound interest, to all true Patriots, involving as it does the destiny of a common country—The subject of *Negro slavery*.

I wish however only to communicate with you on a single aspect of this great question and it is this—The people of this State have called a convention to assemble in June next to revise their Constitution. The question will be presented to the Convention whether or ["no" *interlined*] the right of suffrage shall be extended to the

Blacks with no more restrictions on it than in the case of the whites. And it will I fear be decided affirmatively. The Whig party in view of ulteriour objects, actually took the lead in the legislature, for calling the convention and in conjunction with their convenient allies the Liberty party have since, thoroughly canvassed the State and to a great extent forestalled the public ["sentiment" *canceled*] judgment. While the Democratic Politicians & Presses, have scarcely alluded to the subject and when they have ["done" *interlined*] so it has been in a shuffling & noncommital manner. As an illustration I have taken some pains to get at the state of opinion in this city and it is a fact that I am the only Democrat that dare openly *oppose* it. The result cannot be otherwise[,] the Blacks in this State or as many as may hereafter come into it in, eighteen months hence will be entitled to all the privileges exercised by the whites. What are the consequences? As a Northern Democrat, and fully imbued with the principles of Freedom, as emb[o]died in our Federative sistem, I cannot but look upon it as the most dangerous movement that has ever occurred in this Country.

The particular form which this danger will present itself in, ["it" *canceled*] is at this time difficult to conjecture but that the ultimate result would be to break up our happy & well balanced *Federative sistem* there can be no doubt.

Mr. [Thomas] Jefferson has said that the Northern Democracy were the natural allies of the South (of course he could only mean by the South the slave holders[)]. Yourself or some other southern statesman have declared that, negro slavery was the chief corner stone of our Republican Edifice. As a great practical fact both are right.

I say to my Northern Democratic Friends that Negro Slavery, has been the great barrier[?] of the Free white labouring classes[,] that had it not existed long before this a great National Bank[,] Protective Tariff &c &c ["wh" *canceled*] would have been saddled on the general govt. & that a vast Central sistem, overriding and overruling all State Sovereignity & individual liberty, would have taken the place of our Present Federative sistem.

But to return to the question of Negro suffrage in this State, its immediate effect will be to give the whig ["consoli"(?) *canceled*] *monopoly* party a complete assendency in the State by adding perhaps 15,000 votes to their party and with the 36 Electoral votes of N.Y. possibly controlling the Presidency for half a century, and then Federalism may hope to carry out its long cherished schemes of Legislation, and a time would soon be reached in the developement of that policy, when the peculiar institutions of the States would have to give place to the idea of ["a" *interlined*] *general welfare* when the great bulwark against the monopoly sperit and the great Protection of the Northern labourer, Negro Slavery would be swept away. A true friend of Freedom is he who clearly sees this question in its proper light & thus seeing it dares in the face of a *sickly sentimentality* that would sacrifice the whole race of whites in visionery projects to benefit a few blacks, to stand up for the truth and the great cause of liberty dependent as that cause is on the preservation[?] of the purity of the Anglo Saxon race and our present well balanced Federative sistem.

In conclusion if your duties permit will you do me the favor of replying to this *briefly*, and give me your views of the subject. I am no trading Politician, only a citizen ["and" *canceled and* "and wish to see the opinions of one so eminent and so capable of judging as yourself" *interlined*] & beg to refer you ["to" *interlined*] Gen. [Lewis] Cass or Gov. [William L.] Marcy either of which will I think recollect me. With sentiments of profound Esteem Your Obe[dien]t Serv[an]t, J.H. Van Evrie[?].

ALS in ScCleA; PC in Boucher and Brooks, eds., *Correspondence*, pp. 327–329. NOTE: Though the signature is problematically decipherable, the writer of this letter would seem to be John H. Van Evrie (1814?–1896), a New York physician who was editor of the New York *Day-Book* during 1848–1861 and was the author of *Negroes and Negro Slavery* (New York: N.Y. Day-Book, 1853) and *White Supremacy and Negro Subordination* . . . (New York: Van Evrie, Horton & Co., 1868).

From J[OHN] S. BARBOUR

Catalpa [Culpeper County, Va.,] March 5th 1846

My Dear Sir, We have now the deepest snow, & have been visited, with the severest snow storm, known in the last forty years.

My wife [Elizabeth A. Byrne Barbour] is very unhappy for our son James [Barbour], who is some where in Texas, but we know not where. You kindly gave him a letter to Gen[era]l [J. Pinckney] Henderson & he had others to Gen[era]l [Samuel] Houston, Gen[era]l [Mirabeau B.] Lamar & Gen[era]l [Edward] Burlesson [*sic;* Burleson]. It is most probable that Gen[era]l Henderson will know where he is. But where Gen[era]l Henderson ["is," *interlined*] I am uncertain, & if I knew being wholly unknown to him I could illy ask him ["without your request also" *interlined*] to find out where my son is & forward the enclosed letter.

I feel assured that Gen[era]l Henderson will have seen & been consulted by him & of course will know how to direct a letter to him. And as James will be travelling in several parts of the State he may not be at the point to which Gen[era]l Henderson may direct a letter—and he may afterwards see my son. It is for this cause & to guard James well in his wants, that I have named to him the provision made for him at New Orleans, should any contingency press him for money which I cannot well imagine, as he took with him between 500 & 1,000$. But he has many perils of swindlers & robbers to pass by, *& may need especially in his infirm health.*

Have you read the life of [Henry] Clay by [Calvin] Colton? I have not, but I have seen extracts in the Alex[andri]a Gaz[ette] which make it appear that [James] Buchanan called on Clay [in 1824?] in the presence of [Robert P.] Letcher, [then Representative from Ky.,] and there expressed his preference for Mr. Clay as the Secretary for [Andrew] Jackson. This is the only part of the conversation which is retailed ["by Colton" *interlined*] on the authority, (evidently) of Letcher & Clay. Is it to be believed that this *was all* the conversation held with those three? Clay was intimate with Buchanan & Buchanan the ardent friend of that system which was Clay's *fulcrum* & *lever* for obtaining political power. Clay shows that this conversation did occur. The enquiry returns on us, *when* was it so held? Was it before Buchanan went to Jackson or afterwards? This is most material in the investigation of the part that Clay had in this idle & silly intrigue. It was evidently with Clay before [*partial word canceled*] Buchanan went to Jackson. For Jackson repulsed the proposition so vehemently when Buchanan made it to him, that it is hardly possible to beleive [*sic*] that he wou'd have opened the subject with Clay after the decisive & vehement rejection of all overtures on that subject ["by Jackson" *interlined*]. If he went first to Clay (which is most rational) then Clay must have given such countenance to Buchanan's scheme, as to induce Buchanan to think that consent & approbation by Jackson wou'd effectuate his purpose, and this I have no doubt was & is the truth of the affair.

Clay wished to be President—in default of that his next aim was the department of State. He wou'd have preferred that department under ["Adams" *canceled*] Jackson if he cou'd get it. Numerous circumstances strengthen this belief—But he could not get it under Jackson. *That was impossible.* You and I both know that *was im-*

possible. If there existed no other reason, it is enough to know that if Jackson had been President in 1825, then Mr. [John Quincy] Adams would have been Jackson[']s Secretary of State. No one knowing the relations of the parties, Jackson, Adams, [James] Monroe, the *past* & the *then present,* could pause for a moment in doubt as to Jackson[']s Secretary of State had he been President in 1825. This Clay firmly believed when he told Dr. [Daniel] Drake & others in 1824 at Lexington, that he shou'd vote for Adams. The overture of Buchanan & others after Clay reached Washington in December; raised a momentary hope ["with Clay," *interlined*] that Jackson might not make Adams his Secretary. Accordingly, we find that the evidence *produced by Mr. Clay himself shows* that he professed *to doubt in Jan[uar]y 1825,* for whom he should vote (Jackson or Adams) when by *other portions of his evidence* he *had* ["already" *interlined*] *determined* the question *four months before,* in Lexington!! Buchanan in 1824 was an inferiour man to what he now is. He had neither cast[e] nor character of any moment with any party. Yet he wanted a foreign mission, as [then Representative Thomas P.] Moore of Ky. said of him & that "when he got on his pumps & short breeches & silk stockings he already conceived the commission as in his pocket." Buchanan was no leader of the Penn[sylvani]a delegation *at that time.* He was but a *waif* from the wreck of Federalism, to whom Adams could not give a foreign mission, but Jackson & Clay might and ["it" *canceled and* "this mission abroad" *interlined*] was well secured, if Jackson & Clay could reach power by Buchanan[']s intervention.

Gen[era]l Jackson always thought well of Mr. Adams until *he knew* that he intended to make Mr. Clay Secretary of State. I was with him the night of the 9th Feb[ruar]y after Adams' election by the House; went with him to the leve[e] at Mr. Monroe[']s; stood near him when he met Mr. Adams, & congratulated him (in his happiest manner) on his election. He explained this to me several weeks after by saying that he thought well of Adams; was sincere in his congratulation; but changed his opinion on Clay[']s getting the State dept. from Adams.

If Clay (as he now shows through Colton) knew that Buchanan either came from Jackson to him & did not repulse the offer, he participated in its guilt. And this he does not pretend, for Buchanan went forward with it.

If on the other hand he held such conversation with Buchanan as justified him in going afterwards to Jackson, and justified him too in going forward with the overtures & intrigues, until decisively repulsed by Jackson, why then it proves all that Jackson ever alleged between Buchanan & Clay in the offer made him.

The insincerity in Jackson was in his telling Buchanan "that if the hair of his head knew who he w[oul]d appoint, he w[oul]d cut it off &c." for he as certainly intended ["at that time" *interlined*] to continue Adams, his Secretary of State, as he had hair to cut off. This pattering in a double sense might ["be" *interlined*] a part of that ["sinister" *interlined*] policy, which Jackson was ["as" *canceled and then interlined*] dextrous in playing as any left handed tactician of his times.

I could write you a small volume on this topick. My pen has wandered into it, in the belief that the evidence *now produced* fixes the imputation more strongly than ever, & as Jackson understood it & avowed. Buchanan *was Clay*[']*s friend, & ardently so.* He opened the negotiation with Clay who rec[eive]d it in a way agre[e]able to Buchanan, who persevered with it, until Jackson denounced & repulsed it.

Excuse me. Y[ou]rs with true Regard, J.S. Barbour.

ALS in ScCleA; PEx in Boucher and Brooks, eds., *Correspondence,* pp. 329–331. NOTE: Colton's book mentioned above was *The Life and Times of Henry Clay* (New York: A.S. Barnes & Co., 1846).

From JA[ME]S L[AWRENCE] CALHOUN

Augusta [Ga.,] March 5, 1846

Dear Uncle, Inclosed please find a memorandum [*not found*] from your son James [Edward Calhoun]. I had intended returning home by Washin[g]ton but for a mat[t]er of bus[i]ness at home. You will pleas[e] send me maps also ["as" *interlined*] sent for by Ja[me]s and any other papers you may think proper to send me would be very much valued ["by me" *canceled*]. If you can send me one of your Likeness such as my father had I shou[ld] be much pleased as I have not bin able to get one. Direct your let[t]ers to Cha[r]leston[,] Tallahachy [*sic*] County, Missis[s]ip[p]i and except [*sic*] my best respects for a coppy of your life which was handed to me by sister L[ucretia Calhoun Townes]. My ["Love" *canceled*] Love to Aunt [Floride Colhoun Calhoun]. I hope to see you next somer [*sic*] at your House. I Shal[l] return to Carolina in June next. Your devoted Relatione, Jas. L. Calhoun.

P.S. Please [w]rite soon.

ALS in ScCleA. NOTE: James Lawrence Calhoun was a son of Calhoun's brother William.

From JAMES GADSDEN

Office So. Ca. Ra[il]Ro[ad] Comp[any]
Charleston March 5, 1846

Dear Sir, I understand that Mr. [John M.] Berrien [Senator from Ga.] either has, or will introduce, a Resolution or bill to return to the State of Georgia, and to the Georgia Ra[il]Ro[ad] & B[an]k-[in]g Company, the duty paid the last year on Rail Road Iron; all of which has been appropriated to the Construction of a Road from Augusta, to Connect with other Roads in progress to the Valley of the Mississippi.

This Iron was imported in part through the Agency of this Company; and about the same period a small importation of Rail Iron (the duty on which amounted to Five Thousand & twenty seven ⁹³⁄₁₀₀ Dollars—$5027⁹³⁄₁₀₀) was made with a view to Complete this Road, Connecting, with that at Augusta; on which the main mail to the So. West is transported.

I have now to request; and in Common justice, that on the introduction of the Bill or Resolution alluded to, you will have attached to it a provission to include our claim with that from Georgia. This Amount will enable us to add another Locomotive to the mail service, and thus ensure the *speed* and Certainty so much desired by the Post Master General [Cave Johnson]. Resp[ectfully] Your ob[edien]t Serv[an]t, James Gadsden, Pres[iden]t.

LS in DNA, RG 46 (U.S. Senate), 29A-G5. NOTE: An AEU by Calhoun reads "Duty on rail Road Iron."

Memorial of the heir of John Moore, presented by Calhoun to the Senate on 3/5. Frances Moore asked for repayment of advances made by her ancestor during the Revolutionary War. (The memorial was referred to the Committee on Revolutionary Claims.) Abs in *Congressional Globe*, 29th Cong., 1st Sess., p. 458.

FURTHER REMARKS ON OREGON

[In the Senate, March 5, 1846]
[*The preceding speaker gave way to*] Mr. Calhoun, who wished to correct an erroneous impression which might be conveyed by the remarks of the Senator from North Carolina, [William H. Haywood, Jr., in a long speech in defense of President Polk's course,] in respect to the protocol [of 9/24/1844] which had been spoken of. If Senators would turn to it they would find that it contained simply a declaration on the part of the British minister [Richard Pakenham] stating the reasons why he did not feel authorized to go on with negotiations; and that he had applied to his Government for further instructions: whether those instructions were received or not, he could not say; he presumed, however, that they had been received. The United States never assented to the proposition that any part of Oregon belonged to Great Britain. Our negotiators had always claimed the whole. In his own letter [of 9/3/1844] to the British negotiator he had claimed on the part of the Government the whole valley of the Columbia river. He was not aware that it had ever been acknowledged that the title was not in us.

From the Washington, D.C., *Daily National Intelligencer*, March 6, 1846, p. 2. Also printed in the Alexandria, Va., *Gazette and Virginia Advertiser*, March 7, 1846, p. 2. Variants in *Congressional Globe*, 29th Cong., 1st Sess., p. 459; the Baltimore, Md., *American & Commercial Daily Advertiser*, March 7, 1846, p. 2; the Charleston, S.C., *Courier*, March 10, 1846, p. 2; the London, England, *Times*, April 10, 1846, p. 5.

From J[OHN] S. BARBOUR

Catalpa [Culpeper County, Va.,] March 6th 1846
My Dear Sir, I wrote you last night enclosing a packet for Gen[era]l [J. Pinckney] Henderson of Texas, which was the only mode of communicating with my son James [Barbour] which then occurred.

The mail of this morning brought us a letter from him at Lagrange about sixty miles from Austin, in which he says that his health is improving & that he will be at the seat of Govt. in Texas at the meeting of the Legislature on the 16 ["th" *interlined*] Feb[ruar]y. This letter was mailed at New Orleans the 18th Feb[ruar]y & got there by private conveyance. I presume by this time that mails are established in Texas or will be. Nor do I know which of their Towns is the Seat of Govt. James has travelled over much of the State, & says it is in many parts of it the finest Country he ever saw. He says that our friends [Branch T.] Archer & T[homas] J. Green do not stand well. That as to the Senate for Archer or the Ho[use] of Rep[resentative]s for Green the thing is ridiculous & preposterous. That neither of them have any popularity in any part of the State. That Archer is regarded as a visionary man, honourable but utterly impracticable & worthless. That Green stands low. He thinks that [Samuel] Houston is all powerful in the State, & that he and Gen[era]l [Thomas J.] Rusk will be chosen to the Senate.

In my comments on the Life of [Henry] Clay by [Calvin] Colton, having little to do, I threw out those suggestions & reminiscences which it was possible might interest you. Clay & [William H.] Crawford were the first open intriguers for the Presidency that we have known. [Aaron] Burr's affair was clandestine. He wore the mask of virtue, and in that paid some respect to appearances. Clay has done more to taint the politicks of the Country, both on masses & individuals, than every other publick man we have known.

[In 1824 James] Buchanan wanted a foreign mission. Clay wanted the department of State. Here & *in these*, are the clues to all the mystery in that transaction. The facts now shown by Clay are stronger in corroboration of what [Andrew] Jackson charged on ["Clay" *canceled and then interlined*] *through* Buchanan ["as Clay(')s agent," *interlined*] than all the other proofs presented to the publick. Buchanan was in communication with Clay *on that particular subject.* He went *afterwards* to Jackson. Clay neither reproved nor checked the overture. *Jackson did.* Buchanan must have found it *acceptable to Clay*, else he w[oul]d not have proceeded to Jackson. Jackson[']s denunciation was decisive & he stopt. It is manifest to one at all in the secret of the relations of [John Quincy] Adams & Jackson at that time, that Jackson had no option but to give Adams the office of Secretary of State. Adams had it to give Clay. Jackson had it not, and therefore Clay got it, by giving Adams the Presidency.

I took up my pen to repeat the request that I took the liberty of making—that you will send the package to Gen[era]l [J. Pinckney] Henderson for James & ask him to forward it to James wherever he is, for I am confident that Gen[era]l Henderson will know.

My eldest son [John S. Barbour, Jr.,] speaks of going to Texas & carrying some negroes to settle a plantation about the last of this month. James gives so flattering an account of the Country that his

Brother thinks it judicious to adventure something that way. With all Respect Y[ou]rs Sincerely, J.S. Barbour.

ALS in ScCleA.

From JAMES GADSDEN

Charleston S.C., March 6, 1846

Dear Sir. I send you a few Lithiographic Maps, which present the projected Rail ways to the West, which you can distribute among our Western Friends. Those of Carolina & Georgia stand in Bold relief, and shew the strong natural Position of Charleston in its relations with the West. We need only Railways to the Valley of the Mississippi to realize all our fond & confiding predictions, as to the future prosperity and growth of this City. We have heard nothing from your committee on the Memphis Memorial.

The Postmaster General [Cave Johnson], contemplates with what reason I am unable to comprehend, a material change in the main mail, by which the interests of the So. C. R. R. Company may be seriously affected. I have given to him the decision of this Board, and as much has been said of late of the obst[in]ancy & unaccommodating spirit of Rail Ways, I have thought it proper to place our position before you and Mr. [Isaac E.] Holmes [Representative from S.C.], so that you will be able to correct any impressions which may be attempted to prejudice this Corporations [*sic*] should Mr. Johnson, under his contracted restrickness [*sic*], not accord to our proposition.

The Contract we now have this Company is satisfied with, and we believe few Companies have performed their obligations with more fidelity. Now Mr. Johnson requires Three more performances, Change of hour, night service in part, and *higher speed*. The latter most objectionable as involving greater *hazard* and *expense*. In addition he requires the right to control the hours of departure & arrival of mails, without regard to the inconvenience they may inflict on the interests of the Company and accommodation of Travellers. By the present arrangements our Passenger Trains & mail Train are one, and are made to play in advantageously for the Company; & without this *union* we could not afford to take the mail at present price.

Now we have said to Mr. Johnson we will accord to you all that you require—*higher speed*[,] *change & control of hours as the de-*

partment may require for the *main mail*, provided we are *adequately compensated.* By this arrangement we would propose that the main mail Train be exclusively at the Control of the Post Office Department, to follow all the changes which the public interest may require, and to give all the *dispatch* & *certainty* in mail intellegence that the spirit of the Age would demand.

We are aware what the Commercial Community require, and believe that the whole Community are willing to pay an equivalent for what they receive. By the arrangement proposed the *certainty* & *dispatch* would be ensured, and much of the now just complaint on the irregularities of the mails would be avoided.

To carry out this excellent arrangement would require an extra Train for Passengers, and by this accommodation line we would supply all the smaller Post offices, so that the main mail Train would not be stopped on its course but speed onward with all the desire of those who are awaiting intelligence. When you consider the growth of the West and the increasing mail matter, that is to pass by this main line to the far West—Texas & California, you will see the propriety of the plan proposed, and it is the only plan by which the Post Master General can secure effectually all he requires—The Hours & Speed—By paying for it. The plan would not on our Road involve much more than 8 to 10,000 Dollars additional & for this he will have all the speed & certainty he could desire. I submit the views with respect. Your ob[edien]t James Gadsden.

[P.S.] You will be attracted by the Short Line from Charleston to Mazatlan [Mexico]. We need only enterprise in Charleston.

ALS in ScCleA.

From L[EMUEL] WILLIAMS [JR.], "Confidential"

Boston, March 6th 1846

My dear Sir, Soon after the receipt of your note written on the eve of your departure from Washington, I left this part of the country for Lake Superior, where I remained several months cut off from all means of communication with the civilized portion of the community. Since my return I have often contemplated writing to you, but the expectation of meeting you personally has, from time to time, induced me to postpone the fulfilment of my design. I had some things which I wished to say to you & prefer[r]ed to say it in an interview to committing it to paper. Now that I no longer contemplate visiting Washington, I will delay no longer this mode of communication.

I was entirely satisfied with the contents of your note. It was doubtless the best course. The wisest as well as the most dignified. I had no wish to remain in office [as Collector of Customs at Boston] longer on my own account, but the interests of my friends personal, & political, induced me to hope, that after the pecuniary sacrifices I had made to effect the election of Mr. [James K.] Polk I should not have ["been" *interlined*] so unceremoniously discarded, from an office which I had filled to the entire satisfaction of the mercantile community. My removal is attributable entirely to the influence, & representations of Mr. [George] Bancroft, who on his first return to Boston declared to a friend of his that he had "killed Calhounism, in Boston" by my removal. You are well aware I suppose that those persons who advocated the election of Mr. Polk have generally, in New England, been thrust from office, & their places supplied by those who were offered to him. While I mention these things I must exempt my successor [Marcus Morton] from any imputation of endeavoring to effect my removal. He assured me that he did not seek the office, & only was induced to accept of it upon being assured that my rejection was at all events determined upon. This assurance I presume he received from Mr. Bancroft. I will also do him the justice to say that he has not removed any of your & my friends since he came into the office. I do not intend to express any wish upon the question of his confirmation, to which I feel indifferent[,] ignorant as I am of who will probably be his successor. I should greatly prefer Judge Morton to many whom I have heard named as probable to succeed him, & should prefer some, who have been named, to him. We are on terms of courteous communication, and I am sure I feel towards ["him" *interlined*] nothing like hostility. But very different are my feelings towards Mr. [Isaac H.] Wright who has been nominated as Navy agent for this Port. He is in my opinion entirely unfit for the office. I have no personal acquaintance with him, & cannot have, with a man of his character; [*partial word canceled and* "nor" *interlined*] do I think my opinion has been unduly influenced by the fact that he has always been a most ["virulent &" *canceled*; "zealous" *interlined and then canceled*] indefatigable advocate of [Martin] Van Buren[']s, & a bitter opponent of you. My honest opinion is that as he would have, *as Navy Agent*, ample opportunity to defraud the government without the hazard of detection, the interests of the government would not be safe in his hands.

I know it will give you pleasure to hear that I am now placed in a situation which exempts me from the temptation of office from *pecuniary* considerations. There is not any office in the gift of the President of the U. States, or the People, which I could accept; and should you again be before the people for the highest ["office" *interlined*] in their gift, it will give me pleasure to show that in advocating your cause I am not influenced by selfish considerations. I am dear Sir with great respect & regard your friend, L. Williams.

ALS in ScCleA. Note: President Polk in February had nominated Isaac H. Wright to be Naval Agent in the Customs House at Boston. In June he withdrew the nomination without explanation.

From S[tephen] P. Andrews

Boston, March 7th 1846

Honored Sir, I have the honor to remit to you the enclosed papers which contain a notice of the recent revolutionary movement in the Island of Cuba, and which were to have transpired during the last week. This is the result of a plan well combined and its success will, I believe be complete if it meets with support on the part of the United States.

I have in my possession various letters which proves the favorable state of the public mind, and as the plan contemplates as a principal object, an[n]exation to the United States, I felt it important to communicate these facts to you as the individual to whom the Cubans will look with most confidence in aiding their struggle by your countenance.

In making this communication permit me to apologize for its shortness and imperfections as I hardly yet understand the English [*sic*] language so as to trust myself with it. With the highest respect I am Sir Your most humble serv[an]t, S.P. Andrews.

ALS with En in ScCleA. Note: Enclosed is a newspaper clipping from the Boston, Mass., *Chronotype* of March 7, 1846, containing an article entitled "Cuba," that mentions the possibility of Cuban independence from Spain and a resultant probable connection with the U.S.

From [Napoleon Alcindor] Beaulieu, [Belgian Minister Resident at Washington,] Galabrun's[?] Hotel, 3/7. Beaulieu encloses a package and a letter of introduction for himself from Thomas G. Clemson to Calhoun. He apologises for not delivering them earlier but, being packed in his luggage, they only reached him today. Be-cause of the late hour Beaulieu feels obliged to postpone a personal visit to Calhoun and his wife until a later date. (See Thomas G. Clemson's letter of 1/*ca.* 30 to Calhoun.) ALS (in French) in ScCleA.

From W[illia]m P. Duval

Tallahassee [Fla.,] March 7th 1846

My dear Sir, Yours was duly received and I rejoice that the news from England, so fully and clearly proves your foresight and wis-dom. The sound policy you have so ably maintained on the Oregon question, must prevail unless all common sense and patriotism, are thrown away. I have doubted, whether you will speak on this ques-tion after the mul[t]iplicity of long *talks*, we have received, from both houses of congress. Perhaps you are patiently waiting untill the resolution of notice with all the amendments, shall be brough[t] up & discussed so that you may have all before you in discussion. I confess a strong desire to have the full benefit of your views on this important measure. I think the nation expects this and in this State your sentiments, are anxiously desired.

If you should speak, (as what you deliver will be printed in pamphlet form,) I should like to have many of your speeches sent to me, for distribution in this State. I know all the men of standing and influence in the several counties and would take an interest, in spreading your opinions.

The course taken by both [Lewis] Cass and [William] Allen does not meet the approbation of the democratic party in this State. I consider it undignified and intirely too boasting and insulting to to England. The wordy, chinese, tumbling, and vaulting in the ad-vance of war is too ridiculous for a thinking people—we want no gasconading speech[e]s to back our courage. A great nation sensi-ble of her rights will firmly and calm[l]y maintain them nor for one moment de[s]cend from her high attitude, to bandy expressions, of vulgar abuse, or taunting insult with any nation. The senate of the United States, is surely the last place that such inflam[m]atory speek-ers should receive countenance or support.

Gov[erno]r [John] B[r]anch & myself will in three days meet the Georgia commissioners, at Bainbridge in that State, to consult as to the boundary between their State & Florida. Gov[erno]r [William D.] Moseley, who is one of your devoted friends applied to our senators, to request of the President [James K. Polk] he would furnish to us a competent engineer and the necessary instruments to run the line between our States. The Governor has received no answer to his communications on this subject, and he is evidently mortified at this neglect. He ta[l]ked the other day of writing to you, and Mr. Spait [*sic*; Jesse Speight?, Senator from Miss.] on the subject. I do not know on what terms you are with the President but it seems to me if he was apprised of Governor Moseley['s] desire on this subject, he would not hesitate to send an engineer with the proper mathamatical instruments. Georgia declined to agree as we proposed that the United States should join in appointing a commissioner, but her refusal should not prevent our receiving the aid of one of the United States engineers. Our meeting at Bainbridge is to settle some preliminaries, previous to surveying the boundary. It may be a delicate matter for you to interfere, by asking the President to send us an engineer, and I do not desire you to do any thing in this matter, that may give offence to our Senators [David L. Yulee and James D. Westcott, Jr.]—Allthough, I do not approve of their want of attention to the communications of our Governor, and they will find their neglect will effect them more than any one else.

My brother is in Washington and I take it for granted he has long since called to see you.

I have a son [John Crittenden Duval] in Texas whom you saw once with me at Washington, three years since. He fought for the Independence of Texas, where my eldest son [Burr H. Duval] fell, and was one of the few that escaped the dreadful mas[s]acre at Goliad. He has been for more than [a] year on the western frontier of Texas and was lately attached to the [Texas Ranger] Corps under the command of Maj[o]r Hayes [*sic*; Col. John C. Hays].

He is recommended by the Legislature of this State and the Governor to the President, for a captaincy in the new rifle Regiments proposed to be raised. That my son is deserving of the commission, his bravery, and sufferings in the cause of Texas, proves. Few men are better fitted for the command of a company. His morals and courage, skill, and prudence, combine to place him among the first, as a captain in the service. If you and your South Carolina friends and our kind friend Hon[ora]ble Dixon H. Lewis can aid me in procuring this commission for my son John C. DuVal, it would gratify me much. I am too poor to place my son in business. He is in truth a military man and if he has the opportunity (and should live) he will make himself a name, worthy of his family & country.

I want documents badly here and if you can get some friend to frank them to me, they will be used with effect in our Southern Journal printed here. I am with sincere respect & affection yours, Wm. P. DuVal.

ALS in ScCleA.

From K. H. Fish

New York [City,] 7th March 1846

Dear Sir, In my com[municatio]n of 3rd Inst. through the absence of my documents, I made an error, in stating the former boundaries of Texas to be the Rio Grande, north of the State of Tamaulipas. It appears from [William] Kennedy's history of Texas published in '44 (Sold by Taylor of Baltimore) & which I believe is considered the most authentic extant; that the boundary line between Tamaulipas & Texas was the Neuces: and thence between Coahuila & Texas, there were conflicting claims, some maintaining the Neuces & others the Arasanso, & Medina as the boundary untill it strikes the line of Chihuahua, & thence by the line of that State & the Territory of New Mexico to the 42 deg[re]e of north Latitude. From the Same (page 5) it appears that the only title that Republic ever had *South*, or *West* of those, was derived from their own will, & lacked the assent of the Other Claimants: See act of Congress Dec[embe]r 19th '36 running thus: "Be it enacted by the Senate & House of Representatives of the Republic of Texas in Congress assembled: that from & after the ["pass" *changed to* "passing"] of this Act, the Civil & political jurisdiction of this Republic be, & is hereby declared to extend to the following boundaries; To wit: Beginning at the mouth of the Sabine River, & running west along the Gulf of Mexico, three leagues from land, to the mouth of the Rio Grande, thence up the principal stream of said River to its source, thence due north to the 42nd degree of north latitude, thence along the boundary line as defined in the Treaty between the U.S. & Spain, to the beginning"— all which they have not been able to maintain; see failure of the ill advised Santa Fee expedition. And I trust that our Gov[ern]m[en]t will not sanction, or attempt to maintain such outrageous encroachment on the undoubted Territory of a neighbor Republic: for the safety of the revenue, & the prevention of ag[g]ressions by renegade Indians & other Out-laws, it is a matter of importance that the boundary line between Two Countries, the revenue & internal laws of which are dissimilar, should be as broad and plainly marked as possible. And hence in this case it must be evident that the Rio Grande from its mouth to its nearest proximity to the Colorado mountain, and thence[?] that almost impassable mountain to its nearest approach to the 42 deg[re]e north Latitude would form the most safe & peaceful boundaries between the two Countries. But this can only be obtained Righteously through Enlightened Legislation & Liberal compensation for so much of their Territory as might be found to lie East & north of that ["original" *canceled*] boundary untill it reach the line of Texas proper. Commending this matter to your special attention; Allow me again to call your attention to the expediency of organising several Brigades of cavalry from the numerous tribes of Indians on our western frontier, both to guard against foreign aggression & internal jealousies amongst themselves: their intimate knowledge of the Country, with Horses & forage always at command, would render it a cheap yet efficient force. Their uniform should be light & imposing: a suitable number skilled in martial music, & the whole so arranged as should encourage & foster a scientific & civilized martial spirit, through which we may establish almost invincible "Walls of Fire round about our Citizens."

It appears to me that the fitting out large emigrant expeditions professedly to settle in California, in the present stage of our relations with Mexico, is calculated seriously to widen the breach, & should be discountenanced or suppressed. I have the honor to subscribe myself your very ob[edien]t Serv[an]t, K.H. Fish.

N.B. Let me recommend to your attentive perusal Kennedy's History of Texas. Resp[ectfull]y, K.H.F.

ALS in ScCleA. NOTE: An AEU by Calhoun reads "Mr. Fisk [*sic;*] Relates to the boundary between Texas & Mexico." Kennedy's history referred to was *Texas: its Geography, Natural History and Topography* (New York: Benjamin and Young, 1844).

From BENJAMIN A[LFRED] CALHOUN

Kemper County Missi[ssippi,] March 9th 1846

Dear Uncle, I have settled in Kemper County Mississippi. When I reached here, I could not get immediate possession of quarter section of Land which Doct[o]r Jones had barga[i]ned for for me. Learning that an adjoining quarter section (that embraced my horse Lot and part of the stables that I had beleived were on the pur-

chased quarter) was open for entry under the preemption Law, I
determined to build a house on it, and did so in a fiew days, and
located near the stables for the double purpose of looking after my
Team and procuring preemption. After remaining in the house
about a week I called on two respectable neighbors acquainted with
the facts, and after they had examined the premises took them with
me to Columbus and there made the following proof. 1st I had
built a House—the size of it, and the particulars about it, The time
I had lived in it, That I wanted it for settlement and not for speculation, (My application was for the East half). That there was a
man by the name of Darnall on the west half and had been for 12
months, that I owned no Land—Had never enjoyed the benefit of
the preemption Law—and that I was a single man—over 21 years
old. Upon this proof I was granted preemption, paid it out, and received certificate. After returning home from Columbus learned
there was considerable excitement about it amongst Darnall[']s
relations—and that his Father in Law should say he would spend all
he owned but what he would defeat it. Since then I have been
notified to attend at Columbus to take deposition or prove out preemption[;] again Notified to attend at DeKalb, the first, 70—the other
about 20 miles from me. Thear [*sic*] object seem[s] to me, to keep
it out of the neighborhood where the facts are known, and secondly
to annoy. Under the circumstances, I wish your advice, and that
you may understand the matter fully, will subjoin the following history. The North West of section 6 in Township 10—of Range 19 was
settled some 6 years since by a squatter. He remained on it a year
or so and left, he was followed by a Widdow woman who remained
on it a year or two and on leaving sold her improvements to Joseph
Barnett, who then owned some 1400 acres adjoining. William J.
Darnall shortly after married Barnett[']s daughter and Barnett placed
his son in law Darnall on it and he has remained on it ever since
(some 2 years). This last fall Darnall was trying to get overseers
place, and also trying to sell improvements asking some $250 for it,
acknowledging he had no right but that the man bu[y]ing could get
preemption. I do not beleive he ever designed taking preemption,
or ever would have applied for one had I not made application.
Since I obtained preemption Darnall has put up another house in
some 10 feet of the old one and as I learn under instructions from the
register. I wrote to the Register [of the U.S. Land Office at Columbus, Miss., William Dowsing] that I had understood he had been
instructing and advising means to defeat his own work but could
not beleive it. I received from the Register the enclosed reply [*not*

677

found]. I fear he is a man that can be bought over—and they I fear would be induced to pay his price from the following considerations. The body of good Land in my neighborhood is small, around is un-oc[c]upied Land. Squatters frequently set down upon it and re-main a year or two then sell there [*sic*] improvements to those men for some trifling consideration. The Barnetts and Darnalls hold no little Land in this way, and if the stranger wishes to take preemption on any of it he must first pay them a bonus—before suffering him to do so and if he refuses he is run off by force of armes or threats. If he cannot be run off then a common interest makes a common cause and they combine to defeat him. This then is the situation I am placed in. The preemption I obtained is well timbered, the Land will do for cultivation, and my building site is on it. I have none on the other quarter, it being level black Land. I am now regret[ting] I had not applied for the whole quarter as the man on it cannot ap-preciate the motives which influenced me in not taking it all, for the Register urged me to take it all as Darnall could not (he said) get it if he applied. Again Darnall has proved a different man from what I expected he was. To show you something of his c[h]aracter he is in the habit of wrestling with Negrows. I have enclosed cer-tificate and Register[']s Letter. Pleas[e] get Patent for it if you can and if they will permit it I should now like to have the other Eighth. If you obtain it and will pay the money I will refund it in 30 days, by check from Mobile. I am fearful Uncle you will think this a long and troublesome letter, but you must recollect my want of experi-ence, and to whom could I go to obtain sound advice and useful service sooner than to you. With my ardent wishes for your health, I remain affectionately your Nephew, Benjamin A. Calhoun.

ALS in ScCleA. NOTE: Benjamin Alfred Calhoun (b. 1824) was the youngest son of John C. Calhoun's brother Patrick Calhoun. He married Mary Yarbrough of Miss. and reportedly died at an unknown date in Texas. This letter is post-marked at Gainesville, Ala.

From R[OBERT] J. W[ALKER], Secretary of the Treasury

Treasury Department, March 9th 1846

Sir, I have the honor to acknowledge the receipt of the letters of Mrs. Petrie addressed to you, with the one enclosed therein to this Department. The claim referred to is probably that of an unclaimed dividend now on the loan Office Books for South Carolina in the name of Mary Tucker amounting to $58⁷⁹⁄₁₀₀.

Enclosed you will find a copy of the regulations relative to the payment of such unclaimed dividends. I am Very Respectfully, Your Obed[ien]t Serv[an]t, R.J.W., Secretary of the Treasury.

FC in DNA, RG 56 (Secretary of the Treasury), Letters to Individual Members of Congress, Series E, 1835–1848, 4:117.

From J[oseph] A. Woodward, [Representative from S.C.]

House of Representatives, March 9th 1846

Dear Sir: I am perfectly acquainted with Mr. Jordan Bennett [of Chester District, S.C.], who will come before the Senate for confirmation as *Coiner* to the mint at Charlotte N.C. He is a most excellent man, of great intelligence and distinction as a machanician. I have known ["him" *interlined*] well from early boyhood, and take great pleasure in recommending him to your favourable consideration. Very respectfully & &c, J.A. Woodward.

ALS in DNA, RG 46 (U.S. Senate), 29B-A4, Bennett.

From F[itz]w[illiam] Byrdsall

New York [City,] March 10th 1846

Dear Sir, I have long observed that the distinguishing characteristics of every National administration, produce a corresponding effect upon our political world untill at length a kind of Daguerreotype resemblance is presented. In contemplating the dialogue which recently occurred in the Senate of the U.S. between Senators Heywood [*sic*; William H. Haywood, William] Allen and [Edward A.] Hannegan respecting the real views of the President [James K. Polk] upon the 54th and 49th degrees and the Oregon question generally, I was forcibly struck with the impression of the little confidence the President reposes in any of the Senators, and infer from this, that there is but little confidence between man and man at the seat of Government. That such a Daguerreotype resemblance exists, I am impressed with the belief.

The speech of Senator Heywood has produced a great impression here. It is the subject of general remark with a considerable sprinkling of laughter at the performance of Allen & Hannegan. By the bye, I was much pleased with your mode of treating the personalities of Allen some time ago, when you happily and properly said that you could not notice any remarks that went in that direction.

Your friends generally in this city are desirous that [Michael] Hoffman be not confirmed. This man was one of the correspondents of the secret circular clique who treasonably to the country and the party opposed the annexation of Texas. He is politically merciless besides towards us here. There are some twenty odd appointments in his gift as Naval officer and they are of the same kidney as his own. His rejection would be a wholesome lesson, and it is due to him for the good of all of his kind. It would gall the tricksters and shew them that the game is not wholly their own, and the outcry would be amusing in the behalf of the "Old Admiral" as he is called by way of distinction amongst the "favorite Sons" and "Catos" &c. It might lead to his nomination for Governor next heat. All the better, as Cato is down and the land Admiral might follow.

There was a meeting in Tammany hall the other Evening in favor of Municipal Reform towards the close of which Mr. [John] Commerford whom you personally know, made an excellent speech in the course of which he mentioned your name when some one in the crowd proposed three cheers for John C. Calhoun which were given with great enthusiasm. What Mr. C[ommerford] said of you then was warmly received and I can assure you that amongst the people here you have many sincere friends. But the difficulty is with the leaders who have been again resussitated by the President in being placed in high positions. One of them, Hoffman, we should like to see meted to him measure for measure by the Senate, and it would add to the pleasure to see his tail of appointments go out after him, to make room for those he proscribed. We want no such Land admirals in the public service.

I have lately seen Mr. [Cornelius Van Wyck] Lawrence [Collector of Customs] and am induced to believe that he will repair his mistake in regard to myself. His manner, language and tone gave evidence of sincerity when he said to me, that he was sorry but once, and that was all the time ["since," *interlined*] that had ever removed me. I am inclined to think that he will now feel more a liberty to act fairly by your friends here.

The people of the middle of the nineteenth Century do not desire war—no right minded man does. The destruction of human life, or property is not necessary to vindicate our territorial rights or National honor. The War hawks at Washington will not gain much political capital with the people, and if the Executive plunges the country in war about Oregon, I would not desire his reputation a few years hence, nor for ever after. I have the honor to be yours Resp[ect]f[ull]y, F.W. Byrdsall.

ALS in ScCleA. NOTE: Hoffman's appointment was confirmed by the Senate on 3/23.

From F[RANCIS] LIEBER

Columbia S.C., March 10th [18]46

My dear Sir, Permit me to address you on a subject the nature of which will, I trust, protect me against any charge of intrusion or forwardness.

I am not acquainted with Mr. [Robert J.] Walker's tariff and donot know, therefore, how the importation of books ["is treated" canceled and "has been handled" interlined]. I hope the great cause of exchange of knowledge will be treated, this time, by Congress more liberally, more rationally, indeed more according to our own interest, than it has ever yet been done. If the rude—I had almost said, base principle of protecting home literature, which means no more than protecting dark paper and light ink, must be retained; if the far worse than merely rude principle of protecting piratical printing and literary pilfer, must be retained, be it so; but why should there be a heavy duty on foreign books if not reprinted here? Why should not ["foreign" canceled and "English" interlined] books be free, at least a year and a half after their publication in the ["country" canceled] England, and why should ["not" interlined] all English folios and quartos together with all other foreign books— German, French &c be wholly free? The revenue accruing to the U.S. from the tax on books is paltry for so great a country, while the duty weighs very heavily upon the scholar. But it is useless for me to point out to you ["all" interlined] the objectionable features of our barbarous, clogging and, I donot hesitate to call it, ungentlemanly book-tariff. The U. States acknowledge the principle that knowledge ought to be ["as" interlined] free as the wafting breezes, in the case of Colleges. ["And" canceled and "But" interlined] are books less important when written for by an individual? Is there a College cause of knowledge and a private cause of knowledge, or is

681

there but one great cause of ["know" *canceled*] thought and intellect as there is but one great cause of religion ["to" *canceled and* "of" *interlined*] which the humblest ["private" *canceled*] prayer of a loving child under its bed-clothes is as essential a part as the vastest mission or the hymn of thousands.

Permit me to beg you that you will not forget this subject, when America and Europe look to you with close attention for the management of a subject which seems at least for the moment far more important.

The year 1846 will be a great era, if the British free traders succeed the future historian will begin a new chapter—may be a period—with this year. Have you read the account of the meeting of laboring farmers ["at" *canceled*] on the cross-road ["of" *canceled*] near Goatacre, [Wiltshire, England] in the British papers? It is by far one of the most remarkable occurrences in history. With the greatest respect my dear Sir Your &c, F. Lieber.

ALS in ScCleA. NOTE: At a mass meeting on 1/6/1846 at Goatacre, Wiltshire, poor farmers and agricultural laborers passed resolutions calling for repeal of the British Corn Laws and gave testimony of the hardships brought upon them by the laws and the potato blight.

From [the Rev.] ALEXANDER BLAIKIE

Thompsonville Conn[ecticu]t, March 11th 1846
Sir, Amidst the varied duties of your station, in the discharge of which you are daily engaged, permit me to ask your attention to a small matter.

By the death of [John J.] Peav[e]y Esquire, the office of American Consul at Pictou in Nova Scotia (my native place) is vacant.

Among the candidates for the office, whose applications have been forwarded to His Excellency the President [James K. Polk], is Mr. John Stiles[,] Merchant of Boston. His certificate of business qualifications from several citizens and merchants of Boston has been sent by mail to the President.

Believing him to be a man of high integrity, (having known him from his youth), and every way well qualified for the office named, permit me as an American Citizen to ask of you this favour, or such part of it as your high sense of duty may dictate, namely to give your recommendation and exercise your influence in the proper quarter, to secure his appointment to said Consulate.

Mr. Stiles is no relative of mine, yet believing that the interests
of our Nation can be at least as well subserved by his services in that
office, as by the services of any other incumbent, I make the above
equest.

Any inquiry which you may be pleased to make in relation to
ny character and standing, beyond my introduction to you by Dr.
Pressly, as a Citizen and Christian Minister, General Archibald C.
Niven of the House of Representatives will readily answer.

Your attention in any measure to the above request will confer
a favour on respectfully your friend and fellow Citizen, Alexander
Blaikie.

ALS in DNA, RG 59 (State Department), Letters of Application and Recommendation during the Administrations of James K. Polk, Zachary Taylor, and
Millard Fillmore, 1845–1853, John Stiles (M-873:83, frames 517–519).

Remarks on the reception of an abolition petition, 3/12. Simon
Cameron of Pa. presented a petition from a female antislavery society for a Constitutional amendment to absolve citizens of Pa. from
"participating in perpetuating slavery." It was moved that the petition be tabled, which the Chair declared carried. Several Southern senators insisted that the prior question of reception be considered. "Mr. Calhoun said, the views of the action of the Senate,
as given by the Senator from North Carolina [Willie P. Mangum],
were correct. There was but one practice, which was to raise the
question of reception, and lay that question upon the table. As to
his own course, Mr. Calhoun said he should never vote to receive a
petition which proposed to give to the Federal Government a cogni-
zance over the institution of slavery. Whenever the vote should
come up this would be his position." From the New York, N.Y.,
Herald, March 14, 1846, p. 4. Variant reports in the Baltimore, Md.,
American & Commercial Daily Advertiser, March 13, 1846, p. 2;
Congressional Globe, 29th Cong., 1st Sess., p. 486.

From ALBERT GALLATIN

New York [City,] 15th March 1846

Dear Sir, Mr. [John R.] Bartlett, the bearer of this letter, is my friend
and ["my" *interlined*] colloborator [*sic*] in the attempt to give some
impulse to the pursuits of science and letters in this City which is so
exclusively devoted to Mammon. We are but few, without aid from

the wealthy, and struggle as well as we can amidst many difficulties one of which is the scanty supply of books in our public library. We must procure the most valuable and dearest with our own resources and Mr. Bartlett's object in visiting Washington is to remonstrate against the enormous increase of the duty on the importation of books generally and of that description specially proposed by Mr [Robert J.] Walker [Secretary of the Treasury] whose plan in other respects I do not admire. I beg leave to recommend Mr. Bartlett to you and to pray that you will give him your aid, as far as is con sistent with your views of the subject. The only argument I have to offer is that intellectual food is not a proper object of taxation: it may be doubted whether physical food is.

I take this opportunity of sending you a copy of the first vol. of the transactions of our Ethnological Society. The article I supplied is in some respects the sequel of that on our own Indians, published ten years ago and which met your approbation. I pray you to ac cept the assurance of my distinguished consideration and persona regard. Respectfully Your obedient Servant, Albert Gallatin.

ALS in ScCleA (published microfilm, Albert Gallatin Papers, roll 44, frame 65) PC in Boucher and Brooks, eds., *Correspondence*, pp. 331–332. NOTE: John R Bartlett, corresponding Secretary of the N.Y. Historical Society and a founder of the American Ethnological Society, was a member of Bartlett & Welford, book sellers who dealt largely in importing foreign books. Vol. I of *Transactions o the American Ethnological Society* was published in New York City and Londo in 1845 and contained Gallatin's work, "Notes on the Semi-Civilized Nations of Mexico, Yucatan, and Central America."

From W[illia]m Rysom, "(Confidential)"

New York [City,] March 16: 1846
Sir, There is a person in this City subject to arrest upon a charge involving punishment in the State[']s Prison for a number of years The charge has been preferred in a false and improper manner, by a person belonging to *an organized Gang*, which has made many and frequent attempts to assas[s]inate him, which attempts his sagacity[,] vigilence and activity under a Kind and wise Providence, have en abled him to render abortive.

This Gang I have reason to believe (the soundness of which you may have an opportunity to determine) is connected by links—al most invisible—to sources—almost unapproachable within The Brit ish Cabinet. Now, Sir, great care and circumspection is necessary

ntil this matter shall be satisfactorily determined. I pledge my
best efforts for that object.

If the intrigues and objects are to[o] suddenly discovered and
bruited (they being as I apprehend) war may, perhaps, ensue in
less than ninety days; and there is greater danger—possibly as immediate in not looking into the matter, at all. But, if quietly, wisely
and promptly entered into by an investigation, a power may, possibly, be obtained—(if I am not in error) which may hold in check, if
not subject to direction by the necessities or requirements of this
Country—the action of almost every Government in Europe.

It is very desireable that yourself and Mr. [John Quincy] Adams
[Representative from Mass.] and through you the Cabinet be placed
in possession of such matter as may be deemed important, in the
most discreet and judicious manner.

The application of the subject to Southern Interests may be inferred from the accompanying paper [*not found*].

There is in my judgement a close intimacy of design in the purposes of those organized Gangs and subjects referred to on that
paper.

Do me the favour to shew this letter to Mr. Adams—also the
paper—and in all other respects, consider the Subject confidential.

I shall at some day desire this letter to be returned. Immediately
upon hearing from you I shall either visit Washington for the purpose of placing all matter within my reach before you and Mr.
Adams, personally, or write.

I desire your most patient attention and serious consideration
for the good of your country and Christendom—not one thought or
feather—apart from it. Permit me to subscribe myself Y[ou]r Ob[e-
dient] Ser[van]t, *Wm. Rysom.*

[P.S.] The charge referred to is of assau[l]t with intent to kill.

ALS in ScCleA.

Speech on the Abrogation of the Joint Occupancy of Oregon (First Report)

[In the Senate, March 16, 1846]

Mr. Calhoun, being entitled to the floor, rose and addressed the
Senate very nearly as follows:

The question now under order for discussion is, whether notice

shall be given to Great Britain that the convention of joint occupancy between us and her shall terminate at the end of the year.
To that question I shall confine my remarks, limiting them to that
and to the question immediately connected with it. I shall say
nothing in regard to the title to Oregon. Having been personally
connected with previous negotiations, in which that question was
concerned, it will be seen by all, that I could not do so without impropriety; and, therefore, that it is proper that I should pass it by
without notice. I shall abstain from everything of a personal character, and from everything calculated to wound the feelings of any
gentleman; but, at the same time, I shall express myself freely, fully,
and candidly on all the subjects on which I shall consider it my duty
to touch. With these few prefatory remarks, I shall proceed at once
to the question of notice.

There is one point on which we must all be agreed, and that is,
that a great change has taken place since the commencement of the
session in the importance of this question, and in its bearing upon
peace and war. At that time, this measure of notice was of the greatest and most weighty importance, involving as it did the question
whether peace with Great Britain should or should not continue.
Now, it has become one of comparatively minor importance, and
may be decided either way without exerting any decisive effect on
those important interests. So great, indeed, is this change, that the
very reasons which are urged in the Executive Message in support
of the recommendation that notice shall be given, have no longer
their application. The bearings both of the measure and of the several parties in the Senate which have grown out of it, are entirely
altered. That the Executive recommendation to terminate the notice
is founded on the conviction that, pending such a notice, there can
be no compromise of our difficulties on the Oregon question, must
be, I think, admitted on all sides. Indeed, the language of the
Message is explicit to that effect. It expresses the President's [James
K. Polk's] conviction that no compromise could be effected which
we ought to accept. It announces to us that he made to the British
commissioner [Richard Pakenham] an offer of the parallel of 49°,
but that offer having been rejected, he ordered that it should be immediately withdrawn. And on that same conviction he recommends
to Congress the passage of this notice, with a view to the removal of
all impediments to the assertion of our right to the whole of the
Oregon territory. Assuming that there would be no compromise,
the President tells us that, at the expiration of twelve months, a period will have arrived when our title to that country must either be

abandoned or firmly maintained. Throughout the whole Message there is not the slightest intimation that any compromise is expected; but, on the contrary, the entire document assumes the opposite view. Yet I admit that the grounds on which the President bases this, his conviction, are derived from the negotiation itself, and mainly from the fact that his offer of a compromise on 49° was rejected. I admit that, proceeding on that foundation, it is a fair inference that, if England shall renew on her part the proposition which, when made on ours, she rejected, there would be no impediment in the way to its acceptance; at the same time the President intimates not the slightest expectation that such an offer will be made on her part, or that any compromise will be effected.

Such is the view which I have been constrained to take, after the most careful examination which I have been able to give to the Message of the President; and if I may draw an inference from the opinions of those members of the Senate who believe in the soundness of our title to the whole territory, they concur in this view. Indeed, the grounds on which they place themselves will not admit of their supporting the notice under any other assumption. They go for the whole of Oregon, because they assert that our title to the whole territory, even up to 54°40′, is clear and unquestionable; and they think it better that we should assert that title by arms than abandon any part or portion of it. Hence it is most manifest that if they thought the notice could possibly result in a compromise, they would vote against it.

And this view which I take of the Message, and in which these gentlemen concur, is, as I believe, the view entertained by the country at large. Certainly it is, if we are to draw our conclusions from the general tone of the public press; or if we are to look at what is, perhaps, a still better index of public opinion—the course of our intelligent business men; for the reception of the Message had the most decided effect upon the public stocks. No sooner was its language heard than insurance immediately rose, and, as our vessels returned from their foreign voyages, instead of their being sent out again to sea, they were suffered to remain inactive at the wharves.

Such, too, was the view taken by another portion of the Senate— among which I consider myself as included—and who were opposed to the giving of this notice. They opposed it on grounds directly the reverse of those on which these gentlemen advocated it. Those who advocated the notice did so because they believed there would be no compromise, and could be none. We were opposed to the notice, because we did not agree with them in that opinion. We believed, on the contrary, that a compromise might be effected, and a common ground assumed to which both nations would agree. We did not think that the American title to the whole of Oregon to be so perfectly clear as to be indisputable. We held that the title of neither nation to the whole country was perfect; and, therefore, we could not, and did not, believe that two powerful and enlightened nations, such as Great Britain and the United States, would go to war on such a question, so long as war could by possibility be honorably and properly avoided. This was the view of all who opposed the giving of notice at this time. We wished to give to both parties in this controversy a breathing time—a season for calm and mature reflection; under the influence of which they might come to some just, and honorable, yet pacific conclusion; and because we thought that the immediate giving of such a notice as was proposed would bring Great Britain to one of two alternatives—either to acquiesce in the state of things in which we had placed the question, so as to permit us to get possession of the territory by the gradual results of colonization, or to change the *onus,* and cast the blame of making war from our shoulders upon hers, compelling her to take the attitude of the aggressor.

There were other gentlemen in this body who acted with different views. These were in favor of a compromise. They, too, thought that our title was not perfect, but yet were in favor of giving notice, because they believed, notwithstanding the tone and language of the Message, that the two measures were compatible— that we might give this notice to terminate the convention, and yet effect an amicable compromise of all our difficulties. The grounds on which they come to this conclusion seem to be three. In the first place they think that the language of the Executive shows that he still entertains the hope of compromise. They quote to us his express language, where he says that he hopes an amicable arrangement may be made of the questions in dispute. I am fully aware that the President does use this language, and that the same thing was said twice by [James Buchanan] the Secretary of State, in the course of the correspondence; but it seems impossible to me that, on the plainest and justest rules of construction, the Message can be considered as expressing that meaning. It is a most solemn and weighty State paper, addressed by the Executive of the nation to a co-ordinate branch of the Government, and in which he is bound to hold the plainest and most explicit language—to state with the utmost frankness his real sentiments, and to give the reasons on which they are founded. This is his duty, and this he has performed. And he says, very clearly, that he recommends this notice in order that we may assert our title to the whole territory, and, if necessary, support that title by arms. I cannot look beyond the Message for the President's motives. It is impossible for me to overrule the plain and palpable construction which is on its face by any other which I might feel disposed to place on it. To place any other upon it would, in my judgment, be to disparage the character of the President.

Another ground taken by these gentlemen is, that the President wants to employ this notice as a moral weapon, not a physical one. But no such idea is expressed in the Message. The language of the President is explicit to the contrary. It looks not to a moral, but a physical termination of the difficulty. But, admitting that he wants to use it as a moral weapon, what does that mean? It must mean that he wants to use it for the purpose of intimidation. Now, I submit to the common sense of every gentleman, whether, if this notice should be used in that light, with a great and powerful nation like Great Britain, its effect, instead of leading to a compromise, would not be precisely the reverse. It would be a direct appeal to her fears, to induce her to yield, under such a motive, what she would not yield otherwise.

The third reason is, that the convention of 1818, and renewed in 1827, was wrong from the beginning; that, as a measure of policy, it was a great mistake; that its effect was to fetter the assertion of our rights; and that it would have been better, so far as our rights in the territory were concerned, if there had been no such convention at all. In that opinion I cannot concur: I dissent from it wholly: I hold precisely the opposite opinion: I believe that, but for that convention, the preservation of our rights could have been effected only by an appeal to arms. We must either have gone to war in 1818 and 1827, or must have acquiesced in the hostile claims of Great Britain, (for in that case they would have been hostile.) If we could at that time have obtained the latitude of 49° as a compromise boundary, it would have been wise in us to have done so; but we attempted it in vain. That attempt failing, what other alternative was left us? Either this convention or war. The convention was a substitute for war; and, while it prevented war, it at the same time preserved our rights in Oregon inviolate so long as the convention should continue. I think that those who entered into that treaty acted wisely. It has become but too common at this day for us to sit in judgment on the acts of our predecessors, and to pronounce them to have been unjust, unwise, or unpatriotic, while we pass over the circumstances of their day, and under which they acted. Look at the men concerned.

Look at [James] Munroe [*sic*]—at [Richard] Rush—at [Henry] Clay; it would be hard, indeed, to pronounce men like these to have been either unpatriotic or unwise. Or, if we look at the great names of those who have since acquiesced in the measure they adopted—at [Andrew] Jackson, and at others since—it would be hard to say that such men deliberately acquiesced in an arrangement hostile to the best interests of their country. I do not name the prominent individual concerned [John Quincy Adams?], because his course since that time has cancelled any previous credit to which he might have entitled himself.

Such was the state of things when this resolution of notice was first introduced into the Senate. Since then, as I have said, there has been a mighty change: public opinion has developed itself, not only on this, but on the other side of the Atlantic; and that voice of public opinion has uttered itself most audibly and clearly in favor of a compromise. Here, too, the same change has been manifested, insomuch that I hazard nothing when I say that a large, a very large, majority of this body is at this moment in favor of a compromise—an honorable compromise. And does not all the language and conduct of the British Government itself clearly demonstrate that it is in favor of a compromise; and substantially on the basis which we have ourselves offered? Sure I am that no intelligent and reflecting man can read the language of Sir Robert Peel in reply to Lord John Russell, and not see that he is prepared to act on a proposition substantially the same with that which was rejected by Mr. Pakenham. This declaration of the Premier of Great Britain was made with very great effect; his object in making it was not to censure the able and very faithful representative of Great Britain in this country, but to give emphasis to the assurance that he was ready to make a just and fair compromise of the disputed question. I hope sincerely that our Government has not overlooked that declaration; it was a direct step towards compromise, and I trust it has been met in the same spirit. I trust that intelligence has, before this time, gone abroad to Great Britain to that effect, so as to remove the only difficulty which now lies in the way.

Under the views that I entertain, it is no longer a question whether our difficulties may be pacifically arranged or not; nor is it even a question as to the manner: it is simply a question of time. But there ought to be no delay, because the business of both nations and of the world requires that it should be settled. On great, and momentous, and delicate questions like these, there are the highest public rersons [*sic*] why there should be no delay. Once settle the question of Oregon, and we may then settle the question of Mexico; but till then, Mexico will calculate the chances of a rupture between us and Great Britain; and if she sees any chance of a war against us, she will go over to the Power which makes war upon us. Remove these chances, put an end to such a hope, and Mexico will speedily settle every pending question between her and the United States; and then, I trust, we shall deal generously with her. She is weak—feeble in the extreme—and I trust that we shall adopt no harsh measures with her.

I have now explained the change which has taken place in the bearing of this measure of notice on the questions of peace and war. The change consists in this: that when the notice was recommended, there existed no hope of a compromise; but now the highest and most confident hope is felt by almost all. Now, therefore, there is no great interest connected with our deciding this question of notice, one way or another. Just in proportion as the prospect of compromise was small, the importance of the notice was great; but as the prospect of compromise increases, the measure of notice becomes of less and less importance. We have now reached a point when we can decide the question without much feeling on either side.

I now proceed to another point in my remarks, and to inquire what is the bearing of this measure on the position of the Executive, and what on the position of the parties in this body.

The conduct of the Executive must now be greatly changed. He must act very differently now from what he would have done when he recommended the notice under the persuasion that there could be no compromise, but that we must assert our rights by arms. That he can advise the same thing now which he advised then, is impossible. Then, he had not the remotest expectation of a compromise. If now he has a different view, and thinks that Great Britain is ready to meet us with an offer such as we made, I here say that, if he shall now decline that offer, I do not envy him the consequences that shall follow. The change which has taken place is not a change in the President; it is a change in the state of things. So far from its being any inconsistency, it is, on the contrary, the highest consistency to agree to a compromise when matters have reached a point which was not contemplated when he sent us his Message. There is prevalent among us a great error in regard to this matter of consistency. Some persons think that consistency consists in a uniform adherence to one policy, let the circumstances of the country change or not. Others think that consistency lies in always thinking the same way, after the man has seen the most cogent reasons for changing his opinion. The consistency of these persons is much like the course of a physician who, in the treatment of a malignant fever, should give emetics and calomel at the beginning, and then hold himself bound to continue to give emetics and calomel through every subsequent stage of the disease. Consistency like this would kill the patient; and there is no statesman worthy of the name who would be guilty of the political quackery of advocating always the same course of policy, though the circumstances of his country had completely altered.

But not only has the Executive position changed, but the position of the parties in the Senate has changed in no less degree; and my friends here who go for all of Oregon (friends I will call them, for I have no other than the most friendly feelings towards them) must and do feel that there has been a change. So long as they thought that notice was wholly inconsistent with any compromise, they were its warm and enthusiastic advocates; but now, when they begin to discover that, notwithstanding the giving of the notice, a compromise may still be effected, they find themselves without the same reason for their former zeal; and I shall not be at all surprised if, before this question is finally put, these very gentlemen shall vote against the notice altogether.

But I trust the friends to whom I allude have undergone a still further change besides that of their position. I trust they now begin to see that there are some doubts in regard to our title to the whole of Oregon. That it is unquestionable they cannot now say; for it has been questioned with great ability in their presence on this floor. I know, indeed, that their convictions have been as honest as they have been strong. But, admitting that our title seemed to them ever so clear, is not something due to the changes which have since taken place? Is nothing due to the fact that a majority even of their own political friends think that our title is not so clear but that a compromise may be honorably effected? Is nothing due to their opinion? And does not the mere fact of such a division of opinion among men perfectly honest on both sides present the strongest reason why the dispute need not and ought not to be decided by force? I appeal to these Senators as patriots, as wise and prudent men, to say, when our contest is with so great a Power, whether they are willing to hazard all for a question on which the opinions of good and honest men all over their country are undeniably divided. I appeal to them even as party men, to say whether they will insist on pushing this question to such an extreme as to divide their party.

As to the other portion of the Senate, (in which I consider myself as included,) it is undeniable that a great change has taken place. I feel it myself. Nothing could once have induced me to consent to the notice recommended by the President; but now it is very possible I may give my vote for a modified notice in some form.

And this brings me now, at length, to the direct question to which all I have yet said is preliminary. Shall we give to Great Britain the notice proposed, or shall we not? The question is not free from doubt. But there are two reasons in favor of it.

One reason in its favor is, that it will prevent the continued agitation of this Oregon question being kept up in the country, and carried into the next Presidential election. The measure of notice, if properly qualified, will, I trust, keep all quiet until the year has expired, and then there will be no room for any further difficulty.

Another reason in its favor is, that in all probability Great Britain will not make a final move until Congress shall have acted on the subject; so that we should, as soon as possible, do something in the matter. If it were not for the force of this consideration, I should be for postponing the notice for the present.

And now to the question, in what form the notice shall be given? I will vote, under no circumstances, for a naked absolute notice; because that would be to leave some doubt in the country, and on the public mind generally, whether we preferred to adhere to the state of things which existed when the Message was penned or not. The circumstances of the case have greatly changed. We are not in the same state of things which existed when the Executive Message first came in; and I cannot vote under the remotest impression that there will be no compromise. If any gentleman once hoped so, and would have gone for the notice under that hope, that motive has now passed away.

Nor can I vote for the resolution which has been sent us from the House of Representatives. I have two objections to it. It is equivocal in its meaning. If it means to declare that the President may settle this difficulty by compromise, it means nothing, for the President has that right; but if it is meant as a hint to him to negotiate for a compromise, then I am for speaking more plainly. I am most decidedly against all equivocation in matters of State policy. Let us say plainly what we mean to say. If we mean compromise, let us say compromise; and not send the President a resolution on which he may put just any interpretation that suits him.

If we give this notice at all, I think it should be given substantially as has been proposed by the gentleman from Georgia [Walter T. Colquitt]. If I consent to the notice, it will be, as I have said, to keep this agitation from running into the next Presidential election, and finally to terminate the question; and if we give it at all, let us give it precisely as we intend, expressing the opinion that the difficulty should be settled by compromise. So much I feel inclined to vote for. I say inclined, for I hold this whole question of the notice subordinate to the greater question, viz: the preservation of peace and the settlement of our difficulties without a resort to arms. My vote in regard to notice will rest on the question whether the notice will advance that end or not. And I shall, therefore, reserve myself until I shall be satisfied on that point.

I have thus stated why I am for a compromise, and how far I am in favor of giving notice. I vote on both subjects under circumstances in which I find myself placed, and for which I am not in the least responsible. I am doing the best I can where I find myself, and not what I might have done under different circumstances. I repeat, that for these circumstances I am not responsible. I early resisted that state of things which has now come to pass. In 1843 this question for the first time assumed a dangerous aspect. I then saw, or thought I saw, what was coming, and I examined the question under all its aspects. After the maturest reflection I came to the conclusion which I then stated. I saw that there were two routes before us: one of them was to adhere to the convention of 1827, to do nothing to terminate it, and to adhere strictly and rigidly to its provisions. I saw that although for a time that convention operated beneficially for Great Britain, yet the period was at hand when our turn would come to derive its benefits. Its operation threw into her hands the whole fur trade of that region, and we stood by while the whole of that rich harvest was reaped by her subjects; but I saw that we would soon derive the most important advantages from the provisions of the treaty. The resistless increase of our population and the gradual progress of their enterprise was bringing them fast to the foot of the Rocky mountains. The great South pass had been discovered, and I saw that the settlement of Oregon by American citizens was rapidly approaching.

If we should only adhere strictly to the convention, the progress of things would eventually decide who should have the possession of the territory. Our power to populate the region, and thus to obtain its actual possession, was far greater than that of Great Britain. Its distance from us was far less; the access to it was through an open, grassy country, and, to men so active and hardy as our western pioneers, the journey presented comparatively but small difficulty; whereas to reach Oregon from Great Britain required a circumnavigation of twenty thousand miles, a space but a little short of the circumference of the globe. Of all the spots on the face of the earth, presenting to her the possibility of colonization, Oregon was the most remote. There were hundreds of colonies that lay nearer, and presented a better soil and climate. Even New Zealand was nearer to the shores of England. All, therefore, that we had to do was to stick to the convention, to observe all its provisions with the most scrupulous fidelity, and then let the question of title be quietly and gradually settled by the actual occupation and possession of the country. To this course there was but one impediment: Great Britain might give the notice. But I had no such fear; for I had read the discussions of this question on her side, and I thought I clearly saw that she placed no great value upon Oregon, as a permanent possession of the British Crown, but rather seemed to conclude that, from its geographical position, the United States must ultimately get the whole of it. But, even if her calculation was otherwise, there were great impediments in the way of her giving notice to terminate the convention. She could do so if she pleased, so could we: this was an express provision of the treaty, and could not, in itself, be considered as a hostile movement on either side. But there was another convention which Great Britain contends to be still in existence, but which we insist has expired, and that is the convention of Nootka. This treaty of Nootka is in strict analogy with our convention of 1818; and if she should give us no notice, it could not be set aside unless its provisions were violated. We had observed the terms of our convention, and this foreclosed her from the possibility of such a movement.

It seemed, then, to me, clear as the light of heaven, that it would not do for us to make a movement of any kind. We might, indeed, give our people some facilities in reaching the country; and when they got there, we might extend our laws over them personally, but not territorially. I doubted then, and I still doubt, even the expediency of going so far as that; but, most clearly, we could not set up our laws there territorially; because the moment we should do that, we must establish a custom-house, and levy and collect duties; and if there is anything that can alienate the affections of those people from us, it will be the collection of high duties. Our people have gone there as their fathers came to New England at the beginning, setting aside the religious principle which had so great an influence on their action; and one important end they seek is the enjoyment of free trade. They will contend as earnestly for the free enjoyment of the trade of the Pacific as their ancestors did for that of the Alantic before the Revolution. If we levy high duties on their infant trade, they will soon find a neighboring Power who will extend to them greater advantages in this respect, and whose influence might rend the territory from you. My disposition has been to let them go there and govern themselves. That is a business for which they seem to have a native instinct, that marks their origin. Let them go there and settle the country, and then gradually, and with great judgment and caution, extend our laws over them, as it may become necessary; for here is the most delicate and critical point in the whole affair.

The other course that lay open to us was that pointed out in the bill of 1843, which provided for the practical assertion of our rights in the territory, and the exercise of our sovereignty there to a certain extent, by the passage of certain general laws. I thought this course not to be a fit and proper one. I saw very plainly what would be the consequence; and, indeed, it requires but little reflection to perceive this. To extend our settlements in Oregon, in conformity with the provisions of that bill, would be inconsistent with the terms of the convention, and would speedily bring us either to negotiation or to war. I anticipated that the result would be negotiation. And what then? Negotiation must end either in compromise or war. I never could believe in any other result. I also saw that, if we compromised, it must be on the parallel of 49°. The past history of the whole matter decided that; and, besides, as 49° was the boundary on this side the mountains, most people would think it reasonable and natural it should be the boundary on the other side.

But I would go neither for notice nor for compromise, so long as we could persevere in what I conceived to be the true American policy. Hence I did resist the bill of 1843, in common with many able men in both Houses. It passed here by an equivocal majority of one vote, (the Senator voting under instructions in the affirmative,) but it was lost in the other House. Since then, the proposition for notice has been repeated, with a view to taking possession of the whole country. And so now we are where we are—a position which all ought to have foreseen—where we must compromise or fight.

I say, then, if there is any responsibility attached to the circumstances in which I find myself, I stand acquitted from any participation in it. The responsibility lies among my friends on the right. I doubt not they acted patriotically, but impatiently—in obedience to the impatience of their people. They have suffered themselves to be pushed into their present position without due reflection.

Now, being brought to the alternative by circumstances over

which I have no control, I go for compromise, and against war. But in this course I am actuated by no unmanly fear of consequences. I know that, under the existing state of the world, wars are sometimes necessary: the utmost regard for justice and equity cannot always prevent them. And when war must be met, I shall be among the last to flinch. I may appeal to my past history in support of this assertion. But I am averse from going to war on this question, for the reasons I have given. But not for these only: I have still higher reasons. Although wars may at times be necessary, yet peace is a positive good, and war is a positive evil; and I cling to peace so long as it can be preserved consistently with the national safety and honor; and I am against war so long as it can be avoided without a sacrifice of either. I am opposed to war in this case, because neither of these exigencies exist: it may be, as I conceive, avoided without sacrificing either the national honor or the national safety. But if these dangers did exist, to a certain extent, war is still highly inexpedient; because our rights in Oregon can be sustained with more than an equal chance of success without war than with it. This is a great and weighty reason against war. He who goes so stoutly to war for "all of Oregon or none," may possibly come out of it with "none." I concede to my countrymen the possession of all the bravery, patriotism, and intelligence which can be claimed for them; but we shall go into this contest with great disadvantages on our side. As long as Great Britain has a large force in the east, and is mistress of the sea, she can carry on the war at much less expense.

There is another reason why I am opposed to it: the war would soon cease to be for Oregon; the struggle would be for empire, and it would be between the greatest Power in Europe on the one side, and the greatest and most growing and spirited people of the west on the other. It would be pressed on upon both sides with all the force, vigor, energy, and perseverance of two great and brave nations; each would strike the other in the most vulnerable point, and the blows would be tremendous. Amidst the uproar of such a contest, Oregon would soon be forgotten, utterly forgotten, to be recovered, if at all, on the contingencies of success or the reverse.

My next reason is, that, though it is alleged that we must fight in order to protect our citizens in Oregon, instead of their protection war would ensure their utter destruction. It is the most certain way to sacrifice them. This I will never consent to do. They are American citizens—our brethren and kindred. We have encouraged them to go there; and I never will give a vote the result of which must be their utter and speedy destruction. But if we make a compromise on

697

latitude 49°, they will all be safe; for, if I am rightly informed, there is not a man of them to be found north of that line. This will carry all the points we have in view, instead of sacrificing them all.

I am against war, too, for reasons common to the whole Union. I believe that the most successful and triumphant war we could possibly wage—even if, in ten years, we should get all the most extravagant advocate of war has dared to hope for—if we could take the Canadas, and New Brunswick, and Nova Scotia, and every other British possession, and drive her flag from the whole continent, and prosecute our advantages till we had accomplished the downfall of the British throne, and she should yield up spear and shield and trident at our feet, it would be to us the most disastrous event that could happen. I do not now allude to the ravages and desolations of warfare; to the oceans of blood that must flow, and the various miseries that ever accompany the contest of arms; because I have never observed that the statement of these things had any great effect upon a brave people. No doubt the evils would be very great, because there are no two nations in the world who can do each other so much harm in war, or so much good in peace, as Great Britain and the United States. The devastation would be tremendous on both sides. But all this goes for nothing; for this may all be repaired. The indomitable industry, and enterprise, and perseverance of our widely-spread and still spreading and multiplying population, will soon find ways and means of repairing whatever merely physical disasters war can inflict. But war has far heavier inflictions for a free people; it works a social and political change in the people themselves, and in the character of their institutions. A war such as this, will be of vast extent; every nerve and muscle on either side will be strained to the utmost; every commandable dollar will be put in requisition; not a portion of our entire frontier but will become the scene of contest. It will be a Mexican war on the one side, and an Indian war upon the other. Its flames will be all around us; it will be a war on the Pacific and a war on the Atlantic; it will rage on every side, and fill the land. Suppose Oregon shall be abandoned, we must raise seven armies and two navies; we must raise and equip an army against the Mexicans; and let no man sneer at the mention of such a Power. Under the guidance and training of British officers, the Mexican population could be rendered a formidable enemy. See what Britain has made of the feeble Sepoys of India. The Mexicans are a braver and a hardier people, and they will form the cheapest of all armies. With good training and good pay, they may be rendered a very formidable force. Then, we must have another army to guard our southern Atlantic frontier, and another to protect our northern Atlantic frontier, and another to operate on our northeastern boundary, and still another to cover our Indian frontier. At the least estimate, we shall require a force of not less than two hundred thousand men in the field. In addition to that, the venerable and intelligent Albert Gallatin has calculated the cost of such a war at sixty-five millions of dollars; but that amount is too small. A hundred millions is not an over-estimate; and of this sum, fifty millions must be raised annually, by loans or paper; so that, allowing the war to continue for ten years, we shall have an amount of five hundred millions of public debt. Add to this the losses which must accrue on loans: it will be very difficult to get these loans negotiated in Europe; for, owing to the unfortunate manner in which this affair has been conducted, the feeling in Europe will be generally against us. We cannot obtain the requisite sums under an interest of thirty and forty per cent. Add all these expenses, and our total debt will not be less than seven hundred and fifty millions.

But this is not all. We shall be plunged into the paper system as deeply as we were in the days of the Revolution; and what will then be our situation at the conclusion of the war? We shall be left with a mortgage of seven hundred and fifty millions of dollars on the labor of the American people; for it all falls on the labor of the country at last, while much of the money will go into the pockets of those who struck not a blow in the contest. We should then have the task of restoring a circulating medium of a sounder character, and that from the deepest degradation of the currency. This is a hard job, as all of us know who have gone through with it. Besides, the influence of the war will naturally be to obliterate the line of distinction between the State and General Governments. We shall hear no more about State rights, but the Government will become in effect a consolidated republic. By our very success, it will give a military impulse to the national mind which can never be overcome. The ambition of the nation will seek conquest after conquest, and will soon become possessed by a spirit totally inconsistent with the forms and genius of our Government; and this will lead, by a straight and easy road, to that gulf of all republics—a military despotism. Then we shall have to provide for three or four successful generals, who will soon be competing for the Presidency. Before the generation which waged the war shall have passed away they will witness a contest between hostile generals. He who conquered Mexico, and he who conquered Canada, will each insist upon his right to the seat of power, and they will end their struggle by the sword. Freedom thus lost, institutions thus undermined and overturned, never can be recovered. The national ruin will be irretrievable.

I appeal, then, to gentlemen near me—to my friends, whose separation from us on this question I deeply regret—and I say to them, is it for you, who are Democrats *par excellence*—for you, who are the enemies of paper money and the sworn destroyers of all banks and all artificial classes in society—is it for you to vote for a measure of such very equivocal success?

But I have still higher reasons. I am opposed to war as a friend to human improvement, to human civilization, to human progress and advancement. Never in the history of the world has there occurred a period so remarkable as the peace which followed the battle of Waterloo for the great advances made in the condition of human society, and that in various forms. The chemical and mechanical powers have been investigated and applied to advance the comforts of human life in a degree far beyond all that was ever known or hoped before. Civilization has been spreading its influence far and wide, and the general progress of human society has outstripped all that had been previously witnessed. The invention of man has seized upon and subjugated two great agencies of the natural world which never before were made the servants of man: I refer to steam and electricity, under which, of course, I include magnetism in all its phenomena. Steam has been controlled and availed of for all the purposes of human intercourse. True, the steam-engine had been discovered before that period, but its powers have been subsequently perfected, and by its resistless energies has brought nations together whom nature had seemed to separate by insurmountable barriers. It has shortened the passage across the Atlantic more than one-half, while the rapidity of travelling on land has been three times greater than by the common motive power. Within the same period man has chained the very lightning of heaven, and brought it down and made it administer to the transmission of human thought, insomuch that it may with truth be said that our ideas are not only transmitted with the rapidity of lightning, but by lightning itself. Magic wires are stretching themselves in all directions over the globe, and when their mystic meshes shall at length have been perfected, our globe itself will be endowed with a sensitiveness which will render it impossible to touch it on any one point and the touch not be felt from one end of the world to the other. All this progress, all this growth of human happiness, all this spread of human light and knowledge, will be arrested by war. And shall we incur a result like that which must be produced by a war, for Oregon? And this work is as yet but commenced; it is but the breaking of the dawn of the world's great jubilee. It promises a day of more refinement, more intellectual brightness, more moral elevation, and consequently of more human felicity, than the world has ever seen from its creation.

Now the United States and England are two nations to be pre-eminently instrumental in bringing about this happy change, because I consider them as being the most advanced in the scale of human improvement, and most in circumstances to further this ameliora-tion, because they have the control of the greatest and most extensive commerce at present in existence. We have been thus distinguished by Providence for a great and a noble purpose, and I trust we shall fulfil our high destiny.

Again, I am opposed to war, because I hold that it is now to be determined whether two such nations as these shall exist for the future as friends or enemies. A declaration of war of one of them against the other must be pregnant with miseries, not only to them-selves, but to the world around them.

Another reason is, that mighty means are now put into the hands of both to cement and secure a perpetual peace, by breaking down the barriers of commerce and uniting them more closely in an in-tercourse mutually beneficial. If this shall be accomplished, other nations will, one after another, follow the fair example, and a state of general prosperity, heretofore unknown, will gradually unite and bless the nations of the world.

And far more than that. An intercourse like this points to that inspiring day which philosophers have hoped for, which poets have seen in the bright visions of fancy, and which prophecy has seen in holy vision—when man shall learn war no more. Who can contem-plate a state of the world like this, and not feel his heart exult at the prospect? And who can doubt that, in the hand of an omnipotent Providence, a free and unrestricted commerce shall prove one of the greatest agents in bringing it about?

Finally, I am against war because peace—peace is pre-eminently our policy. There are nations in the world who may resort to war for the settlement of their differences, and still grow great; but that nation is not ours. Providence has cast our happy inheritance where its frontier extends for twenty-three degrees of latitude along the Atlantic coast. It has given us a land which, in natural advantages, is perhaps unequalled by any other. Abundant in all resources; excellent in climate; fertile and exuberant in soil; capable of sustain-ing, in the plentiful enjoyment of all the necessaries of life, a popu-lation of two hundred millions of souls. Our great mission as a people is to occupy this vast domain—there to fulfil the primeval command to increase and multiply, and replenish the land with an industrious and virtuous population; to level the forests, and let in upon their solitude the light of day; to clear the swamps and morasses, and redeem them to the plough and sickle; to spread over hill and dale the echoes of human labor and human happiness and contentment; to fill the land with cities, and towns, and villages; to unite its opposite extremities by turnpikes and railroads; to scoop out canals for the transmission of its products, and open rivers for its internal trade. War can only impede the fulfilment of this high mission of Heaven; it absorbs the wealth, and diverts the energy which might be so much better devoted to the improvement of our country. All we want is peace—established peace; and then time, under the guidance of a wise and cautious policy, will soon effect for us all the rest. I say time will do it, under the influence of a wise and masterly inactivity—a phrase than which none other has been less understood or more grossly misrepresented. By some, who should have known better, it has been construed to mean inaction. But mere inertness, and what is meant by a wise inactivity, are things wide apart as the poles. The one is the offspring of ignorance and of indolence; the other is the result of the profoundest wisdom—a wisdom which looks into the nature and bearing of things; which sees how conspiring causes work out their effects, and shape and change the condition of man. Where we find that natural causes will of themselves work out our good, our wisdom is to let them work; and all our task is to remove impediments. In the present case, one of the greatest of these impediments is found in our impatience.

He who cannot understand the difference between an inactivity like this, and mere stupid inaction, and the doing of nothing, is as yet but in the horn-book of political science. Yes, time—ever-laboring time—will effect everything for us. Our population is now increasing at the annual average of six hundred thousand. Let the next twenty-five years elapse, and our average increase will have reached a million a year, and before many of the younger Senators here shall have become as grayheaded as I am, we shall count a population of forty-five millions. Before that day, it will have spread from ocean to ocean. The coasts of the Pacific will then be as densely populated, and as thickly settled with villages and towns as the coast of the Atlantic is now. In another generation we shall have reached eighty millions of people, and, if we can preserve peace, who shall set bounds to our prosperity or our success? With one foot planted on the Atlantic and the other on the Pacific, we shall occupy a position between the two old continents of the world—a position eminently calculated to secure to us the commerce and the influence of both. If we abide by the counsels of common sense—if we succeed in preserving our constitutional liberty, we shall then exhibit a spectacle such as the world never saw. I know that this one great mission is encompassed with difficulties; but such is the inherent energy of our political system, and such its expansive capability, that it may be made to govern the widest space. If by war we become great, we cannot be free; if we will be both great and free, our policy is peace.

Before I resume my seat, allow me to say a few words which relate personally to myself, and then I will relieve the Senate.

I have been charged with having more inclination for the annexation of Texas than for the retention of Oregon; and it has been said that my partialities are strong for the South, but very weak in comparison for the North. But why is Texas spoken of as particularly connected with the Southern States? I always thought that Texas formed a part, and a very important part, of the valley of the Mississippi, and that the hearts of all who loved the West were particularly set upon its acquisition as a means of perfecting and consummating the Union of our great Western world. I never knew that Texas was confined to a southern latitude. I thought its higher portions extended up to the latitude of 42° north, not far from the great pass of the Rocky mountains; and I have been in the habit of supposing that the southern States proper had not so great an interest in it as had the great West. But it seems I was wrong, and that the annexation of Texas was a purely southern question. Admitting it to be so, I put my defence upon the ground that I have treated both questions—that of Texas and that of Oregon—in a manner best calculated to keep both, and that the course I pursued was the only effectual means to unite Texas and to retain Oregon. If my course was different towards the two, it was because the circumstances of the two were entirely different. In the case of Texas time was against us; in the case of Oregon time was for us: and hence the difference in my policy. Texas has been secured. We were at a point where she must come under our influence, or under that of England. I was anxious to prevent the latter, and secure the former; and I knew that time would be against us. I had to contend against time, which waits for no man. That was no case for a masterly inactivity. I therefore wrestled boldly with the question; and success has proved that the policy was sound. But, in the case of Oregon, time was in our favor. My policy in both cases was the same—to avoid war and to preserve peace. I had no fears of a war with England. I knew that Texas was an independent State, and had so been acknowledged by England herself; so that, if the people of Texas consented to the annexation, the opposition of England had nothing to stand on; and that we had nothing to fear from Mexico, unless she was aided by England; and that England would not aid her unless with a view to the Oregon question. And I thought that, if the Texas question was not settled, there would be bitter feeling between us and England. We are both the descendants of the same stock—both jealous and brave—both fond (too fond) of war; England would have interfered, and then it would cost us a war to recover that which, by a wise and a bold policy, we might have effectually secured.

From *Congressional Globe,* 29th Cong., 1st Sess., pp. 502–506. Also printed in the Washington, D.C., *Daily National Intelligencer,* March 17, 1846, pp. 2–3; the New York, N.Y., *Evening Post,* March 19, 1846, p. 1 (part); the Charleston, S.C., *Mercury,* March 20, 1846, p. 2; the Richmond, Va., *Enquirer,* March 20, 1846, p. 4 (part); the Alexandria, Va., *Gazette and Virginia Advertiser,* March 21, 1846, p. 2 (part); *Niles' National Register,* vol. LXX, no. 3 (March 21, 1846), pp. 42–46; the New York, N.Y., *Observer,* March 21, 1846, p. 47; the New York, N.Y., *Subterranean,* March 28, 1846, pp. 1, 4; the Worcester, Mass., *Bond of Brotherhood,* April 1, 1846, pp. 1–2 (part); the Memphis, Tenn., *Daily Eagle,* April 2, 1846, p. 2, and April 3, 1846, p. 2; the Pendleton, S.C., *Messenger,* April 3, 1846, pp. 1–3; the Greenville, S.C., *Mountaineer,* April 3, 1846, pp. 1, 4; Benton, *Abridgment of Debates,* 15:426–434. Variant in the Alexandria, Va., *Gazette and Virginia Advertiser,* March 17, 1846, p. 3; the New Orleans, La., *Bee,* March 25, 1846, p. 1; the New Orleans, La., *Daily Picayune,* March 25, 1846, p. 1. Another variant in the Baltimore, Md., *American & Commercial Daily Advertiser,* March 17, 1846, p. 2; the Edgefield, S.C., *Advertiser,* March 25, 1846, p. 2. Variant in the Philadelphia, Pa., *United States Gazette,* March 18, 1846, p. 1. Variant in the New York, N.Y., *Herald,* March 19, 1846, p. 3. Variant in the Richmond, Va., *Enquirer,* March 20, 1846, p. 4. Variant in the Charleston, S.C., *Courier,* March 20, 1846, p. 2; the Greenville, S.C., *Mountaineer,* March 27, 1846, p. 1. Variant in the London, England, *Times,* April 10, 1846, p. 5. Another variant is printed below. NOTE: Of this speech, the New York *Herald* issue cited above reported: "Mr. Calhoun sat down. There was no manifestation of applause, as after the war speech of Mr. [William] Allen, but there was a general murmur of approbation and delight pervading the Senate and the galleries."

SPEECH ON THE ABROGATION OF THE JOINT OCCUPANCY OF OREGON (Revised Report)

[In the Senate, March 16, 1846]

Mr. Calhoun, being entitled to the floor, rose and addressed the Senate:

The question under consideration is, whether notice shall be given to Great Britain that the convention of joint occupancy between us and her shall terminate at the end of the year. To that question, and those immediately growing out of it, I shall confine my remarks. I shall say nothing in reference to the title to Oregon. Having been connected with the negotiation in its early stages, it would be indelicate on my part to discuss the subject of title. I shall abstain from all personalities and every thing calculated to wound the feelings of others; but shall express myself freely, fully, and candidly on all the subjects on which I may touch, in the course of my remarks. With these prefatory observations, I shall proceed at once to the discussion of the question of notice.

There is one point in which all must be agreed; that a great change has taken place since the commencement of this session in reference to notice, in its bearings upon the question of peace and war. At that time, notice was a question of the first magnitude, on the decision of which, to all appearance, depended the question of peace or war; but now it is one of comparatively minor importance, and may be decided any way, without any decisive effect on either. The cause of this change will be explained in the course of my remarks. So great, indeed, has been the change that it has not only rendered inapplicable the reasons urged in the message, recommending notice to be given, but has altered materially the position of the Executive [James K. Polk], and that of the several parties in the Senate to which it has given origin, as I shall next proceed to show.

That the recommendation of the message is founded on the conviction that there was no hope of compromise of the difficulties growing out of the Oregon question, is too clear to admit of any rational doubt. Its language is express. It states in so many words the conviction, that no compromise could be effected which ought to be accepted. On that conviction it announces that the offer which had been made to the British minister [Richard Pakenham] to settle the controversy on the 49th parallel of latitude had been withdrawn after its rejection, and our title to the whole asserted. On the same conviction, it recommends to Congress to give the notice in order to annul the convention with the view to remove all impediments to the assertion of our right to the whole of the territory. Assuming, then, that there would be no compromise, it informs us that, at the expiration of the twelve months, a period would arrive when our title to the territory must be abandoned or firmly maintained; and that neither our honor nor our interest would permit us to abandon it; in other words, that we must then assert our exclusive sovereignty to the whole, to the exclusion of that of Great Britain, unless the latter should, in the interval, abandon its claims to the territory. Throughout the whole recommendation there it [*sic*] not the slightest intimation that any compromise is expected. On the contrary, the very opposite is constantly assumed.

But it is alleged that the reasons for believing that there could be no compromise was derived from the evidence which the negotiation itself furnished, and especially by the rejection of the offer to compromise on 49°. Such I admit to be the case, and also that it may be fairly inferred, if England should renew on her part the proposition rejected by her minister, or one substantially the same, our Executive would accept the offer, and settle by compromise the conflicting claims to the territory. But the message intimates nowhere the slightest expectation that such an offer would be made, or, if made, that any compromise could be effected.

Such is the view which I have been constrained to take, after a most careful and candid examination of the portion of the message recommending notice; and such, I infer, is the view taken by the portion of the Senate who believe our title to the whole territory to be clear and unquestionable. On no other view can their warm and decided support of notice be explained. They not only believe that our title is clear and unquestionable to the whole, but also that the honor of the country demands that it should be asserted and maintained by an appeal to arms without the surrender of any part. Acting on this conviction, it is manifest that they can only support notice on the belief that it would not lead to compromise. On the opposite, they would be compelled to oppose it.

Such, also, would seem to be the view taken of the message by the community at large at the time, if we may judge from the tone of the public press, or what perhaps is a still truer index—the conduct of our intelligent business men.

The message had a most decided effect in that respect. Stocks of every description fell, marine insurances rose, commercial pursuits were suspended, and our vessels remained inactive at the wharves.

Such, also, was the view taken by a great majority of that portion of the Senate who were opposed to giving notice, and among whom I include myself. We opposed it on grounds directly the reverse of those on which those who believed our rights to the whole territory to be clear and unquestionable supported it.

They supported notice because they believed there neither ought to be or would be any compromise. We, on the contrary, opposed it because we believed there might be, and ought to be, compromise.

They opposed compromise because, as has been stated, they believed our title to be perfect to the whole; while we supported it because we believed the title of neither to the whole to be clear and indisputable; and that the controversy might be adjusted by a fair partition of the territory. With such impression, we believed that two such powerful and enlightened countries as the United States and Great Britain, would not resort to arms to settle a controversy which might be peacefully and honorably settled by negotiation and compromise.

Entertaining this opinion, we were compelled to oppose notice, because it was necessary to prevent an appeal to arms, and insure the peaceful settlement of the question. By defeating it, a breathing time would at least be afforded to both parties for calm and mature reflection, under the influence of which it was hoped that negotiation might be renewed, and the difference honorably compromised. Or, in case that should fail, things might remain as they have been without a resort to force. In that case, the territory would be left open to emigration, and the question, to whom it should ultimately belong, would be decided by settlement and colonization, unless Great Britain should give notice on her part, in order to prevent it. If she should, we would at least gain the advantage of transferring the responsibility from us to her, should war ensue.

Another portion of the Senate appeared to be in favor both of compromise and notice. Their views were not explicitly expressed; but, as far as they were developed, they, too, seemed to think that our title was not so perfect as to exclude an honorable compromise, and appeared to anticipate it in opposition to the message in recommending it on the three following grounds: first, on the ground of the general declaration of the President in the latter part of the message, that he hoped an amicable arrangement may be made of the question in dispute, in connexion with a declaration of Mr. [James] Buchanan to the same effect, in one of his letters to Mr. Pakenham. It is impossible for me, with every disposition to support the recommendation of the President in favor of notice, to concur in the opinion that a mere general expression of the kind, and inserted in another portion of the message, even when backed by a similar declaration of the Secretary of State, could be fairly construed to overrule the opinion clearly and explicitly expressed by the message in recommending notice, that no compromise which ought to be accepted could be effected. I cannot admit of such a construction, not only because I think it unreasonable, but because I regard the duty of the President, imposed by the Constitution, to recommend measures to Congress, as one of a solemn character, and that it ought to be performed with the utmost candor and sincerity. Being addressed to a co-ordinate department of the government, it ought to express plainly and explicitly his reasons and motives for recommending the measure, omitting none which he regards as material, and inserting none but such as he believes ought to have an influence upon the deliberations of Congress. It ought to be free from the suspicion of being diplomatic. To admit the contrary, would destroy all confidence between the legislative and executive departments to the great detriment of the government. With these impressions, it would be to disparage the character of the President for me to concur in the construction.

The next ground taken by a portion of the Senate referred to is, that notice is recommended to be given by the message, not with the view of giving power to the President to assert our rights to the whole territory, but as a moral weapon, to enforce compromise.

To this construction I have the same difficulty in assenting as to the preceding. There is nothing in the language of the recommendation to authorize it. On the contrary, every word it contains looks expressly, as has been stated, to the enforcement of our rights to the territory on the expiration of the notice. To give a contrary interpretation would be to give a diplomatic character to the message, and be subject to all the objections which have been just suggested. But admitting that it was intended, as alleged, as a moral weapon to effect compromise, I would ask, how could that be effected, but by using it as the means to intimidate Great Britain—to intimidate, by telling her that she must quit the territory within the year, or be expelled at its expiration by force? And what would that be but an appeal to her fear, with the hope of extorting concessions which her reason had refused to yield? Such an appeal in the case of a feeble nation would be hazardous; but in that of one as great and powerful as England, instead of a weapon to enforce a compromise, it would be one calculated to defeat it.

The remaining reason for voting notice on the part of the Senators referred to, is of a very different character. It objects to the convention itself, and condemns the policy of entering into either that of 1818 or 1827, on the ground that instead of being the means of securing and perpetuating our rights in the territory, they have had the very reverse effect, to weaken instead of strengthen our title to the territory. My opinion, I must say, is precisely the opposite. It would, indeed, have been desirable to have settled it then by a compromise on the 49th parallel of latitude; but that, as is well known, was impossible at the time. The offer, in fact, was made on our side, but rejected on the part of Great Britain. The rejection left no other alternative but an appeal to arms, or a surrender of our rights to the territory, or to enter into the convention. To do nothing would have been to acquiesce in the claims of Great Britain, whose subjects were then in actual possession. Her possession, being adverse to ours, would have been gradually maturing, through the long intervening period, into a title too perfect to be opposed by ours. To avoid that, we were compelled to resort to force, or enter into a convention to preserve our rights. We wisely preferred the latter, and the conventions of 1818 and 1827 were the consequence of that preference. They were entered into for the two-fold objects, as substitutes for war, and the means of preserving our rights to the territory, as they then stood, unimpaired. To appreciate the wisdom of the policy, it must be borne in mind that at that time our means of asserting our rights to the territory or of acquiring possession were exceedingly limited, compared to those of Great Britain, but that they were steadily and rapidly increasing. Those who had the management of affairs at that period wisely relied upon time and the rapid spread of population in a western direction, as the means ultimately of acquiring possession of the territory, and entered into the convention with a view of preserving our rights unimpaired until they could operate with full effect.

It is but too common of late to condemn the acts of our predecessors, and to pronounce them unjust, unwise, or unpatriotic, from not adverting to the circumstances under which they acted. Thus to judge, is to do great injustice to the wise and patriotic men who preceded us. In this case, it is to condemn such men as [James] Monroe, [Richard] Rush, [Henry] Clay, and [Albert] Gallatin—all of whom had an agency in directing or conducting the negotiations which terminated in the adoption of these conventions. It would be hard to pronounce men like them to have been unwise or unpatriotic in what they did, or to pronounce President [Andrew] Jackson and others after him so, because they acquiesced for many years under the operation of the convention of 1827, when they could have terminated it at any time by giving a year's notice. I have not named the most prominent individual [John Quincy Adams?] concerned in directing these negotiations, because his course on this occasion has, in my opinion, cancelled any previous credit in that connexion to which he would have been otherwise entitled.

Such was the state of things at the commencement of the session, when the President recommended notice to be given to terminate the joint occupancy; and such the position and grounds assumed by the several portions of the Senate in reference to the notice. Since then, as has been stated, there has been a great change, which has materially affected the question of notice, and the position taken by the different portions of the body in reference to it, as I shall next explain.

Public opinion has had time to develop itself, not only on this, but on the other side of the Atlantic; and that opinion has pronounced most audibly and clearly in favor of compromise. The development has been going on not only in the community, but also in this body; and I now feel that I hazard nothing in saying, that a large majority of the Senate is in favor of terminating the controversy by negotiation, and an honorable compromise. And what is very material, the opinion of the British Government on the subject of compromise has been more clearly and specifically developed than when the message was transmitted to Congress; so much so that there is ground to hope that it is prepared to adjust the difference in reference to the territory substantially on the basis which was offered by the President. It seems to me impossible that any other construction can be given to what Sir R[obert] Peel said in reply to the question put to him by Lord John Russell. His declaration was made under circumstances calculated to give it great weight. The object of making it was clearly not to censure the able and very faithful representative of Great Britain in this country, but to use the occasion to give assurance that he is ready to make a compromise, as it may be inferred, substantially on the basis of the rejected offer. I trust sincerely that such is the interpretation which our Government has put upon it; and that, regarding it as a direct step towards compromise, it has met it with a step on our part, by suitable instructions to our minister in that country. It is to be hoped that a communication has already been transmitted to that effect, which may have the effect of removing what would seem to be the only material difficulty in the way of an adjustment; that is which shall make the first step towards resuming the negotiation.

As things now stand, I no longer consider it as a question, whether the controversy shall be pacifically arranged or not, nor even in what manner it shall be arranged. I regard the arrangement now simply a question of time, and I do trust that, in concluding it, there will be no unnecessary delay. The business of both countries, and of commerce generally, requires that it should be concluded as promptly as possible. There is still another and a higher reason why it should be speedily settled. The question is one of a momentous and delicate character, and like all such, should be settled in order to avoid adverse contingencies with the least practicable delay. A further inducement for despatch in settling the Oregon question is, that upon it depends the settlement of the question with Mexico. Until the former is settled, there is but slender prospect that the latter can be; for so long as the Oregon question is left open, Mexico will calculate the chances of a rupture between us and Great Britain, in the event of which she would be prepared to make common cause against us. But when an end is put to any such hope, she will speedily settle her difference with us. I trust that when we come to settle it, we will deal generously with her, and that we will prove ourselves too just and magnanimous to take advantage of her feeble condition.

It is this great change in favor of the prospect of settling the controversy in reference to Oregon honorably, by negotiation and compromise, which has occurred since the commencement of the session, that has made the great difference in the importance of the bearing of notice on the question of peace and war. What then was apparently almost hopeless, may be now regarded as highly probable, unless there should be some great mismanagement; but just as compromise is more hopeless, notice becomes more important in its bearings on the relations of peace and war; and on the other hand, just as the chances of compromise are increased, notice becomes less important; and hence its importance at the commencement of the session, and its comparatively little importance now.

I shall next proceed to inquire what bearing the increased prospect of compromise has on the position of the Executive, and that of the several portions of this body, in reference to notice, and the Oregon question generally. That it is calculated to effect materially the position of the Executive must be apparent. That he should recommend giving notice to terminate the convention of joint occupancy of the territory, with a view of asserting our exclusive sovereignty to the whole, according to his view of our title, when there was little or no hope of compromise, is not at all inconsistent with his being prepared to adjust the difference by compromise, substantially on the ground offered by himself, now when there is a reasonable prospect it may be effected. Measures of policy are necessarily controlled by circumstances, and consequently what may be wise and expedient under certain circumstances, might be eminently unwise and impolitic under different circumstances. To persist in acting in the same way under circumstances essentially different, would be folly and obstinancy, and not consistency. True consistency, that of the prudent and the wise, is to act in conformity with circumstances, and not to act always the same way under a change of circumstances.

There is a prevalent error on this point. Many think that the very essence of consistency is to act always the same way—adhering to the same party, or to the same measures of policy, without regard to change of circumstances. Their consistency is like that of a physician, who, in the treatment of a highly inflammatory fever, would administer emetics and calomel, not only at the beginning, but at every subsequent stage of the disease. It is the consistency of a quack, which would be sure to kill the patient. The public man who would be consistent in the same way would be but a political quack, and in dangerous cases, his prescription would be not less fatal. If then the Executive is now really in favor of compromise, notwithstanding the strong language used in his message recommending notice, of which I have no information that is not common to all, it ought not to subject him to the charge of inconsistency, but should be put down to the change of circumstances to which I have adverted.

That it is also calculated to alter the positions taken by the different portions of the Senate, in reference to notice, is no less certain; and that my friends (for such I will call them) who go for the whole of Oregon, must, I am sure, feel to be the case with them. They cannot, I am confident, have the same interest in notice now, when there is great reason to believe that the difference will be compromised with or without notice, as they had when there was no hope of compromise. It is clear, that under such change of circumstances, the reason for giving notice with them has, in a great measure if not altogether, ceased, so that I should not be surprised to find their votes cast against it.

But I trust that the change has gone further, and that they, by this time, begin to see that there are some doubts as to our title to the whole of Oregon being clear and unquestionable. It cannot, at least, be regarded as unquestionable, after it has been questioned so frequently and with such ability during this discussion. But if their opinion remains unchanged as to the clearness of our title, I put it to them whether there is not some deference due to the opinion of the great majority of the Senate who entertain different views? Is there not something due to the fact, that the majority even of their own political friends, whose patriotism and intelligence they cannot regard as inferior to their own, think that our title is not so clear but that a compromise might be honorably effected? To put a still stronger question, I ask them, as patriots and friends of Oregon, whether the fact itself of so great a division, even among ourselves, does not afford strong reason why the controversy should not be settled by an appeal to force? Are they willing, as wise and patriotic men, desirous of securing the whole of Oregon, to place the country in conflict with so great a power as England, when the united support and zealous co-operation of all would be indispensable to support the country in the contest? I appeal to them, in the humbler character, as party men, whether they are justified in persisting to push a course of policy which, whether it should end in war or not, must terminate in the division and distraction of their party?

Without pursuing this branch of the subject further, I shall conclude what I had to say in reference to it, by saying that I, for one, feel and acknowledge the change. Nothing could have induced me to vote for notice, in any form, while there was apparently no hope of compromise; but now that there is, I am disposed to do so, if it should be properly modified.

I am thus brought to the question under consideration, to which all the preceding remarks were but preliminary—shall notice be given to Great Britain to terminate the convention of joint occupancy? After what has been said, a few words will suffice to dispatch it.

The question is not free from doubt. After a review of the whole ground, I can discover but two reasons in favor of giving it. The first is, to put an end to the agitation of the Oregon question, which, without it, may run into the next presidential election, and thereby become more difficult of adjustment than ever. The other is the apprehension, that the Government of Great Britain may wait the final action of Congress in reference to notice before it will move on the subject. Were it not for such apprehension, I would be disposed to postpone notice for the present.

The next question is, in what form should it be given, if given at all? I, for one, can, under no circumstances, vote for absolute notice, although I admit it would be less dangerous now than when recommended by the message. I cannot consent to give a vote which might be construed to imply, that there was no hope of compromise, and which might, if given in that form, leave a doubt in the public mind as to the real opinion of the Senate in reference to compromise.

Nor can I vote for notice in the form which has been sent to us from the other House. I object to it as equivocal. If the resolution means simply to declare that the President may settle the controversy by compromise, it means nothing, as the President has that right under the Constitution, and can neither be clothed or divested of it by the authority of Congress. But if it be intended as a hint to him to settle the question by negotiation and compromise, I object to it for not plainly saying so. I am utterly opposed to all equivocation,

713

or obscure expressions, in our public acts. We are bound to say plainly what we mean to say. If we mean negotiation and compromise, let us say it distinctly and plainly, instead of sending to the President a resolution on which he may put whatever interpretation he pleases.

If we give notice at all, it seems to me, for the reasons just stated, it should be substantially as has been proposed by the gentleman from Georgia, (Mr. [Walter T.] Colquitt,) which plainly expresses the desire of the Senate that it should be settled by negotiation and compromise. For it I am inclined to vote, as at present advised; but regarding notice in all its forms as subordinate to settling the controversy without resort to arms, I reserve my decision until I am called upon to vote; and then I shall decide in the affirmative or negative, according as I shall judge that one or the other is best calculated to advance the end I have in view.

I have thus stated my reasons for supporting a compromise, and for favoring, at present, the giving of notice. I have been governed, as to both, by the circumstances under which I find myself placed, but for which I am no ways responsible. I am doing the best I can, where I find myself, and not what I would under different circumstances. So far from being responsible for the present state of things, I early took my stand against that line of policy which has placed us where we are. I refer to 1843. Then the Oregon question for the first time assumed a dangerous aspect. After having been long and frequently brought to the notice of Congress, without exciting attention, I then saw, or thought I saw, that it was destined, at no distant period, to become an absorbing and dangerous question, and accordingly felt it to be my duty, before I decided on my course in reference to it, to examine it in all its bearings with care and deliberation. After much reflection, I came to the conclusion, which I on that occasion explained, in a speech delivered on the subject. I then saw that there were two distinct lines of policy, which might be pursued: one was to adhere to the convention of 1827; oppose every attempt to annul it, and strictly observe its provisions. I saw, that although for a time the convention had operated beneficially for Great Britain, a period was at hand when our turn would come to enjoy its benefits. Its operation had, therefore, thrown into her hands the whole fur-trade of the region; and we had looked on, while she reaped the rich harvest, when it was in our power at any time to annul the convention by giving the year's notice. But I saw that our forbearance would be compensated by the advantages which the convention was about to confer on us, if we should have the wisdom o adopt the proper line of policy to secure them. The increase of our population, and its progress westward were rapidly extending our settlements towards the Rocky mountains, through which a pass had been discovered but a few years before, which greatly increased the facility of colonizing the territory.

In this state of things, it was clear to my mind that if we adhered to the convention, and respected its provisions, the progress of events would ultimately give us possession of the whole territory; as our power to settle the territory, and thereby obtain possession, was far greater than that of Great Britain. Its distance from us was far less, and the approach through an open, grassy, country, affording great facility to the active and hardy pioneers of the West, who emigrate with their families and herds, with little expense or fatigue. Very different was the case with Great Britain. The distance to Oregon, by water, from her shores cannot be much less than twenty thousand miles—a dis[tance] but little short of the entire circumference of the globe; while her approach to it through her American possessions opposes great difficulties to emigration on a large scale. Of all the spots on the globe now open to colonization, and susceptible of being colonized, it is the most remote from her, and the most difficult of access. She has many colonies much nearer to her, to which there is much greater facility of access, with equal soil and climate, as yet very partially settled. Even New Zealand in all these respects is superior to it. With these advantages in our favor in settling the territory, and which were yearly rapidly increasing, it was clear to my mind that all we had to do was to adhere to the convention; to observe all its provisions with the most scrupulous fidelity, in order to obtain the actual occupation and possession of the whole country.

As far as I could perceive, there was but one impediment in the way, and that was, that Great Britain, in order to prevent us from obtaining possession by settlement, might give notice herself to terminate the convention for joint occupancy. But of this I entertained but little apprehension. I had read the correspondence of former negotiations with attention, and my inference was, that she placed but little value on Oregon, as a place for a permanent settlement, and that she had, in a great measure, made up her mind, from its geographical position, that it would ultimately pass into our hands. But be this as it may, I could not but see that there were great impediments in her way of giving such notice, as would preclude us from the right of settling. She has, indeed, the same right to terminate the convention of 1827 that we have, as it is expressly provided

715

that either may give it. But there is another convention which she claims to be still in existence, and to which we, holding under Spain are parties with her. I refer to the Nootka Sound convention. It is strictly analogous with that of 1827, though dissimilar in its language But unlike the latter, it contains no provision for giving notice, and can only be annuled by violation. Under it, we, according to her own showing, have equal rights with herself to joint occupancy and settlement, of which we cannot be deprived on the ground on which she places her rights to the territory, without a breach of faith.

It seemed then to me clear, that our true policy was such as I have stated; to adhere to the convention, and let settlement determine to whom the territory should belong, affording in the mean time whatever facilities we might think proper to our people emigrating to the territory, not inconsistent with the provisions of the convention, and extending our laws over them in like manner, and to the same extent that Great Britain had by act of Parliament. To me it seemed clear that we ought not to go beyond, and that we should by no means extend our laws over it territorially. The necessary effects of that would be to extend our tariff acts to the territory, under an express provision of the Constitution, which requires that all duties and taxes shall be laid uniformly throughout the United States. The restrictions imposed by our high tariff duties, on the infant commerce of the territory, would go far, not only to diminish the inducement to emigration, but to alienate the affection of its people. To enjoy the blessings of free trade over the broad Pacific, with its numerous islands and widely-extended coast, will prove in the end to be the strongest inducement to emigration; and to impose high duties, would do more to check emigration, to alienate its inhabitants, and separate them from our Union, than any other cause. Oregon will be to the Pacific what New England was to the Atlantic in its colonial state; and its people will contend as earnestly for the unrestricted enjoyment of the trade of the Pacific as the New Englanders did for that of the Atlantic before the revolution. It was, indeed, one of the principal causes which led to the revolution. Should we restrict by our high tariff duties their infant trade, they might readily find a power prepared to extend to them all the advantages of free trade, to be followed by consequences not difficult to be perceived. Influenced by these considerations, I came to the conclusion that our true policy was to let our people emigrate and govern themselves for the present with as little interference as possible on our part. In that respect they possess great capacity from their origin and their native instincts. I would let them go there and settle the country in their own way, giving them all the aid, countenance, and support which we could, without extending our authority over them territorially, until it could be properly and safely done. But be it done when it may, great judgment and caution will be required, for there lies the great difficulty of reconciling the interest on the eastern side of the Rocky mountains with that of the western side.

The other line of policy looked to the termination of the convention by giving notice and taking adverse possession of the territory. The bill of 1843, already alluded to, was intended as the first step. I opposed it, not only because I believed that some of its provisions violated the convention, but because I believed that the course it indicated was highly impolitic. It seemed to me, indeed, to require little reflection to perceive that if the bill should pass, and the policy it indicated be adopted, that negotiation or war would necessarily follow; and that, if the former should be resorted to in the first instance to prevent war, it would terminate either in compromise or war. There could be no other result. Nor was it more difficult to perceive, that if the question was compromised, it must be on the basis of the 49th parallel. The past history of the affair, the fact that it had been frequently offered by us substantially as an ultimatum, added to the fact that 49° was the boundary on the side of this Rocky mountains, left no doubt in my mind that, if settled by compromise, it must be on that basis. It is true that our offer heretofore on that basis had been rejected, and that it might thence be inferred that Great Britain could not accede to it consistently with her honor. I am not of that impression. Things have greatly changed since our offers were made and rejected by her. Then the advantages under the convention were all in her favor; but now they have turned in favor of us. Then our capacity to settle the country was small; but now, for reasons already stated, they are great; and what is far from being immaterial, this increased capacity to settle and colonize strengthens the foundation of our claims to the territory. The capacity to settle and colonize a contiguous open region not capable of being settled or colonized by any other power, goes back to the original principles on which all claim to territory is founded.

Seeing that such would necessarily be the consequence of the line of policy indicated by the bill, and wishing to avoid both compromise and war, I took a decided stand against it. I was very ably seconded in my opposition; so much so that notwithstanding the apparently large majority in its favor, when the discussion commenced, it passed this body by an equivocal majority of one. I say equivocal, because one of the Senators felt himself constrained by accidental causes to vote for the measure, after he had avowed his opinion against it. Since then, session after session, measures have been introduced to give notice and extend our authority over the territory, with a view ultimately of taking possession of the whole. As anticipated, negotiation, in order to avoid war, followed; and now we are brought to the alternative of compromise or fighting, as ought to have been foreseen from the beginning. I again repeat, that I am in no way responsible for the present state of things; and if I am compelled in consequence to vote for compromise and notice, the responsibility rests on my friends behind me, whose course has forced the Government into it by the line of policy they have pursued. I do not impeach their patriotism; but I cannot but think that they permitted their zeal in behalf of the territory, and the impatience of those they represent to occupy it, to get the control of their better judgment.

Having been thus brought, by the line of policy to which I was opposed, to choose between compromise and war, I without hesitation take the former. In making the choice, I am actuated by no unmanly fear of the consequences of war. I know that in the existing state of the world, wars are necessary—that the most sacred regard for justice and equity, and the most cautious policy, cannot always prevent them. When war must come, I may appeal to my past history to prove that I shall not be found among those who may falter; but I shall take care never to contribute by my acts to precipitate the country into a war, when it can be fairly avoided. I am, on principle, opposed to war, and in favor of peace, because I regard peace as a positive good, and war as a positive evil. As a good, I shall ever cling to peace, so long as it can be preserved consistently with the safety and honor of the country; and as opposed to war, I shall ever resist it, so long as it may be resisted consistently with the same considerations. I am emphatically opposed to it in this case, because peace, in my opinion, can be preserved consistently with both, and war avoided without sacrificing either. I am opposed to it for the additional reason, because it would be, in my opinion, highly impolitic—a consideration never to be overlooked when a question of the kind is under consideration. I regard it as highly impolitic in this case, because I believe that, should we resort to it, we would lose, instead of securing, the two objects for which it would be avowedly declared, as I shall now proceed to show.

The first is to secure what is claimed to be our rights to the whole of Oregon, under the cry of *"all of Oregon or none."* Those who would go into it for that object will, in my opinion, find in the end that *"none"* is much more probable than *"all."* In coming to this conclusion, I concede to my countrymen the highest bravery, energy, patriotism, and intelligence, which can be claimed for them. But these cannot overcome the great obstacles we would have to encounter, compared to what Great Britain would have in a contest for Oregon. As long as she has a large force in the East, and remains mistress of the Pacific, she will be able to place there a much more efficient force, and at far less expense, than we possibly can at present, which would there decide the contest in her favor.

But were it otherwise, from the nature of the contest, Oregon, though the cause of the war, would be speedily forgotten. The struggle once begun, would soon cease to be for Oregon. Higher and far more powerful motives would soon guide the contest. It would speedily become a struggle for mastery between the greatest power in the world on one side, against the most growing on the other. Actuated by all the feelings belonging to such a struggle, both sides would put forth all their vigor, energy and resources, and overlooking minor points, would aim to strike the most vulnerable, and where each might have the greatest advantage, leaving Oregon to be won or lost as the contingencies of so mighty a contest might decide.

The next object, as is alleged, is to protect our citizens in Oregon. What has just been said is enough to prove how utterly it must fail. Instead of protection, war would most certainly sacrifice them; and that is a strong reason, with me, for opposing it. I feel our obligation to protect them as citizens, and brethern, and kindred. We have encouraged them to emigrate, and I will not give a vote which in my opinion would ruin and abandon them. But what war would fail to effect, would be certainly accomplished by compromise on the line offered by the President. There are none of our citizens, if I am correctly informed, settled north of 49°. Establish that line, and we at once give our citizens in Oregon peace and security, and with them full opportunity to realize their object in emigrating.

But passing from Oregon, I take broader ground, and oppose war for reasons looking to the whole. I see nothing to hope from war, be its result what it may. On the contrary, I believe that the most successful and triumphant war that could be waged—one in which all would be accomplished which its most extravagant advocate could dare hope for—in which we should conquer the Canadas, New Brunswick, and Nova Scotia—in which we should drive the British flag from the continent, and compel Great Britain to yield the whole by treaty, in the short space of ten years, would be disastrous to us. I allude not to its ravages or devastations—to the oceans of blood that must flow, and the manifold losses and miseries which would accompany the war. They are common to all wars; but however vividly painted, they have but little effect in deterring a brave people from a resort to it. No doubt these inflictions would be very great in a contest between two nations of such immense power, and so situated as to be able to do each other the greatest harm in war and the greatest good in peace. But as great as the devastation and destruction of life would be in such a struggle, they are of a nature to be speedily repaired on our side. The indomitable industry and enterprise of our people, with the great resources of the country, would soon repair the former, while our rapidly increasing population would speedily repair the latter. War has far heavier calamities for a free people than these, though less visible—calamities in their nature not easily remedied. I refer to permanent and dangerous social and political changes, which often follow in its train, in the character of the people and their institutions. A war between us and Great Britain, such as has been described, in which every nerve and muscle on either side would be strained to the utmost, and every dollar put in requisition which could be commanded, could not fail, under present circumstances, to work most disastrous, and, I fear, incurable changes in the social condition of our people, and in their political institutions. To realize the consequences in this respect, which must follow, it is necessary to look at the immense extent to which it would rage. It would, in all probability, prove a Mexican and an Indian war, as well as a war with Great Britain, and as such would extend to every portion of our entire frontier, including the Atlantic and the Pacific, the inland and exterior, constituting a circuit of probably not less than 7,000 miles. It would require, in order to conduct it with the energy necessary to bring it in so short a time to the successful termination supposed, especially in a war for mastery, immense exertions on land and water. Two navies—one on the Atlantic and the other on the lakes—and six or seven armies, would be required for the purpose, even on the supposition that Oregon would be abandoned. One army would be required on the Mexican frontier; and let no one sneer at the mention of such a power. Feeble as it now is, when paid and supported by British gold, and trained and commanded by British officers, Mexico would prove a formidable enemy. See what British skill and training have made the feeble Sepoys. The Mexicans are a braver and a hardier people, and, what is no small point, would constitute the cheapest of all armies. There must be in addition, one to guard the gulf frontier; another to guard the southern; another the northern frontier on the Atlantic; another to assail the northeastern frontier on the side of Nova Scotia and New Brunswick; and another to assail the Canadian; and finally another to protect our widely extended Indian frontier. All these, in so mighty a struggle against the greatest of all powers, putting forth her utmost strength, would require a force, including the two navies, of not less, I would suppose, than 200,000 men continually in pay. The expense would be enormous. One of the most venerable and experienced of our citizens, Mr. Gallatin, has estimated it at 65 or 70 millions of dollars annually, if my memory serves me. My impression is that it falls far short of the actual cost, and that $100,000,000 would not be an over estimate. Supposing the sum of $50,000,000 could be annually raised by taxation—a sum far greater than he estimates, and in my opinion much beyond what could be effected—it would leave $50,000,000 annually to be raised by loans, or a forced paper circulation. Now, allowing the war to continue for ten years, there would be incurred a debt in the time of $500,000,000, according to these estimates. Even that, it is probable, would fall much short of the reality, assuming the sum stated should be annually required. It would be difficult to obtain loans in Europe; for owing to the conduct of some of the States in reference to repudiation, and other causes not necessary to state, the feeling of Europe would, I fear, be generally against us, while our own resources would not be sufficient to raise the sum required without a great depreciation of our credit, with a loss of 20, 30, or even 40 per cent., before the termination of the war, in contracting loans, or in consequence of the depreciation of our paper circulation. Including all, our public debt would, at the end of the struggle, be probably not less than six or seven hundred millions of dollars. But this is not all.

We would be plunged into the paper system as deeply as we were in the days of the revolution; and would terminate the war with a mortgage of six or seven hundred millions of dollars on the labor of our people—for on labor the whole must fall ultimately, while a large portion of this vast amount would go into the pockets of those who struck not a blow, nor lost a drop of blood in the contest, and who acquired their gains by seizing upon the distress of the government to drive hard and usurious bargains. In addition, we should have the difficult task to perform of restoring to a sound state a greatly depreciated paper circulation, or of extricating ourselves from it whatever way we might—a task which cannot be performed

without great distress to the country and ruinous effect to that large
and usually the enterprising portion of the community, the debtors.
The effects of all this would be highly injurious to the social relations
of the people. A powerful artificial class would be created on one
side, and a poor and dependent one on the other.

Nor would its effect on our political institutions be less disastrous.
Such a war would obliterate the line of distinction, in a great measure, between the Federal and the State governments, by conferring
on the former vastly increased power and influence. We would hear
no more of State rights. The federal government would then become a great national consolidated government. Our very success
would give a military impulse to the public mind and to the character of the government which it would be hard, if possible, to overcome, and which would seek conquest after conquest until a spirit
would be engendered totally inconsistent with the genius of our
system of government. It would then be in the straight and downward road, which leads to where so many free States have terminated their career—a military despotism. In the mean time, we
would have to provide for three or four successful generals, who
would soon be competing for the presidency; and before the generation which waged the war would have passed away, they might possibly witness a contest between hostile generals for that supreme
office—a contest between him who might conquer Mexico, and him
who might conquer Canada, terminated by the sword.

I appeal to the gentlemen who are the warm advocates for "all
of Oregon or none," regardless of this mighty hazard, and whose
separation from us on this question I regret, and solemnly put the
question to them—is it for you—you, who assume to be democrats
par excellence—you who are the enemies of the paper system, and
of all artificial classes in society—is it for you to support a course of
policy which might lead to such disastrous consequences?

But I oppose war not simply on the patriotic ground of a citizen
looking to the freedom and prosperity of his own country, but on
still broader grounds, as a friend of improvement, civilization, and
progress. Viewed in reference to them, at no period has it ever
been so desirable to preserve the general peace which now blesses
the world. Never in its history has a period occurred so remarkable
as that which has elapsed since the termination of the great war in
Europe, with the battle of Waterloo, for the great advances made in
all these particulars. Chemical and mechanical discoveries and in-
ventions have multiplied beyond all former example, adding with
their advance to the comforts of life in a degree far greater and more

universal than all that was ever known before. Civilization has during the same period spread its influence far and wide, and the general progress in knowledge, and its diffusion through all ranks of society, has outstripped all that has ever gone before it. The two great agents of the physical world have become subject to the will of man, and made subservient to his wants and enjoyments; I allude to steam and electricity, under whatever name the latter may be called. The former has overcome distance both on land and water, to an extent of which former generations had not the least conception to be possible. It has in effect reduced the Atlantic to half its former width, while, at the same time, it has added three-fold to the rapidity of intercourse by land. Within the same period, electricity, the greatest and most diffused of all known physical agents, has been made the instrument for the transmission of thoughts, I will not say with the rapidity of lightning, but by lightning itself. Magic wires are stretching themselves in all directions over the earth, and when their mystic meshes shall have been united and perfected, our globe itself will become endowed with sensitiveness, so that whatever touches on any one point, will be instantly felt on every other. All these improvements—all this increasing civilization—all the progress now making, would be in a great measure arrested by a war between us and Great Britain. As great as it is, it is but the commencement— the dawn of a new civilization, more refined, more elevated, more intellectual, more moral, than the present and all preceding it. Shall it be we who shall incur the high responsibility of retarding its advance, and by such a war as this would be?

I am, in this connexion, opposed to war between the United States and Great Britain. They are the two countries the furthest in advance in this great career of improvement and amelioration of the condition of our race. They are, besides, the two most commercial, and are diffusing, by their widely extended commerce, their blessings over the whole globe. We have been raised up by Providence for these great and noble purposes, and I trust we shall not fail to fulfil our high destiny. I am, besides, especially opposed to war with England at this time; because I hold that it is now to be decided, whether we are to exist in future as friends or enimies. War at this time, and for this cause, would decide supremacy, we shall hereafter stand in that of enemies.* It would give birth to a struggle

---

* Editor's note. This garbled sentence should read, according to the Washington *Daily Union* version: "War at this time, and for this cause, would decide in which of the two relations we shall hereafter stand."

in which one or the other would have to succumb before it terminated; and which in the end, might prove ruinous to both. On the contrary, if war can be avoided, powerful causes are now in operation, calculated to cement and secure a lasting—I hope a perpetual—peace between the two countries, by breaking down the barriers which impeded their commerce, and thereby uniting them more closely by a vastly enlarged commercial intercourse, equally beneficial to both. If we should now succeed in setting the example of free trade between us, it would force all other civilized countries to follow it in the end. The consequence would be, to diffuse a prosperity greater and more universal than can be well conceived, and to unite by bonds of mutual interest the people of all countries. But in advocating the cause of free trade, I am actuated not less by the political consequences likely to flow from it, than the advantages to be derived from it in an economical point of view. I regard it in the dispensation of Providence as one of the great means of ushering in the happy period foretold by inspired prophets and poets, when war should be no more.

I am finally opposed to war, because peace—peace is pre-eminently our policy. There may be nations, restricted to small territories, hemmed in on all sides, so situated that war may be necessary to their greatness. Such is not our case. Providence has given us an inheritance stretching across the entire continent from East to West, from ocean to ocean, and from North to South, covering by far the greater and better part of its temperate zone. It comprises a region not only of vast extent, but abundant in all resources; excellent in climate; fertile and exuberant in soil; capable of sustaining in the plentiful enjoyment of all the necessaries of life a population of ten times our present number. Our great mission, as a people, is to occupy this vast domain; to replenish it with an intelligent, virtuous, and industrious population; to convert the forests into cultivated fields; to drain the swamps and morasses, and cover them with rich harvests; to build up cities, towns, and villages in every direction, and to unite the whole by the most rapid intercourse between all the parts. War would but impede the fulfilment of this high mission, by absorbing the means and diverting the energies which would be devoted to the purpose. On the contrary, secure peace, and time, under the guidance of a sagacious and cautious policy, "a wise and masterly inactivity," will speedily accomplish the whole. I ventured to say "a wise and masterly inactivity," in despite of the attempt to cast ridicule upon the expression. Those who have made the attempt would seem to confound such inactivity with mere inaction. Nothing can be more unlike. They are as wide apart as the poles. The one is the offspring of indolence, or ignorance, or indifference. The other is the result of the profoundest sagacity and wisdom—a sagacity which looks into the operations of the great causes in the physical, moral, and political world; which, by their incessant operation, are ever changing the condition of nations for good or evil; and wisdom, which knows how to use and direct them when acting favorably, by slight touches, to facilitate their progress, and by removing impediments which might thwart or impede their course—and not least, to wait patiently for the fruits of their operation. He who does not understand the difference between such inactivity and mere inaction—the doing of nothing—is still in the horn-book of politics, without a glimpse of those higher elements of statesmanship by which a country is elevated to greatness and prosperity. Time is operating in our favor with a power never before exerted in favor of any other people. It is our great friend; and under the guidance of such a policy, it will accomplish all that we can desire. Our population is now increasing at the rate of about 600,000 annually, and is progressing with increased rapidity every year. It will average, if not impeded, nearly a million during the next twenty-five years; at the end of which period our population ought to reach to upwards of forty millions. With this vast increase, it is rolling westwardly with a strong and deep current, and will, by the end of that period, have spread from ocean to ocean. Its course is irresistable. The coast of the Pacific will then be probably as densely populated, and as thickly studded with towns and villages, in proportion to its capacity to sustain population, as that of the Atlantic now is. At the same rate, we shall have increased to upwards of eighty millions of people at the end of another twenty-five years; when, with one foot on the Atlantic and the other on the Pacific, and occupying a position between the eastern and western coasts of the old continent, we shall be in a position better calculated to control the commerce of both oceans, and to exert an influence over both continents, than any other country in the world. If we avoid war, and adhere to peace, all this will be effected—effected, I trust, without the loss of our free popular institutions. I am aware how difficult is the task to preserve free institutions over so wide a space, and so immense a population; but we are blessed with a Constitution admirably calculated to accomplish it. Its elastic power is unequalled, which is to be attributed to its federal character. The hope of success depends on preserving that feature in its full perfection, and adhering to peace as our policy. War may make us great; but let it never be forgotten that peace only can make us both great and free.

With a few remarks relating to myself personally, I shall conclude. I have been charged with being more strongly inclined to secure the annexation of Texas, than our rights to Oregon. It has been attributed to my greater partiality to the South than to the West. But I am yet to learn why Texas should be considered as belonging to the South rathern than to the West. I always thought that it formed a part, and not an unimportant part, of the valley of the Mississippi; and on that account, as well as for giving greater security to the southern portion of the valley, the West desired its annexation. Besides, I have yet to learn that Texas is confined to a southern latitude. I had supposed that it extended far north and west, up to the latitude of 42° in the neighborhood of the great pass of the Rocky mountains, on which the value of Oregon to us so much depends. I had supposed that what are called the Southern States had not so direct and deep an interest in its annexation as the West; but it would seem, from language held on the occasion, that in all this I was mistaken, and that the annexation of Texas was purely a Southern question, and only supported by the West under the expectation of obtaining in return the support of the South to the whole of Oregon up to 54° 40', and, if necessary, at the certain hazard of a war.

But passing by all this, and assuming that Texas was purely a Southern, and Oregon a Western question, I repel the charge of partiality, and shall now proceed to show, that if a different line of policy was pursued by me in reference to the two, it was because it was right and proper it should be. I treated both questions in the manner best calculated to effect the object in view, and indeed the only one by which both could be secured. The circumstances of the cases were entirely different. In the case of Texas, time was against us, in that of Oregon, time was with us; and hence the difference in my course of policy in reference to them. To understand the difference it is necessary to premise, that Texas had reached that period in her history when it was clear that she would be compelled to form intimate and dependent relations either with us or England, if she continued independent. But it was manifest, if left alone, without any movement on our part, that her connexion must be with England and not with us. She could extend to Texas commercial advantages far greater than we possibly could, and afford her greater facilities in obtaining means to relieve her from her great pecuniary mbarrassments. England saw this, and had actually commenced her movements to avail herself of its advantages. We, too, perceived t; and also that annexation afforded the only means of counteracting her movements, and preventing Texas from being placed exclusively under her control. In this emergency, I was called to the State Department, with a view of taking charge of the pending negotiation or annexation. I saw that the time had arrived when immediate and decided action was required; that time was against us, and that o resist the effects of its operation boldness and decision were indispensable. I acted accordingly, and success proved the soundness of my policy. It was not a case for masterly inactivity. Not so the case of Oregon, where time was with us, and hence the different line of policy which I adopted in reference to it, and which would have secured the whole, had my advice been followed, as has been explained.

In one particular my policy was the same in both cases. I aimed in each to avoid war and preserve peace. I clearly perceived that in annexing Texas there was no danger of a war with England, if managed judiciously. She was an independent state, and had been so acknowledged by England, France, and other powers. She had a right, as such, to dispose of herself, and to unite her destinies with ours, if she saw proper, without any right on the part of England to resist it, or ground or pretext to make war in consequence. I also perceived that there were no just grounds to apprehend a Mexican war in consequence. She was not in a condition to make war, without the aid of England, and there was no reason to apprehend that she would be aided or countenanced in it by the latter; unless, indeed, the Oregon question should terminate in a war between us and her, in which event, I regarded a Mexican war as inevitable, as has been stated. Thus far my anticipations have been realized—Texas annexed, and peace preserved, by the policy which I pursued. A different line of policy—one which would have permitted England to obtain the ascendency over Texas, which she would have acquired without annexation, would have inevitably led to a state of things, involving us and England finally in war. It would have been impossible to prevent feelings of jealousy and enmity from growing up between us and Texas. The very similarity of our character and pursuits, and the rivalry which they would give birth to, would necessarily lead to that result; while the long and ill-defined boundary between the two countries, extending for more than a thousand miles through forests, prairies, and navigable rivers, without a natural boundary in any part, would produce frequent collisions between our people and those of Texas. Controversies and conflicts would have been the result. Texas, as the weaker power, would throw herself upon Great Britain for support; and wars, frequent and bloody wars, between us and her would have followed. Annexation has fortunately removed these causes of war. Should the Oregon controversy terminate in peace, every cause of war between the two countries would be removed, leaving the prospect of lasting peace between them.

From *Speech of Mr. Calhoun, of South Carolina, on the Resolutions Giving Notice to Great Britain of the Abrogation of the Convention of Joint Occupancy* ([Washington: John T.] Towers, printer, [1846]). Also printed in *Congressional Globe*, 29th Cong., 1st Sess., Appendix, pp. 471–476; the Washington, D.C., *Daily Union*, vol. I, no. 274 (March 19, 1846), p. 1077; the Richmond, Va., *Enquirer*, March 24, 1846, pp. 1–2; the Milledgeville, Ga., *Federal Union*, March 31, 1846, pp. 1–2; the Huntsville, Ala., *Democrat*, April 8, 1846, pp. 1–2; the London, England, *Times*, April 18, 1846, pp. 8–9 (part); Crallé, ed., *Works*, 4:258–290; Alderman and Harris, eds., *Library of Southern Literature*, 2:695–702 (part); Wilson, ed., *The Essential Calhoun*, pp. 126–129 (part). NOTE: Two versions of Calhoun's important speech of 3/16 on Oregon have been included herein. They are similar in argument and content, but the dissimilarity in language is revealing about the nature of speech reporting. The first version originated from the Washington *Daily National Intelligencer* report of 3/17; the one immediately above which we have labeled "Revised Report" originated in the Washington *Daily Union* report of 3/19. From Calhoun's letters below to Anna Maria Calhoun Clemson on 3/23/1846 and to Charles A. Clinton on 3/24/1846, it seems that Calhoun went over the notes of the *Daily Union* report before it was published, thus providing a version that he felt reflected the style and the shaping of arguments that he wanted to get before the public. This is suggested by the fact that the later version was printed in the session Appendix to the *Congressional Globe*, though the earlier version had already appeared in the *Globe*; the later version as well was issued in a pamphlet and included in Crallé's *Works*. This revision was a relatively rare practice on Calhoun's part and indicates the importance which he ascribed to his action and position in this speech. It also indicates the degree to which material, in Calhoun's case, was generated by reporters, often unfriendly, who heard and summarized speeches, rather than from prepared texts. The Washington, D.C., *Daily Union*, vol. I, no. 271 (March 16, 1846), p. 1066, reported that Calhoun's "speech is, at his request, withheld for the present, but will appear speedily in our columns." The next day (p. 1072) the same paper again promised a speedy publication of the revised version of Calhoun's speech and added: "Other speeches have also been delayed in like manner, from some apprehension, perhaps, that the speakers would not be distinctly heard in the reporters' gallery." However, the Charleston, S.C., *Mercury*, March 26, 1846, p. 2, seemed to prefer the early unrevised report by the *Daily National Intelligencer* which is printed above in this volume as "First Report." The *Mercury* found the *Intelligencer* version "incomparably the best report ever made off-hand of a speech of Mr. Calhoun. . . . We have since examined the revised report of the speech, and feel bound to say that the report of the Intelligencer is in many respects superior to it in vividness and simplicity and in only one or two passages does it fall short of the full meaning of the speaker."

From MARIA D[ALLAS] CAMPBELL

[Washington, March 17, 1846?]

I go tomorrow morn[in]g at six o'clock & cannot leave here without one more shake of the hand, from you as I fear it may be very long before we meet again. Can you pay me a short visit this afternoon, say 5 or 6–or shall I come to see you? I beg as the only favor, I shall exact from you that you will let me hear from you from time to time, & if I can give you the slightest interest in my letters I promise to reply most faithfully. God bless you[;] let me see you if possible. Y[ou]r old & truest friend, Maria D. Campbell.

ALS in ScCleA. NOTE: This completely undated letter has been assigned a speculative date because of its possible relationship to the immediately following item.

From M[ARIA] D[ALLAS] CAMPBELL

[Washington,] Tuesday Night March 17th [18]46

My dear Sir, I am sorry I did not see you as you promised this eve[nin]g, as I might have avoided troubling you in this manner–which I know amid the multiplicity of your duties, is an annoyance. I wish at parting to remind you of your promised interest for the young friend I named to you. He would prefer you should see the President [James K. Polk], & begs you will take the trouble to read some letters which Mr. Jefferson Davis, of the House, will exhibit to you. Do not fail to send the *Speech*, & all others which may arise interesting to your friends & among those I beg you will include, y[ou]rs very truly, M:D: Campbell.

ALS in ScCleA.

From P. GWINNER

Philad[elphi]a, March 17th/46

Dear Sir, Gen[era]l [John?] Hall ["a frank & honest man" *interlined*] ex Custom House Officer left here yesterday for Washington. He has

a desire to see you, & wished a letter from me which his native mod-
esty (which even your scrutenising eye may not be able to discover)
prevented his asking for. He therefore requested a friend to ask
me to write you & say that he will call & see you; it gives me pleasure
to comply with his request. The Gen[era]l is an active politician,
with ultra tariff notions. Your views on the Oregon [question] is
looked for with much interest. It is rumored that [Henry] Horn
will be rejected. I hope in that event as I intimated in my last, a
friend of yours may succeed him. [Simon] Cameron will make every
effort to strengthen himself & no doubt has his plans matured, but I
think his opposition must destroy his influence with the President,
& Horn[']s immediate friends. Very Respectfully & truly y[ou]rs,
P. Gwinner.

ALS in ScCleA.

From CLEMENT C. BIDDLE

Philadelphia, 18th March 1846
My dear Sir, The meagre outline of your excellent speech in the
Senate on Monday, which I found in our "Ledger," this morning,
makes me most anxious to receive the report of it, *in extenso*, in the
most faithful form, that I may not only again have the pleasure of
perusing it, but also of sending it to a valued friend in England who
looks, with deep interest, to every thing that comes from you, I mean
Mr. Thomas Thornely, the colleague of the Hon. Mr. [Charles Pel-
ham] Villiers, the two members in the House of Commons for Wool-
verhampton; and I may add, that Mr. Thornely has been an able and
earnest advocate for Free Trade for the last twenty years.

I need not say how much gratified I have ["had" *altered to*
"been"], by the manly, statesmanlike, and philosophical views you
take of this perplexing Oregon question, the only obstacle apparently
now in the way of the consummation of our best hopes in the full reali-
zation of the principles, if not in the entire practice, of Free Trade,
and of the national blessings that enlightened policy, when carried
out, will confer on every section of our Union, North, South, East and
West. And when once fully adopted will cause us to feel shame and
mortification that we should so long have been the dupes of designing demagogues and deluded democrats, used by selfish monopo-
lists, to *protect* their own *plunder*, and thus subject *us* to suffering,

by their selfish misrule. Mr. [Robert J.] Walker's report from the Treasury entitles him to high praise, and is a most able and satisfactory document; but his bill, as given in the newspapers, I cannot relish. What, 30 per cent ad valorem? on many articles, in 1846, when by compromise they were brought down to 20 per cent in 1842, and general [Alexander] Hamilton's maximum, as stated by himself in the Federalist, was 3 times 3, or 9 per cent *for protection?* One of *our* most sensible *manufacturers,* a day or two ago, when I asked him what he thought of the tariff bill of Mr. Walker, replied, that *he* had no objection to it, but that he thought 30 per cent on Woolens too high a duty, as, at that rate, they, the manufacturers, would still have to encounter competition with the smug[g]lers; and that, as a permanent rate, that would keep off the smug[g]lers, he would prefer 25 per cent ad valorem on woolen imports. Now, I may add, that this gentleman is doing a profitable, and has been for a long time engaged in the same prosperous, business, namely, that of manufacturing woolen cloths.

I have been so much delighted in reading [George W.F. Howard] Lord Morpeth's speech on his election, that I send you the London Evening Chronicle of Friday, February 6th, the last London paper we have, containing the report of it, & will thank you when you have read it, to return it, as it does not belong to me. I wish, moreover to call your attention to the leaders, especially to that on Lord Morpeth's election. The remarks are admirable, and, you must excuse me for saying, that, with the same justice, they can be applied to one of our own statesmen, whom I must not *to you* name. You will also be amused with Mark Antony's Funeral Speech, abridged and adapted for the use of Protection Meetings; and with a few slight alterations might be adapted to our Manufacturers' Market.

Among my English correspondents is Mr. W[illia]m Brown of Liverpool, who will be the next member for South Lancashire. In his last letter, he expresses fears, that the Lords will not concur in any [free trade] bill passed by the House of Commons, with a majority *less than a hundred,* & that, he thinks, therefore, a dissolution of parliament will take place; but that the bill must pass ultimately. With great regard, & sincere respect, most truly y[ou]rs, Clement C. Biddle.

ALS in ScCleA; PEx in Boucher and Brooks, eds., *Correspondence,* pp. 332–333.

From D U F F G R E E N

New York [City,] 18th March 1846
My dear Sir, I have just read the brief extract of your speech as
given in the Journal of Commerce. Enough is given to satisfy me
that it is the crowning effort of your eventful life. Of all the triumphs which you have accomplished this is the greatest. You are
now, indeed, the benefactor, not only of your own country but of
the civilized world. Had you remained in the Cabinet and accomplished the peaceful adjustment of this question by the acquisition
of the "*whole* of Oregon" your personal fame would have been far
less, but you could not have done this, and you must see that it
would have been very difficult for you to have compromised on 49°.
You would have been assailed by northern fanatics. You would
have been charged with sectional feeling—with having surrendered
the interests of the north for the advancement of southern political
influence. Now the north will hail you as benefactor ["with" *canceled*] of the whole country & especially of the north. The moderate
men of all parties—the religious and moral sentiment of the country
will rally around you, and you will have the thanks of all who desire
peace. The treatment of the President [James K. Polk], and the
movement of [Lewis] Cass & Co. made the crisis for your advantage
& for the advancement of the great cause of peace and civilisation,
and it [*ms. torn*; has] been your good fortune that your enemies &
the jealousy ["&" *canceled*] rivalry ["of" *canceled*] & ambition of
your adversaries have given you the opportunity of developing the
principles which have governed your political life. You have tri-
umphed & no one rejoices more than your friend, Duff Green.

ALS in ScCleA; PC in Boucher and Brooks, eds., *Correspondence*, p. 333.

From D U F F G R E E N

New York [City,] 18th March 1846
Dear Sir, Two of your friends who have been removed from office
here have just left me. They tell me that Mr. [Michael] Hoffman
has some thirty offices in his gift, that he removed five immediately
on coming into office [as Naval officer for the N.Y. Customs district]
and that four of them were known to be sterling democrats but were
guilty of being bold enough to declare themselves to be your po-

litical friends. This was their only known disqualification to hold office under Messrs. Hoffman & [Robert J.] *Walker.*

Mr. Alexander Wells, I know personally. He was nominated by Tam[m]any [Hall] & is *now* a member of the Legislature at Albany, a young Lawyer of talent, & a sound State Rights democrat.

Mr. Daily [is] one of the most respectable democrats in the city.

Mr. [Patrick J.] Devine married a cousin of [former] Gov. Kavanaugh [*sic*; Edward Kavanagh] of Maine [and was] appointed on the recommendation of the Maine Congressional delegation & Albert Smith.

Doctor Baily [is] the Editor of the Jeffersonian and a good Democrat.

I know that Hoffman is of the [Silas] *Wright* Clique & it is said that he was one of the *"secret circular"* men.

His rejection by the Senate would produce a decided effect, and he ought not to be confirmed before you recieve [William L.] McKenzie's book which I am told will contain some developements greatly to Hoffman[']s prejudice.

Hoffman was recommended to Mr. [James K.] Polk by the junto who organised themselves to get possession of the Patronage of this State, and now represents [Martin] Van Buren & [Silas] Wright in the Custom House.

His rejection would gratify many of your friends but it is proper that you should know that the friends of Wright & Van Buren are now for 49° & vindicating your course. I give you facts. You hear [*one word canceled and* "both" *interlined*] sides & can best judge. Yours truly, Duff Green.

ALS in ScCleA.

From JOHN STILES

Boston, March 18th 1846

Sir, The Rev[eren]d Alex[ander] Blaikie, by letter received last evening, informed me that he had written to you on the subject of my application for the U.S. Consulship at the port of Pictou, N[ova] S[cotia]. The petition has been delayed a few days longer than the Rev. Mr. Blaikie anticipated, to obtain the Signatures of Mr. [F.A.] Benson and other Coal dealers interested in the Pictou trade, who were not at home till within a few days. The petition for the Consulship was forwarded today enclosed to Mr. [George] Bancroft.

Trusting you will excuse the liberty taken in addressing you I am Your mo[st] ob[edien]t Serv[an]t, Jno. Stiles.

ALS in DNA, RG 59 (State Department), Letters of Application and Recommendation during the Administrations of James K. Polk, Zachary Taylor, and Millard Fillmore, 1845–1853, John Stiles (M-873:83, frames 520–521). NOTE: An AEU by Calhoun reads "Mr. Stiles desires the app[ointmen]t of consul."

From TILLY ALLEN

New York City, Mar. 19th 1846

My Dear Sir, I have Just got through with reading your sentiments upon the Origun question as express[e]d to the Senate on Monday last, and cannot deny myself the pleasure of expressing to you the profound satisfaction ["is" *altered to* "it"] has given me; so entirely different from any one of the *Political* Speeches heretofore deliver[e]d upon that subject—so filled with pure Philanthropy, and the best interests of all the human family as well as our Country and its Institutions, without a single political taint. This production, my Dear Sir, at this crisis of our national affairs, is like the shadow of a great Rock to a weary traveler in a foreign land, and will go down to posterity, to unborn ages as imperishable as the name of its Illustrious Author. Although I have not been a political ["supporter" *interlined*] for several years past, yet I cannot but indulge the hope, and express the wish, which seems to be nearly Universal here at present, that I may have the opportunity to give my support to the author of such noble, and may I not say from the spirit they breathe *God like* sentiments for the highest office in the gift of this great people, at no very distant period. Be assured Sir, that the course you have adopted from the purest principles, has gained for you many, very many strong friends, throughout the whole community. I am but an humble Individual connected with the Commercial Interests of this Country and unknown to yourself, nor have I any right to expect an acknowled[g]ment of this, although it would be exceedingly gratifying if ever so short. I am Dear Sir Yours very Sincerely, Tilly Allen.

ALS in ScCleA; PC in Boucher and Brooks, eds., *Correspondence*, pp. 333–334.

From FERNANDO WOOD

New York[City,] March 19 1846

My dear Sir, I congratulate you upon the ablest effort of your life—your Speech on Oregon &c. I know my humble praise is of little consequence ["to" *altered to* "when"] whole communities are raising their congratulatory voices but as one of the people—as your friend and as one who feels a deep interest and pride in the success of our institutions and welfare of this great Republic I feel it a duty to say this much. Very Truly &, Fernando Wood.

ALS in ScCleA.

From CH[ARLES] AUG[USTUS] DAVIS

New York [City,] 20 March 1846

My D[ea]r Sir, I have just risen from the perusal of your speech (as reported in the N[ational] Intel[l]igencer) on the "Oregon question" and for the gratification it afforded me and that of my little domestic circle to whom I read it I beg to render to you my sincere thanks.

Among the difficulties that environ public men it has always struck me the greatest must be to reconcile the mass to the fact that what may be [*one word canceled and* "expedient" *interlined*] to day may not be so next year—or rather to prevent the *demagogue* from misleading the mass, by showing them that it is "*inconsistent*" for a man to urge to day what he may have opposed last year. On this point by a very simple illustration you have been most happy in putting this matter on its true footing—for it ever has seem'd to me to indicate a cowardly if not a wicked mind to persevere in one course of political policy for the sake of avoiding the vapid charge of *inconsistency*, whilst changes may have occur'd which render such a course fatal to the best interests of the Country. That "Calomel" *settles* it and the "Emetic" will never fail to "bring up" the folly you so effectually dispose of.

That was another happy hit you made in speaking of sitting in judgment upon the acts of predecessors without regarding the state of times and all the facts that then press'd around for consideration. A Capt. of a ship may at one time save his Vessel by casting anchor and prevent her being driven on shore, whilst at another time such a course would be sure to lead to disaster—if inquired into at the time and not left for enquiry years after, it w[oul]d be found that in one case his cables were new and strong, and his sails and rigging old and weak, and the reverse at the other time. And thus it is in political matters.

The mention you make of the improvements of the age and the contributions now made by science to human advancement and human happiness, is *peculiarly felicitous.* In fact take this speech altogether, I regard it as one of your best—and as it is based on matters which belong to all time and *all interests* (moral and physical) it will be garner'd up by a wider circle than others which appertain more to Special interests. It is a *"Pantheon"* and no one dare demolish it as he may see in it a nitch for his own God. If this speech is publish'd in pamphlet form and ["under" *interlined*] your correction I should be pleas'd to have as many copies of it as I can procure.

There is only one point I wish had been "dove tail'd" in it—and that is the fact of domestic slavery ["as" *interlined*] guaranteed by the Constitution operating as a safe guard to England[']s possession of her Canadian Colonies—which is a fact, for I believe if it were not for the direct influence of our *planting* interest at the South holding as they do a vote in *labor* there—the *agriculturalists* of the north would very soon march into Canada, and by new northern States alter the whole matter. As soon as "John Bull" sees this—as some of them now do—we shall hear less from him in the Shape of senseless rebuke for holding slaves. If our Southern planters had yielded to the morbid action of abolitionists as did the West India planters— at this very day Canada, would be all *Yankee.* This at least is my theory, and I believe there is more prose than poetry in it.

I had written thus far when the Mail p[e]r Steamer from England was distributed and I have been reading some interesting letters from some English friends there. There seems one sentiment in regard to the last publish'd correspondence, in which the offer to refer the question was rejected by our Gov't. This news had just reach'd England and produced a very sad effect—the impression being that our Gov't. is determined to have a quarrel at any rate. Unless this feeling is corrected there (as I presume it will be) that dogged stubborn people may conclude that it is best to give us a chance[?].

What an effect your Speech w[oul]d have and will have when it gets there! But I[']ll detain you no longer—only adding that they are sending off some additional Vessels to the Pacific. Y[ou]r ob[edi-en]t S[ervan]t, Ch. Aug. Davis.

ALS in ScCleA.

From PARKE GODWIN

New York [City,] Friday [March 20, 1846]

Hon[ored] and Dear Sir, I have written to Mr. Donalson [*sic*; Andrew J. Donelson], recently appointed Minister to Berlin, to be permitted to accompany him as Secretary of Legation. As I have no personal acquaintance with him, may I ask you to speak a word for me if it should fall in your way. Understanding both the French and German languages, I could doubtless be of use in many ways in the place I solicit.

Your speech [of 3/16] in favour of Peace, as honourable in its sentiments, to your heart, as the masterly policy it discloses is to your head, has produced a fine and profound impression in the city: and that not only am[on]g the commercial classes, whose interests are too apt to control their judgment, but with thinking and humane men of all classes. Every word of it should be, not fram[e]d in letters of gold, but written on the hearts of the people, which is far better. Had you done nothing else to deserve well of your country, ["you" *canceled*] excuse me for saying that your efforts to prevent the awful calamities of war would have raised you an eternal monument in all noble minds.

I have [heard] indirectly, through a correspondent in London, by the late arrival of to day, that your son in law Mr. [Thomas G.] Clemson was well at the time my friend saw him in Belgium: but the date of his interview is not given. Respectfully Your ob[edient] Serv[an]t, Parke Godwin.

ALS in ScCleA. NOTE: The date for this letter is supplied from the postmark "New-York, 20 March," and the year 1846 is established by context and Godwin's subsequent letter of 4/6/1846.

From W[ILLIAM] H. MARRIOTT

Baltimore, March 20th 1846

My Dear Sir, It becomes my duty as your friend, honestly to give you the opinion entertained here, in relation to your speech on the Oregon question & it gives me sincere pleasure to say that every one, Whig & Democrat, with whom I have conversed, approve, & pronounce it to be unequalled. The speech has elevated you, notwithstanding the high position which ["ha"(?) *canceled*] you have always occupied, and at no period in your history, did ["you" *canceled*] the Republic ever express themselves as well satisfied with any Speech you ever made. Such is the *true* sentiment here.

I hope to have the pleasure to see you soon. Do me the favor to let me have a few ["numbers" *interlined*] of your speech, as soon as printed in Pamphlet form. Very Truly In haste, Your Friend, W.H. Marriott.

ALS in ScCleA.

From WILLIAM S. WAIT

Greenville, Bond Co[unty,] Ill[inoi]s
March 20, 1846

Dear Sir, The situation which you held at the Memphis convention has induced a very large portion of the intelligent people of the Mississippi ["Valley" *interlined*] who are not influenced by aspirations for their own personal advancement to office or political consideration, to hope much from your continued efforts in behalf of the neglected interests of Western commerce.

The West does not yet feel its own strength, and there is no combination among its representatives in Congress to demand justice from the nation. We have many young men in Congress who look principally to executive favor, and some of maturer years who have other studies than an enlarged view of national policy ["and" *changed to* "or"] the true interest and happiness of the mass of the people.

I need not suggest to you that the interest of no considerable portion of the nation can be neglected without injury to the whole; and can any intelligent citizen fail to see ["that" *interlined*] the disbursement of nearly the entire revenue of the union upon one half of its population, is an injustice which demands and should receive a prompt remedy.

I am not the only man in this region who feels that he owes a debt of gratitude to you for presiding at the Memphis convention, or who is happy to acknowledge and has the disposition to appreciate your great talents and worth as a statesman and a citizen. So long as your equanimity remains unruffled, the attempt to place you in a false position before the people upon the Oregon question can have no effect against your well deserved popularity that will be permanent. Without the spur of jealousy, these attacks would ["be" *canceled and* "have been" *interlined*] yet more feeble.

May I hope that your attention will be particularly directed to a Bill offered to the House some weeks since proposing to give up to the States of Ohio, Indiana, Illinois and Missouri the great national enterprise of the Cumberland Road, with a grant of land to each State to make the best of, for completing their respective portions. If this is a national work, why abandon it to the States? If it be a proper subject of appropriation why should it not be made in a legitimate form? Is Congress reduced to the necessity of turning out real estate upon apprisal to meet just claims for specific appropriations? The States have not asked for this donation in land, and it is not probable they would accept it. I think that I can safely answer for Illinois upon this question. The Road is needed now, and should have been completed twenty years since. This land could not be disposed of in less than one generation of men, and the whole avails would probably be dissipated in some complicated, clumsy & protracted system of sale. Moreover no two States ever did or ever could agree upon the prosecution of such a labor. Illinois & Missouri have been at loggerheads upon the subject already. These considerations are enough to show that should this bill pass, not another blow can ever be struck upon this important work until it is repealed.

But this is not the worst view of the case. If our claim to appropriations for works of national utility in the West, are silenced in this instance by so preposterous a grant, which seems in fact but a riddance of a portion, a refuse portion of that domain which is by many eminent citizens[?] considered of no value to the nation, what are we to expect in favor of any claim whatever in behalf of Western interests or Western commerce?

What appears to my mind the true ground for the West to take, and what I have urged in vain for several years upon my friends in Congress, is, to demand just and *sufficient* appropriations for every object truly national in its character—to be ["well" *interlined*] satisfied in their own minds that their demands are reasonable and just, and, *to accept nothing less!*

May I ask your attention to that portion of the "Address of the Democratic State Convention," inclosed [*not found*] which relates to Western interests, the brief constitutional view of a portion of this question may not coincide with your opinion, but your candor and magnanimity will allow ["them" *canceled and* "it" *interlined*] all the weight which ["they" *canceled and* "it" *interlined*] merits or at least your charity will induce you to forgive an honest difference of opinion, should you suspect that bias which interest seldom fails to exercise in warping the purest judgment. With very sincere respect I remain your friend, William S. Wait.

ALS in ScCleA. NOTE: Wait was a Democratic member of the Ill. House of Representatives during the 1830's and 1840's and a delegate to the State constitutional convention of 1847.

From C[HARLES] A. CLINTON

New York [City,] March 21st 1846

My Dear Sir, I have just concluded an attentive perusal of your Speech on the Oregon Question and I cannot refrain from telling you how much I have been pleased and gratified. It is equally honorable to you as a philanthropist, a Statesman and an American. It has given very great and general Satisfaction to all intelligent and reflecting men in this City and I have no doubt of its favorable acceptance by the whole Country.

As my character and position are too well known to allow the possibility of my ever acting from personal, or unworthy considerations, I am sure, that you will not suspect me of flattery, when I assert, that by this last effort, you have placed yourself in the first rank, among the greatest statesmen that this Country has ever produced. Your views and policy are sound, orthodox, and wise; and you have truly indicated the true secret of success ["toward" *altered to* "in"] the great progress now making, in giving free Republican government to all Northern America. I sincerely hope that the day is not far distant, when your high statesmanlike qualities and pure private life, will secure for you the highest reward in the gift of the People. But if this should not be the result, I am sure, that you would, like my father [DeWitt Clinton] and others, who have run their career before you, devote your best talents to the public good, without reference to the ingratitude of the masses, and it is this appreciation of your character and motives, which has given you the uniform support, even under unpropitious circumstances, of that class of gentlemen at the north, who without hope of official emolument [*sic*] and political honors, will always support the policy most conducive to the welfare of the country, and the men whose pure characters and high talents guarantee a consistent: an able and an honest Support of that policy. With great esteem I have the honor to be Your friend & ob[e]d[ien]t Ser[van]t, C.A. Clinton.

ALS in ScCleA; PC in Boucher and Brooks, eds., *Correspondence*, pp. 334–335.

From A. SIDNEY DOANE

New York [City,] March 21 [1846]
My dear Sir, The Directors of the New York & Boston Magnetic Tel[egraph] Association have instructed me to convey to your [*sic*], in behalf of the Association, their thanks for your welcome notice of the Telegraph, in your eloquent & patriotic speech upon the Oregon question. While the erection of Magnetic Telegraphs is rapidly progressing through the country, unaided & unnoticed by our wealthy citizens, we are glad to see that one of the master minds of the Republic is alive to their importance & is disposed to cheer us onward by words of encouragement. With best wishes for your health & prosperity, I have the honor to be Yours very truly, A. Sidney Doane, Pres[ident,] N. York & Boston Mag[netic] Tel[egraph] Ass[oci-ation].

ALS in ScCleA.

From [FRANKLIN H. ELMORE], "(Confidential)"

Charleston, 21 March 1846
My Dear Sir, I have within a few minutes learned that the Pres[iden]t [James K. Polk] has nominated Mr. [Thomas] Gadsden Esq. for Surveyor of this Port. I fear he has done an imprudent thing. He has not been *well advised.* I have it from sources of the highest credibility that Mr. Gadsden[']s habits are such as to render his

capability more than doubtful—but all my purpose now is, not to procure his defeat, only to guard you & Gen[era]l [George] McDuffie [Senator from S.C.] against error. I have no doubt from the manner in which this movement is received here, that you will have in a short time ample evidence from authentic sources. In that I take no part—my action is confined ["simply" *canceled*] to this communication to you & Mr. McDuffie, intended simply to prevent your being imposed on, or hurried into sanctioning what you may regret here after. Take time & you will in all probability be fully advised what should be done.

Several of your *best* & *most* judicious friends have been to see me within a few minutes & have requested me to say this much. In great haste Y[ou]rs faithfully [unsigned.]

ALU in ScCleA. NOTE: Thomas Gadsden's nomination had been sent to the Senate on 3/18 and was confirmed routinely on 4/2.

From DUFF GREEN

New York [City,] 21st March 1846
My dear Sir, It would now seem that that [*sic*] the Ultras desire to take the Oregon question into the next Presidential Election and that therefore they will oppose all further action. Nothing could be better for the country or for you. This will make you the representative of the peace party here and in Europe. If instead of notice you stand on your original proposition of Masterly inactivity as to England and positive action as to colonisation you will control events. If I were permitted to advise or make a suggestion I would go for a rail road from the mouth of the Ohio to the South pass and for such legislation only as will favor Emigration. England cannot in the face of the movement for free trade take any hostile measure. This will rally around you the friend[s] of peace. Your speech will become the platform on which a new organisation will take place & your election and the consequent success of your principles & policy, will be certain. I am for 54° 40 on this ground & so will be the country. Yours truly, Duff Green.

ALS in ScCleA.

From DUFF GREEN

New York [City,] 21st March 1846

My dear Sir, I wrote a hasty note this morning suggesting the reasons why you should go against notice, and adhere to your original masterly inactivity. The reasons are so pressing, obvious and important that I venture to urge them at ["more" *canceled and* "greater" *interlined*] length.

Sir Robert Peel[']s speech was able, but it was a speech addressed to the judgment[,] interest and passions of the English people. Yours was an appeal to the judgment[,] interests and sympathies of mankind. You have the great advantage that henceforth you are placed at the head of the great movement of the age. You are the man of progress and represent the principle of peace, on which it rests. For the first time in your life you fill your true position and you should not forfeit it.

You have not reached that position by a single step or by accident. It is the result of the combination of causes & effects which mark your eventful life. You at this moment concentrate the hopes, the affections & the confidence of the world more than any other living man, and the issue which your political opponents seek to make will demonstrate this.

You were for "masterly inactivity" because you foresaw that we would colonise [Oregon] and that England would not. You agreed to compromise on 49° only because you were compelled to choose between compromise or war. If your political opponents fall back on 54° 40 and oppose notice & go for "masterly inactivity" as a means of obtaining to 54° 40['] they adopt your measure & thus admit that you were right & they wrong.

If ["they" *canceled*] you now oppose "masterly inactivity" they will charge ["that" *canceled*] you with deserting your own measure and with a surrender of our interests. You cannot meet this charge unless you ["do" *canceled*] make it appear that you do it for the sake of peace, and as the only means of avoiding war. War will not follow unless England gives the notice and if so she will be responsible for the war, and it will be a war of aggression on her part. If she desires war and would give the notice as a means of provoking it she will find enough in our Mexican relations for her purpose and we would have conceded all north of 49° for nothing if she takes part openly or covertly with Mexico.

But will England give the notice? If Congress refuses to give the notice we are where we were when you recommended "masterly inactivity["] & with this difference.

I refer you to the speech of Sir Howard Douglass, the member [of Parliament] for Liverpool, who says that the repeal of the Corn laws necessarily involves so great a change of the British colonial system as to make it the interest of England that Canada & the other colonies to [*sic*] become independent states. Such I know to be the opinion of [Richard] Cobden, [John] Bright, Villars [*sic; Charles Pelham Villiers*], [Joseph] Hume & others, the advocates of free trade. Such I know to be the opinion of the Duke of Wellington & such is the opinion of Sir Robert Peel. Would Sir R. Peel who is about to adopt a measure which will make it the interest of England & of Canada that Canada should ["become" *canceled*] be annexed to the United States, give notice to terminate the joint occupancy when that notice will be understood to be a declaration of war? Impossible. Will it not be his interest & his policy so to modify the intercourse between this country and England as to make it more & more the interest of both to preserve peace? Would not the friends of peace demand free trade as a means of preserving peace? Could England go to war for Oregon in the face of such a movement? & would not the apprehension of war compel the the [*sic*] friends of peace in the old world as well as the new to rally on the platform created by your speech as the means of preserving peace, & if the Ultras do oppose you will not the Whigs and the sound portion of the Democracy rally around you as the representative of the great Conservative measures, ["&" *canceled*] Peace & free trade for the sake of Peace?

I need not enlarge on this subject. You will see its bearing. It is all important to defeat the notice, the more especially if by doing so it is to be carried into the next Presidential Election. You cannot wish a better issue. The effect of it will be to prevent any Whig nomination. You will be put forward and in my opinion you will be elected by acclamation. Many things conspire to render the Baltimore Convention & caucus nominations odious. The Ultras will represent the corrupt & factious interest in the Democratic party. The Whigs will not be able to maintain an organisation as against you and your Election will be the commencement of a political millenium which will fill the land with wealth[,] gladness & peace.

But you & your friends ought to meet the most ultra on measures for colonisation[,] Rail Road, forts & bounties[?] of land to Emigrants. England cannot, dare not take exceptions. Your sincere friend, Duff Green.

ALS in ScCleA.

From W[ILLIAM] B. SLAUGHTER

Culpeper C[our]t House [Va.,] March 21st 1846

My dear Sir, I congratulate you and the country upon your *great* speech, on the Oregon question, *the* great speech of the Session—*the* great speech of any session and of the age—for comprehensiveness of thought, for cogency of argument, for clearness of illustration and for touching and thrilling eloquence, it is in my opinion unsurpassed, and unsurpassable. I do hope there is virtue and intel[l]igence enough remaining in our demoralised country to appreciate and appropriate its merits. Enclosed is a letter from our friend [John B.?] Floyd, be pleased to shew it to Mr. [George W.] Hopkins and return it to me by mail. I hope Mr. Hopkins has furnished Floyd with copies of Mr. Martin[']s letters to the President, at least with a statement of its contents.

My papers are in the hands of General [Simon] Cameron of the Senate, perhaps you can suggest some matters in relation to them which may influence him to report favourably. I have heard but one opinion in regard to your speech and that is in harmony with my own. Sincerely y[ou]r friend, W.B. Slaughter.

ALS in ScCleA.

To Mrs. PLACIDIA [MAYRANT] ADAMS, Pendleton

Washington, 22d March 1846

My dear Madam, I regret to say that I have not heard a word in reference to the sale of the mort[g]aged land in Michigan, which was ordered for the 14th Feb. I am entirely at a loss to account for the silence. After waiting a sufficient time to hear, I wrote to Mr. [Isaac E.] Crary about it, informing him of your pressing necessities, & requesting an early answer. I have not had one yet, although it is time I should. I hope I may hear in a few days. If not, I shall write again.

I got a letter [of 2/13] from Mr. [Enoch B.] Benson, in relation to what you owe him, some time since & have written him, that I would see him paid, when I sold my crop of cotton, say by the last of May at fartherst [*sic*], if your debt was not paid before, and expressed a hope that he would indulge you until then.

It would not be convenient for me to pay any part of the principal of the bond just at this time, but in order to relieve you from your embarrassments, if you will see your creditors in the Village and send me on a list of the debt due each, I will endeavour to make arrangements with them to meet ["the payment of" *interlined*] their debts at periods that will suit them, say by the middle of July at fartherst, provided the whole including Benson[']s should not exceed $1000. You may show this to any of them you please. Yours truly, J.C. Calhoun.

ALS owned by Mr. Holbrook Campbell, Springfield, Mass.

From F[RANCIS] W. PICKENS

Edgewood, 22 March 1846

My dear Sir, I enclose the within to Mr. [Thomas G.] Clemson. I have heretofore enclosed them to Mr. [James] Buchanan, but he had occasion to write me a few weeks since and in that he said he had no *franking privaledge* [*sic*] now which I did not know before. I thought the Sec[re]t[ar]y of State had that privaledge.

We have had a very severe and long Winter and stock has suffered much. But things seem now to be changed and we are blessed with almost full Spring all at once. The trees are nearly full out and all kinds of small grain look well. As to planting we are two weeks more backward than last year owing to the floods of rain until within the last 10 days. I have been excessively engaged for three weeks past. I have about 500 acres of my corn planted and my cotton land nearly all bed[d]ed up. I have bed[d]ed up with the hoe far more than I ever did in my life, and I think I have had the most extensive ditching of any man in this country. My first planting of corn is just coming up. This time last year I had a good stand on 600 acres. When I was in Savannah & Charleston my overseer on the Neck[?] place acted the villain and plundered me of a great deal of

corn & other provisions. I have been there for the last three weeks
as I turned him off immediately and had charge of the place myself
for some time.

I wrote you while in Charleston fully & have not heard since.
Present us affectionately to Cousin Floride [Colhoun Calhoun]
& [Martha] Cornelia [Calhoun]. Very truly & Sincerely, F.W.
Pickens.

ALS in ScCleA. NOTE: This letter was postmarked in Charleston on 3/27.

To Mrs. A[NNA] M[ARIA CALHOUN] CLEMSON, [Brussels]

Washington, 23d March 1846

My dear Anna, We were all very happy to learn by the last steamer,
that you had entirely got over the pain in your face, & that Mr.
[Thomas G.] Clemson & the children were well; and I am sure you
will be so to learn, that we are all well. My cough has not entirely
ceased, but is [sic] gradually been decreasing for several weeks, &
now gives me little trouble. My health, otherwise, is good. ["Patrick" *interlined*; Calhoun], John [C. Calhoun, Jr.], James [Edward
Calhoun], Willy [William Lowndes Calhoun], & Andrew [Pickens
Calhoun] & family were all well, when we last heard from them.
John's cough had not ceased, but he was very stout & hearty in appearance. I add, what I am sure will gratify you, James, I infer from
his letters, is improving much, & has acquired a much more decided
taste for his studies.

I enclose you a copy of my speech delivered last week on the
Oregon question. I shall enclose several to Mr. Clemson, but the
one enclosed is intended especially for yourself. Many of my friends
think it the best I ever delivered. It was certainly received in a
manner highly calculated to be gratifying to myself & friends. I
received congratulations on all sides when I sat down, even from
the most violent of the 54° 40 men. Such was the anxiety to hear me,
that the crowd began to collect at 8 oclock, and long before the hour
the galleries & the passages were blocked up. Thousands had to retire for the want of room.

I spoke very late in the debate, after, indeed, it had begun to
drag very heavily, and delicacy forbid me from touching on the subject of title. I felt the difficulty of my position, and could not (know-

ing the great anxiety to hear me) but feel some solicitude; and wa
not a little relieved when all was over, & I could perceive from indi
cations all around, that I had not fell below expectation.

But in the midest of these gratifying indications, I soon saw, tha
I had excited the jealousy of party leaders on both sides. Thei
organs, the Intelligencer & the Union, gave sure indications of that
I had addressed notes to the editors of both in the morning request
ing them not to publish the reports of my speech, until I had an op
portunity to see & correct them; but in spite of all the precaution,
took, the Intelligencer published without regarding my request ɑ
against my remonstrance to its foreman who brought me the repor
["late" *canceled*] at night when it was too late to correct, & what wa
more indicative of party jealousy, inserted it in the midst of othe
matter, without even mentioning it, or giving the least hint, that
had addressed the Senate.   It was with great difficulty I could pre
vent the Union from publishing without my correction, and when i
published, it was done without affording me an opportunity of cor
recting the proof, and then placed on the out side of his paper
where usually matters of no importance are inserted, without ad
verting to it or making any remarks.   I mention these things, no
that they annoy me in the least, but that ["you may know" *interlined*
to what petty jealousy I am subject.   My letter [of 8/12/1844] to
[William R.] King was treated the same way, but it forced its way
against all attempts to keep publick attention from it, & such will be
the case in the present instance, if I may judge from what has already
occurred.

I have said more about myself, my dear daughter, than I would
to any one else, not from any feeling of vanity, but because I know
it would gratify you & Mr. Clemson to learn in what manner my ef
fort on such a question was received by the ["publick" *canceled anɑ*
"audience" *interlined*] on the occasion.   As to the publick at large
if I may judge by the papers & my letters, I never made an effort of
the kind that was received with greater favour, as far as I have had
an opportunity of judging.   The praise of the papers have been in
many instances extravagant, and from quarters which one would not
expect.   I give as an example ["an extract" *interlined*] from Mike
Walsh's paper [*The Subterranean*], which is the organ of what may
be called the ["lowest" *interlined*] strata in the New York population.

As I have many letters to write before the steamer leaves, & a
your Mother [Floride Colhoun Calhoun] writes by that which take:
this, I must conclude with Grandfather's love & kisses to the dea

748

hildren [John Calhoun Clemson and Floride Elizabeth Clemson].
Your affectionate father, J.C. Calhoun.

ALS in ScCleA; PEx in Jameson, ed., *Correspondence*, pp. 684–685.

To [THOMAS G. CLEMSON, Brussels]

Washington, 23d March 1846

My dear Sir, I received by the last Steamer your two letters. As to Mr. [Francis J.] Grund & his publication, which you enclosed, I cannot learn, that they have made the least impression, or that they have been even noticed. I am of the impression, neither deserve notice, as far as you are concerned. My former letters will have informed you of the mistake in relation to the non reception of the treaty & your's & Anna's letters; and that originated with the Secretary. The treaty is now before the Senate, & will be acted on probably this week. Your letter to Mr. [John] Mobley & the package have been forwarded to him; the one by mail & the other by a safe ["private" *interlined*] conveyance. I enclose a letter to you from your Overseer. You will see that all are well, &, I doubt not, your business is going on well. I wrote under so much haste in my last & preceding letters, that I omitted to notice the compliment bestowed on me by Mr. [Philippe] Bourson, the editor of the [Brussels] Moniteur & what you said in reference to republishing my speeches in England. A notice so highly complimentary from so competent a judge is indeed very flattering & acceptable, & I wish you to present one of the copies of my speech on the Oregon question (herewith enclosed) to him in my name, as a mark of my respect. I must refer you to my letter to Anna for particulars, as to its reception on this side of the Atlantick.

I would of course be glad to see the volume of my speeches & & republished in England, including the present & a few others omitted in the American edition. If you find it can be done, I will furnish the additional speeches.

Of the other copies of my speech on the Oregon question, one is intended for yourself & the others to be disposed of as you please. The translation & publication of one in the German language might have a good effect.

I enclose also a pamphlet on the copper mines of Lake Superior, which may be interesting to you. They are said to be rich both in silver & copper; indeed, to be more so than any other known mines. On the subject of politicks, I can say but little that is satisfactory.

Our affairs have become much entangled both at home & abroad You will see in my speech on Oregon, that I have reasoned the question of notice, as it stands on the face of the Message; & have opened a door for Mr. [James K.] Polk, & the 54.40 men to support compromise *now* in the view I take, in consequence of a change of circumstances. But I fear, that the real truth of the case is, that the Message was in its character diplomatick, & that notice was recommended to play the game of intimidation—a desperate game certainly with so great a power as England. The result has proved such, as ought to have been anticipated; great uncertainty as to the real intention of the Executive, & the division & distraction of the party, with the loss of confidence on all sides, & a timid vacillating course on the part of the Executive, afraid to compromise or to take any other step. It is a state of things from which I fear the worst. In the meane time, our relations with Mexico is becoming critical, in consequence of the position, which our army in Texas has been ordered to take on the [Rio] del Norte, below Matamoros, & far in advance of our settlements, without any appearant reason, as far as I can see. Under such circumstances, I cannot but regard the future as uncertain; & the contingency of war & peace as doubtful, while a moderate share of segacity & firmness might in a short time, secure the blessings of the latter & avert the calamities of the former. Your affectionate father, J.C. Calhoun.

ALS in ScCleA; PC in Jameson, ed., *Correspondence*, pp. 685–687.

From S[HADRACH] PENN, JR., *"Private"*

St. Louis, March 23 1846

Dear Sir, I was deceived, or rather in error, as to the action of Col. [Thomas H.] Benton on the Oregon question. Having lost ground by his course in relation to Texas, I inferred that he would disregard previous commitments, and contend for the whole of Oregon, regardless of consequences. His policy has, however, been more prudent, and I must say more praiseworthy. He is almost co-operating with you—but, judging from the tone of his confidential friends here, his personal feelings towards you have undergone no change. He may hate Gov. [Lewis] Cass more at the present juncture, and probably dislikes Mr. [William] Allen, because he views him as setting up for himself—if not as a deserter from *"the cause."*

The report of the conclusion of a treaty on the basis of the 49th deg[ree], which reached here day before yesterday, was pretty well received. Indeed the best informed men here have, for some two or three months, confidently anticipated such a result; and as the failure of the President to recommend any preparation for war, and the action of the anti-blustering portion of the Senate, must have prepared the people generally for such a treaty, the annunciation of its conclusion and ratification, will produce very little excitement—perhaps none, except among politicians.

I was for the whole of Oregon—but not for war—because I believed it was practicable to obtain the whole territory by establishing a road and line of military posts, and properly encouraging emigration and protecting emigrants. The "masterly inactivity" policy would have suited me—and, I think, the nation.

But a "new aspect" was put upon the question by the abandonment of the positions taken in your correspondence with Mr. [Richard] Pakenham; by offering to compromise on the 49th deg[ree]; by taking ground in favor of the notice, and asserting that *the question must be speedily settled.* Now, Sir, I think England is far more anxious than we should be for an early settlement of the boundary. With a line of military posts, a road, jurisdiction as far as the treaty allows, and suitable encouragement to emigrants—a monthly mail, and a supply of arms and ammunition and Indian Agencies, we should ["should" *canceled*] negotiate more effectually than by any other mode. But I suppose the die is cast. That 49 will be the boundary I do not doubt; but why should not the President [James K. Polk] be held responsible for the offer he has made? Why step in to shield him? I think he is only true to those he fears; that he has been guilty of double-dealing, and that, in a short time he will command the respect of a very small portion of the party. I know he has proscribed those who elected him, and truckled to those who denounced his nomination, condemned his views on Texas, and pronounced him a fourth-rate man. When right I shall sustain his measures for the good of the country—but I can never regard him as an elevated, firm or worthy man. His aim is to be re-elected, and to accomplish that object he outrages, friends panders to recent foes, truckles to the Hunkers, violates solemn promises, and outrages every principle of political morality. The picture need not be extended. By and by you will understand him.

I shall publish Judge [David R.] Atchison's speech [to the Senate] and intend to copy yours, so soon as it may reach me through our very uncertain mails. I wish you to be understood and hope you will not forget your promised visit, after the close of the present session, or the route which I suggested as the proper one for you to take.

It strikes me that Gen. Cass has regarded war too certain for his own good. The President was willing to see him make a lofty tumble—and, then, may he not have been willing to see you vote against the notice, or for such a modification of it as his partisans could condemn? I may be too suspicious; but treachery makes a deep impression on one's mind, and ingratitude breaks down confidence. Yours Truly, S. Penn, Jr.

[P.S.] I need Document No. 2 of the House—that is the President's Message and accompanying documents[.] Can you conveniently send them to me[?]

ALS in ScCleA; PEx in Boucher and Brooks, eds., *Correspondence*, pp. 335–336. Note: An AEU by Calhoun reads: "Mr. Penn[,] Send Doc[umen]t no. 2." Penn's letter is clearly dated and postmarked March 1846, which makes his reference to "a report of the conclusion of a treaty" in the second paragraph highly puzzling, since the Oregon treaty was not received and acted on in Washington until June. Perhaps the statement can be ascribed to anticipatory rumor.

To C[HARLES] A. CLINTON, [New York City]

Washington, 24th March 1846

My dear Sir, I am much gratified with your very complimentary notice of my remarks on the Oregon question. The sentiments you express are lofty & patriotick, & well become your name and descent. He is unworthy of the confidence of the people, who is not ready to sacrafice [*sic*] his popularity for their real & durable interest.

I enclose a copy of my remarks in pamphlet form corrected from the notes of the stenographers, which you will please accept as a mark of my sincere respect. Yours truly & sincerely, J.C. Calhoun.

ALS owned by Francis J. Serbaroli, New York City.

To "The President" [JAMES K. POLK]

Washington, 24th March 1846

Dear Sir, I enclose several letters recommending Mr. [James] Webb for the place of district Judge for Texas. They are all Gentlemen of the highest respectability & speak in the highest terms of Mr. Webb's qualifications for the office for which he applies & character & respectability as a citizen.

I have had but slight opportunities of becoming acquainted with him personally, but as far as I have had my impression is very favourable towards him in every respect. With great respect I am & &, J.C. Calhoun.

ALS with Ens in DNA, RG 59 (State Department), Letters of Application and Recommendation during the Administrations of James K. Polk, Zachary Taylor, and Millard Fillmore, 1845–1853, James Webb (M-873:92, frames 474–480, 484–486, and 417–419). NOTE: Enclosed were letters to Calhoun of February 25, 1846 from Mirabeau B. Lamar, February 28, 1846 from Barnard E. Bee, [ca. February 28, 1846] from Abner S. Lipscomb, and March 4, 1846 from J[ames] Hamilton, Jr., all apparently hand-delivered to Calhoun by James Webb.

From ARNOLD BUFFUM

New York [City,] 3 mo[nth] 25, 1846

Esteemed friend, Being personally unknown to thee, I will observe that I am an old man, and have been an observer of political movements in our country for more than fifty years; and although I have never been a politician by profession, yet I have ever felt a deep interest in the manner in which our political affairs have been conducted. I have *not* been among the admirers of the political course which thou hast generally pursued, and until the present session of Congress, candor requires that I should say, I had felt no particular regard for what I had supposed to be the principles which governed thy actions.

But the object of this communication is to let thee know, that on reading thy speech on the Oregon question, it seemed to me to contain evidence of lofty and noble sentiments, which can only spring from a mind endowed with just and holy principles; so that at this late hour, I now avow myself as one, among the *admirers* of the Hon. John C. Calhoun. I enclose herein a small tract on the hor[r]ors of War, to which I solicit thy careful attention. If thy Speech is printed in Pamphlet form, I shall feel very much obliged by the transmission of two or three copies of it. Most respectfully, Arnold Buffum.

ALS in ScCleA. NOTE: AEU's by Calhoun read "Mr. Buffum" and "Send Speech." The tract enclosed has not been identified. Buffum (1782–1859) was known as an antislavery man.

From DAVIS DEVINE

Syracuse [N.Y.,] March 25th 1846
My D[ea]r Sir, You will please pardon this intrusion upon your attention from an entire stranger to you, and one of whom you never heard & may never again be troubled with. Yet sir, you are not unknown to me, neither has your distinguished & Statesman like career in the United States Senate & as Secretary of State during one of the most important negotiations that has ever been carried on—passed unnoticed & unadmired by me. I have long known, admired and approved ["of your" *canceled*] of your political course—and have long wished that politicks and parties would so shape themselves, that this vast & growing Republic might have the honor & benefit of your experience & transcendant talent & foresight to guide the ship of State as the Chief Magistrate thereof. Would to God you occupied that *inestimably important position at the present time.* The country, & the world at large, would be vastly the gainers thereby. It however is not so, and we must therefore endeavor, to make the best use of the means that God and the People have given us to conduct the country through the difficulty into which it has been brought. And Sir the people (& myself as one of them) look with anxiety to you ["in" *canceled*] as preeminently at the head of the United States Senate, and exercising a vast influence over that body, to settle this vexed Oregon question upon *Just* and *honorable* terms, without precipitating the country into an interminable and ruinous war—the effects of which, morrally, politically & physically we should not recover from in a whole century, if ever.

Your speech upon that subject, delivered in the Senate but a few days since, meets with the entire approbation from all thinking & reflecting men in this region of the country, and will have a powerful influence sir, upon the British people & Parliament—for good. It will be hailed with joy there sir, as well as here, with all who are not ashamed to do right. And the 49th paralell after all the offers of that, that have heretofore been made I deem to be Just—as between man & man that would & should estop us from claiming more no matter what our title may be to the remainder. If it *was* "unquestionable" *it is not now*, as we have conceded that the remainder was in doubt by offering it to England so often & quietly permitting her to occupy it for so many years. And how can an *honest* man, make a claim of more than to the 49th without blushing and feeling that by so doing he is degrading himself in his own estimation. But enough of this ["to" *interlined*] one who has the whole subject in his mind[']s ye as familiarly as the school boy his A.B.C. You will smile, I have no doubt, at my writing you upon this subject, and for thinking that you might heed, or care about the feelings & views of an entire stranger. Still all men have their views & feelings—their prejudices & their prefferences & I, like all the rest have mine. And you Sir have for ten years been *my* "Beau Ideal["] & mentor as a *Statesman and a man*. You will therefore pardon me for intruding myself upon your valuable and important time. I am not in the habit of doing such things. You sir are the only stranger that I would ["deign"(?) *canceled and* "stoop" *interlined*] to communicate with in this manner. And I have done it sir, knowing you were a *man* & would take it in the spirit it is intended—as a *Just* tribute, to *talant & genuine worth*—which is not despised by such a man, though it may come from a humble source. I can refer you to Senator [Sidney] Breese, & Judge Douglass [that is, Representative Stephen A. Douglas] of Ill. & Representative] T[imothy] Jenkins of N. York who have known me. Very respectfully Yours, Davis Devine.

P.S. Will you sir, do me the favor to send me your last Speech in the Senate on the Oregon Question, in pamphlet form, if it will not be too much trouble. I very much wish to preserve it. Truly Yours, D.D.

ALS in ScCleA.

From EPHRAIM H. FOSTER, [former Senator from Tenn.]

Marsfield, near Nashville, March 25th 1846

Dear Sir: Since the first commenc[e]ment of the Oregon discussion, I have waited with quite a feverish impatience to hear what you would have to say on ["the" *interlined*] interesting & absorbing topic. True, I could not doubt—considering your previous movements & intimations—as to the broad line you would be likely to pursue: & I rejoiced to believe—as I confidently did—that you would hold up your great aegis over the peace & happiness of the Nation. My inquietude, in fact, proceeded more from a thirst to enjoy the rich and acceptable repast which I knew you would prepare for my appetite, than from any fear or apprehension as to the policy you would promote & advocate.

I am, Sir, at length gratified—let me add, if you please, more than gratified. The Baltimore Patriot of the 17th Inst., copying from the [Daily National] Intelligencer of the day before, reached my table this morning, containing your speech in extenso, & originally printed no question, under your own eye. I have read the paper with infi nite delight; & whilst I desire to give wide & unqualified tribute to many of your previous displays, I must say that I look upon this las as the crowning effort of your life. Had you never spoken before, & should it ["now" *canceled*] be your destiny never to speak again you would still have done enough for fame, & might now safely res your claim to high renown upon ["upon" *canceled*] the judgment o posterity. Pardon, Dear Sir, my freedom. I take great liberties know, when I appro[a]ch you in this fashion, but I beg you to be lieve that I offer no unmeaning or insincere flatteries. My mind i full of what I am saying, & "from the abundance of the heart th mouth speaketh."

The strength & cogency of most of its arguments, constitute bu a poor half of the worth & excellence of the speech. Our profoundes gratitude & admiration are due to the humane patriotism & the kine persuasions that breathe, in eloquent strains, through many burnin; paragraphs, & which benev[o]lently implore, where stern justic would authorise you to rebuke, in strong & indignant terms, the rash ness of many around you. You have, indeed, in a noble and exhalted display of genius, reached the head, &, at the same time, touched th sensibilities of all reflecting men of every party, & I pray how lon you may live to enjoy the harvest of honors you have so recently garnered.

If I add a thought or two on a matter not altogether foreign t my subject, I hope you will not judge me for [*partial word canceled* envy, malevolence, or ["a" *interlined*] great want of charity. I ma deceive myself; but I humbly trust & believe that these unchristia feelings have nothing to do with me on the present occasion. I can not then, for the soul of me—hard as I have tried—sufficiently approv the tender manner you have observed towards [James K. Polk] th President—for altho in this alarming agitation there are many grea & wilfull offenders, we are bound, from his elevated position, to cor sider him the greatest of all. I ought however in equal frankness t confess that in your situation & surrounded by the great respons bility that devolved upon you, I might—notwithstanding my indig nant convictions—have pursued the gentle, uncondemning cours you have adopted. It was, doubtless, the best way to lead him: fc "soft words" we are told, "do away anger," & experience teaches u that respectful professions may charm & subdue a madman. At bo

om—believe me Sir, for I know him long & well: at bottom Mr. Polk
s a small man, & in the case before us, individually he is undeserving
of any apology. He has, in this great national affair, acted, most of
the time, as a party trickster & not as a statesman, & if he backs water
now—and I ardently hope he will—nothing but his ["fears" *interlined*]
will make him do so. He begins to find out that a "Duck river" stump
speech can't be always practically carried out at the Capitol, & I dare
say he regrets ["now" *canceled*] the hasty abandonment, by his party,
of that "masterly inactivity" which some of them have so weakly
denounced. The truth is, the President—tho President he be—is a
little creature, & used to the lowest arts of a demagogue. He is,
verily, too—to further a just condemnation—a parisitical plant with
all the instincts of a creeper, & though he may shoot a high ["lief"
canceled] leaf now, it is from a slender stem & owes its borrowed
elevation to the tenacity which fasten'd the little tendrils of a feeble
vine to the proudest tree of the forest.

Adieu, Dear Sir. I have said more perhaps than I ought to have
said. But I could not restrain, so far as you are concerned, my poor
commendations, & "calamo currante" I dropped the last paragraph
[*partial word canceled*] for the which, if in the least offensive or mis-
placed, I throw myself on your goodness. I neither expect or desire
an answer, but remain Truly your friend, Ephraim H. Foster.

ALS in ScCleA. NOTE: An AEU by Calhoun reads "Hon. Mr. Foster."

From DUFF GREEN

New York [City,] 25th March 1846

My dear Sir, I have been writing several letters for the Journal of
Commerce in which I have reviewed the Oregon question, and commented on the declaration of Douglass [*sic*; Stephen A. Douglas]
that the Texas & Oregon resolution was drawn up by Mr. [Robert J.]
Walker and submitted by Mr. [Benjamin F.?] Butler, and have paid
my respects to Mr. [Thomas] Ritchie. I have requested the Editors
to send the paper to Mr. [Dixon H.] Lewis. I hope he will show it
to you and that you will approve of the ground that I have taken. I
hear it frequently said by leading & influential whigs that they would
vote for you for President in preference to any man, Mr. [Henry]
Clay only excepted. My own opinion is that Clay will be a candidate but I do not think he can carry the whig party. We have no
hope but to move forward regardless of the party. If we do move

boldly forward we will control events but to do this we must expose the intriguers and render a convention so odious that the ultras dare not resort to it.

I have suggested to [James Brooks] the Editor of the [New York] Express & he promises me to get a list of the members of the late convention, to keep it as a standing advertisement showing who of the members have obtained offices for themselves and their friends and connexions. By opening an account current with the Baltimore Convention, the people will come to know the motives which bring these men together and render inoperative their mandates.

In the letters which I am writing for the Journal of Commerce I will refer to this matter, and prove that the effect of measures adopted by [James K.] Polk has been to sacrifice our claim north of 49° and make him responsible for the loss.

I see that some of your southern friends have taken very strong ground against the Harbour bill. I hope that you will vote for it. It will do much to allay party excitement and to bring the north west to acquiesce in the rejection of all notice. Never ["was" *canceled*] did any Government or any party do so foolish or wicked an act as ours have done in relation to Oregon. England is in the position where she would gladly surrender the whole country for a reasonable continuance of the use, ["and" *canceled*] for the revolution in her commercial policy will revolutionise her whole colonial system.

But to return to the Harbor bill. It seems to me that the true ground to take is that the purpose of the Constitution was to charge the federal Government with whatever relates to our intercourse with foreign Governments and with the intercourse between the States. The regulation of commerce and the collection of imposts are ["expess" *canceled*] express grants and under these grants the erection of ["Harbor" *canceled*] the light houses, and the deepening of Harbors have been charged to the federal Government from the beg[inn]ing. Does not the same principle apply to the bringing of the products of the interior to the seaboard that applies to the carrying it from the seaboard to the foreign market? Is not our interior trade part of our foreign trade? The idea started by Gen[era]l [Andrew] Jackson that we can only improve our rivers up to a Custom House is preposterous. There is nothing in the Constitution which would facilitate the importation of a bale of *foreign* goods that does not apply with equal force to the exportation of western beef & pork. If you can place yourself with the west on this question you will do much to control the action of the Government on this subject. Arrest the appropriations you cannot. All that you can do is to prevent improper appropriations. Some is necessary and and [*sic*] opposition to what is right will end in combinations to carry through appropriations that are wrong.

The repeal of the corn laws & food taxes in England creates a new crisis, and [*one word canceled*] the growing wealth & increasing population of our western States brings up the question of these appropriations in a shape that requires that it should ["be" *interlined*] acted upon in the spirit of liberality. It is the part of wisdom to do so and the more especial[l]y as on such questions precedent is used as a construction of the Constitution.

I am sure that you will rightly appreciate what I write. I am your friend and rejoice in the position you now occupy, and venture these suggestions believing that you will see their force, whether you concur with them or not. Yours truly, Duff Green.

ALS in ScCleA. NOTE: The "Harbour bill" referred to by Green was a massive internal improvements measure, with almost fifty projects, mostly in the Mississippi, Missouri, and Ohio valley regions. The bill had passed the House of Representatives on 3/20 by a vote of 109 to 92. For the next several months it was under consideration in the Senate, passing on 7/24 by a vote of 34 to 16, Calhoun in the minority. Polk vetoed on 8/3, and overrides failed in both chambers a week before the end of the session.

To "The President" [JAMES K. POLK]

[Washington, *ca.* March 25, 1846]

Dear Sir, The enclosed contains an application in favour of Mr. [John] Stiles of Boston for the place of Consul at Pictou[,] Nova Socia [*sic*; Scotia], made vacant by the death of the late consul [John J. Peavey].

I am not personally acquainted with the applicant, but the Rev[eren]d Mr. [Alexander] Bla[i]kie, who recommends him, is a Presbyterian Clergyman of high respectability, whose statement may be implicitly relied on.

I would be gratified with a compliance with his wishes, if it can be done with propriety. With great respect yours truly, J.C. Calhoun.

ALS with 2 Ens in DNA, RG 59 (State Department), Letters of Application and Recommendation during the Administrations of James K. Polk, Zachary Taylor, and Millard Fillmore, 1845–1853, John Stiles (M-873:83, frames 515–521). NOTE: Apparently enclosed were letters to Calhoun from Blaikie dated 3/11 and from Stiles dated 3/18.

From E. W. ROBINSON

Baltimore, March 25th 1846

Esteemed Sir, I have read with great pleasure and profit your admired speech on the Oregon question, and should be much gratified if you would send me a copy of it in pamphlet form.

I hope it will not be considered fulsome in me to say to you that I am among your warmest admirers, and have looked to you to preserve in a great degree the peace of the country. From the moment that you announced in the Senate, your belief that the controversy with England would be settled without war, I with many other of your friends, have felt that we might place every reliance on your talents, energy and patriotism to maintain peace.

I hope that nothing has occurred, not even the President's Message of yesterday to change your views. With great respect I remain y[ou]r fr[ien]d & Ob[edien]t S[ervan]t, E.W. Robinson.

[P.S.] A line or two from you, at your convenience acknowledging rec[eip]t of this would be very acceptable.

ALS in ScCleA. NOTE: On 3/24 Polk had replied to a Senate resolution inquiring whether present foreign relations required any increase in military or naval forces. Polk reiterated his annual message to Congress on 12/2/1845 in which he had stated that the "controversy" over Oregon and the "unsettled condition" of Mexican relations were evidence of the need for such an increase.

From JA[ME]S SHIELDS, Commissioner

General Land Office, March 25th 1846

Sir, I have the honor to acknowledge the receipt of your note of the 20th Inst. [*not found*], enclosing the duplicate receipt, No. 31,989 of the Columbus [Miss.] office for the E[ast] ½ N[orth] W[est] ¼ Sect[ion] 6 T[ownship] 10, N[orth] R[ange] 19 E[ast], in the name of your nephew [Benjamin A. Calhoun], and requesting the issue of a patent, if it can be done. You also request to know if a patent could not issue to him for the other half of the quarter section.

In reply I have to state, that the land in question is covered by a location under the Choctaw treaty of 1830, but whether such location is a valid one under that treaty, which would defeat any pre emption claim, or only a "contingent location" which would yield to such claim, the reports from the Indian office do not enable this office to determine. An examination into these Indian locations is now in progress at the Indian office, and final action on the subject, it is expected, may in a short time be had. Until that period no patent could issue on the entry made by your nephew and as the proof filed by him is defective in showing "that he did not remove from his own land in the same *land district*" instead of "in the same *State*" (Mississippi,) additional testimony on this point will be necessary, even if the Indian location should be no bar to his claim. In reference to the other half of the quarter section, I would remark, that, although the law gave him a right to a quarter section, it allowed the entry by him of a half quarter section, and having elected to take the latter, his claim was fully satisfied at the time of his entry and he cannot now be permitted to renew and enlarge it.

His letter to you and that of the Register [in Columbus, Miss., William Dowsing] to him which accompanied your note, would indicate that his right is contested upon other grounds, and that notice has been given him by the contestants of testimony to be taken in reference thereto. Should any such testimony be forwarded to this office, it shall be fully examined.

The duplicate receipt and the letter enclosed by you are herewith returned. With much respect Your Ob[e]d[ien]t Serv[an]t, Jas. Shields, Comm[issione]r.

FC in DNA, RG 49 (General Land Office), Letters Sent: Preemption Bureau, 1846–1847, 21:501–502.

From JOHN A. BOLLES

Boston, March 26, 1846

Dear Sir, I have read with great satisfaction your recent speech on the Oregon question. It will do much towards preserving unbroken our harmonious relations with England. It will do much towards preserving our social & political institutions unimpaired. It is one of those prophetic announcements, uttered occasionally, too seldom by political Seers, which thrill the popular mind & heart, & disclose to common view glimpses of a future so bright & glorious on the one side, or so disastrous & gloomy on the other, that all who discern them are impressed with new & deeper feelings of responsibility as citizens of the Republic.

If your speech is printed, as of course it will be, in a pamphlet form, please favor me with a few copies. Yours most resp[ectfull]y, John A. Bolles.

ALS in ScCleA; PC in Boucher and Brooks, eds., Correspondence, p. 336.

To A. Sidney Doane

Washington, 26th March 1846

Dear Sir, I am much obliged to you for the complimentary manner, which you, as the Organ of your association, have been pleased to notice my remarks on the Oregon question; & in return enclose a corrected copy in pamphlet form. With great respect I am & &, J.C. Calhoun.

ALS in ScU-SC, John C. Calhoun Papers.

From Jeptha Fowlkes

Memphis Ten[nessee,] March 26th 1846

D[ea]r Sir, Presuming upon a slight acquaintance at our Convention on 12th Nov. but more upon your known affability of character & readiness at all times as a public servant, to be approached, I venture this intrusion. I hope to stand excused for this interruption—and beg leave to refer you [to] our immediate representative & personal friend Hon. F[rederick] P. Stanton [Representative from Tenn.] for the claims I may have upon your consideration as a gentleman.

Regarding you as a friend to our public works, I venture to call your attention to a recent difficulty at our yard between Commodore [E.A.F.?] Lavallette & Col. A.B. Warford[,] Civil Engineer. The latter gentleman is our steadfast friend—the gentleman & the competent engineer—he has been the constant object of attack *indirectly* of Mr. Sec[retar]y [of the Navy, George] Bancroft—who is opposed to our works at heart—and is now in my opinion disposed to defeat them. So settled were my convictions to this end, that I drew up & had the Declaration & resolutions passed thro the Gen[era]l Assembly of Tennessee while there this winter—upon this subject. Will you in behalf of many personal & political friends & admirers give ["call" *canceled*] your attention to this controversy now refer[r]ed to the Hon. Sec[retar]y Bancroft between Commodore Lavallette & Col. A.B. Warford—from the correspondence you will gather the facts. I have written to Mr. Stanton & Mr. [Simon] Cameron in the Senate.

I have not seen the *first* man who is not *for* Warford & *against* the Commodore. We have no use for a naval staff here at present—and if they can't come without throwing every thing into *"pie"* as the printers would sa[y], have them if possible sent to their own proper element—the ocean! Col. Warford throughout to my personal knowledge has been mild, discreet & desirous for peace & harmony—and has evinced a willingness to do—to say any thing compatible with character & station to heal the rupture. He has acted throughout the gentleman—and as he is the known & tried friend of our works, it is ["a" *interlined*] duty to sustain him, so long as he is right.

Will you lend it a moment[']s consideration & oblige, Sir, many who cherish for you warm personal regard—and a settled disposition to press forward your political claims to the highest station known to our people—and which you are so eminently suited to occupy. We are for you in this valley! I am, dear Sir, very respectfully & sincerely y[ou]r frie[n]d & ser[van]t, Jeptha Fowlkes.

P.S. Though, but slightly known to you—perhaps entirely forgotten—yet I beg you whenever I can serve you to command me freely—to serve you as a man, & to elevate you politically will give me, ever, the highest gratification to contribute "the widow[']s mite." J.F.

I have read this to my old friend Col. Jos. S. Watkins who is doubtless known to you. He concurs in the sentiments, feelings, & wishes expressed & desires your attention if compatible with your views & feelings.

ALS in ScCleA. NOTE: An AEU by Calhoun reads "See Mr. Stanton."

To ALBERT GALLATIN, [New York City]

Washington, 26th March 1846

My dear Sir, I am much obliged to you for the first Vol: of the Transactions of the American Ethnological Society. I anticipate much pleasure from its perusal.

I entirely concur in the views expressed by Mr. [John R.] Bartlett in reference to the ["duties" *changed to* "duty"] on books & will cheerfully aid in accomplishing them.

I enclose a copy of my speech on the Oregon question, which please to accept as a mark of my high respect & regard. With great respect Yours & &, J.C. Calhoun.

ALS in NHi, Gallatin Papers (published microfilm, Gallatin Papers, roll 44, frame 77).

From S. E. Hood

Phila[delphi]a, March 26/46

Sir, By the recent Message of the President it is manifest that the Crisis is approaching, a Crisis I apprehend that will be more calamitous to the Civilized world but more especially in the destiny of this Country than any event recorded in modern History. Its result will most certainly be the breaking up of our Confederacy with a retrograde movement of some 200 years. Disaster and shameful defeat will and must of necessity crown every effort we make for at least 2 years if the War should continue so long. In the first place the entire destruction ["of" *interlined*] our Atlantic Cities, is as certain as the continued rising and setting of the Sun. 3 to 4 million of our people will in a short time be made houseless beggars, and there is no possible means of preventing it. 12 Steam Frigates will desolate the entire Atlantic Border. 10,000 British troops landed in Texas will revolutionize the entire Southern States, by Arming the Slaves in the South. An Army will pour in upon us from Canada and devastate the Northern frontier. Oregon will be taken from 54 40—to California and we cannot prevent it. Unlike the People of Europe we are not mere machines to be driven hither and yon at the bidding of Political demagogues. We are not and can never be prepared for a war with England unless our Gover[n]ment assumes to despotic form. But apart from all this contemplate for a moment the progress we made in the last war, when England was engaged with the affairs of Europe and had her hands full. Defeat attended all our military opperations on the Canada Borders, and Peace was made without a Single concession, altho at that time Steam was not known as a military appliance, and I presume no rational man of those days will deny that if peace had not then been made a dissolution of this Union would have followed. The Gover[n]ment was bankrupt and its bonds were in the market at 30 p[e]r c[en]t discount. Borrowing was out of the question almost as much then as it will be now, and in order to test the ability of maintaining a war at this time, before we irretrieveably commit ourselves, let Congress at once appropriate 50 millions, and Proposals issue by the [Treasury] department to Borrow. My life upon the issue there would be no loaners; it is true during the last war some 70 millions were borrowed, but no more could be borrowed notwithstanding the Comparative impotency of our adversary and hence it was that peace on any terms was urged upon our Ministers at Ghent, and moreover the doctrine of Repudiation now so rife had not been dreamed of, but in order to make this fact more apparrent in 1842 at Peace with all the World the Gover[n]ment bonds were hawked about the American markets for 6 months begging for a Loan of 6 million at 6% when money in the market was abundant on other Securities at 4% and it could not be obtained. The Bonds were finally sent to England and from thence they were cast back upon us with a Sneer at the impudence of Republican Repudiators. Hence Sir it is apparent that we lack the principle ingredient of war. But you may say the means may be raised by direct taxation. Pardon me sir for Sneering at such a suggestion. What the Republican States that have been repudiating there honest debts on the alleged inability to pay them can they augment their liabilities 20 fold to prosecute a war. Oh no the moment you thurst your hand into the Pockets of freemen directly the train will be laid for Rebellion. For example the State of Pennsylvania is now laboring ["under" *interlined*] and has been the last 4 years ["for" *canceled*] suffering moral degradation from an inability to pay the Interest on 40 million of debt. The Expenses of a war including fortifications the first year would certainly amount to 100 Million, the one sixth part of which would be the share of Penn[sylvani]a—say 17 Million. Is it then Possible for a State to contribute 19 million per annum, who still continues to avow her inability to furnish 2 million, and the same reasoning will apply equally to every other State. It may be said the same difficulties apply as well to our adversary. But no[,] there Gover[n]ment is different[;] there people are differently circumstanced. They must loan her more and Sustain her in all her efforts to secure that which they have loaned. Her immense national debt will always be the largest contributer to her military prowess. If we had a debt of 500 million dollars, more would be loaned to secure that whic[h] is loaned, the debt in its ramifications would be equal to a large military force. To illustrate this in a simple manner A owes B 100 dollars. The former becomes embarrassed and ask[s] for a further loan, will he not lend it with the view of Securing that which is already loaned if the refusal so to do involves the issue. Besides England in time of peace maintains a military force abundantly able without additional means to knock us into a Cocked hat. 30,000 men and 50 Steamers judiciously employed will reduce us to our marrow bones sueing for Peace, without Or[e]gon or any other barren heath.

Now Sir neither argument or even Sophistry can falsify the foregoing facts and conclusions. Hence the necessity of Pausing before we com[m]it ourselves. With all respect and deference I look to you Sir to avert the direful calamity now pending over us. You have the power with the 2 Senators from Texas to frustrate the designs of the most accursed Cabal ever kno[wn] to the Senate of the U.S. As Secretary of State you saved the nation once. Do it again and unborn millions will sing halle[lu]jahs to your memory. The Nursery Songs of ages to come will attune their notes and square their metre to the name of J.C. Calhoun. You will be remembered on the Page of history when the [William] Allens [and James K.] Polks &c will be forgotten. Your friend, S.E. Hood.

ALS in ScCleA.

From Tho[ma]s G. Clemson

Brussels, March 27th 1846

My dear Sir, Your favour of the 25th inst. [*sic*; 2/25] was the only letter we received by the Steamer Cambria. We suppose that our other letters with the Belgian gentleman of whom you speak, with letters from Mrs. [Floride Colhoun] Calhoun to Anna [Maria Calhoun Clemson], was left behind with the mails. It is always a great disap[p]ointment to us when the steamers arrive without letters, for we are always anxiously awaiting fresh arrivals. I do not know how the other Legations are treated by the Department, but from what I can understand I fare no worse than others. No attention appears necessary to us from the Department. My impression ["is" *interlined*] that there is great need for reformation there, as perhaps in many other departments of the public service. There should be a clerk whose duty ought to be, to acknowledge the receipt of every Despatch. Such a course would be a relief to us, and if such acknowledgement was occasional[l]y accompanied with the desires & doings of the Government it would be a great ["relief" *canceled and* "aid" *interlined*] to us abroad, and thus enable us to act with concert and efficiency in promoting the interests of the Government. But as it is no matter what the business pending may be[,] months elapse before we receive intimation of the ["receipt of the" *interlined*] most important documents. Thus since I have been here, or rather since Mr. [James] Buchanan's coming into the State Dept. I have received but the circular, and one single Despatch on business from the Secretary, which were instructions six or eight months after they had received the projet of the treaty of Commerce. A note from [Adolphe Dechamps] the minister of Foreign Affairs here, gave me information through Mr. [Charles] Serruys, that he ["Mr. Buchanan" *interlined*] had received the Treaty ["after signature(?)" *canceled and* "which I concluded in Nov." *interlined*] here. This is all I know about it, save what you had the goodness to write me in your preceeding [*sic*] letter, which gave me considerable anxiety, until the receipt of ["the" *canceled and* "your" *interlined*] last which explained the matter. At all events there must be great negligence in the Department to overlook so large a package as that which contained the Duplicate with the accompanying documents. If all the Departments are so badly arranged and proceed so clumsily it is astonishing that the Government should progress at all. To us who are forced to look close to what is done at home & feel a jealous interest in the proceedings I can assure you, ["we have" *changed to* "there(?) is"] ample cause to regret the course that is often pursued by those in power as well as parties.

We were distressed to hear of your indisposition, but fortunately the information ["of your indisposition" *canceled*] with that of your recovery were received simultaneously. I hope that you have felt no further inconvenience from it, and that you are as well as you would desire to be. If the Weather has been as favourable & mild in Washington as it has been here during the winter, you must have had little cause for complaint. Indeed there has been more severe weather during the past week than in the last three months together. If this cold should continue, considering the unusually advanced state of vegitation [*sic*], serious damage may be done the crops, which up to this period are very promising.

I have had no news from my place since you wrote me from So. Carolina. Not a line from Mr. [Francis W.] Pickens, or Mr. Mowblay [*sic*; John Mobley]. Of course I hope things are doing well. I do not know anything about the expenses, nor do I know who receives the money that is paid for Corn or other articles sold on the place. I fear there will be disorder without you give some directions which I can not give from this distance. I wrote Mr. [John Ewing] Bonneau to give me a statement of moneys that have been received & disbursed on my account.

Necessity commands us to do many things that we otherwise would not. If any one would be so good as to give me, the income dependent on this situation they would be most welcome to the privilege of wearing the coat, and all the trappings of office, for which I have no particular predilection. Whilst I am in the line and doing duty I only regret that the chances for promotion are so small. Could I have been transferred to Berlin (should Mr. [Henry] Wheaton be sent elsewhere) it would have satisfied my ambition for foreign appointments in every sense of the word. The duties there are not more arduous or important than here and the position of minister much more agre[e]able, whilst the increased pay would be a great desiderata acquired. In my case with my family it is impossible to do more than live, and to travel is ["almost" *canceled*] out of the question. The position of Brussels is remarkably fine[;] if we had a little more pay we could run of[f] to the Rhin[e] or Switzerland, Paris, Scotland & London & be returned in a few days from either place but as it is we are tied down. I sometimes conclude that if there be really no chance for promotion that I will return to the United States but in that case I should be depriving myself & family of the accumulation of the interest on my property in the United States which amounts to a couple of thousand dol[lar]s per annum— & which is so much put aside for a rainy day, & which now if I were in the United States would be gone and not suffice living or if it would do so I should be tied to one spot, the income not being large enough to travel or move about which ["is" *canceled*] I look upon as positively essential to health. By remaining here under the circumstances I live, and accumulate the interest of my property at home, and am in the way of chances. Notwithstanding the desire we have to see you & the necessity of my presence at my plantation[,] I am compelled to the conclusion that my duty would not permit me to return.

Mr. Wheaton passed through this city the other day on his return to Berlin. He expressed a desire to go to Paris or London & desired me to remember him particularly to you when I wrote. He thinks that neither Mr. [William R.] King [U.S. Minister to France] or Mr. McLean [*sic*; Louis McLane, U.S. Minister to Great Britain] will remain much longer absent.

The papers appear to think that Mr. Buchanan will retire if the resolution to give notice with the amendment enjoining negotiation

hould pass the Senate. It appears to me to be a decided stricture
n the administration, and it would not be surprising if it followed
he same course with that of [John] Tyler. The United States I
egret to say is now loosing [*sic*] ground in Europe on the Oregon
question. A war would not only be unpopular, but in such an event
is things stand, the entire onus would fall on us. Mr. [Daniel]
Webster[']s view is not without weight. If the Administration do
not intend settling the question by compromising she had better prepare for war & say so. To talk about extending the laws of the U.S.
over all of Oregon to the exclusion of England, and at the same time
to talk about negotiation, War &c is becoming ridiculous. At all
events it is having that effect here. There has been entirely too
much, blustering boasting talk. It looks badly at a a [*sic*] distance
when compared with the deliberate, calm & disspassionate course
pursued by Great Britain. I hope for my country that the concils
[*sic*] of peace, and dignity have prevailed since the receipt of Sir
Rob[er]t Peel[']s measures. I feel firmly convinced if you were to
come to England that you could settle the question to the satisfaction
of all parties, in twenty four hours, and I most sincerely wish that
such an event, as your coming abroad, could be brought about.

I will now state to you a fact in connection with the value of
Vancouvers Island, which I shall feel myself bound to give in my
Despatch which goes out in the steamer with this letter. I have it
from a gentleman who knew the person well & who had visited the
Island several times from the Sandwich Islands where he was consul.
He stated to me that he supposed the United States never would
consent to compromise the question by giving up to England the
Island of Vancouver because it contained *large deposits of Coal*:
the knowledge of which fact gives it a value far beyond what it had
as mere land & would make it infinitely so for steam navigation to
the China[,] the Sandwich Islands & along the Coast.

If there be any possibility of construing motives from conduct
there can scarce be a doubt but that England wishes the question settled amicably. No doubt she considers she has claims and will maintain them, but it [is] equally true, I think, that she attaches less
importance to them than what some of our loud speaking gentlemen
would feign make us believe. My opinion is that she would be
willing to compromise the matter even to our advantage, if we will
satisfy her honour and let her down easy. But blustering and loud
talk will effect nothing. It has a bad effect on this side of the ocean
& it is turned against us by the English press, and has a corresponding
bad effect upon the continent where the American papers are not

seen, and where all the news from America are taken from garbled extracts from English papers & where the last message of Mr. [James K.] Polk produced any thing but a good feeling. That paper wounded the governments of the Continent & had the effect of strengthening the Alliance between England and France instead of weakening it. Still I have no doubt that Louis Philippe desires to see the question closed, for he knows that if England and the United States were unfortunately to engage in a War, it would be next to impossible for France to ma[i]ntain neutrality.

I was very glad to hear that negroes had risen. I hope the rise may be maintained or continue. I think it a natural consequence of the annexation of Texas, and should not be surprised if they would continue to rise without a rise in the price of Cotton, which I regret to say I see no cause to anticipate. However you at home may be better able to foresee events than we here. Tho the last crop is doubtless smaller than was anticipated, the stock on hand is large and the consumption of Cotton has been smaller than usual owing to the smallness of the provision crops in Europe last [year] which has had an influence in diminishing the consumption of Cotton and which will continue [to] be felt in Ireland & elsewhere, and which will most probably produce a large stock on hand when the next new crop comes into market. If our own Government was to use its influence actively to bring about direct trade between the United States and Germany &c it would give an impulse to Consumption that would soon be felt, when we might hope that consumption would pass production and effect price & the general prosperity of American business. Without some such cause should ["should" *canceled*] operate in our favour it is to be apprehended that the essays and the success that attends the growth of Cotton in the East India possessions, (or rather certain parts) will continue to reduce the price of that article below what it has ever been.

But our Secretarys of State have no such extended views. They care little about our foreign relations further than they serve for political capital and each and all of our diplomatic agents are left to pursue such course as they think proper. They become luke warm & finally cease to know what is desired of them or in what way they can serve the cause. Frequently such agents either Diplomatic or Consular do us more injury than good, and so long as we continue in the course heretofore pursued by the Govt. it will continue to be of little moment whether we do or not send agents abroad.

Mr. Pickens in his last letter to me told me that he declined taking the agency of selling my place, because the time was too short and because he would like to be free as he might purchase it for himself or a friend. He also said that I had better not hire the negroes[,] that it would be more to my interest to sell them & if I should conclude to do so he would give the value that might be fixed by disinterested persons and take them from me on the same terms ["that"(?) *changed to* "as"] to time, as I might sell my place for. I wrote him that I had no inclination to sell my negroes, that I wished to have them hereafter if I should feel inclined to plant. I should regret if my neighbours and negroes should take up the idea that they are to be sold. Right or wrong it would make the negroes & overseer careless & make the whole concern a prey to the cupidity of all around.

I should like very well to have Mr. Picken[s]'s view of the value of my plantation as well as the negroes but that would I suppose be difficult to obtain, particularly if he entertains an idea of purchasing the former. About the latter there can be no doubt for he made an offer.

We have an unusu[a]lly important ministerial crisis on hand at this time. The ministers all tendered their resignations to the King [Leopold I] so long since as the 2nd inst. & his majesty has met with great difficulty in constituting another. You know that the country and ["the chambers" *interlined*] are pretty nearly balanced by the two parties Catholics & liberals. Heretofore the country has been governed by cabinets composed of members from either party. The difficulties have been great & the changes frequent. The present cabinet divided on the law of Instruction. On the 25th inst. the chambers were prorogued until the 20th of April so that all publi[c] business has been brought to stand. The country is perfectly tranquil, but if difficulties were to occur in France troubles might arise here.

We are all very well. Anna has written you I see by this mail. You will have an opportunity hereafter of writing more frequently as the steamers hereafter will commence running twice a month. Your affectionate son, Thos. G. Clemson.

ALS in ScCleA; PEx's in Boucher and Brooks, eds., *Correspondence*, pp. 336–337.

From DAVID H. DAVIDSON

Express Office[,] Utica N.Y., March 27th 1846
Sir, Would you have the goodness to let me have two Copies of your speech on the Oregon question[?]

My reason for asking two copies is this—I consider from what I have seen in the paper's you[r] Speech a Death blow to the war Spirit in the House and a wish to forward one Copy to a member of the House of Keys (or Legislature) in the Isle of Man[,] he wishing to know my candid oppinion if there would be War between England and this Country[.]

Would also thank you to let me have a Copy of the report of Committe[e] on the bill making appropriations for certain Rivers & Harbors past [*sic*] in the House—if such is printed[.]

Hopeing that you will not be offended with the liberty I have taken in thus troubling you[,] I remain Sir Your's Most Respectfully, David H. Davidson.

ALS in ScCleA.

From FRANCIS LIEBER

Columbia S.C., March 27th [18]46
My dear Sir, May I be so bold as to request you to let me have a copy of your admirable Oregon speech, should it be printed in pamphlet form, so that I can preserve it?

I have read part of it to our Senior Class in ["my" *interlined*] lectures on political economy, from the National Intelligencer, and commented upon.

Accept my thanks for this speech. However humble they may be, I know I offer them in the name of innumerable fellow-citizens.

We are going on well, here, with our new president [of South Carolina College, William C. Preston]. With the highest regard My Dear Sir Your very obed[ien]t, Francis Lieber.

ALS in ScCleA.

From JAMES M. MACDONALD

Jamaica, L[ong] I[sland,] 27 Mar. 1846
Sir, I wish to thank you, not only in my own, but in the name of the whole community, in which I reside, for your late Speech on the Oregon question, in the Senate of the U.S. I think I can truly say, that I have never heard so general an expression of the warmest approbation from men of all parties & creeds, as has been called forth by the perusal of that able production.

May wisdom from on high be largely bestowed on you in performing the important part which you are called to act in the present critical juncture of our public affairs. Yours, with very great respect, James M. Macdonald, Minister of a Presb[yteria]n Cong[regation].

ALS in ScCleA.

From P. A. READING

Lambertville, N.J., March 27th 1846
Respected & Esteemed friend, I have just read your remarks made in the Senate upon the Oregon Resolutions, as reported in "the Daily Union" of the 19th inst. and a more explicit, correct and convincing statement of the matter, I have never before read. It is replete with interest & instruction, and I can not see how the vote of the Senate when taken, will be other than in support of the principles and views advanced and supported in that speech, and I am persuaded the Senate will confer a great favour and lasting benefit on the nation, by sustaining the course you so ably advocate. Thereby continuing to us as a people the blessings of peace, instead of the manifold evils of war, with all its train of ills, and obstacles which such an event will throw in our onward path of Freedom and the principles of "*State Rights*." That was a glorious & well timed hit. Your rebuke to our "par excellent" friends, was a kind thrust given in *brotherly* kindness. They no doubt *felt it*, and will *appreciate* it. Indeed, it is a solemn & momentious question further to consider of, and well is it for them, that they have a friend in the Senate chamber who will apprise them of the suicidle and ruinous course they seem disposed to take. These views are contracted.

Your *past* position, as well as the present, was well defined and sustained, and told well for the friends of *Texas* and of *peace*. And I can not but think that some of our friends will now better understand & comprehend the force of the language "masterly in-activity," than they appeared to do before they listened to your speech.

In fact you acquitted yourself in such an admirable statesmanlike manner on this occasion, that I could not withhold my warm approbation of your course, and not only in this instance, but on all proper occasions. You exhibit in your public life, the *true and vital interests of the nation*. The time will come, when a nation will manifest her gratitude for such useful services, in a still more prominent and honorable manner than heretofore.

I am now a citizen of New Jersey, (["formerly" *canceled*] my native State) having removed from Philadelphia to this village last spring. You may have some knowledge of its locality, when I tell you it is immediately opposite the village of New Hope, the residence of our friend L[ewis] S. Coryell—The Delaware only separating us, and our intercourse facilitated by a Bridge. He is absent from home, and with his friends at Washington. How I almost envy him the rich mental feast he has enjoyed of late, in listening to the debates in Congress. We are daily expecting his return. I was with his family last evening. They were well, and with others of his fr[ie]nds, will be glad to see him on his return.

Should your speech be published in pamphlet form, please send me a copy, as also any similar matter which you may think will ["be" *interlined*] interesting, and not too much trouble to transmit.

I need not add, it will always give me pleasure to hear from you, and learn of your health & happiness, and may I say, of the success of our favourite Doctrine—The cause of "States Rights," that Glorious *anchor* of the *Constitution*.

I have this moment learned by a friend just from the City of Phila[delphia], that the President [James K. Polk] (in reply to a call from the Senate) has sent in a special message recommending an increase of the navy and other war preperations. Can it be basised upon recent information from abroad, a refusal by England to *renew* negociations? I trust not. But merely carrying out his views as stated in his first annual message to Congress.

I shall now look for Mr. Coryell[']s return with some anxiety as he can inform me upon the subject of this *special* message.

I am inclined to think the *friends* of Mr. J.K. Polk will get him into an unpleasant situation in reference to the all engrossing subjects now before Congress.

Pardon me for this tresspass upon your time, and believe me as formerly Your sincere friend, P.A. Reading.

ALS in ScCleA.

From CHA[RLE]S S. J. GOODRICH

Brooklyn N.Y., March 28th/46

Hon. and Dear Sir, Though a stranger to you, I have long known you in the public councils of the Republic as one of those rare and gifted ones who dare be independent, and permit me to add, dare be honest, amid the sycophancy and venality of a corrupt age and country. When I witness these traits of character, so rare in our public men, I cannot but admire them; and though I may differ in opinion on some matters of public policy, still I cannot but hold in high regard one who, I doubt not is conscientious & fearless in the discharge of his public duties—a sure reward sooner or later attaches to such.

I observe that on the Oregon question you have recently made one of your great efforts. We have had very imperfect reports of it and supposing that you may have had it published under your own eye, I have ventured to trespass on your goodness to send me a copy. When my relative & cousin Mr. [John] Forsyth was in the Senate & State department, I was indebted to him for many valuable pub[lic] Doc[uments]. My other friends in Congress knowing that I am somewhat heretical do not always favor me except with articles wholly whig or loco. With the Oregon question I am not fully conversant and any thing on this great & interesting question & especially any thing emanating from yourself, I should value exceedingly.

I had an introduction to you in Charleston, I think in 1824, but of course you would not recollect me. My father I believe was with you in "Yale" some few years before I was born. Excuse the liberty I have taken and accept assurances [of] the esteem and high regard of your oblig[e]d & humble ser[van]t, Chas. S.J. Goodrich.

ALS in ScCleA. NOTE: Elizur Goodrich, professor of law at Yale from 1801 through 1810, was the only person named Goodrich at Yale during Calhoun's years there.

From CHARLES JARVIS

Ellsworth [Maine,] March 28th 1846

Sir, You are addressed on a subject of State and National Interest. If asked why not then, have addressed a Member of the Maine Delegation, my answer is; that your action in the premises, if favorable, would not be liable to the imputation, of being influenced by a sectional interest.

A Farmer, and having no property vested in trade, or in navigation of any description, my opinion has not been influenced by private considerations; and may be considered as indicating the sentiments of the democracy of Maine.

Though in theory an ultra free trade man, yet under present circumstances, I am in favour of a tariff, graduated on revenue principles, in strict conformity with the genius of our institutions, imposing the highest duties on the luxuries, and the lowest, on the necessaries of life, without the slightest regard directly, or indirectly to protection.

A Tariff of duties on all imported articles, irrespective, of whether any of them are produced in certain States, is the extreme limit of protection which ought to be asked; or which can be granted, on any principle of equity. Such a tariff by the enhancement of prices, might not only relieve the producing States, from their portion of the burthen of the government of the Union; but might even render, their Sister States tributary to them; and that in proportion, to the extent of their consumption of the articles of the producing States, which pay duties when imported. On this account all imported articles, of general consumption, not produced in any State of the Union, are emphatically, the proper subjects of as high a duty, as they will bear, without inducing smuggling.

On this principle, the exemption of Tea & Coffee from duty, is objectionable, as being, in general use throughout the United States, a duty upon them would be paid in proportion to population; or if varying from that, would bear more heavily, on the manufacturing States; which had been relieved, by the operation of the duties on foreign articles, of the same description, as their manufactures. A Tariff exempting Tea and Coffee from duty, is virtually protective; as the duties on other articles, must be higher, to afford an adequate revenue. Though not material, it would have been better, if all the agricultural products, which constitute the staple exports of the United States, had been included in the list of free articles. The proposed duty of twenty per cent on such articles, is a mockery of the Agricultural Interest. The free exportation of those articles, is conclusive evidence that they neither require, nor can receive protection; and the proposed exemption of Cotton from duty, is an acknowledgement of the principle.

With the exceptions above noted, and the recommendation to abolish the bounties on the fisheries, I am not aware of any material objection, to the project submitted by the Secretary of the Treasury [Robert J. Walker]; and it not being my purpose to analyze that Tariff, I proceed to the leading object of this letter.

Consulting only her own interests, Maine would be an ultra free trade State. She can derive no incidental protection from any tariff. With a sea bo[a]rd of near three hundred miles, a soil of hardly medium fertility, and a winter of five months, she depends upon her navigation, fisheries and lumber, for no inconsiderable portion of her bread stuffs, and the supply of almost every article of manufactures. Her navigation, burthened with heavy duties on articles, used in ship building, has to enter into competition, with that of the whole world. Her lumber, being largely exported to foreign markets, can receive no protection; and its great bulk, and consequent expence of transportation secure to it, the market of the other States of the Union. On her fisheries, she in common with the other New England States, has hitherto received a bounty, which it is now proposed to repeal.

Even under the proposed tariff, the enhanced price of the foreign and domestic articles which Maine will consume, cannot be estimated at less than one and a half millions of dollars; one third of which may go into the treasury of the United States; but two thirds would go to other States as incidental protection to their productions. Allowing then, which is far from being the truth, that the bounty on the fisheries, is so much paid exclusively to Maine, from the common treasury; it does but tend to equalize, in a small degree, her contribution to the support of the General Government; it does not amount to more than one tenth of the contribution levied upon her, as incidental protection to the Irorn [*sic*] of Pen[n]sylvania, the Lead of Missouri, the Hemp of Kentucky, the Sugar and Molasses of Lou-[i]siana, and the Manufactures of Massachusetts and Rhode Island.

But in consequence of the bounty, the price of fish has been reduced to the lowest rate, at which the fisheries can be prosecuted; repeal the bounty and fish would rise in price, many now engaged in the laborious occupation abandoning the business. The fisheries are now carried on exclusively by men of small means, who do the labor within themselves; they are carried on not by hired labor, but by fathers of families, with the aid of their boys, or of those who engage for a share in the fishing cruise. Those who do the labor are the recipients of the bounty; unlike in that respect, to the operatives in a manufactory, who work for stipulated wages, regulated by the rate of wages, in other employments, deriving no advantage, from the enhanced price of the manufactured articles; resulting from the incidental protection of duties; the whole of which is engrossed by the capitalist.

The fisheries now afford no field for the employment of capital, even if the law would permit, they could not be carried on with profit by hired labor. From the great uncertainty of the business, they are most appropriately the subject of bounties; fisherman[']s luck is proverbial; when unfortunate, the bounty intervenes, to save the fisherman from utter ruin.

In consequence of the bounty, greater numbers have engaged in the business; and dry fish, which is almost exclusively consumed, by the poorest class, is thus furnished at a lower rate. The consumer of fish wherever located, is virtually a recipient of the bounty on the fisheries; and that too in proportion to his consumption of the article; for the proposition is as undeniable, that a bounty, reduces; as that a duty, enhances the price of a commodity.

For the reasons above stated the justice, as well as the expediency of repealing the bounty, may well be questioned; but weighty as they are, in a national point of view, there is one, still more deserving of consideration.

The Navy is now recognized as the strong arm of defensive as well as of offensive war. The materials being on hand, ships of war may be built in a few months time; but to man them we must have Sailors. The days of the Roman and Cartheginian Galleys have long since gone by; nautical skill and experience are indispensable to the Sailor. A Soldier can be made in the course of six weeks; the Conscripts of France, raw country lads, fresh from the plough and the workshop, in that space of time, were converted into disciplined Soldiers. Not so with the Sailor; months will hardly suffice to give a lands-man, the use of his sea legs; years are required to make the Sailor. France was not deficient in Ships; but to man those Ships, was the insuperable difficulty, she had to encounter, in her Navy. To surmount this difficulty all the mighty energy of Bonaparte was exerted in vain; he could construct a road over the Alps, but to convert a Lands-man into a Sailor was beyond his power. Notwithstanding the extent of her mercantile marine, England has met with the same difficulty, which has been only partially surmounted, by the odious practice of impressment, from the Merchant Service.

The bounty when granted was advocated as indispensable for the carrying on of the fisheries, which in time of war would furnish men for the Navy. The bounty was not granted merely as a drawback of the duty on Salt, for it greatly exceeded that amount; but as a drawback also, of the duties on the Iron, Cordage & Canvass, required in the construction of the Vessels, and the duties on the other articles used in the prosecution of the business; all which would probably far exceed the amount of the duty on the Salt, consumed in the curing the fish.

The repeal of the bounty, cannot therefore be considered as a necessary consequence of the repeal of the duty on Salt; but as an abandonment, of what has been the settled policy of the government from its establishment.

Thomas Jefferson then Secretary of State, in his report on the Fisheries Feb[ruar]y 2d 1791 uses this language. "This rapid view of the Cod Fishery enables us to discern, under what policy it has flourished or declined in the hands of other nations, and to mark the facts, that it is too poor a business to be left to itself, even with the nations most advantageously situated." Irrespective of the well known facts in the case, this is high authority to warrant the assertion, that the repeal of the bounty would be the destruction of the Fisheries; and the alternative presented, is its continuance or their abandonment.

It is conceded that the Fisheries make the best and hardiest of Sailors; unless some substitute can be devised, better at once abandon the Navy, and save the idle and expensive pageantry of Ships and Officers, than destroy its efficiency, by cutting off its surest resource for men, when their services are most required.

In time of war the fisheries must be suspended, the fishermen would then be thrown out of employment; the foreign merchant service, and the coasting trade will then require no additional hands; but as they both can and will be carried on, neither will be able to furnish an increased number of men for the service of the Navy. Once wonted to a sea-faring life, fishermen like other Sailors, are averse to, if not unfit for occupation on the land; they would then be compelled, almost from necessity to seek refuge on board of our National Ships for the means of subsistence. Fishermen may be considered as a Sea Militia; but the Fisherman, unlike the Militia-Man, who has not learnt the simplest duty of the regular Soldier, is fully prepared to discharge the duty of a Sailor on board of a Man of War.

Even if the bounty was in every other respect, a tax upon the community, it is the cheapest way of supporting this Sea Militia, always ready for service in the hour of need. As a School for Sailors, for the service of the Navy, at the time when their services are most required, the Fisheries, are as important, as the West Point Institution for the instruction of Officers of the Army.

The point being conceded that Fish, as a food for man, is worth the average of the labor it costs, the bounty does not subtract a dollar from the productive industry of the country, it merely enables the fishermen to afford the article at a cheaper rate; its tendency is thus to releive the poor in a measure from the capitation tax imposed by duties on articles of their consumption.

For the reasons assigned the repeal of the Bounties on the Fisheries is opposed as injurious to Maine, by causing a violent revolution in the industry of a large and useful class of her citizens, throwing many of them out of employment, and compelling them to seek other means for support; and as injurious to the United States, by greatly reducing the number of that description of Seamen, who in time of war, would furnish the best men for the manning of our National Ships, and thereby impairing, if not destroying the efficiency of the Navy.

Most respectfully submitting the foregoing observations for your consideration I am Sir with sentiments of the highest esteem, Y[ou]r Ob[edien]t Serv[an]t, Charles Jarvis.

ALS in ScCleA.

From SILAS REED

St. Louis, March 28th 1846

Dear Sir, Your late speech on the Oregon question has been rec[eive]d & read here by your friends with great satisfaction—and, although the party in this State are generally for the 54th parallel, even at the hazard of war, yet most admit the truth and fitness of your opinions. Indeed, *my* mind has undergone some change on this subject since I had the pleasure of conversing with you this winter, and I am satisfied that you now have with you, in the position you occupy, a large majority of the American people. I have therefore to congratulate you upon the favor with which the wise policy you advocate has been received by the country at large, and trust that nothing will occur to interrupt the increasing confidence in the ultimate triumph of your views. I have the honor to be With great respect Your Ob[edien]t Serv[an]t, Silas Reed.

ALS in ScCleA.

From A. P. STINSON

St. Joseph Mich., Mar[ch] 28, 1846

My dear Sir, I have just finished the reading of your Speech on the Oregon question, Deliver[e]d in the Senate on the 16th Inst., as Published in the N.Y. Courier & Enquirer, which Paper a friend was Kind Enough to Loan me for Perusal, being the only Paper containing It in Town. If I had any Doubts before, as to the true Policy of our Government Relative to that all absorbing question, I have none now. They are dissipated & were so, while Reading your masterly Speech, which Speech I Predict will *tell on the Senate*, & in the Nation. As there was no other paper which Contain[e]d It, and all were Deserous of hearing It, all having been waiting Impat[i]ently your views, I took It & went to a Public Place & there Read It with Satisfaction to my self & Admiration to *All*.

Pardon me my Dear Sir, for the *frank manner which I write*— when I say, & while I say It, I but Reiterate the almost united voice of our Citizens, that it is the Master Speech of the Session & is in fact *The Speech*. Your views meet, as they merit, a Hearty Response Here. I hope to have the Speech to *preserve*[?]. I have written sundry Communications for Different Papers, over Different Signatures & as often Dating at *Washington* as Else where, with a view of Promoting you. To day I have written one for my *son in Law's* paper the Milwaukie (W.T.) Courier, over the Signature of "Reas Effendi" which If Published will mark & send you.

In my Last, I desired to be kept Advised of your wishes & Intentions (Politically) to the End, that I might in Some humble manner coop[e]rate.

The "Granite State" (N.H.) where for more than 20 years I Resided, has It would seem, gone *Whig* in her recent Election! I am in no wise disappointed, I had Expected as much. The "*Political Jug[g]lers*" have done It. "New tests" of Democr[ac]y had been introduced & old Democrats "Read out of the Party" by the *New fangled Democ[ra]ts* & Hence their overthrow. I tell you Sir, The "Central Cliques", The "Political Jug[g]lers", are Down. Their

Dynasty ["are" *changed to* "Is"] Dead Dead Dead. *The People* are arising In their might & Majesty Determined Hereafter to do their busin[e]ss in their own way & *Woe* be to the Men, or set of men, who shall attempt to Circumvent them. When Leisure will afford, shall always be Happy to hear from you. Your friend Ever, A.P. Stinson.

ALS in ScCleA.

From F[ITZ]W[ILLIAM] BYRDSALL

New York [City,] March 29th 1846

Dear Sir, I cannot but regret the passage of the Resolution by the Senate which called out the President's [James K. Polk's] late message; and when all circumstances both at home and abroad, in relation to the Oregon question, are considered, I cannot see how he could well avoid giving such a message in reply to that Resolution. He was compelled to re-assume the positions taken in his annual message or to recede from them. Could he have done the latter with such consistency as would be compatible with the public interests?

But the quarter from whence the Resolution came is of the high Protective School, and therefore the belief is induced that the real object in view was such expenditures as would keep up the Tariff to the present high pressure system. The Whigs of New Jersey are the most inveterate Protectionists in the Union.

It is fortunate however for the Country that the message has had but little effect upon the business people here. There was a slight change in the stock market, but they have rallied again much as they were before. For a day or two ["busness" *changed to* "business"] men felt chagrined and condemned in no measured terms both the President and the Senator from New Jersey for what appeared in their view, as unnecessary and as injurious to the present favorable prospects of business. A little reflection coupled with the confidence now reposed in the majority of the Senate, dispelled their apprehensions. The Speeches of Messrs. [William H.] Heywood & Calhoun were of that character and ability that the impressions made by them could not be removed by the message although it did give "note of dreadful preparation."

We had some talk of getting up a public meeting here to sustain those Senators in Congress who are desirous of maintaining the National rights and honor of the Country by peaceable measures if possible. But seeing the little effect of the message, we do not deem a public meeting necessary. I profess myself to be one of those who go for the "whole of Oregon," for I believe we have the best claim to it; but the "whole of Oregon or none" presents an alternative that no sensible man can agree to. I am not in favor of giving up any spot that is confessedly ours, because we cannot get a portion that is in dispute, or that does not indisputably belong to us. But this great Nation should never go to war unless clearly in the right, and for that which is strictly right.

My object in writing this is simply to inform you of the state of feeling here in relation to the recent message of the Executive—that considerate persons blame the call upon him at this juncture in matter and purport ["as" *interlined*] improper, because it was cornering him upon the Oregon question at an inappropriate time when it is involved in circumstances of importance and more especially of intricacy, or such at least as are calculated to induce ["a" *canceled*] rather a message consistent with diplomacy than any other character. And also to inform you that the message has not, so far as I have learned, altered any impression created by your recent speech. I am Dear Sir with the greatest respect Your ob[edien]t Ser[van]t, F.W. Byrdsall.

ALS in ScCleA; PEx in Boucher and Brooks, eds., *Correspondence*, p. 338. NOTE: Byrdsall's reference to "the Senator from New Jersey" means William L. Dayton, a Whig, who on 3/2 had introduced resolutions calling on the President to inform the Senate whether the current state of foreign affairs required increases in the military and naval establishments.

To T[HOMAS] G. CLEMSON, [Brussels]

Washington, 29th March 1846

My dear Sir, As I have written you and Anna [Maria Calhoun Clemson] by the steamer, which sales [*sic*] on the 1st April, I now write simply to inform you, that the treaty [of commerce with Belgium] has been ratified by the Senate in a manner highly honorable to you. There was but one vote against it, & that only on general grounds, opposed to all reciprocal treaties in reference to Navigation. It seems to be generally admitted, not only that the treaty was highly advantageous, but that it was the best treaty of the kind we had ever made. The result was, the more hon[or]able from the fact, that when first taken up, a few days since, I had great fears from the extent of the opposition indicated, & the quarter from which it came, that it would not be ratified. Some objections were made to the details, but the main were directed ag[ai]nst all treaties of the kind, & ground taken that none of the existing should be renewed. So strong was the opposition, that there appeared no prospect of ratification without material amendments, especially by limiting its duration to a short period, say three years. But at the next meeting discussion brought out fully the merits of the treaty, when it passed with the smallest possible minority. I had to take a part in the discussion. The vote was highly gratifying to me and does great credit to you.

I enclose a letter received by mail.

We all continue well & join love to you & Anna & children [John Calhoun Clemson and Floride Elizabeth Clemson]. Your affectionate father, J.C. Calhoun.

[P.S.] I enclose a few copies more of my speech on the Oregon question.

ALS in ScCleA; PEx in Jameson, ed., *Correspondence,* pp. 687–688.

From JOHN A. NORTON

Worcester (Mass.), March 29th 1846
Dear Sir, I have been highly gratified by the perusal of a portion of the Speech delivered by yourself in the Senate on Monday March 16th upon the Oregon question. I am a young & ardent Whig, but the noble & lofty sentiments contained in the extract of your speech which I read created a strong desire in my mind to read the whole of it, & if you can snatch a moment from your busy & arduous labors to send me a copy of it I shall ever hold the act in grateful remembrance. As a friend of Peace & human progress, & as an American citizen I tender you my sincere thanks for the noble advocacy of the cause of both by yourself. With the best wishes for your health & happiness I am with sincere respect Your friend & servant, John A. Norton.

ALS in ScCleA.

From J[ohn] C. C. Carroll

Cincinnati, March 30, 1846

Dear Sir, I beg leave again to trouble you in relation to the matter of Thomas Auten's application for a Pension. I received your documents of date February 26, 1846, and in accordance to the directions therein contained I wrote to Charles G. McChesney Esq. Sec[re]t[ar]y of State of New Jersey at Trenton in relation to the deficient points in Thomas Auten's application or declaration for to be placed upon the pension list and get his back pension with the interest accruing thereon since March A.D. 1831, or in accordance with the act of June 7, 1832. Mr. McChesney has been kind enough to examine and I herein enclose to Your Honor all the papers he has been pleased to send me [for] the old man. Thomas Auten is so feeble and so deaf as stated in his declaration and the *left side* of his face nearly all eaten away with a Cancer that it is nearly impossible to get an answer from him to any thing[;] on account of his difficulty in speaking I mis-understood the name of one of his Captains, Capt. [Jacob] Ten Eyck, which I believe I spelled "Denyke." The old man told me of his Brothers &c in the service at same time with himself. Those are their names I presume in Mr. McChesney's letter to which I respectfully direct your attention. Auten does not recollect the year he entered the service, but I presume that it was in 1776 or 1777. Your Honor will perceive by refference to Mr. McChesney's letter to me that the Roll is without date. The old man Mr. Auten swore to his Declaration that his monthly pay was $8.00 or about that if I recollect the money he says being *British* then. Your Honor will perceive that the letters &C of the Sec[re]t[ary] of Stat[e] of New Jersey corroborate all the old man's, Auten's, statements. He says that he well put[?] in the service &c about three years steady without being at home more than a few days at any one time, which doubtless is true from every concomitant circumstance.

And now Dear Sir permit me once again in behalf of one of the few survivors of that memorable struggle to trouble you to attend to this a little more. I hope the Honorable Commissioner of pensions [James L. Edwards] will accept these documents from New Jersey as an Amendment to his Declaration. I am afraid that I am too troublesome to you[;] if so you will please excuse my zeal in behalf of a Revolutionary Soldier. All I do in the matter is at the many solicitations of tenderhearted people who see the distress and pity the misfortunes of the old veteran. Will Your Honor pleas[e] request the Honorable Commissioner to further direct me if any thing yet essential is still lacking. Auten *cannot* recollect even the year or *month* of the year he entered the service nor when he was discharged, though he is willing to swear that he was about three years in the service at one tour except probably a few days leave of absence at any one time. The papers may all be directed to me as I have all the trouble, attention and whatever little expense there is to bear in this respect. I submit this to its fate humbly hoping it may be that Your Honor will affect its object. I do not know what else I can procure or do in the matter. Hoping that if in any time a [*sic*] can do any thing in return for your kind attention to me I will most cheerfully comply.

Probably I may seem awkward to the Honorable Commissioner of pensions but I trust he will excuse me for it is done without experience in this behalf and but little means of obtain[in]g it. I most respectfully remain Your most obliged Serv[an]t at Command, J.C.C. Carroll.

ALS with Ens in DNA, RG 15 (Veterans Administration), Revolutionary War Pension and Bounty-Land Warrant Application Files, 1800–1900, R329 (M-804:93, frames 878–879, 889, and 891–892). NOTE: McChesney's letter of March 23, 1846 to Carroll states that Auten was in the Somerset County militia, "probably 1776 or 77," and encloses a certificate to that effect.

From ABBOTT LAWRENCE

Boston, March 30th 1846

My Dear Sir, I have two special friends who leave us this afternoon for Washington where they intend to pass a few days. Mr. William H. Prescott the historian and Mr. Charles ["H." *canceled*] Sumner, of the legal profession. These gentlemen are both well known in the literary world, and as such I have felt that they should make your acquaintance. Whatever may be the differences between you and myself, upon political questions, I trust we are both too liberal, to allow mere opinions upon National questions to sunder the ties of comity due to each other, or those with whom we are associated. I begin however to think that we are coming nearer together upon the great questions that now agitate the Country—and I assure you with entire frankness that I know not the man in the United States, with whom I desire to have social converse more than with yourself. I have to ask the favor of you to call on Messers. Prescott & Sumner, with whose simplicity of manners and high intelligence you cannot but be pleased ["with" *canceled*]. These gentlemen I beg to say have the highest opinion of your personal character and eminent abilities. I pray you dear Sir to believe I remain Very faithfully Your Ob[edien]t Ser[vant], Abbott Lawrence.

P.S. I have almost threatened a visit to Washington for the purpose of conversing with you—upon topics, of interest in the future.

ALS in ScCleA; PC in Jameson, ed., *Correspondence*, pp. 1079–1080.

Petition of Gilbert Stalker and N.B. Hill, presented by Calhoun to the Senate on 3/30. This document, which is undated, asks compensation for the petitioners' steamboat, the *James Boatright*, which was lost in 1838 on the coast of Florida while being used by the U.S. Army as a transport in the Seminole war. Seventeen supporting documents are enclosed. (The petition was referred to the Committee on Claims, which later reported a bill which was not acted upon.) DS in DNA, RG 46 (U.S. Senate), 30A–H2.

From J[OHN] S. BARBOUR

Catalpa [Va.,] March 31st 1846

My Dear Sir, Tomorrow my eldest son [John S. Barbour, Jr.,] will leave us on a visit to Texas. He will call on you at Washington. We have heard nothing of James [Barbour] for six or eight weeks & Mrs. [Elizabeth A. Byrne] Barbour is uneasy about him.

Will you give my son an introductory note to Gen[era]l [Thomas J.] Rusk of the Senate? and a letter, to Gov[erno]r [J. Pinckney] Henderson?

My correspondence is so frequent a tax on you that I ought to feel compunction for it.

I am glad that your speech has made so deep an impression upon the public mind.

The President [James K. Polk] is embarrassed with great difficulty in meeting the wishes of the two parties into which his friends have segregated. I do not think that his publick acts are the true exponents of his real sentiments. Left to himself his instincts are cautious & patriotic. Goaded by the incentives of faction and selfishness; he has unmoored his judgement from its haven; & his conduct is the sport of the wave that plays its freak upon his duties.

I rec[eive]d a letter from Mr. [Thomas] Green[,] the son in law of [Thomas] Ritchie a day or two past. He may be regarded as reiterating the views of the organ [the Washington *Daily Union*] as they look behind the scenes. Read it & throw it in your fire.

There is one thing that you will excuse me in saying—that all the Whig compliments bestowed on your present position & labours, will never be followed by any other testimonial of approbation than empty praises. This is of the party, and the party that speaks by the voice of its leaders.

They will commend & condemn you.

I learn from the best sources that our extra Gov[erno]r [William ("Extra Billy") Smith] avowed "that he had cut himself loose from the Calhoun party." I give you the words as they are reported credibly through an honourable channel to me. Whether he means to remain with you whilst he cuts himself loose from your party is a question of casuistry which a sharp witted moralist may answer.

One cause for distrust you may keep constantly by your side with this individual. That he has ["neither" *canceled*] neither a high nor a firm sense of Honour, & ["secondly"(?) *canceled*] that he is an open & declared applicant for office from the federal Executive; and that this is indispensable to recruit his broken fortunes.

You will not forget this & if you do not you are in no peril of being deceived or betrayed. The magnet is true to its pole, & the Executive will is the guide & the key to the politicks of all such men.

I have thought these cursory lines might not be without their use. With sincere Respect & Regard, Y[ou]r friend, J.S. Barbour.

[P.S.] My son who will go now to Texas, has no other objects than to see the country, Look after & take care of his Brother, and if he like the prospe[ct] he may buy some lands in it. J.S.B.

ALS in ScCleA.

From W[illia]m P. Duval

Tallahassee [Fla.,] March 31st 1846

My dear sir, I have read over your speech on the Oregon question, deliberately three several times, and find it out of the compass of my language to express my opinion of the wide and statesmanlike views you have delivered to the nation. Throughout this State but one opinion prevails on the wisdom and far-seeing judgement, you have displayed on this important and dangerous question, so well calculated by intemperate politicians to involve, the peace if not the ruin of our institutions.

Here Democrats and Whigs unite in commending your profound reasoning on this vital question, and in acknowledging no man in our national Legislature has so clearly and so ably, discussed the effect and consequences that would result from a violent and partizan action, demanding "all of Oregon." I wish one at least of this able speech of yours corrected by yourself sent to me, as your friends are anxious to have it republished *here*, and distributed over our State. I wrote to you some time since that I desired to be in the next congress; now if Mr. [David Levy] Yulee [Senator from Fla.] is your friend, as Mr. [James D.] Westcott [Jr., Senator from Fla.] now pretends to be, they should at once urge their friends to call for my services— since it is certain Mr. [William H.] Brockenbrough [Representative from Fla.], cannot be reelected, and if he is brought out again as the Democratic candidate a Whig will be elected.

I care nothing for a seat in congress on my own account, for under no contingency would I consent to remain longer than one congress. It is alone my object to sustain our great Southern principles in the coming contest for another President. If these men are sincerely your friends they should at once write to those they confide in to unite in support of my election. No man in this State could do more, if as much, in congress as myself in times of trouble & difficulty.

I have recently received a letter from my son Thomas who was the former Secretary in this territory, now residing at Austin in Texas. He is the warm friend of my early and valued friend Judge [James] Webb, and is as solicitous as myself in desireing he should receive the appointment of Federal Judge in that State. You could not render a greater service to the people of Texas & to our country at large in any appointment to be made by the President than in using your influence, for Judge Webb. A paper called, "The new Eara" [*sic*] edited by John C. Chalmers Esq. in which Judge Webb is proprietor in part, is now established at Austin, and in the absence of Mr. Chalmers my son Thomas is the acting Editor. In a letter to me he says "I have consented to edit this paper untill Doct[o]r Chalmers['s] return from Washington with the understanding, that I would write nothing of a partizan character, so far as relates to the politics of the State. There are in truth no politics here as yet, men— and not measures, are the theme of our new[s]paper discussions. Being a stranger in the country, with nothing to depend upon for a living, but my profession, and the good will of the people, I don[']t choose to make enimies of one half, and embroil myself in difficulties,

789

by taking sides for this, or that man. I may hereafter do so, but it would be of no service to me just now. Whatever I may write therefore of a political cast, shall be in praise of *Democracy* in general, and *Mr. Chalhoun [sic] in particular.*"

This is the language and feeling of myself and my sons and must ever be such.

Your speech is destined to have a powerful effect on Parli[a]ment, and throughout great Brittain. The Statesmen of that nation will accord to you a station preeminent among the highest of the age. I long to see the notice of your speech from the British press. May God bless and preserve you for your country many years. Your friend, Wm. P. Duval.

ALS in ScCleA.

Remarks on war with Great Britain over Oregon, 3/31. Lewis Cass of Mich. in the course of a long speech ridiculed Calhoun as a "Cassandra" for having spoken of "the horrors of war" of ten years' duration, and suggested that "such an exhibit ought" not to be made in the Senate. "Mr. Calhoun asked the privilege of a moment to explain. In reference to the most successful war that we could wage against Britain, in driving her from Canada and from Oregon, and in displacing her flag from this continent, twenty to thirty years would be demanded, and every dollar of money that we could raise. If the Senator thinks that we could do it in ten years, he is most mistaken. It would, perhaps, require at least twenty years to effect her expulsion. He had argued upon the most successful war, and he had said nothing hypothetically disparaging to his own country." Cass disclaimed any inference that Calhoun had disparaged the country. From the New York, N.Y., *Herald*, April 2, 1846, p. 4. Variant report in *Congressional Globe*, 29th Cong., 1st Sess., p. 578.

From J[OHN] S. SKINNER

New-Orleans, 31 March 1846

My dear Sir, Your kind letters over took me at Charleston, where, and elsewhere South & S.W. of that, the hospitalities of my friends, so numerous and so kind beyond my deserts, have detained me so much on the way, that I now begin to apprehend it will be impossible for me to call in person on those in Alabama whose civilities you bespoke for me.

I have visited some fine sugar estates "on the coast" of Louisiana & passed the last week in the neighbourhood of Natchez. Your speech on the Oregon question I procured there at the moment of leaving and [had] the pleasure to read it to a delighted audience on board the Steamer coming down. For views enlarged & profound and for true eloquence and philosophy liberal & enlightened it must enlarge the circle of your admirers and friends not at home only, but wherever the friends of christianity & civilization exist. Already I hear many Whigs say with such politics and such philosophy moral & political we are content.

I do not yet despair altogether, but much fear that I cannot encounter the greater delay of the *detour* I had marked out for myself thro Alabama. With cordial regard & best wishes, your friend, J.S. Skinner.

ALS with En in ScCleA. NOTE: Skinner enclosed a notice from an unidentified newspaper, dated 3/31, calling attention to the publication in its pages of Calhoun's Oregon speech.

To W[ILLIAM] B. WILSON, W[ILLIAM] H. PARKER, and W[ILLIAM] H. LOGUE, South Carolina College, Columbia

Washington, 31st March 1846

Gentlemen, In answer to your note, informing me, that a Resolution has been adopted by the Clariosophic Society, requesting me to consent to have my Portrait taken for their ["hall" *canceled*] Hall, I have to say that I feel honoured by the request & with pleasure give my consent. With great respect I am & &, J.C. Calhoun.

Contemporary copy in ScU-SC, Clariosophic Society Papers, ms. vol. entitled "Minutes, Letter Book, and Constitution, 1842–1849," p. 225. NOTE: Compare Calhoun's letter of 4/6/1846 to William Kenedy Barclay.

SYMBOLS

▥

The following symbols have been used in this volume as abbreviations for the forms in which documents of John C. Calhoun have been found and for the repositories in which they are preserved. (Full citations to printed sources of documents can be found in the Bibliography.)

Abs	—abstract (a summary)
ADS	—autograph document, signed
AEI	—autograph endorsement, initialed
AES	—autograph endorsement, signed
AEU	—autograph endorsement, unsigned
ALI	—autograph letter, initialed
ALS	—autograph letter, signed
ALU	—autograph letter, unsigned
CC	—clerk's copy (a secondary ms. copy)
CtY	—Yale University, New Haven, Conn.
DLC	—Library of Congress, Washington
DNA	—National Archives, Washington
DS	—document, signed
DU	—document, unsigned
En	—enclosure
Ens	—enclosures
EU	—endorsement, unsigned
FC	—file copy (usually a letterbook copy retained by the sender)
LS	—letter, signed
M-	—(followed by a number) published microcopy of the National Archives
MoSHi	—Missouri Historical Society, St. Louis
NcD	—Duke University, Durham, N.C.
NcU	—Southern Historical Collection, University of North Carolina at Chapel Hill
NHi	—New-York Historical Society, New York City
NjMoN	—Morristown National Historical Park, Morristown, N.J.
NNPM	—Pierpont Morgan Library, New York City
PC	—printed copy
PEx	—printed extract
PHi	—Historical Society of Pennsylvania, Philadelphia
RG	—Record Group in the National Archives
Sc-Ar	—South Carolina Department of Archives and History, Columbia
ScC	—Charleston Library Society, Charleston, S.C.
ScCleA	—Clemson University, Clemson, S.C.
ScU-SC	—South Caroliniana Library, University of South Carolina, Columbia

Symbols

TxU	—Barker Texas History Center, University of Texas at Austin
Vi	—Virginia State Library, Richmond
ViLxW	—Washington and Lee University, Lexington, Va.
ViW	—College of William and Mary, Williamsburg, Va.

BIBLIOGRAPHY

◫

This Bibliography is limited to sources of and previous printings of documents published in this volume.

Alderman, Edwin Anderson, and Joel Chandler Harris, eds., *Library of Southern Literature*. 17 vols. Atlanta, Ga.: the Martin & Hoyt Company, 1907–1923.

Alexandria, D.C. and Va., *Gazette*, 1808–.

Ambler, Charles Henry, ed., *Correspondence of Robert M.T. Hunter, 1826–1876*, in the *American Historical Association Annual Report* for 1916 (2 vols. Washington: U.S. Government Printing Office, 1918), vol. II.

The Autograph Album: a Magazine for Autograph Collectors. New York City: Thomas F. Madigan, publisher, vol. I, no. 2 (October 1933).

Baltimore, Md., *American*, 1799–.

Baltimore, Md., *Constitution*, 1844–1845.

Benton, Thomas H., ed., *Abridgment of the Debates of Congress*. 16 vols. New York: D. Appleton & Co., 1854–1861.

Bond of Brotherhood, The. Worcester, Mass.: 1846–1867.

Boucher, Chauncey S., and Robert P. Brooks, eds., *Correspondence Addressed to John C. Calhoun, 1837–1849*, in the *American Historical Association Annual Report* for 1929 (Washington: U.S. Government Printing Office, 1930).

Charleston, S.C., *Courier*, 1803–1852.

Charleston, S.C., *Mercury*, 1822–1868.

Cincinnati, Ohio, *Daily Enquirer*, 1841–.

Cincinnati, Ohio, *Daily Gazette*, 1827–1883.

Columbia, S.C., *South-Carolinian*, 1838–1849?.

Columbia, S.C., *The State*, 1891–.

Congressional Globe . . . 1833–1873 . . . . 46 vols. Washington: Blair & Rives and others, 1834–1873.

"Convention of Texas, 1845," in *William and Mary Quarterly*, 1st series, vol. XV, no. 1 (July, 1906), pp. 41–42.

Crallé, Richard K., ed., *The Works of John C. Calhoun*. 6 vols. Columbia, S.C.: printed by A.S. Johnston, 1851, and New York: D. Appleton & Co., 1853–1857.

Curtis, George Ticknor, *Life of James Buchanan, Fifteenth President of the United States*. 2 vols. New York: Harper & Brothers, 1883. Reprint: Freeport, N.Y.: Books for Libraries Press, 1969.

Davis, Varina Howell, *Jefferson Davis, Ex-President of the Confederate States of America, A Memoir by his Wife*. 2 vols. New York: Belford Company, Publishers, 1890.

"Documents. 1. John C. Calhoun on the Division of the Methodist Church in 1844," in *Gulf States Historical Magazine*, vol. I, no. 3 (November, 1902), p. 212.

Edgefield, S.C., *Advertiser*, 1836–.

Fulkerson, H.S., *Random Recollections of Early Days in Mississippi.* Baton Rouge: Otto Claitor, 1937.

Greenville, S.C., *Mountaineer,* 1829–1901.

Huntsville, Ala., *Democrat,* 1823–1853?.

Jackson, Miss., *Mississippian,* 1832–1865.

Jackson, Miss., *Southern Reformer,* 1843–1846.

Jameson, J. Franklin, ed., *Correspondence of John C. Calhoun,* in the *American Historical Association Annual Report* for 1899 (2 vols. Washington: U.S. Government Printing Office, 1900), vol. II.

Journal of the Proceedings of the South-Western Convention, Began and Held at the City of Memphis, on the 12th November, 1845. Memphis, Tenn.: 1845.

Journals of the Convention, Assembled at the City of Austin . . . for the Purpose of Framing a Constitution for the State of Texas. Austin: Miner & Cruger, Printers to the Convention, 1845.

"Letters from John C. Calhoun to Francis W. Pickens," in *South Carolina Historical Magazine,* vol. VII, no. 1 (January, 1906), pp. 12–19.

Lexington, Ky., *Observer and Reporter,* 1831–1873.

London, England, *Times,* 1785–.

McIntosh, James T., et al., eds., *The Papers of Jefferson Davis.* 7 vols. to date. Baton Rouge: Louisiana State University Press, 1971–.

Memphis, Tenn., *Daily Eagle,* 1843–1851.

Milledgeville, Ga., *Federal Union,* 1830–1872.

Mobile, Ala., *Daily Advertiser,* 1833–1861.

Mobile, Ala., *Register and Journal,* 1841–.

Moore, John Bassett, ed., *The Works of James Buchanan, Comprising his Speeches, State Papers, and Private Correspondence.* 12 vols. Philadelphia and London: J.B. Lippincott Company, 1908–1911.

Nashville, Tenn., *Union,* 1835–1875.

Nashville, Tenn., *Whig,* 1838–1855.

Natchez, Miss., *Mississippi Free Trader and Natchez Gazette,* 1835–1861?.

New Orleans, La., *Bee,* 1827–1917?.

New Orleans, La., *Daily Picayune,* 1836–1914.

New Orleans, La., *Louisiana Courier,* 1807–1860.

New York, N.Y., *Evening Post,* 1832–1920.

New York, N.Y., *Herald,* 1835–1924.

New York, N.Y., *Observer,* 1823–1912.

New York, N.Y., *The Subterranean,* 1843?–1847.

Niles' Register. Baltimore: 1811–1849.

Pendleton, S.C., *Messenger,* 1807–?.

Philadelphia, Pa., *United States Gazette,* 1789–1847.

Raleigh, N.C., *North Carolina Standard,* 1834–1870.

Richmond, Va., *Enquirer,* 1804–1877.

Speech of Mr. Calhoun, of South Carolina, on the Resolutions Giving Notice to Great Britain of the Abrogation of the Convention of Joint Occupancy. Washington: [John T.] Towers, printer, [1846].

Springfield, Ill., *Illinois State Register,* 1836–1918.

Tuscaloosa, Ala., *Independent Monitor,* 1837–1872.

U.S. Senate, *Senate Documents,* 29th Congress.

U.S. Senate, *Senate Journal,* 29th Congress.

Vicksburg, Miss., *Daily Sentinel,* 1838–1851?.

Vicksburg, Miss., *Daily Whig,* 1839–1863.

Vicksburg, Miss., *Sentinel and Expositor*, 1836–1846.

Walmsley, James Elliott, "The Return of John C. Calhoun to the Senate in 1845," in the *American Historical Association Annual Report* for 1913 (2 vols. Washington: U.S. Government Printing Office), 1:159–165.

Washington, D.C., *Constitution*, 1844–1845.

Washington, D.C., *Daily National Intelligencer*, 1800–1870.

Washington, D.C., *Union*, 1845–1859.

Wheeler, Henry G., *History of Congress, Biographical and Political: Comprising Memoirs of Members of the Congress of the United States, drawn from Authentic Sources; Embracing the Prominent Events of their Lives, and their Connection with the Political History of the Times.* 2 vols. New York: Harper & Brothers, 1848.

Wilson, Clyde N., ed., *The Essential Calhoun. Selections from Writings, Speeches and Letters.* New Brunswick, N.J., and London: Transaction Publishers, 1992.

INDEX

◧

Abbeville District, S.C.: 29–30, 47, 53–54, 74–75, 93, 159, 178–180, 248–249, 328, 367, 420, 469–470, 633–635, 645.

Abbey, Richard: from, 440; mentioned, 349.

Abdullah, Sultan of the Comoro Islands: mentioned, 598.

Aberdeen, Lord: mentioned, 211, 304, 404–406, 460, 465, 627, 646.

Abingdon, Va.: 279.

Abingdon, Va., *Banner*: mentioned, 295.

Abolition: ix–x, xiii, 3, 12–14, 17, 31–32, 50–51, 67, 70–72, 79–83, 89, 97–101, 118, 128–129, 132, 154, 156–158, 161, 171–173, 175, 177, 184, 218, 231, 270, 354–356, 364, 376, 387, 390, 417–418, 463–464, 473–474, 495, 504, 510–511, 516, 529, 571, 588–589, 593–595, 603, 614–616, 653, 660–662, 683, 690, 736, 753, 764. *See also* Slavery.

Ackley, Lyman: from, 351.

Adams, John Quincy: mentioned, xiii, 225, 237, 390, 463–464, 495, 510, 517–518, 521, 589, 603, 663–665, 668, 685, 690, 709.

Adams, Placidia Mayrant: mentioned, 313, 587; to, 585, 745.

Adams, Richard: from, 236.

Address on Taking the Chair of the Southwestern Convention: text of, 276–285.

Africa: 10, 130, 356, 473–474, 553, 597–598.

Agnew, John O.: from, 258; to, 296.

Agriculture: in Calhoun/Clemson family, xviii, 3–4, 11, 30, 33–35, 42–43, 47–48, 51–54, 67–68, 70–71, 78–79, 87, 93, 101–110, 115, 141–143, 145–146, 155, 159, 166, 178–180, 189, 202, 233–234, 238–241, 301–303, 307–308, 314, 326, 331–337, 339–343, 349–351, 440–441, 452–453, 503, 507, 538, 541, 570, 574, 622, 627, 634–635, 745, 749, 767–768, 770–771; mentioned, 11–12, 32–33, 35, 50–51, 63, 79, 103–104, 122, 152, 155, 159, 161, 166, 171, 173–174, 190, 212, 273–274, 320, 380, 384, 391, 395–397, 437, 451, 483, 490–491, 495, 500, 526, 598, 601, 606–608, 610, 620, 655, 678, 682, 702, 724, 736, 776–777; Southern, 8–9, 11, 27, 35–41, 48, 69–73, 78, 82, 101, 116, 118–125, 144, 190–195, 209–210, 214, 217–219, 240, 258, 276–284, 288, 290, 300, 305–306, 309–310, 327, 352, 354–356, 362, 364, 407, 425–426, 440–441, 462, 479, 481, 485, 497, 528, 537–538, 551, 559, 574, 580, 603, 608–610, 613, 625–626, 643, 668–669, 736, 746, 770, 776–777, 788, 791.

Aiken, S.C.: 36, 326.

Aiken, William: from, 201, 328; mentioned, 205, 208, 218.

Alabama: xviii, 4, 27, 42–44, 47–48, 52, 54, 65, 68, 92–94, 100, 105, 107, 134, 143–146, 148, 166, 171, 176, 180, 183, 186, 189, 192–195, 208–209, 214, 216, 221, 229–230, 235, 238–240, 242, 247, 249, 254–255, 278–279, 292–293, 296–297, 300–301, 314, 327–328, 331–332, 334, 339, 343–344, 349–350, 367, 412, 452–453, 456, 460, 463, 478–479, 491, 533, 570, 573–574, 582–583, 611–612, 634, 645, 790–791; Senators from (*see* Bagby, Arthur P.; Lewis, Dixon H.). *See also* Mobile, Ala.

242, 274, 308, 313, 335, 341, 365,
504, 510, 533, 621, 623, 628, 747–
749, 784.

Clemson, John Calhoun: mentioned,
10–11, 18, 44, 68–69, 133, 147,
187, 242, 274, 308, 313, 335, 341,
365, 504, 510, 533, 621, 623, 628,
747–749, 784.

Clemson, Thomas G.: from, 16, 69,
104, 303, 331, 537, 543, 623, 640,
766; mentioned, xiv, 3, 9–11, 33–
34, 47, 66, 78–79, 84, 131–133,
159, 187, 247, 272–274, 302–303,
312–314, 325–326, 342, 350–351,
503, 505, 510, 548, 634, 672–673,
737, 746–748; to, 42, 67, 146, 238,
339, 365, 532, 621, 749, 783.

Clemson University Library: documents in (more than 320 included
herein).

Cleveland, Ohio: 183, 317.

Clifton, C.R.: from, 268; to, 297.

Clinch, Duncan L.: mentioned, 339,
475.

Clinton, Charles A.: from, 740; mentioned, 728; to, 752.

Clinton, DeWitt: mentioned, 740–
741, 752.

Coal: 380, 574–577, 600, 651, 733,
769.

Cobb, Howell: mentioned, 378, 457.

Cobden, Richard: mentioned, 744.

Cochin China: 600–601.

Cochran, John: from, 254.

Coddington, John: mentioned, 22, 92.

Coffee: 124, 158, 210, 219, 776–777.

Coffee, John: mentioned, 8.

Cogdell, John S.: from, 563.

Colhoun, James Edward: from, 420;
mentioned, 53, 159, 315, 633–635;
to, 29, 54, 195, 342, 454.

Colhoun, John Ewing: mentioned,
333.

Colhoun, Martha Maria: mentioned,
313–314, 455–456.

College of William and Mary: document in library of, 562; mentioned, 243–244.

Collier & Pettis: mentioned, 571.

Collier, George: from, 291; to, 292.

Colonization: 80, 472–474.

Colorado: 676.

Colquitt, Walter T.: mentioned, 148,
378, 456–457, 463, 632, 693, 714.

Colton, Calvin: mentioned, 237–238,
663–665, 668.

Columbia, Ky.: 450.

Columbia River: 87, 211, 316, 401,
406, 423, 429, 458, 466, 509, 560,
567, 585, 615–616, 655–656.

Columbia, S.C.: 36, 79, 115, 141–
142, 179–180, 196–197, 302–303,
319–320, 327, 344–345, 352, 397,
431, 525.

Columbia, S.C., *South-Carolinian*:
document in, 276; mentioned, 33,
67, 87, 319, 345–346, 397–398,
431.

Columbia, S.C., *State*: document in,
144.

Columbus, Christopher: mentioned,
160, 310.

Columbus, Ga.: 134, 144, 461.

Columbus, Miss.: 98–100, 677–678,
760–761.

Columbus, Ohio: 118, 317, 432, 434–
435.

Columbus, Ohio, *Ohio State Journal*:
mentioned, 293.

Columbus, Ohio, *Ohio Statesman*:
mentioned, 116, 184.

Combs, Leslie: mentioned, 321.

Commerford, John: mentioned, 680.

Comoro Islands: 598, 601–603.

Concordia, La., *Intelligencer*. See Vidalia, La., *Concordia Intelligencer*.

Concordia Parish, La.: 191, 309.

Confederate States of America: 385,
416, 577.

Conger, Thomas: mentioned, 640.

Congressional Globe: documents in,
368, 371, 423, 424, 427, 428, 439,
443, 446, 477, 493, 514, 561, 569,
631, 636, 666, 667, 683, 685, 704,
790.

Connecticut: 381, 394–396, 463, 589,
682–683.

Conner, Henry W.: from, 174, 209,
414; mentioned, 37–39; to, 463.

Conner, Samuel: to, 242.

Conn, Joseph H.: from, 258; to, 296.

Consistency: 691–692, 711–712, 735.

Constantine: mentioned, 499.

Consumption: 55.

Glass: 603.

Glenn, D.C.: from, 268; to, 297.

Glenn Springs, S.C.: 54, 66, 68, 87.

Goblet, Albert Joseph: mentioned, 133.

God: 26, 31–32, 66, 72, 77, 99, 129, 269, 319, 338, 350, 357, 392, 422–423, 437, 498, 500, 508, 512, 526, 536, 542, 545, 563, 589, 602, 607, 609, 653, 754. See also Providence.

Godwin, Parke: from, 737; mentioned, xvi–xvii, xx, 648.

Gold: 73–74, 146–147, 314, 378–380, 433–434, 586–587, 598, 619.

Golding, ——: mentioned, 178, 180.

Goliad, Tex.: 674.

Goode, William O.: mentioned, 161–162, 318, 345.

Good, George W.: from, 291; to, 292.

Goodrich, Charles S.J.: from, 775; mentioned, xx.

Goodrich, Elizur: mentioned, 775.

Goodwin, William: from, 351.

Gordon, William F.: from, 653; mentioned, 654.

Gouge, William M.: mentioned, 37.

Gourdin, Henry: from, 209.

Grain: 146, 166, 607, 620, 635, 746.

Grand Gulf, Miss.: 278–279, 491.

Grand Rapids, Mich.: 639.

Grason, William: from, 558.

Gray, Cyril: mentioned, 170, 227, 295.

Grayson, William J.: mentioned, 35, 37–38, 118–121, 195, 209, 589; to, 83.

Great Britain: and abolition, 31, 70, 89, 128–129, 154, 161, 172, 177, 184, 354–356, 364, 417, 516, 529, 588–589, 653, 736, 764; mentioned, 10, 17–18, 46, 59–61, 64, 70, 73, 78, 102, 125–126, 130, 132–133, 146–147, 149, 158–161, 164–165, 167, 173–175, 181, 211–212, 228, 244, 259, 267–268, 282, 288, 303–306, 326, 331, 347–348, 350–351, 389, 393–394, 408–409, 417, 419, 443, 460, 476–477, 484, 490, 498–499, 505–506, 509–510, 523, 537–539, 541, 543, 549–556, 568, 577–578, 598–602, 608, 625, 627–628, 642, 681–682, 684–685, 704, 749, 772, 778–779; Minister of

to U.S. (see Pakenham, Richard); U.S. Minister to (see McLane, Louis). See also Corn Laws; Oregon.

Great Lakes: 8, 280–282, 288, 325, 480, 482–485, 489, 535, 551, 576, 670, 720, 749.

Greece, ancient: xix, 64, 196, 203, 357, 476, 496, 499, 546, 565, 567, 790.

Greece, modern: 496, 499, 516.

Greek Orthodox Church: 499.

Green, Duff: from, 169, 221, 222, 321, 614, 732, 742, 743, 757; mentioned, xx, 46, 91, 189, 269, 548, 648; to, 233.

Greene, B.H.: mentioned, 331.

Greene County, Ala.: 292, 583.

Green, Eliza M.: mentioned, 170, 234.

Greenleaf, Simon: mentioned, 338–339.

Green, Lucretia Maria Edwards: mentioned, 170, 234.

Green, Mary: mentioned, 314.

Green, Thomas: mentioned, 24, 787–788.

Green, Thomas J.: from, 154, 269; mentioned, 668.

Greenville, Ill.: 738.

Greenville, S.C.: 141, 179.

Greenville, S.C., *Mountaineer*: documents in, 276, 371, 423, 685; mentioned, xii.

Gregg, Josiah: mentioned, 415.

Grey, Lord: mentioned, 536, 619.

Grieb, F.: mentioned, 155, 202.

Grisham, William: mentioned, 378, 586.

Groves, John: mentioned, 640.

Grund, Francis J.: mentioned, 505, 539, 625–626, 640–643, 749.

Grundy, Felix: mentioned, 270.

Guaymas, Mexico: 415.

Gulf of Mexico: 7, 58, 158, 164, 251, 276–283, 479–480, 482–489, 491, 528, 675, 721.

Gunnegle, Wilson: mentioned, 371.

Guthrie, James: from, 479.

Gwinner, P.: from, 48, 399, 619, 729.

Gwin, William M.: from, 100; mentioned, 23, 98–99.

Henderson, J. Pinckney: mentioned, 631, 662–663, 667–668, 787.
Henry, Patrick: from, 268, 617; to, 297.
Henshaw, David: mentioned, 116, 557.
Hercules: mentioned, 476.
Heriot, William B.: mentioned, 39.
Hernandez, Joseph M.: mentioned, 339.
Hibernian Benevolent Association: 514.
Hiern, R.A.: mentioned, 261–262.
Higgins, Francis B.: mentioned, 342, 350.
Hill, John D.: from, 258; to, 296.
Hill, N.B.: from, 787.
Historical Society of Pennsylvania: documents in, 30, 97, 202.
H. Kinney (steamboat): 251.
Hoban, James, Jr.: mentioned, 501–502, 512.
Hoffman, Michael: mentioned, 112, 321, 383, 680–681, 732–733.
Hogan, John: from, 160; mentioned, 28–29, 97, 210, 418, 524.
Hogs and bacon: 33–34, 166, 174, 746, 758.
Hoit, Lucius: mentioned, 640.
Holcombe, Henry P.: from, 255.
Hollick, Frederick: mentioned, 570–571.
Hollingshead, ——: mentioned, 369.
Holmes, Isaac E.: from, 298; mentioned, 204, 269, 327, 438, 569, 669.
Holmes, Nathaniel: from, 258; to, 296.
Holt, Robert S.: from, 285; to, 297.
Holt, Thomas H.: from, 322.
Holy Alliance: 517, 519.
Homer: mentioned, 64.
Hominy: 178.
Hompeth, Count ——: mentioned, 110.
Hong Kong: 601.
Hood, Abner: from, 258; to, 296.
Hood, S.E.: from, 764.
Hopkins, George W.: mentioned, 745.
Hoppin, Charles A.: from, 254; mentioned, 252–253.
Horn, Henry: mentioned, 399, 442, 620, 730.

Horses: 19, 40, 47, 72–73, 103, 107, 109–110, 122, 155, 174, 178, 180, 191, 240–241, 252–253, 266, 300, 335, 340, 488, 608, 676–677.
Horsewhipping: 137–138.
Horton, Albert C.: from, 247.
Houk, George W.: from, 244.
House of Representatives, U.S.: Calhoun in, 168, 347, 366, 512, 697; mentioned, 67, 77, 148, 170, 211, 225, 312, 317, 321, 387, 410, 412, 427, 431, 446, 453, 506–508, 516, 533, 561, 569, 589, 612, 631, 654, 664, 668, 679, 683, 693, 696, 713, 739, 759, 772.
Houston, Samuel: mentioned, xi–xii, 7, 557, 648, 652, 659–660, 662, 668, 766.
Houston, Tex.: 250, 658–660.
Houston, William: from, 285; to, 297.
Howard, John H.: from, 461; mentioned, 134.
Howell, Joseph D.: mentioned, 299.
Howell, Margaret L.: mentioned, 299.
Hoyt, Jesse: mentioned, 46, 176, 225, 227.
Hubbard, ——: to, 247.
Huddell, Robert: from, 610.
"Hudibras": mentioned, 388.
Hudson Bay Company: 88, 167, 366, 404, 406, 466.
Hudson, Thomas B.: from, 258; to, 296.
Huger, Daniel E.: from, 290; mentioned, xi, 145, 148, 155–157, 159, 165–166, 182, 190, 196–197, 204, 219–220, 298, 328.
Hughes, Christopher: from, 186.
Hughes, Margaret Smith: mentioned, 187.
Hume, Joseph: mentioned, 744.
Hunkers: 17, 48–49, 85–86, 156–157, 184–185, 232–233, 315, 324, 402, 440, 460, 534, 536, 751. See also Albany Regency.
Hunter, John L.: from, 254.
Hunter, Robert M.T.: from, 230; mentioned, xii, 23–24, 56, 77, 591, 605.
Hunt, John: from, 359.
Huntsville, Ala., *Democrat*: document in, 704; mentioned, 13.
Hurtel, John: from, 254.

McChesney, Charles G.: from, 786; mentioned, 635–636, 785–786.
McComas, William: mentioned, 161–162.
McDonald, A.: from, 254.
McDowall, A.: from, 209; mentioned, 39.
McDowell, James: mentioned, 169.
McDuffie, George: from, 493; mentioned, 89–90, 96, 117, 145, 148, 155–157, 159, 165–166, 182, 197, 204, 220, 246, 318, 327, 351, 414, 420, 432, 456, 463, 501, 529, 660, 742.
McGinnis, E.G.: from, 426.
McKay, James I.: mentioned, 23, 118, 148.
McKean, Samuel: mentioned, 96.
MacKenzie, Roderick: from, 235.
McKibbin, John: from, 323.
McLane, Louis: from, 393, 403, 464, 568, 646, 654; mentioned, 17, 20, 163, 294, 390, 618, 624, 627, 768; to, 393.
McLane, Robert M.: from, 618.
McLean, John: mentioned, 118, 163.
McLemore, John: mentioned, 23.
McLeod, Alexander: mentioned, 350.
McLeod, Hugh: from, 247, 248, 415.
McNab, J.: from, 254.
McNutt, Alexander G.: mentioned, 45.
McPheeters, W.M.: from, 291; to, 292.
McVay, William: from, 359.
McWillie, A.A.: from, 268; to, 297.

Macaulay, Thomas B.: mentioned, 172, 177.
Macdonald, James M.: from, 773.
Machinery: 34, 102–103, 115, 141–142, 155, 178–180, 202, 380, 492, 597, 679, 700, 722.
Mackay, Alexander: from, 547; mentioned, 393–394.
Mackenzie, William Lyon: mentioned, 170–171, 204, 223, 226, 733.
Maclay, William B.: mentioned, 329.
Macon, Ga.: 457.
Macpherson, William: mentioned, 542.
Madagascar: 598, 601.

Madison County, Fla.: 84–86, 127, 215–216.
Madison County, Miss.: 617–618.
Madison, James: mentioned, 368.
Magee, Stewart: from, 351.
Magrear, J.W.: from, 258; to, 296.
Maguire, George: from, 258; to, 296.
Magwin, John: from, 291; to, 292.
Maine: 156–158, 168–169, 338–339, 475–478, 733, 776–780; Senator from (*see* Fairfield, John).
Mallary, Rollin C.: mentioned, 516.
Mammon: 683.
Manchester, England: 409.
Mangum, Willie P.: mentioned, 683.
Manning, A.W.: from, 258; to, 296.
Manufactures: 35–36, 38–41, 69, 71, 120–124, 152, 173, 175, 192, 210, 282, 288, 302, 305–306, 322, 355, 362, 370–371, 395, 401–402, 407, 451, 459, 483, 485–488, 506, 538, 559, 574–577, 597, 603, 607–608, 649, 651, 731, 776–778.
Manure: 32, 51, 72, 82, 105, 173, 239, 341.
Marcy, William L.: mentioned, 19, 46, 91–92, 112, 139, 152, 207, 321, 348, 383, 414, 549, 662.
Marengo County, Ala. *See* Cane Brake (in Marengo County, Ala.).
Maria (steamboat): 265, 267, 271, 275, 296–300, 349.
Marietta, Ohio: 605.
Marine hospitals: 468–469, 480, 482, 484, 487.
Marion, Ala.: 144.
Marius: mentioned, 423.
Markoe, Francis: mentioned, 133, 581, 622.
Marl: 32.
Maronite Church: 499.
Marriott, William H.: from, 738.
Marshall, Mich.: 113–115, 639–640.
Marshall, Mich., *Democratic Expounder*: mentioned, 114–115.
Marshall, Thomas F.: mentioned, 80.
Martello towers: 7, 552.
Martin, ——: mentioned, 745.
Martineau, Harriet: mentioned, 589.
Martin, Hugh: mentioned, 588.
Martin, James: from, 351; mentioned, 588.
Martin, John B.: from, 291; to, 292.